Behavior in Organizations

**The Irwin Series in Management
and
The Behavioral Sciences**

L. L. CUMMINGS and E. KIRBY WARREN   Consulting Editors
JOHN F. MEE   Advisory Editor

Behavior in Organizations

H. JOSEPH REITZ
University of Florida

1977

Richard D. Irwin, Inc. Homewood, Illinois 60430
Irwin-Dorsey Limited Georgetown, Ontario L7G 4B3

© RICHARD D. IRWIN, INC., 1977

All rights reserved. No part of this publication may be
reproduced, stored in a retrieval system, or transmitted,
in any form or by any means, electronic, mechanical,
photocopying, recording, or otherwise, without the prior
written permission of the publisher.

5 6 7 8 9 0 K 5 4 3 2 1 0 9

ISBN 0-256-01792-1
Library of Congress Catalog Card No. 75–39358
Printed in the United States of America

Preface

THIS BOOK is about behavior—the behavior of men and women at work in organizations of all kinds. By all kinds we mean not only business and industrial, but also government, military, service, educational, health care, and even entertainment organizations.

The book is intended for use at the undergraduate or introductory graduate level for courses in organizational behavior, behavioral science in administration, and management. Every effort has been made to keep the writing style concise and readable, to avoid unnecessary jargon, and to provide abundant examples of behavioral concepts and processes at work in a variety or organizations. To further assist the student, each chapter begins with a set of objectives and a chapter outline and concludes with a summary, questions for review and discussion, and a list of key words.

The focus is on behavior, not concepts—the kinds of behavior practicing managers must deal with every day. The content is based on research and theory from the behavioral sciences. The text revolves around this research and theory and their applications in contemporary organizations. It does not concentrate on the people who developed the research, theory, and applications. Theories and models are identified with the behaviors they describe, rather than with the individuals who derived them. It has always seemed that describing expectancy models as "Vroom's model" or "Porter and Lawler's model" has contributed to the disinterest and confusion rather than the education of students at this level.

Because the book focuses on behavior, it covers many behavioral topics in greater detail than most comparable books. The focus allows for the development and discussion of the processes and effects of a variety of individual and group behaviors, and of the personal, environmental, and organizational factors that influence those behaviors. Several topics which would seem to be of critical importance in contemporary organizations are discussed in some depth, in contrast to the short shrift they typically receive. Among these topics are performance evaluation, creative and innovative behavior, group decision making, helping behavior, imitation, cooperation, competition, and intergroup conflict.

There has been a deliberate attempt to organize the subject matter in some logical fashion, so that later parts of the book build on and progress from earlier parts. Thus we progress from simple to complex individual behaviors, then from simple to complex group behaviors.

Part One describes the general nature of managerial activity in organizations and the kinds of behavior managers are likely to encounter. It then provides a foundation for understanding the material which follows by describing and evaluating the various sources of knowledge about behavior in organizations.

Parts Two and Three deal with individual behavior in organizations. Part Two presents a small set of theoretical approaches and models for understanding behavior in general and individual behavior in particular. Part Three discusses specific individual behaviors including perceiving and evaluating, decision making, creating and innovating, and expressing satisfaction and dissatisfaction.

Parts Four and Five deal with group and social behavior in organizations. Part Four provides a basis for understanding group behavior by describing why and how individuals form groups, the processes of group development, and group structure. Part Five covers specific group and interpersonal behaviors including communications, group decision making, helping, cooperating, competing, conflicting, influencing, and conforming.

Part Six concludes the book by discussing two major topics which incorporate much of the previous material on individual and group behavior: leadership and changing behavior in organizations.

Acknowledgments

Writing a textbook as sole author has its advantages and disadvantages. The major advantage is avoiding the problems of differences in time schedules (and inclinations to adhere to them), in opinions, in professional and pedagogical philosophies, and in writing styles which cause many a joint author to cry, "Never again!" when the manuscript is finally finished. The major disadvantage, of course, is that the responsibility for everything from conceiving the outline to securing permissions falls on one set of shoulders. If the sole author doesn't do it or doesn't see that it gets done, it doesn't happen. The buck starts and stops here.

In the writing of this book, however, the disadvantages of sole authorship were offset to a large degree by the assistance of a number of people. Many of them provided help which was highly professional in its expertise yet very personal in the willingness with which it was given. I think I may have stumbled onto a new variable in helping behavior. We know that a victim is more likely to receive assistance from a small rather than from a large group of observers. Perhaps it is also true that individuals needing help elicit more assistance than groups in similar plights.

Among those who helped shape whatever is good about this book are Bob Duncan, who reviewed early portions of the manuscript, and Larry Cummings, James G. Hunt, Paul Thompson, Kirby Warren, and Ross Webber, who read the entire manuscript and provided valuable comments on both content and organization.

Mike Mastandrea and Don Eckert assisted with much of the review of literature that preceded the writing of each chapter. Linda Jewell helped in many ways through the final stages of manuscript preparation, including a final critical review and proofreading. Fran Frketic, Sandy Long, and Liz Vincent had a hand in typing various drafts of the manuscript. The task of typing the final draft was done very capably and painstakingly by Mary Fearn.

Finally, a special word of thanks to Larry Cummings, Roger Ross, and Ira Horowitz. Larry and Roger first conceived the idea for this project and never failed thereafter to provide the support, evaluation, feedback, encouragement, and occasional sympathetic ear that one needs throughout the course of a major effort. Ira provided the kinds of support and encouragement which all too rarely come from administrators but which characterize his support for the professional activities of his faculty.

Gainesville, Florida
December 1976

H. JOSEPH REITZ

Contents

tional Communications: *Functions of Communications. Directions of Communication.* Communications in Research and Development Organizations: *Channels of Communication. Factors Affecting the Use of Channels. Communication Networks. The Role of Technological Gatekeeper.*

part one
Introduction to Behavior in Organizations

1
Managers and Behavior in Organizations

2
Sources of Knowledge about Behavior in Organizations

PART ONE discusses a problem which is faced by all managers in all organizations: the need to understand, predict, and influence human behavior.

Chapter 1 considers how frequently most managers encounter the behavior of other people in organizations and discusses the variety of behaviors that is possible. Organizations are defined, as well as the different categories of people with whom a manager must interact. The chapter concludes with a description of how this book is organized.

Chapter 2, which discusses the various sources of information about human behavior which are available to managers, presents three criteria to be used in evaluating a source of information. The dangers of relying solely on personal experience are discussed, and a case is made for systematic methods of obtaining information. Different methods, ranging from case studies to experimentation, are described, and an example of each is presented. The advantages and shortcomings of the various methods are reviewed.

OUTLINE OF CHAPTER

chapter one

Managers and Behavior in Organizations

At approximately 7:30 a.m. on Tuesday, June 23, Chet Craig, manager of the Norris Company's Central plant, swung his car out of the driveway of his suburban home and headed toward the plant located some six miles away just inside the Midvale city limits. It was a beautiful day. The sun was shining brightly and a cool, fresh breeze was blowing. The trip to the plant took about twenty minutes and sometimes gave Chet an opportunity to think about plant problems without interruption.

The Norris Company owned and operated three quality printing plants. Norris enjoyed a nation-wide commercial business, specializing in quality color work. It was a closely held company with some 350 employees, nearly half of whom were employed at the Central plant, the largest of the three Norris production operations. The company's main offices were also located in the Central plant building.

Chet had started with the Norris Company as an expediter in its Eastern plant just after he graduated from Ohio State. After three years Chet was promoted to production supervisor and two years later was made assistant to the manager of the Eastern plant. Two years ago he was transferred to the Central plant as assistant to the plant manager and one month later was promoted to plant manager, when the former manager retired.

Chet was in fine spirits as he relaxed behind the wheel. As his car picked up speed, the hum of the tires on the newly paved highway faded into the background. Various thoughts occurred to him and he said to himself, "This is going to be the day to really get things done."

He began to run through the day's work, first one project, then another, trying to establish priorities.

Chet's thoughts were interrupted as he pulled into the company parking lot. When he entered the plant Chet knew something was wrong as he met Al Noren, the stockroom foreman, who appeared troubled. "A great morning, Al," Chet greeted him cheerfully.

"Not so good, Chet; my new man isn't in this morning," Noren growled.

"Have you heard from him?" asked Chet.

"No, I haven't," replied Al.

Chet frowned as he commented, "These stock handlers assume you take it for granted that if they're not here, they don't have to call in and verify it. Better ask Personnel to call him."

Al hesitated for a moment before replying. "Okay, Chet, but can you find me a man? I have two cars to unload today."

As Chet turned to leave he said, "I'll call you in half an hour, Al, and let you know."

Making a mental note of the situation, Chet headed for his office. He greeted the group of workers huddled around Marilyn, the office manager, who was discussing the day's work schedule with them. As the meeting broke up Marilyn picked up a few samples from the clasper, showed them to Chet and asked if they should be shipped that way or if it would be necessary to inspect them. Before he could answer Marilyn went on to ask if he could suggest another clerical operator for the sealing machine to replace the regular operator who was home ill. She also told him that Gene, the industrial engineer, had called and was waiting to hear from Chet.

After telling Marilyn to go ahead and ship the samples, he made a note of the need for a sealer operator for the office and then called Gene. He agreed to stop by Gene's office before lunch and started on his routine morning tour of the plant. He asked each foreman the types and volumes of orders they were running, the number of people present, how the schedules were coming along, and the orders to be run next; helped the folding-room foreman find temporary storage space for consolidating a carload shipment; discussed quality control with a pressman who had been running poor work; arranged to transfer four people temporarily to different departments, including two for Al in the stockroom; talked to the shipping foreman about pickups and special orders to be delivered that day. As he continued through the plant, he saw to it that reserve stock was moved out of the forward stock area; talked to another pressman about his requested change of vacation schedule; had a "heart-to-heart" talk with a press helper who seemed to need frequent reassurance; approved two type and one color order okays for different pressmen.

Returning to his office, Chet reviewed the production reports on the larger orders against his initial projections and found that the plant was running behind schedule. He called in the folding-room foreman and together they went over the line-up of machines and made several necessary changes.

During this discussion, the composing-room foreman stopped in to cover several type changes and the routing foreman telephoned for approval of a revised printing schedule. The stockroom foreman called twice, first to inform him that two standard, fast-moving stock items were dangerously low; later to advise him that the paper stock for the urgent

Dillon job had finally arrived. Chet made the necessary subsequent calls to inform those concerned.

He then began to put delivery dates on important and difficult inquiries received from customers and salesmen. (The routine inquiries were handled by Marilyn.) While he was doing this he was interrupted twice, once by a sales correspondent calling from the West Coast to ask for a better delivery date than originally scheduled; once by the personnel vice president asking him to set a time when he could hold an initial training and induction interview with a new employee.

After dating the customer and salesmen inquiries, Chet headed for his morning conference in the executive offices. At this meeting he answered the sales vice president's questions in connection with "hot" orders, complaints, the status of large-volume orders and potential new orders. He then met with the general manager to discuss a few ticklish policy matters and to answer "the old man's" questions on several specific production and personnel problems. Before leaving the executive offices, he stopped at the office of the secretary-treasurer to inquire about delivery of cartons, paper, and boxes, and to place new orders for paper.

On the way back to his own office, Chet conferred with Gene about two current engineering projects. When he reached his desk, he lit a cigarette, and looked at his watch. It was ten minutes before lunch, just time enough to make a few notes of the details he needed to check in order to answer knotty questions raised by the sales manager that morning.

After lunch Chet started again. He began by checking the previous day's production reports; did some rescheduling to get out urgent orders; placed appropriate delivery dates on new orders and inquiries received that morning; consulted with a foreman on a personal problem. He spent some twenty minutes at the teletype going over mutual problems with the Eastern plant.

By midafternoon Chet had made another tour of the plant after which he met with the personnel director to review with him a touchy personal problem raised by one of the clerical employees, the vacation schedules submitted by his foreman, and the pending job evaluation program. Following this conference, Chet hurried back to his office to complete the special statistical report for Universal Waxing Corporation, one of Norris' best customers. As he finished the report he discovered that it was ten minutes after six and he was the only one left in the office. Chet was tired. He put on his coat and headed through the plant toward the parking lot; on the way he was stopped by both the night supervisor and night layout foreman for approval of type and layout changes.

With both eyes on the traffic, Chet reviewed the day he had just completed. "Busy?" he asked himself. "Too much so—but did I accomplish anything?" His mind raced over the day's activities. "Yes and no" seemed to be the answer. "There was the usual routine, the same as any other day. Any creative or special project work done?" Chet grimaced as he reluctantly answered, "No."[1]

WHY STUDY BEHAVIOR?

June 23 was probably an average day for Chet Craig in the above case; as a typical young manager he is doing things considered normal for someone in his position. If you review Chet's day, you will find that most of his activities have something in common. In fact, they have something in common with the majority of activities of nearly all managers on that June 23rd, or any other working day. The common denominator is the behavior of people.

This book is about the behavior of people in organizations—the kinds of behavior which you, as a prospective manager, are going to encounter in the course of your work. Regardless of the type of organization you join, whether it's an industrial organization like Chet's or a school, a hospital, a ship, a labor union, a bank, a carnival, an infantry brigade, or a commune, you will probably spend more of your time encountering and dealing with human behavior than in any other type of activity. The purpose of this book is to help you understand human behavior so you can deal with it effectively.

Wait a minute! you may be thinking. I'm not going to be a foreman. I'm studying to be a professional manager, one who can go out and apply expertise in making decisions and solving problems.

Well, it may be true that you are being professionally trained, and perhaps you are acquiring certain technical skills in financial analysis, inventory control, cost accounting, market research, or production scheduling. Nevertheless, you will be applying these skills in some organization. That means you'll be working with and through people, regardless of your position or level in the organizational hierarchy. Even if you *try* to isolate yourself from others, the chances are that you, like Chet, will find yourself constantly involved with people.

---

[1] This case was abridged by permission of Thomas J. McNichols from *Policy Making and Executive Action* (New York: McGraw-Hill Book Co., 1967), pp. 745–50.

What Managers Do

Although hundreds of books and thousands of articles have been written about management and about what managers *ought* to do, very few have been written about what managers *actually* do. From most books and articles about management (and from the curricula of most schools of management) it is easy to get an impression that managers spend most of their time in air-conditioned offices reading reports, thinking, planning, scheming, organizing, creating, and solving. It sounds very cozy and orderly. In reality, however, Chet Craig's workday probably comes much closer to describing the routine activities of actual managers.

Those few systematic studies of managerial behavior that have been published support the Chet Craig image rather than the reflective-thinker image of a manager. Perhaps the best single book on the subject, Henry Mintzberg's *The Nature of Managerial Work*,[2] draws the following conclusions from reviewing the research on what managers actually do.

A manager's day typically consists of brief, varied, and fragmented activities. How brief? How varied? Foremen studied by one researcher averaged between 237 and 1,073 incidents *per day!*[3] Most of these incidents lasted less than a minute; few lasted more than two minutes. They consisted of giving orders, answering questions, dealing with crises, seeking information, evaluating work, answering phones, coordinating with supervisors, settling disputes, listening to complaints, getting instructions, checking on compliance, soliciting ideas, complaining, seeking permission, denying permission, giving permission and so on throughout the day, with virtually no letup.

The manager's routine gets a little better as one moves up the ladder in an organization—but the pattern of brief, varied, and fragmented activity persists. An in-depth study by Mintzberg of chief executives in consulting, research and development, hospital, manufacturing, and educational organizations revealed the same behavioral patterns.[4] These executives engaged in more than 50 dis-

---

[2] Henry Mintzberg, *The Nature of Managerial Work* (New York: Harper & Row, 1973).

[3] R. H. Guest, "Of Time and the Foreman," *Personnel*, vol. 32 (1956), pp. 478–86.

[4] Henry Mintzberg, "The Manager of Work—Determining His Activities, Roles, and Programs by Structured Observation," Ph.D. thesis, M.I.T. Sloan School of Management, 1967.

tinct activities every day, half of which lasted less than nine minutes. The variety of activities included receiving reports, processing mail (usually skimming it and throwing it away), scheduled
meetings, unscheduled meetings, telephone calls, ceremonies, tours
of the plant, dealing with subordinate and client crises—all in what
appeared to the researcher to be random fashion. That is, the only
pattern was that there was no pattern; significant events were interspersed with trivial events; client contacts were interspersed with
superior and subordinate contacts, all in rapid-fire fashion.

Is there no validity to the reflective manager image, then, alone
in a quiet, private, tastefully decorated office ("No calls, please, for
the next few hours—I'm thinking"), leaning back in a large, soft
leather chair, chewing thoughtfully on a pencil, conjuring up a new
sales program or devising some innovative solution to a client program? Such behavior does occur, of course—but more likely at
home than at the office.[5] None of the systematic studies found managers behaving this way more than rarely. For example, one researcher, in studying 160 managers over a four-week period, found
that the typical manager was able to enjoy only nine uninterrupted
periods of at least 30 minutes' duration during all four weeks.[6]

*Managers spend most of their time—by preference—engaged in
verbal, nonroutine, current activities.* The chief executives studied
by Mintzberg spent only one fifth of their time at desk work—and
complained that that was too much time. Meetings accounted for
70 percent of their time, unscheduled meetings averaged only 12
minutes' duration, and scheduled meetings a little more than an
hour. The rest of their time was spent on the telephone (calls averaged 6 minutes each) and on plant tours, which averaged only
11 minutes; this was the one activity in which the executive could
avoid being interrupted.

Mail (both the reading and the writing of it) seemed to be uni-
versally unpopular. The executives received a good deal of mail,
averaging 36 pieces a day, but they often postponed and then spent
little time reading it and even less time responding to it. Less than 1
in twenty pieces of mail evoked a reply from these executives.

A study of Swedish executives found the same aversion to the
written media; some chief executives wrote no more than one or
two letters per week. The researcher noted that "The picture of a

---

[5] For many managers, home is the place to think about work.

[6] Rosemary Stewart, *Managers and Their Jobs* (London: Macmillan, Ltd., 1967).

chief executive as a man who is busy dictating and signing letters was not borne out by any of our studies."[7]

Managers may spend little time in writing or reflection at work, but they devote much time to talking and listening to others. Mintzberg's chief executives said they spent 78 percent of their time in verbal interactions; he reports this was comparable to managers studied by other researchers, 80 percent of their time being devoted to verbal interaction by one group of middle managers,[8] 67 percent by one group of senior and middle managers,[9] and 89 percent by a third group of middle managers.[10]

What do managers do then? The same things you will most likely be doing if your next job is managing: working with other people in a never-ending succession of usually brief, mostly varied, and seldom dull encounters. Even if you happen to find yourself in a staff position on your first job, in which your work is more analytical and advisory than supervisory, you will still have to deal with human behavior to a greater extent than you probably expect— seeking information from others, communicating with others, influencing and being influenced by others.

If your ambitions include rapid promotion and advancement, the chances are that you will not remain in a staff position for very long. A large-scale study of managerial careers showed that the most upwardly mobile managers were in their initial specialty of staff positions (sales, accounting, personnel, engineering, etc.) for a relatively short time.[11] The typical executive-level manager (one who had made it beyond the middle-management level) was in a technical specialty less than three years before moving up to direct supervisory position. The most rapidly advancing manager (one who had reached the executive level before the age of 40) spent an average of only 18 months at the technical specialist level before moving into a direct supervisory position. And virtually all of these executives

---

[7] Sune Carlson, *Executive Behavior: A Study of the Work Load and the Working Methods of Managing Directors*, cited in Mintzberg, *Nature of Managerial Work*, p. 40.

[8] E. E. Lawler, L. W. Porter, and A. S. Tannenbaum, "Managers' Attitudes toward Interaction Episodes," *Journal of Applied Psychology*, vol. 52 (1968), pp. 432–39.

[9] Stewart, *Managers and Their Jobs*.

[10] Tom Burns, "The Directions of Activity and Communication in a Departmental Executive Group," *Human Relations*, vol. 2 (1954), pp. 73–97.

[11] E. E. Jennings, *The Mobile Manager* (Ann Arbor: University of Michigan Bureau of Industrial Relations, 1967).

spent 10 to 15 years directly supervising others before moving to the executive level.

Kinds of Behavior Managers Encounter

What types of behavior can you expect to encounter as a practicing manager in an ongoing organization? What kinds of things do subordinates, supervisors, peers, co-workers, clients, customers, suppliers, concerned citizens, taxpayers, voters, inspectors, and politicians do that you are going to have to understand and deal with?

My father, who has been a manager for more than 30 years, once told me, "Nothing surprises me anymore. If you stick around long enough, you'll have to deal with every kind of human activity there is." I think one of the things he liked best about managing is the never-ending variety of situations and activities with which a manager must cope. Regardless of expertise or level, a manager ultimately deals with the most variable commodity of all—human beings.

It turned out that my father was right. In the five years I spent as a manager, I found myself dealing with a variety of behaviors I would not have thought possible—all the way from unsuspected sacrifice to incredible selfishness. Like you, I once figured my professional training (in industrial management) would put me above the everyday problems of dealing with people. Like Chet Craig, I found that every plan I dreamed up, every decision I made, had to be carried out by people. Not only that, but all the data and information I needed to solve problems and make decisions was not neatly provided for me in a case or textbook; I had to go out and get it (or try to get it) from people.

When you consider that people who work spend more of their time at work than any other single activity, it should not be surprising that they exhibit the wide range of behavior they do. As William Faulkner put it, "You can't eat for eight hours a day nor drink for eight hours a day nor make love for eight hours a day— all you can do for eight hours is work." And in the course of those eight hours at work, people are going to produce work and sabotage it, learn and forget, make decisions and procrastinate, create and conform, exult and despair, come early and not at all, avert catastrophe and cause accidents, get drunk and sober up, fight and reconcile, get excited and become bored, form cliques and get left out, reveal confidences and clam up, understand and misinterpret, take risks and avoid them, accept others and stereotype them, empathize and discriminate, help others and stab them in the back, cooperate and compete, bargain and threaten, lead and follow, harmonize and disrupt, grow and die.

That's what this book is about—the kinds of human behavior you're going to deal with, both the productive and the counterproductive, the pleasant and the unpleasant, as it occurs in today's organizations.

ORGANIZATIONS AS SOCIAL UNITS

Organizations are the major social unit humans have devised for getting things done. In this country, more than 90 percent of those who work do so in some organization.

An organization can be defined as a social unit which has been deliberately designed to achieve some specific goal or goals. Examples of organizations and their goals include the following:

Organization	Goal
Corporation	Profit
Hospital	Healthy community
Army	Secure nation
School	Educated children
Political party	Community power
Police force	Secure community
Civic symphony	Musically cultured community
Prison	Rehabilitated criminals
Church	Saved sinners

Characteristics of Organizations

The important feature of an organization which distinguishes it from other social units such as groups or communities is a deliberate design and specific goals. An organization, therefore, is a human instrument created for some purpose.

During its lifetime an organization's design may change and its goals may expand, contract, or become obscured. For example, an institution designed to protect society from the criminally insane may evolve into an institution designed to socially rehabilitate the criminally insane.

Regardless of such changes, organizations are distinguished from other social units, such as mobs, families, races, tribes, and classes, by their design and objectives. Certain characteristics of organizations promote the achievement of their objectives. These include the division of labor, systems for coordinating and controlling the activities of members, and the ability to change membership. The

division of labor has permitted organizations to produce goods or
services on a large scale, with increasing sophistication. At the same
time, requirements for systems to control or coordinate these activities have increased. Because an organization can acquire and lose
personnel as well as change job assignments, it typically acquires
an identity independent of its members. This identity is usually reinforced by some formal name, such as Hallmark Incorporated, Research Hospital, United States Marine Corps, Rockhurst High
School, Conservative Party, Jackson County Sheriff's Department,
Kansas City Philharmonic, Leavenworth Federal Penitentiary, or
St. Patrick's Church. Not only do such social units acquire an identity
separate from their membership, but the organizations and their
identities typically survive several generations of members.

Interactions of People and Organizations

A manager must learn to deal with many different groups of
people who interact with the organization, as shown in Figure 1-1.

FIGURE 1-1
Groups with Whom a Manager Must Interact

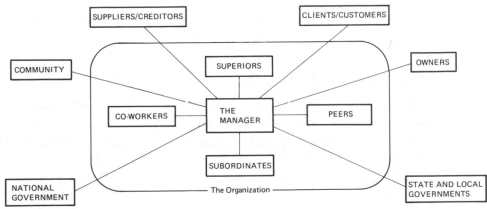

First, of course, there are the people the manager supervises—his or
her *subordinates*. Then there are the manager's *superiors*, including
the boss, the boss's boss, and others at higher levels of the organization. There are also the manager's *peers*, fellow managers at or
near the manager's level in the organization, and *co-workers*, members of the organization at different levels outside the manager's
direct line of authority.

A manager's contacts are not limited to those within the organization. Outside the organization there are the *clients* or *customers* who seek the goods or services the organization provides. There are *suppliers* and *creditors* who provide the organization with the materials, energy, and other resources it needs to function. There are the *owners* of the organization—the stockholders of a corporation; or the taxpayers who support a public institution like a school, a hospital, or an army; or private donors in the case of foundations, museums, and symphony orchestras. There are members of the *community* in which the organization operates, whose interests in the organization may range from aesthetics to preventing pollution. There are the numerous professional and governmental *agencies* that will inspect, investigate, and influence the activities of the organization for reasons of health, sanitation, safety, civil rights, security, or politics.

A manager may be called upon to interact with members of these groups at any time. Each will have a claim on the manager's talent and time, whether he or she is experienced or inexperienced, line or staff. As a manager in one of today's organizations, you will find yourself spending a good deal of your time working through, around, against, over, and with the behavior of others.

PLAN OF THE BOOK

This book is organized around the behavior of people in organizations. It is divided into six parts, as shown in Figure 1–2.

The purpose of Part One is to arouse your interest in learning about behavior in organizations. The first chapter provides an idea of the content and scope of the book, and the second describes the different sources of our knowledge of behavior.

Parts Two and Three deal with individual behavior in organizations. Part Two provides a basis for understanding behavior in general, and individual behavior in particular. It describes three major theoretical approaches to understanding human behavior and presents the major models of individual performance. Different sets of factors which can influence that performance are discussed. Part Three deals with other specific individual behaviors, including perceiving and evaluating, decision making, creating and innovating, and expressing satisfaction and dissatisfaction.

Parts Four and Five deal with group and social behavior in organizations. Part Four provides a basis for understanding group be-

FIGURE 1–2
Organization of the Book

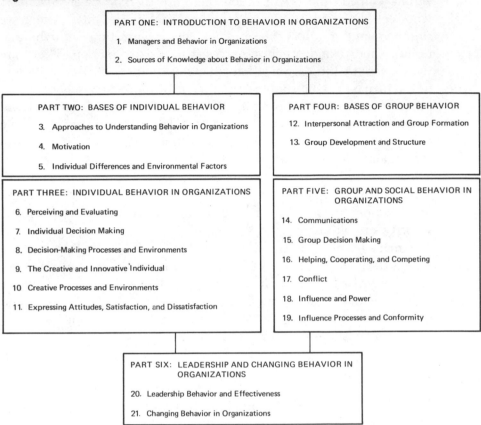

havior, describing why and how individuals form groups, the processes of group development, and characteristics of group structure. Part Five deals with specific group and interpersonal behaviors, including communications, group decision making, helping, cooperating, competing, conflicting, influencing, and being influenced.

Parts Three and Five are designed to provide three sets of information about the behaviors discussed: a description of the behavior and the processes through which it occurs, factors which lead to or affect that behavior, and results, outcomes, or consequences of the behavior. For most of the topics this is accomplished in one chapter, but some information is separated into two chapters to make it easier to grasp.

Part Six discusses two major topics which incorporate much of the material already presented on individual and group behavior: leadership and changing behavior in organizations. The chapter on leadership describes the nature, determinants, and effects of leadership behavior. The final chapter discusses the problem of changing behavior in organizations and describes several behavior-change techniques currently used in organizations.

QUESTIONS FOR REVIEW AND DISCUSSION

1. Do you think that Chet Craig is a good manager? Why or why not?

2. Name the different groups of people with whom the following managers might interact: (*a*) a production supervisor in an assembly plant, (*b*) the director of a public hospital, (*c*) the captain of a commercial airliner, (*d*) the director of a municipal zoo, (*e*) the project leader of an advertising campaign, (*f*) the campaign manager of a local political candidate.

3. What distinguishes an organization from (*a*) a group, (*b*) a mob, (*c*) a family?

Objectives

1. To provide criteria for evaluating different sources of information about behavior in organizations.
2. To present and describe the various sources of information which enable us to learn about behavior in organizations.
3. To give an example of each source.

OUTLINE OF CHAPTER

Criteria for Evaluation of Knowledge about Behavior

Personal Experience as a Source of Knowledge

Methodological Approaches to Studying Behavior

Relatively Less Systematic Approaches
 Cases
 Participant Observation

Systematic Assessment
 One-Time Systematic Assessment
 Longitudinal Assessment

Experimentation
 Laboratory Experiments
 Field Experiments
 Natural Experiments

Summary

Questions for Review and Discussion

chapter two

Sources of Knowledge about Behavior in Organizations

The competitive spirit . . . is the inner drive that for two centuries has made the American workingman unique in the world, that has enabled him to make this land the citadel of individual freedom and of opportunity.

The competitive spirit goes by many names. Most simply and directly, it is called the work ethic.

As the name implies, the work ethic holds that labor is good in itself; that a man or woman at work not only makes a contribution to his fellow man but becomes a better person by virtue of the act of working.

That work ethic is ingrained in the American character. That is why most of us consider it immoral to be lazy or slothful—even if a person is well off enough not to have to work or deliberately avoids work by going on welfare.

I read a report recently about some on welfare in one of our cities who objected to taking jobs that they considered menial. As I read that report, I thought of my own father. During the years that I was growing up, he worked as a streetcar motorman, an oil field worker; he worked as a farmer; he worked also in a filling station.

Let us recognize once and for all—no job is menial in America if it leads to self-reliance, self-respect, and individual dignity.

We must make it possible for workers to try "refresher courses" and "second careers" to open up the chance for a new variety in work.

We must reinstill a pride of craftsmanship, a pride in good service, that results in quality workmanship.

And we must make sure that technology does not dehumanize work, but makes it more creative and rewarding for the people who will operate the plants of the future.

These are the needs of the American worker, taking their place alongside the needs we are more familiar with: the need for real wage increases that actually lead to a better life rather than wage increases which are completely eaten up by price increases, the need for steady employment, the need for a safe and clean place to work, the need for medical care and a secure retirement.

In our quest for a better environment, we must always remember that the most important part of the quality of life is the quality of work. And the new need for job satisfaction is the key to the quality of work.

As the American economy moves toward meeting the new needs of the American worker, what should it look for in return? The answer can be summed up in a single, often misunderstood word: productivity.

That word, productivity, puzzles and sometimes frightens people. It sounds like the old "speedup" or some new efficiency system that drives people harder.

Productivity really means getting more out of your work.

When you have the latest technology to help you do your job, it means you can do more with the same effort. That's why we say investment in modern equipment will increase productivity.

When you have the training you need to improve your skills, you can do more. That's why we say job training will improve productivity.

When you are organized to do away with red tape and duplicated effort, you can do more. That's why we say better management techniques will increase productivity.

And when you have your heart in what you're doing, when it gives you respect and pride as well as a good wage, you naturally do more. That's why we say job satisfaction is a key to productivity.

And so these are the four elements of productivity: investment in new technology, job training, good management, and high employee motivation. Taken together, they raise the amount each worker actually produces.[1]

—Richard M. Nixon

THE ABOVE ADDRESS contains a number of propositions about human behavior in organizations:

- Competition increases productivity.
- Most Americans like to work.
- Most Americans consider work a moral obligation.
- New technology increases productivity.
- Training increases productivity.
- New management techniques increase productivity.
- Job satisfaction increases productivity.
- Satisfaction increases motivation.
- All jobs—even the most menial—are potentially rewarding, respectable, and dignified.

These are important propositions, especially when broadcast by the President of the United States. Each statement has significant implications, both for business policy and for national policy. But are the propositions valid?

[1] From former President Richard M. Nixon's Address to the Nation on Labor Day, September 6, 1971.

There is room for disagreement with virtually every one of these propositions. The disagreements stem from a variety of sources of knowledge about human behavior in organizations. Some come from the evidence of systematic research: "There is little evidence in the available literature that employee attitudes bear any simple—or, for that matter, appreciable—relationship to performance on the job."[2] Some disagreements come from the evidence of personal experience:

> This Nixon was sayin' he don't see nothin' wrong with people doin' scrubbin'. For generations that's all we done. He should know we wants to be doctors and teachers and lawyers like him. I don't want my kids to come up and do domestic work. It's degrading. You can't see no tomorrow there.[3]
>
> —Maggie Holmes

Which is right? Does job satisfaction increase productivity, or not? Who is right—Richard Nixon or Maggie Holmes? Is there dignity in menial work, or isn't there?

These are important questions for people in organizations, both managers and nonmanagers. Therefore they are important questions for you. How do we find the answers to these questions? Where can we go to learn about the behavior of people in organizations?

CRITERIA FOR EVALUATION OF KNOWLEDGE ABOUT BEHAVIOR

In evaluating any method or source of knowledge about behavior, three questions must be asked:

1. *Is it reliable?* That is, will the same situation, if repeated, have the same results? A clock is reliable if it records 60 minutes every single hour, day and night. A performance evaluation is reliable if it gives the same scores to people who perform equally well.

2. *Is it valid?* That is, does it really describe what is going on, does it measure what it is supposed to measure? A clock is a valid indicator of time if it is reliable and has been set properly. A performance evaluation is valid if it is reliable and in fact evaluates performance, if it gives higher scores to better performers than to poorer performers, and if it does not measure something else, such as the evaluator's biases toward the performers.

---

[2] A. H. Brayfield and W. H. Crockett, "Employee Attitudes and Employee Performance," *Psychological Bulletin*, vol. 52 (1955), p. 424. Job satisfaction, its causes and effects, will be discussed in Chapter 11.

[3] A domestic worker, quoted in Studs Terkel, *Working: People Talk About What They Do All Day and How They Feel About What They Do.* © 1972, 1974 Pantheon Books, A Division of Random House, Inc., p. 116.

3. *Is it generalizable?* That is, can what is learned be applied safely to other situations? Under what other conditions is it reliable and valid? Clock time is generalizable on earth; in space or on other planets, it is another matter. A performance evaluation may be generalizable only within a department, a company, or an industry. In other situations, it may not be either reliable or valid.

Unless a source is reliable, it cannot be valid. If it is not valid, it cannot further our understanding. If it is valid but cannot be generalized, it is useful, but its usefulness is restricted. When a source is both valid and generalizable, then it can significantly advance our understanding of behavior.

To give you an idea of how a single subject can be examined by a variety of methods, all the examples of experience and research cited in this chapter deal with the general topics of the behavior of managers and how they achieve success. Other topics have been examined by all these methods; managerial behavior was chosen as an example here for its potential interest to students of organizational behavior.

PERSONAL EXPERIENCE AS A SOURCE OF KNOWLEDGE

Every person derives knowledge of human behavior from personal experience—actually dealing with others in a face-to-face situation. The major advantage of personal experience as a source of information is that knowledge so derived is not easily forgotten. The disadvantages of personal experience generally derive from our limitations as human beings. First, our work experiences, for example, are necessarily limited by our jobs, contacts, and tenure. Second, our interpretations of these experiences can be limited or biased by our individual characteristics, expectations, and previous experiences. Third, our learning from others' experiences is limited by their ability to communicate them to us. Therefore, while personal experiences are often relevant, their usefulness is limited by questions of scope and accuracy.

Two examples of what famous people in the field of management say they have learned about effective managerial behavior from personal experience are given below. As you read them, ask yourself how reliable, valid, and generalizable their knowledge is.

The first example is from the late Douglas McGregor, a well-known psychologist and lecturer in management. Having taught and researched management for several years, he left his positions as professor of psychology and executive director of the Industrial Relations Section at M.I.T. to become president of Antioch College. An essay he wrote on leadership near the end of his six-year tenure reflects his personal experiences:

> Before coming to Antioch I had observed and worked with top executives as an advisor in a number of organizations. I thought I knew how they felt about their responsibilities and what led them to behave as they did. I even thought that I could create a role for myself that would enable me to avoid some of the difficulties they encountered. I was wrong. It took the direct experience of becoming a line executive, and meeting personally the problems involved, to teach me what no amount of observation of other people could have taught.
>
> I believed, for example, that a leader could operate successfully as a kind of adviser to his organization. I thought I could avoid being a "boss." Unconsciously, I suspect, I hoped to duck the unpleasant necessity of making difficult decisions, of taking the responsibility for one course of action among many uncertain alternatives, of making mistakes and taking the consequences. I thought that maybe I could operate so that everyone would like me— that "good human relations" would eliminate all discord and disagreement.
>
> I could not have been more wrong. It took a couple of years, but I finally began to realize that a leader cannot avoid the exercise of authority any more than he can avoid responsibility for what happens to his organization. In fact, it is a major function of the top executive to take on his own shoulders the responsibility for resolving the uncertainties that are always involved in important decisions. Moreover, since no important decision ever pleases everyone in the organization, he must also absorb the displeasure, and sometimes severe hostility, of those who could have taken a different course.
>
> A colleague recently summed up what my experience has taught me in these words: "A good leader must be tough enough to win a fight, but not tough enough to kick a man when he is down." This notion is not in the least inconsistent with humane, democratic leadership. Good human relations develop out of strength, not of weakness.
>
> I am still trying to understand and practice what is implied in my colleague's statement.[4]

---

[4] Douglas McGregor, *Antioch Notes,* May 1, 1954, *31,* No. 9.

The second example of personal experience is J. C. Penney's comments in a book written when he was in his nineties.[5] Penney started his first cash and carry store in Kemmerer, Wyoming, in 1902. Although he was nearly wiped out in the Depression, he succeeded in building J. C. Penney's into a chain of 1,700 stores in 48 states by 1960. He worked until the day he died in 1971 at the age of 95. His book provides a medium for his views on management, based on his 60 years of experience.

Penney's global theory of management is best summarized in his code of Christian Principles in Business. These principles, he said, are not only moral but, happily, effective in business: "Experience has shown their power to be positive . . . they win."[6] He defined these principles as:

1. *Hard work wins.* To paraphrase, managerial success and happiness are directly and positively related to effort. "Clock watchers never seem to be having a good time." (p. 72)
2. *Honesty wins.* To paraphrase, honest managers are more successful than dishonest managers.
3. *Confidence in men wins.* To paraphrase, giving managers increasing responsibility improves their effectiveness.
4. *The spirit wins.* "Business is therefore as much religious as it is secular" (p. 74). To paraphrase, managers who serve others in their work will be more successful than those who serve only themselves.
5. *Practical application of the Golden Rule wins.* To paraphrase, managers who administer by Christian principles will be more successful than those who do not.

These two men convey their experiences in a forceful, convincing fashion. But are their experiences reliable, valid, and generalizable? Had McGregor never been president at Antioch when he was, would he have believed that a leader cannot avoid the exercise of authority? If J. C. Penney had in fact been wiped out by the Depression, would he have believed that hard work and honesty always win?

Are McGregor's convictions generalizable to leaders of communes, as well as colleges? Do Penney's principles "always win"—for disadvantaged persons as well as for WASPs? These are some things their

---

[5] J. C. Penney, *View from the Ninth Decade* (New York: Thomas Nelson & Sons, 1970).

[6] Ibid., p. 69.

personal experiences cannot tell us. While personal experience can provide valuable insights about possible relationships, for validity, reliability, and generalizability more systematic methods of obtaining data about human behavior in organizations are necessary.

METHODOLOGICAL APPROACHES TO STUDYING BEHAVIOR

The methods of studying behavior to be described here have several things in common. First, the researchers attempt to carry out their observations in a manner which minimizes the effects of their own personal characteristics and biases. This is usually referred to as objectivity: the researchers try to report what actually occurred rather than what they would have liked to occur.[7]

Second, the researchers focus on some *variables* of particular interest. They may specify certain variables as being independent, dependent, or moderating. An *independent* variable is thought to affect a dependent variable, while a *dependent* variable is thought to be affected by an independent variable. For example, a researcher studying the relationship between age and senility would specify age as the independent variable (age is not dependent on senility) and senility as the dependent variable (senility is thought to depend on age). A *moderating* variable moderates the effects of the independent variable on the dependent variable. For example, health moderates the effects of age upon senility: A healthy person is less likely to become senile than a sick person.

The more systematic methods of research state one or more hypotheses. A *hypothesis* is a description of the relationship the researchers expect to find between the variables being studied. For instance, it might be hypothesized that women are less likely to become senile than men.

Another thing these methods have in common is their reference to *previous research*. A good method is based on what other studies have discovered about some of the variables in question and is designed to build on that previous knowledge.

Research reports specify how the variables of interest were *observed, investigated, or measured*—what particular techniques or devices were used. This provides other researchers with the opportunity to test the researchers' findings themselves and thus to investigate the reliability and validity of the knowledge provided.

---

[7] Factors which distort or influence perception, judgment, and evaluation are discussed in Chapter 6.

Research reports also describe the *subjects*—the people whose behavior was observed. This is important not only for replicating the research to determine its reliability and validity, but also to give an idea of its generalizability. If certain relationships have been found to hold for male and female, young and old, black and white, student and worker, educated and uneducated, urban and rural subjects, we would feel confident in their generalizability to many populations. If a relationship has been found only with college sophomores, we might wait for additional evidence before generalizing it to senior factory workers.

Systematic research will report the *findings* and/or *conclusions* of the research—what the researcher's observations were about the variables of interest. Finally, such research will lead to *suggestions for further research* to help answer questions raised by the research or to improve the data's reliability, validity, or generalizability.

RELATIVELY LESS SYSTEMATIC APPROACHES

Cases

The case method is the detailed, in-depth observation of a behavioral process in an ongoing organization. The focus is usually narrow, and there are usually only one or two subjects. The researchers usually specify one or more dependent variables of interest and then attempt to describe the subject's entire situation in order to uncover one or more independent variables. The researchers typically act as detached observers and gather most of the data by structured and unstructured interviews and from organization records and files.

Cases are excellent methods for exploring or describing organizational processes. They often provide many suggestions for future research. However, because they usually focus on a small group of subjects in a single organization, their reliability and generalizability cannot be demonstrated. Further, the researchers' objectivity is often strained.

An example of the case method is a study of the early careers of two young managers.[8] The focus of the case was upon the events, characteristics, and impressions of these young men in their first years in business, and the purpose was to uncover some of the fac-

[8] W. R. Dill, T. L. Hilton, and W. R. Reitman, *The New Managers* (Englewood Cliffs, N.J.: Prentice-Hall, 1962).

tors that make for successful managers. Much *previous research* had focused upon the reflections of senior managers, in a more personal-experience approach. Other research had concentrated on the manager's personality characteristics, while excluding those of peers, subordinates, and superiors. In this study, the intent was to examine all of these factors in depth in hopes of discovering key elements in the process of becoming successful as a manager.

The *subjects* of the case were two alumni of the prestigious master of science program in industrial administration at the Carnegie Institute of Technology. Both were young men of superior intellectual ability, ambitious to get ahead and anxious to do well.

The *variables* of interest were managerial success and its causes. Success was *measured* by advancement. One of the subjects, Olin Larson, was advancing rapidly in a large manufacturing organization. He was viewed by superiors and peers as a young man whose promotion possibilities were unlimited. The other subject, Tony Rodwell, had recently been demoted. He had blown an opportunity to become chief of production scheduling in a large factory and instead had been demoted to assistant to the superintendent of shipping.

Factors leading to managerial success were *investigated* by two in-depth, open-ended interviews of two to four hours' duration with each subject. Additional interviews were conducted with friends, associates, and superiors of each subject.

One of the *conclusions* of the case was that a new manager's sensitivity to his surroundings is a key factor in determining his early success. "Comparison of differences in orientation and attitude between Larson and Rodwell suggests some important factors relating man's assumptions about the environment to his managerial effectiveness" (p. 2).

Larson was described as being very sensitive and aware. He treated each assignment "as food for thought and an opportunity to learn" (p. 2). As evidence, the case described how Larson handled an early assignment—maintaining a file of reports for the vice president of control and planning. While others viewed this assignment as routine and uninteresting, Larson described it as important and challenging. Not content merely to maintain files, he used his initiative: He set up an index, made decisions about when to revise and update the file, anticipated changes and additions, and sought outside help in increasing the value of the file to the vice president.

He used the assignment as a means of learning more about the company and increasing his visibility with top management.

Rodwell, on the other hand, was described as less sensitive. He "had difficulty at first in assessing his environment well enough to make use of his other abilities" (p. 2). Rodwell's first assignment was as assistant to the chief of production scheduling; he was led to believe that within a few months he would replace the chief. Instead of using the assignment as an opportunity to learn, Rodwell viewed it as an unimportant, short-term job. In his own words, he made no attempt to gain the confidence or liking of his chief. Instead, he used the opportunity to demonstrate to the chief his own superior technical competence in scheduling.

From such incidents the observers made their conclusions about key factors in early career success. A *suggestion for further research* might be to test their conclusions more systematically on a large sample of new managers. For instance, the sensitivity of managers who were relatively equal in opportunities for advancement and other relevant characteristics could be measured and then, over the span of a few years, it could be observed whether the more sensitive managers actually advanced more rapidly than their less sensitive counterparts. While this case, like others, was useful in uncovering possible independent variables in a process, more systematic research on larger populations is necessary before it could be said that "Sensitivity to one's environment is a key determinant of managerial success."

Participant Observation

Participant observation is a variant of the case method in which the researchers carry out the study from their positions as members of an organization, rather than as detached observers. Participant observers feel their data are more reliable and valid if their roles as researchers are masked by their roles in the organization. Detached observation runs the risk that subjects will manipulate their behavior so as to mislead observers; that is, subjects tell the researchers what they want them to hear and let them see what they want them to see—they do not act "natural." By first becoming a member of the organization, a researcher can use subtle and covert methods to minimize the effects of conducting research on a subject's behavior.

There are certain problems with participant observation. First, there is an ethical aspect to researching naive subjects. The researcher must take pains not to embarrass, discomfort, or endanger subjects. For example, an observer of unethical or illegal behavior is faced with the problem of protecting the subject's identity. Second, becoming involved as a participant may affect the researcher's objectivity. Thus, while participant observation enables us to learn about behavioral processes to which we may otherwise have no access, its reliability and validity are difficult to demonstrate.

An example of participant observation is a study of managerial careers which was part of a larger investigation of managerial behavior.[9] The *research question* for this study was: What are the bases on which managers are chosen and promoted? *Previous research* had focused on the relationship between individual traits and rank and had found that certain characteristics, such as education and social group, are often related to selection for promotion in the management hierarchy.

The *subjects* of the research were the 226 managers of a manufacturing plant with 8,000 employees, located in a heavily industrialized urban area of the central United States. There were 36 staff members, 36 superintendents, 61 general foremen, and 93 first-line foremen in the managerial group.

The *variables* of interest were selection to and promotion within management, and the factors that appeared to contribute to selection and promotion. The *dependent* variables of selection and promotion were *measured* by data collected from the company's personnel files and organizational chart.

Factors influencing selection and promotion were investigated by observation of the researcher, who managed to acquire a staff position in the plant. This position enabled him to acquire information about promotion and selection policies by developing personal relationships with 70 managers and 11 workmen in the plant. Informal discussions with these "intimates" provided the bulk of his information. In addition, he interviewed another 113 managers and 27 nonmanagers at the plant. His position as staff member gave him access to personnel files and let him observe managers in action, attend meetings, and overhear remarks. Events, gossip, and discussions were recorded in a daily work diary. Socializing with the other managers at the local yacht club and at lodge meetings, and with managers and workers on days off, was another source of information.

_____
[9] Melville Dalton, *Men Who Manage* (New York: John Wiley & Sons, 1959).

Discussions and interviews led to conflicting suggestions as to why certain people were selected for or promoted within management while others were not. High-ranking company officials and the suggestions in supervisory manuals and handbooks generally agreed that ability and hard work, coupled with traits such as honesty, flexibility, and integrity, determined success. The high officials denied, without being asked, that informal factors affected advancement. However, discussions with intimates among skilled workers, first-line foremen, and staff suggested that ability was less important than other, less formal characteristics, particularly membership in the Masonic order and in the local yacht club.

Assuming that if ability determined advancement, then factors affecting ability such as age, education, and work experience should be similarly related, the researcher collected data on these factors from personnel files. He found such great variation in age, education, and experience within and between ranks that he hypothesized other forces might be at work. He therefore examined four other factors as possible "aids" to career advancement: (1) being a Mason and not being a Catholic (the Church prohibited Catholics from becoming Masons); (2) being of Anglo-Saxon or German descent; (3) belonging to the yacht club; (4) being a Republican.

The researcher's *conclusions* were that such informal factors were indeed related to managerial selection and advancement. Although it was estimated that a substantial majority of the city's population was Catholic, 69 percent of the plant managers were Masons. A random sampling suggested that persons of Anglo-Saxon or German descent comprised less than 38 percent of the city's population, but they made up some 85 percent of the managerial group.

The researcher further found that almost all managers were Republicans, or pretended to be: managers carried only "Republican" newspapers into the plant; all managers who had previously held public office did so as Republicans. Finally, the researcher reported that while membership in the yacht club appeared less related to management rank than ethnicity and religion, 114 of the 226 managers were members.

A *suggestion for further research* would be to investigate whether informal factors are important to managerial success in other kinds of organizations and in other regions of the country. It would also be of interest to investigate whether organizations in which informal factors determine success are more or less effective than organizations in which managerial advancement is based on merit.

SYSTEMATIC ASSESSMENT

Whereas case studies and participant observation are usually carried out over a period of weeks or months, systematic assessment attempts to measure variables of interest at a particular point in time. It typically includes the use of questionnaires to measure attitudes, expectations, values, and beliefs. Large numbers of subjects are usually involved.

One-Time Systematic Assessment

Systematic assessment is a good method for determining the strength of the relationship between two variables. Because large numbers of subjects can be studied, it is often possible to demonstrate high reliability and to assess the generalizability of the data. However, because one-time systematic assessment involves the measurement of several variables at the same time, it is difficult to infer cause-effect relationships among the variables. If, for example, questionnaires reveal that persons with family problems spend more time at work, we cannot infer whether the problems affect their work habits, or whether their work habits cause the problems, or whether problems and work habits are caused by one or more unobserved variables. There are sometimes problems with the validity of questionnaire research. When a worker is asked questions about his fellow workers, for instance, the researchers may be measuring something other than the worker's sociability attitude, such as his perceptual complexity.

An example of a one-time systematic assessment is a study of absenteeism of managers.[10] The *research question* was: What is the relationship between the needs of managers and their rate of absenteeism? *Previous research* had suggested that managers whose needs are satisfied are less likely to resign, and managers at higher levels tend to be more satisfied than those at lower levels.

The *subjects* of this research were 40 managers selected by sampling from four hierarchical levels of a state liquor control board. Their responsibilities ranged from supervisor to board member. The *variables* studied were the need satisfaction of the managers and their rate of absenteeism. Need satisfaction was *measured* by a

---

[10] L. G. Hrebiniak and M. R. Roteman, "A Study of the Relationship between Need Satisfaction and Absenteeism among Managerial Personnel," *Journal of Applied Psychology*, vol. 58, no. 3 (1973), pp. 381–83.

questionnaire completed by the managers. Each question asked the respondent manager how much of a certain quality (e.g., job security, opportunity for independent thought and action) there was for his position, and how much he felt there should be. The difference between how much the manager said there should be and how much he said there actually was provided a measure of need dissatisfaction. Absenteeism was *measured* by recording from official payroll records the number of days each manager had been absent during a year.

The *hypothesis* being tested was that absenteeism is positively correlated with need dissatisfaction among managers. Note that the hypothesis does *not* state that dissatisfaction *causes* absenteeism, because a one-time systematic assessment cannot determine causality; it can only determine if two or more variables are related.

The *results* of the study supported the hypothesis. The correlation between need dissatisfaction scores and absenteeism rates was .53. There is less than one chance in 100 of obtaining a correlation as high as .53 if the two variables were not related, so we accept the data as supporting the hypothesis. Managers with higher levels of need dissatisfaction had greater rates of absenteeism than managers with lower levels of need dissatisfaction. In fact, further statistical analyses revealed that the relationship held true regardless of hierarchical level: for board members and unit supervisors alike, dissatisfaction and absenteeism were correlated.

A *suggestion for further research* from the study would be to test the relationship between need dissatisfaction and absenteeism for managers in other types of organizations (manufacturing, educational, and service, for example). This would enable us to see whether the results are applicable to managers in general or only to those in certain organizations.

Longitudinal Assessment

A variant of systematic assessment is a longitudinal assessment, in which the variables of interest are measured at two or more points in time. This method, when coupled with certain techniques for statistically analyzing data, makes it possible to cope with one of the major problems of one-time assessment—determining cause-effect relationships. By examining the strength of relationships among variables at different points in time, we can often infer which variables are independent and which are dependent, as the example below will demonstrate. One problem with this type of study is that the researcher must study the same subject at every point in time. If a subject is present for one measurement and not for another, the data for that subject are worthless.

An example of a longitudinal assessment is a study of manager satisfaction and performance in which the *research question* was: What are the relationships among merit pay, satisfaction, and performance of managers?[11] *Previous research*, an experimental laboratory study of workers, had indicated that merit pay improves performance, while bonuses in general, even if not merited, improve satisfaction. Thus satisfaction and performance are not necessarily related.

The *subjects* chosen were 62 first-line managers in marketing and finance for a large equipment manufacturer. Each manager had at least four subordinates. The variables studied were the job satisfaction and performance of these managers, and the merit salary increases they received. Satisfaction was *measured* by a ten-item questionnaire asking each manager to express satisfaction or dissatisfaction with certain aspects of his job. Performance was measured by asking two of each manager's peers to rate the quantity and quality of his performance on a scale from 1(low) to 7(high). Merit pay was measured by obtaining from company salary records each manager's annual salary increase minus cost-of-living adjustments and expressing this difference as a percentage of his previous year's annual salary. Each of these variables—merit pay, satisfaction, and performance—was measured for each manager at the time of the company's annual salary-performance review in one year (time 1) and at the same time one year later (time 2).

The *hypotheses* being tested were that merit pay affects both job satisfaction and performance, but that job satisfaction does not affect performance. Note that in this systematic assessment, the effect of one variable on another could be tested because the research was longitudinal—measures were taken at different points in time. Special statistical techniques[12] can be used in these studies to infer cause-effect relationships by examining the relative size of correlation coefficients between variables across time periods. For instance, if the correlation between merit pay in 1969 and performance in

---

[11] C. N. Greene, "Causal Connections among Managers' Merit Pay, Job Satisfaction, and Performance," *Journal of Applied Psychology*, vol. 58, no. 1 (1973), pp. 95–100.

[12] Cross-lagged correlational analysis and frequency of change in product-moment correlation techniques.

1970 was greater than the correlation between pay in 1970 and performance in 1969, and greater than the correlation between both pay and performance in 1969, we would feel it more likely that pay causes performance and less likely that performance causes pay.

The *results* supported some of the hypotheses. Managers who received merit pay became more satisfied than those who did not, supporting the hypothesis that pay is a cause of satisfaction. Managers who were satisfied did not outperform managers who were less satisfied, supporting the hypothesis that satisfaction is *not* a cause of performance. Regarding cause-effect relationships between pay and performance, however, the results were equivocal. Managers who received more merit pay at time 1 outperformed their lesser paid peers at time 2. However, managers who were rated high performers at time 1 received more merit pay than their lower performing peers at time 2. Apparently, merit pay leads to good performance, but good performance also leads to merit pay.

A *suggestion for further research* would be to test the results of this study in an experimental field design in order to determine more clearly the extent of the cause-effect relationships suggested by the research. Another suggestion would be to investigate what organizational rewards besides pay (e.g., recognition, promotion, fringe benefits) affect managerial performance and satisfaction.

EXPERIMENTATION

The key factor in experimentation is the *manipulation* of one or more variables by the researchers. It is usually hypothesized that one or more independent variables have certain effects on a dependent variable. Then an experiment is designed which allows the researchers to change the independent variables systematically and measure the effect of those changes on the dependent variable. This can be done by allowing the independent variable to vary for each subject and measuring the change in each subject's behavior. For example, the intensity of noise in a room could be varied and the researchers could observe how subjects' work rates changed as a function of the noise. This is called a *within-subjects* design. Researchers can also apply different levels of the independent variable to different groups of subjects and observe differences in behavior between the groups. For example, some subjects might work in a very noisy room, some in a slightly noisy room, and some in a perfectly quiet room. This is called a *between-subjects* design.

Because experimentation usually involves the passage of time (the work rate is noted, the noise level is changed, and then the work rate is noted again) *control groups* are often used to test whether the changes in the experimental groups' behavior were due to the experimental manipulation of the independent variable or simply to the passage of time. The behavior of the control group is usually measured just like that of the experimental group, but independent variables are not manipulated.

Laboratory Experiments

The key word in laboratory experimentation is control. The researchers usually have a limited number of variables they want to manipulate or observe. By conducting the experiment in some artificial setting under their control, they can eliminate many random errors caused by changes in variables which they do not want to measure or study. If temperature or noise or age or education might affect the variables they are studying, they can control these effects by conducting the study in a room where temperature and noise can be regulated and by selecting subjects of only a certain age range and educational background.

Laboratory experiments have certain problems. One is that in controlling so many variables the researchers may unwittingly disclose their hypotheses to the subjects, who then alter their behavior accordingly. These *demand characteristics* of the laboratory situation sometimes induce the subjects to behave just as the researchers hoped, but contrary to the way the subjects would have normally behaved. This, of course, can diminish the reliability, and thus the validity, of the research. A second problem is with generalizability. Some question whether behavior under artificially controlled conditions is the same as behavior under natural, uncontrolled conditions. Replication of laboratory experiments in ongoing organizations gives us confidence in the generalizability of findings of such research.

An example of a laboratory experiment is a study of managers' and union representatives' perceptions of each other.[13] The *research question* was: How is the perception of someone's personality affected by the role in which he is believed to be functioning? *Previous research* had indicated that individuals' roles affect the way

---

[13] Mason Haire, "Role Perceptions in Labor-Management Relations: An Experimental Approach," *Industrial and Labor Relations Review*, vol. 8 (1955), pp. 201-16.

they are perceived. For instance, college students had a difficult time perceiving a factory worker as intelligent.

The *subjects* for the study were 76 members of a union's central labor council and 108 industrial relations and personnel managers. All union representatives and management representatives lived and worked in San Francisco. *Independent variables* were the role of the perceiver (union or management) and the role of the perceived (union or management). The independent variables were *manipulated* by giving each subject two pictures and descriptions of men, one described as the secretary-treasurer of a union, one as a local manager of a small branch manufacturing plant. The pictures were of "ordinary" middle-aged, moderately dressed men with neutral expressions. The descriptions contained the information that the man was around 46, was healthy, was married, had a family, had several successful jobs, had few hobbies, read newspapers, and fixed things around the house.

Pictures, roles, and descriptions were rotated among the subjects so that each combination of picture, role, and description was seen by an equal number of subjects among both the 76 union representatives and the 108 management representatives. The *dependent variable* was how the subject described the men in the pictures. The *measure* was a list of 290 adjectives describing personality characteristics. Each subject was told to look at the picture, role, and description and then check the adjectives he thought best described that person's personality.

The *hypothesis* was that, regardless of picture or description, both groups of subjects would describe the "union secretary-treasurer" as greatly different from the "local plant manager."

The *results* soundly supported the hypothesis. The 108 management representatives described the man in the picture much more favorably when they were told he was a plant manager than when they were told he was union secretary-treasurer. For instance, the adjectives most frequently used by the management representatives to describe the plant manager were "honest, conscientious, dependable, adaptable, sincere." However, the adjectives they used to describe the union secretary-treasurer included "aggressive, argumentative, opinionated, outspoken."

The 76 union representatives described the man in the picture differently, depending on whether they were told he was a plant manager or a union secretary-treasurer. If told he was a plant manager, the union representatives were less likely to describe him as "active, friendly, honest." If told he was union secretary-treasurer, they were more likely to describe him as "aggressive, ambitious, active, efficient."

A *suggestion for further research* from this study might be to investigate the causes of these differences in perception: Do managers view union men less favorably because of their own experiences or because other managers expect them to hold such views? Another suggestion would be to investigate the effects of these differences in perceptions. Do they affect communications, bargaining, and trust? Both suggested studies would likely require further experimental designs.

Field Experiments

The major difference between a field experiment and a laboratory experiment is that field experimenters relinquish some of their control over "extraneous" variables in order to conduct their experiments in an ongoing organization. This enhances the generalizability of findings.

In addition to variations caused by uncontrolled variables, field experimenters have other problems, not the least of which is ethical. Because work is such an important part of people's lives, often involving their self-concepts as well as their livelihoods, the extent to which researchers are justified in manipulating variables which will significantly affect the subjects' work behavior is open to question. This, plus the reluctance of many organizations to allow researchers to "fiddle around" with their systems, accounts for the relative scarcity of field experiments.

An example of a field experiment is a study of the effects of human relations training on the leadership behavior and performance of managers.[14] The *research question* was: How will the behavior and performance of managers be affected by their participation in a human relations training program? *Previous research* on the effects of such programs had not been very convincing. Much of it had focused on the effects of such training on attitudes, and most studies had failed to observe a control group (a group which does not participate in the program) to provide a basis for evaluating change in the experimental group.

---

[14] H. H. Hand and J. W. Slocum, Jr., "A Longitudinal Study of the Effects of a Human Relations Training Program on Managerial Effectiveness," *Journal of Applied Psychology*, vol. 56, no. 5 (1972), pp. 412–17.

The *subjects* of this research were 42 line and staff managers randomly selected from the same hierarchical level of a Pennsylvania steel plant. Half of the managers were randomly assigned to the experimental group which would undergo the human relations training, and the remaining 21 became the control group, which did not receive the training. Both groups were very similar in important characteristics, such as education, length of service in present position, and position in the company hierarchy. The similarity of the groups is important; otherwise, we could not tell whether differences in their posttraining performance were due to the training or to differences in other characteristics.

The *variables* investigated were as follows. The *independent* variable was the human relations training program: half the managers participated, half did not. The program consisted of 90-minute training sessions given once a week for 28 weeks. It included discussion of managerial styles, individual and group exercises in group dynamics, and lectures on theories of motivation. The *dependent* variables included the manager's attitudes toward self and others, his leadership behavior, and his effectiveness.

Attitudes were *measured* by a 64-item questionnaire. Leadership behavior was measured by questionnaires administered to both the managers themselves and to their subordinates. Both leadership questionnaires asked the respondent to describe how often the manager performed 40 different activities (e.g., emphasizing work, treating subordinates as his equal). The manager's effectiveness was measured by ratings from his superiors on his knowledge, aggressiveness, reliability, cooperation, and organizing ability. All measures were taken prior to the training program, 90 days after completion of the program, and 18 months after completion of the program.

The *hypothesis* was that as a result of the training program managers would develop attitudes more sensitive to themselves and others, would more frequently structure their subordinates' work and show their subordinates consideration, and would be rated as more effective by their superiors.

The results supported most of the hypotheses—over the long run. No significant differences in either attitudes or behavior were found between the experimental group and the control group of managers 90 days after the program was completed. However, 18 months after program completion, the members of the experimental group (those who had participated in the program) revealed more sensitive attitudes toward themselves and others, more frequently showed consideration to their subordinates, and were rated as significantly more effective than the members of the control group. In fact, in showing consideration to subordinates and in ratings of effectiveness, the control group regressed, while the experimental group improved over the 18 months. Although no changes in structuring subordinates' work were reported for either group over either the short run or the long run, the program was considered successful.

One *suggestion for further research* would be to investigate whether it really takes two years for changes in managerial attitudes and behavior resulting from human relations training to become evident, and, if so, why, and how the process might be speeded up. Such research would probably require a similar design—a longitudinal field experiment.

Natural Experiments

A somewhat rare variant of experimentation is the natural experiment. Like a field experiment, it is conducted in an ongoing organization. Unlike other types of experiments, in a field experiment the independent variables are not manipulated by the experimenters but are allowed to occur as a natural function of the organization's process. The major advantages of natural experiments are that they are natural and thus more acceptable to organizations and other skeptical researchers, and they relieve the researchers of ethical problems in manipulation. The major disadvantage is the researchers' loss of control as to when and how the independent variables change.

An example of a natural experiment is a study of the performance of managers at AT&T over a five-year period.[15] The *research question* was: How do a company's initial expectations for a young manager affect his subsequent performance and success? *Previous research* had found that managers who had been assigned challenging goals improved their performance, while those assigned impossible or easy goals did not improve as much. Other research had found that managers tend to improve their performance when it falls short of company expectations.

The *subjects* of the study were 62 college graduates originally hired as management trainees by AT&T. Of these, 44 had been hired

---
[15] D. E. Berlew and D. T. Hall, "The Socialization of Managers: Effects of Expectations on Performance," *Administrative Science Quarterly*, vol. 11, no. 2 (1969), pp. 207–23.

by subsidiary B of AT&T; 18 had been hired by subsidiary D one year later. Most had joined AT&T directly after graduation, although a few had served in the armed forces or had worked briefly for another company.

The *independent variables* were the expectations of AT&T for each manager's performance. This is called a *natural* field experiment because the independent variables were not manipulated by the experimenters but occurred in the natural course of the company's operations. The independent variables were *measured* by interviews with each manager's superior and later with the manager himself. They covered 18 categories of expectations, including such factors as technical competence, communications skills, self-development, productivity, and initiative. The company's expectations for a given manager were rated from 1(low) to 3(high) on each of the 18 categories.

The *dependent variables* included measures of both success and performance. Success was measured by obtaining from company records each manager's increase in salary over the course of the study (five years), and by rating each manager from 1(low) to 10(high) based on end-of-study interviews with his superiors. Performance was measured by averaging the manager's company performance evaluations over the course of the study and by comparing his rated contributions to those expected of him by the company. All measures were repeated every year for five years.

The *hypothesis* tested was that new managers given demanding and challenging assignments for their first jobs would have greater success and better performance records than those given less demanding initial assignments.

The *results* generally supported the hypothesis. In subsidiary B, managers who had been given demanding first-job assignments received a significantly greater overall contribution and performance index, a better overall appraisal and potential, and greater salary increases than those whose initial jobs were less challenging. In subsidiary D, managers with demanding initial jobs were significantly higher on all performance and success criteria after four years than those with less demanding initial assignments.

A *suggestion for further research* from this study would be to investigate why certain managers receive initially demanding job assignments, while others do not. A second suggestion would be to investigate why initial company expectations are so important. Do they affect the manager's motivation or evaluation, or both?

SUMMARY

In this chapter we have reviewed several methods of deriving knowledge about human behavior in organizations. Each method has its advantages and disadvantages, especially concerning the criteria of reliability, validity, and generalizability of the findings. Personal experience leaves lasting impressions but is weak in all three criteria. Most of "what we know" comes from more systematic methods.

Case studies are rich in detail but lack generalizability. In practice they are seldom based on theoretical principles. Cases provide insights, but it is nearly impossible to prove or disprove anything via the case method. Participant observation is a method of improving the reliability and validity of such in-depth approaches, but it still lacks generalizability.

Systematic assessment can be both reliable and generalizable, but it cannot confidently test cause-effect relationships. Longitudinal assessment can uncover possible cause-effect relationships, but reliability often suffers from the time lapses between assessments.

Experimentation is superior for determining causes and effects. Laboratory experiments offer the greatest control and confidence in their findings, but this control decreases their generalizability. Field experiments sacrifice some control for greater generalizability but often raise ethical questions. True natural experiments have one major shortcoming—they occur so infrequently that few researchers ever have the opportunity to investigate them.

Most of the research on which this book is based comes from the more systematic methodologies: assessment and experimentation. It is hoped that occasional references to participant observations and case studies will illuminate some behavioral processes. Personal experiences (only a few of which are the author's) will be used as examples to assist your understanding of the concepts and processes which have been uncovered by systematic research.

QUESTIONS FOR REVIEW AND DISCUSSION

1. What criteria should be used in evaluating sources of information?

2. What are the shortcomings of personal experience as a source of knowledge? What are its advantages?

3. What are the weaknesses of cases and participant observation?

4. What is the difference between an independent and a dependent variable? Give an example of a relationship between two variables and state which is independent and which is dependent.

5. What are the advantages of experimentation over systematic assessment? What are the advantages of systematic assessment over experimentation?

6. Which of the methods discussed might pose special problems for researchers?

7. Analyze some recent decision made by the federal government or your local governments. What sources of information were used? Evaluate the reliability, validity, and generalizability of those sources.

KEY WORDS

Reliability   Participant observation
Validity   Systematic assessment
Generalizability   Longitudinal assessment
Independent variable   Laboratory experiment
Dependent variable   Field experiment
Objectivity   Hypothesis
Case study

part two
Bases of Individual Behavior

3
Approaches to Understanding Behavior in Organizations

4
Motivation

5
Individual Differences and Environmental Factors

PART TWO develops a framework for understanding the behavior of individuals in organizations.

Chapter 3 discusses three different approaches that have been taken in promoting understanding of behavior in organizations: the cognitive approach, the reinforcement approach, and the psychoanalytic approach. The basis for each approach is presented, its key concepts and processes are defined, and brief examples of applications are given. The chapter concludes with a review and comparison of the three approaches.

Chapter 4 proposes that individual performance should be regarded as a function of ability and motivation. Two different models of the motivation of behavior in organizations are described in some detail: expectancy models which are derived from the cognitive approach discussed in Chapter 3, and the operant model, which is a reinforcement approach. The chapter concludes with a comparison of the expectancy and operant models in terms of the variables they emphasize, research evidence, and differences in predictions.

Chapter 5 emphasizes the importance of differences among individuals and how the environment affects ability and motivation. Classifications of needs which assist understanding of individual differences in motivation are presented, and their importance in certain kinds of performance is reviewed. Both the physical and social environments are shown to be capable of affecting individual motivation and abilities. The chapter concludes with a summary of the roles of abilities, motivation, and the environment in performance and a discussion of some implications for managers.

Objectives

1. To present three different sets of assumptions about behavior in organizations: the cognitive approach, the reinforcement approach, and the psychoanalytic approach.
2. To compare the three approaches.
3. To discuss the relevance of each for understanding behavior in organizations.

chapter three

Approaches to Understanding Behavior in Organizations

Toby dropped a cube of sugar into his coffee and ambled over to the table where two of his co-workers waited.

"You know," said Toby as he eased his bulk into a chair, "what Marilyn did today was really something. Not many managers would stick their necks out for us the way she did."

"You better believe it," replied Lenny moving over to make room for Toby. "I thought old Herbert was gonna choke when she dumped the blame for that shortage right back in his lap. You know he wanted her to make us come in this weekend to cover up for his mistake."

"Yeah, and he wasn't about to see us get paid double time, either; you can bet on that," added Jeri, the third member of the trio.

"No way," agreed Lenny. "You know something? I've never worked for anybody who sticks up for us like Marilyn. This isn't the first time she's kept one of the big boys off our backs. Most other bosses I've had would've just said, 'Yes, Mr. H," and come back to us with one of those 'I can't help it, gang, you know how vice presidents are' numbers. And we'd be here this weekend correcting his errors on our time."

"I wonder what makes Marilyn like that?" mused Toby. "You know—willing to risk her job for us when she thinks we're right."

"I think she's just a person with a strong conscience," offered Lenny. "She's the type that'd just feel too guilty letting Herbert get away with something like that. I mean, she has the thing about getting ahead, all of them do. But she also has this view of herself as a person who looks out for her people first, and she could no more let us hang than she could fly."

"I don't know about conscience and ideals and all that," replied Toby. "I think she's just got a good attitude toward us, and a kind of hostile attitude toward Herbert and his kind. I think she expects that if she lets people push us around, she'll lose the old man's respect—and ours. She believes that respect is a key to getting ahead in this company."

Jeri stubbed out her cigarette and stood up to leave. "It could be

simpler than either of you think," she said. "Marilyn acts that way because
it works. When she sticks up for us, we put out for her harder than ever.
We've got the best production record in the company now, and everybody knows it. Besides, have you ever seen how the brass reacts when
she's stood up to one of them? They don't give her any guff for a long
time, believe me."

"Well, whatever the reasons, let's hope she keeps it up," said Toby,
hoisting himself out of his chair." "Let's get back to work."

THE IMPORTANCE OF ASSUMPTIONS ABOUT BEHAVIOR

IN THE SITUATION described above, Toby, Lenny, and Jeri are trying
to understand the behavior of their supervisor. To all of them, it is
important behavior which they would like to see continue, but each
understands it in a different way.

To Lenny, Marilyn's behavior is a function of her personality. In
his eyes, she stands up for her workers because her conscience and
her self-concept will not allow her to do otherwise. Lenny is taking
what is called a *psychoanalytic* approach to understanding Marilyn's
behavior. That is, he believes her behavior is a result of certain
enduring characteristics of her personality.

To Toby, Marilyn's behavior is a reflection of her attitudes and
beliefs. She stands up for her department because she has favorable
attitudes toward her workers and hostile attitudes toward those who
would abuse them. She demands respect because she believes respect leads to success in the company. Toby is taking a *cognitive*
approach to understanding Marilyn's behavior. That is, he perceives
that her behavior results from mental concepts such as beliefs, attitudes, and expectations.

Jeri explains Marilyn's behavior in terms of its outcomes or results. She believes Marilyn stands up for her workers because that
behavior usually results in outcomes which reward or please her:
the employees work harder, and superiors show her respect. Jeri is
taking a *reinforcement* approach to understanding Marilyn's behavior. That is, she sees Marilyn's behavior as being influenced by
its consequences, by what happens to Marilyn's environment (in
this case, by changes in the behavior of her subordinates and
superiors).

In the course of their discussion, Toby, Lenny, and Jeri reveal
some of their assumptions about the nature of people. These assumptions are likely to have developed from their own experiences in

organizations, their training and education, and their discussions with others. They serve as general guidelines for their understanding of others' behavior and their own behavior toward others.

Every person has probably developed a set of assumptions or a theory of human behavior. Whether people can clearly express this theory or not, it guides their understanding of how they should behave toward others. These assumptions are also important, even crucial, because different assumptions yield different clues as to how they ought to react to others' behavior.

For example, suppose you were Toby, and you believed that behavior is a result of beliefs and attitudes. You would try to maintain Marilyn's favorable attitude toward you by being friendly or helpful. You might also try to support her belief that she is successful because of the respect others have for her.

If you were Jeri and you believed that behavior is the result of its outcomes, then you might try to reproduce those outcomes that followed Marilyn's previous support of her department. You would work extra hard, encourage your colleagues to do likewise, and try to keep her superiors off her back.

If you were Lenny and believed that behavior is a function of personality, your options in this case would be somewhat limited. You might express views that the ideal supervisor was one who supported his or her workers. If Marilyn let you down, you might try to make her feel guilty or sympathetic. And you would probably hope that Marilyn's personality never changed while she was your supervisor.

Assumptions about the nature of human behavior influence not only our understanding of and reactions to others but the study of behavior as well. In this chapter we will examine the three of the most common sets of assumptions: the cognitive, reinforcement, and psychoanalytic approaches to studying and understanding behavior in organizations.

There are three main reasons why it is useful for you to understand these approaches. First, an understanding of the different assumptions about the causes of behavior will make individual studies or theories about behavior in organizations more meaningful. For instance, if you understand the cognitive approach, you can see why perceptions of reward systems are thought to be at least as important as the reward systems themselves. If you understand the reinforcement approach, you can see why punishment is thought to be a relatively ineffective device for maintaining behavior in organizations. If you understand the psychoanalytic approach, you can see why groups are thought to develop in stages from immaturity to maturity.

A second reason for studying the various approaches to understanding behavior is that they can provide you with a means for classifying what you will learn about organizational behavior. If you can recognize certain theories or studies as influenced by one or another of the three approaches, you will find it easier to understand those theories and studies.

Finally, as you progress through this book, you will be able to decide how useful each approach is in understanding the different types of organizational behavior. Analyzing these assumptions may make you aware of your own assumptions about the nature of behavior. It is hoped you will gain some insight about the usefulness and accuracy of the assumptions you hold.

THE CAUSES OF BEHAVIOR

There is a basic proposition that human behavior is a function of both the person and the environment. We may be concerned with a parking lot attendant's driving, a mail carrier's delivery, a mechanic's repairing, an insurance agent's selling, a medical attendant's nursing, a supervisor's managing, or an executive's decision making. In each case, it can be said that the behavior is a function of both the individual who is behaving and the environment in which he or she is behaving. That is,

$$B = f(P, E),$$

where B stands for behavior, P for the person or individual, and E for the environment.

The speed and efficiency with which the parking attendant parks cars is partly determined by his own characteristics—his driving skill, experience, and health, and how much effort he is willing to expend. His efficiency is also partly determined by characteristics of the environment—the arrival rate of cars to be parked, the number and speed of other attendants, the layout of the parking lot or garage, and the weather.

Likewise, a nurse's patient care is affected by both personal and environmental characteristics. Her nursing skills, her experience with patients, her health, and her effort will affect the speed and quality with which she carries out her routine duties, such as giving medication, collecting information, and monitoring patient conditions. Environmental factors such as the number of patients and other nurses on the ward; the physical arrangements of the ward; demands of the head nurse, doctors, and patients; the nature of patients' conditions; and the availability of medication and monitoring devices will also affect the regularity and quality of her caring for patients.

It would be a useful exercise at this point to list some personal and environmental characteristics which affect job behavior in two or three different occupations, such as:

- The examination performance of a student.
- The supervisory performance of an assembly-line foreman.
- The concert performance of a rock star.
- The flying performance of an airline pilot.
- The decision-making performance of a battlefield commander.
- The racing performance of a jockey.

As you list factors which can affect the rate and quality of a student's exam answers or a commander's decisions or a jockey's rides, you should see how both individual and environmental factors are influential. In addition, you may recognize that individual and environmental factors can *interact* in their determination of individual behavior. Not only does the environment directly affect behavior, but it can alter some individual characteristics, such as effort or health. For example, too much cold and snow may cause the parking attendant's arthritis to flare up, as well as making cars more difficult to park. A change in policy disallowing tips may make him unwilling to put as much effort into care and courtesy. An improved nursing station may permit nurses to put more effort into patient care.

Similarly, the individual may alter the environment in which he behaves.* The parking attendant can scatter sand and rock salt on an icy lot to give himself and the cars he parks more traction. A nurse can establish a set of informal rules for her patients to follow to make her job easier.

So the basic equation $B = f(P, E)$ should read "Behavior is a function of the *interaction* between a person and his environment."

---

* In this book the individual is regarded as being either male or female, whether the reference is to managers, subordinates, or people in general. The occasional use of masculine forms of expression is in the indefinite sense, and they should be interpreted as applying equally to men and women.

This means that the person and his environment determine his behavior both directly, and indirectly by their effects upon each other.

The three approaches to understanding behavior discussed below are all consistent with the proposition that both individual and environmental characteristics affect behavior. However, there are differences among them in the emphasis each places on the person and his environment.

THE COGNITIVE APPROACH

Basis

The cognitive approach heavily emphasizes the role of P (the person) in the equation $B = f(P, E)$. It maintains that conscious mental activities, such as thinking, knowing, and understanding, and mental concepts, such as attitudes, beliefs, and expectations, are major determinants of human behavior.

In the cognitive approach, as in the psychoanalytic approach, there is a strong interest in the behavioral effects of covert (not directly observable) responses. Because we cannot directly observe thinking and understanding, because we cannot touch or see attitudes, values, and beliefs, cognitive theorists must use indirect means to measure what they see as important determinants of behavior. Questionnaires and attitude surveys, for example, are important tools of the cognitive approach.

While there is no single, overall theory of behavior to which all cognitive theorists would agree, there are certain propositions that are common to (or at least not inconsistent with) most cognitive theories. These can be grouped under the headings of cognitive elements, cognitive structure, and cognitive functions.[1]

Cognitive Elements

Cognitive and reinforcement theorists agree that behavior is initiated by a stimulus—a physical object which affects the person in some way. However, cognitive theory is mostly concerned with what occurs between the stimulus and the individual's response to it, or how the stimulus is processed by the person, while reinforcement theory is more interested in the stimulus and the response per se.

---

[1] For a more detailed discussion of the cognitive approach, see M. E. Shaw and P. R. Costanzo, *Theories of Social Psychology* (New York: McGraw-Hill Book Co., 1970), chap. 7.

For instance, if someone offered you $10 to burn this book, and you complied, a reinforcement theorist would concentrate on the observable elements of that sequence (the person who made the offer, the offer itself, the $10, the book, your burning of it, and any subsequent outcomes such as approval of or recognition for your actions). In trying to explain why you burned the book and to predict if you would do it again, a cognitive theorist, however, would concentrate on processes which might apply between the offer and the burning, such as your attitude toward the person and the book, your relative values of education and money, your beliefs as to how the person viewed you, and your expectations for actually receiving the promised $10.

According to cognitive theory, all behavior is organized. The individual organizes his or her experience into cognitions which are then fitted into his or her existing cognitive structure. This structure in turn determines the individual's response.

Cognition　A cognition is the basic unit of cognitive theory—an item of information. It is the internal representation of an experience which occurs between a stimulus and a response and which can affect that response. This relation is depicted below:

$$\text{Stimulus} \longrightarrow \text{Cognition} \longrightarrow \text{Response}$$

An individual perceiving a stimulus processes it into a cognition, which precedes and may affect his response. For instance, a creaking sound may be perceived as the noise made by a loose board being stepped on by a burglar. This interpretation may lead to responses of perspiration, clammy hands, and a quickening heartbeat.

Cognitive Structure

According to cognitive theory, cognitions do not exist in isolation. Instead, they are associated with, modify, and are modified by other cognitions. These associations and relationships among cognitions develop into cognitive structures or systems. The exact nature of a cognitive system depends upon (1) the characteristics of the stimuli which are processed into cognitions and (2) the experience of the individual.

For example, two cognitions, "I fell in the lake" and "I became cold," might join to form a simple cognitive system, "The lake is cold." Here the association is due to characteristics of the stimuli:

wetness and cold occurred almost simultaneously. The two cogni
tions "John was in my room" and "My latest James Brown record
album is missing" might be joined to form the cognitive system,
"John is a thief." Here the association is made because of previous
experiences when John's presence was followed by some object's
absence, or perhaps because of warnings by a third person to "Look
out for light-fingered John." In this example, the cognitive structure developed out of experience, either with John or with a third
person.

Cognitive structures can take various forms. They have a number
of properties and can result in different consequences.

Properties of Cognitive Structure[2]   One property of cognitive
structure is differentiation or multiplexity, which is determined by
the number and variety of different cognitions which make up a
particular system. A system composed of two cognitions, as in the
examples given above, is *simple*. A system composed of cognitions
about war, for example, might contain hundreds or thousands of
cognitions, particularly for a person who has experienced combat.
Such a system would therefore be considered *complex*.

A second property of cognitive structure is a system's unity or
consonance. If the cognitions in a system are basically in agreement,
the system is high in consonance; if a system contains cognitions
which are contradictory, the system is low in consonance. If everything we know about John is unpleasant or derogatory, that system
is highly consonant. A person who has had both good and bad experiences in war and associates with both "hawks" and "doves" will
have a cognitive system about war which is likely to be low in
consonance.

A third property of cognitive structure is the interconnectedness
of a system, or the degree to which it is integrated with other systems. When many cognitive systems are interrelated, they form an
ideology. For example, a person who has negative cognitive systems
regarding war, capital punishment, abortion, drunk driving, and
euthanasia could be said to have a prolife ideology. Where there is
little or no interconnectedness among cognitive systems, the person
is said to have *compartmentalized* systems. A student's cognitive
system regarding ethics for politicians may be completely unrelated
to his cognitive system regarding ethics for students, for example.

---

[2] For more detail on cognitive structures, see David Krech, R. S. Crutchfield, and
E. L. Ballachey, "Cognition," in *Individual in Society: A Textbook of Social Psychology* (New York: McGraw-Hill Book Co., 1962), chap. 2.

Cognitive Functions

Cognitive systems are said to have several functions. Among these functions are giving meaning to new cognitions, generating emotions, forming attitudes, and providing motivation for behavioral consequences.

Meaning According to cognitive theorists, meaning occurs when a new cognition is related to an existing cognitive system. The cognition acquires certain attributes, depending upon how it interacts with one or more cognitive systems. For instance, if you try an entirely new food, the stimulus of that taste acquires meaning as you relate it to similar tastes, or tastes of similar foods, or notions of sweet, sour, hot, or cold. An experience which cannot be related to a cognitive system is said to be meaningless. Most students have experienced some cognitive fact in a course which failed to have any meaning for them because they could not associate it with any existing system.

Emotional or Affective Consequences The interaction between a cognition and cognitive systems not only gives meaning to the cognition but may have affective consequences as well. That is, it may generate feelings of like, dislike, good, or bad. If the new food you are given to eat results in a stimulating and pleasant taste, you may feel "good" about the food and also about the person who gave it to you.

Attitudes When a cognitive system about something acquires affective components, an attitude toward that object is formed. The merger of the cognitive and affective components is thought to generate behavioral tendencies toward the object (e.g., to approach or to avoid it). Attitudes are said to have cognitive (knowledge), affective (emotional), and action (behavioral tendency) components. Your attitude toward cigarettes includes cognitive components: cigarettes are said to be bad for one's health; you may have known heavy smokers who died of lung cancer; you have unpleasant aftertastes after smoking; some of your friends smoke; about one half a cigarette after a heavy lunch produces a pleasant sensation; you cannot concentrate well when smoking. It also includes affective components (you may mostly dislike the effects of cigarette smoking) and an action tendency (you may seldom buy cigarettes).

Motivation The relevance of cognitive theory for the analysis and understanding of observable human behavior lies in the motivation of behavior. First, behavior is said to consist of not only overt actions but also internal factors such as thoughts, emotions, perceptions, and needs. Second, behavior is said to be generated by inconsistencies which arise in the cognitive structure. An inconsistency generates both feelings and tensions which are reduced by behavior, and this behavior can include overt actions or reorganization of cognitive systems. Thus, most cognitive theorists assume that man has an innate need for both cognitive organization and cognitive consistency.

As an example of the dynamics of behavior according to cognitive theory, consider the plight of Jean Johnson, who returns to her apartment after a sales trip late one night. Certain cognitions (a growling stomach, a feeling of emptiness, knowledge that she hasn't eaten since lunch) cause her to conclude that she's hungry. However, a quick search of the refrigerator and cupboards yields the cognition that there is nothing edible in the apartment. Tension arises from inconsistencies between the cognitions of "I am hungry" and "There is no food." Jean could resolve the tension by going next door to ask for food, with a goal of obtaining food which could be eaten and thus satisfying her hunger. In this case, the tensions lead to overt behavior. However, suppose she felt that borrowing food would create greater tensions (embarrassment); so might going to the corner delicatessen (fear). Then the tension could be reduced by cognitive reorganization, such as convincing herself that she is not hungry, or by conjuring up mental images of eating food (obviously a short-term solution), or "forgetting" about her dilemma by doing something else, such as reading the newspaper or watching television.

To summarize, in cognitive theory the individual's response to events is determined by conscious mental activity, and the response can involve either overt behavior or covert organization and reorganization of that which is "known." All behavior is said to be organized; an innate human need for organization and consistency is assumed. Behavior is also regarded as complex, and as comprised of physical, mental, and emotional components.

Some Applications of Cognitive Theory to Organizational Behavior

By its nature, cognitive theory lends itself particularly to human processes such as perception, motivation, and decision making. You will find the influence of cognitive theory in several chapters of this book; the following topics are examples.

Routine Individual Behavior   One of the general models of productive behavior which will be developed in Chapter 4 is the expectancy model. In this model, the effort one puts into performance is said to be a function of one's expectations as to what that level of effort will bring in the way of improved performance and its accompanying rewards.

Decision-Making and Problem-Solving Behavior   Existing cognitive systems are thought to have a heavy influence on problem identification and selection of problem-solving techniques. Cognitive theory has also greatly influenced research into how and why individuals search for additional information, both prior to and after making decisions. These topics will be taken up in Chapters 7 and 8.

Attraction and Association   Much of the material to be discussed in Chapter 12 is related to cognitive theory. Cognitive consistency is often used to explain and to predict attraction between individuals. It is also helpful in understanding the cohesiveness of a group (the attraction of a group for its members) and some of the effects of high cohesiveness on members' behavior.

Perceiving and Evaluating   The area of social perception, discussed in Chapter 6, is heavily influenced by cognitive theory. The chapter will introduce a cognitive model of the perceptual process and will show how cognitive approaches are useful in explaining attribution, judgment, prejudice, and stereotyping.

Influence Processes   One section of Chapter 19 discusses imitative behavior, in which an individual uses the behavior of a model to provide cues for his own behavior in similar situations. One analysis of this process theorizes the use of cognitive processes by which the model's behavior is recorded for future reference by the imitator.

THE REINFORCEMENT APPROACH

Basis

Reinforcement theory grew out of the experimental analyses of behavior by two distinguished psychologists, Ivan Pavlov and Edward Thorndike. Pavlov's research on the digestive processes in dogs eventually led him to formulate the principles of *classical conditioning,* by which a particular response (salivation by a dog) is conditioned to follow a previously unrelated stimulus (the ringing of a bell) by associating the unrelated stimulus to a related one (giving the dog a piece of meat). Thorndike's research on learning led him to postulate his famous *law of effect,* which similarly attempts to explain the association between certain stimuli and responses.

Thorndike's law, which still serves as the basis for contemporary theories of reinforcement, can be paraphrased as follows:

> If a behavioral response to a particular stimulus is rewarded, that response is more likely to be repeated. If a behavioral response to a particular stimulus is not rewarded or is punished, that response is less likely to be repeated.

To illustrate, suppose that an army recruit is presented with a particular stimulus—a request from his drill instructor for volunteers. The recruit's response—volunteering—is rewarded by words of praise from the DI and further rewarded because the chore is to go to the air-conditioned PX for ice cream for the DI, while the rest of the recruits are conducting close-order drill on a hot parade ground. The law of effect predicts that subsequent presentations of the same stimulus, a request for volunteers, would be very likely to elicit the same response from the recruit: he would again volunteer. On the other hand, suppose that his initial volunteering effort was completely ignored, or he was berated for his stupidity in ever volunteering for anything, or his chore consisted of remaining on the hot parade ground to police the area of litter while his fellow recruits are sent to an air-conditioned classroom for a movie on sex education. In this case, the law of effect predicts that subsequent requests for volunteers by that DI would be less likely to elicit a volunteering response by this recruit.

Reinforcement theory tends to stress the E part of the equation $B = f(P, E)$. This emphasis is one characteristic which distinguishes it from both the psychoanalytic and the cognitive approaches, which tend to place more emphasis on the P part of the equation. Whereas psychoanalytic theory and cognitive theory place a great deal of importance on factors *inside* the individual (i.e., personality systems or cognitive systems) to explain behavior, reinforcement theory places a great deal of importance on factors outside the individual (stimuli and outcomes, rewards and punishments).

As with the other two approaches, there is no single "reinforcement theory" which could be stated to the satisfaction of all reinforcement theorists. However, reinforcement approaches are primarily concerned with directly measurable processes—stimuli, responses, and outcomes that are accessible to observers, that is, able to be systematically and reliably measured. The reinforcement approach can be described as follows:

$$S \longrightarrow R \longrightarrow O,$$

where an observable stimulus (S) leads to an observable response (R) which is followed by some measurable outcome (O). The outcome in turn affects the likelihood that the same stimulus will elicit the same response.

Reinforcement Concepts

There are several concepts common to all reinforcement approaches to understanding human behavior.[3]

Stimulus   A stimulus is anything that happens to change the behavior of an individual. A stimulus must be physical or material, observable and measurable. All stimuli are found in the environment of the individual.

Response   A response is any change in the behavior of an individual. In the reinforcement approach, a response occurs because of a stimulus; thus, a stimulus always produces a response, and a response is always brought about by a stimulus.

Reinforcer   A reinforcer is any outcome of a response which results in increasing the relationship between the response and the stimulus which produced it. That is, a reinforcer increases the probability that the stimulus will elicit the same response again. There are two types of reinforcers, positive and negative.

A *positive reinforcer* is an outcome of a response which strengthens the association between the response and the stimulus which produced it whenever the outcome is presented or occurs. For instance, laughter is a positive reinforcer for a comedian. If he tells a joke and the audience roars with laughter, he is likely to repeat that joke before his next audience. Expressions of admiration and graditude are positive reinforcers for most people. If a lawyer takes an afternoon off to try a case without pay for some indigent clients, and she finds herself showered with praise and thanks for her success, she is likely to develop a habit of taking on clients who cannot ordinarily afford a lawyer. An outcome which strengthens a response or makes the response more frequent when the individual experiences it is a positive reinforcer.

A *negative reinforcer* is an outcome which, when *removed*, strengthens the association between a response and the stimulus which produced it. If an individual is experiencing something un-

---

[3] For a more detailed analysis of these concepts and applications of the reinforcement approach, see Albert Bandura, *Principles of Behavior Modification* (New York: Holt, Rinehart & Winston, 1969).

pleasant and his response to a certain stimulus causes the unpleasant experience to stop, the association between the stimulus and his response will be strengthened. The unpleasant experience is called a negative reinforcer.

For example, suppose a street maintenance crew member who suffers from the noise of traffic and machinery is given a special set of earplugs by his supervisor. If he discovers that wearing earplugs eliminates the noise, he is increasingly likely to wear those earplugs when at work in the street. The noise is a negative reinforcer—it strengthens the association between the stimulus (working in the street) and his response (wearing the earplugs).

A supervisor who is continually ignored by her workers may discover that her employees stop ignoring her after she fires one of them. If their ignoring her is unpleasant, her response of firing people may become more frequent. The workers' hostility is a reinforcer for her response of firing someone.

In the same manner, much of what is called *avoidance behavior* is strengthened by negative reinforcers. We tend to walk in the shade in the summer, because moving to shade from direct sunlight removes the negative reinforcers of heat and perspiration. A father changes a baby's wet diaper because it removes the negative reinforcer of the baby's screaming. A worker goes home early because doing so removes the negative reinforcer of bad working conditions. A professor shuts his door because this removes the negative reinforcer of students interfering with his writing. Any outcome which strengthens a response or makes a response more frequent when the individual stops experiencing it is a negative reinforcer.

Extinction   Extinction is the weakening of the association between a stimulus and a response. Extinction occurs because the response is not reinforced; that is, the response neither produces a pleasant experience nor causes an unpleasant experience to cease. The response to the stimulus has no relevant outcome for the individual.

As a response continues to elicit no outcome, the response is weakened, becoming less frequent or less powerful. Eventually, as nonreinforcement persists, the response will cease entirely, be dropped from the individual's repertoire of behaviors, and be "forgotten." It becomes extinct.

Several explanations are given for extinction. One is that nonreinforcement means that the response is ineffective in the attainment of reward, and the individual turns to more rewarding forms of behavior. Sometimes the term *reactive inhibition* is used to explain extinction. This is psychology's version of Newton's third law: For every action there is a reaction. For every response there is a negative psychological reaction, which might be something like fatigue. If the response continues to go unrewarded, the individual will avoid the negative reaction by ceasing the response.

Many examples of extinction can be cited in everyday human interactions. A salesman who never receives an order from a customer eventually stops calling on him. A student who never finds the professor in his office ceases his visits. A suitor whose love is unrequited stops pressing his advances. An engineer whose innovations are ignored becomes less innovative. A girl whose parents turn a deaf ear no longer confides in them. A wide receiver who keeps dropping passes finds the quarterback throwing to him less and less. Television viewing declines in the summer, partly because of the multitude of reruns. A cook whose culinary efforts draw no response from the family turns away from Julia Child. When Willie Mays's swings no longer produce base hits, he retires.

The processes of reinforcement and extinction will be discussed in greater detail in Chapter 4. The concepts of negative reinforcements and extinction inevitably raise the issue of punishment, however, and this will be discussed here briefly.

Punishment Punishment is either the withholding of a reward or the application of an unpleasant stimulus in an attempt to extinguish a response. As positive reinforcement is the administration of a reward, punishment can be the withholding of a reward; and as negative reinforcement is the removal of an unpleasant stimulus, punishment can be the application of an unpleasant stimulus. The object of reinforcement is to strengthen a response; in contrast, the object of punishment is to weaken or extinguish a response.

Punishment can take many forms. A parent spanks a child for running into the street (object: extinction of running into the street; punishment: administration of painful stimuli). A wife rebuffs her drunken husband's sexual advances (object: weakening of alcoholic drinking responses; punishment: withholding of pleasurable stimuli). Criminals are administered corporal punishment or deprived of freedom in an attempt to extinguish their criminal behavior (stop stealing!). A boss yells at a secretary who mistyped a letter (stop making mistakes!). A child hits a playmate who is teasing her (stop pestering!). A coach embarrasses a player by "chewing him out" in front of the crowd (stop fumbling!). Congress votes down funding for a pet Presidential program (stop bombing Cambodia!). The President withholds funds from congressional-backed programs (stop voting down my programs!). A pathology department delays the processing of a certain physician's work (stop insisting on non-routine work!). A physician blocks the refurbishing of the pathology laboratory (stop delaying my work!).

To summarize, the reinforcement approach emphasizes the role of the environment in behavior. The environment of the individual is the source of the initial stimulus which produces a behavioral response. It is the individual's interaction with the environment which results in some outcome. The nature of this outcome (which we could consider a response of the environment) affects the relationship between the stimulus and response, thus affecting the individual's future behavior.

The stimulus produces a response, the response has an outcome for the person, the outcome affects the S–R relationship. If the outcome is the application of a positive reinforcer or the removal of an unpleasant state, the S–R relationship is strengthened.

Some Applications of Reinforcement Theory to Organizational Behavior

The reinforcement approach has wide application to the study of human behavior in organizations. The concepts of reward, behavioral outcomes, and environmental stimuli are relevant to every chapter in this book. A sampling of the reinforcement approaches to organizational behavior to be discussed includes:

Routine Productive Behavior Chapter 4 will describe how variations in administering rewards (called varying reinforcement schedules) can affect the quantity of work produced.

Learning Behavior Reinforcement theory is often referred to as a theory of learning. Chapter 4 discusses how different schedules affect rates of learning, as well as rates of forgetting what was learned (extinction).

Leadership Behavior One application of the reinforcement approach to understanding leadership behavior is the doctrine of *reciprocal causation*, which shows how a group can exert as much influence on a leader's behavior as the leader exerts on the group. This is discussed in Chapter 20.

Conflict One reason why conflict between groups is difficult to resolve is that members often reinforce one another for demonstrating loyalty to their own group and for expressing hostility toward the outgroup. The problems such behavior creates for reducing conflict are discussed in Chapter 17.

THE PSYCHOANALYTIC APPROACH

Basis

The psychoanalytic approach takes the position that human behavior is dominated by the personality. The chief architect of the psychoanalytic approach was Sigmund Freud, whose revolutionary work in the field of psychology included his concept of an unconscious level of mental activity. He claimed that most mental activity is unknown and inaccessible to the individual, but such activity nevertheless strongly influences human behavior.

A second Freudian innovation was in methodology of research. He applied the analysis of dreams to the study of the unconscious; dreams, he said, are a form of wish gratification which provide access to an individual's unconscious mental activity. Dream analysis became an important part of Freud's method of collecting data for the development of his theories.

Freud's concept of the nature and importance of unconscious levels of mental activity, together with his methodologies for studying that activity and his analyses of abnormal behavior, form the bases for the psychoanalytic approach.[4] His inferences about the structure and functioning of the personality are important to the psychoanalytic approach to understanding behavior.

The Structure of the Personality

The central feature of the psychoanalytic approach is the personality, which is described as a dynamic system providing the basis of all behavior. The personality is said to consist of three subsystems: the id, the ego, and the superego. The libido provides the energy for the system.

The Id The id is the original subsystem of the personality. It is the reservoir and source of all the psychic energy which causes the system to function.

---

[4] For more extensive discussion of the psychoanalytic approach, see C. S. Hall and Gardner Lindzey, "The Relevance of Freudian Psychology and Related Viewpoints for the Social Sciences," in *The Handbook of Social Psychology* eds. Gardner Lindzey and Elliot Aronson, 2nd ed. (Reading, Mass: Addison-Wesley Publishing Co., 1968), vol. 1, chap. 4.

The id is often depicted as a "seething cauldron" of wishes or desires demanding immediate gratification. These wishes are derived from the psychological instincts with which each person is endowed from birth. Psychological instincts are based in part on biological instincts and are said to be inherited from the repeated experiences of previous generations. For example, if murder and cannibalism were indeed somewhat common practices for our ancestor *Austra- lopithecus,* as evidence uncovered in the Olduvai Gorge suggests, then such violent aggressive instincts commonly reside in the ids of modern-day people. To Freud, an individual's id is the respository for the psychological instincts inherited from the instincts and practices of all his or her ancestors.

In seeking gratification of these desires, the id is said to be un- burdened by such limiting factors as ethics, morals, reason, or logic. Thus contradictory desires can abide in a single id; for example, the desire to respect one's father and the desire to kill him, or curiosity and fear of the unknown, could exist simultaneously. Although the id is said to be in a constant state of excitation, the contents never change. The instincts or wishes are all present at birth; they are always present; they neither diminish nor multiply; they are never forgotten.

The purpose of the id is to supply psychic energy for operation of the personality system. It does this by providing desires or wishes to be fulfilled, operating on the basis of the pleasure principle. The pleasure principle aims to reduce tensions, whether they be externally caused (as through the deprivation of air) or they arise internally (as a sudden urge to strike something). The goal is to reduce tension to a minimum by providing an immediate gratification of the wish or desire. This is accomplished through the *primary process* of discharging tension as soon as it arises in the id.

The id, then, is an unconscious storehouse of inherited psycho- logical instincts which provides energy to the personality system by generating wishes.

The Ego   The ego is the subsystem that both serves and governs the other two systems by interacting with the outside world. The ego develops from the id's necessity to look to the outside world for gratification of desires. In this sense, the ego acts as an inter- mediary for the id. Its nature is determined in part by the id and by its experiences with the outside world.

The purpose of the ego is to protect life by interpreting and exploiting the outside world. As the ego becomes aware of that world and experiments with it (the infant, for example, gradually becomes aware of its mother as a source of hunger gratification and discovers that crying speeds up the gratification of its hunger needs), it develops a facility for judgment and learns to adapt to and to act upon its environment. The ego reacts to the wishes of the id by deciding whether or not it can gratify them. If the decision is yes, the ego must discover the means to do so. If the decision is no, the ego must either suppress the wish or direct it to a "safer" or more feasible area.

The ego carries out its functions under the *reality principle,* which serves the pleasure principle. By the reality principle, the ego interprets the outside world and exploits that reality at the best time to reduce the tensions of the id. Thus the ego functions to perceive, understand, and evaluate reality. In the course of its service, it may strive to delay the gratification of the particular desire from the present to a more appropriate time. For example, given an urge to reduce inner tension by screaming, the ego may interpret the outside world as being unfavorable at that time. At a wedding, the expected hostility of the wedding party could *increase* inner tension to a degree exceeding the reduction resulting from the scream. The ego may then decide to delay the scream until the service is over, or until the reception, or it may try to divert the energy into kicking the person in front or pinching oneself.

The ego, then, is the conscious, organized, executive subsystem of the personality which translates the wishes of the id into activity and interacts with the outside world.

The Superego   The superego is the moral arm of personality. It is a basically an unconscious source of standards or norms by which the activities of the ego are judged. It is also the mediator of punishments for deviating from those norms.

The superego develops from the interactions between the ego and society, particularly one's parents. As the child develops, he or she comes to identify with his or her parents (or guardians, in the case of absent or deceased parents). This process of identification includes the adoption of the parents' enforced notions of "right" and "wrong." Those things that are encouraged or reinforced by the parents become the *ego ideal,* the child's concept of perfection. Those that are discouraged or punished by the parents become the *conscience.* It is important to note that the child's superego does not develop directly from the parents' behavior; it stems from parents' superego. The developing superego becomes a model of what the parents say is right and wrong and what the parents reward or punish the child for, rather than a model of how the parents themselves behave. According to Freud, it is through this direct superego-to-superego process that the values of a society are passed from generation to generation.

The superego is to the ego what the parent is to the child. The superego's function is to limit the instinctual gratification of the person according to the principles of the parents or guardians. It operates on neither the pleasure principle nor the reality principle but on the *perfection principle,* which holds that all behavior must conform to the ego ideal. Since its mental activity is primarily unconscious, and since it does not operate on the reality principle, the superego, once developed, remains essentially unchanged.

The Libido   The libido is the energy which makes the system dynamic and causes it to function. Libidinal energy is psychic in nature, not biological.

The sources of libidinal or psychic energy are the psychological instincts known as life or self-preservation instincts. These instincts are not totally sexual, although they have commonly been construed as such. They include both sexual and ego instincts and those instincts that attract us to and cause us to identify with anything in the outside world. Attempting to clarify the concept of libido, Freud described it as:

> The energy, regarded as a quantitative magnitude (though not at present actually measureable), of those instincts which have to do with all that may be comprised under the word "love." The nucleus of what we mean by love naturally consists (and this is what is commonly love, and what the poets sing of) in sexual love with sexual union as its aim. But we do not separate from this—what in any case has a share in the name "love"—on the one hand, self-love, and on the other, love for parents and children, friendship and love for humanity in general, and also devotion to concrete objects and abstract ideas.[5]

While Freud said that libidinal energy springs from the life instincts, he also postulated a separate set of instincts, the death or self-destruction instincts, but did not name the energy derived from them. Libido is the vital energy or life force which circulates throughout the three subsystems of the personality and is distributed among them.

---

[5] Sigmund Freud, *Group Psychology and the Analysis of the Ego,* trans. James Strachey (2d ed.) (New York: Bantam Books, 1965), p. 29.

Functioning of the Personality

The functioning of the personality is graphically represented in Figure 3–1. Libido, or psychic energy, originates in the id and cir-

FIGURE 3–1
Functioning of the Personality

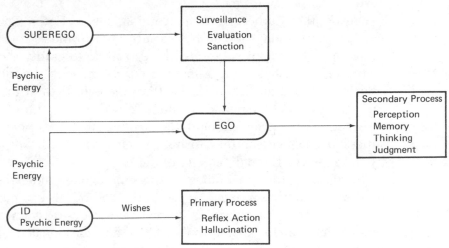

culates throughout the system, energizing each of the three subsystems—id, ego, and superego. The amount of energy in a subsystem determines its relative strength.

Wishes are generated by the id. Operating on the pleasure principle, the id strives to reduce the inner tension created by the wish through immediate discharge of that tension via the primary process. Gratification can be obtained in one of two ways: either by a reflex action (such as gulping for air when oxygen is deprived) or by hallucination, if a reflex action is either not available to reduce the particular tension (as when no food is available to assuage hunger) or the reflex action would be likely to increase tension (like gulping for air while under water). Thus a person dying of thirst in a desert may produce a hallucination of a cold stream or cool lake of water as a means of reducing tension.

In the event that the primary process (reflex action or hallucination) fails, energy flows to the ego for transformation into the various mental activities of the *secondary process* (perception, memory, judgment, thought). These activities are carried out under the reality principle and are thus constrained by time and place. Through these mental activities the ego strives to decide whether particular actions toward particular objects will be reasonable means of reducing the tensions produced by the id. Thus the desert wanderer strives to discover whether the pool ahead is a mirage or reality, whether it is better to walk toward the mountains or sit and wait for possible rescue, and whether or not he should drink the bottle of hair oil in his pack.

During these processes of perception, memory, thinking, judgment, and decision, the ego is also subjected to the scrutiny of the superego. That is, not only must the ego strive to gratify the wishes of the id, it must do so in a manner consistent with the ideals and rules established and enforced by the superego. If the ego successfully integrates the demands of both id and superego, the result is satisfaction and pride. Should the ego violate some norm of the superego (behave contrary to his conscience), it will be punished by the superego through feelings of guilt.

To illustrate the functioning of the superego, consider the plight of a pilot who has survived a crash in the desert. His ego may judge the best method for obtaining gratification of desires for water and relief from heat to be simply to wait beside the downed plane for rescue. Suppose, however, that his ego ideal contains notions that his ideal self is an active, take-charge person whose fate is under his own control. If so, the decision to wait passively for rescue, to place his fate entirely in the hands of others, may meet with disapproval of the superego, requiring either a modified plan or some form of rationalization for this departure from the ideal self. Or suppose there were a passenger in the plane who had his own canteens of water but who was badly injured. One alternative for the pilot's ego to consider would be to drink the injured man's water. If he did so, it is likely that his conscience would react by assaulting him with strong feelings of guilt.

In summary, it should be clear why the psychoanalytic theory is referred to as a theory of tension. Inner tensions initiated by the wishes of the id cause the system to function. The ego is under pressure to gratify these wishes both quickly and at low cost, while it is under the tension of close scrutiny by the superego.

The three subsystems of the personality are intimately related: in turn, the ego develops from the id, and the superego from the ego. Yet each acquires the distinctive characteristics that are summarized in Table 3–1.

TABLE 3–1
Characteristics of the Subsystem of the Personality

	Id	Ego	Superego
Basis	Biological	Psychological	Social
Acquired through	Inheritance	Experience	Socialization
Goal	Pleasure	Reality	Perfection
Function	Wish generation	Self-preservation	Wish inhibition
Quality of mental life.	Unconscious	Conscious	Unconscious

Process	Primary:
	  Reflex action
	  Hallucination
		Secondary:
		  Perception
		  Memory
		  Thinking
		  Judgment
			Surveillance:
			  Evaluation
			  Sanction

Some Applications of Psychoanalytic Theory to Organizational Behavior

Because of its roots in the study of neurotic behavior, psycho-analytic theory has been considered irrelevant to the study of the "normal" behavior of humans in organizations. However, increasing interest in an expanded concept of mental health and "mentally healthy behavior" has provided an entry for psychoanalytic theory into the analysis of organizational behavior, although its influence is not as extensive as either the cognitive or the reinforcement approach.

Some of the areas of organizational behavior which have felt the influence of psychoanalytic theory and which will be discussed in later chapters include the following:

Creative Behavior   Chapter 10 proposes that certain stages of the creative process are unconscious in nature. Defensiveness and certain fears are thought to inhibit the expression of creative ability. Hypnosis has been used as a tool for removing such mental blocks.

Dissatisfaction   Behaviors such as daydreaming, forgetting, apathy, rationalization, and even some sickness, disability, and pain are often analyzed in psychoanalytic terms of reactions to frustration, anxiety, and conflict. Certain behavior patterns, including absenteeism and tardiness, aggression, and alcoholism, are described as "games people play" in the psychoanalytic approach of the late Eric Berne. Chapter 11 will discuss such approaches to the understanding of dissatisfaction.

Group Development   Descriptions of the stages which groups must go through to become "mature" are heavily psychoanalytic in nature, as will be discussed in Chapter 13.

Leadership and Influence   Freud's great interest in authority and power is reflected in psychoanalytic approaches to the study of the emergence of leadership, the nature of the leader's relationship to his followers, and styles of leadership, as described in Chapter 20. Topics in Chapter 19 relevant to psychoanalytic theory include conformity and imitative behavior.

SUMMARY: COMPARING THE THREE APPROACHES

As a summary to this chapter, some of the major characteristics of the cognitive, reinforcement, and psychoanalytic approaches to understanding human behavior will be compared.

Emphasis

The cognitive approach emphasizes internal mental processes such as thinking and judgment. The individual's interpretation or perception of the environment is considered more important than the environment itself. The reinforcement approach emphasizes the role of the environment in human behavior; the environment is seen as the source of stimuli which both produce and reinforce behavioral responses. The psychoanalytic approach emphasizes the role of the personality system in determining behavior. The environment is considered only insofar as the ego interacts with it to satisfy the wishes of the id.

Causes of Behavior

In the cognitive approach, behavior is said to arise from imbalances or inconsistencies in the cognitive structure, which can result from perceptions of the environment. The reinforcement approach holds that behavior is determined by environmental stimuli, both prior to the behavior (eliciting responses) and subsequent to it (reinforcing responses). According to the psychoanalytic approach, behavior is activated by tensions generated by unfulfilled wishes arising from the id.

Processes

The cognitive approach holds that cognitions (knowledge and experiences) are mentally processed, modifying and being modified by the existing cognitive structure. Resulting imbalances or inconsistencies in the structure generate behavior to reduce those inconsistencies. In the reinforcement approach, the environment acts on the individual, eliciting a response which is determined by genetic endowment and past reinforcement history. The nature of the environment's reaction to that response (positive, negative, or neutral) determines the individual's future behavioral tendencies. In the psychoanalytic approach, wishes or desires are generated in the id, then processed by and acted upon (satisfied, diverted, or suppressed) by the ego, under the scrutiny of the superego. Behavior results from the ego's decision of how to satisfy the id's wishes and the superego's constraints.

Importance of the Past in Determining Behavior

According to the psychoanalytic approach, an individual's past can be a relatively important determinant of his behavior. The natures of the id and the superego are both hereditary, and the relative strengths of the id, ego, and superego are determined by their past development and interactions. Nevertheless, the psychoanalytic approach holds that an individual's behavior is the result of the current state of his personality system, regardless of how that state was developed. In this sense, the psychoanalytic approach is ahistoric.

The cognitive approach is likewise ahistoric. Certainly past experiences determine the cognitive structure. However, behavior is said to be a function of the current state of one's cognitive systems, regardless of how they came to be. Reinforcement theory, on the other hand, is historic. An individual's response to a given stimulus is said to be a function of his reinforcement history—how often and in what way that response has been rewarded in the past.

Level of Consciousness

In the cognitive approach, various levels of consciousness are said to exist, but conscious mental activities, such as knowing, thinking, and meaning, are considered most important. In reinforcement theory, no distinction is made between conscious and unconscious. In fact, mental activity is usually considered to be another form of behavior and is not endowed with any special causal powers; that is, mental activities such as thinking and feeling may accompany overt behavior but do not cause it. In the psychoanalytic approach, most mental activity is unconscious. It is the unconscious activities of the id and the superego which largely determine behavior.

Data

In the cognitive approach, data on attitudes, values, understanding, and expectations are collected, primarily through surveys and questionnaires. The reinforcement approach measures observable environmental stimuli and physical or material responses. This may be done through direct observation or with the help of technological devices. The psychoanalytic approach uses as data expressions of wishes and desires and evidence of blocking or suppression of those desires. These data are revealed through analysis of dreams, free association, projective techniques, and hypnosis.

Determining the Right Approach

At this point you may be asking which of these three approaches is right. The science of human behavior has not yet progressed to a stage where we can answer that question. Advocates of any given approach will stoutly defend it, even to the exclusion of others. It is possible that all three approaches are valid in certain respects. It is even possible that none of them is "right," and the answers lie somewhere else.

The best strategy would seem to be to delay evaluation of these approaches until you see what they have to offer. Each has been useful in generating theory and research which has contributed to an understanding of organizational behavior. By the time you have finished this book you can decide for yourself if any one approach seems to be more useful than the others. In the meantime, do not reject any approach, particularly just because it is not consistent with your own views about the nature of man. "No theory changes what it is a theory about; man remains what he has always been."[6]

QUESTIONS FOR REVIEW AND DISCUSSION

1. Which of the three approaches discussed in this chapter places the most emphasis on environmental determinants of behavior?

---

[6] B. F. Skinner, *Beyond Freedom and Dignity* (New York: Alfred A. Knopf, 1971), p. 206.

2. In the cognitive approach, when does a cognition acquire meaning?

3. Which of the three approaches places the most emphasis on conscious mental activity as a determinant of behavior?

4. What is the difference between reinforcement and extinction? Between extinction and punishment?

5. Why is the psychoanalytic approach said to be a theory of tension?

6. Suppose you were trying to deal with a "problem" worker whose productivity and attendance were erratic. What differences might it make if you subscribed to the cognitive approach rather than the reinforcement approach?

7. Given the same problem as in Question 6, what differences might it make if you subscribed to the reinforcement approach rather than the psychoanalytic approach?

KEY WORDS

Cognition
Cognitive structure
Ideology
Law of effect
Stimulus
Response
Reinforcer

Extinction
Punishment
Personality
Id
Ego
Superego
Libido

OUTLINE OF CHAPTER

72

chapter four

Motivation

The visitor allowed his eyes to wander around the room. I've seen a lot fancier coaches' offices than this, he thought. No plush carpeting or expensive panelling, just a comfortable-looking old desk, a handful of chairs, and a couple of metal filing cabinets. The one concession to comfort appeared to be a large rug woven in the school colors.

No, what made this office impressive were not its size and furnishings, he concluded, but a select few momentos which adorned its walls. Even from his chair the visitor recognized them: plaques in recognition of College Coach of the Year for 1969 and 1975; action photographs from the coach's 100th and 200th victories; a picture with the President of the United States in the team dressing room following a bowl game which clinched the national championship.

The visitor started to slip his writing pad back into his briefcase, then hesitated. "One last question," he said. "Almost every coach I know has the same slogan posted somewhere in his players' locker room. It reads, 'Football is 10 percent ability and 90 percent effort,' or something like that. Do you believe that saying is true?"

"Of course I do," replied the old coach amiably. "First, we only play as well as we practice. A kid needs to be motivated to put on the kind of concentration and effort we require for an efficient and effective practice session, particularly after a full day of classwork. Second, most games between top teams are won in the fourth quarter, when that extra ounce of effort pays off, especially when everybody is fatigued. Third, injuries are part of the game. If everybody who was hurt came off the field, you'd see some mighty lonely referees out there come November. Playing with pain isn't a talent, it's something a kid does because he wants to play bad enough."

The visitor nodded as if in agreement, although he'd heard it all before. But as he stood up to go, he just couldn't resist the temptation. "Tell me, Coach," he said, "if football is only 10 percent talent, why are your recruiting expenses 30 percent of your budget?"

The coach rose to escort his visitor to the door. Clapping his hand on the visitor's shoulder, he said, with just a hint of a smile, "Because that's my secret of success. I discovered a long time ago that motivation and effort may be 90 percent of the game, but you win a lot more games motivating big fast kids than little bitty slow ones."

THE ROLE OF MOTIVATION IN PERFORMANCE

THE "SECRET" the old coach revealed in the interview described above was his recognition that there are two major factors an individual contributes to task performance: ability to perform the task and motivation. Ability includes the physical and mental skills and the knowledge and experience that a person applies to a task. Motivation has to do with the effort with which this ability is applied to the task.

Had the visitor asked the coach to diagram his secret on the board, the latter might have written:

$$P = f(A x M),$$

where P stands for an individual's performance, A for ability, and M for motivation. The equation suggests that individual performance is affected by the interaction between ability and motivation.

There are two reasons why it can be suggested that performance is a function of ability interacting with motivation. The first is that in the dynamics of behavior there are many instances in which ability affects motivation. A person who discovers he has a unique ability to play football or influence people or give speeches may be motivated by that discovery to exploit his talent. Another who finds she has little ability to teach or to play the piano or to run a lathe may be inclined to put little effort into teaching, piano playing, or woodwork.

Similarly, motivation can affect ability. Girls who wanted to be jockeys were sufficiently motivated to get jobs working with horses and to teach themselves how to ride in races or to learn with the help of others. As their ability improved, they became capable of competing successfully with male jockeys. The reverse is also true; one who is no longer motivated to use a skill will find it deteriorating from lack of practice.

The second reason performance can be considered a function of ability interacting with motivation is that research evidence has indicated such an interactive effect. A typical finding is graphically represented in Figure 4–1, which indicates differences in the way motivation affects the performance of high- and low-ability people. When people of both low ability and high ability are unwilling to put any effort into their performance, the differences in the performances will be minimized.

Imagine that I am capable of running long distances at a sustained rate of one mile every five minutes, while your best sus-

FIGURE 4–1
How Ability Moderates the Effects of Motivation on Performance

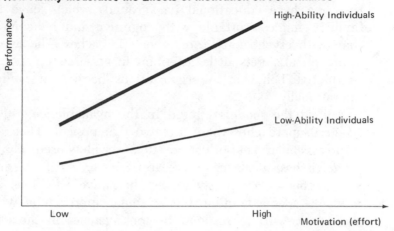

tained rate is one mile every six minutes. One hot, muggy afternoon we decide to run for an hour. The heat and lack of incentive result in minimal effort from both of us—say only enough to run at 25 percent of our ability. So I run at 25 percent of 12 mph, or 3 mph. At the end of the hour I have covered a distance of three miles. You, running at 25 percent of 10 mph, or 2½ mph, cover only 2½ miles, one-half mile less than I do.

The next time we run it is clear and cooler, and you and I wager $100 that I cannot run two miles farther than you in one hour. The perfect weather conditions and size of the wager provide the incentive for each of us to run to 110 percent of our ability (if college football players can give 110 percent every time, as their coaches claim, why can't we do it once?). At 110 percent of 12 mph, I cover 13.2 miles in the hour. At 110 percent of 10 mph, you cover only 11 miles. The difference between the distances we have run has increased from one-half mile to over two miles. (You owe me $100, by the way.)

In this way, changes in level of effort make more of a difference in the performance of high-ability people than in that of low-ability people. As the coach found, "You win a lot more football games by motivating big fast kids than little bitty slow ones."

MODELS OF INDIVIDUAL MOTIVATION

In the literature of organizational behavior, approaches to understanding individual motivation are largely cognitive and reinforcement in nature. This is partially because most of the researchers in the area have educational backgrounds which leave them more familiar and comfortable with cognitive and behavioral research than with psychoanalytic or other approaches. The psychoanalytic approach also gets little attention in research on motivation and productive behavior in organizations because it is hard to use operationally.

Among the models offered in the available cognitive and behavioral approaches there are two that prevail. These models are quite dissimilar, yet both are useful and widely used. The *expectancy model* is basically a cognitive approach in which the individual is said to choose consciously among alternative behaviors. The *operant model* is a noncognitive reinforcement approach in which the individual is said to respond to contingencies in the environment; thinking is not held to be a cause of behavior.

At this time, neither model is clearly superior to the other in terms of predicting or understanding behavior. Each has certain strengths and weaknesses. We will describe the expectancy and operant models and make some comparisons between them.

EXPECTANCY MODELS

Sources for the expectancy model can be traced back 30 or 40 years through the work of psychologists such as Edward Tolman, whose cognitive theory of learning contradicted the prevailing reinforcement approach, and Kurt Lewin, whose "field theory" of behavior emphasized internal psychological processes and deemphasized the importance of one's past in determining behavior. One version of modern expectancy theory emphasizes the importance of attitudes in determining how a person intends to behave.

An Attitude Model of Behavioral Intentions[1]

The attitude model strives to explain why an individual will tend to behave in a certain way. This tendency, or behavioral intention, is said to result from:

1. The individual's belief in the probability that the response would lead to some consequence.

[1] See Martin Fishbein, "The Search for Attitudinal-Behavioral Consistency," in Joel Cohen, ed., *Behavioral Science Foundations of Consumer Behavior* (New York: Free Press, 1972), pp. 245–52.

2. His attitude toward that consequence.
3. His belief about what he is expected to do by society.
4. His motivation to do what he thinks he should do.

The model proposes that one's *intention* to act a certain way is a function of one's attitude toward the act, plus one's perception of the norms governing the act. For example, whether I work late or go home early tonight is a function of my attitude toward working late (I don't like to work late, I don't like to miss dinner), and relevant norms (I believe I should work as hard and as long as necessary to complete this task), (I think society expects fathers to eat dinner with their families whenever possible).

Of particular interest to the development of expectancy theory is the concept of the individual's attitude toward any possible behavioral act. This concept is expressed algebraically as:

$$A_{\mathrm{act}} = \sum_{i=1}^{n} B_i a_i$$

where B_i = The individual's belief i about the act; that is, the probability that performing the act will lead to some outcome, i

  a_i = His evaluation of outcome i

  n = The number of beliefs he has about the act

In other words, an individual's attitude toward performing some act of behavior is the sum of his beliefs about what will happen to him if he performs that act, times the value he places on those things that might happen to him. For example, my attitude toward working late would be the sum of:

My belief that, if I work late: times My feeling about:

- I'll get my work done (high probability)
- I'll get very tired (moderate probability)
- I'll miss the rush-hour traffic (certain)
- My dinner will be cold (high probability)
- My family will be angry with me (almost certain)

- finishing my work (very positive)
- being tired (slightly negative)
- missing traffic (moderately positive)
- cold dinner (moderately negative)
- angry family (very negative)

Suppose this combination of beliefs and feelings resulted in a neutral attitude—I was indifferent. The model would then predict that whether or not I worked late would primarily depend upon the weight I give to my personal norms (I ought to finish my work) and societal norms (I ought to go home for dinner).

To summarize, according to the attitude model an individual's beliefs about what will happen to him if he performs some act influences his attitude toward performing the act. This attitude in turn influences his intention to perform the act. The relationship is illustrated in Figure 4–2.

However, the model does *not* say that attitudes are consistently good predictors of behavior. First, personal and societal norms may influence behavioral intentions as much as, or more than, attitudes do. Second, there are important determinants of behavior other than

FIGURE 4–2
An Attitude Model

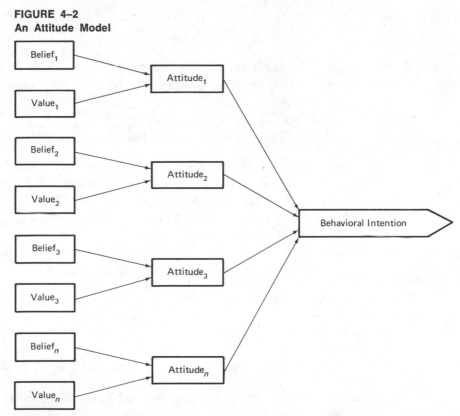

An individual's intention to perform an act is a function of his or her attitudes toward the act. The individual's attitudes, in turn, are a function of his or her beliefs about the results of the act and of how he or she values those results.

behavioral intentions, such as the situation (environment) and individual differences (abilities). Thus this model is really an attempt to predict only behavioral intentions, which can be considered equivalent to motivation in the equation $P = f(A \times M)$.

A Basic Expectancy Model[2]

A basic expectancy model has been developed from a theory of motivation especially adapted to the behavior of people in organizations. Essentially, it views behavior in organizations as largely voluntary. That is, an individual in an organization usually has several alternative behaviors from which to select, and he chooses one of them, based on the expectations he has about that alternative.

The key concepts in this model are force, expectancy, and valence.

Force   The force on a person to perform an act, or his motivation to exert a certain amount of effort in performing that act, is the dependent variable in this model. Force might be considered as similar to the concept of attitude in the attitudinal model.

Expectancy   An expectancy is the individual's belief at a particular time about the probability that a given act will be followed by a particular outcome. An expectancy is somewhat similar to the concept of belief. Expectancies can range in strength from 0.0 (impossible for the act to obtain some outcome) to 1.0 (certain that the act will result in some outcome).

For example, consider a corporate recruiter looking for a new manager to supervise a group of employees. One alternative is to spend a couple of days recruiting at State College campus, 150 miles away. The college usually graduates some 200 students in business, about 20 percent of whom have a technical background. The recruiter, who will be competing with other recruiters from surrounding states, believes he can interview 20 students during his visit. He estimates his chances of finding a qualified candidate in that large a group to be about 5 out of 10. His *expectancy* that the act of visiting State College would result in the outcome of finding a qualified candidate is 0.5.

He might also consider visiting the local community college. However, it graduates only a handful of students in business each quarter. Although half of them have technical backgrounds, many already have jobs with local companies. The recruiter believes he

[2] See Victor H. Vroom, *Work and Motivation* (New York: John Wiley & Sons, 1964).

might find only one or two of these graduates available and estimates his chances of interviewing a qualified candidate at no better than 1 out of 10. His expectancy that the act of visiting the local community college would result in the outcome of finding a qualified candidate is 0.1. Thus his expectancy for recruiting locally is much lower than his expectancy for recruiting at State College.

Valence   Valence is a measure of the individual's feelings about a particular outcome—whether he is indifferent toward it, is attracted to or likes it, or is repelled by or dislikes it. Thus valences can be zero, positive, or negative.

The valence of an outcome can be expressed in the form of an algebraic equation:

$$\text{Valence } j = f_j \left[\sum_{k=1}^{n} (V_k I_{jk}) \right] (j = 1 \ldots n)$$

where valence j = The valence of some outcome, j

$\qquad V_k$ = The value of result k to outcome j

$\qquad I_{jk}$ = The perceived likelihood that outcome j will obtain result k (the *instrumentality* of outcome j)

I_{jk} can be either positive or negative, ranging from -1 through 0 to $+1$. If outcome j is perceived as being certain to have result k, then $I_{jk} = +1$. If outcome j is perceived as having no effect on result k, then $I_{jk} = 0$. If outcome j is seen as making result k impossible, then $I_{jk} = -1$.

The valence of an outcome for a person depends upon what results can come from the outcome and how the person feels about these results. The more positive the individual feels about possible results of an outcome, the greater the valence of the outcome. The more instrumental the individual perceives an outcome as being in obtaining these results, the greater the valence of the outcome.

To return to the recruiter's problem, one outcome of visiting State College is finding a qualified candidate. This outcome (outcome 1) has three possible results. Result 1 is that the recruiter feels pleased to find a qualified candidate. Result 2 is that he successfully hires the candidate. Result 3 is that other companies hire all the qualified candidates, leaving the recruiter empty-handed.

The recruiter places different values on each of these results. Result 1 has a mildly positive value. Result 2 has a value 10 times greater. Result 3 has a very negative value. Putting numbers on these values, he might estimate that $V_1 = 1$, $V_2 = 10$, and $V_3 = -7$.

The recruiter also perceives different instrumentalities for the outcome in getting results. The probability that finding a qualified candidate will please him is virtually certain: $I_{11} = 1.0$. The probability that he can hire the candidate, once found, he estimates to be fairly certain, say, $I_{12} = 0.7$. The probability that other companies will hire all the candidates, $I_{13} = 0.3$.

Given these values and instrumentalities, it is possible to determine the valence of outcome 1—finding a qualified candidate—as:

$$\text{Valence}_1 = (V_1 I_{11}) + (V_2 I_{12}) + (V_3 I_{13})$$
$$= (1 \times 1.0) + (10 \times 0.7) + (-7 \times 0.3)$$
$$= 1.0 + 7.0 - 2.1$$
$$\text{Valence}_1 = +5.9$$

The valence of outcome 1 is moderately positive.

Of course, every act has more than one possible outcome, and each outcome has its own valence. In this example, visiting State College might have several relevant outcomes for the recruiter, such as monetary costs (O_2), time away from home (O_3), seeing a football game (O_4), and visiting friends on campus (O_5). Costs and time away from home would probably have negative valences; seeing the game and visiting friends would have positive valences. Different expectancies that the act would lead to these outcomes would also exist.

This model would use the expectancies and valences of these outcomes as independent variables to predict the dependent variable, the amount of force impelling the recruiter to visit State College:

$$F_i = f\left[\sum_{j=1}^{n} (V_j E_{ij}) \right]$$

where F_i = The force to perform some act, i

V_j = The valence of outcome j

E_{ij} = The strength of the expectancy that act i will lead to outcome j

That is, the force on a person to perform some act, i, is a function of the algebraic sum of the products of the valences of the possible outcomes for act i times his expectancies that the act will achieve these outcomes.

In the example above, visiting State College has five relevant outcomes. Outcome 1, finding a qualified candidate, has a valence of +5.9 and an expectancy of 0.5. Multiplying the expectancy times the valence for each of these outcomes and summing the total would give the force impelling the recruiter to visit State College. If that force were greater than the forces impelling him to act differently (such as recruit at the local community college), the model would predict that the recruiter would indeed go to State.

Figure 4–3 diagrams an expectancy model. By comparing Figures

FIGURE 4–3
An Expectancy Model

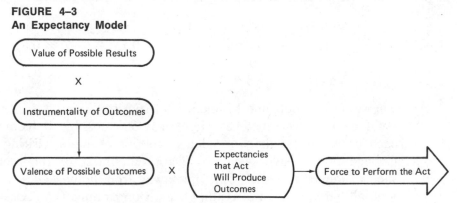

The force to perform an act is a function of the valence of its possible outcomes and the expectations that the act will have those outcomes. The valence of an outcome, in turn, is a function of the value of its possible results and its perceived instrumentality in obtaining those results.

4–3 and 4–2, you can see many similarities between the expectancy model and the attitude model. Both emphasize as determinants of motivation (force or intention) the perceived value (valence) of outcomes to some act and the perceived likelihood (expectancy or belief) that the act will obtain those outcomes.

One difference is that the expectancy model does not explicitly include personal and societal norms. However, we could simply include the effects of those norms as additional outcomes to an act.

You can see that the expectancy model is cognitive, in that motivation is said to be a function of conscious choice among alternative forms of behavior. It is also subjectively rational, in that it assumes an individual will be more inclined toward an act that he expects will have greater value than any other act. These assumptions seem to be straightforward and logical. However, they cause some problems in the model's generalizability and testability, as you will see.

A Perceptual Model[3]

An alternate form of the expectancy model, a perceptual model, differs from the basic form in four ways. First, it is expressed diagramatically, rather than mathematically. Second, it attempts to represent some of the dynamics of human motivation. Third, it includes more variables. Fourth, it explictly emphasizes the importance of perception in motivation.

FIGURE 4–4
A Perceptual Model of Motivation

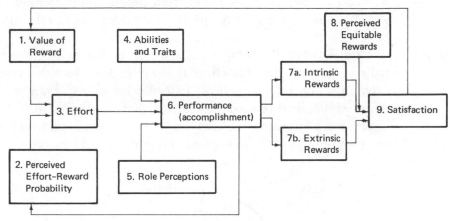

Source: Adapted from Lyman W. Porter and Edward E. Lawler, III, *Managerial Attitudes and Performance* (Homewood, Ill.: Richard D. Irwin, 1968), p. 17.

In the complete perceptual model, as presented in Figure 4–4, performance is seen as a function of abilities and traits, role perceptions, and effort. Abilities and traits will be discussed in the next chapter. Role perceptions are the activities that an individual believes are necessary for him to perform his job successfully.

Our major interest in the model is in the variable *effort,* which is similar to *behavioral intention* and *force.* According to the model, the effort a person puts into performance is a function of the value he places on the possible rewards he might receive and his perception of the probability that his effort will lead to these rewards.

Value of Rewards The variable labeled value of rewards is similar to the expectancy concept of the value placed by the in-

---

[3] See Lyman W. Porter and Edward E. Lawler III, *Managerial Attitudes and Performance* (Homewood, Ill.: Richard D. Irwin, 1968).

dividual on the possible results of an outcome. Note that the value of a reward is dependent both on the reward and on the individual. For example, I may place more value on a $500 bonus than on an additional one-week vacation. However, you may place more value on a $500 bonus than I do.

Note that for variable 7 in the model (rewards), a distinction is made between intrinsic rewards and extrinsic rewards. *Intrinsic* rewards are those that are received directly from work and do not come from someone else. A sense of accomplishment or pride and pleasure in the task one is performing are examples of intrinsic rewards. *Extrinsic* rewards come from others; they include such rewards as pay, praise, promotion, recognition, time off, and fringe benefits.

Effort-Reward Probability   According to the model, the individual's perception that his effort is likely to lead to some rewards is a combination of two beliefs. In order for one to believe that his effort will lead to rewards, he must believe both that his effort will improve his performance *and* that his improved performance will be rewarded. That is, for a given individual:

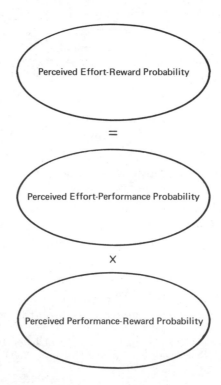

The concept of a perceived effort-performance probability is equivalent to the concept of expectancy. Perceived performance-reward probability is equivalent to instrumentality.

This is an important concept in the expectancy model, particularly in its implications for management. We will discuss those implications later; first we want to make sure you understand the concept thoroughly.

Suppose that you are in a staff position and you have the opportunity to give a market report to the top executives in your company. You believe that a good presentation will give you increased visibility and recognition from this group, and it will increase your value to your boss (you perceive a high performance-reward probability). You also believe, however, that no matter how much preparation you put into the presentation, you are unlikely to make a good presentation because you are nervous and have been allotted only a small amount of time (you perceive a low effort-performance probability).

According to the model, in these circumstances you will not put as much effort into preparation as you would if you believed that the more you prepared, the better you would perform. You will put a lot of effort into preparation only if you believe that effort is likely to improve your performance *and* if you believe that improved performance will bring you rewards (see Figure 4–5).

Like other models, the perceptual model also proposes that effort or motivation depends on the degree to which the individual values the possible rewards for his effort. That is, even though you believe that effort in preparation will improve your presentation, and that a good presentation will lead to increased recognition and esteem from your superiors, your effort will *not* be great if you are indifferent toward recognition and esteem from your superiors.

This model thus proposes that three factors directly affect effort or motivation, and all three must be high to induce an individual to exert great effort. In Table 4–1 some possible combinations of these factors and the effort which the model predicts will result from each combination are presented.

See if you can think of an example to fit each of the eight combinations in Table 4–1. For instance, there are few attempted escapes from maximum security prisons, even though a successful escape would result in a highly valued reward (freedom), because the prisons are designed to make the probability of successful escapes almost zero.

FIGURE 4–5
Effort-Reward Probability

The effort put into performance depends on the perceived rewards for that performance and the belief that effort will affect performance.

Equity   Variable 8 in Figure 4–4, perceived equitable rewards, suggests that the satisfaction one derives from a reward is moderated by whether or not one perceives the reward as equitable or just. According to the model, one source of dissatisfaction with rewards is the degree to which actual rewards fall short of rewards to which one believes he is entitled. A soldier who is awarded the Silver Star

TABLE 4–1
Some Possible Combinations of Variables Affecting Effort, according to the Perceptual Model

Perceived Probability that:			
Effort Will Affect Performance	*Performance Will Affect Rewards*	*Value of Rewards*	*Resultant Effort*
High	High	High	Very high
High	High	Low	
High	Low	High	Less high
Low	High	High	
High	Low	Low	
Low	High	Low	Low
Low	Low	High	
Low	Low	Low	Minimal or none

for bravery in combat may feel proud yet be somewhat dissatisfied because he feels he deserves the Medal of Honor. A career diplomat who is rewarded for distinguished service by being named deputy ambassador to the United Kingdom may be less than satisfied because the ambassadorship is given to someone else, not for career service but for a large campaign contribution to the party in power.

Dynamics of the Model In addition to predicting that effort is a function of one's perception of effort-reward probabilities and one's evaluation of possible rewards, the perceptual model suggests how the results of one's efforts will influence subsequent effort. In Figure 4–4, the arrow going from point 6 back to variable 2 indicates that if the performance of an act is in fact followed by some rewards, this will in turn increase the individual's perception that subsequent effort exerted in the performance will likely be rewarded.

A second dynamic characteristic of the model is the arrow from variable 9 back to variable 1. This arrow indicates that the satisfaction one derives from rewards received for performance will in turn affect the subsequent effort one is willing to put into performing that act.

To demonstrate the two dynamic characteristics of the model, go back to the example of your preparation of a presentation for the executive board. Suppose that, despite your originally pessimistic expectancies, your spouse convinces you to spend the night working on your presentation. The next day the presentation seems to go well, and upon concluding it you are enthusiastically congratulated by the president and other executives. Your own boss is obviously delighted and suggests that a better job assignment may soon follow. Because your performance was immediately followed by rewards, the model suggests, there will be an increase in your perceived probability that effort leads to rewards, and thus an increase in the effort you would be willing to exert the next time you find yourself in that situation.

Suppose that you additionally find the praise, congratulations, and attention to be warm, flattering, and very satisfying. The model suggests that your satisfaction with the rewards increases their value to you, and thus the effort you would be willing to exert the next time is increased. Experiencing rewards and the satisfaction derived from them influence subsequent levels of effort.

Like the other expectancy models of motivation, the perceptual model describes an individual's motivation to perform his job as being a cognitive product of a subjectively rational, hedonistic nature. That is, the individual does what he consciously decides to do, and he decides to do the things that he expects will maximize his satisfaction. The model is also ahistoric: effort is determined by the state of one's perceptions or expectations at the instant of decision. True, expectations may be a function of previous performance outcomes and the satisfaction experienced from those outcomes. However, expectations may also be influenced by other factors; for example, one may be duped by a con artist or an unscrupulous supervisor into believing one will be rewarded.

According to the model, if you know someone's perceived effort-reward probabilities and the value he places on those rewards, you can predict his level of effort regardless of *how* he came to perceive those probabilities or value those rewards. This is one of the major differences between expectancy models and the operant model.

AN OPERANT MODEL

Origins of the operant model most widely used to study behavior in organizations can be traced back to the 1910s. A psychologist, John B. Watson, had become very frustrated by the subjective, introspective theories of behavior espoused by his colleagues. Such theories, he claimed, were making no progress because they were based on hypothetical, scientifically unmeasurable constructs such as imagination, reason, images, will, and mind. Most psychologists, he said, erroneously "claimed that consciousness is the subject matter of psychology."[4]

Casting about for a more objective approach to studying behavior, one which he hoped would be more similar to the approaches of sciences like physics and chemistry, Watson was attracted by the work of the reinforcement theorists described in Chapter 3. Watson was most influenced by Pavlov's studies of physiological responses and Thorndike's studies of learning. He was also attracted by the attempts of another Russian psychologist, V. M. Bechterev, to establish a more objective approach to psychology through the study of observable behavior.

With these foundations, Watson established an American objective psychology called *behaviorism*. Comparing his approach to introspective techniques, he said that "Behaviorism holds that the subject matter of human psychology is the behavior of the human being."[5] The behaviorist's approach is to limit his study to things

---

[4] John B. Watson, *Behaviorism*, rev. ed. (Chicago: University of Chicago Press, 1930), p. 2.

[5] Ibid.

that can be most reliably observed: behavior, what a person says or does. The operant model used today follows that tradition.

This model is based on two simple assumptions. First, behavior is essentially determined by the environment. It does not necessarily deny the existence of internal, mental processes; however, because they are difficult to measure reliably, and because behaviorists believe they play no important role in predicting overt behavior, they are not included in this model of human behavior. Second, human behavior, like the behavior of physical and chemical elements, is held to be subject to certain laws, which can de discovered through observation.

The basic operant equation describing behavior is

$$R = f(S, A),$$

where R stands for reflex or response, S for the physical environment (stimuli) in which the response occurs, and A includes environmental variables outside the immediate physical environment, such as time and prior reinforcement history.[6] The operant model is diagrammed in Figure 4–6.

FIGURE 4–6
An Operant Model

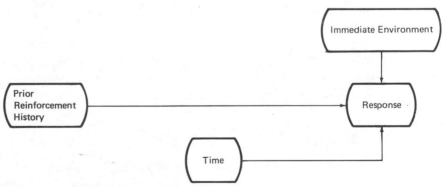

An individual's response is determined by his or her immediate environment, prior reinforcement history, and time.

The Response

Behavior, broken down into an observable unit of analysis called a response or reflex, is said to result directly from some environ-

[6] B. F. Skinner, "The Concept of the Reflex in the Description of Behavior," *Journal of General Psychology*, vol. 5 (1931), pp. 427–58.

mental stimulus. In the previous chapter response was defined as
any change in the behavior of an individual.

Responses have several measurable characteristics of interest to
behaviorists. The term *strength of response* is used to describe several of these characteristics, such as intensity, duration, latency,
frequency, speed, and rate. The response of pulling on a rope can
be used to differentiate among these response characteristics.

Suppose a person has been conditioned to pull a rope upon command by the use of money as a reinforcer. The intensity of his
response could be measured by the maximum force he exerts on the
rope when he pulls it. The duration of his response would be the
number of seconds he exerts some minimum force on the rope during
a response. Latency would be the time lag between the issuing of
the command and his beginning to pull on the rope. Frequency
might be the number of times he pulls on a rope after a command
or after his last reinforcement. Speed could be the time it takes his
hands to move a certain distance in pulling the rope for a unit of
time. Each of these characteristics might be subject to the control
of an experimenter through variations in stimuli, reinforcers, and
reinforcement schedules.

A *conditioned response* is one that is not naturally elicited by a
stimulus but becomes associated with that stimulus by reinforcement. Saying "thank you" when food is passed to you is a response
you have been conditioned to use by reinforcement (smiles, words
of praise) administered by your parents when you were learning
"proper" table manners. Turning on a fan on a hot night is a response
you have been conditioned to use by the reinforcement of a drop
in temperature which follows it.

The Stimulus

We have defined a stimulus as anything that happens to change
the behavior of an individual; that is, anything that produces a
response. According to the operant model, only external, physical,
or material stimuli are appropriate for the scientific analysis of
human behavior, because only such stimuli can be reliably measured and experimentally manipulated. These stimuli serve the
functions of eliciting, reinforcing, and discriminating.

Eliciting   An element in the environment (or a change in that
element) may directly produce a specific change in behavior as a
response. Such a stimulus is said to elicit the response. For example,
presenting a stimulus of a loud, sharp noise will elicit the response

of wincing. A stimulus of a sudden slap on the cheek will elicit the response of crying out. Such responses are referred to as *unconditioned responses*. Unconditioned responses require no conditions other than the eliciting stimulus—they almost invariably occur as a result of that stimulus.

Reinforcing An element in the environment (or a change in that element) may occur as a consequence or outcome of a response to some stimulus. Outcomes which strengthen the response are said to reinforce the stimulus-response relationship. In Chapter 3 we described the $S \rightarrow R \rightarrow O$ process, where O is an outcome following a response to a stimulus. If O makes subsequent responses to that stimulus more intense, more frequent, longer, or more likely, O is said to be a reinforcing stimulus. For example, candy might be a reinforcing stimulus for a child who has just obeyed an order; a drop in temperature might be a reinforcing stimulus for a person who has just turned on a fan; the cessation of noise might be a reinforcing stimulus for shutting the door to one's room.

Discriminating An element in the environment (or a change in an element) may act as a signal to an individual that a conditioned response is likely to be reinforced.

A discriminating stimulus is said to set the stage for a conditioned response. It is the condition under which a conditioned response will occur. If a child's whining and complaining are reinforced (e.g., by candy, toys, or hugging) only when a certain person (e.g., a grandparent) is present, that person will serve as a discriminatory stimulus for the conditioned response of whining and complaining. If a dog is reinforced for attacking only when it hears the word "Attack!" then the word serves as a discriminating stimulus for the aggressive response. In the same way, darkness is a discriminating stimulus for turning on your car headlights, ringing is a discriminating stimulus for picking up your telephone receiver, and Friday is a discriminating stimulus for going to the pay window.

Time and Prior Reinforcement History

Variables outside the immediate environment which can affect the $S \rightarrow R$ relationship, in addition to reinforcing stimuli (discussed above), are time and prior reinforcement history.

Time Time affects the $S \rightarrow R$ relationship through fatigue. If one has been continually responding to a series of stimuli for a long period of time, the strength, intensity, or frequency of responses tends to decline, even if the stimuli are virtually unchanged. Your rate of reading this book may decline after two hours of continuous reading. Your response of looking intently at all the words to the stimuli of printed pages may decrease in frequency from 500 to 50 words per minute.

The rate of response itself may be a factor affecting the strength of response. A high rate of response may lead to a rapid decline in the strength of response. A worker may respond less strongly after sustaining an assembly rate of 50 parts per minute than after a rate of 20 parts per minute. A boxer may throw fewer punches after a flurry than before.

Prior Reinforcement History   It has been shown that an important variable determining the strength of a response to a stimulus is the kind of reinforcement previously experienced for so responding to the stimulus. In Chapter 3 we noted that the outcomes for a response could be positive (pleasant), negative (unpleasant), or neutral. If the outcome to a response is neutral (the individual is indifferent to it), or if there is no outcome, extinction begins to occur; that is, response strength decreases.

By experimentally varying the outcomes to responses, researchers have discovered three patterns of reinforcing which have different effects on subsequent response rates.[7] These patterns, called schedules of reinforcement, are:

1. *Continuous reinforcement.* Under a continuous-reinforcement schedule, *every* response is reinforced. Continuous reinforcement is often used in training: Every time the student correctly performs what he has been taught, the teacher rewards him.
2. *Extinction.* Under an extinction schedule, *no* responses are reinforced. Extinction is also used in training: Whenever the student incorrectly performs what he has been taught, he is not rewarded, or he is ignored.
3. *Intermittent reinforcement.* Under an intermittent schedule, some responses are rewarded, some are not, based on a preplanned schedule. The basic intermittent schedules are described below.

In the *fixed-ratio* schedule, every Nth response is reinforced; one might reinforce every other response, or every seventh response, or every 100th response. Some sales commissions are fixed-ratio sched-

---

[7] C. B. Ferster and B. F. Skinner, *Schedules of Reinforcement* (New York: Appleton-Century-Crofts, 1957).

ules of reinforcement: The salesperson is given a bonus for every 25th sale of a certain item during a special sales drive.

In the *variable-ratio* schedule, every Nth response, *on the average,* is reinforced. The average is achieved by using a series of random ratios whose mean is the average desired. For instance, a variable ratio of 20 might be achieved by a series of reinforcements consisting of a ratio of 10 responses to 1 reinforcement (10:1), followed by 2:1, 30:1, 8:1, and 50:1. Gambling devices like slot machines are examples of variable-ratio schedules: a machine is set to pay off one jackpot for every N pulls of the lever, on the average. Sometimes there may be as few as 15 pulls between jackpots, sometimes as many as several hundred, but over the long run the machine pays off on a predetermined ratio of pulls to jackpots.

In the *fixed-interval* schedule, reinforcement is administered to the first response occurring after a predetermined interval of time has elapsed since the last reinforcement. Many pay schedules are fixed-interval schedules. You might get paid every Friday (one week after the last pay day) or every month (30 days after the last pay day).

In the *variable-interval* schedule, reinforcement is scheduled according to a random series of time intervals which vary about a mean. For instance, a variable interval of one week might be achieved by reinforcing responses occurring after 2 days, 2 weeks, 1 week, 1 day, and 11 days. Sometimes inspections are scheduled so as to reinforce performance on a variable-ratio basis. The inspecting agency visits each unit every six weeks, on the average, and the unit is rewarded on the basis of the inspector's report, but the time interval between inspections may vary from one to ten weeks.

Intermittent schedules are capable of maintaining high rates of responses. In addition, behavior reinforced intermittently is less easily extinguished than behavior reinforced continuously.

Contingencies of Behavior

Perhaps the clearest distinction between the expectancy and operant models is that expectancy models place the causes of behavior prior to the behavior, while the operant model places the causes of behavior after the behavior. In expectancy theories, one's expectancies and values regarding future behavioral outcomes determine effort. In the operant model, behavior occurs or persists because of environmental contingencies; that is, what happens after the behavior. Two basic kinds of human behavior are defined in the operant model: innate and operant.

Innate Behavior   Any behavioral responses or reflexes which humans exhibit due to their genetic endowment or the processes of natural selection are referred to as innate behavior. We "inherit" behavioral tendencies because our ancestors who exhibited them were more likely to survive than those who did not. The survival of the species is contingent upon these behaviors—such as ingesting food and water, breathing, expelling wastes, mating, defending one-self and one's family, and so forth. These behaviors enabled those who exhibited them, or who performed them best, to outsurvive those who were deficient in them. The reason for their survival value is the long-term environment in which the species evolved.

Operant Behavior   The process which supplements natural selection in survival is called operant behavior. According to B. F. Skinner, "Important consequences of behavior which could not play a role in evolution because they were not sufficiently stable features of the environment are made effective through operant conditioning during the lifetime of the individual, whose power in dealing with the world is thus vastly increased."[8]

The individual's power is increased because he can learn how to react to changes in his environment and to manipulate his environment in ways which improve his chances for survival. The results reinforce him. As humans we inherit the capacity to be reinforced by certain things—salt, sugar, sexual contact, physical freedom. We use that inherited capacity to be reinforced in learning ways to deal with our world effectively. One who is deprived of salt learns to do things to the environment to obtain it—like go to a store, recognize a salt container, take the container to a checkout stand, and produce sufficient money. Similarly one who is held prisoner is likely to be reinforced by behavior which can lead to escape or release.

In operant behavior, the key to behavior lies in its consequences: what happens to the individual and his environment as a result of the behavior, and what has happened in the past. Purpose and intention are not possessions of the individual, they lie in his environment. One does not work to earn a living. One works because working is behavior which has been reinforced in ways which make it possible to live.

Innate behavior results from the environment acting on the

---

[8] B. F. Skinner, *About Behaviorism* (New York: Alfred A. Knopf, 1974), p. 46.

individual. Operant behavior is the individual acting on the environment.

MAJOR DIFFERENCES BETWEEN EXPECTANCY AND OPERANT MODELS

Variables of Interest

Both expectancy and operant models have been developed to explain, predict, and influence behavior. Users of one model go about these tasks in ways quite different from users of the other, however.

The expectancy model focuses on the mental life of the individual. Attitudes, values, satisfaction, expectancies, valences, beliefs, and subjective probabilities of future events are studied for their interrelationships with behavior and with each other.

If you were interested in understanding, predicting, or influencing another's behavior, you could not directly observe, analyze, or measure that person's attitudes, values, satisfaction, expectancies, and so forth, because these aspects of mental life occur or exist inside the other person. You would have to rely on indirect measures for your data, either inferring them from the other's behavior or inducing the person to report data about himself to you. For example, you may infer another's values from the decisions he makes or from the way he spends his money or his time.

We often try to obtain such self-reports by asking questions such as: "Do you like your job? What do you think your chances are for promotion? How would you feel about a 10 percent salary increase?" A more systematic method used by researchers and managers of numbers of people employs questionnaires and surveys. This method makes it possible to compare the responses of different individuals more accurately and to collect and analyze data on large numbers of people, and the reliability and validity of the data are improved.

Users of expectancy models often become interested in mental and emotional data in itself. They study the nature of expectancies or valences and assess the impact of satisfaction on values or of beliefs on attitudes.

The operant model focuses on variables which can be observed or measured directly. It does not deny the existence of mental activity; it simply treats it as another form of behavior. The operant model does not credit attitudes, values, feelings, and other cognitive or emotional variables with the ability to cause overt behavior.

If you were interested in explaining, predicting, or influencing another's behavior using an operant model, you would collect data on his environment and his past reinforcement history. For example, if you wanted to find the causes of someone's behavior, you might carefully reccrd what happens to him as a result of that behavior for a certain number of responses. If you wanted to predict his behavior, you would collect data on the frequency and pattern of past consequences he has experienced for that behavior. If you wanted to change his behavior, you would try to change his environment and the consequences of his behavior.

Evidence for the Models

Evidence testing and either supporting or failing to support the validity of both expectancy and operant models fills thousands of pages of scholarly journals and books. Much of the research described in later chapters is based, either explicitly or implicitly, on one or the other of these models. Some of the research directly testing the models is discussed below.

Research on Expectancy Models Several field studies of the expectancy model have tried to predict actual production output or performance ratings of workers and managers. A typical approach has been to measure instrumentalities, valences, and other perceptions of work, effort, and outcomes by questionnaires, and then test the relationships between these variables and subsequent measures of performance. In general, the evidence has found instrumentalities, valences, and role perceptions significantly related to measures of subsequent performance.[9]

A recent summary of research and theory on the expectancy model indicates that while different parts of the model have been tested and supported in research, few adequate tests of the complete model have been carried out.[10] Several studies have found that people prefer occupations with high valences to those with lower valences, as the model predicts. Other studies have found

---

[9] For a review of such research, see H. G. Heneman III and D. P. Schwab, "Evaluation of Research on Expectancy Theory Predictions of Employee Performance," *Psychological Bulletin,* vol. 78 (July 1972), pp. 1–9.

[10] T. R. Mitchell, "Expectancy Models of Job Satisfaction, Occupational Preference, and Effort: A Theoretical, Methodological, and Empirical Appraisal," *Psychological Bulletin,* vol. 81 (1974), pp. 1053–77.

that people's satisfaction with their jobs is a function of their perception that those jobs are instrumental in obtaining outcomes which they value highly. Still other research shows that workers' attitudes toward performance are a positive function of the perceived instrumentalities and valences of good performance. Thus there is a good deal of evidence that people are attracted to and prefer things that they expect to be rewarding.

Studies attempting to predict the effort one puts into a job, using expectancy models, have yielded mixed results. Most of the studies found that workers or subjects who perceived high instrumentalities and valences in their jobs exerted more effort than those who perceived lower instrumentalities and valences in their jobs. However, about one third of the studies reviewed did not find instrumentalities and valences significantly related to measures of job effort.

One of the conclusions drawn from reviewing research on the expectancy model is that it is very difficult to test accurately because it is so complex. This problem is confounded by the fact that it includes many variables which are not directly observable and measurable, such as valences and instrumentalities. Any measures of such variables are at best only partial. Considerable work needs to be done on devising techniques for measurement which are highly reliable and valid. E. E. Lawler, one of the architects of expectancy theory, admits that "the theory has become so complex that it has exceeded the measures which exist to test it."[11] This is one reason some are more attracted to the operant model.

Research on the Operant Model   Since the operant model has had a longer history, there is a greater accumulation of evidence regarding it. The operant model also requires no mental or emotional data, and a good deal of research (including all the early evidence) has been conducted on the behavior of nonhuman subjects.

Much evidence supports the concept that different schedules of reinforcement have predictable effects on behavior. It has been shown that an extinction schedule will reduce response strength, that initiating a continuous reinforcement schedule will increase responses, and that intermittent schedules will maintain response strength more effectively than continuous schedules will. Simple behavioral changes can be predictably effected by changing the environment and altering the contingencies of reinforcement for be-

[11] E. E. Lawler III and J. L. Suttle, "Expectancy Theory and Job Behavior," *Organizational Behavior and Human Performance*, vol. 9 (1973), pp. 482–503.

havior—rearranging the consequences of behavior—with no attempts to assess or alter mental or emotional variables.[12]

One example of the different effects of variable and continuous schedules of reinforcement is a study of workers who were hired to score answer sheets to student exams.[13] One group of workers was paid under a continuous-reinforcement system (CRF) in which each worker was paid 25 cents every time she completed scoring a batch of 60 answer sheets. Another group of workers was paid under a variable-ratio reinforcement system (VR) in which each worker was paid 50 cents on a random basis which averaged out to every second batch she completed scoring. Thus both groups were paid, on the average, 25 cents per batch, one group continuously and the other according to a variable-ratio schedule.

Operant theory predicts that VR schedules of reinforcement produce higher response rates than CRF schedules, and the prediction was supported in this study. Workers under the VR schedule increased their productivity by nearly 60 percent more than workers under the CRF schedule, over a one-week period. The VR group went from an average of 250 to 362 answer sheets per hour, an improvement of 112 per hour, while the CRF group went from 197 to 269 answer sheets per hour, an improvement of 72 per hour. The two groups were equally satisfied with the system under which they were paid.

An imaginative study of the effects of reinforcement schedules attempted to reduce absenteeism rates in a manufacturing plant.[14] In one department of 215 workers, a lottery system was devised to reinforce coming to work on time on a variable schedule. Every day a worker came to work on time, he was given a chance to win a weekly prize of $20. Any day he did not come to work on time, he forfeited his chance for the prize.

Over the six weeks of this phase of the program, absenteeism decreased 18 percent. This compared to a 14 percent increase in absenteeism in four comparison groups totalling 508 employees who were not participating in the lottery system. In a second phase of

---

[12] Ferster and Skinner, *Schedules of Reinforcement.*

[13] Gary Yukl, K. N. Wexley, and J. D. Seymore, "Effectiveness of Pay Incentives under Variable Ratio and Continuous Reinforcement Schedules," *Journal of Applied Psychology,* vol. 56 (February 1972), pp. 19–23.

[14] Ed Pedalino and V. U. Gamboa, "Behavior Modification and Absenteeism: Intervention in the Industrial Setting," *Journal of Applied Psychology,* vol. 59 (1974), pp. 694–98.

the program, the lottery was run every other week. This process is known as "stretching" a reinforcement schedule by increasing the interval between reinforcements or ratios of responses to reinforcement. According to the operant model, once a reinforcement schedule has produced a certain response rate, it is possible to maintain that rate while stretching the schedule of reinforcement—that is, while increasing the number of responses before reinforcement.

In this study, there was no significant increase in absenteeism from phase 1, in which the lottery was held every week, to phase 2, in which the lottery was held every other week. A final demonstration of the effects of the reinforcement was to discontinue the lottery program altogether. After the program was discontinued, absenteeism climbed back to its original rate.

Differences in Predictions

Both the expectancy and the operant models have received substantial support in research. The two models, however, present substantially different views of human behavior. One reason why neither model is clearly superior is because few direct comparisons have been made between the two. Recently, however, some distinct and testable differences between the models have been pointed out,[15] and this may lead to research which can tell more about the relative merits of the expectancy and operant models.

One of the major differences in predictions is what happens to performance when the frequency with which the individual is rewarded changes. The expectancy model says that if one's expectations of reward decrease, one's effort or motivation to perform will likewise decrease. Suppose a salesperson made a sale every time he called on a customer, so that his expectancy of a rewarding outcome to calling on a customer was 1.0. Then a recession sets in and customers buy less frequently, say on the average of every other call. The expectancy model would predict that the salesperson's effort would decrease during the recession as his expectancy of reward declines. This decrease in effort should result in a decrease in the rate of calling on customers. The operant model, on the other hand, would predict *no* decrease in the salesperson's rate of calling on customers. According to this model, a variable-ratio reinforcement

---

[15] T. C. Mawhinney and Orlando Behling, "Differences in Predictions of Work Behavior from Expectancy and Operant Models of Individual Motivation," *Proceedings of the 33rd Annual Meeting of the Academy of Management*, 1973, pp. 383–88.

schedule such as the salesman experiences during the recession is sufficient to maintain a rate of response produced by a continuous-reinforcement schedule such as he had experienced prior to the recession.

No direct tests have yet been made of these competing predictions about the effects on human performance of changing reinforcement schedules (expectancies). One study did, however, directly compare the predictive accuracy of the two models in a simulated situation. The study of test graders described above tested a high-expectancy (CRF) system against a low-expectancy (VR) system.[16] One group of workers was paid 25 cents apiece for every batch of tests graded—a system in which $E = 1.0$ (continuous reinforcement). A second group of workers was paid 25 cents apiece on a random basis, averaging to about two out of every five batches of tests they scored—a system in which $E = 0.4$ (variable-ratio reinforcement).

Expectancy theory would predict less effort, and thus less productivity, for the low-expectancy group. An operant model would predict no such differences. The results failed to support the expectancy model. Workers under the CRF schedule who received 25 cents every time they completed a batch showed a productivity increase of 72 units per hour during the study. But workers under the VR schedule who received 25 cents only two out of every five times they completed a batch showed a productivity increase of 76 units per hour.

Of course, this single study is not conclusive, but it does illustrate differences in the predictions of the two models, and it suggests one case in which the operant model may be a better predictor of human performance. It is hoped more research of this type will be carried out on a variety of job situations which will directly test competing predictions of the two models.

SUMMARY

Individual performance in organizations is a function of both ability and motivation. Motivation is usually measured by the effort, intensity, or persistence with which an individual applies his or her abilities to the job.

Several models have been developed to explain and predict individual motivation in organizations. These include expectancy

---

[16] Yukl, Wexley, and Seymore, "Effectiveness of Pay Incentives."

models, which follow the cognitive approach to understanding behavior, and the operant model, which follows the reinforcement approach.

In the expectancy model, motivation is determined by the individual's expectations about his behavior and the satisfaction or value he will derive from the outcomes to his behavior. The past is important only insofar as it affects the individual's present beliefs, attitudes, or perceptions. According to expectancy theory, an individual is likely to exert high effort when he (1) believes that effort can improve performance, (2) believes that performance will affect outcomes, and (3) values the outcomes.

In the operant model, motivation is determined by the individual's present environment and past history of reinforcement. The environment serves both to produce a response and to reinforce it. The pattern or schedule by which the individual's behavior has been reinforced affects his tendency to repeat that behavior. According to the operant model, an individual is likely to exert high effort when he is in an environment in which performance has previously been reinforced.

These models can suggest different strategies for managers interested in increasing levels of effort in their organizations. The expectancy model suggests that managers should attempt to change the beliefs, attitudes, expectations, or values of their personnel. The operant model suggests that they should change the environment of the organizations and the contingencies under which personnel are reinforced.

QUESTIONS FOR REVIEW AND DISCUSSION

1. How important is motivation in performance? What other factors affect individual performance?

2. How would you measure the motivation of an hourly worker? A piece-rate worker? A salaried employee?

3. How do expectancy models fit into the cognitive approach to understanding behavior?

4. How important are the individual's perceptions in the expectancy models? Why?

5. In the expectancy models, how can an individual's past affect his current level of effort?

6. According to the operant model, in what ways does the individual's environment affect his behavior?

7. How might an individual's past affect his current level of effort, according to the operant model?

8. What is the difference between a continuous and an intermittent schedule of reinforcement? Which is said to be more effective in maintaining a current level of effort?

9. Describe a situation in which the expectancy and operant models would both suggest the same managerial strategy for dealing with an employee problem.

10. Describe your recent reinforcement history for watching television. Is it continuous or intermittent? If intermittent, is the schedule of reinforcement fixed or variable?

KEY WORDS

Motivation

Attitude

Expectancy

Valence

Effort-reward probability

Conditioned response

Eliciting stimulus

Discriminating stimulus

Reinforcing stimulus

Continuous reinforcement

Intermittent reinforcement

Ratio schedule

Interval schedule

Operant behavior

Objectives

1. To discuss the importance of accounting for individual differences in trying to understand and predict human behavior.
2. To describe possible individual differences in motivation and ability.
3. To discuss the importance of environmental factors in determining performance.
4. To identify the characteristics of the physical and social environments that are important to individual motivation and performance.
5. To examine implications for managers.

chapter five

Individual Differences and Environmental Factors

"*Sometimes I wonder what makes him tick.*"

Drawing by Modell:
© 1975 The New Yorker Magazine, Inc.

MOTIVATION, or the effort with which a person applies his or her abilities to a job, is a crucial determinant of that person's performance. The general models of motivation described in Chapter 4 should help you understand the role of motivation in performance. However, trying to explain, predict, understand, or influence human behavior in organizations requires something more. It is necessary to take into account not only general models of motivation but specific characteristics of the individual and his environment.

Figure 5–1 depicts the roles of individual differences and environmental factors in performance. Performance is determined by indi-

FIGURE 5–1
Effects of Individual Characteristics and Environmental Factors on Performance

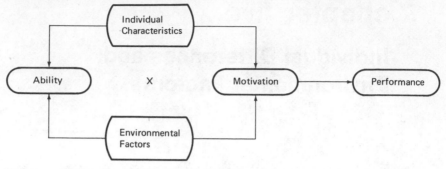

Performance is a function of ability and motivation. Both ability and motivation are
affected by individual characteristics and environmental factors.

vidual ability and motivation. Differences between individuals in
certain characteristics can result in differences in their abilities and
in the things that motivate them. Characteristics of the environment
can likewise affect both individual abilities and motivation.

INDIVIDUAL DIFFERENCES

The models described in Chapter 4 may be reasonable and
helpful in understanding behavior, but their application in trying
to predict the motivation and performance of individuals is com-
plicated by individual differences. These include both differences
in motives or reinforcers and differences in ability.

Differences in Motives or Reinforcers

Rewards or performance outcomes have been considered only
in the general terms of the expectancy and operant models. In
applying these models, managers and administrators must specifically
consider the different kinds of things that reward or reinforce human
behavior.

Psychologists have identified scores of different rewards and
reinforcers and have arranged them into categories to aid understanding. Cognitive psychologists and psycholanalysts have provided most of these categories, which they refer to as classes of
needs or motives. They define a need or motive as an inner force

which impels a person to behave in a particular way. Behaviorists refer to these categories as classes of reinforcers. For simplicity's sake, we will use the terms of the psychologists who provided the original categories.

Five Categories of Needs   The most widely known classification of needs was compiled by a psychologist who described human motivation as arising from five categories of needs.[1] These categories are:

1. *Physiological needs*—needs basic to the survival of the human species, such as hunger, thirst, respiration, and sex.
2. *Safety needs*—needs basic to the physical and psychological protection of the individual, such as needs for shelter, protection from threat and danger, orderliness, consistency, and predictability in one's environment.
3. *Social needs*—needs basic to one's association with and acceptance by other humans, such as needs for friendship, love, and affiliation.
4. *Esteem needs*—needs having to do with one's self-worth, such as needs for recognition, power, and self-respect.
5. *Self-actualization*—the need to fulfill one's potential, to test one's limits, to become whatever one can become.

Some psychologists propose that these needs reside inside a person as forces capable of energizing and directing his behavior. A behaviorist would identify counterparts to all these needs in the person's environment and would attribute the energizing and directing to these objects. For instance, behaviorist counterparts to the physiological needs would be food, liquid, oxygen, and members of the opposite sex, all objects in the environment which are highly reinforcing to human behavior. It would be a useful exercise to identify objects in the environment which would be behaviorist counterparts to the other four categories of needs.

Two theories springing from these categories of needs have received much attention. One states that the categories of needs can be arranged in a hierarchy of priorities or prepotency, as depicted in Figure 5–2. According to this theory, physiological needs dominate human motivation until they are somewhat satisfied, at which point safety needs become most potent. Only when both physiological and safety needs, which are referred to as "lower

---

[1] See Abraham H. Maslow, *Motivation and Personality* (New York: Harper & Bros., 1954), chap. 5.

FIGURE 5–2
A Hierarchy of Needs

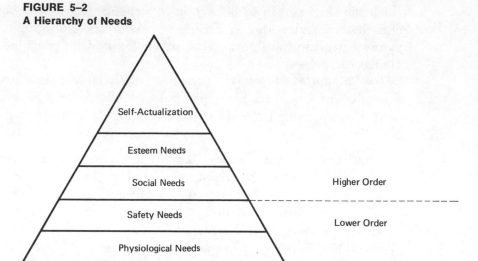

Higher order needs are said to become important in an individual's motivation only after his or her lower order needs have been at least partially satisfied.

order" needs, have been satisfied will "higher order" needs become important in determining an individual's motivation. Thus an individual will be unlikely to be motivated by the need for self-actualization until his physiological and safety needs have been essentially taken care of and he has achieved a measure of satisfaction of his social and esteem needs.

This theory is intuitively appealing and has been widely used to interpret certain kinds of behavior. For instance, certain isolated tribes in tropical climates have never developed any culture, music, literature, or history. This failure is often attributed to their inability to ever satisfy their physiological and safety needs because of the environment in which they live. Because they have no means of preserving food, their lives are a continual series of searches for the next meal.

However, the need hierarchy remains essentially an untested theory. Further, the hierarchy has been literally interpreted as applying to all humans in the specific order suggested in Figure 5–2. Such interpretations fail to account for differences between individuals or cultures.

A second theory growing out of the need hierarchy proposes that needs which essentially have been satisfied are not effective motivators of behavior. That is, an individual will not direct his behavior toward the satisfaction of a need which is already satisfied. For example, food is not likely to be an effective means of energizing or directing the behavior of someone who has just finished a big meal.

These theories make it evident that individuals can differ in the kinds of things that motivate or reinforce them. Even within a single department in an organization, there may be some people who value recognition and esteem more than any other available rewards, some who value power, some who value friendship, some who value the opportunity to express themselves in their work, some who value security, and some who value monetary rewards. Few people are motivated or reinforced by a single need or object; most are capable of responding to a variety of rewards, although they may prefer one more than others.

Other Types of Needs   Besides the hierarchy of needs, several other categories have been proposed as capable of motivating human behavior in organizations. The most prominent of these is the need for achievement, proposed and researched by psychologists at Harvard.[2] According to this theory, a human need to accomplish challenging goals is developed in early childhood. The development of this need is said to result largely from encouragement and reinforcement of autonomy and self-reliance in children by their parents.

Motivational researchers have developed a set of projective tests for assessing an individual's need for achievement and have designed and carried out programs for developing achievement motivation in adults. They report that businessmen and executives who undergo achievement training greatly increase entrepreneurial activities such as expanding businesses and investments.[3]

Some other motives which have been proposed as particularly meaningful to human behavior include needs for competence and mastery, satisfaction of curiosity, activity, and aesthetic fulfillment. Competence needs are said to be reflected in the quest to control one's environment, curiosity needs in the unending search for knowledge, activity needs in restlessness and boredom, and aesthetic needs in the attraction for beauty over ugliness.

People are capable of being motivated by a large, complex set of motives or reinforcers which deal with physiological survival, secur-

---

[2] See David C. McClelland, *The Achieving Society* (Princeton, N.J.: D. Van Nostrand Co., 1961).

[3] David C. McClelland, "Achievement Motivation Can Be Developed," *Harvard Business Review*, vol. 43 (November–December 1965), pp. 6–24.

ity, affiliation, esteem, self-actualization, achievement, competence, curiosity, activity, and beauty. The range and variety of these factors make it imperative to account for individual differences in dealing with individual behavior.

No individual will respond with equal intensity to all these motives or reinforcers. In any group of individuals there will be differences in the strength of individual responses to a given reward. Thus it is essential for managers and administrators to recognize that any power or influence they have to reward or reinforce an individual's behavior is restricted to their control over the things that particular individual finds rewarding or reinforcing. A pat on the back is unlikely to bring a favorable response from someone who is indifferent to social recognition. More responsibility will probably not be viewed as rewarding to someone who perceives himself as already overworked or overburdened.

A Two-Factor Theory of Motivation in Organizations[4] One other classification of factors which are important to motivation has generated a large amount of interest and research. From studies of job satisfaction in industrial settings, a group of researchers concluded that there are two sets of these factors which differ in their effects on people at work.

Some factors were said to be necessary to maintain a reasonable level of satisfaction; without them, people would be dissatisfied at work. However, these factors were said to be incapable of energizing and directing behavior other than showing up at work and performing at minimum levels. These were labeled *hygiene* factors; they include:

- Company policy
- Supervision
- Relations with fellow workers
- Job security
- Salary
- Working conditions
- Status
- Job effects on personal life

A second set of factors was said to be not essential to satisfaction but necessary to energizing and directing effort and behavior above minimum levels. These factors, which were said to be capable of strongly motivating people at work, were labeled *motivators*:

- Achievement
- Recognition
- Advancement

[4] See Frederick Herzberg, Bernard Mausner, and Barbara Snyderman, *The Motivation to Work*, 2d ed. (New York: John Wiley & Sons, 1959).

- The nature of the work itself
- Responsibility
- Opportunities for professional and personal growth

The two-factor theory, while intuitively appealing and eagerly accepted by many practitioners, has suffered a great deal of criticism for certain weaknesses in the methods used in its research. Failure to reproduce the findings with different research methods is one such criticism. Researchers and practitioners have become quite skeptical of the notion that certain factors are capable of affecting only job satisfaction, while only a limited number of other factors are capable of affecting motivation and effort. Many are particularly critical of the proposition that salary or money is incapable of affecting motivation or performance. There is much evidence that money is capable of energizing and directing a wide variety of human behavior, largely because it can be used to satisfy a wide variety of human needs.

A further problem with this theory is that it is too simplistic—it overlooks individual differences. To say that people at work are capable of being motivated only by achievement, recognition, advancement, responsibility, growth, and the job itself is to ignore the wide range of individual differences which are found in any organization. While "motivators" may be very rewarding to many people, there are nevertheless many others who, because of their experience or state, respond strongly to improvements in "hygiene" factors such as money, status, and working conditions.

Differences in Ability

We have proposed that human behavior is a function of characteristics of the person and his environment; further, a person's performance is a function of his ability and motivation. We have devoted a good deal of space to discussing the complex question of human motivation, and it is equally important to consider the role that ability plays in an individual's ultimate performance. In fact, differences among individual performances of certain types may be dominated by differences in the individuals' abilities. No matter how intense your motivation, it is unlikely that any of you would fight better than Muhammad Ali, act better than Glenda Jackson, write better than William F. Buckley, volley better than Chris Evert, or talk more than Howard Cosell.

For our purposes ability is a broad term encompassing all personal characteristics, other than motivation, which can affect performance. Ability includes physiological, intellectual, and personality characteristics, aptitudes and skills, knowledge and experience. Each of these ability factors can play a major role in performance.

Physiological, Intellectual, and Personality Characteristics   Physiological characteristics such as height, weight, stamina, and coordination may be the dominant factors in physical tasks such as lumberjacking, construction, dancing, and moving furniture. Intellectual characteristics may largely determine academic performance, problem solving, and research. Personality factors may strongly affect bargaining or decision-making behavior, sales performance or success in entertainment fields.

Aptitudes and Skills   Aptitudes are individual characteristics which facilitate the learning and acquisition of new skills. Thus, aptitudes can affect the rate at which one learns a new job and the level of performance one is able to maintain. Skill, or the acquired ability to perform a specific task well, is a function of physiological characteristics, knowledge, and experience. Skill may be the single most important determinant of a person's performance of complex tasks such as computer programming, surgery, or piloting an aircraft.

Knowledge   An understanding of how and when tasks should be performed, as well as what tasks should be performed, is classified as knowledge. Many deficiencies in human performance in organizations can be traced to people who did not know the scope of their task responsibilities. The performance of a quality control inspector may be unsatisfactory if he is unaware that his job includes the task of reporting excessive variances in product quality to production control. The performance of a supervisor may be deficient if she is unaware that she should be preparing her subordinates for advancement to new jobs, as well as managing the performance of their present tasks.

Experience   Surprisingly, experience can have either a positive or a negative influence on performance. An individual's experience in dealing with a particular stimulus or situation leads him to develop certain tendencies to react to that stimulus in a particular way. Eventually, experience leads to the development of dominant responses or habits—behavior which the individual displays almost invariably and without hesitation in a particular situation.

If the dominant response is the most appropriate one that could be used in that situation, then experience has facilitated performance. For example, a manager might develop the tendency to ignore the gripes and complaints of one of his departments, because his experience has shown their griping and complaining to be unrelated to their work situation and simply a way to pass the time of day. His dominant response to a gripe or complaint from that department, therefore, is to acknowledge hearing it and then return to more profitable work.

However, all experience does not lead to appropriate dominant responses. A person who develops an inappropriate response may continue to use it when confronted with a similar situation. The inappropriate response interferes with trying out new and perhaps better responses. For example, a new salesperson, anxious over his first meeting with a customer, nevertheless successfully sells a reasonable quantity of low-profit-margin items. The salesperson is relieved and pleased by the outcome to this response—a nice order. In subsequent visits the salesperson is usually successful in obtaining the same order from that customer. Eventually, he tends to respond to the customer with a request for the same order. His experience leads him to say, with satisfaction, "Old Jones Hardware is a customer good for 75 bucks almost every time." His sales pitch to Jones becomes so comfortable and so frequently reinforced by an order that the salesperson fails to try other responses, such as asking for a larger order or an order for higher margined products.

Of course, customers develop the same kinds of experience-based tendencies. "Brand loyalty" simply refers to a customer's habit of responding to a stimulus situation. Finding herself in need of a certain product, she purchases the brand that has been reasonably satisfactory in the past. This tendency may lessen her chance of trying a new or competing product which may actually be better than the familiar brand.

Experience can also have a negative influence on performance when the individual fails to distinguish subtle changes in the situation which render a previously appropriate response inappropriate. A defensive lineman in football is strongly reinforced by early successes in charging through the offensive line to tackle an opposing quarterback behind the line of scrimmage, but a clever quarterback may exploit that tendency. He could counter with plays which look like those in which a hard defensive rush pays off but which instead trap the defensive player, and then he could run the ball through the place the lineman should have been.

Similar problems arise from previous experience in problem

solving. One who learns that a certain heuristic or method is successful and efficient in solving a certain class of problems may continue
to use that method on problems which appear similar but which in
fact call for a new or different one. Former President Nixon's foreign
policy spectaculars were successful as a method of coping with
public uneasiness over domestic problems and declines in Presidential popularity in the opinion polls during his first term. But the
Watergate scandel evoked a public loss of confidence which additional trips to the U.S.S.R. and Egypt could not reverse.

ENVIRONMENTAL FACTORS

The environment in which the individual performs can affect his
performance in several ways. Certain elements of the environment,
such as technology, can ease or hinder performance; in fact, they
can virtually prevent it from falling below some minimum level or
exceeding some maximum level. The physical and social environments can also indirectly influence performance by affecting the
motivation or effort of the performer.

The Physical Environment

Certain elements of the physical environment affect individual
behavior on the job; these include general working conditions and
specific elements such as tools, technology, and task design. These
physical elements can affect both the ability and the motivation of
people to perform their jobs.

The landmark in research and application of knowledge to
improving human performance through changing the physical environment was Frederick Taylor's work with the Bethlehem Iron
Company several decades ago. Hired to improve worker efficiency,
Taylor set about studying task design and work methods in the belief
that there was "one best way" to perform every task. He was interested in methods and tools which conserve human energy and
reduce fatigue. By standardizing work methods, introducing
programmed rest periods, and inducing worker cooperation
through higher wages, Taylor produced a 362 percent increase in
productivity![5]

The current state of knowledge about the role of the physical
environment could fill several volumes. A number of professional

[5] F. B. Copley, *Frederick W. Taylor* (New York: Harper & Row, 1973).

journals are devoted to research in the area. It would be impossible to summarize all such research here, but a few examples will illustrate some of the physical elements which influence human performance in organizations.

The effects of noise and lighting have long been recognized in many jobs, particularly those involving repetitive tasks. Above-normal or continuous noise can interfere with learning and decrease performance. For example, one group of students received typewriting training under normal noise conditions for 32 sessions, while a similar group was trained under above-normal noise conditions.[6] Both groups learned at about the same rates for the first 16 sessions, after which the group exposed to abnormal noise learned at a significantly slower rate than the normal group. Differences between the two groups were greatest at the end of the training sessions.

Noise does not always hinder performance, however. Housewives and professional persons were subjected to intermittent and continuous broad-band noise while performing repetitive tasks.[7] Both types of noise produced errors, which were reduced by providing the subjects with ear protection. However, gaps in productivity were 50 percent less frequent during intermittent noise than under continuous noise. Intermittent noise can thus sometimes be beneficial because it reduces monotony in repetitive tasks.

Changes in the amount or character of lighting can affect a broad range of performance, particularly difficult visual tasks. For example, persistent decreases in major league batting averages, despite livelier baseballs and lower pitching mounds, can be attributed in part to the greater number of games played at night, as well as other environmental changes such as larger parks, bigger fielders' gloves, and more relief pitchers. Improvements in lighting have produced greater assurance and reliability in visual inspection in all sorts of organizations, from steel factories[8] to optometry offices.

Other physical factors in the design of tasks can alter human performance by affecting the arousal, boredom, or fatigue of per-

---

[6] L. Sebek and K. Brenk, "Influence of Noise on Degree of Development of Typewriting Skill," *Revijer in Psikologyie,* vol. 3, nos. 1–2 (1973), pp. 57–61.

[7] L. R. Hartley, "Performance during Continuous and Intermittent Noise and Wearing Ear Protection," *Journal of Experimental Psychology,* vol. 102 (March 1974), pp. 512–16.

[8] J. Moraal, "Effects of Training and Sleep Deprivation on Visual Inspection of Static and Dynamic Patterns," *Ergonomics,* vol. 16, no. 3 (1973), pp. 332.

formers.[9] Because fatigue can impair motor and mental skills as well as effort, it has been the subject of a good deal of applied research. The aviation industry has been particularly involved in such research as technological advances have increased the work loads and task durations of pilots and air traffic controllers. Such factors as night flying, crossing several time zones, and schedules which result in frequent changes in sleep habits lead to fatigue. This fatigue manifests itself in such performance problems as disturbance of timing, neglect of necessary information, exaggerated vigor of response, and failure to respond at all.[10]

Tasks requiring the simultaneous performance of more than one activity may hinder the performance of the acts involved. In one experiment, three groups of subjects listened to news bulletins. One group did nothing else, a second group carried out a simultaneous motor activity, and a third engaged in a simultaneous mental activity. The results revealed that the first group correctly recalled 58 percent of the news items; the second group, only 39 percent; and the third group, only 29 percent, or half of what the first group recalled. Such effects obviously can cause problems in jobs where the necessity to monitor information sources continually is coupled with demands for simultaneous mental and motor activity, particularly in military, hospital, police, and transportation organizations.

The introduction of background music has frequently been successful as a means of decreasing boredom and increasing alertness, particularly in jobs requiring the continual repetition of tasks, such as assembly-line work.[11] In fact, a general approach to the problem of monotony and boredom has been to introduce variation into the task through the use of music, frequent short rest periods, rotation of job assignments, and other relatively minor changes in the physical environment.

The Social Environment

The elements of the social environment which can affect the behavior of people in organizations include both other people (such as supervisors, co-workers, subordinates, clients, and customers) and

---

[9] For an excellent summary of such factors and a theoretical discussion of their effects, see W. E. Scott, Jr., "Activation Theory and Task Design," *Organizational Behavior and Human Performance,* vol. 1 (August 1966), pp. 3–30.

[10] C. Cameron, "Fatigue Problems in Modern Industry," *Ergonomics,* vol. 14 (1971), pp. 713–20.

[11] J. E. Fox, "Background Music and Industrial Efficiency: A Review," *Applied Ergonomics,* vol. 2 (1971), pp. 70–73.

social systems (such as laws, rules, policies, and incentive programs). This book devotes much attention to consideration of the social environment under such topics as satisfaction, leadership, group influence, competition, and creative behavior.

The social environment, like the physical environment, can either facilitate or hinder performance. A common complaint of many people in service organizations is that company policies or supervisors prevent them from providing the kind of service their clients really need. For example, college dormitory counselors have said that housing administration policies force them to serve more as custodians of property and enforcers of rules than as counselors of the students who live in the dormitories.

The system with which an organization chooses to reward its members is a crucial determinant of the direction in which they will expend their efforts. It is unfortunately true that reward systems sometimes stray from organizational goals, and workers are thus confronted with conflicting pressures from their social environment. In one study of such conflict, workers were exhorted to concentrate on the quality of their work and told that quality would determine their wages.[12] The actual reward system, in which workers were paid on the quantity they produced, was not changed, however. For a short time the quality of work improved, but it soon reverted to previous lower levels as workers redirected their efforts toward quantity of production. Thus they responded more to the reward system than to company policies and announcements.

Authority figures are one source of social influence on performance, but competitors, co-workers, and customers also can alter the levels of effort put into a job. Work restriction is a well-known industrial phenomenon in which a work group disregards company policies and incentives and establishes its own moderate work pace. The group prevents any member from exceeding that pace by social or physical sanctions. On the other hand, the pressures resulting when other people are performing the same task can induce competition and increase levels of effort and performance, depending upon the reward system and task involved.

The mere presence of a social environment can sometimes produce significant changes in performance; this is called the *social facilitation effect*. Research shows that the presence of an audience

---

[12] G. S. Johnson, "Control of the Quality and Quantity of Human Performance: An Experimental Analysis," *Dissertation Abstracts International*, vol. 32 (February 1972), p. 4941.

or crowd as witnesses facilitates the performance of well-learned responses, but it seems to interfere with learning or performing newly learned responses.[13]

The theoretical explanations for these different effects is that an audience increases the arousal level of a performer and makes dominant (well-learned) responses more likely to occur. It has been observed that certain entertainers, professional musicians, and athletes perform best before large crowds and only indifferently during practice sessions.

Sometimes, however, the presence of an audience is a problem. One who is performing a novel task or trying to change a behavior pattern may tend to slip back to the old, dominant pattern of responding when faced with the arousing effects of a crowd. Managers of boxers, for instance, have problems getting them to change their tactics to adapt to a particular opponent's strengths and weaknesses. Despite coaching and training, they tend to revert to their accustomed styles in the presence of a crowd and their opponents. Those of you who have to appear before a large audience have probably experienced the difference between your rehearsal performance and the moment of truth on opening night.

SOME IMPLICATIONS FOR MANAGEMENT

According to the general model we have proposed, human performance in organizations is a function of characteristics of both the individual and his environment. The individual's performance is a function of his or her abilities and motivation, both of which can be affected, enhanced, or limited by the physical and social environment.

The principal implication of this model for managers and administrators is that there are several sets of determinants of human performance in organizations. The degree to which a given manager can influence these determinants varies from case to case, but managers should at least be aware of some of the possibilities that exist.

Managers and administrators affect the ability levels of their organizations through their recruitment, selection, and training practices. One obvious approach to improving performance is to recruit more talented or capable people. This approach requires a recognition of the abilities most needed by the organization, an ability to identify potential recruits who possess these needed abilities, and

[13] R. B. Zajonc, "Social Facilitation," *Science*, vol. 149 (1965), pp. 269–74.

the resources necessary to attract them to the organization. Selecting talented or capable people and placing them in jobs where they can best use their talents is the crucial aspect of such a program. The success of any program designed to increase performance by bringing in new talent depends on the validity of the criteria on which the organization bases its selection process.

Research indicates that there is plenty of room for improvement in the selection processes of most organizations. Many of the traditional approaches have been found deficient. The personal interview, a device used by virtually every organization, has proven to be notoriously unreliable as a predictor of performance. Written personality, intelligence, and aptitude tests often are unrelated to performance, and sometimes they discriminate against certain groups of potential employees. In recent years the federal government has required organizations to demonstrate, with hard evidence, that their selection procedures can distinguish between efficient and less efficient employee performance and do not systematically discriminate against the members of any ethnic or demographic group.

Training is another way of improving performance through raising ability levels. It can include programs run by the organization itself, performed in the organization by outside consultants, or conducted independent of the organization, as in trade schools and degree granting institutions. Less formal methods include on-the-job training and apprenticeships. Regardless of the type, training requires an identification of needed skills, the selection of individuals capable of acquiring and applying these skills, and the use of programs capable of imparting them. To demonstrate the value of training to the organization, there must be evidence that it does, in fact, increase the necessary skills. Ideally, this evidence would come from comparisons between the performance of trained and untrained personnel.

Theoretically, there are two basic approaches to influencing levels of motivation or effort in organizations. One is to recruit or select members who are likely to put greater effort into their performance than others. Unfortunately, there are few reliable and valid tests for assessing effort potential. Managers are forced to rely on the assessments of personal references in attempting to gauge the effort potential of job candidates, and this type of assessment has provided little evidence of validity.

The other approach is to develop reward systems which reinforce people for the effort they put into their work and to eliminate, as much as possible, factors which deter performance and effort. An appropriate guide might be, "If you want effort from people, make it matter." Those who find that extra effort makes no difference in their work or outcomes will find other channels for their energy. Those who find that extra effort pays off in improved job performance and rewards will be encouraged to continue exerting high levels of effort.

One way in which recruitment and selection can influence motivation and effort in organizations is that managers can strive to recruit employees who are likely to enjoy the kinds of work they will be expected to do and who are likely to be reinforced by the kinds of rewards that will be available to them. Some industries have developed (with some success) tests for assessing the degree to which a job applicant will be "turned on" by the available job and job outcomes. Most organizations, however, have no such tests, and probably the best approach is for the manager and the job applicant to be candid with each other. The manager explains as accurately as possible the nature of the job, its everyday details, and the specific rewards available. Given such information, the candidate should be able to assess his own potential for reinforcement, effort, and performance in the organization. At least he should have a realistic set of expectations about the job, thus lessening the chances for the debilitating effects that disillusionment can have on effort and motivation.

Testing, training, and reward systems are all factors in the environment of an organization which can affect levels of ability and effort. Careful attention to the immediate work environment also can yield clues to factors which influence performance. One obvious way to improve performance is to provide workers with better tools and the information necssary to do the job. The performance of farmers is improved by making available better farm implements, superior seed, effective fertilizers and insecticides, and technical information from agricultural experts. The performance of doctors is improved by access to information and improved diagnostic procedures, surgical instruments, and medicines. The performance of traffic controllers is improved by radar, of vaulters by fiberglass poles, of engineers by computers, and of managers by the assignment of assistants.

Performance can also be improved by identifying and removing obstacles in the environment which hinder performance. Physical barriers between people are removed to improve their communication. Inferior products are removed from a salesperson's line, unnecessary activites from a job description, red tape from a counsellor's procedures, germs from an operating room, noise from a classroom, distractions from a researcher, and outside interruptions from an executive conference. All of these make it easier for people to perform their jobs.

SUMMARY

Performance in organizations is a function of motivation and ability. In attempting to understand, predict, or influence behavior, managers must take into account the fact that individuals differ in their abilities and in the things that motivate them.

Individuals can be motivated by a variety of motives or rewards. These include survival, security, affiliation, esteem, self-actualization, achievement, competence, curiosity, activity, and beauty. However, the chances are that any two individuals will respond differently to any given reward. Further, no individual will respond with equal intensity to different rewards.

Individual differences in ability may show up in physiological or intellectual characteristics, in aptitudes and skills, and in knowledge and experience. Despite the care with which organizations select and train new members, individual differences in ability will always be sufficient to produce a range of performance levels in any job category. Some people will always have more ability than others.

Because behavior is a product of the interaction between the individual and the environment, the role of the physical and social environment cannot be overlooked. The physical environment of work, including technology and working conditions, can either complement or inhibit individual abilities. The social environment, including supervisors, peers, subordinates, and nonmembers of the organization, plays a major role in individual motivation. Recognizing the impact of the physical and social environment on ability and motivation may enable managers to find ways that make it easier and pleasanter for individuals to perform their work.

QUESTIONS FOR REVIEW AND DISCUSSION

1. How can individual differences affect performance?

2. Explain why a satisfied need is not an effective motive for performance. If this is true, what are the implications for the manager of highly paid technicians?

3. What are the shortcomings of the two-factor theory of motivation?

4. Describe a job for which you would expect ability to be more important than motivation and one for which you would expect motivation to be more important than ability.

5. "Experience is the best teacher." Discuss this statement.

6. Describe a situation in which the physical environment has a greater effect on performance than individual differences in ability or motivation do.

7. What elements of the social environment might affect the performance of a (*a*) research worker, (*b*) police officer, (*c*) minister, priest or rabbi, (*d*) first-line supervisor?

8. How can recruitment and selection processes of an organization affect the motivation of its members?

KEY WORDS

Need or motive	Hygiene factors
Lower order need	Aptitude
Higher order need	Dominant response
Need for achievement	

part three
Individual Behavior in Organizations

PART THREE describes four individual behavior processes which are important to organizations and explores their implications for management.

Chapter 6, on the perceptual process, examines the influence of physical and social environments on perception and evaluation. It describes several perceptual tendencies and notes individual differences in perception. The implications of perceptual processes for management are discussed, particularly as regards performance appraisal.

Chapters 7 and 8 are concerned with individual decision making. Chapter 7 discusses three elements of the decision process: the decision, the problem, and the individual. Criteria for evaluating decisions are reviewed, and certain problem characteristics which can affect the decision process are discussed. Two models of the individual as decision maker are presented, and individual characteristics which are related to differences in the way people make decisions are described. Chapter 8 considers the influence of the physical and social environments on individual decision making. It describes a seven-step normative model of decision making and examines several ways in which managerial decision making typically deviates from the normative model.

Chapters 9 and 10 deal with creative and innovative behavior in organizations. Chapter 9, which emphasizes the need for such behavior in contemporary organizations in all fields, examines the nature of creativity and describes some methods by which creative potential can be measured. Characteristics of creatively behaving individuals are discussed, and some suggestions are made for managers concerned with increasing creative behavior in their organizations. Chapter 10 examines the four phases of the creative process and gives examples of each. A number of factors which have been found either to disrupt or to advance the creative process are discussed. The chapter suggests that some managerial practices interfere with the creative process and concludes by discussing ways in which organizations can facilitate creativity and innovation.

Chapter 11 deals with attitudes, particularly those expressing job satisfaction and dissatisfaction. The nature, sources, and functions of attitudes are described. Job satisfaction is analyzed, with consideration of how it is measured and the factors that affect it. The chapter concludes by discussing the implications of job satisfaction and dissatisfaction for such organizational problems as absenteeism, tardiness, turnover, and productivity.

Objectives

1. To examine different factors which affect human perception.
2. To describe several common perceptual tendencies.
3. To discuss the implications of perceptual processes for management, especially as regards performance appraisal.

OUTLINE OF CHAPTER

chapter six

Perceiving and Evaluating

The senior partners of the law firm of Schmidt and Snodgrass decided to automate the preparation of routine legal documents. Mr. Knock, a junior member of the firm who also acted as office manager, was assigned the task of accomplishing this. Originally, Ms. Lohman, a woman with three years of prelaw training, was selected to implement the program. She had quickly proven too technically incompetent and socially incompatible to do the job.

Somewhat in desperation, Mr. Knock then chose Ms. Jones, one of the younger and more capable secretaries, as her replacement. The system implementation was then successful to the satisfaction and surprise of all concerned. Ms. Jones, through special schooling and diligent effort, had learned the intricacies of the relatively complex system and managed to convert many of the standard documents into forms such that they could be readily produced automatically.

At the end of the year, which was review time for all office personnel, Ms. Jones was given a minimum raise. Ms. Jones was of the opinion that her dual efforts, as secretary and system operator, were worthy of a greater reward and stated this to Mr. Knock. His explanation was that due to her past raises, resulting from her excellence as a secretary, she was already approaching the pay standard of the secretaries of long tenure and that a more substantial increase would create dissension and dissatisfaction among these women. Ms. Jones responded by refusing the small raise, claiming that it was an insult.

While it was not stated in so many words, Mr. Knock read this as a precursor to her resignation.[1]

A CLASSIC CASE of superior-subordinate conflict is described above. The conflict is centered around one of the outcomes of Jones's performance—a raise. Her performance consisted of serving capably as a secretary and implementing a system for automating the preparation of legal documents. The outcome of her performance considered here was a raise—a minimum raise.

[1] J. V. Murray and T. J. Von der Embse, *Organizational Behavior: Critical Incidents and Analysis* (Columbus, Ohio: Charles E. Merrill Publishing Co., 1973), p. 14.

Preceding chapters have noted that good performance must be rewarded if it is to be continued. The problem in this case is whether the outcome was rewarding for Jones.

Knock perceived the raise as a reward. He viewed Jones as nothing other than a secretary, capable, no doubt, but still a secretary, and a young one at that. He perceived a larger raise as out of the question, because she had received such large raises for her excellent performance in past years that she was already making as much as the most senior secretaries. The older secretaries, he believed, would perceive a large raise for Jones as inequitable.

Jones, on the other hand, does not perceive the proferred raise as a reward. She sees herself as not just a secretary, but the key person in implementing a new system. In terms of the expectancy model described in Chapter 4, Jones exerted extra effort in her work during the year to perform above and beyond a normal secretary's duties, all in expectations of some rewards. The result of her extra effort was the highest performance of her career at Schmidt and Snodgrass, and for this she received the lowest raise of her career. From her perspective, the raise is not a reward for her efforts, but an insult to her performance.

Whether she will resign, as Knock fears, we cannot predict. As Chapter 11 will demonstrate, resignation is a function of not only dissatisfaction but other alternatives as well. However, we could predict that her subsequent levels of effort will be considerably diminished. In terms of the expectancy model, her perception that effort leads to rewards has all but vanished. In terms of the operant model, exerting extra effort and performing well have failed to be reinforced.

This case points out quite clearly one fact of organizational life: people often see the same things in very different ways. These differences in perception can be the cause of a good deal of poor communication, misunderstanding, misinterpretation, confusion, lack of cooperation, hostility, and even conflict.

In this chapter we will describe the processes of perception and the factors which affect the way people perceive the world around them. We will discuss a number of perceptual tendencies which are common sources of misunderstanding or misperception, and their implications for management. Finally, we will concentrate on one area of managerial behavior in which perception plays a vital role: performance appraisal.

PERCEPTUAL PROCESSES

Perception includes all those processes by which an individual receives information about his environment—seeing, hearing, feeling, tasting, and smelling. All are important, but in the behavior of individuals in organizations the first three—seeing, hearing, and feeling—are the dominant senses. The study of these perceptual processes shows that their functioning is affected by three classes of variables—the objects or events being perceived, the environment in which perception occurs, and the individual doing the perceiving.

THE ROLE OF THE OBJECT IN PERCEPTION

Obviously, perceptions are affected by the object being perceived. Your perceptions of this page are partly a function of the texture of the paper and the quality and placement of the printing on that paper. Jones's perceptions of the raise offered her were partly a function of the words used to convey the offer.

One of the basic characteristics of human perception is *selective organization*. Perception is selective in that only some of the available perceptions are important to a given individual's behavior. In cognitive terms, only some cognitions are perceived by the individual; others are excluded or rejected. In operant terms, only some of the characteristics of an object or event affect a given individual; others are ignored or have no effect.

Perceptions are organized in that individual stimuli are perceived to be related to each other in recognizable or familiar patterns. You do not perceive this page as a collection of uppercase and lowercase letters of the alphabet. Rather, it is a collection of letters which you organize into familiar words (aided by the grouping of some letters closer together than others), words into sentences, and sentences into paragraphs conveying information.

A number of characteristics of objects have been found which affect the way perceptions are selectively organized.[2] They can be characterized as related to either selection or organization.

Selection

Any characteristics which make the object or event stand out from others enhance the probability that it will be perceived. Ob-

---

[2] See David Krech, R. S. Crutchfield, and E. L. Ballachey, *Individual in Society* (New York: McGraw-Hill Book Co., 1962), pp. 20–34.

jects or events which are intense, frequent, or numerous, for example, are more likely to be perceived than those that are dull, infrequent, or few.

An intense light is more likely to be seen than a dim one; a complaint department will pay more attention to a shouting customer than a quiet one. Coming late to work occasionally may not be noticed, but coming late to work frequently—such as every other day—is sure to draw someone's attention. One misspelled word in a letter may be overlooked; numerous misspellings will be obvious.

Objects which move, change, or contrast also have a higher probability of being perceived than those that are stationary, unchanging, or blend in. A fugitive hiding in the shadows becomes visible when he moves; a billboard with moving parts draws more attention than a painted sign. A flashing neon sign is an effective advertisement; employees are quick to sense a change in their supervisor's behavior toward them. Criminals often select the most popular colors of common models of lower priced cars to make their identification and detection more difficult; a woman or black in an executive group gets more than an equal share of attention.

Organization

Certain characteristics of objects or events affect the way they are organized in perception. These include similarity and dissimilarity, proximity in space, and proximity in time.

Similarity and Dissimilarity   Things that have similar physical characteristics are associated; those that are dissimilar are separated. On a football field, 22 players are perceived as 11 blue-shirted players and 11 white-shirted players. In a hotel lobby they are perceived as a group of football players amidst a crowd of normal-sized people. At Schmidt and Snodgrass, Knock perceived the members of the firm as secretaries and lawyers.

Proximity in Space   Objects or events may be perceived as related because of their proximity in space. A man, woman, and two children standing together at a bus stop are perceived as a family. If several people in the same department happen to quit their jobs, others will perceive their departures as related and will invent causes, such as low morale or poor supervision, to explain what might very well have been coincidence.

Proximity in Time   Objects or events may also be perceived as related because of their proximity in time. If three national leaders die within a short time, there is talk of conspiracy. Two events which occur sequentially are often perceived as cause and effect. If a sudden increase in productivity follows the assignment of a new manager, he is usually given credit for being responsible for the increase, even though it is unlikely that he could have had such a dramatic effect. "Being in the right place at the right time" often means being present when something good happens, so that your presence is associated with that good, whether or not you are responsible for it.

THE ROLE OF THE ENVIRONMENT

The environment in which an object or event is being perceived can have a dramatic effect on the way it is perceived—or even whether it is perceived at all. Both physical and social environments play an important role in perception.

The Physical Environment

Whether an object is perceived or not may depend upon whether it can be distinguished from its environment. A leopard stretched out on the shaded branch of a tree may be invisible at 50 feet, but the same leopard in a barren cage could be highly visible at 100 yards. An urgent letter may be lost in the shuffle of daily mail; the same message in a telegram could be the first correspondence to be read.

The physical environment can create a particular perspective which affects the way an object or event is perceived. A city viewed from an airplane at 10,000 feet may appear neat, clean, and well ordered, but at city street level it may be chaotic and dirty. A telephone ringing at 10 A.M. may sound pleasant and cheerful, whereas the same ring at 3 A.M. sounds harsh and ominous.

The Social Environment

The changing social environment of organizational activities can lead to widely different perceptions of the same objects or behavior. A manager who "constructively criticizes" an employee in the presence of others may be perceived as cold and unfeeling, and the message is likely to be lost on the employee, whose attention may be more on how fellow employees are reacting than on what the boss is saying. The same constructive criticism in the privacy of the manager's office has a better chance of being received and understood by the employee, and it may have a more positive effect on the employee's perceptions of the manager.

Similarly, the social environment creates a perspective which directly affects perception. If a manager drinks two bourbon-and-waters at lunch, this may be perceived as part of his job; if he does the same thing in his office at 9 A.M., it could be perceived as symptomatic of his alcoholism. A 5 percent raise will be perceived more favorably by someone whose colleagues are averaging 2 percent raises than by someone whose colleagues' raises are averaging 15 percent.

THE ROLE OF THE OBSERVER

The same physical stimulus in the same physical and social environment may be perceived differently by different individuals, or differently by the same individual at different times. Human perceptual tendencies and individual differences account for a good deal of subjectivity and unreliability in perception. Even in the legal system it has become apparent that eyewitness accounts of crimes and activities are not the positive sources of evidence they once were thought to be.

As an example of the magnitude of error possible, in one 1974 case 17 witnesses identified a man as having shot a police officer, but other evidence revealed that the man identified was, in fact, innocent.[3] In an experiment designed to test the reliability of eyewitness accounts, a professor was "attacked" in front of his class of 141 students.[4] When, seven weeks later, all those present at the attack were asked if they could identify the assailant, 60 percent identified the wrong man. One innocent bystander was pointed out by 35 students, and even the professor picked out the wrong person as his attacker.

Perceptual Tendencies

Studies of human perceptual processes have revealed several tendencies which are so common they have been accorded specific labels. These include perceptual readiness, the halo effect, implicit

---

[3] W. J. Cronice, "What You Think You See You May Not See at All," *Gainesville Sun,* January 6, 1975, p. 3A.

[4] R. D. Buckhout, "Determinants of Eyewitness Performance on a Lineup," *Bulletin of the Psychonomic Society,* vol. 4 (1974), pp. 191–92.

personality theory, projection, first impressions, stereotypes, and attribution.

Perceptual Readiness   There is a general tendency for people to perceive what they expect or want to perceive. Humans do not play merely passive roles in perception; they actively select and interpret stimuli on the basis of past perceptual and reinforcement history and current motivational state. This tendency is called perceptual readiness.

Saying that people see what they *expect* to see is another way of saying that their past perceptual histories affect their present perceptual processes. For example, you have undoubtedly perceived decks of playing cards consisting of two black suits, clubs and spades, and two red suits, diamonds and hearts. If you were confronted with a hand containing a red jack of spades, you would tend to see either a red jack of hearts or a black jack of spades, until someone called your attention to the change. Since all your experience with cards has been with red hearts and black spades, you would expect to see that same pattern, and that is what you would "see."

Similarly, one person's past experience may have taught him to attend to certain characteristics of an object which are different from the characteristics to which another pays attention. For example, training and occupation influence the way a person views a problem. In discussing a new plant location, marketing representatives will attend to sales figures, market potential, and distribution problems, while production representatives will be more sensitive to supplies, the labor pool, plant layout, and local antipollution laws.

Saying that people see what they *want* to see is another way of saying that motivation affects perception. A hungry person is more sensitive to stimuli related to food, such as picures of food, odors of food cooking, and discussions about food. He is also more likely to interpret ambiguous stimuli as being related to food than is a person who has just eaten his fill.[5] Similarly, those who are motivated by power are more likely to perceive or read into situations certain aspects of power. A personality test has been designed to exploit this perceptual tendency in humans.[6] Subjects are shown a picture of one or more individuals in a situation (e.g., an engineer sitting at a desk) and then are asked to write a story about what is

[5] R. I. Levine, Isidor Chein, and Gardner Murphy, "The Relation of the Intensity of a Need to the Amount of Perceptual Distortion," *Journal of Psychology*, vol. 13 (1942), pp. 283–93.

[6] D. C. McClelland, J. W. Atkinson, R. A. Clark, and E. L. Lowell, *The Achievement Motive* (New York: Appleton-Century-Crofts, 1953).

happening in the situation depicted. Those who are highly achievement oriented tend to see the situation as depicting an individual achieving or planning to achieve goals. Those who are more socially oriented tend to see the same situation as depicting an individual satisfying or seeking to satisfy social needs.

At very high levels of motivation, such as might occur when the incentive to do something is very strong but a problem prevents the person from doing that thing, perception can become distorted by imagination or hallucination. A person deprived of water may begin to see or hear it as the hours of deprivation go by. Daydreaming may replace striving for one who has tried to succeed but has been frustrated. A person striving for but unable to acquire power may have "delusions of grandeur" and may see himself as able to wield much more power than he actually can.

Halo Effect   There are a number of specific perceptual tendencies related to the general process of perceptual readiness. The halo effect refers to the tendency for an individual's evaluations of specific characteristics of another to be strongly influenced by his overall impression of the other. For example, people tend to overestimate the performance and good qualities of others they like and to underestimate the performance and good qualities of others they do not like.

This tendency can result in such situations as a professor giving an unwarranted high grade to a well-liked student. It is not so much conscious bias on the professor's part; rather, because she likes the student she wants him to do well, and her perceptions of the student's exam are influenced by what she wants to see. A common phenomenon in communication is the tendency for a receiver to evaluate information by evaluating its source. For example, an idea proposed by a low-status member of a group tends to be discounted; the same idea coming from a high-status member tends to be overrated and is more likely to be accepted.

Implicit Personality Theory   In judging and making inferences about others, the individual's perceptions are influenced by his belief that certain human traits are associated with one another. Implicit personality theory deals with the tendency to perceive trait X in a person who possesses trait Y. For example, many people associate the traits *industrious* and *honest*. They perceive all hardworking people to be honest, without any information as to their honesty.

In an experiment which demonstrated the effects of implicit

personality theory, students were told that a guest lecturer would be conducting one of their classes.[7] They were given written descriptions of the lecturer before his appearance; half received descriptions which made the lecturer out to be warm and personable, and the other half were given identical descriptions, except that the lecturer was described as being cold and aloof. After the lecturer had made his appearance, he was evaluated by the students. Those to whom the lecturer had been described as warm rated him as more considerate, better informed, more sociable, more popular, and more humorous than did those to whom he had been described as cold. These students held implicit personality theories which associated personal warmth with consideration, knowledge, and humor.

Projection   Under certain conditions, people tend to see in another person traits that they themselves possess. That is, they project their own feelings, tendencies, or motives into their judgments of others. This may be particularly true regarding undesirable traits which the perceiver possesses but fails to recognize in himself. For example, an individual who is himself not very energetic may see others as lazy or may explain their lack of achievement as resulting from their unwillingness to work hard. One who is dishonest may be suspicious of others and may perceive dishonest intentions in others where they do not exist. People who are afraid may interpret others' behavior as fearful or anxious.

First Impressions   Are first impressions really lasting impressions? The evidence says yes, unless the first impressions are strongly contradicted. Information obtained early in the stages of forming an impression about another is an important determinant of the way subsequent information about that person is perceived and integrated. The tendency is to place more importance on early information and less on later information, particularly if the latter is not compatible with the former. A person's first impression of another makes him perceptually ready to see the other person in a particular way.

In a series of experiments testing the effects of first impressions, groups of subjects were given two paragraphs describing the behavior of a boy named Jim.[8] One paragraph described Jim as be-

---

[7] S. E. Asch, "Forming Impressions of Personality," *Journal of Abnormal and Social Psychology,* vol. 41 (1946), pp. 258–90.

[8] A. S. Luchins, "Primary-Recency in Impression Formation," in *The Order of Presentation in Persuasion,* vol. 1, ed. C. I. Hovland (New Haven, Conn.: Yale University Press, 1957).

having like an extrovert, being friendly, talking to several acquaint-ances on his way to school. The other paragraph described Jim as behaving like an introvert, walking home alone, crossing the street to avoid a girl, and remaining aloof from other students.

Some subjects were first given the paragraph describing Jim as an extrovert, followed by the paragraph describing him as an intro-vert. They then gave their own impressions of Jim and predicted his behavior in several situations. Jim was described as extroverted by 52 percent of these subjects, while only 36 percent described him as introverted.

Other subjects were given the paragraphs in reverse order, so that Jim was described first as an introvert, then as an extrovert. In giving their subsequent impressions of Jim, 56 percent of these subjects described him as introverted. Although both groups read exactly the same information, the order in which it was presented significantly affected their impressions of Jim.

Stereotypes Stereotyping is the tendency for a person's per-ceptions of another to be influenced by the social group to which the other belongs. In perceiving and forming impressions of an-other, a person is likely to categorize the other according to some salient characteristic, such as sex, race, religious group, nationality, occupation, or organizational affiliation. The individual's experiences with others in the category in which he has placed them lead him to believe they have certain traits in common. Thus he is ready to per-ceive the other as possessing the same trait. He is not ready to perceive the other as possessing some trait which is uncharacteristic of the category in which he has placed the other.

Some examples of common stereotypes are that redheads are short tempered, Americans are materialistic, Japanese are extremely nationalistic, Germans are industrious, blacks are musical, truck drivers love country music, politicians are self-serving, and judges are wise.

Not all stereotypes are negative, and not all of them are wrong. There is evidence that certain traits are more likely to be found among members of one social group than another. However, not all members of a group possess the trait which is typical of the group. Although a college faculty may be more liberal than many other occupational groups, not all college professors are liberal. Although Germans may be more industrious than people of many other na-tionalities, some are lazy.

Stereotyping leads to perceptual distortion in that the individual is ready to attribute to another the traits that he believes are characteristic of the other's group. A policeman may perceive a young, long-haired, erratic driver to be high on drugs or alcohol, when in fact the driver is ill or injured. A student may perceive a policeman arresting a black as a racist, when in fact the arrest is for mugging and terrorizing inhabitants of a black neighborhood.

Stereotyping can not only make one ready to see certain traits in an individual, it can also make it more difficult for one to see other traits not characteristic of the other's group. In one study college students at Berkeley were given the following description of a man: he works in a factory, reads a newspaper, goes to the movies, is of average height, cracks jokes, is intelligent, strong, and active.[9] In writing a description of what sort of person they thought this man was, the students had a very difficult time seeing the man as intelligent. Some denied that he was intelligent, since he worked in a factory. Some modified their perception, saying that he lacked initiative. Some refused to see a mere worker as intelligent and described him as a foreman instead. Only a few were able to see him as both a common worker and intelligent. For most of the students, the stereotype that factory workers are not particularly intelligent was too powerful to overcome.

Attribution   Attribution refers to the process by which the individual assigns causes to the behavior he perceives. People are interested not only in observing behavior in organizations, for example, but in determining its causes. Their evaluations of and reactions to others' behavior may be heavily influenced by their perception that the others are responsible for their behavior. When plant productivity increases, the manager responsible will be evaluated less favorably if the increase is attributed to new machines installed at the order of the home office than if it is attributed to his handling of employees. A nurse who drops a tray of medicine will be excused if the incident is perceived as caused by a slippery floor, chastised if it is viewed as caused by her clumsiness, and perhaps fired if it is viewed as deliberate.

There are those who argue that considerable perceptual distortion occurs because too much credit or blame for behavior is placed on persons rather than on the environment. There is, they contend, "a pervasive tendency for actors to attribute their actions to situational

---

[9] Mason Haire and W. F. Grunes, "Perceptual Defenses: Processes Protecting an Original Perception of Another Personality," *Human Relations*, vol. 3 (1950), pp. 403–12.

requirements, whereas observers tend to attribute the same actions to stable personal dispositions."[10]

In other words, in the equation $B = f(P, E)$, there is a tendency to emphasize P as the cause of behavior rather than E. Certainly B. F. Skinner and other behaviorists view this tendency as a major perceptual error. Even attributing creative behavior such as invention and innovation to the scientist or artist who produced it is in error, because, according to Skinner, "the possibility arises that contingencies of reinforcement may explain a work of art or the solution to a problem in mathematics or science without appealing to a different kind of creative mind or to a trait of creativity."[11]

Nevertheless, people do seek the causes of others' behavior, tend to attribute behavior to the individual rather than the environment, and evaluate or react to behavior based on their perceptions of its causes.

Status. One factor which strongly influences the attribution process is the status of the individual whose behavior is being perceived (the actor). High-status persons are perceived to be more responsible for their actions than low-status persons. In one study, subjects were asked to persuade a graduate student (high status) and a freshman (low status) to donate blood.[12] After the students both agreed to donate, the subjects were asked to give their opinions as to why the students had agreed. The subjects perceived that the freshman had done it because he was persuaded, but the graduate student had done it voluntarily. The high-status student was seen to be more responsible for his actions than the low-status student.

Intentions. Status also influences the perception of the actor's intentions. People are more likely to attribute good intentions to high-status actors than to low-status actors.[13] A valuable worker putting in overtime will be seen as doing it for the good of the company, while a poor worker putting in overtime will be seen as doing it for the money or to finish work that should have been done earlier. A

――――――
[10] E. E. Jones and R. E. Nisbett, *The Actor and the Observer: Divergent Perceptions of the Causes of Behavior* (Morristown, N.J.: General Learning Press, 1971), p. 2.

[11] B. F. Skinner, *About Behaviorism* (New York: Alfred A. Knopf, 1974), p. 224.

[12] J. W. Thibaut and H. W. Rieckin, "Some Determinants and Consequences of the Perception of Social Causality," *Journal of Personality,* vol. 24 (1955), pp. 113–33.

[13] Albert Pepitone, "Attributions of Causality, Social Attitudes, and Cognitive Matching Process," in *Person Perception and Interpersonal Behavior,* ed. Renato Tagiuri and Luigi Petrullo (Stanford, Calif.: Stanford University Press, 1958), pp. 258–76.

vice president taking the afternoon off for golf will be viewed as only getting away from the tremendous pressures of the job. A foreman who does the same thing will be viewed as goofing off, evading responsibilities.

Obviously, people's perceptions of an actor's intentions can influence their reactions to his behavior. If an act is viewed as intended to gain some reward, it is likely to be valued less than if it is viewed as caused by "less selfish" motives. This happens often in upward communication. Consider a young manager who suggests a reorganization of her department. If her intent is perceived as improving the department's efficiency, she and the suggestion will be valued more highly than if her intent is perceived as striving for attention or power.

Opportunity for Surveillance. Whether or not it is possible to supervise an actor's behavior can affect other's perceptions of his responsibility or intentions. Workers who do well when they cannot be closely supervised are given more credit than those who do well when they are closely supervised. The former are viewed as doing well because they want to, or because they are good workers. The latter are viewed as doing well because they have to, or because they fear reprisal.

For example, one experiment required supervisors to monitor and evaluate a worker's performance.[14] Some supervisors monitored a regular worker, others a blind worker. Although the blind and the sighted workers performed equally well, the blind worker's performance was rewarded much more often than that of the sighted worker. The sighted worker could see that his performance was being monitored, while the blind worker could not. The sighted worker's performance was attributed to the supervisor's surveillance and thus did not deserve rewards, while the blind worker's performance was attributed to the worker's personal motivation, which "deserved" rewarding.

Consequences. Attributions of an actor's responsibility also can be influenced by the consequences of his behavior. The worse the consequences, the more likely the individual is to be viewed as responsible for the act.[15] If a machine breaks down at 4:30 P.M. Friday, little work time will be lost and the foreman can pass it off

[14] L. D. Baker, Nicholas DiMarco, and W. E. Scott, Jr., "Effects of Supervisor's Sex and Level of Authoritarianism on Evaluation and Reinforcement of Blind and Sighted Workers," *Journal of Applied Psychology*, vol. 60 (1975), pp. 28–32.

[15] Leon Mann, *Social Psychology* (Sydney, Australia: John Wiley & Sons, 1969), p. 103.

as an unexplained malfunction. If it breaks down at 9 A.M. Monday, resulting in two days' lost production, the operator will be viewed as guilty of neglecting machine maintenance. Accidents are accidents, except when they are disasters. People believe so strongly that disasters can be prevented that, sooner or later, a human scapegoat will be found.

Individual Differences

Because perceptions can be influenced by prior experiences and motivation, and because each individual's experiences and motivation are somewhat unique, it is not surprising that different people perceive the same thing differently. Beyond this, several individual characteristics have been studied to determine whether they have consistent effects on human perception. The characteristics studied most frequently are sex, personality, and culture.

Sex   Consistent differences between the perceptual processes of men and women have been reported.[16] The evidence is too complex to say which sex, if either, tends to be more accurate in perception. However, women differ from men in certain perceptual tendencies. Women appear to be more intuitive, to stereotype more, and to rely more on visual cues. Although they have been reported to be less analytical, women seek more information about others than men do. Because neither sex is demonstrably more accurate, these findings simply suggest that we would expect the perceptions of men and women to differ.

Personality   A number of studies have attempted to find a relationship between certain personality characteristics of observers and the way they perceive other people. However, as yet no consistent relationships between personality variables and perceptual processes have been found.[17]

Certain personality characteristics seem to be indirectly related to perception, however. One important factor in perception can be the influence of other people. Sometimes in perceiving new, subjective, or uncertain objects or events an individual's perceptions may be influenced by what others say they are perceiving. And certain personality traits—low self-esteem, high anxiety, low self-

---

[16] Renato Tagiuri, "Person Perception," in *The Handbook of Social Psychology,* vol. 3, ed. Gardner Lindzey and Elliot Aronson (Reading, Mass.: Addison-Wesley Publishing Co., 1969), p. 428.

[17] Ibid., p. 430.

confidence, and strong needs for affiliation—are indicative of persuasibility. For example, a new employee, uncertain of his job and anxious about his future, may easily be influenced in his perceptions of his supervisor. If the older employees tell him the supervisor is mean, aggressive, and constantly criticizing mistakes, the new employee's perceptions of his supervisor's behavior will be heavily influenced in that direction. Their influence makes him perceptually ready to see his supervisor's behavior as mean, aggressive, and critical.

Culture   We have noted that prior experience and reinforcement history affect perceptual processes. Because people from the same culture have some similarities in their experiences, and people from different cultures have entirely different experiences and live and work in entirely different environments, we would expect culture to affect perception.

Effects of culture on perception are largely due to three factors: functional salience, familiarity, and communication systems.[18]

Functional Salience.   The environment in which a person lives causes him to attend to certain things more than others. This is the concept of functional salience. When the person is reinforced for discriminating among certain stimuli and not reinforced for other discriminations, he learns from his environment certain ways of selecting and organizing his perceptions. For example, a physician who normally practices in a large city may be unable to diagnose certain diseases common to an isolated rural area. Having never been reinforced for perceiving certain differences in symptoms, he is unable to see what the rural doctor can.

Familiarity.   Individuals from one culture may be totally unfamiliar with certain activities or designs common to another culture. For example, workers in an industrialized culture consider the concept of time as an important factor and expect appointments at a definite hour and minute. Workers from a less developed culture may perceive an order to do something immediately as meaning to do it tomorrow, or next week, or at the next convenient time.

Communication Systems.   Each culture develops a system for communicating, including language, symbols, and art, which can influence perceptual processes by stressing some aspects of the environment over others, or by emphasizing certain ways of classifying the environment. For example, there is no Portuguese word for

---

[18] Henri Tajfel, "Social and Cultural Factors in Perception," in Lindzey and Aronson, *Handbook of Social Psychology*, pp. 357–79.

warm; temperatures are perceived as being either hot (*quente*) or cold (*frio*).[19]

Very close, technologically oriented work groups develop their own culture and language, so that members of the group perceive problems in special ways that differ from the perceptions of outsiders. Many occupational specialties develop work cultures which include their own norms, values, rituals, uniforms, and languages and which can influence their perceptions. Hospital attendants may classify patients according to their medical problems, seeing them not so much as men or women, young or old, black or white, but as hernias, hysterectomies, and heart cases. Police officers may classify people in general according to their role in the war on crime as cops, criminals, or civilians, or sometimes as just cops and civilians, with all civilians being perceived as actual or potential criminals.

A MODEL OF INDIVIDUAL PERCEPTION

Figure 6–1 graphically summarizes the discussion of perception thus far. An individual's perception of an object or event is affected by characteristics of that object or event. In addition, his perception

FIGURE 6–1
Factors Affecting Individual Perception

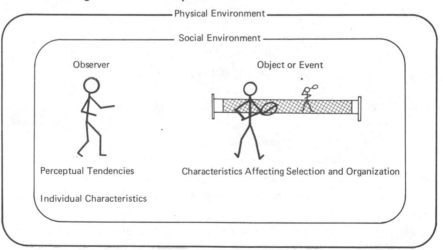

Characteristics of the observer, the object or event being observed, and the physical and social environments all have an effect on perception.

[19] E. H. Lenneberg and J. M. Roberts, "The Language of Experience," *Supplement to the International Journal of American Linguistics*, vol. 22 (1956), pp. 1–33.

is affected by his own perceptual tendencies and individual characteristics and by the physical and social environments of both the
object and the observer.

SOME IMPLICATIONS OF PERCEPTUAL PROCESSES

The nature of human perception has a number of implications
for organizational activities. Obviously, some of these implications
deal with communications; as we note in Chapter 14, perceptual
differences account for many communication failures.

Communications may fail because the sender fails to take into
account the receiver's physical and social environment. The complexities of a detailed combat order written up in the comfort of an
air-conditioned headquarters may be lost on a battlefield commander receiving the order in the heat and frenzy of an enemy
counterattack.

Communications may fail because the receiver is perceptually
ready for a message different from the one actually sent. An example
came from a purchasing agent who normally ordered 5,000 card-
board packing boxes every month from the same supplier. One
month, due to an extremely large order for the product packed in
these boxes, the agent upped his usual order from 5,000 to 15,000.
To his surprise, the shipment he received in return contained only
5,000 boxes. In a hurried, angry phone call to the shipper, he discovered that the supplier had perceived the 15,000 order to be a
typographical error, since the order had never before exceeded
5,000. Without checking with the agent, the supplier had simply
"corrected" the order and sent the usual number of boxes.

Communications may fail because the sender has no words to
express what he perceives. An incident illustrating this point occurred at an ROTC summer training program. In marching from
the barracks to the drill field, the cadets were required to cross
seldom-used railroad tracks. The third man in each outside rank had
been drilled to break ranks upon command, race ahead of his platoon to the tracks, come to parade rest facing down the tracks, and
sing out, "All clear on the starboard (port) side, sir!"

The routine worked smoothly for several weeks, until one fateful
day when a track guard found himself facing not an empty track,
but a passenger train bearing down on the crossing at a moderate
clip. Having been conditioned to use only proper military terminology, and having been given only the terminology to use when the

tracks were empty, the guard stood frozen and mute astride the tracks. From his position back near the middle of the troops, the cadet in charge of the platoon could not see the train and continued to chant the cadence, which the cadets obeyed by marching toward the crossing.

Fortunately, a drill instructor approaching from the opposite direction saw what was happening, halted the column, and dragged the still mute cadet from the tracks just before the train rumbled through the crossing. Without his intervention, I am confident that the incident would have ended in disaster.

In addition to communications, another major management area in which perception plays a significant role is in the evaluation of employee performance. The rest of this chapter will deal with performance appraisal methods.

PERFORMANCE EVALUATION[20]

A manager's evaluation of employees' performance is one of his or her most important tasks. Measuring employee performance provides the manager with information necessary for the success of the organization. It can reveal strengths and weaknesses of the personnel and indicate areas in which training or recruitment are needed. It can provide feedback about the effectiveness of the manager's directives and policies.

Performance evaluation can also aid the manager in influencing and directing the performance of employees. First, whatever facets of performance are measured tend to become goals. In manufacturing organizations where the number of units produced is the central measure of performance, productivity tends to become the goal at the expense of quality, unless quality is measured too. If a social worker is evaluated solely on the number of cases handled per month, a teacher by the number of students taught, a school by the number of degrees awarded, a hospital by the percentage of beds occupied each day, a police officer by the number of tickets written, an infantry unit by body count, we would expect them to concentrate on those aspects of their performance. Very different behavior would be likely if the social worker were evaluated by the satisfaction or improvement of the people receiving the services, the teacher

---

[20] This section draws on L. L. Cummings and D. P. Schwab, *Performance in Organizations: Determinants and Appraisal* (Glenview, Ill.: Scott, Foresman & Co., 1973). For a clear and more detailed presentation of appraisal methods and problems, this book is an excellent source.

by the increase in student learning, the school by the job success of its graduates, the hospital by the average time from patient admission to dismissal, the police officer by the number and severity of accidents on his or her beat, and the infantry unit by the amount of territory under its control.

Performance evaluation is important to those who are being evaluated for several reasons. As suggested above, it provides them with a target for their behavior by indicating exactly what aspects of their behavior are important enough for management to measure. It can influence the amount of effort they put into their performance by making it clear that effort increases performance and, ultimately, rewards.

Performance evaluation provides the employee with feedback on changes in his performance. A salesperson who works extra hard one month and finds that she has moved up from 17th to 10th among the company's salespeople learns that effort can affect performance. A basketball player who concentrates on passing rather than shooting learns only that such effort decreases his point production if individual assists are not recorded.

Performance evaluation also clarifies the links between employee performance and organizational rewards. All too frequently an employee who receives a promotion or a raise has only a vague idea of what aspects of his performance have earned it. Without clear measures of performance, organizational rewards may be attributed to error, luck, favoritism, sympathy, or aspects of performance other than those desired by the organization. If organizational rewards are to be effective, employees must perceive a link between performance and rewards. Accurate and timely performance evaluation enhances that perception.

Unfortunately, performance appraisal is often performed sloppily, if at all, in some organizations. Vague, inaccurate performance measurement can create a number of behavioral problems for a manager. Inaccurate appraisal can result in employee confusion over what behavior is desired or what "good" behavior really is. If poor performers receive higher evaluations than they deserve, feelings of inequity can lead to dissatisfaction and turnover among good performers.

Ambiguous and imprecise measurement can even lead the organization to reward undesired behavior and punish desired behavior. For example, suppose a manager evaluates employees solely on his overall impressions of their value to the organization. It is possible that a very mediocre performer could create a very favorable impression by appearing to work hard when the boss is around and by arranging to take credit for others' contributions. If this employee is in fact overrated, others might pick up the example and work harder at managing their supervisor's impressions than at carrying out their assigned duties.

Perceptual Inaccuracies in Performance Appraisal

Performance may be appraised by one person, usually the employee's immediate supervisor, or by several people. For example, a movie star's performance is evaluated by the director, independently by various movie critics, and jointly by his peers in the Academy Awards program. A graduate student's course performance is evaluated by each of her instructors, while her overall performance is evaluated by a committee of departmental faculty. A manager is typically evaluated by both his immediate superior and his superior's superior; he may additionally be evaluated by a committee. Some professional people, particularly in education and medicine, may be evaluated by committees composed of their peers. Perceptual inaccuracies in performance appraisal may be due to individual tendencies and to special problems in multirater appraisal, such as a general evaluative set.

Individual Tendencies   All of the perceptual tendencies discussed earlier in this chapter may present problems for accurate performance appraisal. The most common problems are the result of halo effect, time, and attribution.

Halo Effect. There is a tendency for an individual rated high on one characteristic to be rated high on all characteristics. If the employee is well liked or has tried hard, he may be overrated on other aspects of work, particularly if the rated aspects are somewhat vague criteria such as integrity, loyalty, cooperation, willingness to learn, friendliness, and so on. The halo effect often makes using multiple criteria for evaluation meaningless, because an individual is typically rated the same on all criteria.

Time. One factor which can lead to inaccurate evaluation in several ways is time. Because first impressions are difficult to overcome, they can exert an undue influence on the evaluations of employees during their first several months on the job. Managers also tend to develop a perceptual set about an employee who has been around for a long time. The employee is labeled as consistently good, or perhaps as always mediocre, and changes in his performance may not register with his superior because of his past history. Finally, performance appraisals carried out very infrequently may exceed the capability of the manager's memory. A supervisor who evaluates 75 employees only once a year may find it difficult, if not impossible, to recall each individual's performance accurately. The manager may be hard pressed to do more than rank the few best and few poorest performers, leaving all sorts of room for error in the evaluation of the great majority of the employees.

Attribution. Perceptual tendencies in attribution can affect the accuracy of appraisal. Individuals, particularly those high in need for achievement, tend to internalize success and externalize failure.[21] That is, they tend to see themselves as the causes of organizational success and other factors as the causes of organizational failure. Such tendencies can result in underevaluating the contributions of employees. In his baseball memoirs manager Leo Durocher recounted his experiences with Houston pitcher Jerry Reuss, who won 16 games one season under Durocher, his best season ever:

> So over the winter I read in the paper that Jerry Reuss called me a dummy. Well, I'll tell you one thing. This dummy don't throw the balls. That other dummy on the other end of the wire is throwing the ball. I couldn't have been such a dummy when he won. I must have left him in pretty good, I must have made some right guesses, because sixteen was the most he had ever won anyplace.[22]

Another attributional tendency can create problems in performance evaluation involving changes in performance levels. When an actor succeeds after repeated failure, an observer is more likely to attribute the success to luck or effort rather than ability. Similarly, an observer is more likely to attribute to luck and effort an actor's failure after repeated success.[23] That is, observers tend to see ability as remaining constant, with variations in luck or effort accounting for unprecedented changes in performance.

General Evaluative Set   Some people are predisposed to be harsh or severe in their evaluations of others; the highest evaluations they give are "adequate," "acceptable," or some other moderate rating. Others are predisposed to be easy or lenient in their evaluations; the lowest evaluations they give are "average," and they rate almost

[21] Bernard Weiner and Andy Kukla, "An Attributional Analysis of Achievement Motivation," *Journal of Personality and Social Psychology,* vol. 15 (1970), pp. 1–20.

[22] Leo Durocher with Ed Lenn, *Nice Guys Finish Last* (New York: Simon & Schuster, 1975), p. 429.

[23] Irene Frieze and Bernard Weiner, "Cue Utilization and Attributional Judgments for Success and Failure," *Journal of Personality,* vol. 39 (1971), pp. 591–605.

everyone "above average." These individual predispositions to evaluate everyone low or high obviously create problems in performance
appraisal. When evaluations are clustered at one end of a scale, it
is difficult to make distinctions among them for the purposes of giving employees feedback or administering rewards.

Sometimes the organizational reward system influences managers
to develop a certain evaluative set. For example, the armed services
require each officer to be evaluated each year by his or her superior
on a scale of 1 (incompetent) to 9 (outstanding). Over the years it
became apparent, in some services, that there was a strong tendency
for superiors to assign high ratings. As a result, an officer receiving
a rating of 7 was likely to be passed over for promotion. This put
pressure on superiors to inflate their ratings so as not to jeopardize
the careers of their subordinates. As a result, most officers receive an
8 or 9 rating—everyone is "above average."

Performance Appraisal Methods

Two basic types of performance appraisal or evaluation have
evolved: evaluation by comparison and against absolute standards.[24]
Each lends certain strengths and weaknesses to the problem of accurate appraisal. A third system has been designed to reduce ambiguities in evaluation.

Evaluation by Comparison   One method is to evaluate each person in comparison with others. A variation of this method is to rank
the appraisees in order along some dimension; for example, each
employee is ranked according to his or her perceived contribution to
the department. A second variation is to assign each person being
appraised to some relative category of predetermined size. Grading
on a curve is such a method; the instructor determines that a certain
percentage of the class will receive As, Bs, Cs, and so forth.

Evaluation by comparison has certain advantages. In most cases it
takes little time, unless the number to be ranked is large. Comparisons tend to reduce the effects of a general evaluative set. One way
to overcome an evaluator's tendency to judge everyone high or low
is to insist that the appraisees be ranked.

Comparison also has several drawbacks. First, it is difficult to rank
order a large number of people. It may be easy to rank the top few
and bottom few, but meaningfully comparing the majority in between is a problem. One method which copes with this problem is

---

[24] Cummings and Schwab, *Performance in Organizations,* chap. 7.

paired comparisons, whereby each person is compared against every other person being appraised, one by one. Unfortunately, the number of comparisons required by this method increases geometrically as the number of appraisees increases, so that ranking 5 employees requires only 10 paired comparisons, but ranking 10 employees requires 45 comparisons, and ranking 50 employees requires 1,225 comparisons!

Another problem with comparisons is that it does not reduce attributional tendencies or halo effect. Further, it is difficult to compare rankings made by different evaluators or rankings of different groups of appraisees. For example, suppose you happen to get in a class of dull students but your roommate is in a class of high achievers, and both classes are graded on the curve. He may learn twice as much as you and yet receive a D to your B.

Evaluation against Absolute Standards   Individual performance can also be compared against some set of absolute standards. For example, one way to get into the Baseball Hall of Fame is to pitch a no-hitter. Regardless of what other pitchers do or have done, every pitcher who meets that absolute standard of a no-hitter is immortalized in the Hall of Fame. Similarly, an instructor may give an A to everyone who averages 90 percent on all work, regardless of others' performance.

One advantage of evaluation against standards is that people can be evaluated on several criteria rather than one global characteristic, as is the tendency with comparisons. Another advantage is flexibility in methods of evaluation. A person may be appraised on whether or not he has met some criterion (e.g., whether or not he pitched a no-hitter), or on the degree to which he has met some criterion (e.g., to what extent he has improved over last year, how much he helps or cooperates with others).

Unfortunately, most types of evaluation against standards are susceptible to several types of inaccuracy. Halo effect, attributional tendencies, general evaluative set, and outright prejudice or bias are possibilities. One specific variation designed to reduce some of these errors is the behaviorally anchored rating scale.

Behaviorally Anchored Rating Scales   A system designed to reduce ambiguities in evaluation utilizes behaviorally anchored rating scales. Basically, the appraiser is assisted in judging the degree to which the person being evaluated possesses some trait or how well he performs some task by being given a specific example of behavior corresponding to each level of the trait or performance.

For example, suppose an organization wanted to evaluate the degree to which several managers were promotable. Conventionally, it would ask the appraisers to evaluate each manager's promotability on a scale from 1 (definitely not promotable) to 9 (overdue for promotion). Unfortunately, this question leads to ambiguities as to what is meant by "not promotable" and "overdue" for promotion. These ambiguities make the evaluations susceptible to halo effect (He's honest, and we have too few honest managers, so he should be promoted) and evaluative sets (In my opinion, nobody is promotable until they've been here ten years).

To overcome these tendencies, the judgments and opinions of knowledgable managers can be used to develop specific examples of behavior which serve to "anchor" each point on a rating scale, such as the one in Figure 6–2. A behaviorally anchored rating scale has

FIGURE 6–2
A Behaviorally Anchored Scale for Rating Manager Promotability

Description	Scale	Behavioral anchor
Overdue for promotion	9	
		Has had other recent job offers; salary in top 5 percent of age bracket
Ready for promotion	8	
		Has had two or more employees promoted out of department in last year
Probably promotable next year	7	
		Has department above average two consecutive years
Possibly promotable next 1–2 years	6	
		Department currently above average; in present assignment less than 1 year
Unsure of promotability	5	
		Seeks help with problems should be able to handle alone
Unlikely to be promotable next 1–2 years	4	
		Consistently works overtime just to keep up
Definitely not promotable next year	3	
		Has attended no development programs last three years
Probably not promotable foreseeable future	2	
		Department below average; in present assignment more than five years
Unlikely to ever advance beyond present assignment	1	

several advantages. First, it focuses on behavior and performance rather than personalities. Second, it is possible to get a high degree of interrater agreement using such scales. Third, it provides excellent feedback to appraisees who wish to improve their evaluations. The scale provides concrete examples of what they need to do or to avoid in order to improve their evaluations.

Of course, the development of behaviorally anchored scales requires a good deal of time and effort. Like any other evaluation tool, they must be validated from time to time to ensure that the behaviors specified are still relevant to the job and predictive of performance. If developed and validated with care, such scales can help alleviate some of the perceptual biases to which most employee evaluations are susceptible.

SUMMARY

Human perception is an important part of all organizational behavior. Perception is a fairly complex process in that what we perceive can be influenced in a variety of ways, and this leads to the possibilities of perceptual distortion and misunderstanding.

Perceptions are selectively organized. The ways we select and organize them depend in part on characteristics of the object, person, or event being perceived, such as its intensity, contrast, similarity, and proximity in time and space. In addition, both the physical and social environments in which perception takes place can influence what is perceived and how it is perceived.

The role of the observer is reflected in common perceptual tendencies and individual differences. Several common tendencies increase the chances of misunderstanding and perceptual distortion. Among these are perceptual readiness, halo effect, projection, and stereotyping. One of the most important is the attribution process through which people seek to determine the causes of others' behavior. Observers are inclined to attribute an actor's behavior to some stable characteristic of the actor, particularly his personality. Actors, on the other hand, are likely to attribute their own behavior to the environment or the situation.

As for individual differences, some consistent differences have been found between the perceptions of observers of different sexes and from different cultures. Cultural differences in perception can be attributed to differences in reinforcement history, environments, and communication systems.

One of the implications of what we know about human perception is that managers ought to be tentative in accepting at face value the observations of a single individual about another person or some event. This is particularly true in cases in which that single observer is highly emotional about what he has observed. On the other hand, the manager should not be surprised to find disagreements in observations of the same event by two or more honest, well-intentioned individuals. A person who can consistently report his or her observations accurately is a real asset.

Human perceptual tendencies have major implications for managers in the appraisal of employee performance. Perceptual selectivity and organization can result in inaccurate evaluations, and this can mean loss of feedback and influence for the organization. Halo effect, time, attribution, general evaluative sets, and lack of agreement among those who appraise performance are common problems in this area.

Performance appraisal methods in current use vary in the effectiveness with which they cope with perceptual errors. Comparative evaluations reduce the effects of general evaluative sets but are susceptible to other distortions. Absolute evaluations permit appraisal on more than one characteristic or dimension but are particularly vulnerable to halo effects and general evaluative set. Although more difficult to design than other methods, behaviorally anchored rating scales can reduce the effects of many perceptual inaccuracies, thus increasing the chances for accurate performance appraisal.

QUESTIONS FOR REVIEW AND DISCUSSION

1. What do we mean when we say that perceptions are selectively organized?

2. Give an example showing how the different work environments of a superior and a subordinate might cause them to perceive the same event differently.

3. What is the difference between a stereotype and an implicit personality theory? Give an example of each.

4. What are the implications of attribution processes for (a) managers whose work force includes minority workers, (b) a review board judging the conduct of a police officer?

5. Think of some ways that cultural differences might affect the perceptions of two army recruits, one from a large, industrialized urban area, the other from a farm community.

6. What perceptual tendencies might create special problems in evaluating the performance of high-level managers?

7. What problems might the general evaluative set of foremen cause for their supervisor? How might the supervisor alleviate those problems?

8. What are the advantages and disadvantages of evaluating performance against absolute standards?

9. What are some advantages and disadvantages of evaluating performance by comparison?

10. What specific performance appraisal problems can behaviorally anchored rating scales alleviate?

KEY WORDS

Selective organization	Stereotype
Perceptual readiness	Attribution
Halo effect	Functional salience
Implicit personality theory	General evaluative set
Projection	Behaviorally anchored rating scale
First impressions	

Objectives

1. To outline the elements of individual decision making.
2. To present criteria by which decisions are evaluated.
3. To discuss types of problems calling for management decisions and characteristics of those problems which affect decision processes.
4. To describe two models of man as decision maker, and to discuss individual differences which affect decision processes.

chapter seven

Individual Decision Making

What do I do now, mused Chris Carter, as he flopped onto his bed, the letter still in his hand. The excitement with which he had torn open the envelope and his elation at the first words, "We are pleased to offer you a position . . . ." had subsided into uncertainty. He was uncertain as to how he felt, let alone how he should decide.

On the one hand, it was great to get a firm job offer. More than half his graduating class, he knew, still had no offers. And RBC *was* a prestige company, well up in *Fortune*'s list of the 500 largest corporations in both sales and profits.

On the other hand, their salary offer was nearly $1,000 less than he had hoped for. And almost as important (more important? less important? he couldn't decide which) the position was in their Cincinnati office. He had been led to believe that he would be assigned either to Houston or Denver, either of which he would have looked forward to eagerly.

To top it off, the letter more or less insisted on a firm answer within two weeks! That really made it tough, because he'd just come back from what he felt was a successful interview with another good company. Not as prestigious as RBC, for sure, but their openings were in San Francisco and Boston, two of his favorite cities. They might come through with a good offer, but it seemed unlikely to Chris that he would hear from them before RBC's two-week deadline was up.

So many things to consider, he sighed, laying the letter aside and staring up at the ceiling. He knew little about Cincinnati, except that it was on some river and allegedly had good restaurants. Nothing like Boston, he guessed. True, it was within a few hundred miles of his fiancée's hometown, but Chris wasn't sure if that was a plus or a minus.

The position itself was good, and he'd get to use some of the stuff he had studied in college, believe it or not. There seemed to be good chances for promotion—but you probably never really knew about that until you had been there awhile.

The salary bothered him. It wasn't bad, about what other graduates he knew were being offered. But he had hoped that his college record and military service would get him an offer substantially above average.

Should he take it or not? If he took it, all the worry would be over, and he and his fiancée, Pat, could start planning. But, then, if the other com-

pany came through with a comparable offer, he might regret it. And what if
he turned down RBC? Suppose no other offers came through? Then he'd
be back where he started several months ago: sifting through company
brochures and enduring the agony of preliminary interviews, writing letters
and hoping.

"Well, I'd better call Pat and let her know," he muttered unenthusi-
astically, rolling off the bed and heading for the kitchen. One thing for
sure, he thought, it's going to be a long two weeks.

IN THE SITUATION described above, Chris Carter is facing a decision not unlike one you may be facing before long—an important
decision with limited information. The kind of decision he ultimately makes will depend on several factors, and the process he
uses to make the decision may take one of several forms.

The decision Chris faces has several characteristics—it is not
routine, it is fairly complex, it contains considerable uncertainty
and some elements of risk. The environment in which he is making
the decision has several relevant characteristics: He is under time
pressures, he has access to only limited information, and his decision is subject to influence from others, notably his peers and his
fiancée.

Some of Chris's own characteristics may influence his decision:
his age, intelligence, and certain personality characteristics. The
process he uses to make the decision may have the biggest impact.
For instance, right now he is considering only two alternatives, to
accept the offer or reject it. Will he allow himself to be limited only
to those alternatives, or will he look for other possibilities, such as
asking RBC for an extension of its deadline, trying to negotiate a
larger salary, asking the other company for a quicker decision, or
trying to get an offer from some third company?

This chapter and the one following are about individual decision
making and problem solving—the kind of behavior Chris will be
engaged in for the next two weeks, and the kind of behavior he
will constantly be involved in, whatever organization he finally joins.
We will look at the various elements of decision making: the problem, the individual making the decision, the decision process, the
decision itself, and the environment in which the decision is being
made. Each of these elements has several characteristics which can
affect the way decisions are made. Then (in Chapter 8) we will
describe a normative model which outlines how, in the opinion of
many writers, decisions ought to be made, breaking the process
into seven sequential steps. A descriptive model will compare typical

individual decision processes with the normative model, and the differences between what should happen and what usually does happen when individuals make decisions will be explored.

ELEMENTS OF DECISION MAKING

Management is sometimes called the art (or science) of decision making. This definition is too narrow, however; organizational success depends on recognizing problems which need decisions and on implementing decisions as well as making them.

Nevertheless, making decisions, and related activities such as seeking information and searching for alternatives, accounts for significant portions of many a manager's day. The related activities are particularly time-consuming. In Chet Craig's case, which introduces Chapter 1, most of the time he spent discussing problems with subordinates and supervisors involved seeking and giving information and discussing possible solutions.

Whether a decision is a crisis (how to handle a threatened walkout) or long term in nature (what new markets should be developed); whether the decision is about people (whether an employee is ready for promotion) or about things (whether to buy or lease new equipment), decision making is comprised of several elements. In Figure 7–1, these elements are designated as the decision maker,

FIGURE 7–1
Elements of Decision Making

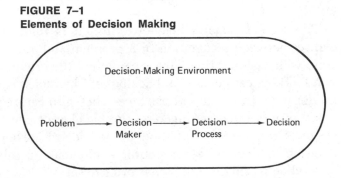

the problem, the environment, the decision process, and the decision itself. These elements form the basis for discussion in Chapters 7 and 8. The product of decision making—the decision itself—is discussed first, and then the effects of the other elements on the decision are considered.

THE DECISION

What characteristics of decisions are important to the organizations in which they are made and to the people who are affected by them? That is, how is a decision evaluated as being either "good" or "bad"? Decision criteria can be classified as related to either efficiency or effectiveness.

Efficiency Criteria

Efficiency is a measure of what an organization gets out of a decision relative to what it puts into it. If organization A takes two man-days to make the same decision that organization B made in ten man-days, organization A's decision has been much more efficient.

One major efficiency criterion is the *cost* of making the decision. Relevant costs might include man-hours spent in researching, discussing, and deciding. Other costs might be for information processing and distribution (computer analysis and photocopying, for example) and outside help (consultants and advisers). The costs of decision making are particularly relevant today; trends toward participative and group decisions and increased use of machine-aided information processing can result in very expensive decision making processes for relatively unimportant decisions. We can only marvel at organizations that spend $30,000 to make a decision worth $25,000.

The second major efficiency criterion is *time*—the time which elapses between recognition of a problem and a decision on how to cope with it. Long time lapses can affect the organization in several ways. They can create a backlog of decisions whose delay can hinder organizational performance. They also can require the acquisition of more decision makers; the backlog of court cases in many counties requires the creation of new courts. They can render a decision ineffective; a competitor could make a sale while the organization is still deciding what price to set.

Effectiveness Criteria

Effectiveness in decision making is the extent to which a decision solves a problem. Suppose a manager decides to hire temporary workers to reduce a backlog of orders. If, as a result, the backlog is reduced, the decision has been effective. If the backlog is only partially reduced, the decision has been partially effective.

The criterion most often used to evaluate a decision is its *accuracy*. Accuracy includes the extent to which the decision maker correctly evaluated the information, assessed the costs and benefits of alternatives, and computed the optimal alternative. The accuracy of some decisions is more easily determined than others, as by "proving" a decision correct through mathematics or logic. It may be possible to determine the precise accuracy of certain decisions in finance, inventory control, accounting, production, transportation, and similar areas subjective to quantitative analysis.

A second criterion important to the effectiveness of a decision is its *feasibility*. The most accurate decision will be useless if the organization is incapable of carrying it out. The most accurate assessment of U.S. dependence on foreign oil might conclude that our best interests would be served by becoming independent. However, it may be impossible for the United States to generate enough energy on its own to meet future demand if current trends continue.

Finally, most organizational decisions require *support* before they are truly effective—others must cooperate in carrying them out. A decision to automate information processing may be financially accurate and feasible, yet it will be ineffective if employees sabotage it. A decison to market a new product may fail if salesmen are not sold on it themselves.

Cost, time, accuracy, feasibility, and support are the major criteria by which decisions are evaluated. The problem, the decision-maker, the process, and the environment will determine how well a decision meets those criteria.

THE PROBLEM

All decisions begin with a problem. The problem may be as specific as a breakdown in machinery or as general as limited resources. From a manager's viewpoint, a problem is best defined as an obstacle to a goal.

Viewing problems as obstacles to goals has several advantages. First, it helps the manager distinguish problems from symptoms. For example, a manager may be bothered by excessive griping and complaining. Is griping a problem or a symptom? It is difficult

to conceive of griping as an obstacle to a goal. However, it is easy
to conceive of griping as an expression of problems employees are
having—obstacles to their goals.

Second, defining a problem in terms of the goal it is blocking
suggests criteria for evaluating the effectiveness of alternative solutions. To what extent does an alternative improve the chances of
achieving the goal which is being impeded by the problem?

Finally, defining the problem in terms of the goal may in itself
suggest possible alternatives and help avoid restricting the set of
alternatives considered. For example, the Allied command in World
War II was confronted with scores of heavily defended Japanese-
held islands. One approach to winning the war would have been to
invade and capture each of these islands. Viewing these islands as
obstacles to the goal of Japanese surrender rather than as objectives
in themselves enabled the Allies to simply bypass several of them,
rendering them ineffective by cutting them off from their sources of
supply. Thus the losses of life and time which would have resulted
from invasions were avoided.

Types of Problems

What kinds of problems do managers and administrators typically face? Most of them require decisions involving either evaluation, or allocation, or both.

Evaluation   In a sense, all decisions require evaluation. Theoretically, a decision maker determines the worth or value of alternative
solutions to problems before deciding what to do. However, in
actual practice decision makers sometimes neglect the evaluation
process altogether.

There are certain decisions, however, which are almost wholly
evaluative in character. Performance and program appraisal are two
examples. In *performance appraisal* (see Chapter 6), managers evaluate the worth of an employee's performance, ideally against some
set of objective standards, and decide whether that performance
is satisfactory or not. Performance appraisals may also be used in
other decisions, such as determining future job assignments, promotions, and pay increases. In *program appraisal,* managers evaluate the worth of some program or activity, ideally against some set
of objective standards. For examples, a hospital administrator may
want to decide whether to change the accounting system, a school
administrator may want to evaluate the new math, a television pro-

ducer may want to evaluate his evening news program, a production manager may want to evaluate the four-day work week.

In evaluation, decisons are ideally made through accurate judgment of persons or program performance and comparison against objective criteria. This ideal is more easily obtained for some evaluations than for others. It is easy to evaluate the performance of a baseball pitcher. Statistics are recorded on his won-lost record and earned run average and are easily compared against historical norms, his previous records, and the performance of other pitchers. It is easy to evaluate the mandatory 55 mph speed limit of 1974. Gasoline mileage improved 10 to 20 percent for highway travel, and automobile fatalities dropped by more than 10 thousand.

Other evaluations are not so easily made, particularly when criteria are unclear or performance is not easily measured. For example, how would you go about evaluating the performance of a military chaplain, a college professor, a conservation agent, high school counselor, or Vice President of the United States? Or what about evaluating a human relations training program, a half-way house for convicts or addicts, a continuing education program, or the relative evils of inflation and recession?

Allocation   Ultimately, all decisons are made with an eye toward allocation of resources. If we lived in an infinite world where time and resources were never-ending, we would need to make no decisions. However, because we live and work in a world where money, materials, people, and time are finite, we must decide how to allocate them—which project or department will get the most money, how much and what materials to buy, who is to be hired or promoted or fired or trained, when to act and how much time to devote to this program or that group.

Even evaluative decisions are made with an eye toward eventual allocation decisions. People or programs in trouble are likely to be allocated more time, until they change, are abandoned, or replaced by more urgent problems. People or programs doing well are likely to be allocated more promotions, praise, money, or other resources.

Individual and Organizational Decisions   We have been discussing decision making from the organization's point of view: is a person or program productive or profitable or effective for the organization? However, many decisions in organizations involve only the individual and his own values and criteria. A manager may evaluate an employee's performance highly because he likes the employee personally; factors involved in perception and evaluation were discussed in Chapter 6. An administrator may decide to scrap a program not because of its lack of effectiveness but for personal reasons.

Consultants and staff personnel eventually recognize this fact of organizational life. At a recent conference, computer experts spoke of the problems of getting governmental decision makers to use their expertise. As one urban planner put it, "Administrators make political decisions, and sometimes they don't like the facts to get in the way."[1]

The Decision to Join or to Exert Effort   Two types of individual decisions crucial to any organization are the decision by outsiders to join the organization and the decision by members to exert effort in performing organizational tasks. The expectancy model of motivation described in Chapter 4 is a model of both choice and effort. According to the model, choice among alternatives (like which organization to join or which job to take) is a function of the relative outcomes of each alternative, the values of those outcomes, and the expectations of obtaining them, all as perceived by the decision maker. The decision to join is analyzed as the basic subject of Chapter 12.

The decision on how much effort to exert was also described in Chapter 4 in relation to the expectancy model. Effort is seen as a function of the perceived probabilities that additional effort will improve performance and that improved performance will increase rewards, plus the value placed on those rewards.

Problem Characteristics Affecting Decision Making

There are certain characteristics of problems which have important effects on decisions and the way they are made. Three characteristics which have received a good deal of attention in research literature are the novelty, uncertainty, and complexity of decisions.

Novelty   Some decisions become very routine and familiar to a decision maker. The situation, alternatives, and criteria may vary only slightly from one decision to the next. A purchasing agent may face the same requirements, the same vendors, and the same constraints every week. For example, he needs to buy 1,000 hogs, there are only three suppliers in the area, he always looks for the lowest price, acceptable quality, and reliable delivery. Similarly, quarterbacks face zone defenses, symphony conductors face tight budgets,

---

[1] *The New York Times,* January 26, 1975, Weekly Review section, p. 5.

nurses face reluctant patients, students face midterm exams, and detectives face homicides so often that dimensions of the problem, and their responses, become familiar and routine. They have developed programs, rules of thumb, or decision processes with success rates satisfactory to them, and they feel comfortable in falling back on these routines.

Sometimes, however, a problem situation or criterion may change so drastically that routine or previously learned responses are inadequate. The problem of getting a man to the moon and back before the Russians did so was so novel that it required totally new concepts in both scientific and managerial methods. The problems of guerilla warfare were so novel as to require totally new concepts in weapon systems and military tactics for American forces in Vietnam. Current problems of the energy crisis, food shortages, inflation and recession occurring simultaneously are so novel as to make previous approaches of questionable value.

One of the effects of introducing novelty is that delays and uncertainty in decision processes may result. Typically, routine processes or solutions are first tried without success, with the results being confusion, buck-passing, or rationalization. Only eventually is the situation reassessed and a search for new alternatives undertaken. This pattern holds true for the space program, Vietnam, and current economic problems.

Another result of novelty is a change in the effectiveness of previous problem solvers. Those who have been successfully involved in routine solutions may find it extremely difficult to change to totally new lines of attack. Traditionally valued individual abilities may not be good predictors of success in novel situations; even high intelligence may be of little help. In one study, in which 100 men were given 30 minutes to solve a completely novel problem, 46 successfully solved the problem.[2] The 46 problem solvers did not differ from the 54 failures in individual abilities and intelligence. However, the problem solvers were different in their behavior—they attempted significantly more solutions to the problem than the failures did. Apparently effort and high levels of activity, rather than ability, paid off in solving this novel problem.

Novelty and its requirements for creativity and innovation have become prominent factors in organizational life today. These will be taken up in Chapters 9 and 10.

---

[2] Kjell Raaheim and Geir Kaufmann, "Level of Activity and Success in Solving an Unfamiliar Task," *Psychological Reports,* vol. 30 (1972), pp. 271–74.

Risk and Uncertainty   Every decision can be viewed as having three components: the stake or investment, the probabilities of outcomes, and the outcomes themselves. A gambler's decision to bet that the next flip of a coin will be heads consists of his stake (say $5), the outcomes (heads—he wins $5, tails—he loses $5), and the probabilities (0.5 for success, 0.5 for failure). Risk is usually defined as the chance of failure, which in the gambler's case is 0.5, or 50 percent. A high-risk decision is one in which chances of failure are high; a low-risk decision is one in which chances of failure are low. Many activities related to decision making in organizations are carried out to reduce the risks of a particular decision. For example, a doctor who decides to operate on a patient will seek assistance from attendants, nurses, an anesthetist, a pathologist, and a radiologist and perhaps will consult with other surgeons to reduce the risk of the operation (lessen the chances for failure).

Unlike the gambler's bet, in which the stake, possible outcomes, and their probabilities are known for certain, most decisions also involve degrees of uncertainty. Uncertainty exists when one or more of the components of a decision are not certainly known. Consider a company's decision to develop a training program for newly hired managers. There is uncertainty about the investment: Exactly how much time, money, and administrative effort the program will require is uncertain. There is uncertainty about the possible outcomes: No one is sure how much better a successfully trained manager will be or what effects a poor program will have on the new managers or the rest of the organization. Finally, there is uncertainty about the probabilities of various outcomes: No one can state the precise probability that a certain percentage of managers will benefit from the program.

Research has shown that risk and uncertainty are significant variables in decision making. There is evidence that individuals are willing to take more risks in decisions they judge as relatively unimportant. In one study, subjects rated the importance of 12 decisions and indicated how much risk they were willing to take in each. Among male subjects, the more important the decision, the less risk they were willing to take.[3] No such relationship was found for females (this difference will be discussed in the section on personal characteristics of decision makers).

There is also evidence that outcomes to decisions affect the

---

[3] Kenneth Highbee and Terence Lafferty, "Relationships among Risk Preferences, Importance, and Control," *Journal of Psychology*, vol. 81 (June 1972), pp. 249–51.

amount of risk taken. In a series of three experiments subjects were asked to decide among several dosages of drugs.[4] They were led to believe that high dosages had possible high payoffs but also involved greater risks of unpleasant side effects. In each of the three experiments, subjects who were told the drug would be administered within 30 minutes of their decision chose smaller dosages than those who were told the drug would not be administered for several hours. For example, subjects who believed the drug would be administered in 20 minutes chose an average dosage of 94 milligrams, while subjects who believed the drug would not be administered for 3 to 24 hours chose average dosages of 146 to 175 milligrams. According to the researchers, the negative consequences of a decision may become more important to the decision maker than the positive consequences when both are soon to occur.

Uncertainty itself affects the degree of risk the decision maker will take. In an experimental study individuals made a series of bets.[5] The amount they bet was up to them. Uncertainty varied over the series of bets, from a pure risk bet to one involving high uncertainty as to the stake, chances of winning, or outcome. Individuals risked more money as uncertainty decreased. The average amount risked in bets with no uncertainty (pure risk) was 15 percent more than the average amount risked on bets with a small degree of uncertainty, and 25 percent more than the average amount risked on bets with a large degree of uncertainty.

Faced with decisions involving great uncertainty, organizational decision makers are willing to invest money and time in methods for reducing uncertainty. Governments, political parties, armies, and sports teams use espionage, spies, or scouts to reduce uncertainty about the activities of their rivals. Industrial companies buy up suppliers to reduce uncertainty about raw materials, use market research to reduce uncertainty about public acceptance of products, and employ quality control to reduce uncertainty about the reliability of their manufacturing processes.

Complexity The complexity or difficulty of a decision has some predictable effects. Individuals tend to take longer to make complex decisions than to make simpler ones. In part this is because there is more information to be processed in complex decisions. However, it

---

[4] E. E. Jones and C. A. Johnson, "Delay of Consequences and the Riskiness of Decisions," *Journal of Personality,* vol. 41, no. 4 (1973), pp. 613–37.

[5] D. G. Marquis and H. J. Reitz, "Effect of Uncertainty on Risk Taking in Individual and Group Decisions," *Behavioral Science,* vol. 14 (July 1969), pp. 281–88.

may also be due to the greater uncertainty individuals have about complex decisions. For example, two groups of girls were given either easy or difficult decisions in choosing among art prints. Those confronted with the difficult decision felt less certain about their decisions and took more time to make them.[6]

Organizations often respond to complex decisions by assigning them to groups. In theory, groups would take less time because they could divide the tasks among their members. Further, group discussion could reduce uncertainty. Unfortunately, groups do not always work to such an advantage in decision making. Nevertheless group decision making has become an integral part of organizational behavior (groups as decision makers are the focus of Chapter 15).

INDIVIDUALS AS DECISION MAKERS

The role of the individual in the decision-making process has been studied from two different perspectives. One method has attempted to discover behavioral tendencies common to most people in most decision-making situations. From this research different models of decision making have been developed. The second method has tried to find individual characteristics which are related to specific aspects of people's decision-making behavior.

Models of Man as Decision Maker

Decision making is one form of behavior which has been extensively studied and analyzed through the use of models. Models have been created to describe human decision making and to improve it. Some models are very formal and heavily mathematical. They are applicable to computer-assisted studies of economic and financial decision making and are used for activities such as forecasting the economies of nations and the prices of commodities, stocks, and bonds.

Every formal model has as its basis, either explicitly or implicitly, some more general model of man as decision maker. The most prominent of these are the economic-man and administrative-man models. All the models commonly include the concept of decision

---

[6] Leon Mann and Valerie Taylor, "The Effects of Commitment and Choice Difficulty on Predecision Processes," *Journal of Social Psychology*, vol. 82 (December 1970), pp. 221–30.

making as a *rational* activity—rational in the sense that a decision maker will select an alternative which is consistent with his or her own value system. In a broad sense the criteria for rationality are "the existence of an objective and the selection of some alternative that promises to meet the objective as seen by the decision-maker."[7]

Rationality does not rule out emotion. Emotion may be involved in selecting an objective for a decision (e.g., in deciding whether to take a new job offer, is my objective to further my own career or to look after the best interests of my family?). However, when emotion interferes with the selection of an alternative which otherwise meets the decision maker's objective, then nonrationality replaces rationality.

Economic Man The economic-man model of decision making is based on a concept of complete rationality. In this model, the decision maker facing a problem is assumed:

1. To recognize all possible alternative solutions to the problem.
2. To be aware of all possible consequences of each alternative.
3. To be able to evaluate the consequences against his value system.
4. To be able to rank the alternatives in the order in which they are likely to meet his objectives.
5. To select the alternative which maximizes his objectives.

The important features of economic man are that he has perfect information (knows all alternatives and their possible consequences), and he seeks to maximize some expected value.

The main quarrels with this model come from those who maintain that people do not really have perfect information, and the model is not a good predictor of human behavior. Critics also argue that the economic-man model is normative rather than descriptive—it is based on how decision makers ought to behave rather than how they actually behave.

Supporters of the model contend that its value lies in its practical utility. Although individuals may not be perfectly rational, to build other assumptions into the model would make them too cumbersome to be of use. Further, the assumptions of the model are best for predicting aggregate behavior—of market economics and prices, for instance. While individuals may not have perfect information

---

[7] E. F. Harrison, *The Managerial Decision-Making Process* (Boston: Houghton Mifflin Co., 1975), p. 61.

and may not continually seek to maximize expected gain, it can be assumed that markets do behave this way.

The evidence to support the practical utility of maximizing models is mixed. In fact, economic forecasting as a whole remains somewhat less than successful, even with today's massive amounts of data and sophisticated computer technology. A recent study of forecasts of both government and private economists of inflation rates over a 13-year period found plenty of room for improvement. Forecasts of rises or declines in prices were generally right in four years, wrong in four years, and ambiguous in five. The study concludes "One could do as well and with less ambiguity by tossing a coin."[8]

Administrative Man   Responding to what he viewed as unrealistic assumptions of the economic-man model, Herbert A. Simon developed a set of alternative assumptions which have come to be labeled administrative man.[9] According to Simon, man as decision maker is guided not by perfect rationality but by *bounded rationality*, under which principle he is assumed to:

1. Recognize only a limited number of possible alternatives.
2. Be aware of only a few of the consequences of each alternative.
3. Have access to only a limited, approximate, simplified model of the real situation.

A decision maker's awareness of alternatives and their consequences is limited by his own fallible and limited cognitive abilities and by the fact that whatever information he can get will be less than perfect. It is also limited because acquiring comprehensive knowledge requires both money and time, and these are finite resources.

Further, man is viewed as striving not for maximization of values but for *satisficing*. That is, he selects an alternative which meets or exceeds some minimal level of criteria, rather than a maximal level. For instance, if salary were the sole criterion in job selection, man as maximizer would seek to discover all the jobs for which he is capable and would select the one with the highest salary. Man as satisficer would seek to discover one or more jobs which meet or exceed some minimal standard he has set for himself and would be content to select from among that limited set. According to the satisficing concept, "Most human decision-making, whether indi-

---

[8] G. H. Moore, "Economic Forecasting—How Good a Track Record?" *The Morgan Guaranty Survey*, January 1975, pp. 5–8.

[9] H. A. Simon, *Models of Man* (New York: John Wiley & Sons, 1957), p. 198.

vidual or organizational, is concerned with the discovery and selection of satisfactory alternatives; only in exceptional cases is it concerned with the discovery and selection of optimal alternatives."[10]
The authors of this statement argue that maximizing is excessively
more complex than satisficing. They describe the differences between
the two as analogous to the differences between searching a haystack for the sharpest needle and searching a haystack for a needle
sharp enough to sew with.

These concepts of bounded rationality and satisficing will seem
much more plausible if you analyze your own decision processes.
When you decided upon the college or university you are now attending, did you exhaustively consider each of the 2,200 or so institutions of higher learning in the United States and list the possible
consequences of attending each one? Given your list of alternatives,
did you select the one which maximizes your expected values, then
continue to search for better alternatives? As important a decision
as college is, most of you considered a very limited number of possibilities and a few of the consequences, such as cost, available
majors, and location, and you picked the one that satisfied these few
standards and was likely to accept your application.

Like any other kind of behavior, decision-making behavior is
partly a function of the characteristics of the individual. Personality
traits, personal characteristics, and physiological factors have all
been found to affect decision-making behavior.

Personality Factors

Among the personality factors that affect decision-making ability
are confidence, and self-esteem, and dogmatism.

Confidence and Self-Esteem Two personality factors which
have obvious implications for decision making are confidence and
self-esteem. We would expect confident people with high self-esteem
to differ from those who are less confident in the way they process
information. They also would be expected to make decisions more
quickly.

Research tends to support these expectations. For example, individuals with *high* self-esteem are relatively slow to lower their expectancies of future success after a *failure* to solve a problem. On

[10] J. G. March and H. A. Simon, *Organizations* (New York: John Wiley & Sons, 1958).

the other hand, individuals with *low* self-esteem are relatively slow
to raise their expectancies of future success after *successfully* solving a problem.[11]

Dogmatism Dogmation is a tendency to persist in beliefs or
doctrines, even in the face of contrary evidence. Highly dogmatic
individuals also tend to accept authority more readily than those
low in dogmatism. Researchers have long suspected that highly dogmatic individuals differ in decision making from those who are less
dogmatic. The evidence has been mixed.

One study investigated the way dogmatic individuals accepted
new information relevant to a decision. High and low dogmatics
were given a difficult novel problem to solve. They were also given
"hints" or new information on how to solve the problem, some of
which, they were told, had been endorsed by expert problem solvers.
Some of the hints were "good" hints in that they facilitated solving
the problem. Others were "bad" hints—they actually hindered problem solving.

Results showed how high and low dogmatics differed in receiving
new information. Highs tended to accept it because it was endorsed
by experts. Thus their problem solving improved when good hints
were endorsed by experts but suffered when bad hints were endorsed. Low dogmatics, on the other hand, tended to reject expert
endorsment. Thus their problem solving suffered when good hints
were endorsed, and it improved when bad hints were endorsed.[12]

However, differences in decision making between dogmatics and
nondogmatics appear to be specific, as found in the studies above,
and not diffused over all facets of decision making. For example,
one study simply compared a series of 48 decisions made by the 60
least dogmatic students to those made by the 60 most dogmatic
among 650 tested students whose differences in dogmatism were
extreme. Significant differences between the two groups occurred on
only 1 of the 48 decisions.[13] Thus dogmatism may be an important factor only in certain kinds of decisions and decision-making
activities.

[11] R. M. Ryckman and W. C. Rodda, "Confidence, Maintenance, and Performance
as a Function of Chronic Self-Esteem, and Initial Task Performance," *Psychological
Record*, vol. 22 (Spring 1972), pp. 241–47.

[12] C. B. Schultz and F. J. DiVesta, "Effects of Expert Endorsement of Beliefs on
Problem Solving Behavior of High and Low Dogmatics," *Journal of Educational
Psychology*, vol. 63, no. 3 (1972), pp. 194–201.

[13] W. J. Beausay, "A Study of Decision-Making as a Function of the Authoritarian Personality," *Dissertation Abstracts International*, vol. 33A (no. 11), p. 6082-A.

Personal Characteristics

Personal characteristics which can have an effect on decision-making behavior include age and sex. It has been difficult to establish a generalizable relationship between intelligence and decision-making ability, however.

Age   The catch phrase of the under-30 group of the late 1960s, "Never trust anyone over 30," implied differences in values between younger and older Americans. It also suggested that individual faculties such as judgment, reasoning, and decision making begin to decline as one approaches middle age.

If decision-making ability did deteriorate at such an early age, the implications for organizations would be tremendous. Individuals rarely reach top positions in large organizations until their forties or fifties, in part because they may prolong formal education through graduate school, it takes several years to gain experience in a sufficient number of the organization's activities, and the size of the organization's hierarchy requires several promotions to reach the top.

However, while there is some evidence to suggest a gradual decline in decision-making ability in the age ranges found in most organizations (namely, 25–65), this evidence is neither overwhelming nor completely consistent. For example, a study of memory and reasoning among four age groups, 21–35, 36–50, 51–65, and 66–80, found effects of age on only one of four memory variables tested, and this effect was significant only for those over 50.[14] The average number of problems solved was as follows:

Age	Number of Problems Solved
21–35	21.3
36–50	20.2
51–65	15.0
66+	13.1

There was, however, a decline in scores on tests measuring the efficiency of reasoning beginning in the 36–50 age groups.

A very different kind of study was carried out on professional airline pilots, whose tasks require a high degree of perceptual sensitivity and decisiveness.[15] The evidence indicated that visual and

---

[14] J. F. Brinley, T. J. Jovick, and L. M. McLaughlin, "Age, Reasoning, and Memory in Adults," *Journal of Gerontology*, vol. 25 (March 1974), pp. 182–89.

[15] J. A. Szafran, "The Effects of Ageing on Professional Pilots," in *Modern Trends in Psychological Medicine*, ed. J. H. Price (New York: Appleton-Century-Crofts, 1970).

audio perception, signal detection, and high-speed sequential decision-making ability among pilots 20–60 years old were more dependent on physiological characteristics such as the efficiency of the lung-heart system than upon age per se.

Sex   In some recent public discussions about women's rights, it has been argued that females are not only equal to males in decision making but would actually be better, particularly in governmental and policy positions. It is alleged that superiority would result from the greater insight, empathy, and compassion women would apply in decision making.

Unfortunately, sex differences in empathy and compassionate decision making have not been studied. Direct tests of problem-solving abilities, however, have yielded only a few differences, which may tend to diminish with age. For instance, one study of undergraduates found that females performed more poorly than males on certain deductive reasoning problems, due to the females' greater reluctance to change the way the problems were represented.[16] Males solved 56 percent of the problems; females 45 percent. However, a study of decision making among people 41–76 years old found differences declining with age. Among those in their forties, men outscored women on solving heuristic problems. Among those in their fifties men were more efficient than women on simple problems but not on difficult problems. Beyond the age of 60, there were few differences between the sexes in problem-solving performance.[17] Thus there is little evidence that sex differences are critical in individual decision making.

Intelligence   One of the things about decision making which is usually surprising is that there is little clear-cut evidence to directly relate intelligence and decision-making ability. A review of research and summaries of research yields statements such as:

> Information regarding the intellective correlates of decision-making has been quite sparse.[18]
>
> If mental ability plays a part in success in decision-making, it is not a prominent factor.[19]

---

[16] S. M. Schwartz and D. L. Fattaleh, "Representation in Deductive Problem Solving: The Matrix," *Journal of Experimental Psychology*, vol. 95 (October 1972), pp. 343–48.

[17] M. L. Young, "Age and Sex Differences in Problem-Solving," *Journal of Gerontology*, vol. 26, no. 3 (1971), pp. 333–36.

[18] Nathan Kogan and M. S. Wallach, *Risk Taking* (New York: Holt Rinehart & Winston, 1964), p. 10.

[19] L. W. Barber, "Decision-Making and Level of Intelligence," *Character Potential: A Record of Research*, vol. 4 (1968), pp. 85–86.

Even in research where relationships between intelligence and decision-making ability have been found, there are too many exceptions to conclude that there is a generalizable connection. In one study, 32 male and 41 female subjects were given five different problem-solving tasks and a general intelligence test.[20] Intelligence and problem-solving success were clearly related for the male subjects but not for females. Even studies of specific aspects of decision making have found little evidence of consistent effects of intelligence. One study of elementary school children found IQ to be unrelated to creativity in decision making, and only marginally related to risk taking.[21] A larger study of psychiatric patients, surgical patients, and physicians found that while risk taking was significantly related to age, it was not related to intelligence.[22]

If intelligence is unrelated to decision making, why is this so? It would seem intuitively reasonable that they would be related. Indeed, organizations are inclined to include measures of intelligence among the standards they use for selecting people to fill decision-making positions.

One explanation for the lack of a relationship is that intelligence is a very complex characteristic. In Chapter 9 a model of human intellect composed of 120 different abilities will be discussed. Different kinds of decision making require different sets of these abilities, such as cognition, memory, information generation and manipulation, deduction, and evaluation. Since standard intelligence measures typically reveal only a few of these abilities, it should not be surprising that it is so difficult to relate intelligence to decision-making success.

Physiological Factors

Among the physiological factors which can affect decision-making behavior are fatigue, and alcohol and drugs.

Fatigue You must have had to make some decision while fatigued. After driving all night to get home or studying several hours for an exam, you probably felt less able to cope with decisions, particularly if they were complex. You may remember your father

---

[20] Kjell Raaheim and Geir Kaufmann, "Is There a General Problem-Solving Ability?" *Journal of General Psychology*, vol. 90 (1974), pp. 231–36.

[21] Ethel Pankove and Nathan Kogan, "Creative Ability and Risk Taking in Elementary School Children," *Journal of Personality*, vol. 36 (1968), pp. 420–439.

[22] John Steiner, "A Questionnaire Study of Risk-Taking in Psychiatric Patients," *British Journal of Medical Psychology*, vol. 45 (1972), pp. 365–74.

or mother sighing "I'm too tired to think about it right now" when you pressed them for a decision after a hard day.

Does fatigue inhibit decision making? If so, how? These are questions of obvious importance to organizations in activities such as scheduling shifts and timing decision-making activities. For example, how would decision making be affected by a four-day, ten-hour-a-day work week? Does the fatigue of cross-continental jet travel impair the decision-making performance of executives and diplomats?

While fatigue is generally accepted as inhibiting certain decision-making activities, such as long-term recall and concentration, research indicates that these effects are not simple. For example, subjects in one experiment pedaled bicycles for varying amounts of time and were then tested for mental performance.[23] Moderate amounts of exertion (less than maximum—not fatiguing) actually improved performance on tests of attention which relied heavily on short-term memory. However, extreme (fatiguing) exertion impaired attentiveness. The evidence suggests that exertion raises arousal levels. Moderate amounts of arousal will facilitate mental activity, but severe arousal interferes with mental activity, thus inhibiting decision making.

Airline pilots have been the subject of considerable research on the effects of fatigue. This research has attempted to distinguish between physical fatigue, such as results from strenuous or continual physical effort, and mental fatigue, which results from tension or loss of sleep. Differences appear to be minimal, however. Fatigue, whether physically or mentally induced, leads to neglect of necessary information and wide variations in responses to situations calling for immediate decisions—sometimes overvigorous responses, sometimes failure to respond at all. The evidence indicates that fatigue does lead to increasing levels of arousal, which in turn affects decision-making activities. It suggests that, in the airline industry, as much attention should be paid to job improvements which will reduce mental fatigue as to technical improvements which will reduce physical fatigue.[24]

Alcohol and Drugs There is increasing evidence that abuse of alcohol and drugs by individuals in modern organizations is rela-

[23] C. P. Davey, "Physical Exertion and Mental Performance," *Ergonomics,* vol. 16 (September 1973), pp. 559–99.

[24] C. Cameron, "Fatigue Problems in Modern Industry," *Ergonomics,* vol. 14 (November 1971), pp. 713–20.

tively widespread. Estimates of the numbers of problem drinkers and drug users range as high as 1 in 10 to 1 in 7 employees. All levels of personnel, from part-time blue-collar worker to big-time executive, are affected.

Despite the contentions of heavy users of alcohol and drugs that a little drink or a little pill helps them get their minds straight, the evidence is strongly to the contrary. Reviews of research on drug use indicate that the inhibition of decision-making activities depends on the type of drug used. For instance, amphetamines give the feeling that there has been a shorter lapse of time than actually occurs, while narcotics have the opposite effect. Narcotics adversely affect attentiveness and short-term memory.

The effects of alcohol appear to be quite general. For example, in one study, 20 subjects received 2.5 milliliters of 100-proof vodka or 101-proof bourbon per kilogram of body weight (about 5–6 ounces for an average person).[25] Tests conducted one to two hours after drinking showed the alcohol significantly increased the time required and errors made in 5 of 11 different tasks. In another study, 40 males between 21 and 35 received either .41 or 1.23 milliliters of 95-proof alcohol per kilogram of body weight.[26] Tests conducted 30 minutes after drinking found those who received the larger dose required more time and made more errors in a sorting test, and the visual performance of both groups was significantly reduced. Further, although both groups eventually improved their performance over time, the rate of improvement was diminished for the group receiving the larger dose.

SUMMARY

Decision-making behavior is affected by human tendencies and individual characteristics, by the type of problem confronting the decision maker, and by the decision-making environment. Other elements of decision making are the decisions themselves and the decision process. Decisions can be evaluated by both effectiveness and efficiency criteria, such as accuracy, feasibility, support, cost, and time.

[25] W. D. Chiles and A. C. Jennings, "Effects of Alcohol on Problem Solving Tasks," FAA Office of Aviation Medicine Report No. 72–11, March 1972.
[26] E. G. Lewis, "Influence of Test Length and Difficulty Level on Performance After Alcohol," *Quarterly Journal of Studies in Alcohol,* vol. 34 (March 1973), pp. 78–88.

In organizations, most decisions revolve around evaluation or allocation problems. Certain characteristics of these problems, particularly their novelty and complexity, and the risk and uncertainty
surrounding the decision can significantly affect decision-making
processes.

Of the two major models of man as decision maker, administrative man seems the more plausible. In this model, the decision
maker is guided neither by perfect information nor by a desire to
maximize outcomes. Instead, he considers a limited number of
available alternatives and strives to satisfy some minimum criteria,
while employing a simplified model of the situation and less-than-
perfect information. .

Studies of individual differences in decision making have uncovered certain characteristics which are related to decision-making
tendencies. These include personality factors, personal characteristics, and physiological factors. Of these, physiological factors appear
to be more important to decision-making behavior than the others.

In the next chapter we will examine the effect of the environment
on decision making, describe a normative model of how decisions
should be made, and compare typical individual decision processes
with the model.

QUESTIONS FOR REVIEW AND DISCUSSION

1. How would you evaluate the effectiveness of (a) a gambler's decision to bet, (b) a student's decision to attend college, (c) a manager's
decision to fire an employee?
2. What criteria would you use to evaluate the efficiency of a particular
decision by a local government official?
3. What are the important variables in an individual's decision to exert
effort?
4. List two evaluation problems and two allocation problems commonly
faced by managers. For each problem, how might a manager's personal evaluation criteria differ from organization criteria in making
a decision?
5. How do decision makers tend to react to (a) increasing risk and
uncertainty, (b) increasing complexity of a problem?
6. What are the advantages and disadvantages of prior experience in
problem solving?
7. What are the major differences between the economic and the administrative models of man as decision maker?
8. Review a recent important decision that you made. In what respects

did your behavior fit the economic-man model? In what respects did it fit the administrative-man model?

9. If you were about to hire someone for a position which primarily involves decision making, what individual characteristics would you look for?

KEY WORDS

Efficiency	Dogmatism
Effectiveness	Economic man
Problem	Administrative man
Risk	Bounded rationality
Uncertainty	Satisficing

OUTLINE OF CHAPTER

chapter eight

Decision-Making Processes and Environments

© 1974, Reprinted by permission of
The Wall Street Journal *and Bo Brown*

THE IMPORTANT ELEMENTS of individual decision making are the problem, the decision maker, the decision process, the decision itself, and the environment in which it takes place. Chapter 7 discussed the characteristics of decisions, problems, and individuals important to managerial decision making. This chapter will describe how the individual's environment can affect decision making, and two models of decision-making processes will be presented.

THE DECISION-MAKING ENVIRONMENT

Like any other form of behavior, decision making occurs in a complex environment which influences and is influenced by the process and outcomes of the behavior. Much of the research on the decision-making environment has investigated factors which are thought to inhibit or disrupt decision processes.

The Physical Environment

Physical factors which can affect decision making include time pressures and discomforts and distractions resulting from such things as noise and temperature.

Time   The pressures of time tend to change decision-making processes. For example, three groups of 35 men were given five pieces of information (selling price, ease of handling, maintenance costs, styling, and riding comfort) to use in deciding which of 30 automobile models they would like to buy.[1] One group was under no time pressure, one under low pressure, and one under high pressure. Men under high time pressures tended to attach greater weight to negative information than positive information in arriving at their decisions. Men under little or no time pressure showed no tendency to attach greater weight to either negative or positive information about the cars from which they chose.

Time and confidence in decisions affect each other. When there is little time to make a decision, one can evaluate only some of the available information, and thus one may feel less confident about the decision. If there are no time pressures, one who lacks confidence in making a decision will delay the decision to search for and evaluate the new information, perhaps in hopes that something will happen to make the correct alternative more apparent. In one study interviewers had to decide how each of several job applicants should be rated according to four personality variables, based on interviews of varying lengths.[2] The results showed that confidence in the decision increased with the amount of available information and the time spent making the decision. For example, interviewers who had only eight-minute interviews with each applicant took an average of five minutes to make their decisions and rated their confidence at only 2.4 on a scale of 5.0. Interviewers who had 32-minute interviews with each applicant took an average of 7.5 minutes to make their decisions and rated their confidence at 3.1 out of 5.0, significantly higher than the first group.

Other Physical Factors   The unnatural working conditions under which some people must function have prompted a good deal of research into the effects of physical disturbances on decision-making. The overall question of this research is whether excessive noise or temperatures or other distractions might significantly impair the decision making of people in jobs like heavy construction, transportation, traffic control, mining, engine maintenance, deep sea diving, and high-altitude piloting.

---

[1] Peter Wright, "The Harassed Decision-Maker: Time Pressures, Distractions, and the Use of Evidence," *Journal of Applied Psychology*, vol. 59, no. 5 (1974), pp. 555–61.

[2] Bo Ekehammer and David Magnusson, "Decision Time as a Function of Subjective Confidence and Amount of Information," *Perceptual and Motor Skills*, vol. 36, no. 1 (1973), pp. 329–30.

In general, physical discomforts and distractions can impair decision making by causing the decision maker to overlook or ignore relevant information. In the study of men evaluating automobiles which was described earlier, three additional groups of 35 men were asked to decide which model they preferred.[3] FM music played in the background while one group made their decisions (low distraction), a radio talk show was heard at low volume for a second group (moderate distraction), and a talk show was heard at high volume for the third group (high distraction). The moderately distracted group attached greater weight to negative information than the other two did, and the highly distracted group ignored more information than the other groups; members of this group paid attention to only about half the automobile characteristics the other groups considered.

Other studies of noise and vibration indicate that excesses in these conditions produce stress or excessive arousal which impairs decision making. A study of military jet pilots found they took significantly longer to respond correctly to a series of arithmetic and memory problems when exposed to sinusoidal vibrations of 5 to 7 cycles per second.[4]

A more extensive study of the effects of altitude exposed eight military volunteers to atmospheric pressures equivalent to those encountered at 15,000 feet.[5] During their 48 hours of exposure, these volunteers performed a variety of sorting tasks after 3, 20, 24, and 45 hours of exposure. The results showed that speed and accuracy were reduced more for cognitive tasks than for psychomotor tasks. Complex decision-making tasks were more affected than simple tasks, and speed was sacrificed to maintain accuracy. However, the greatest decrements in performance occurred in all tasks after three hours of exposure, after which performance improved as the volunteers learned to adapt to the tasks and the atmospheric effects.

An explanation for the detrimental effects of extreme physical conditions on decision making is suggested by Dr. H. F. Huddleston of the Royal Air Force Institute of Aviation Medicine: "Man has finite capacity for information handling and if some is devoted to persistent anxiety about his organic integrity a lesser capacity remains for carrying out tasks."[6]

---

[3] Wright, "Harassed Decision-Maker."

[4] H. F. Huddleston, "Vertical Sinusoidal Vibrations as a Psychological Stress," *Nature*, vol. 211 (July 1966), pp. 324–25.

[5] R. L. Cahoon, "Simple Decision-Making at High Altitudes," *Ergonomics* (vol. 15, no. 2 (1972), pp. 157–64.

[6] Huddleston, "Vertical Sinusoidal Vibrations," p. 325.

The Social Environment

The environment in which decision making occurs is not only physical but social. The social environment can alter, impede, or facilitate decision making in many ways. We have described how bounded rationality and the satisficing principle operate to produce less than "optimal" decisions in real-life situations by limiting the number and evaluation of alternatives considered. Other concepts related to the social environment which can affect decision making are the concept of bounded discretion, feedback, and the influence of others.

The Concept of Bounded Discretion[7]   In the list of alternatives a decision maker generates, some will be restricted by the social environment. For example, one alternative for students faced with the problem of final exams is to cheat. However, most students feel restrained from selecting that alternative because of personal or social sanctions against cheating, even if expected rewards in terms of grades are highest and expected costs in terms of time spent and risk of being caught are minimal.

FIGURE 8–1
The Concept of Bounded Discretion in Decision Making

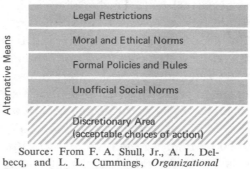

Source: From F. A. Shull, Jr., A. L. Delbecq, and L. L. Cummings, *Organizational Decision Making* (New York: McGraw-Hill Book Co., 1970), pp. 18–19.

Figure 8–1 depicts the concept of bounded discretion as operating as sets of social constraints which limit the discretion of a decision maker in selecting among his alternatives. Realistically, most people recognize that their alternatives are limited by laws, ethics, rules,

---

[7] See F. A. Shull, Jr., A. L. Delbecq, and L. L. Cummings, *Organizational Decision Making* (New York: McGraw-Hill Book Co., 1970), pp. 18–19.

and norms to which they must adhere. In fact, individuals are often expected to adhere to the concept of bounded rationality so strongly that we are upset if they even *consider* an illegal or unethical alternative, let alone select it. Most of this nation's people were dismayed to learn from the Watergate tapes that former President Nixon was even willing to discuss paying hush money to cover up the incident.

Feedback   Feedback in decision making is the information one receives about the accuracy or quality of decisions one is making. Organizations often do a rather haphazard job of arranging for their decision makers to get feedback about their performance. For example, personnel departments may get little systematic information about the performance of job candidates they decide to employ relative to the performance of candidates they decide not to employ. This haphazard approach to feedback is unfortunate, as there is considerable evidence that feedback can significantly alter decision making.

For example, research on the difficulty of the goals an individual sets for himself shows rather clearly that such decisions are directly affected by the information the decision maker receives as to whether he has succeeded or failed in achieving previous goals. The usual consequence of failure is to decide to lower or maintain the previous level of goals, while the usual consequence of success is to decide to increase the level of difficulty of future goals.

One study which demonstrated the effects of different kinds of feedback employed 80 students to add up monthly time sheets of hourly employees.[8] During a rest period, each student's work was evaluated for quantity and accuracy. Twenty students were given accurate, complete feedback about their performance, 20 were given incomplete feedback (quantity only), 20 were given incorrect feedback (errors were exaggerated), and 20 received no feedback at all. All were then asked to decide how many time sheets they expected to complete during the next time period (future goals).

The results showed that goal decisions were significantly affected by feedback regarding past performance, even when the effects of actual previous performance were accounted for. The 20 students who received complete, accurate feedback set significantly higher goals than all the other students. There were no significant differences in goal setting among the groups with incomplete, inaccurate,

[8] L. L. Cummings, D. P. Schwab, and Marc Rosen, "Performance and Knowledge of Results as Determinants of Goal Setting," *Journal of Applied Psychology*, vol. 55, no. 6 (1971), pp. 526–30.

or no feedback on performance. However, those whose feedback exaggerated their actual errors (erroneously low feedback) actually set lower goals than those who received no feedback.

Influence of Others   The influence of other people on individual decision making is not limited to formal feedback on performance. Like any other kind of behavior, decision making can be influenced by social reinforcers such as praise and criticism and by other features of the social environment. Later chapters (18 and 19) of this book are devoted to the influence of other people on behavior in general. A few studies directly relevant to decision making will be mentioned here.

To study the effects of praise and criticism on problem-solving performance, three groups of fifth-grade boys worked on a moderately difficult set of anagrams.[9] After completing the set, some of the boys were praised, and some were criticized. The results showed that, regardless of previous performance, those who were praised performed more effectively on a subsequent set of problems than those who were criticized. For most people (not only children), criticism produces stress which can interfere with certain kinds of behavior if it becomes too strong.

A very different kind of study examined the effects of a number of factors on the decisions of soldiers to fire in combat.[10] Five factors were found which could significantly influence the decision to fire. Three of these were risk from enemy fire, ability to identify the target, and proximity to target. The other two factors are examples of the influence of others: whether or not others were firing, and whether or not one had been ordered to fire. The decision to fire was most influenced by whether or not one had been ordered to fire, and least influenced by proximity to the target.

The finding that decisions to fire are significantly influenced by whether others are firing is an example of a common process of social influence called modeling or imitation, in which individuals in novel or anxiety-producing situations often simply "do what others are doing." A field experiment testing the effects of others' behavior on decisions to violate the law is a good example of imitation.

Pedestrians were observed making a decision to cross or not to

---

[9] L. C. Randolph, "A Study of the Effects of Praise, Criticism, and Failure on the Problem Solving Performance of Field-Dependent and Field-Independent Individuals," *Dissertation Abstracts International*, vol. 32B, no. 5, (1971), pp. 3014–15B.

[10] Randy Olley and H. H. Krauss, "Variables Which May Influence the Decision to Fire in Combat," *Journal of Social Psychology*, vol. 92, no. 1 (1974), pp. 151–52.

cross an intersection with sparse traffic against a red light.[11] A male confederate of the observer, standing next to the pedestrian, sometimes obeyed the law (did not cross against the light) and sometimes violated the law (crossed against the light). Observations of over 2,500 cases revealed that the behavior of the confederate significantly affected the pedestrians' decisions. When the confederate was present and crossed against the light, more pedestrians crossed than when there was no confederate available to imitate. When the confederate refused to cross against the light, fewer pedestrians crossed. Although both male and female pedestrians were significantly influenced by the confederate, females conformed slightly more than males. This finding is consistent with other research on influence which will be discussed further in Chapter 19.

Thus both the physical and social environments can significantly affect a decision maker's behavior. In the next section we will discuss a model of how decision makers *ought* to behave. The physical and environmental factors we have discussed go a long way toward explaining why decision makers often fail to follow the normative model.

PROCESSES OF DECISION MAKING

Confusion between normative models of decision making (the way people should make decisions to maximize some value) and descriptive models (the way people actually make decisions) has often led to misinterpretation of the literature on decision-making processes. While research on decision-making processes has been dominated by normative models, we will discuss both in order to compare what should be done with what is usually done.

A Normative Model of Decision Making

Normative models usually assume that decision making involves a sequence of several phases of activity. In organizational decision making five or six phases are usually prescribed. Our normative model will include seven phases, as depicted in Figure 8–2. These are:

Setting Objectives   Ideally, decision making in an organization starts with a set of predetermined objectives. These may include

---

[11] Lionel Dannick, "Influence of an Anonymous Stranger on a Routine Decision to Act or Not to Act: An Experiment in Conformity," *Sociological Quarterly*, vol. 14, no. 1 (1973), pp. 127–34.

FIGURE 8–2
A Normative Model of the Decision-Making Process

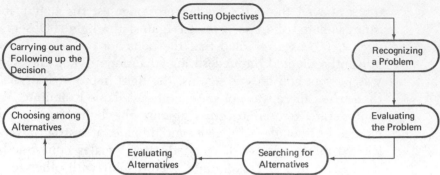

Objectives are used in recognizing and evaluating problems and in evaluating alternatives.

overall organizational objectives, such as maximizing expected return on investment, providing high patient care at low cost, minimizing violent crime within budgetary restrictions, or maintaining military supremacy. There may also be subunit objectives, such as increasing profitable sales, decreasing the amount of accounts receivable, increasing public knowledge of security systems, or developing a new naval weapons system.

Starting with clear, predetermined objectives facilitates the decision-making process in two ways. First, it makes it easier to recognize when a decision is required. Second, it provides standards for evaluating alternatives.

Recognizing the Problem   One phase that is often left out of normative models is recognizing that a decision is required. In fact, much of the formal training managers undergo deals with problem-solving methods rather than problem-finding methods. This may create the unfortunate illusion that all problems that need to be solved will somehow present themselves to the manager.

Realistically, however, problems are not always neatly presented or readily apparent to managers. In fact, fear of reprisal may induce employees who are aware of problems to cover them up rather than call attention to them. Wiretapping by the police department may be a problem no one wants the chief to recognize. Customer dissatisfaction with a new product or newly discovered defects which might endanger consumers may be kept from high-level executives. Tactical defeats which jeopardize an entire military operation may be glossed over in reports to the commander in chief.

Ideally, then, the second phase of decision making should include methods for searching for problems. This would require monitoring organizational activities and comparing them against standards or expectations. This is one area with which phase 1, setting objectives, interacts.

A warning signal of possible problems is a discrepancy between actual performance and goals. If profitable sales are 50 percent below monthly goals, there is a problem requiring a decision (such as the decision of automobile manufacturers to give cash rebates on new-car purchases in early 1975). If accounts receivable increase rather than decrease, if burglaries jump 25 percent over the preceding year, if delivery dates in a new weapons system are 12 months past the agreed-upon deadline, it is likely there are problems that require decisions.

Evaluating the Problem   Having identified a problem, the decision maker begins looking for a solution. Ideally, however, he or she first evaluates the problem to determine whether (1) the problem is important enough to try to solve, and (2) the problem has a feasible or possible solution.[12]

Problem evaluation is another phase which is often missing from normative models. Nevertheless, managers operating in a real world are confronted not only with problems which are not always readily apparent but with limited resources for solving those problems they do discover. As Chapter 1 suggests, time is one of a manager's most precious resources, and the manager (and subordinates) cannot solve all problems, at least not immediately. Therefore the manager must establish priorities for dealing with those that are most important.

Establishing and following such priorities may not be easy. Problems which are the most aggravating to a manager or adminstrator may be of only minimal importance to the success of the organization. Therefore the manager may have to live with certain problems while attempting to solve more important ones. For example, though moonlighting (working at second jobs) by certain employees may annoy the manager, it may leave little obvious impact on the organization's success. In this case the manager may have to live with the problem of employees who sometimes appear tired, are impossible to reach at home, and talk about their other jobs while at work.

---

[12] The concept of a problem evaluation phase is discussed in R. F. Mager and Peter Pipe, *Analyzing Performance Problems* (Belmont, Calif., Fearon Publishers, 1970), chap. 2.

Not only should managers distinguish between important and unimportant problems, they should recognize which problems are unsolvable. An appropriate prayer reads, "O God, give us the serenity to accept what cannot be changed, courage to change what should be changed, and wisdom to distinguish the one from the other." Applied to the organizational context, this suggests that a manager, with finite amounts of time, talent, and resources, may have to decide that some problems, even though important, may be currently insoluble and thus are better put off. Of course there may be a fine distinction between procrastination or indecision on difficult problems and realistic delay of insoluble ones. But sometimes, for example, a manager may discover the source of a problem to be an organizational policy which will not be changed even if he puts his job on the line. In such a case he must decide whether he should continue "to fight city hall," quit, or register his complaint and get back to work.

Searching for Alternatives   Once an important, possibly solvable problem has been recognized, the manager ideally generates a list of alternatives from which to pick an optimal solution. Normative models differ on the criteria for this activity. According to some, the decision maker should try to uncover all possible solutions to a problem *and* to assess the possible outcomes to each solution. According to others, the decision maker should first assess the costs of searching (time and money, for instance) versus the gains possible from better alternatives, and then search until expected costs from further search equal or exceed expected gains from better alternatives.[13] This approach is analogous to the economic decision to produce goods up to a quantity where marginal costs equal marginal revenue.

Normative models usually include a formal method of searching for alternatives. A formal search process would include predetermination of a list of information sources, evaluation of the credibility and expected usefulness of each source, and estimation of the cost in terms of money and time of using each source. This information would lead to a plan including strategies for exploiting each source and the timing of a sequence of activities in the search process. Finally, a formal search would include a predetermined set of criteria for deciding when the search should end.

Several arguments for a formal rather than an informal search

---

[13] For a lucid discussion of this approach, see Ira Horowitz, *An Introduction to Quantitative Business Analysis* (New York: McGraw-Hill Book Co., 1965), pp. 72–77.

method have been offered. Listing sources beforehand may generate ideas about other sources of information which might be overlooked. Estimating source credibility and usefulness may result in a more efficient search process. Establishing a timetable and criteria for ending the search may decrease the likelihood of procrastination and indecision.

Evaluating Alternatives Normative models require the decision maker to amass, or to try to amass, a rather extensive amount of information in evaluating alternatives. While this information may be acquired in the process of searching for alternatives, an additional search for information about alternatives already uncovered may be necessary.

First, the decision maker must recognize all possible outcomes from each alternative solution—not just positive outcomes but negative ones as well. An analysis of several foreign policy decisions by the United States suggests that some of the better known blunders (the Bay of Pigs, Pearl Harbor, the Vietnam escalation) were partially due to a failure to consider all the possible outcomes of the decision. For instance, in deciding to attempt a secret invasion of Castro's Cuba with Cuban exiles, the Kennedy administration failed to consider the possibility of a military disaster, of outrage among friendly Latin American countries, of denunciation from much of the rest of the world, and of forcing an alliance between Castro and the U.S.S.R.[14]

Second, the decision maker must be able to assess the value of each outcome, both positive and negative. For instance, in deciding to invade Cuba, a high positive value was placed on the outcome "successful covert invasion leading to counterrevolution and overthrow of Castro regime." However, a high negative value should have been placed on the outcome "invasion fails, landing forces captured, United States humiliated, Castro embraces Soviet Union."

Finally, the decision maker must assess the likelihood of each possible outcome to each alternative. Considerable effort has been devoted to assisting decision makers to assess the probabilities of future events more accurately. One approach is to estimate the probability of a future event by determining the likelihood it will occur, given other conditions, then estimating the likelihood of occurrence of those conditions. In weather forecasting, for instance, a meteorologist may determine that, historically, the arrival of a cold front is preceded by rain 80 percent of the time. Estimating that the

---

[14] Irving L. Janis, *Victims of Groupthink* (Boston: Houghton Mifflin Co., 1972).

chances that an approaching cold front will reach the local area in the next 24 hours are about 3 out of 4, the forecaster calls for "a 60 percent chance of rain tomorrow" ($80\% \times 3/4$).

Recognizing, evaluating, and estimating the likelihood of each outcome to all alternatives prepares the decision maker to evaluate and compare the alternatives. Normative models suggest that all alternatives must be evaluated in some common framework so that logical comparisons can be made. If the decision is purely an economic one, the common framework can be money. That is, investment A has an expected payoff of k dollars, investment B an expected payoff of n dollars, and so forth.

However, many decisions have alternatives with outcomes that are not readily comparable. In deciding how to allocate expenditures for the coming year, a hospital administrator may be forced to choose between a new radiomammography machine and additional workers in laundry and dietary services. In such cases normative models suggest that the decision maker should assess each outcome in terms of its *utility* to the organization and compare alternatives on the basis of their expected utility.

Choosing among Alternatives   Even when outcomes can be evaluated on some readily comparable basis, choice can be difficult. Those who study decision-making processes have described five types of alternatives:

1. A *good alternative* has a high probability of positively valued outcomes and a low probability of negatively valued outcomes.
2. A *bland alternative* has a low probability for both positively and negatively valued outcomes.
3. A *mixed alternative* has a high probability for both positively and negatively valued outcomes.
4. A *poor alternative* has a low probability of positively valued outcomes and a high probability of negatively valued outcomes.
5. An *uncertain alternative* is one for which the decision maker cannot assess the relative probabilities of outcomes.[15]

Some combinations of these types of alternatives will produce more difficult choices than others. For example, consider a decision maker faced with only two alternatives. If one alternative is good and the other is bland, mixed, poor, or uncertain, then his decision is easy. However, choosing between two alternatives of the same

---

[15] J. G. March and H. A. Simon, *Organizations* (New York: John Wiley & Sons, 1958), pp. 113–14.

type is difficult, although it would be preferable to be faced with two good alternatives than with two poor ones.

It is difficult to choose between a bland and a poor alternative because both are unacceptable. It is difficult to choose between a mixed and an uncertain alternative because of their uncertainty. It is difficult to choose between a bland and a mixed alternative because of their incomparability. Consider for instance the decision of a symphony orchestra to hire a guest conductor for the upcoming season. One alternative (mixed) is a brilliant conductor who is likely to conduct an exciting season but whose temperament is so volatile that the chances are high of his alienating important financial backers of the symphony. The other alternative (bland) is a conductor who is unlikely to produce anything other than an average season in terms of both music and public relations.

To assist the decision maker who is encountering difficult choices of this sort, decision theorists have suggested several strategies.[16] They argue that consistent use of decision-making strategies will yield a better return than a nonstrategic approach, over the long run.

The Principle of Insufficient Reason. One strategy deals explicitly with the *uncertain* alternative. When the decision maker is unable to estimate the likelihood that certain outcomes will occur, the *principle of insufficient reason* states that he should assume that each outcome is equally likely to occur. This strategy will transform an uncertain alternative into a good, mixed, bland, or poor alternative. An example might be Feedapak, a small animal-food company faced with two proposals for marketing a new synthetic dog food. Proposal A is a high-budget mass media advertising campaign, while proposal B is a modest-budget test-market approach. If proposal A works, sales and profits will soar; if it fails, the company may face bankruptcy. If proposal B works, sales and profits will increase slowly; if it fails, profits will be down temporarily. If the company were unable to forecast the likelihood of occurrence of A's outcomes, according to the principle of insufficient reason each outcome to that alternative should be considered equally likely. Therefore, the chances of soaring profits or bankruptcy should be considered equal for proposal A. By using this principle, proposal A is transformed from an uncertain alternative into a mixed alternative.

Maximin and Minimax Strategies. A strategy applicable to decisions with alternatives of widely differing payoffs is the maximin

---

[16] For numerical examples and further explanations of decision-making strategies under conditions of uncertainty, see Horowitz, *Quantitative Business Analysis,* chap. 5.

strategy—maximizing minimum potential gain. Under this approach, the decision maker selects the alternative whose worst possible outcome has the highest positive value of all alternatives. This strategy would be of use in selecting among a set of good alternatives. A similar strategy is minimax—minimizing maximum loss. Under this approach, the decison maker selects the alternative whose worst possible outcome has the least negative value of all alternatives. This strategy is useful in selecting among mixed, bland, and poor alternatives or combinations thereof. For example, using minimax, Feedapak Company would select proposal B.

Maximax Strategy. Both maximin and minimax strategies are decidedly pessimistic. They assume the worst will happen and select the alternative that will turn out best, given the worst. A contrary strategy is maximax—to maximize the maximum possible gain. Under this strategy the decision maker selects the alternative with the outcome offering the highest positive value of all. If Feedapak used a maximax strategy, it would select proposal A.

Minimax Regret Strategy. A fifth strategy is useful to those who find themselves reflecting wistfully over lost opportunities. In any decision involving more than one alternative with at least one positively valued outcome, the decision maker risks losing the potential gain of rejected alternatives when he finally makes his choice. If Feedapak Company selects proposal B, it risks losing the possible gain from proposal A. A strategy has been devised to deal with situations in which the decision maker wishes to minimize lost opportunities—*minimax regret.* This strategy requires the construction of utility tables in which each outcome of each alternative is assigned a numerical value, based on its utility to the decision maker. Suppose Feedapak assigns utilities of 100 to the success of proposal A and 0 to its failure, 40 to the success of proposal B and 30 to its failure, as depicted in the following payoff table:

	Success	Failure
Proposal A	100	0
Proposal B	40	30

From this payoff table an opportunity-loss table can be constructed by subtracting each utility figure from the highest utility in its column. In the success column, 100 is the highest utility; in the failure column, 30 is the highest utility. Thus the opportunity loss table is:

	Success	Failure
Proposal A	$100 - 100 = 0$	$30 - 0 = 30$
Proposal B	$100 - 40 = 60$	$30 - 30 = 0$

Proposal A has a maximum regret (opportunity loss) of 30, and proposal B has a maximum regret of 60. Using a minimax regret strategy, Feedapak Company would select proposal A.

Carrying Out and Following Up the Decision   Obviously, the best decision is worthless if it is never enacted. A good deal of this book, particularly Chapters 4, 16, 18, and 21, is concerned with concepts and behavior relevant to implementing decisions—motivation, cooperation, leadership, influence and control, for example.

Ideally, the decision maker not only carries out a decision but monitors the results to see how good a decision it actually turned out to be, or to determine if modifications or even reversals need to be made. This is another phase which is facilitated by setting objectives. Ideally, the alternative is selected to make some contribution to one or more objectives. Measuring actual results against expected objectives is one way of evaluating the success of a decision and determining whether changes or adjustments in the decision are necessary. If Feedapak Company selects proposal A, and a severe recession drastically curtails consumer interest in new dog foods, the company might abandon its mass media campaign or postpone it until economic conditions change.

A Descriptive Model

Unlike normative models of how people ought to make decisions, descriptive models of how they actually do make decisions are neither precise nor neat. Despite strong arguments that individuals and organizations could significantly improve their decision making by following the normative prescriptions of management scientists, most decision making continues to be less than optimal.

Setting Objectives   Programs like management by objectives (MBO) are designed to create and maintain a routine of joint goal setting at all levels of management, in order to facilitate motivation, evaluation, and decision making. Unfortunately, such programs have not been widely adopted, partially because of resistance from within companies and partially because hard evidence of their success has been below expectations.[17]

In most cases, decision makers have some overall objective (maximizing expected profit, gain, or utility) in mind when confronted with a decision task. However, the establishment of a firm set of clear operational objectives prior to decision making is clearly the

---

[17] Robert Albanese, *Management: Toward Accountability for Performance* (Homewood, Ill.: Richard D. Irwin, 1975), pp. 90–93.

exception. In fact, the objective may evolve out of the decision making process itself. As decision makers discover what alternatives and outcomes are available, they may begin to formulate an idea of what a realistic objective is in particular circumstances.

Recognizing and Evaluating the Problem   Research is not clear about how an individual recognizes when a problem exists or how he decides to tackle it. It is likely that few managers actively seek problems. The varied activities and demands of a typical manager's day provide enough data to convince him he has all the problems he can handle.

For especially active managers such as first-line supervisors, problem evaluation is usually based on three criteria. First, problems are handled in the order in which they are encountered. Second, problems that can be dealt with immediately receive priority over those requiring more time. Third, problems whose symptoms indicate a crisis or emergency take precedence over all others. Thus a self-description by a manager might be, "I've got no time for contemplation; I spend all my time putting out fires."

Searching for and Evaluating Alternatives   The principle of bounded rationality (see Chapter 7) is descriptive. Operating under pressures of time and with limited resources and information, a typical decision maker conducts a limited search for alternatives. Instead of an exhaustive search for the optimal solution, he feels compelled to search only until he has uncovered a small number of alternatives which meet a limited set of criteria. Instead of gathering exhaustive information about each alternative, he compares a given alternative against one or two crucial criteria and rejects or accepts it as a further possibility on that basis. For example, in considering alternative proposals for investment, two crucial criteria might be size of initial investment (must be less than X dollars) and time until payoff (must be less than Y years). The investor would compare each alternative found against these two criteria and would reject outright those that failed to meet them and set aside for further study any that did meet them.

There is evidence that search does not necessarily stop with the first acceptable alternative. The job-seeking behavior of graduate business students who were subjects in a longitudinal study of decision processes displayed this tendency.[18] As these students approached graduation, they began to seek jobs through formal inter-

---

[18] Peer Soelberg, "Unprogrammed Decision Making," *Industrial Management Review*, vol. 8 (Spring 1967), pp. 19–29.

views and plant visits. Although some of them described several criteria as crucial to their job selection, the typical graduate screened job alternatives on the basis of only two—starting salary and initial location. However, even if he received a firm offer which met or exceeded both of these criteria and which he was inclined to accept, he typically continued to interview and visit until he had received one more acceptable firm offer. The researcher labeled this behavior as searching for a "confirmation candidate"—an alternative which enabled the graduate to confirm the wisdom of his decision by comparison.

Choosing among Alternatives The act of choosing among alternatives appears to be a much simpler process than is envisioned in normative models. Most decision makers do not actually assess the utility of each possible outcome to an alternative, estimate the probability of occurrence of each outcome, and compute the expected utility or determine the subjective expected utility of each alternative.

Some decision makers are most heavily influenced by risk. Some "risk avoiders" tend to choose the alternative with the most likely positive outcome, regardless of its expected value. Some consistently select high-value alternatives with moderate amounts of risk.

Some decision makers are undeterred by risk and probabilities. A few will go for the big payoff, regardless of the odds against them. A few will avoid high-payoff alternatives, assuming that the investment or risk will be too high.

Indeed, most decision makers do not process information about probabilities, expectancies, and risk very well. Too many studies have shown that individuals make inconsistent choices in series of decisions involving uncertainty and risk. There is too much evidence that decision makers pay little or no attention to useful and available information. Two researchers who have experimentally studied individual decision making for several years came to the following conclusion about humans making decisions: "[They] have a very difficult time weighing and combining information—be it probabilistic or deterministic in nature. To reduce cognitive strain, they resort to simplified decision strategies, many of which lead them to ignore or misuse relevant information."[19]

Carrying Out and Following Up the Decision Once a decision has been made and carried out, ideally decision makers should con-

---

[19] Paul Slovic and Sarah Lichtenstein, "Comparison of Bayesian and Regression Approaches to the Study of Information Processing in Judgment," *Organizational Behavior and Human Performance*, vol. 6 (1971), pp. 649–744.

tinue to evaluate their chosen alternatives in order to determine just how good their decisions were and whether they perhaps should be changed or modified. However, evidence of postdecision behavior indicates that most decision makers are neither careful nor unbiased in following up their decisions.

Cognitive Dissonance Theory. One approach which has shed some light on postdecision behavior is cognitive dissonance theory.[20] This theory states that if an individual has cognitions which directly conflict with one another, he will experience an uncomfortable state or feeling (dissonance) which he will be motivated to reduce. "Cognitions which directly conflict" means two or more pieces of information which contradict each other. For example, consider a homicide detective trying to solve a murder. One piece of evidence, a motive or weapon, indicates that individual X committed the murder; another piece of evidence, an airtight alibi, indicates that this person could not have committed the murder. These two cognitions contradict one another, creating a state of psychological discomfort for the detective which arouses him to continue his investigation until the discrepancy between the cognitions can be resolved.

The popular television series "Columbo" can be interpreted as a study of the effects of cognitive dissonance. Columbo inevitably encounters some small piece of information which contradicts either the airtight alibi of the real murderer or the evidence planted by the murderer to frame an innocent person. That discrepancy always serves to motivate Columbo ("Pardon me, Ma'm, but there's just one thing that really bothers me . . . just one little thing I need to clear up") to entertain us for 90 minutes while resolving the discrepancy and nabbing the real murderer.

According to cognitive dissonance theory, if dissonance is sufficiently noxious to motivate people to reduce it, it is also sufficiently noxious to motivate people to avoid it. Applied to decision making, this suggests that once a person has selected an alternative he will be motivated to avoid information which might suggest he made a poor or suboptimal choice. He has one cognition that says the alternative he has selected is the best possible one. Subsequent information which might be unfavorable to his chosen alternative, or favorable to an unchosen alternative, would result in dissonance. Knowing this, and being anxious to avoid dissonance, he is not inclined to evaluate thoroughly the decision he has already made.

---

[20] Leon Festinger, *A Theory of Cognitive Dissonance* (Stanford, Calif.: Stanford University Press, 1957).

Dissonance theory predicts that he would pay more attention to subsequent information which supported his decision and would disregard discrepant or dissonant-producing information which might disconfirm it.

There is conflicting evidence to support such a theory. Marketing research on the behavior of consumers who have purchased one brand of a product has shown that they tend to pay more attention to subsequent information (such as advertisements) that is favorable to their purchase than to that favoring other brands.

For example, the behavior of new-car buyers was observed after they had purchased a car.[21] Advertisements about the car they had purchased were considered information supporting their decision; advertisements about other cars were considered information not supporting their decision. The new-car buyers showed a clear preference for reading advertisements about the car they had already purchased. However, they did not avoid reading ads about cars that they had considered but had not purchased. Although they read more ads about their purchase than about any other car, in reading ads about other cars they did not distinguish between cars they had considered but did not buy and other cars.

Such evidence supports the first prediction of cognitive dissonance effects on postdecision behavior: that decision makers welcome information which supports their decision. The second prediction, that decision makers avoid information which opposes their decision, is not well supported.

In two separate studies, college students were given a choice between taking an objective test or an essay test. After their decision, they were given lists of articles about the two types of exams and asked which they would most prefer to read. For some groups of students, the articles gave favorable information about one or the other type of exam; for other groups, the articles gave unfavorable information. Students confronted with favorable articles preferred those about the type of exam they had chosen, consistent with the predictions of cognitive dissonance theory. However, students confronted with unfavorable articles showed no clear preference for articles about either type of exam.[22] In fact, there was some indica-

---

[21] Danuta Ehrlich, Isaiah Guttman, Peter Schönbach, and Judson Mills, "Post-Decision Exposure to Relevant Information," *Journal of Abnormal and Social Psychology,* vol. 54 (1957), pp. 98–102.

[22] Judson Mills, Elliot Aronson, and Hal Robinson, "Selectivity in Exposure to Information," *Journal of Abnormal and Social Psychology,* vol. 59 (1959), pp. 250–53.

tion that students sought additional information about their choice, even if that information was adverse. Two thirds of these students, given a choice, preferred an article recommending a change *from* the type of exam they had chosen to an article recommending a change *to* the type of exam they had chosen.[23]

SUMMARY

Decision making is a common type of organizational behavior which is as yet not thoroughly understood because the factors which influence it are complex.

Both the physical and social environments play important roles in decision making. Time pressures and extreme physical conditions can interfere with effective decision behavior. Research in this area has important implications in military, transportation, construction, and maintenance organizations and other fields where decision making often occurs in extreme conditions. In particular, evidence that decision makers can adapt to some extremes suggests that training programs should include decision-making exercises under extreme physical conditions.

An important feature of the social environment is that it can significantly restrict the decision maker's freedom of choice. Organizations dissatisfied with the quality of decision making might do well to examine the availability of information and feedback provided for their managers. They might further review company policies, rules, and norms for possible detrimental effects on organizational decision making. Decision makers themselves ought to be aware of those elements of the social environment that interfere with their decision processes and look for ways to insulate themselves against unnecessary restrictions and distractions.

Those who study decision making recommend a sequence of several steps as a model process. These include setting objectives, recognizing the problem, evaluating it, searching for alternatives, evaluating and then choosing among alternatives, and carrying out and following up the decision.

However, individual abilities are imperfect, and individual tendencies are somewhat varied. These characteristics, together with pressures from the physical and social environments, result in actual decision behavior which typically fails to meet the standards of the

---

[23] Sidney Rosen, "Post-Decision Affinity for Incompatible Information," *Journal of Abnormal and Social Psychology*, vol. 63 (1961), pp. 188–90.

normative model. The biggest discrepancies between the ways decision makers should act and the ways they actually do act are in stating the problem, searching for alternatives, and following up on the decision.

QUESTIONS FOR REVIEW AND DISCUSSION

1. What factors in the physical environment are likely to affect the decision-making behavior of a (a) production-line foreman, (b) surgeon, (c) advertising account executive, (d) bank loan officer, (e) college quarterback?

2. What factors in the social environment are likely to affect the decision-making behavior of a (a) newspaper publisher, (b) television network censor, (c) criminal trial lawyer, (e) marketing manager, (f) college president?

3. What kinds of environmental factors might a manager want to insulate himself against in making an important decision? What are some possible drawbacks to insulating oneself?

4. How does setting objectives help a manager recognize a problem?

5. What criteria should a manager use to evaluate a problem before searching for alternatives?

6. Theoretically, how long should a manager continue to search for alternative solutions to a problem? In practice, when does the search for alternatives usually stop?

7. How do managers usually fail to meet the standards of the normative model in carrying out and following up on a decision?

8. If you had to pick one single factor as the most likely cause for managers' departing from the normative model in their decision making, what would it be? Suggest some ways of dealing with that factor.

KEY WORDS

Bounded discretion	Mixed alternative
Feedback	Uncertain alternative
Normative model	Principle of insufficient reason
Good alternative	Maximin strategy
Poor alternative	Minimax regret strategy
Bland alternative	Cognitive dissonance

OUTLINE OF CHAPTER

chapter nine

The Creative and Innovative Individual

One morning last summer Ron and I had to have some advertising ready to show at nine o'clock in the morning. We both got to the office at seven o'clock and neither of us had any idea what we wanted to say. The subject was institutional investing, and we had to have a campaign ready to run in a magazine called *The Institutional Investor*. That magazine is read by guys who have lots of dollars to spend in the market. Our client was Hirsch & Company, the stockbrokers, and through *The Institutional Investor* they were trying to reach the guy who is working for the ILGWU who's got maybe a million dollars of union funds to invest in the market. He has discretionary power over a lot of money and the idea is to get him to buy his blocks of stock through Hirsch & Company. How do you talk to this guy? That was the problem.

Sitting there at seven o'clock in the morning we were really desperate, I mean desperate, because the guy is coming in at nine o'clock to see advertising and he doesn't want to know from anything else. As far as he's concerned he's to be shown a campaign and he doesn't want to know that we've been backed up and busy as hell. It's a funny feeling; what are we going to do? Ron and I always work up to the wire but this time was the closest we ever were. Maybe, we thought, this will be the time when we won't make it.

Well, we started out talking about sex. Seven o'clock! "How are you?" "Fine, how are you?" "Boy, did you see Norma walk by here last night? Wow, what a body!" Comes 7:30 A.M. and nothing's happening. Like at about quarter of eight I say, "What are we going to do with this problem?" Ron says, "Aw, don't worry, we'll make it." All of a sudden he says, "I've been thinking about it all morning." We started feeling sorry for ourselves. "You know, it's really a pain in the ass," I say. "You never can go home and like just think of nothing, right?"

Ron says, "Yeah. That's interesting, isn't it? That you always think of your job. I bet these guys in the institutional investing business feel the same way about themselves. I bet they think that they're heroes the way we think we're heroes for being here this early."

I say "Yeah, that's interesting. I'll bet they really think they're hot stuff because they don't get to go to lunch because they're working so hard. Hey, did you ever notice when you don't go to lunch you really feel better because you think you're working so hard?"

Ron says, "Yeah, I know. I feel great when I'm working like a son of a bitch and I don't go to lunch. I bet these guys feel the same way, sitting there with their millions of dollars to spend, they must really feel like they're something when they miss lunch or they have to order a hamburger sent in."

And I say, "Hey, a hamburger. Remember that day we were working with that guy Dave and he ordered a hamburger and it got cold? Remember how proud he was that he didn't even have the time to eat?"

Ron says, "Yeah, what a headline—'The Glory of the Cold Hamburger.' That could be it, the whole campaign. 'The Glory of the Cold Hamburger.' " That was the concept for the entire campaign, not just a single ad. The ideas started coming right out of the concept. The guy shaving in the morning saying that he thinks about stocks even in the bathroom and like he's putting in a 24-hour day. We know that we want to show the readers of *The Institutional Investor* a picture of a hamburger and we want to say to him, "You know, we understand exactly what it's like. You've got too much money and there are too many people depending on you for you to run out and have a big expense-account lunch. So you order a hamburger in and it gets cold and you know what? You get a big charge out of it. You really think you're hot stuff for eating this cold hamburger and you know, you're right."

The campaign started to grow from the guy feeling the way he does because he works so hard. The fact that he doesn't get a chance to see his kids. The fact that he shaves and thinks about work. One by one the ads start to come: "The Glory of the Cold Hamburger"; "The 24-Hour Workday."

Ron is drawing like a madman at this point. Now, how do we tie it all together? Well, why are these people working like this? Why are they breaking their necks? Because a lot of people are depending on them. Fine. That's the whole thing. "Call Hirsch & Company because a lot of people are depending on you."

By this time Ron is drawing with one hand and lettering in headlines with the other. There are four stages in making an ad: A thumbnail, which is just a tiny sketch; a rough, which is like a thumbnail, but big; a comp, which means the headline is lettered in and the drawing is much more detailed; and the finish.

"How do you like this?" he said. "We've got a nice shot of the hamburger, with a couple of potato chips on the side, and we've got a little piece of type." I'm sitting there writing copy now, mentally, and also talking it out. The excitement in the room is fantastic. Now we can't sit down. We're jumping up and down because we've a deadline to make and now we've got it and we know we're going to make it. There is an electric feeling in the room and this is what this business is all about as far as the creative person is concerned. Ron finishes his comp at 9:15. The man from Hirsch showed up at 9:20. We had five ads ready to show him—five complete layouts with the headline comped in, the body copy roughed in, with a slogan line that they live with and go along with forever. It was ready.

The feeling in that room between 8:30 and 9:00 is like insanity. Ron is drawing as fast as he can, throwing papers around, and I'm chattering like a maniac. That's when an ad comes together, this is how it happens. No one has ever written about it. No one's ever come close to describing what it is. They talk about it as though it's magic. There's really no magic, nor is it very creative. You know what it's like? It's like two salesmen sitting down trying to find a handle on how they're going to sell the car this morning. It's nine o'clock and the door's going to open, people are going to come in, and what are we going to say to get them to buy this car? That's really the whole thing. People shouldn't try to make it into a writer and an art director. It's two salesmen sitting there trying to figure something out and coming up with an idea.

When the Hirsch guy came in he said, "What have you got?" We said, "Well, what we have is, these guys all want to be heroes, right?" He said, "Right." "And some of these guys," we said, "they really feel sorry for themselves when they work like dogs, right?" "Right." "Right." "Well, let's do a campaign glorifying them for breaking their ass, making them know that we know that they work hard. It's institutional, it's long-run. It's not going to mean a guy is going to call up Hirsch and Company and say, 'I want you because you ran that ad.' It means that maybe he's got his choice between Hirsch and Company and some other schnook he's never heard of before, he'll vaguely remember that Hirsch and Company did something he was really happy with." The Hirsch man took one look at the ads and said, "I buy it."

The campaign ran, and it has been one of the good, successful campaigns in this area because the guys it was directed at—they can feel for it, it's them, it's their life. Some of these investment guys have even called Hirsch up asking for reprints of the ad. They want to hang it up in their offices. "That's me, you know?" they say. They show it to their wives and say, "You know why I come home late at night? Here's why." They want to frame it. People are like that. They really do react to advertising.[1]

THE NEED FOR CREATIVE BEHAVIOR

ORGANIZATIONS NEED creative behavior. For some organizations, like the advertising agency in the story above, the need has always been

---

[1] Jerry Della Femina and Charles Sopkin, *From Those Wonderful Folks Who Gave You Pearl Harbor.* Copyright © 1970 by Jerry Della Famina and Charles Sopkin. Reprinted by permission of Simon and Schuster.

obvious, but the need for creativity is no longer the sole province of Madison Avenue.

Organizations in all fields—industry, science, education, the military, government, medicine, entertainment, public welfare, labor—today demand more creative behavior. Even staid, venerable institutions like professional baseball no longer dismiss as crackpots people with revolutionary ideas. The multicolored uniforms, white shoes, and night-time World Series games which are part of today's Major Leagues were the brainchildren of Charles O. Finley, a man who has been persona non grata among baseball's hierarchy for his eccentric ideas and behavior.

This growing interest in creativity reflects the current view that it is both necessary for survival and capable of providing opportunities for growth. Every organization is, in a sense, competing with hundreds of other organizations—not just for money but for a host of other resources it needs to survive and grow. There is competition for markets, audiences, students; for talent and manpower; for raw materials; for attention and public support; for favorable legislation and taxation. As competition increases the costs of expanding or maintaining its share of resources, an organization must come up with new ways to use the resources it has. The adoption in baseball of Charlie Finley's gimmicks was precipitated not by new expressions of his personality but by the accelerating success of professional football, a rival sport.

The public's experience with increasing change and improvement shortens the life expectancy of the profitability of products, processes, and services already in the market. Prime-time television shows seldom last two seasons. Today's Broadway hit is next year's bore. Hemlines and necklines go up, down, sideways, disappear. Textbooks must be revised every four years. Divorce rates skyrocket. The "offense of the 70s" cannot score in '74. "What's new?" is a standard greeting.

In the face of such demand, creativity is not only necessary for survival, it acquires great incentive power in the opportunities it can provide those organizations that can use it effectively. With an affluent public conditioned to expect and seek innovation, the organization that publishes the best novel, produces the Academy Award winner, comes up with the best-tasting cigarette, discovers a cure for cancer, or figures out how to stop fallout or retard pollution or recycle cow manure can amass for itself enormous rewards in the way of recognition, markets, finances, talent, adulation, or envy.

And yet, organizations have historically understood little about creative behavior. As late as 1964, a seminar on "the creative organization" was conducted by the prestigious University of Chicago Graduate School of Business. These academicians and professionals from creativity-concerned organizations were able to reach very few conclusions as to the character of creative organizations or ways to maximize creative behavior in organizations.[2] (These topics will be discussed in Chapter 10.)

Fortunately, as demand for and interest in creative products has grown, so has interest in creative behavior as a subject for study. From 1925 to 1950, less than two tenths of 1 percent of the publications in psychology was devoted to creativity—about five to ten articles per year. In 1965, nearly 100 articles on theory and research in creativity were published. By 1970, over 20 percent of 160 educational research projects around the country included creative development as one of their major objectives.[3] In 1972, some 250 publications in psychology focused on creativity. Today, centers for research on creativity are located at the universities of Southern California, California at Berkeley, Georgia, Utah, and New York at Buffalo, and at Macalester College in Minnesota.

Chapters 9 and 10 respond to this interest in creativity based on theory and research on the topic, which have mushroomed in the past 25 years. These chapters are directed, as fas as current research and theory can go, toward the questions managers, administrators, directors, educators, and creative individuals themselves have been asking: What is creativity? How can creative talent be identified? Can creative ability be improved? What factors influence creative behavior?

This chapter is designed to provide you with a basic understanding of the nature of creativity and an ability to infer some ways in which creative behavior can be enhanced and influenced. We will first describe the differences between creative ability and creative behavior and between creative ability and intelligence. We will consider whether creative ability can be measured or improved, and whether or not it is a common trait. Common characteristics of highly creative individuals will be described. Chapter 10 will analyze the various elements of the creative process. It will identify factors

---

[2] G. A. Steiner, ed., *The Creative Organization* (Chicago: University of Chicago Press, 1965).

[3] J. P. Guilford, "Creativity: Retrospect and Prospect," *Journal of Creative Behavior*, vol. 4 (Summer 1970), pp. 149–68.

which appear to inhibit or facilitate creative behavior and present a few implications for those concerned with using or developing creativity.

Throughout these chapters, examples from the lives of creative people will be used for illustration. The incident which began this chapter was chosen not only to pique your interest but to illustrate certain points to be made later: Creativity requires preparation. It can be facilitated by goals, deadlines, and understanding of the process. And it does not require an extravagant budget.

THE NATURE OF CREATIVITY

Like any other behavior, creative behavior is attributable to personal ability and other factors. In this sense, creative behavior operates under the same general principles set forth for individual behavior in Chapters 4 and 5. Thus we propose that creative behavior is a function of ability and motivation, and like other behavior, is influenced by the physical and social environments. It is important to stress this, because creativity has been viewed as such a mysterious process that there is a tendency to regard creative behavior and creative ability as one and the same thing.

The demands placed on industry in World War II for innovation in war matériel resulted in the first significant efforts to bring research and development laboratories into the industrial setting. After the war, many companies decided to retain research and development personnel in the hopes that their skills would transfer to peacetime production, and the result would be innovative consumer products which would help take up the slack in production as the war ended. Unfortunately, in many companies the management of research and development consisted of some such attitude as: "Stick those research guys off in a corner somewhere until they come up with something we can use. Whatever you do, keep 'em away from the rest of the plant. We don't want those weirdos giving our regular people any strange ideas." Management was basically ignorant of creativity and somewhat fearful of creative people, and yet it felt that somehow the same creative ability that helped win the war could contribute to peacetime prosperity. These managers behaved as if creative ability could be translated into creative behavior simply by putting a group of scientists together in a laboratory until, by some mysterious process, a new and better product appeared.

This misconception resulted in disappointed managers and frustrated, dissatisfied scientists. Today we know enough about creativity and the creative process to enable organizations concerned with such things to make more enlightened use of talented people. The first step in dissolving some of the mystery surrounding creativity, then, is to distinguish between creative ability and creative behavior.

Creative Behavior and Creative Ability

Creative behavior is the production of ideas that are both new and useful. "Production" implies translating the new and useful ideas into something which others can perceive, either verbally, as by singing, writing, or talking, or nonverbally, as by building, dancing, or demonstrating. "Useful" qualifies the new product somewhat. To be creative, behavior must be of some value to someone sometime. For instance, a beginning piano student experimenting during his practice session may happen to hit a set of ten notes that *never* has been heard before—and hopefully, to the rest of his family, will never be heard again. The combination is new, and even deliberate, but not what could be called creative.

Creative ability is the capacity to produce ideas that are both new and useful. Students of creative ability describe it as a set of talents which enable the individual to make new combinations and associations. The literature on creativity stresses two features of creative ability. First, it appears to be not a simple, unidimensional capacity but a complex set of abilities. Second, a great deal of creative ability has to do with coming up with new associations between concepts which others have never made before.

Regarding the complexity of creative ability, J. P. Guilford, who has devoted his career to investigating and directing research in the nature of human intelligence, recently concluded that, "Creative talent is not a single, broad ability parallel to but distinct from intelligence, but, like intelligence, is composed of numerous abilities. Creative performance draws on a large number of these abilities for different purposes and on different occasions."[4]

We will discuss the general relationship between creative ability and intelligence later. First we should consider the concept of creative ability as a capacity for making new associations or combinations, or *divergent thinking*. While it may be a cliché to say "There's

---

[4] J. P. Guilford, "Some Misconceptions Regarding Measurement of Creative Talents," *Journal of Creative Behavior*, vol. 5 (Second Quarter 1971), p. 86.

nothing new under the sun," much of what we call creative is simply the product of one individual's associations between two or more known elements which others before him had never associated. It is easy to see this in music. For example, all of the orchestral instruments and all of the sounds produced by those instruments and the human voice were known before Mozart combined them into his opera *Don Giovanni*. The piano, vibraphones, and the counterpoint technique existed long before George Shearing combined them to create his own distinctive musical style.

This aspect of creativity has been labeled the *bisociative act*—the act of combining two previously unconnected cognitive matrices. A number of famous creative acts have been broken down into separate elements to illustrate the bisociative act. For instance, Newton's concept of gravitation has been broken down into the following two elements:

1. *Element A.* It was known that the moon's path deviated from the straight line it would have taken had it not been for the earth. This rate of deviation was also known.
2. *Element B.* It was known that an object falling toward the earth accelerated. This rate of acceleration was also known.

Associating A and B led to the idea that there was a relation between A and B. Further investigation revealed that the rates were equal. This led to conclusion C: The same force acts on both the moon and a falling object. This force is called gravity.[5]

Creativity and Intelligence

Divergent thinking and bisociative abilities are important capacities associated with creative ability, but they are not the only ones. In particular, there exists a rather complex association between creativity and intelligence.

It is a common error to think of creativity and intelligence as one and the same thing. Those who speak of "creative genius" fall into the perceptual trap laid by their own rhetoric. They equate creative genius with intellectual genius, under the assumption that only persons of very high intelligence can be creative.

This misconception has initiated a great deal of research into the relationship between intelligence and creative ability. At the risk of oversimplifying the findings of that research, the relationship can

[5] J. W. Haefele, *Creativity and Innovation* (New York: Reinhold Publishing Corp., 1962), p. 30. Haefele provides a number of similar examples.

FIGURE 9–1
Relationship of Creative and Intellectual Abilities

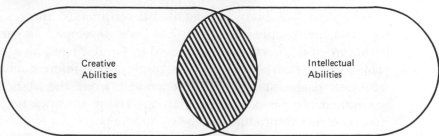

The degree of overlap between the two sets of abilities, creative and intellectual, is apparently not large.

be depicted as in Figure 9–1. That is, some of the abilities involved in creativity are intellectual abilities, and some intellectual abilities are creative. The degree of overlap between creative ability and intelligence is not precisely known, but it is apparently not large. Most studies which have found creativity and intelligence to be related have also found that intellect can explain no more than 10 percent of the variance in creativity. One summary of research concluded that studies with children, in other countries as well as the United States, generally support the independence of creativity and intelligence.[6] Other researchers have reinforced the notion of relative independence by citing evidence that creativity can be fostered by particular environmental changes which have little or no effect on intelligence.[7]

However, most researchers are not quite prepared to claim that the two abilities are completely independent. For instance, many studies which report *no* correlation between creative potential and intelligence have been conducted among groups of subjects with superior intelligence, including groups such as scientists and other professional people.[8] However, assessments of the creativity of individuals encompassing the whole range of intelligence (generally with IQ scores of 60 to 150) usually find a significant positive correlation between the two abilities. Guilford implies that a "threshold" of intelligence—a minimum level—may be necessary for significant creative behavior to be possible.

[6] W. C. Ward, Nathan Kogan, and Ethel Pankove, "Incentive Effects in Children's Creativity," *Child Development,* vol. 43 (June 1972), pp. 669–76.

[7] Serena Wade, "Differences between Intelligence and Creativity: Some Speculation on the Role of Environment," *Journal of Creative Behavior,* vol. 2 (Spring 1968), pp. 97–101.

[8] Guilford, "Measurement of Creative Talents," pp. 77–87.

Creative Abilities and the Structure of the Intellect

The most ambitious and detailed description of the set of abilities commonly called creativity has been developed as part of the *structure-of-intellect theory* proposed by Guilford and his associates.[9] This theory asserts that humans display 120 different intellectual abilities, each functionaliy independent from the rest. Each is composed of one of five mental operations manipulating one of four contents to produce one of six products ($5 \times 4 \times 6 = 120$), as depicted in Figure 9–2.

FIGURE 9–2
The Structure-of-Intellect Model

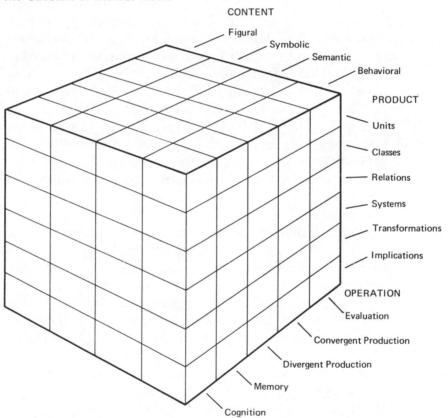

Source: Reproduced from J. P. Guilford, *The Nature of Human Intelligence* (New York: McGraw-Hill Book Co., 1967), p. 63. © 1967 McGraw-Hill Book Co., Inc.

---

[9] J. P. Guilford, *The Nature of Human Intelligence* (New York: McGraw-Hill Book Co., 1967).

In the structure-of-intellect model, *operations* are four major kinds of intellectual activities or processes; that is, an operation is what the person does with information he receives. Cognition includes discovery and awareness. Memory is storage of information. Divergent production is generating information from other information to produce variety and quantity and searching for alternatives, such as new combinations and associations. Convergent production is generating information which is fully determined by giving or searching for logical imperatives, as in deduction. Evaluation is comparing information against standards, such as looking for consistency.

Contents are classes or types of information. Figural content is images, like faces or shapes. Symbolic content takes the form of signs, like letters and numbers. Semantic content is meaningful information which usually can be verbalized, like *hot* or *high*, but also including meaningful pictures. Behavior content is nonverbal and is involved in human interactions.

Products are ways of classifying the forms that information takes while the person is processing it. A unit is a single segregated item, like "a feather." A class is a set of concepts grouped by common properties, like "black feathers and white feathers." A relation is a concept of connections between items of information, like Newton's concept of the relation between the rate of fall of an object and the rate of curvature of the moon's orbit. A system is an organized or structured item of information, like $9 \times 2 \div 3 = 6$. A transformation involves changes in existing information—redefinitions, revisions, or modifications, as in "That's not a penguin, that's a bird in a tuxedo!" Implications involve extrapolations such as predictions or consequences.

Using a battery of tests to assess these 120 abilities and a statistical technique known as factor analysis,[10] Guilford has conducted numerous studies to demonstrate that the abilities do exist in humans and are, in fact, independent. The tests suggest that certain abilities are much more applicable to creativity than others. *Divergent production* may be the most important creative operation. Abilities to manipulate figural and symbolic content are characteristic of many creatively behaving individuals, and transformations are valuable products in the creative process.

---

[10] The statistical validity of the support of this evidence for Guilford's theory is currently being debated. See J. L. Horn and J. R. Knapp, "On the Subjective Character of the Empirical Base of Guilford's Structure-of-Intellect Model," *Psychological Bulletin,* vol. 80 (July 1973), pp. 33–43.

Intelligence tests, on the other hand, rely heavily on convergent production and evaluation, semantic content, and relations and systems. Still other abilities, such as those involving cognition, implications, and memory, may be involved both in intelligence and in creativity. For instance, both Tchaikovsky and Mozart had the eidetic ability to recall music in greatest detail. Mozart described that ability as follows:

> Those ideas that please me I retain in memory, and I am accustomed, as I have been told, to hum them to myself . . . provided I am not disturbed, my subject enlarges itself, becomes methodised and defined, and the whole, though it be long, stands almost complete and finished in my mind, so that I can survey it, like a fine picture or a beautiful statue, at a glance. Nor do I hear in my imagination the parts successively, but I hear them, as it were, all at once. . . . When I proceed to write down my ideas, I take out of the bag of my memory, if I may use that phrase, what has been previously collected into it . . . and it rarely differs on paper from what was in my imagination.[11]

Thus it can be concluded that Figure 9–1 crudely but realistically portrays the relationship between creative ability and intelligence. A recent study of nearly 1,000 students, using a battery of Guilford's tests and various measures of intelligence, indicated that both IQ and creativity are broad, loosely defined abilities which encompass a multiplicity of traits, only some of which are interrelated.[12]

Developing Creativity

One of the most encouraging and promising results of recent research in creativity has been the success of various programs designed to enhance creative ability and behavior. There has been considerable evidence that creative ability, as measured by various tests, can be significantly increased. Of 40 studies reviewed, some 90 percent described various successes in improving ability through training, for both youth and adult groups.[13] Further, improvements have been found in the creative ability of both creative

---

[11] Edward Holmes, *The Life of Mozart* (London: J. M. Dent & Sons, Ltd., 1912), pp. 255–56.

[12] Anne Anastasi and C. E. Schaefer, "Note on the Concepts of Creativity and Intelligence," *Journal of Creative Behavior,* vol. 5 (Second Quarter, 1971), pp. 113–16.

[13] S. J. Parnes and E. A. Brunelle, "The Literature of Creativity, Part I," *Journal of Creative Behavior,* vol. 1 (Winter 1967), pp. 52–109.

individuals and those who are less creative, although their relative abilities remained about the same.

The success of these programs has bred further interest and success. In 1967, a review of known methods and educational programs for enhancing creativity contained 27 different entries.[14] A subsequent review in 1971 listed 49 methods and programs.[15] A sample of these methods includes:

1. *"Delphi" technique*—a joint decision process (see Chapter 15).
2. *Bionics*—discovery in nature of ideas related to solutions of man's problems.
3. *Synetics*—practical use of analogy and metaphor in problem solving.
4. *Morphological analysis*—methodological interrelating of all elements of a problem to discover new solutions.
5. *Purdue creativity training program*—use of audio tapes and printed exercises.

Other methods range from creative workshops to sensitivity training, all with varying degrees of success.

Success in itself has not been the sole reason for the growing interest and development of creativity training programs. Another stimulus has been the gradual realization that, contrary to conventional wisdom, creative ability is not the exclusive possession of a few gifted individuals. To the contrary, it appears that creative ability is widely distributed throughout the general population, and significant increments in creative behavior in organizations may be possible without massive, expensive searches for especially gifted individuals. This is not to deny that, as with other individual characteristics, some individuals have considerably more creative ability than others. Nevertheless, great changes in attitudes regarding the distribution and nature of creative ability have come about in the past several years, among not just those who study the process but those who manage it as well. When 331 managers surveyed by the Creative Education Foundation were asked to respond to the statement: "Innovation is a born capability; it cannot be taught or developed," 91 percent, including 93 percent of the research

---

[14] S. J. Parnes, *Creative Behavior Guidebook* (New York: Charles Scribner's Sons, 1967), pp. 300–302.

[15] D. J. Treffinger and J. C. Gowan, "An Updated Representative List of Methods and Educational Programs for Stimulating Creativity," *Journal of Creative Behavior*, vol. 5 (Second Quarter, 1971), pp. 127–39.

and engineering managers and 100 percent of the personnel managers, disagreed with the statement.[16]

MEASURING CREATIVE POTENTIAL

Any manager, educator, or administrator concerned with making use of or developing creative behavior must be interested in measuring creative potential. Advertising executives whose success depends upon the creative output of artists and copywriters seek to staff the agency with individuals likely to be creative; they would like to be able to assess the creative potential of all prospective employees. Many educators, particularly at the elementary school level, want to identify children with creative ability in order to encourage creative behavior, and also to identify children with low creative ability in order to help them develop it. Administrators seeking to increase the frequency or quality of creative and innovative behavior often employ training programs; they want to be able to test the effectiveness of such programs by measuring the creative ability of the trainees before and after program administration.

Methods

This demand for means of assessing creative potential has led to the development of a number of methods. One early method for estimating creative potential uses intelligence tests. However, as we noted earlier in this chapter, the relationship between intelligence and creativity is so tenuous as to render IQ a poor measure of creative talent. Another obvious method of assessing talent is to rate the individual by the work he or she has produced. That is, a good predictor of future creative behavior is often past creative behavior. A study of famous creative people in a variety of fields indicated that many of them had given early, even preteen, evidence of their talent.[17]

The need remains for more direct methods of assessing creative potential. For one thing, the absence of creative behavior does not necessarily mean the absence of creative potential. A given individual may have never had an opportunity to express his talent, or may not have understood how to do so, or may have been frus-

---

[16] Bruce G. Whiting, "Manager Opinions on Creativity," *Journal of Creative Behavior*, vol. 5 (Third Quarter, 1971), pp. 166–68.

[17] H. C. Lehman, *Age and Achievement* (Princeton, N.J.: Princeton University Press, 1953). This study will be discussed in some detail in the section on Characteristics of Creatively Behaving Individuals.

trated otherwise. Vincent van Gogh was such a person. As a young man, he once wrote his brother that he was like a man "whose heart is eaten out by an anguish for work, but who does nothing because it is impossible for him to do anything. . . . Such a man often doesn't know himself what he might do, but he feels instinctively: Something is alive in me! What can it be!"[18] Van Gogh at that time had not yet found the means of expressing the creative compulsion he felt, which was eventually manifested in his painting. Who knows how many others of talent have felt it wither for lack of recognition or expression?

The three basic means for assessing creative potential are personality tests, biographical measures, and tests of verbal and nonverbal ability. The proliferation of assessment procedures is documented by a 1971 bibliography listed 48 commercially available instruments for measuring creative potential and talent and 23 noncommercially available instruments.[19]

The personality and biographical instruments grew out of studies of the characteristics of creatively behaving individuals, as discussed more fully later in this chapter. We will concentrate here on more direct assessments of creative ability, particularly the more popular tests.

Simple Tests Tests for assessing creative potential are based on the theories of a particular researcher about the nature of creative ability. Those that hold that this ability is a simple or unitary construct have devised simple tests for measuring it. The most famous of these is the Remote Associates Test (RAT).

The RAT requires the subject to form mutually distant associative elements into new combinations by providing mediating links. Each test item provides the subject with three different words, and the task is to find a fourth word that can link these three. For example, the three stimulus words might be:

chair   horse   time

A word that could link them all would be *high*. Try to find a word to link the members of each of the following two sets:

cup   silence   heart
fishing   baseball   trousers

---

[18] Brewster Ghiselin, *The Creative Process* (Berkeley, Calif.: University of California Press, 1952), pp. 3–4.

[19] Bill Kaltsounis, "Instruments Useful in Studying Creative Behavior and Creative Talent," *Journal of Creative Behavior*, vol. 5 (Second Quarter, 1971), pp. 117–26, and G. A. Davis, "Instruments Useful in Studying Creative Behavior and Creative Talent,"*Journal of Creative Behavior*, vol. 5 (Third Quarter, 1971), pp. 162–65.

The RAT test is popular because it is short (30 items) and easy to score and to administer. It requires only 40 minutes, and it is fun to take. However, it has been criticized for viewing creative ability too narrowly. One of the more vocal critics argues, "Since creative talent, from the standpoint of aptitudes, is composed of numerous special abilities, and since criteria of creative performance in everyday life are also complex, no one test of a creative ability can be expected to correlate highly with those criteria."[20]

Complex Tests   The Torrance Tests of Creative Thinking are modeled on a different concept of the creative thinking process.[21] These tests are designed to assess the subject's aptitudes for fluency, flexibility, originality, and elaboration. Examples of some of the tests included in the battery are:

1. *Ask and Guess.* Subjects are shown a picture, then asked to respond to questions such as: What is happening? How can you tell? What do you need to know what is happening for sure, what caused it, and what will result?
2. *Product Improvement.* Subjects suggest as many ways as they can to improve a product. For example: How can you change this toy rubber duck so that it will be more interesting and fun for children?
3. *Unusual Uses.* Subjects list as many interesting and unusual uses as they can for some common object. For example: old bathtubs.
4. *Just Suppose.* Subjects think of all the possible consequences of an improbable situation. For instance: Suppose all male humans were suddenly struck dumb.

Other tests in the Torrance battery include Imaginative Stories and a Figural Battery (picture construction, figure completion, etc.). In many of the tests quality of originality of responses, rather than quantity, is the major criterion for judgment.

Another battery of creativity tests is based on the structure-of-intellect model.[22] The tests are particularly concerned with certain aspects of the model. For instance, there are six tests of different divergent-production abilities, based on the six products or concepts of information. Some of the subject's tasks are:

---

[20] Guilford, "Measurement of Creative Talents," p. 86.

[21] E. P. Torrance, "Predictive Validity of the Torrance Tests of Creative Thinking," *Journal of Creative Behavior*, vol. 6 (Fourth Quarter, 1972), pp. 236–52.

[22] Guilford, *Nature of Human Intelligence.*

1. *Generating behavioral units.* Example: List as many different things as possible you might say if you were both disappointed and jealous.
2. *Reclassification.* Example: Think of several different groupings of objects based on common characteristics (a list of ten objects is given).
3. *Transformation.* Subjects are given a set of drawings of a face, each of which bears a different expression, and are then asked to select an expression to go with each step in a series of three related events, such as: A man asks a girl to dance, she snubs him, he tries another girl.
4. *Elaboration.* Subjects are asked to suggest different feelings and actions for a person in a given situation. Example: Your spouse has just received a fantastic job offer which would require you to move from a neighborhood you love to a foreign country.

Modeling tests after complex notions of creative ability is, in itself, a very difficult task. Further, administering such tests requires a great deal of skill, time, and effort. Even evaluation is a problem, as the criteria may change from test to test and may vary between objective and more subjective processes.

Validity of Measurement

Obviously, no test is worth much if it fails to measure what it purports to measure. Studies are therefore carried out to determine the validity of a test—the extent to which it really measures what it claims to measure, as we discussed in Chapter 2. For instance, if a test for home-run hitting potential were devised, and then it was discovered that on the test Dean Chance (a former pitcher who once struck out 13 consecutive times and went an entire season without a hit; sometimes called "the father of the designated hitter") outscored Henry Aaron (who should need no introduction), we would question the test's validity. This would be called a test of *concurrent validity.* On the other hand, suppose a test for leadership potential was devised and administered to a high school graduating class. If it was found, say five years later, that a large proportion of high scorers were in leadership positions in various fields, while only a small proportion of low scorers were in such positions, our faith in the validity of the leadership potential test would be strengthened. This would be a test of the instrument's *predictive validity.*

Concurrent Validity   Each of the three tests described above has
been shown to have concurrent validity; that is, test scores have
been found to be significantly related to the rated creativity of
various groups of persons tested. For example, the research creativity
of 43 graduate psychology students was rated by their faculty, and
these students were then administered the RAT test for creative
ability.[23] Statistical analysis revealed a significant positive relation
between the RAT scores and the research creativity ratings of these
students ($r = .55$). In similar kinds of studies, the Torrance tests
have been found concurrently valid for rated creativity of such diverse groups as industrial arts students and salespersons in a national
sales organization.[24] Both the Guilford battery and the RAT have
demonstrated concurrent validity with the rated creativity of research scientists.[25]

Predictive Validity   Of course, the most crucial demonstration of
a test's usefulness is to show that it can be used to increase the
accuracy of behavior prediction. The most demanding test of predictive validity is a longitudinal study in which the test is administered and then the behavior is measured at intervals over a long
period of time. This makes it possible to distinguish between the
short-term and the long-term predictive ability of a test.

The most notable analyses of the predictive validity of creativity
tests have been done with the Torrance tests. In one study, a battery
of five creativity tests was given to seventh graders in 1964.[26] These
test scores were combined to form a single composite predictor of
creative behavior. Five years later, in 1969, the creative achievements of 111 of these students were evaluated. Data on their creative
output in art, music, drama, and literature were combined into a
single index of nonacademic creative behavior. Statistical analyses
showed a significant positive relationship between the creativity
predictor (combined test scores) and subsequent creative behavior
($r = .51$).

In a similar but even longer study, the Torrance Tests of Creative
Thinking were given to 144 teen-agers in 1959.[27] Records were kept

---

[23] M. T. Mednick, "Research Creativity in Psychology Graduate Students," *Journal
of Consulting Psychology*, vol. 27 (June 1963), pp. 265–66.

[24] E. P. Torrance, "The Minnesota Studies of Creative Behavior: National and International Extensions," *Journal of Creative Behavior*, vol. 1 (Spring 1967), pp. 137–54.

[25] R. J. Shapiro, "The Identification of Creative Research Scientists," *Psychologia
Africana*, vol. 2 (1966), pp. 99–132.

[26] A. J. Cropley, "A Five-Year Longitudinal Study of the Validity of Creativity
Tests," *Developmental Psychology*, vol. 6 (January 1972), pp. 119–24.

[27] E. P. Torrance, "Predictive Validity of 'Bonus' Scoring for Combinations on Repeated Figures Tests of Creative Thinking," *Journal of Psychology*, vol. 81 (May
1972), pp. 167–71.

for 12 years on the post–high school achievements of these individuals. In 1971 measures of creative behavior, such as number of creative achievements and quality of peak creative achievement, were calculated for each student. Correlations between the 1959 test scores and measured creativity from 1959 to 1971 were all significant, ranging from $r = .39$ to $r = .54$.

Other studies have demonstrated the predictive validity of the Torrance Tests over the short term (one week to nine months) as well. Groups studied included second graders, graduate students, and high school teachers. Behavior predicted included rated creativity of humor, ideas, stories, and solutions to problems.[28]

Results of the Testing of Creativity

As a result of this research over the past 20 years, it can now be said with some confidence that creative ability can be measured. Obviously we are not to the point where we can accurately assess 100 percent of a person's creative potential, but a variety of valid tests can be used to give some idea of people's creative talents.

Another result of this testing has been the conclusion that creative ability is widely distributed throughout the general population. Some individuals have more talent than others, to be sure. But apparently nearly everyone has some creativity—children as well as adults; men and women; black, white, and brown; intelligent and less intelligent; educated and uneducated. This conclusion in itself has some obvious managerial policy implications, from a national level down to the level of individual companies and even families.

Improvements in testing for creative ability have facilitated the development of creativity training programs. A good example of the use of such programs in industry is that carried out by the AC Spark Plug Division of General Motors Corporation. When the division became interested in enhancing the creative behavior of its personnel, the suggestion department and the education department cooperated to develop a training program.

One way to assess the program's effectiveness was through the use of tests.[29] A group of 39 automotive engineers was given the AC Test of Creative Ability and then was put through a series of creative-thinking seminars. Similar tests were administered to the group after the seminars had been completed. The data were broken

---

[28] Torrance, "Predictive Validity of the Torrance Tests of Creative Thinking."

[29] J. E. Walters, *Research Management: Principles and Practices* (Washington, D.C.: Spartan Books, 1965), p. 143.

down into two groups for analysis: the high group (engineers who had more than 80 ideas on the first test) and the low group (those who had fewer than 80 ideas). Both high and low groups improved after training. The high group improved an average of 27 ideas per engineer, or 25 percent, while the low group improved an average of 40 ideas per engineer, or 67 percent.

AC also experimentally tested the effectiveness of its program on productive creative behavior. Two groups were selected for a ten-week training program. Group A consisted of 18 individuals whose history included frequent contributions of profitable suggestions; group B consisted of 13 individuals whose suggestion records were weak. The number of annual suggestions and the amount of money awarded for accepted suggestions was computed for group A, group B, and the plant as a whole for the year prior to the training program. After groups A and B completed the program, similar records on suggestions were kept for another year. The results revealed that both training groups improved on their past performances substantially more than the rest of the plant. The number of suggestions submitted by groups A and B increased 40 percent, compared to 3 percent for the rest of the plant. The average dollar value of suggestions accepted increased by over 100 percent for groups A and B, compared to 17 percent for the rest of the plant. Thus training can affect creative and innovative behavior.

CHARACTERISTICS OF CREATIVELY BEHAVING INDIVIDUALS

Who are the creative people? Are they geniuses or freaks, young or old, tall or short, introverts or extroverts, from happy homes or broken homes, well educated or dropouts, mentally healthy or unbalanced?

This section deals with what we know about people who have been identified as especially creative through their work. What we know about these people generally comes from a research strategy known as the *actuarial approach*. The goal of this approach is to discover measurable traits or characteristics which can be used to identify among the general population those individuals who are particularly apt to perform some target behavior.

The actuarial approach is used in analyzing many types of behavior. For instance, much heart research has been devoted to studying traits and characteristics common to those who have heart disease and common in those who are free of it. This much-publicized research has reported a number of distinguishing traits and characteristics "linked" to heart disease victims, including heavy smoking, obesity, stress, and diet.

Actuarial methods are popular because they are relatively easy to use in research, particularly with today's sophisticated data processing methods and equipment. They also provide a relatively simple managerial strategy for manipulating the amount of behavior in question: Find people who are likely to perform that behavior and bring them into the organization if the behavior is desirable (like leadership or innovation) or keep them out if the behavior is undesirable (like failing or troublemaking). Thus there is a constant demand from organizations for actuarial research to identify individuals who, for example, are particularly likely to sell insurance well, supervise effectively, perform under stress, conform, or create.

A good deal of the research on creativity has been directed toward discovering characteristics which distinguish what some refer to as *highly creative individuals* from the rest of the population. We will use the term *creatively behaving individuals* (*CBIs*) to describe the individuals studied. These people were selected for study because they had actually employed their creative abilities to produce creative outputs in science, business, and the arts.

This research has generally involved two methods. In the first, characteristics of a group of people whose performance has been distinctively creative are compared to characteristics of the general population or of a group of people whose performance is undistinguished. Thus one might compare artists whose works hang in the National Gallery to artists whose work goes unsold. A second method is to obtain ratings of the creativity of a large group of individuals and then search for characteristics which are highly correlated with those ratings. Here one might rate the creativity of the products of a number of inventors, then correlate such characteristics as intelligence, years of education, or number of younger siblings with rated creativity. Actuarial research on creativity has involved characteristics of CBIs which can be classified as demographic, behavioral, and personality characteristics.

Demographic Characteristics

Family background and age are two of the demographic characteristics of creatively behaving individuals that have been studied most frequently.

Family Background   Of particular interest to a number of researchers has been the home environment in which the CBI grew up. In addition to obvious and easily assessable characteristics such as size of family, socioeconomic status, and father's occupation, researchers have analyzed child-rearing practices of parents, family pride, cohesiveness of family, and other more dynamic (and more difficult to assess) characteristics of the backgrounds of CBIs.

Much of this evidence has been equivocal.[30] In some studies the CBIs tended to come from broken homes, but in others they were more likely to come from integral families. Some studies report CBIs are more likely to be found among first-born or only children; others found them as likely to be younger siblings. Some have proposed that CBIs were apt to have suffered many or prolonged childhood illnesses, like Beethoven; others found them to have been relatively healthy. Some CBIs reported that their parents exercised a great deal of control over them as children; others reported their parents allowed them considerable freedom.

On certain characteristics of family background, however, there has been some consensus. For instance, CBIs often have described home and school life as experiences in which parents and teachers trusted them to act reasonably and responsibly. There is common evidence among CBIs of feelings of either personal or family superiority on a social or an intellectual basis.

Age and Other Characteristics   As we discussed earlier in this chapter, the relationship between intelligence and creativity is complex and not fully understood. They appear to be distinct, but slightly overlapping, sets of abilities. In a like manner, studies of differences in the creative behavior of males and females are not yet conclusive. Such differences as may exist are possibly cultural rather than genetic in nature.

For example, few differences are reported between creative performance of American girls and boys at early ages. After fourth grade, however, girls consistently outperform boys on all verbal and some figural tests.[31] Studies in India, on the other hand, have found boys consistently more creative than girls on both verbal and creative tests.[32] These results have been interpreted as reflecting

[30] T. Christie, "Environmental Factors in Creativity," *Journal of Creative Behavior*, vol. 4 (Winter 1970), pp. 13–31.

[31] E. P. Torrance and N. C. Aliotti, "Sex Differences in Levels of Performance and Test-Retest Reliability on the Torrance Tests of Creative Thinking Ability," *Journal of Creative Behavior*, vol. 3 (Winter 1969), pp. 52–57.

[32] M. K. Raina, "A Study of Sex Differences in Creativity in India," *Journal of Creative Behavior*, vol. 3 (Spring 1969), pp. 111–14.

strong cultural differences in behavior deemed appropriate for male children in the United States and in India.

Studies of the relationship between creative behavior and age have not been so equivocal. The largest study is based on volumes of data on the frequency of creative products among thousands of scientists, physicians, scholars, and artists in all fields.[33] One recurring finding is that the greatest frequency of creative products occurs rather early, between the ages of 30 and 40, for most of these people.

Examples from this research can be both illustrative and interesting. The data pinpointed the age of the individual for each of his or her notable contributions to the field.

In science, peak creativity occurred between the ages of 30 and 34 for chemists, as it did for mathematicians and physicists. The most productive age of inventors was 30 to 34. Even Edison, who produced over his 60-year career nearly 1,100 patents, was close to this norm. Between the ages of 33 and 36, Edison took out a total of 312 patents—over one fourth of his career total! In entomology, genetics, agricultural chemistry, and psychology, productivity peaked around age 35. Only astronomy was at variance with the rest: The highest frequency of contributions for astronomers came between ages 40 and 44.

The consistency of the findings in medicine is remarkable. In bacteriology, physiology, pathology, anatomy, surgical techniques, goiter chronology, classic descriptions of disease, and advances in medical and public hygiene, peak productivity occurred between ages 35 and 39.

In music, the peak period for the production of grand operas, superior orchestral works, and chamber music was ages 35 to 39. More symphonies were produced by authors 30 to 34 years old, although there is some bias here in that four of the most productive musicians, Chopin, Mendelssohn, Mozart, and Schubert, all died in their 30s.

In art, the most prolific age for sculpture and important paintings was between 35 and 39. The bulk of the paintings rated as the world's greatest, from artists including Botticelli, da Vinci, Raphael, Rembrandt, Titian, Van Dyck, Van Eyck, and Valazquez, was produced when the artists were between 32 and 36 years of age.

In literature, most of the best books of 52 major famed philosophers were written between ages 35 and 39. The greatest number

---

[33] Lehman, *Age and Achievement.*

of 2,250 miscellaneous literary works came between ages 35 and 39, of the 71 "most influential" books between 35 and 39, of short stories between 32 and 36, and of 60 "best sellers" between 40 and 44. Only poets broke the thirties' barrier—the most productive age for poets was 25 to 29.

Other research, both in the field and in the laboratory, has suggested that on the average creative behavior tends to decline with age after the age of 40. This is, of course, not true for all fields. The most productive period for architects was 40 to 44, for instance. It is obviously not true for all individuals. In fact, there is some evidence to suggest this decline does not continue unabated: There appears to be a resurgence of creative production at great age.[34] In several fields of medicine, for instance, the average creative production of individuals in their seventies and even eighties exceeded their average creativity of earlier periods. Further research in this area may justify a second look at society's increasing tendency toward forced retirement at age 65. It may also make us wonder whether that "second childhood" syndrome (as we so flippantly label bizarre behavior among the elderly) might not be symptomatic of a rebirth of creative energy rather than senility.

Before we dismiss all those under 30 and over 40, moreover, it should be pointed out that creative achievements have been recorded at both childhood and old age. Mozart produced minuets at 5, and Paul Morphy was a chess champion at 12. Bizet, Robert Burns, Samuel Colt, Galileo, Mendelssohn, Milton, Pascal, Pope, and Schubert all made notable creative achievements during their teens. At the other extreme, Bellini produced great art for ten years *after* his 75th birthday, Cervantes wrote the second part of *Don Quixote* at 68, and Galileo continued productivity into his 70s. Thomas Hardy, Laplace, Tennyson, and Verdi all continued to create at least into their 70s.

The relationship between age and creative productivity that is generally found is depicted in Figure 9–3. Initial evidence of creativity (A) may be found at an early age, even in the preteens. The first significant contributions (B) typically occur near the age of 20, and peak productivity (C) is usually between the late 20s and early 40s. Creativity then declines with advancing age to D with a final upsurge to E late in life. Note that the rate of acceleration from B to C is much greater than the rate of decline from C to D.

---

[34] Ibid., p. 235.

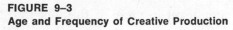

FIGURE 9–3
Age and Frequency of Creative Production

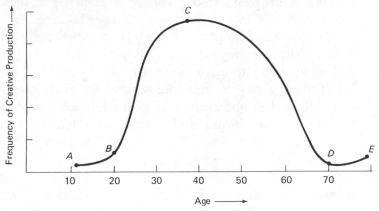

That is, given a long life, a CBI usually turns out more after his peak period than before. Can you suggest some testable hypotheses which might explain this phenomenon?

Behavioral Characteristics

A number of studies of CBIs have discerned distinct behavior characteristics, such as perceptual openness, flexibility, resistance to premature judgment, closure, reliance on intuition and hunches, and a tendency to discern relatively more complexity.[35] Such characteristics are closely related to the creative process itself, and are discussed more fully in that section of Chapter 10. Other behavioral tendencies of CBIs, however, are not so obviously related to the process of creativity. Some of these are of particular interest to managers of creative processes.

High Turnover CBIs are often described as demonstrating great tenacity of purpose when confronted with a creative problem. This "stick-to-itiveness," however, is not characteristic of CBIs when it comes to organizational membership. Observations of identified CBIs in seven quite dissimilar colleges indicated that from 50 to 80 percent of these individuals dropped out of college before graduation.[36]

---

[35] Frank Barron, "The Dream of Art and Poetry," *Psychology Today*, vol. 2 (December 1968), pp. 18–23.

[36] P. O. Heist, "Creative Students: College Transients," *The Creative College Student: An Unmet Challenge* (San Francisco: Jossey-Bass, Publishers, 1968), chap. 3.

This may not seem significant in view of the fact that the national average of dropouts among college students is at least 50 percent anyway. But in five of the seven colleges included in this analysis, the proportion of identified CBIs who dropped out was significantly higher than the dropout rate among the rest of the student body.

This tendency to leave may not be solely confined to academia. A longitudinal study of individuals rated for their creativity in high school included observation of post–high school job performance. Surprisingly, significant and positive correlations were found between various measures of creativity and frequency of job changes.[37] That is, CBIs changed jobs more often than their ex-classmates. Whether they quit out of dissatisfaction, were fired, or simply moved to better opportunities is unknown. Nevertheless, it appears that a manager who allows himself to be influenced negatively by a job applicant's history of dropping out, switching schools, or changing jobs may risk excluding some very creative behavior.

Nonconformity   Of particular interest to students of CBI behavior is their susceptibility to social influence. Organizations have long been accused of preferring conformers to creators, and a negative relationship between conformity and creativity has been suspected. Conventional wisdom depicts the two behaviors as incompatible. Some would even equate counterconformity with creativity.

The evidence, however, does not suggest such simplistic or extreme positions. On the one hand, some studies indicate that CBIs are less susceptible than most to social evaluative cues. That is, CBIs may not conform in certain situations, for a couple of reasons. If the pressures to conform concern their work, they may be much more concerned with the quality of their solution than with outsiders' opinions of it. Thus they resist conforming. On the other hand, if the pressures to conform are peripheral to their work, such as dress or eating habits, they may be so unconcerned about that behavior as to miss the "signals" others give them in an attempt to change their behavior.

And yet there is evidence that CBIs are susceptible to social influence. One study even found highly creative subjects to be significantly more persuadable than less creative subjects on matters not related to their creative talent.[38] It is possible that these seem-

[37] E. P. Torrance, "Is Bias against Job Changing Bias against Giftedness?" *Gifted Child Quarterly*, vol. 15 (Winter 1971), pp. 244–48.

[38] J. R. Raia and S. H. Osipow, "Creative Thinking Ability and Susceptibility to Persuasion," *Journal of Social Psychology*, vol. 28 (December 1970), pp. 181–86.

ing contradictions can be explained if the tendency of CBIs to become intensely involved in their work,[39] perhaps to the neglect of other behavior, is taken into account. It is easy to envision a creative novelist, or painter, or innovator in any field wrapped up in some challenging and perplexing problem. While such people remain open to others' ideas and suggestions, they do not tolerate pressures to deviate from what they consider to be the best solution or the best approach to that solution. In this, they are nonconforming. At the same time they may neglect their appearance, miss appointments, or work at odd hours; they are so wrapped up in their work that they fail to notice the discomfort this aberrant behavior can bring to their colleagues or families. In this respect, too, CBIs are nonconforming. Eventually, however, someone gets through to them and brings to their attention the distress of their associates. As long as the behavior change does not interfere with their work, they may be all too willing to change, even apologetic about their social behavior. They conform.

An excellent analysis of this *apparent* dilemma between conformity and creativity relates to the idea of differentiating between what, to the CBI, is important and what is unimportant behavior. It has been suggested that both the CBI and the organization need to decide which norms or behavioral rules are *pivotal,* in the sense that the prescribed behavior is directly related to the organization's success.[40] For instance, a pivotal norm of professional sports is that athletes and owners refrain from openly betting on games, particularly against their own teams. Other organizational norms may be *peripheral,* in the sense that the prescribed behavior is desirable but not essential. Many professional sports organizations might prefer their players to keep their hair short, avoid flashy clothes, and stay away from public bars; in the 1969 Super Bowl, Joe Willie Namath successfully demonstrated those norms to be peripheral. This suggests a policy allowing for creative individualism, in which the person conforms to the pivotal norms but adopts peripheral norms only when they do not interfere with his own sense of identity and creativity.

An account of advertising organizations and their sometimes agonizing distinctions between pivotal and peripheral norms points out that pivotal norms in one industry may be completely ignored

---

[39] Barron, "Dream of Art and Poetry."

[40] E. H. Schein, *Organizational Psychology,* 2d ed. (Englewood Cliffs, N.J.: Prentice-Hall, 1970), p. 78.

in another. In a chapter appropriately entitled "Give Me Your Drunks, Your Weirdos . . . ," the authors comment:

> We get a great number of nutsy guys. Let's say that there are hundreds—maybe thousands—of guys in this business who, if they were working for Bankers Trust right now, would have found themselves committed. You know, their boss would have sat back and decided "This guy is really going," and he would call the guy's wife up and say, "I think it's time we committed him because, you know, he's doing strange things."[41]

This suggests another type of behavior often attributed to CBIs: "weird" behavior. It has been alleged that creative behavior is often associated with aberrant behavior, which in turn may be symptomatic of "mental illness." You can find positions on all sides of this question in the literature on creativity. Some argue that creative behavior is the manifestation of perfect mental health—that the mentally healthy individual is free of hang-ups which might inhibit the use of his innate creativity. Indeed, some research evidence suggests strong positive associations between behavior involved in the creative process and mental health.[42] Others have reported significant positive correlations between rated creative ability of subjects and mental illness rates of both subjects and their parents.[43] On balance, I think we must accept for the time being that no consistent relationship between creative behavior and either mental health or mental illness can be demonstrated. We had best evaluate the creative behavior on its own merits and let the nature of the organization mission, rather than abstract indices of mental health, dictate whether CBIs who stab telephones with scissors, come to work stoned, write copy in stairwells, or throw desks at windows[44] are violating peripheral or pivotal norms.

Personality Characteristics

One of the foremost researchers in the personality of CBIs described the method of personality assessment as one which "attempts to delineate the person as a whole through use of a multi-

[41] Della Femina and Sopkin, *Those Wonderful Folks,* p. 66.

[42] S. J. Garfield, H. A. Cohen, and R. M. Roth, "Creativity and Mental Health," *Journal of Educational Research,* vol. 63 (December 1969), pp. 147–49.

[43] T. F. McNeil, "Prebirth and Postbirth Influence on the Relationship between Creative Ability and Recorded Mental Illness," *Journal of Personality,* vol. 39 (September 1971), pp. 391–406.

[44] Della Femina and Sopkin, *Those Wonderful Folks.*

plicity of procedures and emphasizes the more favorable and positive aspects of personality and its potentialities for effective functioning."[45]

In one series of personality assessments of CBIs, both tests and the ratings of trained observers were used to describe the personality of the creative architect.[46] Subjects were American architects whose creativity was measured (1) by the combined ratings of the editors of the 11 major American architectural journals and (2) by the ratings of the architects themselves, who rated the architectural creativity of their peers. A statistical process known as Q-sort was applied to derive a set of 100 characteristics related to creativity ratings.

Among the items ranked as *most* descriptive of the creative architect were:

1. Enjoys aesthetic impressions; is aesthetically reactive.
2. Has a high aspiration level for self.
3. Values own independence and autonomy.
4. Genuinely values intellectual and cognitive matters.
5. Has a wide range of interests.

Among the items ranked as *least* descriptive of the creative architect were:

1. Feels a lack of personal meaning in life.
2. Is self-defeating.
3. Feels cheated and victimized by life; self-pitying.
4. Is emotionally bland.
5. Is genuinely submissive; accepts domination comfortably.

Of course, halo effect might account for some of these descriptions. Nevertheless, many of the characteristics descriptive of highly creative architects have been applied to CBIs in other fields as well. A study of physics teachers rated for the creativity of their teaching methods described the innovative teachers as high on aesthetic and theoretical values, high on need for autonomy, and low on need for affiliation.[47] A summary of studies of CBIs cites aesthetic values, autonomy, an ability to force closure when working on problems,

---

[45] D. W. MacKinnon, "Assessing Creative Persons," *Journal of Creative Behavior*, vol. 1 (Summer 1967), pp. 303–4.

[46] Ibid.

[47] H. J. Walberg and W. W. Welch, "Personality Characteristics of Innovative Physics Teachers," *Journal of Creative Behavior*, vol. 1 (Spring 1967), pp. 163–71.

insatiable curiosity for facts, and feelings of confidence and self-destiny as descriptive of CBIs in general.[48]

We may be tempted to dismiss these findings as simply describing a superpersonality, but it must be pointed out that almost all researchers of the CBI personality conclude that it is complex and full of seeming inconsistencies. Some of the inconsistencies that have been pointed out include:

- *Values.* The CBI values both aesthetics and functional practicality.
- *Traits.* The CBI is confident and independent, yet sensitive and vulnerable to criticism.
- *Needs.* The CBI is autonomous, aware of talents and self-identity, yet needs recognition and approval of accomplishments.
- *Knowledge.* The CBI thrives on information yet can ignore this information, seeks all the facts yet relies on intuition.

Perhaps the difficulty of the problem of successfully describing, understanding, and even managing the creative personality is best summed up in a study by another leader in the field of personality assessment. His review of the literature concluded that CBIs not only have more complex personalities than the average person, they thrive on and have a preference for complexity. As if these characteristics do not pose enough problems for managers of creative processes, CBIs are said to be not only independent but self-assertive and dominant, and to reject suppression to control impulses (stab telephones?).

This perplexing description concludes: "Thus the creative genius may be at once naive and knowledgable, being at home equally to primitive symbolism and to rigorous logic. He is both more primitive and more cultured, more destructive and more constructive, occasionally crazier and yet adamantly saner than the average person."[49]

SUMMARY

Contemporary organizations in all fields need creative and innovative behavior. Only in the past few years has enough research

---

[48] F. E. Williams, "Intellectual Creativity and the Teacher," *Journal of Creative Behavior,* vol. 1 (Spring 1967), pp. 173–80.

[49] Frank Barron, *Creativity and Personal Freedom,* rev. ed. (Princeton, N.J.: D. Van Nostrand Co., 1968), p. 224.

been accumulated to provide managers with a body of knowledge to guide the management of creativity.

Creative behavior, like other behavior, is a function of both ability and motivation. Creative ability is really a complex set of abilities which is only partially related to intelligence. It appears to be widely distributed over the general population, although individual differences in creative behavior are great.

Valid tests have been developed to measure creative potential. These tests have been useful in identifying both individuals high in creative potential and those whose creative abilities need to be developed. Experimental evidence in both laboratory and field suggests that creative behavior can be learned and developed.

Certain demographic, behavioral, and personality factors tend to be characteristic of individuals whose behavior is especially creative. Among these are family backgrounds which encouraged creative and/or intellectual activities, complex personalities, and a tendency to move from organization to organization.

There is considerable evidence that for most individuals in most fields the peak period of creative productivity occurs between the ages of 30 and 40. However, outstanding creative contributions have been made by some individuals as early as their preteens and as late as their eighties.

The research summarized here suggests that we have advanced to a stage where it is profitable for managers to try to identify creative talent, both within and outside their organizations. It further suggests that training and educational programs can aid the development of creative potential in organizations. However, creative behavior is a function not of personal ability alone, but of the person and his or her environment. In the next chapter we will discuss creative processes and organizational and environmental factors which influence creative behavior.

QUESTIONS FOR REVIEW AND DISCUSSION

1. What is the difference between creative ability and creative behavior? What might a person with high creative ability need in order to produce creatively?

2. What is the relationship between creative ability and intelligence? What particular intellectual abilities might be involved in creative behavior?

3. Can creative potential be identified and developed?

4. One study of creativity and age classified 90 percent of five-year-old children as creatively behaving individuals (CBIs). The same study found that the percentage of CBIs in the population dropped sharply with each succeeding year. Derive some testable hypotheses to explain this phenomenon.

5. At what ages does peak creative productivity tend to occur? What implications does this have (a) for management, (b) for CBIs?

6. What could be some reasons for high turnover among CBIs in organizations?

KEY WORDS

Creative ability   Predictive validity
Creative behavior   Actuarial approach
Structure-of-intellect model   Pivotal norms
Divergent production   Peripheral norms
Concurrent validity

Objectives

1. To examine the creative process.
2. To discuss factors which can aid or hinder the creative process.
3. To describe how organizations influence the creative process, both positively and negatively.

chapter ten

Creative Processes and Environments

DOONESBURY

Copyright 1973, G. B. Trudeau/ Distributed by Universal Press Syndicate

THE CREATIVE PROCESS

MUCH OF THE MYSTERY surrounding creativity derives from the creative process. Because that process is largely mental and involves such activities as manipulating figures and symbols or trying various combinations and associations, it is difficult to observe directly. The nature of creativity is so hard to get at that it has been popularly attributed to mysterious agents such as muses or demons.

Serious researchers into the creative process, however, have succeeded in removing at least some of the mystery which has enshrouded it. They have observed people involved in creative behavior and studied the activities of famous creative persons, either by interviews or less personal assessment techniques. These researchers have concluded that the creative process can be broken down into elements or stages.

Although there is some variety in the precise words used to describe the process and in the suggested number of elements involved, all the descriptions seem to center around the following concept: The *creative process* involves the mental manipulation of elements already known to the individual and results in some new and useful combination.

The manipulation is usually symbolic and nonverbal; the elements may be known either consciously or otherwise. Indeed, many of the researchers into the process stress the role of "unconscious" information processing in creativity. One pattern observed is described as "free manipulation of symbols, nonverbal and fast; insight at a relaxed time, in a flash."[1]

There appear to be four phases in the process: preparation, incubation, insight, and verification. We might describe these phases as analogous to a cooking procedure:

1. *Preparation.* The ingredients are assembled and combined.
2. *Incubation.* The combinations are allowed to simmer.
3. *Insight.* It is discovered that one or more combinations, or some entirely new combination, appears to achieve the desired taste, consistency, and so on.
4. *Verification.* The dish is tested, refined, and served to guests.

This analogy, while illuminating, should not be taken too literally. Though there is general agreement that these four phases comprise the creative process, it is not clear that they are entirely separable or occur in this precise sequence. Verification or testing may be going on during preparation, as associations or combinations are evaluated or discarded. Incubation may occur during verification, leading to new and better insights. Insights may occur during preparation or verification, improving these two processes. Nevertheless, the phases can be discussed separately.

Preparation

One of the most unfortunate fallacies about creativity is that it just happens. Notions of muses and demons have allowed people, some with considerable talent, to vegetate (either by choice or by direction) for months on end, waiting for an "inspiration" to reveal the path to creative production. Unfortunately, "the creative artist, philosopher, or scientist, who locks himself in isolation and waits for the creative urge to strike, may be very disappointed after he has sat there for several months with no Godot in sight."[2]

Exposure   Creativity is usually preceded by a great deal of hard work in assembling the materials or information to provide the

---

[1] J. W. Haefele, *Creativity and Innovation* (New York: Reinhold Publishing Corp., 1962), p. 5.

[2] R. W. Malott, *Humanistic Behaviorism and Social Psychology* (Kalamazoo, Mich.: Behaviordelia, Inc., 1973), p. 19.

groundwork for the ultimate insight. This involves the reception and processing of new information, as well as the practice of the particular ability involved.

Information may be either verbal, like the written or spoken word, or nonverbal, like symbols, figures, or behavior. It may be received passively, as in reading or watching, or actively, as in experimenting or exploring. Information reception is often spoken of as *exposure*—stimulation of the senses toward a point of saturation.[3] Writers travel, observe, and experience life: Truman Capote becomes a habitué of death row. Actors read, study, observe: George C. Scott immerses himself in the biographies of General Patton. Scientists read, experiment, discuss: B. F. Skinner observes the behavior of rats and pigeons. Athletes observe, imitate, improve, experiment: Lou Brock studies Maury Wills, pitchers, catchers, and umpires.

Work Because preparation means work, some of the mystery and glamour are removed from the process. To most observers, it is clear that original contributions involve considerable work. Many creative writers write a thousand words a day—every day—whether they are working on a book or not. Thomas Wolfe wrote a million words in one four-year period. Van Gogh repeatedly sketched the same model. Edison's experiments knew no hours. The anthropologist Leakey worked the Olduvai Gorge site in Tanzania for over 30 years. Julius Irving ("Dr. J." for the creative way he "operates" on his opponents) played basketball from dawn to dusk. Energy and work are part of the creative process.

Motivation If creation requires preparation, and preparation means work, then creation also requires effort and motivation. Behavior is a function of motivation as well as ability, and intense behavior requires great motivation. The sources of motivation in the creative process can be varied, but the creative process starts with an individual wanting to create something for some reason.

The reason may be simply the desire to meet a challenge. A perplexing or "impossible" problem, be it in medicine (curing cancer), music (producing a "new" sound), literature (sharing an emotional experience), industry (reducing pollution), science (surviving in space), or sports (beating the Athletics), may provide the incentive required. A goal such as putting a man on the moon by 1970 can spark tremendous creative effort. A desire to "beat the competition" has fostered and accelerated much scientific research, as in the race of Watson and Crick against Pauling to describe the structure of DNA.

---

[3] I. A. Taylor, "A Transactional Approach to Creativity and Its Implications for Education," *Journal of Creative Behavior,* vol. 5 (Third Quarter, 1971), pp. 190–98.

In industry, experience has altered the notion that creativity and innovation result from merely amassing talent and waiting for something to happen. Motivation and guidance in the form of needs or goals are the starting point for the vast majority of technological advances. A recent report analyzed 567 technical innovations in products or processes which occurred in 121 companies in five manufacturing industries.[4] These 567 innovations were selected for study because they had been rated the most successful and important innovations by their respective companies. Of these, 75 percent had been initiated by the recognition of a need.

One type of "need" capable of triggering such innovation is a market demand. For example, market research might conclude that a cereal which supplied 100 percent of adult minimum daily requirements in vitamins and iron would be eminently salable, provided the taste were moderately good. This "need" could be translated into a product research goal of developing such a cereal within 18 months, and this would provide the impetus for substantial, concentrated creative activity involving a search not only for the right combinations of ingredients and methods for processing them but also for the possibilities in packaging and promoting the new product.

A second type of need is a production need—recognizing the necessity for a new way of producing a given product. For example, the availability of an improved alloy may trigger a search for ways to incorporate that alloy into refrigerators, requiring innovations in the way certain parts are cast or assembled.

In any event, a recognized need is a major incentive for industrial innovation. Of the 567 innovations included in the study described above, only 20 percent came about in the way fiction usually conceives of innovation: A researcher working independently invents a new gimmick and then tries to find some use for it.

Incubation

Incubation is usually described as a period of relaxation of conscious effort following an intensive amount of preparation. Exactly what occurs during incubation is unknown, as whatever is going on is inaccessible to outsiders. It is easier to describe what is *not* going on; the individual, having read, observed, studied, experimented,

---

[4] D. G. Marquis, "The Anatomy of Successful Innovations," in *Managing Advancing Technology,* 2 vols. (New York: American Management Association, 1972), vol. 1, chap. 3.

associated, experienced and otherwise prepared himself, via sensory stimulation and information processing, to wrestle with the problem at hand, ceases visible effort.

This relaxation of effort may be due to exhaustion or frustration at not being able to solve the problem. It may involve only a re-direction of effort, even toward some completely unrelated activity, including recreation. Examples of the incubation process in the lives of famous CBIs abound in the literature. Coleridge composed "Kubla Khan" after a nap. Mozart found carriage rides and after dinner walks a good prelude to much composition. D. H. Lawrence liked to paint. The poet Hart Crane drank and joked with friends. The pattern of preparation followed by periods of relaxation or re-directing of effort is well established.

Again, why or how this stage is important is yet unknown. It is popular to speculate that "unconscious thinking" is going on during incubation. Unfortunately, if there is an "unconscious," and if in-cubation is unconscious thinking, we are doomed to ignorance about it. By its very definition, the unconscious is inaccessible to the individual. Some methods of probing the unconscious were discussed in Chapter 3 under the psychoanalytic approach. Even if they were reliable and valid, however, these methods are beyond the scope of the typical manager and his or her staff.

For the present, we must simply describe incubation as involving relaxation or redirection of effort and report the apparent frequency of its occurrence before insight. Yet even this little knowledge can have implications for managing the creative process.

Insight

Insight occurs when the individual first becomes aware, or con-scious, of a new and valuable idea or association. It is the raison d'être of preparation and incubation—the solving of the problem, the breakthrough after which thinking is different from what it has been.

Insight is often an emotion-packed element of the creative pro-cess. It can encompass satisfaction of accomplishment, pride of perserverance, a release of tension, a sense of separateness stemming from the achievement of something that has never been done be-fore, anxiety to share and communicate the insight to others.

Insight comes in many forms. It may appear as a flash of inspira-tion, as with Newton; or as a gradual awareness growing out of repeated hard work, as often occurs in poetry and art; or as the result of an apparent accident, as with the discovery of penicillin. It may be a word or words, symbols, figures, or feelings. It may come at any time or in any place, although some CBIs recognize certain times or places or other environmental characteristics as being associated with their greatest insights. In this regard, there is considerable speculation that especially creative periods can be observed and then calculated for a given individual. There is, for instance, some notion that creative behavior occurs most frequently when body temperature is high.[5] Continued research into this aspect of creativity may provide startling and useful insights.

Verification

Preparation and verification are the hard work of creativity. Insight results in the gem of an idea, while verification is the cutting, polishing, and finishing of that gem to its most brilliant form. Verification involves testing the insight for its veracity and usefulness and putting it into a form which allows it to be shared by others.

Testing may require comparison against certain known laws, as in the proof of a new mathematical theorem, or against standards, as in a new argument in logic or a stanza of poetry. It may involve physical demonstration, as in testing a new chemical process or physical concept. It may demand the judgment of trusted colleagues or experts, as often happens with a manuscript of poetry or fiction. It may call for construction, as in architecture or engineering. It may simply need to be written down, or played, or sung, or danced.

For many talented people, verification must immediately follow insight, or the creative breakthrough may be lost. Coleridge is one of the most famous and saddest examples. According to his own account, he awoke from a dream with the poem "Kubla Khan" streaming into his brain. The words practically leapt from his pen, and then he was interrupted by a visitor. Upon the visitor's departure, Coleridge found to his dismay that the rest of the poem had vanished beyond all but dim recall. Of the two or three hundred lines he estimated were available to him, only a handful survived the visitor's call.

Others can apparently postpone verification to their leisure. Neither Beethoven nor Mozart, being eiditic, had problems with recall. Nor did Thomas Wolfe, nor Poincaré, who postponed verifi-

---

[5] Haefele, *Creativity and Innovation*, p. 98.

cation of momentous mathematical identifications until the completion of a journey. Nevertheless, without verification there can be no creativity as we have defined it. Verification confirms the newness of the idea and communicates it to the relevant audience.

The phases of the creative process are summarized in Figure 10–1. Remember, however, that the distinctions between phases are conceptual, and that stages can be occurring simultaneously. New insights can occur during verification. Verification may suggest further preparation. New information may be received during incubation. Insight may provide additional motivation. Nonetheless, the

FIGURE 10–1
The Creative Process

concept of phases in the process is helpful in suggesting ways of enhancing creative behavior.

THE ORGANIZATION'S ROLE IN CREATIVITY

As the study of the nature and process of creativity and of CBIs themselves has progressed, some of the mystery which has obscured creativity has been dissolved, along with the muses and demons formerly associated with the presence or absence of creativity. This process has resulted in the identification of more tangible factors which appear to facilitate or hinder creative behavior. While the list is by no means exhaustive, it serves to illustrate the idea that creativity can be influenced. It is particularly important from the manager's point of view that many of these factors are affected by the organization. Creative behavior in organizations is not simply a matter of selection and training. The organization itself can impede or facilitate the creative process.

Impediments to Creative Behavior

As we have seen, creative behavior is the expression of creative ability. One reason for the absence of creative behavior may be that the individual feels inhibited from expressing his talent. Anxiety, fear of evaluation, defensiveness, and cultural inhibition have all been suggested as blocks to the realization of creative potential. There is some recent evidence to support this speculation.

Fear and Anxiety Studies have found anxiety to be related to creative behavior; high anxiety is associated with low creativity, and vice versa. For instance, individuals with low levels of anxiety have been found to perform significantly better on divergent-thinking tasks than those with high levels of anxiety.[6]

Fear of Evaluation Some speculations in this area have been somewhat vague. "Personal insecurity" and "lack of confidence" are often blamed for inhibiting creativity. More helpful and testable have been propositions that fear of evaluation often retards creative responses. While intuitively plausible, this relationship has yet to be supported, however. One study of 146 fifth- and sixth-graders is illustrative. The students were divided into three groups, one in which evaluation of creativity was played down, one in which eval-

---

[6] Kinnard White, "Anxiety, Extraversion-Introversion, and Divergent Thinking Ability," *Journal of Creative Behavior*, vol. 2, no. 2 (Spring 1968), pp. 119–27.

uation of creativity was emphasized, and a third in which it was not mentioned. Analysis of creative performance under the three conditions revealed no effect of evaluation set—there was as much creative behavior in the highly evaluated group as in the other two groups.[7]

One interesting offshoot of the proposal that fear of evaluation inhibits creativity was the development of the brainstorming process. The process itself will be discussed in greater detail in Chapter 15, as it is primarily a group decision-making device. One of the rules of brainstorming is that no idea brought forth in group session should be subjected to any criticism, in order to reduce the inhibiting effects of fear of evaluation. This notion of "deferred judgment" has received both popular and empirical support. Evidence cited in one summary suggests that deferred judgment—that is, avoiding both positive and negative evaluation of ideas—can lead to improved quality and quantity of ideas for individuals as well as groups.[8]

Defensiveness   Those who postulate the role of an "unconscious" in creativity contend that defensiveness or desire to protect one's ego inhibits creative behavior. This position is consistent with the psychoanalytic approach discussed in Chapter 3. An imaginative study involved the use of hypnosis to test the proposition.[9] Female college students were divided into two groups, one of which was hypnotized. Instructions designed to reduce defensiveness were given to both groups. After the session, tests requiring both creative and noncreative responses were administered to both groups. Women who had been hypnotized (and who were thus theoretically more receptive to defense reduction) scored significantly higher than those who had not been hypnotized on the creative portions of the test, but no differently on the noncreative portions.

Cultural Inhibition   Some writers have suggested that cultural factors may inhibit creativity. For instance, certain norms of certain cultures may increase fear of risk or desire for familiarity, or may inhibit expression, as compared to other cultures. While there is no doubt that such cultural differences exist, their inhibiting effects

---

[7] G. H. Warren and Zella Luria, "Evaluation Set and Creativity," *Perceptual and Motor Skills,* vol. 34 (April 1972), pp. 436–38.

[8] S. J. Parnes, "The Literature of Creativity, Part II," *Journal of Creative Behavior,* vol. 1 (Spring 1967), pp. 191–240.

[9] P. G. Bowers, "Effect of Hypnosis and Suggestions of Reduced Defensiveness on Creativity Test Performance," *Journal of Personality,* vol. 35 (June 1967), pp. 311–22.

on creative behavior have not been directly tested. The hypothesis seems, however, quite plausible. If it is confirmed by research, cultural inhibition has obvious implications for multinational corporations and other organizations whose membership and activities transcend cultural boundaries.

How Organizations Hinder the Creative Process

If fear, anxiety, and defensiveness inhibit creative behavior, then managerial practices or organizational policies which foster such individual reactions will hinder the expression of creative talent. Therefore, we would expect that an oppressive organizational climate manifested by close, punitive supervision would inhibit creative behavior. Because creativity and innovation involve risk, organizations which stress the consequences of failure rather than the rewards for success will inhibit the expression of new ideas.

Likewise, organizational instability can inhibit creative behavior. Unstable organizations are unpredictable to their members, and unpredictable environments can breed insecurity and anxiety. An individual who must be continually concerned about changes in job assignment, working relationships, supervision, policies, and procedures will have little energy or time left for preparation and incubation of creative and innovative ideas.

Stability, however, is often achieved through excessive formalization of rules, policies, relationships, and procedures. There is evidence that formalization can inhibit certain phases of the creative process.[10] In particular, high formalization can interfere with communications and the exposure to new information and ideas characteristic of the preparation phase. If formal rules make it difficult for individuals to experiment, or to suggest, discuss, or seek new alternatives or methods, then these restraints will impede creativity.

Likewise, a highly centralized organizational structure may inhibit early stages of creativity and innovation. Centralized communication networks make it difficult for lower level members of the organization to communicate with individuals outside their immediate departments. Thus the free exchange of information is restricted, and communications may be slowed down, as we shall see in Chapter 14. In addition, centralized structures require decisions to be made at high levels of the organizational hierarchy.

---

[10] Gerald Zaltman, Robert Duncan, and Jonny Holbek, *Innovations and Organizations* (New York: John Wiley & Sons, 1973), pp. 138–43.

Because creative and innovative ideas are often generated at low levels of the organization, this requirement means that new ideas must travel through several bureaucratic layers before a decision is reached.[11] As Chapter 14 points out, the more levels of hierarchy communications must overcome, the greater the chances are that information will be lost or distorted.

Finally, an organization which leaves its members little time for thinking and experimenting will inhibit creative behavior. The creative process takes time; how much it takes we can only speculate at this point. There may be times, particularly during incubation, when it appears that nothing is happening.

If creativity is viewed as an unprogrammed activity, then certainly the proposition that "programmed work drives out unprogrammed work" leads to the possibility that if people are encumbered with myriads of day-to-day work, they will have no time for creative effort. This is not to suggest, however, that time constraints, particularly when attached to the accomplishment of creative efforts, cannot facilitate creativity, as will be shown below.

Aids to Creative Behavior

Certain aids to creative behavior have been identified. They include reinforcement, goals and deadlines, extended effort, and freedom and autonomy.

Reinforcement   Like other types of behavior, creative behavior is influenced by its outcome. If creativity is ignored or punished, if creative efforts are stifled, threatened, mocked, or stolen, one should not be surprised that creativity diminishes. There is some reason to suspect that such outcomes are all too frequently society's response to creative behavior, particularly among school-aged children. To parents, creative behavior may seem another intrusion by the child into the adult's free time, or the parents may fear their child is being "different." To teachers, getting children to conform and cooperate may be a full-time job. The emotional aspects of creative behavior may be more than they are willing to tolerate.

Even if creative talent has lain dormant, it can manifest itself through training and reinforcement. Perhaps it is too often assumed that creativity, like virtue, is its own reward, and thus there is no need to provide extrinsic rewards for creative responses. No doubt

---

[11] H. A. Shepard, "Innovation-Resisting and Innovation-Producing Organizations," *Journal of Business,* vol. 40 (1967), pp. 470–77.

there are powerful intrinsic rewards in the satisfaction and feelings of accomplishment which accompany a creative insight. Yet CBIs, from scientists to toddlers, respond to extrinsic reinforcement as well.

The reinforcers need not necessarily be monetary, of course. There is evidence that CBIs not only respond to recognition and praise but often demand it; one characteristic of CBIs is a high need for recognition. Few novels and no scientific articles are published anonymously; composers immediately copyright their music; artists and sculptors sign their works. The creative person identifies so strongly with his work that in effect he is his product. Thus praise and recognition of the work can be powerfully reinforcing to the individual.

Beyond recognition and praise, rewards like status, fringe benefits, and money have been shown to have reinforcing effects on creative behavior at all levels, even the highest. Much of the world's great art, sculpture, and music have been produced on commission, including what are considered by many to be the world's greatest operas, Mozart's *Don Giovanni* and Verdi's *Aida*.

Goals and Deadlines   Commissions facilitate creativity not only by providing monetary incentive but by setting some guidelines as to what is to be produced and when it should be completed. Massive efforts in technological innovation grew from President John F. Kennedy's goal of sending a man to the moon and returning him safely by 1970. Great movies are produced under strict time pressures caused by the necessity to employ highly paid technicians. Publishing companies find that many writers work better under pressure of time deadlines. Mozart finished *Don Giovanni* by working through the night before its premiere performance. In many fields time pressures can often be fantastic and at the same time productive. The incident which was used to introduce Chapter 9 described how two people put together a complete advertising campaign from scratch in the two-hour period before the customer walked in the door to pick it up. Its authors used the story to make the following point: "Creative people in all agencies work best under the gun. If you were to give an agency three years to do something, they would wait until the last minute to do the work."[12]

Extended Efforts   Obviously, the imposition of tight deadlines can be carried too far, forcing acceptance of the first creative re-

[12] Jerry Della Femina and Charles Sopkin, *From Those Wonderful Folks Who Gave You Pearl Harbor* (New York: Simon & Schuster, 1970), p. 169.

sponse that is produced. There is evidence that conscious efforts to avoid the immediate acceptance of obvious solutions can enhance creative effort, particularly in problem solving. For example, in one study groups worked on problems until they arrived at a solution; they were then instructed to discard that solution and derive a second one.[13] Analysis revealed that second solutions tended to be better than first solutions. This technique forced the creative unit to process and discard habitual "safe" responses, which are likely to be produced first, until it came up with a truly original one.

Freedom and Autonomy   It is often proposed that individuals must be free to create. While a strong desire for autonomy is often characteristic of a CBI, freedom and autonomy can be interpreted in vastly different ways. No doubt freedom from fear of ridicule or repression is important. No doubt the opportunity and time to engage in preparation, incubation, and other elements of the creative process are necessary. Yet freedom and autonomy do not mean the complete abandonment of guidelines or constraints.

We have discussed the positive effects of goals and deadlines on creativity. It also appears that, contrary to earlier popular belief, CBIs can live within budgets: They do not need unlimited expenses to produce creatively. There is even evidence that greater productivity is associated with moderate as opposed to affluent (or, of course, severely restricted) budgets. Important technological creativity can come from modest budgets. Of the 567 successful technical innovations discussed earlier in this chapter, fully two thirds cost less than $100,000. Only 12 of the innovations (2 percent) cost over $1 million.[14]

Thus there seems to be general agreement that creative people want freedom and autonomy, but those with *complete* freedom do not necessarily perform better than the rest. Particularly among scientists and engineers, goals, budgets, and guidelines facilitate rather than hinder creative behavior. As one well-known student of the research process concludes, "There must be freedom, but freedom restricted to the pursuit of the individual job assignment as it relates to organizational goals."[15]

---

[13] N. R. F. Maier, "Screening Solutions to Upgrade Quality: A New Approach to Problem Solving under Conditions of Uncertainty," *Journal of Psychology*, vol. 49 (April 1960), pp. 217–31.

[14] Marquis, "Anatomy of Successful Innovations," p. 42.

[15] D. G. Pelz, "Freedom in Research," *International Science and Technology*, no. 26 (February 1964), pp. 54–66.

How Organizations Facilitate the Creative Process

If reinforcement, goals and deadlines, extended effort, and a measure of freedom and autonomy facilitate creativity, then organizations which take pains to provide these aids should find creative potential well used by their members. Like any other desired behavior, creativity must be identified, actively encouraged, recognized, rewarded, and used. If the organization ignores, belittles, or punishes creative expression, then creative ability will not be used.

Organizations which have clear, operational objectives should be able to provide their members with goals and guidelines which can facilitate creativity and innovation. It is said that "necessity is the mother of invention." If an organization's members do not know what is necessary, creative and innovative solutions to the organization's problems will be infrequent at best.

Organizations which provide their members with support and which tolerate risk taking and even failure provide the kind of climate in which high levels of creativity and innovation can be developed. Creative behavior deals in uncertainty, which requires support and communications at the interpersonal level.[16] Organizations which provide such a climate foster open exchange of information and exposure to new ideas.

There is evidence that both flexibility and complexity can facilitate creative behavior in organizations.[17] Flexibility permits the organization to adopt new, different ways of doing things. Complexity in organizations promotes specialization and autonomy. It also usually means that the organization will be made up of individuals from diverse backgrounds and specialties, and this diversity enhances creative productivity.[18] Diversity provides members with opportunities to come up with new combinations and associations of ideas, provided they are encouraged or at least permitted to interact across the boundaries of their special expertise.

SUMMARY

The creative process can be viewed as going through four phases: preparation, incubation, insight, and verification. Preparation and verification are the most visible phases of creativity. Preparation,

---

[16] Zaltman, Duncan, and Holbek, *Innovations and Organizations,* pp. 146–47.

[17] Ibid., pp. 128–29 and pp. 134–38.

[18] D. G. Pelz and F. M. Andrews, *Scientists in Organizations: Productive Climates for Research and Development* (New York: John Wiley & Sons, 1966).

which involves the assembly of materials and information necessary for the creative insight, requires exposure and study, work and effort. Incubation involves a relaxation or redirection of effort which is said to allow the CBI to manipulate the material assembled in the preparation phase. Insight occurs when the individual first becomes aware of a new and valuable idea or association. Verification is the necessary hard work which tests, refines, and exploits the idea generated in the insight phase.

Because creative behavior, like other behavior, is a function of the individual interacting with his or her environment, organizations can aid or impede creative and innovative expression through the environments they create for their members. Managerial practices and organizational policies which provoke fear, anxiety, or defensiveness among members hinder creativity. Organizations which are unstable, or excessively formal, or highly centralized can also impede.creativity, particularly in its early phases.

On the other hand, organizational flexibility and complexity appear to enhance creative expression, particularly in the early stages. In addition, organizations which actively seek and identify creative behavior, which support, recognize, reward, and use it, increase the probability that creative talent in the organization will not be wasted.

QUESTIONS FOR REVIEW AND DISCUSSION

1. What are the key elements of the preparation phase of the creative process?

2. What activities might be required in verification of an insight concerning (a) an innovative method for teaching elementary mathematics, (b) a new medicine for treating mononucleosis, (c) original lyrics for a popular song, (d) a creative package for a consumer product?

3. How might an individual's co-workers inhibit his or her creative productivity?

4. Describe two things which an organization (educational, military, business, voluntary) you have been in did to stimulate your creative or innovative process.

5. Describe two things which an organization you have been in did to discourage creative behavior.

6. How can goals and deadlines facilitate the creative process?

7. Excessive formalization and centralization can interfere with the early stages of the creative process. How can centralization facilitate the verification phase? (Hint: NASA might provide some examples).

KEY WORDS

Preparation   Insight
Exposure   Verification
Incubation   Cultural inhibition

Objectives

1. To describe the nature and functions of attitudes.
2. To examine job satisfaction and dissatisfaction as attitudes of particular interest to managers.
3. To discuss the implications of job satisfaction for several kinds of employee behavior.

chapter eleven

Expressing Attitudes, Satisfaction, and Dissatisfaction

Lordstown, Ohio (AP)—Beyond the chain link fence and acres of yellow-lined parking lots, the fastest, most automated automobile assembly line in the world stood silent and unmoving.

Dan Dearing and a half dozen other men were picketing the east gate of the plant. But the picketing was casual. Dearing, in fact, sat on the hood of his car, talking quietly in the warm summer night.

"Look," he explained earnestly, "I got a house now, a house and a mortgage and a baby. It makes a difference. I didn't have them two years ago. Besides, being hotheaded never got us anything either."

Two years ago in March, Local 1112 of the United Auto Workers struck Lordstown's General Motors complex of Chevrolet van and Vega plants. It was a militant, attention grabbing strike. On the table were local grievances and contract language. But sociologists said the problem was much deeper—a phenomenon they called the "blue collar blues."

Now, this July 12, about 7,800 members of Local 1112 went on strike again. Grievances were back on the table. But the attitudes and atmosphere had changed. Talk about the "blues"—the monotony of assembly line work and the dehumanizing effects of the pace set by machines—had turned into concern about the economy and job security.

And the militancy?

"Back in '72," said Dan Dearing, 27-year-old relief man in the body shop on an assembly line that makes Vegas, "people were saying 'the hell with the company. Let's change things. Let's walk out and let them steam for a while.'

"And now people are more worried about their jobs. The way the economy is you have to be. Besides, a lot of men laid off then were never called back. I think it scared a lot of people."

Like many Lordstown workers now, Dearing says he can live with his job. There are petty harassments to put up with, but the pay and benefits are good, and that seems the major consideration to most. Assembly line workers make $5.50 an hour, maybe $12,000 a year with a little overtime.

"As far as the boredom and monotony thing, I don't think that will ever change," Dearing said. "I don't have that problem, not on my job. The rest of the people, maybe they just resigned themselves to it."

Lordstown is near the eastern end of the Cleveland-Youngstown industrial axis in northeastern Ohio. Its GM complex spreads over 975 acres next to the Ohio Turnpike. The workers are largely second generation industrial workers—sons and daughters of Mahoning Valley steel workers— or first generation off the farm. There are 550 women and about 1,100 minority employees, mostly black—about the same percentages as in 1972.

The trouble at Lordstown began after a high speed Vega assembly line was installed in 1970. It was the assembly line of the future: 100 cars an hour, 40 more than other lines.

It was designed to make work easier. It moved up and down to reduce bending and stretching. Automatic welders and other machines took over some of the more difficult or delicate jobs. But because it was fast, the average worker had—and still has—35 seconds to perform his task as the line moved inexorably forward.

The workers on the line were young, mod and militant, longhaired and little awed by management, the work ethic or its discipline.

In October, 1971, GM removed the Chevrolet Division and Fisher Body management that had run the plant. The General Motors Division—the "G-MADs" to the workers—was sent in. The new management ordered reductions in the work force.

Too much work per man, said the union. Some cars began coming down the line with internal engine parts stacked on top of the motor block. Other cars came through with slashed electrical cables and cracked instrument panels. Sabotage, said management.

In the months before the 1972 strike, there were often as many as 1,800 cars in the repair yard at the Vega plant. Day after day, the line was shut down after one or two hours because the repair yard was full.

When the 1972 strike finally came it was settled in three weeks and few people in the union say they got much out of it.

But the shutdowns for repairs didn't happen this year. Before this year's strike, there were seldom more than 20 cars in the repair yard, said John Grix, G-MAD's public relations manager at the plant.

It is an unfounded fear, said Grix, but many workers are concerned that repetition of the 1972 tactics would cause GM to pull Vega production out of Lordstown. GM did open a Vega plant in Canada late in 1972 and soon will be producing Vegas at South Gate, Calif.

There have been other changes at Lordstown, too. According to company records, disciplinary lay offs declined from more than 500 in the month before the 1972 strike to about 200 in the month before this year's walkout.

Fender hangers and motor mount men may complain about arbitrary discipline and unfair foremen, but fewer are now willing to risk going out the door for a day, a week or a month without pay.

And the Lordstown work force has turned 30. The average age of the workers was 29.1 in 1972. It was 31.4 years last January. Again and again, company and union officials and the workers themselves talk about wives, children and mortgage payments.

"Right now, a lot of these people are so establishment they are unbelievable," said Grix. "We got a lot of guys out there with long hair and mod clothes. But even that guy, he might be saying, 'I don't buy your lifestyle,' but he's willing to work for us."

Workers' conditions on the line have not improved since 1972, says Ford. "As a matter of fact, they are maybe a little worse." It is not that people don't feel something has to be done about it, he said, but they are going about it in different ways.

The absentee rate has risen from 8 per cent in 1971 to 10.5 per cent in 1973 to 12.7 per cent in June, 1974.

Sometimes 10 per cent of the work force misses Mondays and Fridays.

Many of those who do punch in every day have their own ways of coping. On the picket line or in bars a few miles away, it is easy to find auto workers who tell of going to work stoned on alcohol or marijuana.

Workers might not be any happier at Lordstown these days, but they are more inclined to file a grievance than organize a protest.

Before the 1972 strike, members of Local 1112 had filed 6,000 grievances over work standards, discipline, health and safety conditions and other matters covered by their contract. There were 16,000 grievances on file when they struck this July.

There were more motorcycles than Vegas in the parking lot when, this August, Local 1112 members came in to pick up their weekly strike benefit checks—$40 maximum for a married worker with two children.

Bob Hunt got $30. He is 24 and single and wore white double knit slacks and dark glasses. He is a relief operator on the Vega line and insists on working exactly according to the contract.

"I've been tossed out of the plant umpteen times just because I stick by the book, 100 per cent by the book," he explained. "I just want people to stick up for what they believe is right.

"Some day, I want to see the union defeat management," said Hunt. "I don't mean stomp them on the ground. All I mean is going in to work and not being a number, a robot, a piece of machinery."[1]

IF YOU HAD to sum up the overall attitude of the Lordstown workers toward their jobs from this report, you would probably choose a word like *dissatisfied*. Yet if you read the report very carefully, you might conclude that "dissatisfied" is too simple a description of a

---

[1] Terry Ryan, Associated Press, September 2, 1974. Reproduced by permission.

more complex attitude. For instance, the Lordstown workers appear to feel that the pay and fringe benefits are good, but many feel that the working conditions and work standards are unsatisfactory.

Attitudes appear to vary from worker to worker. Because of rising unemployment, many feel that pay and benefits are the most important aspects of their work. Others are more concerned with the boredom and monotony of assembly-line work or the pressures and dangers of working around high-speed machinery. There are indications that older workers are less dissatisfied (or more resigned) than younger workers.

Expressions of satisfaction and dissatisfaction are likewise complex. While satisfaction in general appeared to be no better in 1974 than it was in 1972, performance as measured by shutdown time for repairs had dramatically improved. Disciplinary layoffs, instead of increasing, had dropped 60 percent. On the other hand, the rate of absenteeism was up 60 percent and the number of grievances filed had almost tripled!

Thus to describe worker attitudes at Lordstown as simply negative or dissatisfied is misleading. Their attitudes, and the attitudes of most people who work in organizations, are complex and varied. Further, the relationships between their attitudes and such important behavior as turnover and performance are neither as simple nor as consistent as was once believed.

This chapter will investigate employee attitudes and related behaviors. It will begin by describing the nature of attitudes in general—their components, characteristics, sources, and functions. The rest of the chapter will focus on work-related attitudes—their nature, their measurement, and the factors that affect them. It will examine research on American workers for evidence of variations among groups of workers and changes over time in job satisfaction. The chapter concludes by describing the relationships between worker satisfaction and absenteeism, turnover, and performance.

THE NATURE OF ATTITUDES

The word *attitude* describes a persistent tendency to feel and behave in a particular way toward some object. Two aspects of this definition should be stressed. First, attitudes persist or endure. That is, in the absence of forces to change, the individual's attitude toward a certain object will remain the same. For example, if you have a very negative attitude toward school and tend to avoid classes and studying, we would expect that attitude to persist in the absence of forces to change (e.g., some change in you or your environment). Attitudes do change, of course. The kinds of attitudes we are interested in here, however, are usually important enough to the individual that they not only persist but are somewhat resistant to change.

Second, a person's attitude is directed toward some object, about which he has both feelings and beliefs. If a Lordstown worker is described as having a bad attitude, the implication is that he or she has negative feelings and beliefs about the wages, working conditions, supervision, co-workers, responsibility, or specific task requirements of the work.

Components of Attitudes

Attitudes are said to have three components. Theorists and researchers believe that three different but related psychological tendencies toward an object make up what is called an attitude. These component tendencies are affective, cognitive, and behavioral.

Affective   The affective component includes a person's emotional feelings about an object, his like or dislike of it. This component can vary from weak to strong in its intensity. For example, Dan Dearing's attitude toward the monotony of his job at Lordstown was not particularly emotional; he expressed no strong feelings about it one way or the other. His emotions toward the security of his job, however, were more intense. The affective components of your attitudes toward school probably vary widely in their intensity. You may really like this class, be indifferent toward another, and moderately dislike a third.

Cognitive   The cognitive component is made up of the beliefs and information a person has about the object. Regardless of whether his information or beliefs are accurate or inaccurate, these cognitions are part of his attitude. The cognitive component of a Lordstown worker's attitude toward her supervisor might include information that he is black, 43, has a B.S. from Ohio State, has been with the company 18 years, and is making twice her salary. It may also include beliefs that he exploits people, is unsympathetic to the problems of women, and discriminates between workers according to their race. Of course, not all her cognitive elements may be true. Her supervisor may really be 50, may be making only slightly more than she is, and may discriminate neither on sex or race. Nonetheless, her cognitions, right or wrong, make up the cognitive element of her attitude toward supervision.

Behavioral The behavioral component consists of a person's tendencies to behave toward the object in certain ways. For example, the worker described in the preceding paragraph may tend to avoid her supervisor whenever possible, to refuse to discuss her problems with him and to be highly skeptical of his suggestions or advice.

It is important to note that, of the three components, an observer can perceive only the behavioral elements of an actor's attitude. He cannot directly observe another's feelings of like or dislike but can only infer them from behavior such as facial expressions, conversation, and approach or avoidance. He also cannot directly observe another's cognitions but can only infer them from behavior such as verbal discussions or written questionnaires.

Consistency of Attitudes

Strictly speaking, then, a person's affective and cognitive components are inferred from his behavioral expressions of an attitude. Further, it is assumed that there is consistency among these components, particularly between the affective and cognitive elements. Positive feelings toward an object are usually associated with beliefs that the object can be of use to the person in getting things he wants or values and in avoiding things he does not want. For example, an executive may like his job because his subordinates provide him with respect, attention, and status, and they distract him from his family problems. Conversely, negative feelings toward an object are usually associated with beliefs that the object interferes with the person's getting things he wants. The executive may not like going home because he believes his wife and children do not give him the respect and admiration he deserves.

In stating that consistency between beliefs and feelings is to be expected, we should make a distinction between two types of belief: belief *about* an object and belief *in* an object. By belief *in* an object, we mean belief that it exists. For example, one may believe *in* God, life on other planets, an international communist conspiracy, padding expense accounts, racial discrimination at work, or merit pay systems. One may also have beliefs *about* these objects; for instance, that God is all-merciful, that extraterrestial life and communist conspiracies threaten human existence, or that merit pay systems exploit workers. The reason for making the distinction is that beliefs *about* objects and feelings toward them are likely to be correlated, while beliefs *in* objects and feelings toward them are not necessarily correlated. One can believe in the existence of expense account padding or racial discrimination and feel either good, bad, or neutral about them.[2]

Attitudes which are internally consistent are stable and not easily changed. Further, attitudes tend to become linked with other attitudes and values in a complex and mutually reinforcing set or cluster. For example, one worker's negative attitude toward minority group workers may be associated with belief in racial superiority, fears of reverse discrimination, values of segregation, dislike for the federal government, mistrust of those who are different, and nostalgia for the good old days. Attitudes like this which become part of so interrelated a system are extremely stable and resistant to change.

Sources of Attitudes

Attitudes are learned, not inherited. The person acquires attitudes in the course of his experiences, and he maintains them when they are reinforced. Acquisition can occur in different ways.

Direct Experience with the Object   Attitudes can develop from a personally rewarding or punishing experience with an object. A truck driver whose route takes him through Nevada is cited for speeding by the highway patrol, fined for overloading his truck, has an accident on a poorly marked curve, gets a lousy meal at a diner, and has to pay 3 cents more for a gallon of diesel fuel than in adjoining states. This driver is likely to develop a very negative attitude toward that state, to be receptive to negative information about it, and to tend to avoid it whenever possible.

Association   Attitudes toward one object may develop from associating that object with another object about which attitudes have been previously formed. The truck driver may develop negative attitudes toward drivers of cars bearing Nevada license plates, associating them with his experiences in that state. He could become hostile toward them, be particularly aware of any driving idiosyncracies he observes, and tend to behave aggressively toward them by passing, cutting them off, and tailgating.

---

[2] Martin Fishbein and B. H. Raven, "The AB Scales: An Operational Definition of Belief and Attitude," *Human Relations*, vol. 15, no. 1 (1962), pp. 35–44.

Learning from Others   Attitudes may also develop from what the person is told by others about the object. The truck driver may pass his negative attitudes toward Nevada on to his colleagues through conversations at truck stops in other states. His family may pick up similar attitudes from listening to his complaints, or more subtly, from observing that he treats people from Nevada in an especially hostile manner.

In general, attitudes which are acquired through personal experience tend to be more resistant to change than those learned from association or from others. However, attitudes acquired in ways other than personal experience can likewise be very stable and resistant if they are part of a mutually reinforcing cluster of attitudes and values.

Functions of Attitudes

A person maintains an attitude for a reason: it does something for him. According to the functional theory of attitudes,[3] attitudes can serve four different functions for an individual:

The Knowledge Function   An attitude can help a person to organize and make sense of his knowledge, experiences, and beliefs. It can provide definiteness and stability to what he perceives by serving as a standard or frame of reference. For example, a stereotype is an attitude in which one attributes to all members of a group (social, ethnic, religious, etc.) certain traits and characteristics. The Watergate scandal resulted in the development of very negative attitudes of the public toward politicians in general, widespread feelings of mistrust, and behavioral tendencies to refrain from campaign contributions and voting.

The Instrumental Function   An attitude may develop because either the attitude or the object of the attitude is instrumental in helping the individual to obtain rewards or avoid punishments. In some cases the attitude is a means to an end. A worker finds that when he expresses a negative attitude toward his boss, his co-workers pay attention to and sympathize with him, but when he expresses a positive attitude, he is ignored or chastened. The negative attitude is instrumental in obtaining rewards (acceptance) and avoiding punishment (rejection). In another case, the object is a

---

[3] See Daniel Katz, "The Functional Approach to the Study of Attitude Change," *Public Opinion Quarterly,* vol. 24 (1960), pp. 163–204.

means to an end, and the attitude develops from association of the object and its outcome. For example, a car salesman may develop favorable attitudes toward blue-collar workers, to whom he can easily sell, and negative attitudes toward doctors, who he finds are always searching for a bargain and difficult to sell. He associates success and profit with blue-collar workers and failure and difficulty with doctors, and thus he develops appropriate attitudes toward those objects through association.

The Value-Expressive Function   Attitudes may give positive expression to a person's central values or to his self-image. One whose central value is the freedom of the individual may express very positive attitudes toward decentralization of authority in the organization, flexible work schedules, and relaxation of dress standards. One who views herself as a liberated female may express negative attitudes toward housewives, authority exercised by males, and sexist humor, as a means of expressing the value she places on women's role.

The Ego-Defensive Function   Finally, attitudes may serve to protect one's ego from unpleasant or threatening knowledge about oneself or one's environment. Accepting threatening information can produce anxiety; developing certain attitudes can distort or block out such information and reduce anxiety. A doctor who treats his nurses without regard for their feelings or capabilities may develop an attitude that nurses are poorly trained, improperly motivated, and uninterested in patients' welfare. This attitude may protect him from being aware that his treatment of nurses is an expression of his feelings of superiority and dominance over women. A manager who develops an attitude that his work is just a game may be trying to protect himself from awareness of the possible consequences of his personal indebtedness, large family, and shaky position in the company.

JOB SATISFACTION

Anyone who works in an organization soon develops a set of attitudes about work which are usually referred to under the general term *job satisfaction*. Like other attitudes, job satisfaction is composed of affective, cognitive, and behavioral elements, can vary in intensity and consistency, can be acquired from a variety of sources, and serves a number of functions for the individual.

Suppose you have recently been hired as a management trainee of a large corporation. After a few weeks you have gradually come to like the program, believe that what you learn will make you a better manager, and tend to take your assignments, both at work and for study, seriously. Since the components are all positive, your attitude is internally consistent. However, you are not particularly pleased with your salary, have not made any real friends in the organization yet, and your spouse does not like the city where you work or the long hours you put in. Therefore your attitude is not externally consistent with other attitudes, and it is only mild in intensity. Your satisfaction from the program has developed from your own experiences in it, from being told by middle managers that the program is an excellent way to learn, and from sensing from others that they envy your position. Your satisfaction may be instrumental in that it makes it easier for you to get out of bed at 6 A.M. every day to make the long trip across town in rush-hour traffic. It may also be ego defensive in helping you cope with the fact that you picked this job over a higher paying position with a smaller firm in your spouse's home town.

Managerial Interest in Job Satisfaction

Should managers worry about how satisfied the members of their organizations are? Don't they have enough to do maintaining the effectiveness, efficiency, and survival of their organizations without being concerned whether their people are satisfied or dissatisfied? You should be able to answer these questions for yourself by the time you have finished this chapter. Many managers are concerned about job satisfaction, and for a variety of reasons.

Some managers worry about job satisfaction for what they consider to be very practical reasons. That is, they believe that job satisfaction directly affects worker productivity. These managers feel that a happy worker will be more efficient, innovative, careful, or compliant and will exert more effort than an unhappy worker.

Some managers, likewise practical, believe that employee satisfaction is a key factor in maintaining low rates of absenteeism or turnover. They feel that satisfied employees will arrive on time more frequently and will miss work or quit their jobs less frequently than dissatisfied employees. We could say such managers' attitudes toward job satisfaction serve instrumental functions for them.

There are some managers who like to keep everyone happy because they themselves find it more pleasant to work in an organizational climate where people are happy and managers are well liked. (These managers' attitudes are likewise instrumental.)

Finally, there are managers who feel morally responsible for maintaining a reasonably high level of job satisfaction in their organization. As one executive put it,

> I have over 500 people who spend 60 percent of their waking hours in my plant five, six, sometimes seven days a week, and I don't know how much more time traveling to and from work and thinking about their jobs. If they're basically unhappy with their work, that means I'm responsible for one helluva lot of human misery, particularly if they go home and take it out on their families.[4]

Whether you believe the moral argument is a valid or sufficient cause for concern about job satisfaction is, of course, up to you. The validity of practical considerations of job satisfaction because of its perceived effects on absenteeism, turnover, and performance will be discussed in detail later in this chapter.

Measuring Job Satisfaction

The interest of both managers and researchers in job satisfaction has led to the development and refinement of instruments designed to measure, in reliable, valid, and systematic ways, the satisfaction levels of people at work. In the course of developing and testing these instruments, researchers have found that people are capable of expressing their satisfaction or dissatisfaction with specific aspects of their work, as well as with their work in general.

Accordingly, researchers have developed more sophisticated instruments, usually in the form of multiple-item questionnaires, which are capable of distinguishing among the different aspects of work with which people are concerned. Such refinements have made job satisfaction surveys more useful to organizations concerned with employee morale by pinpointing those areas in which employee dissatisfaction is greatest.

Managers and researchers currently can choose from a score or more of such questionnaires. We will discuss two of them here: the semantic differential scale and the Job Descriptive Index. Both are widely used, but they differ both in format and in the components of job satisfaction that they measure.

---

[4] Personal communication.

Semantic Differential Scale   A semantic differential scale for measuring job satisfaction is based on the assumption that job satisfaction (or "morale") is a complex function of an individual's attitudes toward the various specific aspects of his work surroundings.[5] The semantic differential is a paper-and-pencil attitude questionnaire which provides pairs of bipolar adjectives (e.g., good-bad, interesting-boring) which the respondent uses to describe his feelings toward a particular object.

FIGURE 11–1
A Semantic Differential Scale for Measuring Job Satisfaction

ME AT WORK

	Extremely	Quite	Slightly	Neither One nor the Other	Slightly	Quite	Extremely	
Appreciated	____	: ___	: ____	: _____	: ____	: ___	: _____	Unappreciated
Excitable	____	: ___	: ____	: _____	: ____	: ___	: _____	Calm
Efficient	____	: ___	: ____	: _____	: ____	: ___	: _____	Inefficient
Penalized	____	: ___	: ____	: _____	: ____	: ___	: _____	Rewarded
Interested	____	: ___	: ____	: _____	: ____	: ___	: _____	Bored
Uncooperative	____	: ___	: ____	: _____	: ____	: ___	: _____	Cooperative
Satisfied	____	: ___	: ____	: _____	: ____	: ___	: _____	Dissatisfied
Unproductive	____	: ___	: ____	: _____	: ____	: ___	: _____	Productive
Encouraged	____	: ___	: ____	: _____	: ____	: ___	: _____	Discouraged
Attentive	____	: ___	: ____	: _____	: ____	: ___	: _____	Inattentive
High Strung	____	: ___	: ____	: _____	: ____	: ___	: _____	Serene
Valuable	____	: ___	: ____	: _____	: ____	: ___	: _____	Worthless
Unreliable	____	: ___	: ____	: _____	: ____	: ___	: _____	Reliable
Spirited	____	: ___	: ____	: _____	: ____	: ___	: _____	Lifeless
Useless	____	: ___	: ____	: _____	: ____	: ___	: _____	Useful
Listless	____	: ___	: ____	: _____	: ____	: ___	: _____	Alert
Relaxed	____	: ___	: ____	: _____	: ____	: ___	: _____	Tense
Ineffective	____	: ___	: ____	: _____	: ____	: ___	: _____	Effective
Informed	____	: ___	: ____	: _____	: ____	: ___	: _____	Uninformed
Unimportant	____	: ___	: ____	: _____	: ____	: ___	: _____	Important

Reproduced by permission, © Dr. William E. Scott, Jr., Graduate School of Business, Indiana University.

One of the scales in this instrument is shown in Figure 11–1. Here the respondent checks that point between each of 20 bipolar adjectives which best describes the way he feels at work. Respondents similarly describe their feelings toward ten other aspects of

[5] W. E. Scott, Jr., "The Development of Semantic Differential Scales as Measures of Morale," *Personnel Psychology*, vol. 20, no. 2 (1967), pp. 179–98.

their organization. These aspects, and examples of adjective pairs used to describe them, are:

1. My opportunities for advancement (limited-unlimited; known-unknown).
2. Company benefits (vague-clear; inadequate-adequate).
3. My pay (reasonable-unreasonable; superior-inferior).
4. My pay in comparison with what others get for similar work in the company (fair-unfair; high-low).
5. My pay in comparison with what others get for similar work in other companies (superior-inferior; unreasonable-reasonable).
6. My supervisor (strong-weak; effective-ineffective).
7. My fellow workers (pleasant-unpleasant; cooperative-uncooperative).
8. Top management (helpful-obstructive; distant-close).
9. My job (exciting-dull; routine-varied).
10. My working conditions (comfortable-uncomfortable; safe-dangerous).

Testing and refinement of this instrument have brought it to a level of reliability which makes it useful for both researchers and managers. For example, statistical techniques have demonstrated that the different components of satisfaction measured are quite similar among diverse groups of workers, including design and development engineers in manufacturing,[6] civil service employees in an ammunition depot,[7] and managerial personnel in a bank.[8] Managers have used the instrument to compare the satisfaction of their employees against industry norms or to compare the satisfaction of various departments within their organization. Using this instrument, a large bank discovered the satisfaction of its keypunchers was significantly lower than that of the rest of its staff. The dissatisfaction was primarily due to lack of eating facilities in the building and the inaccessibility of places to eat in the area near the bank's computer facilities. Pinpointing the source of the problem led the bank to construct adequate cafeteria facilities, and there was a subsequent significant improvement in morale.

[6] Ibid., pp. 179–98.

[7] W. E. Scott, Jr., and K. M. Rowland, "The Generality and Significance of Semantic Differential Scales as Measures of 'Morale,'" *Organizational Behavior and Human Performance*, vol. 5 (November 1970), pp. 516–91.

[8] H. J. Reitz, "Managerial Attitudes and Perceived Contingencies between Performance and Organizational Responses," *Proceedings of the Academy of Management, 1971*, pp. 227–38.

The Job Descriptive Index[9]   A widely used scale is the Job Descriptive Index (JDI), developed by a group of industrial psychologists over a period of several years. This scale measures worker satisfaction or dissatisfaction with five aspects of work: supervision, pay, promotions, co-workers, and the work itself. The scale consists of a series of adjectives or phrases for each of the five aspects; some examples are shown in Figure 11–2. The worker is asked to indicate

FIGURE 11–2
Sample Items from the Job Descriptive Index

Work

_____ Fascinating

_____ Frustrating

Supervision

_____ Hard to please

_____ Praises good work

Pay

_____ Adequate for normal expenses

_____ Less than I deserve

Promotions

_____ Promotion on ability

_____ Dead-end job

Co-workers

_____ Stimulating

_____ Talk too much

Source: The Job Descriptive Index © 1975, Dr. Patricia C. Smith. For further information, write Dr. Patricia C. Smith, Department of Psychology, Bowling Green State University, Bowling Green, Ohio 43403.

how these adjectives and phrases describe his job by placing a Y (yes), N (no), or ? (undecided) alongside each one.

This scale has proved to be an immensely popular measure of job satisfaction and dissatisfaction because of its demonstrated reliability, its simplicity, and the ease with which it can be administered. An example of its use in research is a study of the job attitudes of employees working for a state division of corrections.[10] Previous research with telephone company employees had found that certain "core" dimensions of workers' jobs were significantly related to their

---

[9] P. C. Smith, L. M. Kendall, and C. L. Hulin, *The Measurement of Satisfaction in Work and Retirement* (Chicago: Rand McNally & Co., 1969).

[10] A. P. Brief and R. J. Aldag, "Employee Reactions to Job Characteristics: A Constructive Replication," *Journal of Applied Psychology*, vol. 60 (1975), pp. 182–86.

satisfaction with work. These dimensions were variety (in equipment or operations), autonomy (in scheduling, equipment selection, and procedures), task identity (doing a complete job and seeing its results), and feedback (information on performance).

This study hypothesized that workers whose jobs were high on these core dimensions would be significantly more satisfied with supervision, co-workers, pay, promotion, and the work itself than workers whose jobs were low on the core dimensions. The results supported the hypothesis. Significant positive correlations were found between the four job dimensions (variety, autonomy, task identity, and feedback) and worker satisfaction with the five specific aspects of work measured by the JDI.

Factors Affecting Job Satisfaction

So much has been written about causes of job satisfaction that perhaps it is best to start with a simple basic proposition: Job satisfaction is the result of experiencing rewards at work. Remember (from our earlier discussion) that "rewards" is a broad and variable term; what is rewarding to one person may not be rewarding to another. Nonetheless, worker satisfaction increases when workers have rewarding experiences. For example, in one study 90 workers were promised bonuses based on their productivity.[11] In fact, bonuses were awarded randomly to half of the most productive workers and half of the least productive workers. Subsequent measures showed that, regardless of productivity or prior satisfaction, those who received bonuses expressed increased satisfaction and significantly greater satisfaction than those who did not receive bonuses.

This study demonstrated the simple relationship that:

$$\text{Rewards} \rightarrow \text{Satisfaction}$$

However, determining just what people at work will find rewarding is somewhat more complex.

As we noted in Chapter 5, what is rewarding depends upon the individual's levels of need importance and need satisfaction. For example, one who places a great importance on security needs (maybe he is concerned about losing his job or getting out of debt)

---

[11] D. J. Cherrington, H. J. Reitz, and W. E. Scott, Jr., "Effects of Contingent and Non-Contingent Reward on the Relationship between Satisfaction and Task Performance," *Journal of Applied Psychology*, vol. 55, no. 6 (1971), pp. 531–36.

will be rewarded by obtaining things at work relative to these needs (a guaranteed work contract, a monetary bonus, a raise) but may not find other things rewarding (additional responsibility, praise, a bigger office). Further, according to the theories discussed in Chapter 5, if a need is fully satisfied, no matter how important, obtaining additional things relevant to that need will not be rewarding or satisfying. We also discussed the contention that a satisfied need is not a motivator of behavior. We can paraphrase that to say that rewards directed toward satisfied needs may be neither efficient nor effective means of increasing satisfaction. If employees who have the best fringe benefits in the industry have low job satisfaction, increasing fringe benefits would be an ineffective, or at least inefficient, means of improving their morale.

Characteristics of Work Affecting Satisfaction   Another way of looking at job satisfaction is to examine specific characteristics of work with which employees are concerned. Chapter 5 described the two-factor theory of motivation, which lists a number of characteristics thought to be important to either worker satisfaction or motivation. These include company policy, supervision, relations with fellow workers, job security, salary, working conditions, status, effect of the job on one's personal life, achievement, recognition, advancement, responsibility, opportunities for professional and personal growth, and the nature of the work itself.[12]

One of the most controversial propositions of the two-factor theory is that pay (salary) is not particularly important to workers. A number of researchers, skeptical of both the research methodology and the conclusions drawn from the two-factor theory, have tested some of its propositions with different, more systematic methods. A review of these studies indicates that pay is more important to workers than the two-factor theory suggests. The importance workers place on pay relative to other aspects of their jobs indicates they tend to rank pay relatively high:

> . . . its average rank is closer to third than to sixth, and 27 percent of the studies found that pay ranks first in importance among job facets. The data also show that there is indeed substantial variance in the importance of pay, since it varies in rank from ninth to first.[13]

The increasing interest of the U.S. Department of Labor in job

[12] Frederick Herzberg, Bernard Mauser, and Barbara Snyderman, *The Motivation to Work,* 2d ed. (New York: John Wiley & Sons, 1959).

[13] E. E. Lawler III, *Pay and Organizational Effectiveness: A Psychological View* (New York: McGraw Hill Book Co., 1971), p. 39.

satisfaction has led to recent national surveys of workers, both blue collar and white collar, on the importance they assign to various aspects of work. Some of the results of the 1969–70 survey[14] are given in Table 11–1. For each of 23 different aspects of work, the percentage of workers sampled who rated that aspect as "very important" to them is indicated.

According to this survey, a number of aspects of work are very

TABLE 11–1
Percentage of Workers Rating Job Facets as "Very Important" to Them

	All Workers (N = 1500)*	White-Collar Workers (N = 730)*	Blue-Collar Workerst (N = 685)*
Resources			
I receive enough help and equipment to get the job done	68.4	64.5	71.9
I have enough information to get the job done	68.1	67.4	68.5
My responsibilities are clearly defined	61.2	57.6	64.6
My supervisor is competent in doing his job	61.1	59.7	63.0
Financial Rewards			
The pay is good	64.2	57.4	72.5
The job security is good	62.5	54.2	71.5
My fringe benefits are good	50.6	39.7	62.4
Challenge			
The work is interesting	73.0	78.5	68.2
I have enough authority to do my job	65.6	66.8	63.5
I have an opportunity to develop my special abilities	63.3	69.4	57.2
I can see the results of my work	61.7	60.0	63.8
I am given a chance to do the things I do best	54.3	54.0	55.0
I am given a lot of freedom to decide how I do my work	52.9	56.4	49.8
The problems I am asked to solve are hard enough	30.4	31.2	29.3
Relations with Co-workers			
My co-workers are friendly and helpful	63.4	60.9	67.0
I am given a lot of chances to make friends	44.0	39.3	48.6
Comfort			
I have enough time to get the job done	54.4	47.7	60.3
The hours are good	50.8	41.0	61.6
Travel to and from work is convenient	46.2	42.4	49.7
Physical surroundings are pleasant	40.2	32.3	47.8
I am free from conflicting demands that other people make of me	33.1	25.8	40.0
I can forget about my personal problems	30.8	26.5	35.3
I am not asked to do excessive amounts of work	23.0	15.7	29.5

* Base *N*'s vary slightly from row to row due to nonresponse to individual questions.
† Farm workers have been excluded.
Source: Robert Quinn, Stanley Seashore, Robert Kahn, Thomas Mangione, Douglas Campbell, and Margaret McCullough, *Survey of Working Conditions (1969–70),* Document 291-6-0001 (Washington, D.C.: U.S. Government Printing Office, 1971).

---

[14] Robert Quinn, Stanley Seashore, Robert Kahn, Thomas Mangione, Douglas Campbell, Graham Staines, and Margaret McCullough, *Survey of Working Conditions* (1969–70), Document 2916–0001 (Washington, D.C.: U.S. Government Printing Office, 1971).

important sources of satisfaction (or dissatisfaction) for a significant majority of American workers. Having an interesting job, enough help and equipment, the necessary information and authority to do the job, and being paid well were rated very important by 64 percent of all workers sampled. Aspects of the job dealing with comfort were rated as least important by the workers.

Differences between white-collar and blue-collar workers in the importance attached to certain aspects of rank were apparent from the survey. A ranking of the different aspects according to the percentage of workers who rated them very important indicates that pay ranked first among blue-collar workers, followed closely by sufficient help and equipment, job security, information, and interesting work. Among white-collar workers, interesting work was clearly ranked first, followed by opportunity to develop special abilities, information, authority, and help and equipment.

The sample indicates that the satisfaction of American workers depends on a number of different aspects of work. The Department of Labor concludes from the survey that

> Good pay was indeed of considerable importance to workers, but at the same time they desired jobs that were highly concerned both with the economical and noneconomical aspects of the job.[15]

> Because the "average" American worker appears to seek things simultaneously (e.g., good pay, interesting work) from each job, there may be no *one* way to increase job satisfaction.[16]

Characteristics of Organizations Affecting Satisfaction If job satisfaction is a function of the experiences of people in organizations, then it is to be expected that certain characteristics of organizations affect job satisfaction. There is evidence that both administrative and technological changes can produce corresponding changes in worker satisfaction.

A field experiment conducted among four clerical divisions of a large company demonstrated the effects of administrative changes on satisfaction.[17] The decision processes of two divisions were changed to allow the clerical workers more autonomy and greater voice in decisions affecting them. The decision processes of the

[15] U.S. Department of Labor, *Job Satisfaction: Is There a Trend?* Manpower Research Monograph No. 30 (Washington, D.C.: U.S. Government Printing Office, 1974), p. 17.

[16] Ibid., p. 2.

[17] Nancy Morse and Everett Reimer, "The Experimental Change of a Major Organizational Variable," *Journal of Abnormal and Social Psychology*, vol. 52 (1956), pp. 120–29.

other two divisions were simultaneously changed to a more hierarchically controlled program in which the clerical workers had a diminished decision-making role. As a result, satisfaction increased in the two autonomous divisions but decreased in the two hierarchical divisions.

A review of empirical field studies in business and industrial organizations found several properties of organization structure to be significantly related to job satisfaction.[18] An employee's position in the hierarchy of the organization is strongly related to his job satisfaction. First, managers tend to be more satisfied than nonmanagers. Second, higher level managers are more satisfied than lower level managers. These findings are not surprising in view of the things that blue- and white-collar workers say are important to them (see Table 11–1). As one moves up the organizational hierarchy, jobs tend to be more interesting and challenging, better paying, and more likely to provide one with adequate resources. Thus they are more satisfying to the incumbent. There are individual exceptions, of course. For some people, the increasing responsibilities and pressures of higher level jobs more than offset increases in pay, prestige, and resources, leaving them less satisfied than they were at more junior levels. In some organizations, higher level positions do not provide greater satisfactions than lower level positions. For example, a professional baseball coach may enjoy only a fraction of the security, prestige, and salary of one of his star players.

Other research on organizational factors has consistently found line managers to be more satisfied than staff managers. Can you speculate why a position of direct authority and responsibility for operations would be more satisfying than a consulting and advising position? Could it have something to do with differing opportunities for satisfactions related to power, a sense of achievement and importance, and rapid advancement? Finally, workers in small groups and departments are more satisfied than those in large units. This will be explained in Chapters 12–14, on interpersonal attraction and communication.

One of the best known and least understood books on job satisfaction also described a relationship between technology and satisfaction. Robert Blauner's *Alienation and Freedom*[19] is often cited

---

[18] L. W. Porter and E. E. Lawler, III, "Properties of Organization Structure in Relation to Job Attitudes and Job Behavior," *Psychological Bulletin*, vol. 64 (July 1965), pp. 23–51.

[19] Robert Blauner, *Alienation and Freedom: The Factory Worker and His Job* (Chicago: University of Chicago Press, 1964).

as generally describing the American worker as alienated and highly dissatisfied, due to the impact of technology. What Blauner's studies really showed, however, was that alienation and dissatisfaction are more complexly related to technology. In industries with moderate technology, such as automobile and textiles, he indeed found workers alienated, isolated, and resentful. But in industries where technology had advanced to a more sophisticated stage, such as the printing and chemical industries, he found both freedom and integration. In these latter industries, automation had in fact increased the worker's control over his job and checked the further division of labor, with correspondingly high levels of job satisfaction. Even Blauner admits, "Empirical studies show that the majority of industrial workers are satisfied with their work and with their jobs."[20]

How Satisfied Are Workers?

"Despite being the highest-paid worker in the world, the average American worker today is grossly dissatisfied, largely as a result of the dehumanizing aspects of modern technology applied to his work." This statement is not a direct quote but a paraphrase of speculations by public figures and educators on the lot of workers today, particularly as compared to the "good old days" of the 1940s and 1950s. Such comments, particularly when incorporated into campaign speeches, press releases, and publications, attain notoriety in painting a grim picture of modern-day work. An example is:

> This book, being about work, is, by its very nature, about violence— to the spirit as well as to the body. It is about ulcers as well as accidents, about shouting matches as well as fistfights, about nervous breakdowns as well as kicking the dog around. It is, above all (or beneath all), about daily humiliations. To survive the day is triumph enough for the walking wounded among the great many of us.[21]

The Department of Labor, however, has cited the results of seven national surveys of worker satisfaction conducted between 1958 and 1973 as evidence that worker satisfaction had not declined precipitously over that period.[22] The surveys, conducted by the National Opinion Research Center, the University of California Survey Re-

[20] Ibid., p. 183.

[21] Studs Terkel, from the Introduction to *Working* (New York: Pantheon Books, 1972), p. xi. © 1972, 1974 Pantheon Books, a Division of Random House, Inc.

[22] For a more pessimistic interpretation of these data, see H. L. Sheppard and N. Q. Herrick, *Where Have All the Robots Gone?: Worker Dissatisfaction in the 70's* (New York: Free Press, 1972).

search Center, and the University of Michigan Survey Research Center, all asked workers how satisfied they were with their jobs. The results of these surveys are given in Figure 11–3.

As this figure shows, the percentage of workers reporting that

FIGURE 11–3
Percentage of "Satisfied" Workers, 1958–1973, Based on Seven National Surveys

Date and Source	70%	80%	90%	100%

1958
Survey Research Center,
U. of Michigan
81%
81%

1962
National Opinion
Research Center
83%
84%

1964
Survey Research Center,
U. of California
91%
90%

1964
National Opinion
Research Center
92%
92%

1969
Survey Research Center,
U. of Michigan
85%
88%

1971
Survey Research Center,
U. of Michigan
91%
91%

1973
Survey Research Center,
U. of Michigan
90%
91%

All Workers (except for the 1958 Michigan and the 1964 NORC surveys, which were based on men only)

Men Only, Ages 21 through 65 (except for the 1958 survey, which was based on men 21 or older and which was not available for reanalysis)

Note: "Don't know" answers were excluded from the percentage bases.

Source: U.S. Department of Labor, *Job Satisfaction: Is There a Trend?* Manpower Research Monograph no. 30, Manpower Administration, 1974, p. 4.

they are satisfied with their jobs did not decline but was in fact substantially higher in 1973 than it was in 1958. Despite a slight decline in 1969, at least 90 percent of the workers sampled described themselves as either satisfied or very satisfied with their jobs in 1971 and 1973. The Department of Labor also cites the evidence of eight Gallup polls taken from 1963 to 1973 which showed the percentage of satisfied workers to be fluctuating between 86 and 92 percent. It concludes "There has been no substantial change in overall levels of job satisfaction over the last decade."[23]

Relative Satisfaction of Types of Workers

The Department of Labor also summarizes studies comparing the relative satisfaction of various types of American workers. It concludes that occupation and age are significantly related to job satisfaction, but education and sex are not.

Table 11–2 presents the results of a 1973 University of Michigan survey[24] in which respondents are categorized by occupation. It shows, as other studies have, that professional, technical, and managerial personnel are the most satisfied, and operative and nonfarm laborers are the least satisfied with their jobs.

TABLE 11–2
Mean Job Satisfaction by Major Occupational Group

Occupational Group*	Mean Job Satisfaction†
Professional and technical (N = 323)	25
Managers, officials, and proprietors (N = 319)	19
Sales (N = 112)	11
Craftsmen and foremen (N = 270)	8
Service workers, except private household (N = 238)	−11
Clerical (N = 364)	−14
Operatives (N = 379)	−35
Nonfarm laborers (N = 72)	−42

* The following categories have been omitted due to small numbers of cases: farmers and farm managers, farm laborers, and private household workers.

† Mean values are based on a 28-question measure of overall job satisfaction. A higher numeric score indicates greater job satisfaction. The mean of this measure in 1973 was −2; its standard deviation was 84.

Source: *Job Satisfaction: Is There a Trend?* Manpower Research Monograph no. 30, U.S. Department of Labor, Manpower Administration, 1974, p. 10. Data taken from: R. P. Quinn and L. J. Shepard, *The 1972-73 Quality of Employment Survey: Descriptive Statistics, with Comparison Data from the 1969-70 Survey of Working Conditions* (Ann Arbor, Mich.: Survey Research Center, 1974).

Surprisingly, few differences between men and women in job satisfaction have been observed, and differences that have been reported are small and inconsistent. For instance, in 1971, the difference between the percentage of women and men who were satisfied with their jobs was only 2 percent, with more women satisfied;

[23] U.S. Department of Labor, *Job Satisfaction: Is There a Trend?* Manpower Research Monograph no. 30, Manpower Administration, 1974, p. 6.

[24] Ibid., pp. 9–13.

in 1973, the difference was again only 2 percent, but this time more men were satisfied.

Most studies agree that older workers tend to be more satisfied with their jobs than younger workers (see Table 11–3). This rela-

TABLE 11–3
Mean Job Satisfaction by Age

Age	Job Satisfaction*
16–20 (N = 175).	–41
21–29 (N = 584).	–27
30–44 (N = 657).	10
45–54 (N = 443).	9
55 or older (N = 292).	23

* A higher numeric score indicates greater job satisfaction. The mean of this measure was –2; its standard deviation was 84.
Source: *Job Satisfaction: Is There a Trend?* Manpower Research Monograph no. 30, U.S. Department of Labor, Manpower Administration, 1974, p. 12. Data taken from: R. P. Quinn and L. J. Shepard, *The 1972–73 Quality of Employment Survey: Descriptive Statistics, with Comparison Data from the 1969–70 Survey of Working Conditions* (Ann Arbor, Mich.: Survey Research Center, 1974).

tionship between age and job satisfaction has been confirmed both by national surveys and by studies of workers within a single organization. In fact, studies over the past 15 years have shown that older workers are more satisfied than younger ones. The generation gap in job satisfaction may be due in part to higher expectations among younger workers, which become tempered by the realities of personal experience as they grow older. It is probably of more importance that better jobs tend to be based on experience, and thus they tend to go to older workers. Since the older workers get the better jobs, they are more satisfied.

Although it might be expected that more educated workers would be more satisfied because of their ability to obtain better jobs, there is little evidence to support this. Most studies show no simple linear relationship between educational level and job satisfaction. In fact, the seven national surveys discussed earlier suggested that the most satisfied workers were those who either had not gone beyond eighth grade or who had not only been to college, but had done some graduate work. In the 1973 survey, for example, the highest percentage of satisfied workers was among those with a college degree or more, followed in order by those with eight years or less of education, those with a high school diploma, those with some college, and those with some high school.

Finally, there is evidence of some differences in overall job satisfaction between white workers and minority workers. These differences, although consistently in favor of whites over the eleven years for which we have data, have not been dramatic. The greatest difference was recorded in 1969, when satisfied white workers exceeded satisfied black workers by 9 percent. In 1973, that difference was 5 percent, with 90 percent of the white and 85 percent of the black workers sampled reporting satisfaction with their jobs.

JOB SATISFACTION, DISSATISFACTION, AND WORKER BEHAVIOR

Absenteeism and Tardiness

The tendency for individuals to associate with people whose presence is reinforcing and to avoid people whose presence is punishing will be discussed in Chapter 12. The same approach or avoidance tendencies hold true for work. Individuals who are not satisfied or happy at work—that is, who find little reinforcement in their jobs—will tend to miss work or show up late occasionally. This is because from time to time some alternative more attractive than going to work will arise, such as taking a three-day weekend trip or staying in a warm bed on a cold, rainy morning. Individuals who are really unhappy at work—that is, who are punished by certain aspects of their jobs—will tend to avoid these punishments through chronic tardiness or absenteeism.

Even if you have not worked regularly, you have probably experienced the same tendencies in attending classes. Some class you may find reinforcing. You are interested in the subject, or you like the instructor's approach, or you sit with close friends, or the classroom is comfortable, or there is some combination of these factors. You tend to "get in the habit" of going to that class every day. Another course you may find neither reinforcing nor punishing. The subject is neither very dull nor very interesting, the instructor's approach is neither exciting nor repelling, none of your friends are in the course. You tend to go to class because you've paid for it, because you're afraid you'll miss something which will be on the next exam, because most people go, because you feel you need to learn the material. However, you don't mind being late once in a while (the instructor never starts on time, anyway), and if friends come up with a boat and skis some warm spring afternoon, you'll probably be long gone and hard to find when class time rolls around. Occasionally you have a course which you feel is pure torture, usually a required course outside your major field of interest. The instructor lectures right out of the book, or perhaps he turns each class into a rap session, which you feel forces you to listen to the irrelevant babblings of students who know less about the subject than you do. The room is uncomfortable, the building clear across campus, and the class meets at 8:00 in the morning (or 4:30 in the afternoon). Two or three times the instructor has failed to show up for class—always unannounced. In this case you will probably welcome excuses for cutting class, including slight headaches, doctor's appointments, and studying for other exams.

In the same way, studies of absenteeism have shown that workers whose job satisfaction is low tend to have higher rates of absenteeism than their more satisfied colleagues. Research has found that relatively dissatisfied workers record a greater number of absences per year and also have a greater number of one-day absences. For example, one study investigated the satisfaction of 160 nonsupervisory female employees in a regional office of a national insurance company.[25] The employees were all at least high school graduates, ranging in age from late teens to early sixties. Employee satisfaction with specific facets of work (such as job itself, pay, co-workers, achievement, supervision) and overall satisfaction were measured by two attitude scales. Frequency of absences was recorded for each employee for the following year. The results of correlational analysis showed that overall satisfaction was significantly related to subsequent frequency of absences. Dissatisfied workers had significantly higher rates of absenteeism than satisfied workers ($r = .28$, $p < .01$).

Turnover

Dropping out of school is a considerably more extreme form of withdrawal or avoidance of dissatisfaction than cutting a few classes. In the same way, quitting a job is a much more extreme step than merely being late or taking a day off. The major difference to the employee is that he needs to consider both the psychological and material costs of quitting, together with possible alternatives to that job—that is, whether he can get work somewhere else.

A theory of interpersonal attraction which we discuss in Chapter 12 provides a framework for examining the relationships between

---

[25] L. K. Waters and Darrell Roach, "Relationship between Job Attitudes and Two Forms of Withdrawal from the Work Situation," *Journal of Applied Psychology*, vol. 55, no. 1 (1971), pp. 92–94.

satisfaction and turnover. Briefly, this theory states than an individual's tendencies to leave a relationship depend upon the rewards and costs he thinks he is getting from the relationship (outcomes), the rewards and costs he thought he was entitled to from the relationship (comparison level), and the rewards and costs he thinks he could obtain from another relationship if he left the present one (alternatives). According to the theory, a person is dissatisfied when his outcomes are below his comparison level. However, he is unlikely to leave the relationship unless his alternatives exceed his comparison level. Applying this theory to job turnover, we would expect both satisfaction and the availability of alternatives to affect rates of turnover.

All the major reviews of research on satisfaction and turnover indicate that high turnover is associated with job dissatisfaction. For example, the study of female insurance employees reported above also investigated turnover.[26] Excluding employees who resigned because of pregnancy, there was a significant negative correlation between measures of job satisfaction and termination during the following year. That is, those employees who expressed greatest dissatisfaction were most likely to quit. A subsequent study by the same researchers of two more groups of female clerical workers yielded similar results.[27] Employee dissatisfaction among workers in both groups was a reliable predictor of both frequency of absences and quitting. The consistency of this relationship is emphasized in a recent review of research in this area.[28] Of 13 studies reviewed, including populations of insurance salesmen, student nurses, lower level managers, retail store employees, and Air Force pilots, only one failed to find dissatisfaction related to turnover.

Research evidence also supports the idea that one's alternatives play a significant role in making a decision to quit. If turnover due to death, disability, and being drafted is excluded, it is found that turnover increases during periods of rising employment. Looking at national trends in employment, the Bureau of Labor Statistics finds that annual fluctuations in the rate at which manufacturing workers quit their jobs are strongly related to changing rates in job oppor-

---

[26] Ibid., pp. 92–94.

[27] L. K. Waters and Darrell Roach, "Job Attitudes as Predictors of Termination and Absenteeism: Consistency over Time and across Organizational Units," *Journal of Applied Psychology*, vol. 57 (June 1973), pp. 341–42.

[28] L. W. Porter and R. M. Steers, "Organizational, Work, and Personal Factors in Employee Turnover and Absenteeism," *Psychological Bulletin*, vol. 80 (August 1973), pp. 151–76.

tunities.[29] According to the Department of Labor, "It is possible to account for more than 80 percent of the variation in rates of turnover by considering the business cycle alone."[30]

There is no doubt from the evidence, then, that satisfaction and turnover are *related*, particularly when other job opportunities are readily available. As you may recall from Chapter 2, however, longitudinal or experimental research gives us more confidence in stating that one variable *causes* another. One such set of studies has demonstrated not only that dissatisfaction leads to higher rates of turnover but also that the effects of dissatisfaction vary for different groups of workers. These studies have followed a large group of workers for several years, collecting data on their satisfaction and job history, including changing jobs and unemployment.

The researchers found that job satisfaction expressed by women 18 to 25 years old is an excellent predictor of whether or not they changed jobs. Women, both black and white, who said they like their jobs only "fairly well" were much more likely to change jobs than those who liked their jobs "very much."[31] Among women 30 to 44 years old, satisfaction expressed in 1967 was a reliable predictor of job changing during the next three years.

However, the tendency for dissatisfied women to leave their jobs diminished as their tenure with the company increased.[32] Tenure also lessened the effects of dissatisfaction on turnover for male workers with less seniority.[33] It is likely that senior workers in this group perceived the costs of leaving and losing seniority as greater, and perhaps their chances of obtaining a better job as lower, than their colleagues with less seniority.

Another longitudinal study also found that individual differences moderated the satisfaction-turnover relationship.[34] For men, dissatisfaction with pay was the best predictor of turnover, but for women,

---

[29] Harold Wool, "What's Wrong with Work in America?: A Review Essay," *Monthly Labor Review*, vol. 96 (March 1973), pp. 38–44.

[30] U.S. Department of Labor, *Job Satisfaction: Is There a Trend?* p. 25.

[31] Roger Roderick and Joseph Davis, *Years for Decisions: A Longitudinal Study of the Educational and Labor Market Experience of Young Women* (Columbus: The Ohio State University, 1973), pp. 29, 32.

[32] Sookoon Kim, Roger Roderick, and John Shea, *Dual Careers: A Longitudinal Study of the Labor Market Experience of Women* (Washington, D.C.: U.S. Government Printing Office, 1973), vol. 2, pp. 55–56.

[33] Herbert Parnes, Gilbert Nestel, and Paul Andrisani, *The Pre-Retirement Years: A Longitudinal Study of the Labor Market Experience of Men* (Washington, D.C.: U.S. Government Printing Office, 1973) vol. 3, p. 37.

[34] Thomas Mangione, *Turnover—Some Psychological and Demographic Correlates* (Ann Arbor, Mich.: Survey Research Center, 1973).

the best predictor was dissatisfaction with working conditions. Workers with more than three years' seniority were most likely to quit when they expressed dissatisfaction, not with pay but with the interest and challenge of the job itself.

Productivity

"A happy worker is a good worker" is a persistent belief of many practicing managers. In Chapter 20 it will be shown how such a belief induces some managers to practice "country-club" leadership. They concentrate their managerial efforts on making workers as happy and comfortable as possible, expecting high effort and productivity in return. But is job satisfaction actually related to productivity? And if so, does satisfaction lead to productivity, or instead, does productivity lead to satisfaction?

The notion that job satisfaction leads to performance grew out of interpretations of early social-psychological research in industry. In the most famous of these studies, the Hawthorne studies, it was found that the productivity of a group of telephone equipment assembly women improved over time, regardless of increments or decrements in the quality of their working conditions. The only variable measured which seemed to increase with productivity was the workers' morale. From these studies, students of management and managers themselves leapt to the erroneous conclusion that "there is greater production . . . when workers are satisfied with their jobs. Improve the morale of a company and you improve production."[35]

Unfortunately, the conclusion was so appealing that a sound theoretical explanation as to why satisfaction should lead to performance was never developed. Without this theory, the research tended to consist of a large number of systematic assessments of satisfaction and performance. As Chapter 2 noted, such systematic assessments can tell us whether relationships among two or more variables exist, but they cannot determine causality.

While some early studies did find positive correlational links between satisfaction and productivity, subsequent and somewhat more rigorous research yielded mixed results. In some studies the two variables were positively related, in some they were negatively related, and in others they were not related at all. A major review

[35] W. E. Parker and R. W. Kleemeier, *Human Relations in Supervision: Leadership in Management* (New York: McGraw-Hill Book Co., 1951), p. 10.

of that research led to the conclusion that the evidence did not suggest a consistent relationship between satisfaction and productivity.[36] A review of 20 subsequent studies reached the same conclusion: Satisfaction and productivity are not necessarily related.[37] Certainly there is no theoretical or empirical basis for continuing to believe that satisfaction leads to improved performance.

There is, however, some support for the argument that, under certain conditions, performance leads to satisfaction. In Chapter 4, the expectancy model diagrammed in Figure 4–4 suggests that the effort the individual puts into performance is, among other things, a function of the perceived probability that that effort will lead to some reward. If one were working in a system which in fact rewards good performance, one would therefore expect performance and satisfaction to be positively related. Indeed, one would expect that high performance eventually would lead to high satisfaction, as a result of the rewards obtained for high performance.

For example, consider a number of recruiters competing against each other for the same group of recruits. These recruiters, who value both winning in competition and money, are paid bonuses based on their relative success over a recruiting season. At the end of the season, those who have signed the best crop of recruits obtain the greatest satisfactions, both from winning and from their bonuses. Those who have signed the poorest group of recruits are relatively deprived, both from losing in competition and from missing out on the bonuses. In this case it would be possible to predict satisfaction from prior performance.

There is evidence that performance does lead to subsequent satisfaction but only under certain conditions, not all of which have at this time been specified. Studies have found that the effects of performance on satisfaction depended upon occupation,[38] organization level, and skill level.[39]

A study described earlier clearly demonstrates the variability of the nature of the relationship between satisfaction and perfor-

[36] A. H. Brayfield and W. H. Crockett, "Employee Attitudes and Employee Performance," Psychological Bulletin, vol. 52 (1955), pp. 396–424.

[37] Victor Vroom, Work and Motivation (New York: John Wiley & Sons, 1964).

[38] R. E. Doll and E. K. E. Gunderson, "Occupational Group as a Moderator of the Job Satisfaction–Job Performance Relationship," Journal of Applied Psychology, vol. 53 (1969), pp. 359–61.

[39] J. W. Slocum, R. B. Chase, and D. G. Kuhn, "A Comparative Analysis of Job Satisfaction and Job Performance for High and Low Skilled Operatives," Experimental Publication System, April 1970.

mance.[40] The researchers argued that there is no sound theoretical basis for a causal relationship between satisfaction and performance. Instead, they argued, both satisfaction and performance result from other variables; satisfaction results from being rewarded, and performance results from being rewarded for prior performance. Therefore, depending upon conditions, satisfaction and performance might appear to be positively related or negatively related, or might not appear to be related at all.

To test these propositions, workers were hired to score some aptitude tests. The workers were told that, in addition to everyone being paid an hourly rate, the best workers would receive a bonus doubling their pay. After working for one pay period, performance and satisfaction measures were taken for all workers. However, bonuses were given, not to the best workers, but randomly to half the best workers and half the poorest workers. The workers then went back to work for the second period, after which performance and satisfaction were measured, and bonuses were awarded as before.

The researchers hypothesized that receiving a bonus would increase satisfaction, regardless of performance. They further hypothesized that performance during the second period would depend on whether one's bonus for the first period had been related to performance. For purposes of analyses, then, there were four groups of workers, as depicted in Figure 11–4.

FIGURE 11–4

First-Period Performance \ Bonus at End of First Period	Awarded	Not Awarded
High	1	2
Low	3	4

There were equal numbers of workers in each category. Workers in categories 1 and 3 (those who received bonuses) indicated significantly greater satisfaction in general, and with pay, fellow workers, the task itself, and their own competence, than did workers in categories 2 and 4. Clearly satisfaction depends on rewards and not

---

[40] Cherrington, Reitz, and Scott, "Relationship between Satisfaction and Task Performance."

on performance. During the second pay period, as hypothesized, workers in categories 1 and 4, who were appropriately reinforced, significantly outproduced workers in categories 2 and 3, who were inappropriately reinforced.

Table 11–4 shows that satisfaction and performance were clearly

TABLE 11–4
Prior Characteristics and Subsequent Performance

| Category | First Period | | | Second Period |
	Performance	Bonuses	Satisfaction	Performance Rank
1	High	Yes	High	2
2	High	No	Low	4
3	Low	Yes	High	3
4	Low	No	Low	1

unrelated in this experiment. Workers in categories 1 and 3 were most satisfied at the end of the first period, and workers in categories 2 and 4 were least satisfied. Yet workers in categories 1 (most satisfied) and 4 (least satisfied) performed best in the second period, while workers in categories 2 (most satisfied) and 3 (least satisfied) performed least in the second period. In fact, the greatest increase in productivity came from the least satisfied group, category 4.

SUMMARY

An attitude is a persistent or enduring tendency to feel and act in a particular way toward some object. An attitude is composed of beliefs, emotional feelings, and behavioral tendencies. We acquire attitudes through direct experience with an object, by associating it with other objects, and by learning them from other people. Attitudes can be reinforcing, help organize information and experience, express values, and sometimes serve to protect the individual from anxiety.

Job satisfaction and dissatisfaction are attitudes of particular interest to managers. Individuals are capable of expressing their satisfaction or dissatisfaction with many different aspects of their work. Various reliable and useful instruments for measuring these attitudes are currently available to researchers and managers.

People experience job satisfaction from rewarding aspects of their work. These may include performing interesting and challenging work; receiving money, recognition, or esteem; achieving goals; working with compatible supervisors and co-workers; and having pleasant working conditions.

Large-scale studies of worker satisfaction in the United States suggest that, contrary to many opinions, workers in general appear to be at least as satisfied today as they were 15 years ago. For the past several years, some 90 percent of workers sampled have reported that they were satisfied with their jobs. Among these workers, managers and technical and professional people report greater satisfaction than blue-collar workers do, and older workers tend to be more satisfied than their younger colleagues.

Job satisfaction is of concern to managers because it is related to important employee behaviors. Satisfied workers have lower rates of absenteeism than dissatisfied workers and tend to quit or change jobs less frequently. Tardiness, apathy, and sabotage are often expressions of dissatisfaction. However, research evidence does not suggest that satisfied workers are necessarily more productive than dissatisfied workers. Productivity is affected by many factors other than satisfaction, as we discussed in Chapters 4 and 5.

QUESTIONS FOR REVIEW AND DISCUSSION

1. What kinds of attitudes are most difficult to change? Give an example of such an attitude.

2. Describe the affective, cognitive, and behavioral components of your attitude toward big business.

3. How confident are you of the accuracy of the cognitive components of the attitude you expressed for Question 2? From what you learned about perception and evaluation in Chapter 6, how might some affective components of your attitude have affected the cognitive components?

4. What is your attitude toward working for industry? What were the sources from which your attitude developed? What functions does it serve for you?

5. How would you go about the task of assessing the satisfaction and dissatisfaction of the students on your campus with their courses?

6. What specific factors might affect student satisfaction with a course?

7. What are some ways in which students express their satisfaction and dissatisfaction with courses?

8. List the factors which are most likely to affect a student's performance in a course.

9. What are the differences between your answers to Questions 6 and 8?

KEY WORDS

Attitude
Affective component
Cognitive component
Behavioral component
Consistency
Job satisfaction

Stereotype
Knowledge function
Instrumental function
Value-expressive function
Ego-defensive function

part four
Bases of Group Behavior

12
Interpersonal Attraction and Group Formation

13
Group Development and Structure

PART FOUR builds a foundation for understanding the behavior of groups and the behavior of individuals as members of groups in organizations.

Chapter 12 examines the nature of groups and describes types of groups commonly found in organizations. It suggests why groups are prevalent features of organizational life by describing the functions groups perform for individuals. It enumerates the variables that attract individuals to established groups or encourage them to form new groups. The chapter concludes by presenting a model of the factors that influence an individual's attraction to and dependence upon an interpersonal relationship.

Chapter 13 describes the processes through which groups develop, from formation to maturity. It discusses certain characteristics which evolve as groups develop: roles, status, and cohesiveness. It presents the implications of these characteristics for organizations, particularly role conflict, status inequities, and the effects of cohesiveness on group relations and performance.

Objectives

1. To examine the nature of groups and types of groups commonly found in organizations.
2. To discuss the importance of groups for individuals and the bases for interpersonal attraction.
3. To present a model which describes factors influencing individual attraction to a relationship.

chapter twelve

Interpersonal Attraction and Group Formation

Tallahassee, Fla. (AP)—An 18-year-old Florida State freshman nearly killed after being dragged 80 feet by a car following a fraternity hazing incident says he sees nothing wrong with the tradition and still hopes to join the fraternity.

"I think there should be a certain amount of pledging hassle to make you show your desire for joining the fraternity," said Steven Butdorf, who faces six more weeks in the hospital after being admitted in critical condition on April 20.

Butdorf, who had both legs broken, underwent skin graft surgery Tuesday for deep abrasions received when he was thrown out of a moving car and dragged underneath the vehicle.

The West Palm Beach youth said he and another pledge—candidates for fraternity admission—were dragged out of the Theta Chi fraternity house and taken on a "road trip" by four fraternity members who left them stranded on a deserted road outside the city.

The two youths began hitchhiking back to campus when Butdorf was picked up by a car of youths, who sped off without taking the other candidate, Butdorf said.

He said he was taken a short distance when he was pushed out of the car, caught underneath the vehicle and dragged. He was discovered by the other youth.

The Leon County sheriff's office has impounded the van used by the fraternity in the hazing trip but investigators refused comment on why.

"It was the first road trip I have ever been taken on and all the other fraternity members feel real bad about what happened," Butdorf said. "Road trips are just a part of the game of pledging."

All fraternities on campus engaged in various forms of hazing despite college rules against the practice, Butdorf said.

He said he hoped to return to Florida State, where he is a pre-veterinary major, next fall.

"I hope at that time I will be able to join the fraternity," he said. "I was so close to initiation I want to go ahead and finish."[1]

---

[1] *Gainesville Sun*, May 1, 1974. Reproduced by permission of the Associated Press.

MOST PEOPLE who read the news story above will marvel at Steven's desire to join a fraternity—a desire seemingly intensified, rather than diminished, by his close brush with death. Yet his behavior demonstrates two fairly common human tendencies.

One is that most people, particularly upon becoming members of a large organization (like a state university) are strongly inclined to seek membership in some smaller group. This inclination, which we will consider in this chapter, is part of the reason for the development and continued existence of fraternities, sororities, clubs, and other social organizations on most college campuses. It is also demonstrated by the pervasive existence and influence of informal groups in all organizations—educational, military, religious, governmental, industrial, or oriented to health or service.

A second point Steven's experience demonstrated is that severe initiation rites often increase the attractiveness of a group for its members. This tendency, demonstrated both in laboratory research and in the field, is recognized and capitalized on by certain groups and organizations which purposely make entrance requirements stringent in order to attract and hold members. This tendency will be discussed and explained in the next chapter.

Chapters 12 and 13 provide a basis for understanding the social and group behaviors to be discussed in Part Five. This chapter describes the nature of groups and different types of groups commonly found in organizations. It examines the reasons why people form groups and factors which attract individuals to groups and organizations. The next chapter describes the processes of group development and certain characteristics of group structure which evolve as a group develops.

THE NATURE OF GROUPS

This chapter could have been entitled "Gregarious Behavior." *Gregarious* means sociable, companionable, being fond of the company of others. The fields of anthropology, psychology, and sociology all agree that human beings are gregarious—they are social animals. People are attracted by others and seek out their companionship. They are particularly reinforced by lasting, face-to-face relationships with a small number of people like themselves. Such relationships are called groups; they can be found in every area of human activity, including work and organizational behavior.

The essential characteristics of a group are: (1) two or more people, who (2) interact with one another, (3) share some common ideology, and (4) see themselves as a group.

Characteristic (2) means that the members at least occasionally meet, talk, and do things together. They do not all have to meet at the same time, but in order to be a group member, a person must have occasional contact with one or more of the others.

Characteristic (3) means that the group members have something in common. They might share a goal, such as protecting their jobs; or a concern, like security; or the same prejudices or values; or they might face a common threat. Whatever its basis, the group has something in common which gives it and its members some identity.

Characteristic (4) results from (2) and (3). People who interact with one another and who share some common ideology are usually attracted to one another. The reinforcement they receive from interacting with one another leads them to identify with one another and eventually to perceive themselves as something special, as a unique group. As we will note throughout the rest of this book, group membership has very important implications for the behavior of those who belong.

Types of Groups

Sociologists and psychologists who study the social behavior of people in organizations identify several different types of groups. Examples of each of these types of groups can be found in most large organizations.

Formal and Informal Groups   A formal group is one that is deliberately created to perform a specific task. Members are usually appointed by the organization, but this is not always the case. A number of people assigned to a specific job form a formal group. One example of such a group is a committee, and other examples are work units, such as a small department, a research and development laboratory, a management team, a small assembly line, or a clean-up crew. Examples of nonindustrial formal groups include an operating room team, an artillery gun crew, a police special weapons unit, the defensive unit in football, and the string section of an orchestra.

An informal group is one that arises out of the interactions, attractions, and needs of individuals. Members are not assigned; rather, membership is voluntary and depends upon the mutual attraction of the individual and the group for each other. Informal groups often develop within formal groups out of certain values or concerns which some members find they share. They may also develop across or outside of formal groups. For example, a nurse may find herself in a small informal group within a surgical team because certain members share a fear and dislike of a certain surgeon. She may belong to a group of nurses and other medical personnel who share a respect for life which unites them against hospital practices such as abortion and euthanasia. She may be the only nurse in a third group of people who share a common interest in parachute jumping.

A classic study of industrial organizations described three types of informal groups.[2] The most common type in the organizations studied were called *horizontal cliques*. Membership was restricted to people of similar rank and the same work area. The operating room clique to which the nurse in the example above belongs is an example of a horizontal clique.

A *vertical clique* is composed of people from different hierarchical levels within the same department. Such groups often develop out of a shared need for security or accomplishment, or a common interest which overcomes the social distance between superiors and subordinates. For example, during periods of high turnover, the old-timers may have more in common with one another, regardless of rank, than they would have with newcomers of similar rank. Their experiences and knowledge of the way things are really run form a bond.

A *random clique* is composed of people of various ranks, departments, and locations. Often such an informal network is composed of people who "get things done" and who share a common interest in avoiding red tape, bypassing the bureaucracy, and enhancing one another's power. Such cliques can become very powerful. Sometimes membership is facilitated by common membership in other organizations; the members may all happen to belong to the same political party, or lodge, or church. For example, it was found that members of a random clique of managers all belonged to the local yacht club and the order of Masons.

Open and Closed Groups   Another basis for classifying groups is whether they are open or closed.[3] At one extreme is the completely open group, which is in a constant state of change; at the

[2] Melville Dalton, *Men Who Manage* (New York: John Wiley & Sons, 1959).
[3] R. C. Ziller, "Toward a Theory of Open and Closed Groups," *Psychological Bulletin*, vol. 64 (1965), pp. 164–82.

other extreme is the completely closed group, which is quite stable. Open groups differ from closed groups along four dimensions: changing group membership, frame of reference, time perspective, and equilibrium.

Changing Group Membership. An open group is constantly adding and losing members. A good deal of time is devoted to socializing new members. A closed group maintains a relatively stable membership, with few additions and losses in members over time. Power and status relationships are usually well established and fixed. One result of these differences is that new members have relatively more power in an open than a closed group.

Frame of Reference. The high rate of turnover in an open group helps it to expand its frame of reference. New members bring new perspectives to the group's activities and problems. Because new members of open groups are somewhat more powerful than their counterparts in closed groups, they may be less hesitant to challenge current perspectives of the group. The expanded frame of reference in an open group also can enhance creativity. The stability of membership in closed groups, on the other hand, usually results in a relatively narrow frame of reference. Lacking the challenge from new members who bring in fresh ideas, a closed group can become very unlikely to change its established perspectives.

Time Perspective. The instability and constant change of an open group make it difficult for the group to maintain long time horizons. Since membership may be brief, members' perspectives for group activities are oriented toward the present or very near future. In contrast, the stable membership of a closed group enables it to maintain a much longer time horizon. Many of the members recall the history of the group, and their expectations for continued long association enable them to use long-term planning. Orientation to the future is aided by the group's historical perspective; as the saying goes, "The past is but a prologue to the future."

Equilibrium. Equilibrium is the extent to which a balanced system, after having been disrupted, returns to a state of balance or stability. A constant state of disequilibrium, imbalance, or disruption is obviously detrimental to group performance. Thus an open group must develop methods for counteracting the disequilibrium of constant change. Increasing the size of the group is suggested as one method of maintaining equilibrium.[4] The larger the group, the less it will feel the impact of any one member's leaving or joining. The

---

[4] Ibid.

more heterogeneous or diverse the membership, the more easily it
can absorb new members; the possibility of a new member finding
others with which he is compatible is increased. Another means of
increasing equilibrium may be through associations of former members, such as alumni associations and veterans organizations, or associations of prospective members, such as the Junior Chamber of
Commerce, fraternity and sorority pledge classes, Young Republicans and Democrats, and Future Farmers of America.

Any organization may have both open and closed groups. Many
groups whose function is evaluation or review may be relatively
open. For example, membership on a promotion committee is often
limited to one or two years, and terms are staggered so that half the
members are replaced every year. Student groups may also be
relatively open, as most students have sufficient time or interest for
only a couple of years, and they typically maintain short time horizons relative to the group's activities. Boards of directors typically
are relatively closed groups; they have been described by critics as
"self-perpetuating cliques" whose members hold sufficient votes or
proxies to reelect themselves each year. The closed nature of such
groups enables them to develop a historical perspective and to engage in long-term planning, often at the cost of developing new
perspectives.

Differences between open and closed groups can generate quite
different perspectives and values, and this can lead to conflict. This
outcome will be discussed in Chapter 17.

Reference Groups   One characteristic of individuals discussed
in Part Three is their tendency to seek feedback about themselves.
Each person from time to time feels a need to evaluate himself and
his performance: Am I doing well or doing badly? Am I right or
wrong? Is my behavior acceptable or offensive to others? Are my
attitudes typical or unique?

A reference group is any group to which an individual belongs
(or sometimes aspires to belong) and which he uses as a standard
for self-evaluation and/or as a source of his personal values and
attitudes. The group is said to provide two functions for the individual: *social comparison*, in which he evaluates himself by comparing himself to other members, and *social validation*, in which he
uses the group to evaluate his attitudes, beliefs, and values.

In serving these two functions, reference groups wield a good
deal of influence on behavior in organizations. This influence can
be observed in prejudice and stereotyping, in work restriction and

rate busting, in mutiny and conformity. It can be both productive and counterproductive for individuals as well as for organizations, as we will note in the discussion of groups and social behavior in Part Five.

An extreme example of how reference group processes operate was provided by an aspect of the Korean War. The importance of such groups to individual functioning was understood and dramatically demonstrated by the Chinese Communists in their treatment of U.S. prisoners during that war.[5] The apparent goals of their treatment of U.S. POWs were to reduce escapes and attempts to escape and to "reeducate" them to accept the Communist philosophy. The overall approach was to reduce or eliminate the interpersonal bonds which had previously united POWs against their captors, as evidenced in true and fictionalized accounts of U.S. POWs in World War II executing mass escapes, harassing their captors, and generally resisting attempts to induce cooperation with the enemy. The Chinese wished to avoid such prisoner behavior and set out to undermine such group solidarity systematically.

For example, all leaders and key personnel around whom the men could rally were segregated. Mail was screened, allowing only bad news (union strikes in defense industries, deaths and illness at home, "Dear John letters") to filter through to the prisoners. Opportunistic prisoners were used to spy and sow doubt and suspicion among other POWs. Organized activities such as religious services, sports, social gatherings, and classes were strictly forbidden. Individuals were tricked into small "confessions" which were then used to further doubt and suspicion among POWs that "everybody else" was collaborating with the enemy.

As a result, "the systematic manipulation of communications and social relationships among prisoners produced a degree of social alienation which was characterized in most men by a systematic withdrawal of involvement from *all* social situations . . . giving up attempts to establish relationships with other persons."[6] Lacking group solidarity, the POWs made few attempts to escape or to harass their captors. Organized resistance was almost nil. Without reference group pressures, many collaborated with the enemy, giving information and signing confessions. A few refused repatriation to the United States at the end of the war.

---

[5] See E. H. Schein, "Interpersonal Communication, Group Solidarity, and Social Influence," *Sociometry*, vol. 23 (1960), pp. 148–61.

[6] Ibid., p. 151.

While the overall results were not the great military disaster many in this country claimed them to be, they shook the morale of both the military and the civilian population. Rumors of mysterious "brainwashing" and "thought control" techniques spread, but these mysterious forces were revealed to be nothing more than a sophisticated understanding of reference groups and a systematic method for reducing their influence. Deprived of such groups for social support and evaluation, many prisoners became doubtful, insecure, and susceptible to the influence of their captors. Significantly, those whose reference group identifications were strong and transcended the boundaries of the camp, and those to whom the enforced solitude and time for meditation could serve as sources of strength and improved self-concepts (such as strongly religious individuals) tended to be most resistant to attempts to induce collaboration.[7]

JOINING GROUPS

Groups are everywhere. They pervade every facet of organized and unorganized human activity, from the nuclear family to the scientific laboratory. The universal nature of groups raises two questions: Why do people join groups? Why does a given individual join a particular group?

Reasons for Joining Groups

Basic explanations for people's propensity to form and join groups are as varied as the approaches to understanding any human behavior. A psychoanalytic approach might suggest that group formation is an instinct inherited from the primal family of the earliest forms of Homo sapiens, when protection and survival were the motivating forces. A cognitive approach might suggest that people join groups because they have expectations that membership will benefit them, or because they associate groups with positive outcomes, or because they have developed favorable attitudes toward groups. An operant approach would simply explain that most people have experienced positive reinforcement from social and group behavior.

Whatever basic approach is taken, it is possible to outline any

[7] For greater detail in the theory and analysis of the Communist Chinese indoctrination program, see E. H. Schein, Inge Schneier, and Curtis Barber, *Coercive Persuasion* (New York: W. W. Norton Co., 1961).

number of reasons for forming and joining groups. We will limit our discussion here to reasons for forming or joining groups in organizations. Several reasons can be discovered by examining the various needs or categories of rewards considered in Chapter 5: affiliation, security, esteem, power, identity, and accomplishment.

Affiliation   One reason why people join groups is that they enjoy the regular company of other people, particularly those with whom they share something in common. Their experiences with others indicate that they are likely to obtain friendship, friendly interaction, and acceptance by others if they are "in" with some group. People at work as members of organizations are as reinforced by such things as they are outside of work. Many people who work long hours every day may have little opportunity for social interaction off the job. Their requirements for affiliation must be satisfied on the job, or not at all.

Security   Perhaps the strongest basis for group formation among the first humans was security and satisfaction of physiological needs for food and shelter. Even in modern organizations, people experience feelings of insecurity which can be alleviated by group membership. An individual joining a large impersonal organization can experience anxiety because he realizes he is giving up some control over his behavior and is uncertain how the system works. Joining a group whose members have already experienced and survived the initial period of organizational life is an effective means of reducing such anxiety. One can learn the ropes and become a part of an established information network faster by joining a group than by going it alone. In fact, this capacity for informal groups to socialize new members into the organizational routine gives them a good deal of power over new members—even if the new member is formally their leader. "Well, we've got to break in a new supervisor this week," is not a rare comment among established work groups during changes in managerial assignments.

Studies of American infantrymen in combat have revealed an often fanatic devotion among small groups of men.[8] A soldier's associations with other members of his squad or fire team enable him to alleviate anxieties about the uncertainties of war by discussing rumors and self-doubts and by discovering that others are basically as afraid as he is.

---

[8] S. A. Stouffer, A. A. Lumsdaine, M. H. Lumsdaine, R. M. Williams, Jr., M. B. Smith, I. L. Janis, S. A. Star, and L. S. Cottrell, Jr., *The American Soldier*, vol. 2: *Combat and Its Aftermath* (Princeton, N.J.: Princeton University Press, 1949).

Esteem   An individual can increase his self-esteem through group membership. First, one can gain esteem by becoming a member of a high-status group. Getting in with the "in" crowd is both intrinsically and extrinsically rewarding. Associating with high-status people is reinforcing, and one who belongs to such a group is usually accorded high status by outsiders.

Second, the close relationships an individual can develop as a group member provide opportunities for recognition and praise that are not available outside the group. If the members hold similar attitudes and values, individuals may be highly reinforced for expressing their opinions and views. The group provides an atmosphere in which members feel safe, even encouraged, to express themselves, whereas outside the group they would be reluctant or apprehensive about such self-expression. A worker may feel free to gripe and complain about his work, his boss, or his pay to his group, knowing that others will agree and he need not fear that anyone will contradict him or that his complaint might get back to his supervisors.

Power   Group membership can be a source of power in two different ways. First, there is the notion that "united we stand, divided we fall." Student groups organized as a means of gaining and exercising some control over their fate in the college environment have had varied success in changing curricula and academic and administrative regulations and in giving students a sense of power. This same advantage has been the driving force behind unionization: Collectively, workers enjoy much greater power than they do as individuals. Even belonging to an informal group gives the individual a sense that his group will not let him be overcome by the impersonal bureaucracy of the organization.

Informal groups also provide individuals with opportunities to exercise power over others. By becoming the leader of an informal group, a person can exert influence over group members even if he does not occupy a formal position of authority in the organization. One attractive feature of informal group power is that such a leader can avoid the responsibilities that usually go with formal positions of power.

Identity   Group membership contributes to the individual's eternal quest for an answer to the question "Who am I?" According to the psychological concept of the looking-glass self, we do not see ourselves directly, but only as reflected in the behavior of others toward us. Most of our information about ourselves comes from other people. If people laugh at my jokes, I come to think of myself as a funny person. If people are attentive to my words, I see myself as important. If I have trouble getting dates, I see myself as unattractive.

As a member of a group, I can get more of this information for several reasons. First, my experience with other members gives me confidence in interpreting their reactions. I can distinguish good-natured kidding from serious criticism, for instance. Second, the group members' experience with me gives them a better basis for evaluating my personality and behavior. I feel they can distinguish short-term from long-term changes, for example. Finally, I feel that friends will be more willing to give me information that others might not. The remark, "Even her best friend won't tell her" suggests that only in extreme cases will someone close to us refrain from giving us important feedback about ourselves.

Accomplishment   Groups may form simply because it takes more than one person to accomplish a certain task, or because the task is made easier through cooperative effort. Several people may form a group to share knowledge about a common problem. They may need to pool their talents, their tools, their contacts, or their power to get something done. Even if the task is only temporary, as long as they are interacting and share the common ideology of accomplishing the task, they will come to see themselves as a unit. Thus they will meet our definition of a psychological group.

The Bases of Interpersonal Attraction

The reasons why particular individuals are attracted to one another and are led to form a specific group can be described as the bases or determinants of interpersonal attraction. These determinants include opportunity to interact, status, similar backgrounds, similar attitudes, personality characteristics, and success.

Opportunity to Interact   The most important basis for interpersonal attraction and group formation is, simply, the opportunity to interact. Obviously, people who never see or talk to one another are unlikely to be attracted to one another. But beyond such obvious effects, research has indicated that environmental factors which increase or decrease the opportunity to interact directly affect interpersonal attraction and group formation.

Physical Distance.   Other things being equal, people who live close to one another or who work close to one another have more opportunities to interact than people who are physically distant. Thus we would expect to find more close relationships among people who are located close to one another than among those located far apart.

Observations of people at work confirm this expectation. When clerical workers in a large corporation were observed and interviewed, it was found that the distance between their desks was the most important determinant of the rate of interaction between any two employees.[9] In turn, employees who interacted frequently developed bonds of friendship. Identical relationships among physical distance, interaction, and attraction have been found in research and development laboratories and college faculty office buildings. Even in bomber crews, members showed greater attraction for those whose seat locations allowed most frequent interactions.[10]

Architecture and Psychological Distance. Physical distance is not the only barrier to social interaction. Architectural arrangements also affect opportunities to interact and ultimately have an influence on interpersonal attraction. Some architectural factors create physical or psychological barriers between physically close individuals; others promote interaction.

Studies of office layouts, for example, reveal that clusters of offices with doors opening into a central location, such as a reception area, secretary's work space, or elevator waiting area, promote interaction and attraction among occupants of the offices (see Figure 12–1). Arrangements in which offices are placed side by side discourage interaction, especially between occupants of offices at opposite ends of the corridor (see Figure 12–2).

Psychological distance is often a result of other opportunities to interact. Occupants of offices A and G in Figure 12–2 are less likely to interact, not only because of the physical distance between them but because offices B through F provide alternative opportunities to interact which they may feel they must bypass in order to interact with each other.

Architectural arrangement also affects the development of friendships and cliques at home. Figures 12–3 and 12–4 depict the patterns of social interaction which developed among neighbors in rental units and private homes in Park Forest, a large suburban development outside Chicago.

---

[9] John T. Gullahorn, "Distance and Friendship as Factors in the Gross Interaction Matrix," *Sociometry*, vol. 15 (1952), pp. 123–34.

[10] D. M. Kipnis, "Interaction between Members of Bomber Crews as a Determinant of Sociometric Choice," *Human Relations*, vol. 10 (1957), pp. 263–70.

FIGURE 12–1
Offices Arranged to Promote Interaction

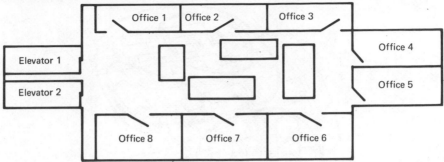

All offices open onto the secretarial-reception area, and there is common access to elevators.

FIGURE 12–2
Offices Arranged to Discourage Interaction

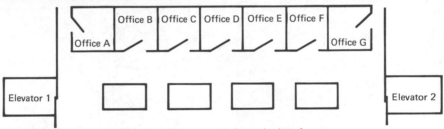

Common areas are minimized; offices A and G are isolated.

Status Once individuals are provided with an opportunity to interact, status is often an important factor in determining who will be attracted to whom. There are two tendencies in this area—individuals are attracted by others of similar status, and individuals like to interact with people of high status, given the opportunity to do so.

As an example of the effects of status, researchers observed the interaction of individuals attending a one-day professional conference.[11] High-prestige members preferred to interact with one another, but those low in professional status were more attracted by the high-prestige members than by one another.

Similarity of Backgrounds Do "opposites attract," as the saying goes, or do "birds of a feather flock together," as another saying

[11] J. I. Horowitz, H. F. Zander, and Bernard Hymovitch, "Some Effects of Power on the Relations among Group Members." In Dorwin Cartwright and Alvin Zander, *Group Dynamics*, 2d ed. (Evanston, Ill.: Row, Peterson, 1960), pp. 800–809.

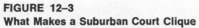

FIGURE 12–3
What Makes a Suburban Court Clique

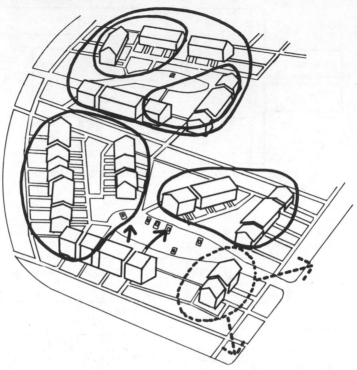

In the rental courts formed around parking bays social life is
oriented inward. In the large court at the bottom, for example,
wings whose backdoors face each other form natural social units.
Buildings sited somewhat ambiguously tend to split the allegiance
of their inhabitants, or else, like the lonely apartment unit at lower
right, isolate them. Smaller courts like the one at the top are
usually more cohesive; and though there may be subgroupings,
court people often get together as a unit.

suggests? Relationships between interpersonal attraction and similarity in demographic characteristics such as age, sex, religion, educational attainment, race, nationality, and socioeconomic status
have been extensively investigated. Reviews of this research generally provide evidence that individuals tend to be attracted to
others of the same or similar socioeconomic status, religion, sex, and
age.[12] However, the effects of similarity on attraction are neither
overwhelming nor universal. Individual characteristics which de-

[12] H. J. Lott and B. E. Lott, "Group Cohesiveness as Interpersonal Attraction:
A Review of Relationships with Antecedent and Consequent Variables," *Psychological Bulletin*, vol. 64 (1965), pp. 259–302.

FIGURE 12–4
How Suburban Homeowners Get Together

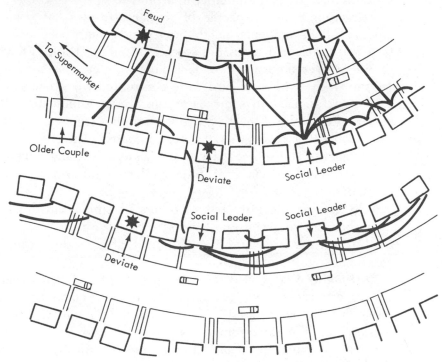

(1) Individuals tend to become most friendly with neighbors whose driveways ad-
join theirs. (2) Deviates or feuding neighbors tend to become boundaries of the
gang. (3) People in the most central positions make the greatest number of social
contacts. (4) Street width and traffic determine whether or not people make friends
across the street. (5) People make friends with those in back of them only where
some physical feature creates traffic—such as the short-cut pavement one woman
on the lower street uses on her way to the supermarket.

Source: W. H. Whyte, Jr., *The Organization Man*. Copyright © 1956 by William H.
Whyte, Jr. Reprinted by permission of Simon and Schuster.

termine interpersonal attraction may vary from situation to situation. For example, the same person may be most strongly attracted
to people with similar job tenure at work and people of the same
religion away from work.

Similarity of Attitudes   One reason for attraction between people
of similar demographic characteristics may be similarity of attitudes. As we noted in Chapter 11, personal experience and experiences related to one person by others are important sources of
that person's attitudes. People of similar backgrounds are more
likely to have had similar experiences and personal contacts than

people of dissimilar backgrounds. Therefore, similarity of backgrounds may indicate similarity in attitudes.

Attraction between people of similar attitudes has been found among college students, neighbors, friends, married couples, military personnel, and industrial workers. Similar attitudes have been found to overcome major socioeconomic differences such as race. In one study, white subjects were confronted by either a white or a black stranger.[13] In some cases the stranger indicated attitudes agreeing with the subject's attitudes, ranging from religion to television; in other cases, the stranger indicated attitudes contrary to the subject's. The subject's feelings toward the stranger were found to be a direct function of attitude similarity and unrelated to racial similarity.

Why are people attracted to others of similar attitudes? Most likely because they consider support for their attitudes to be highly reinforcing, particularly those attitudes that are value expressive or ego defensive in nature.

Personality Characteristics   Are people attracted to others with similar, opposite, or complementary personality characteristics? The research evidence suggests that personality compatibility is an important factor in determining the strength and duration of interpersonal relationships. Compatibility may result from personality similarity, such as the attraction between two individuals high in dogmatism, or from complementarity, such as the attraction between an individual high in dominance and another high in subservience. It has been suggested that the important factor in personality is that one is attracted to others whose personalities confirm one's own self-concept. A person who sees himself as one who needs to be dominated will be attracted to others who are dominant.[14]

Success   "Nothing succeeds like success." One basis for this observation is the fact that successful groups and individuals attract others and their resources. Successful companies attract new employees; successful colleges attract faculty, students, and donations. Winning teams find that recruiting is relatively easy—a matter of selecting the best of those who are eager to join a successful program. A college recruiter with a good chance to land a local basketball superstar once revealed that his greatest fear was that the

[13] Donn Byrne and T. J. Wong, "Racial Prejudice, Interpersonal Attraction, and Assumed Dissimilarity of Attitudes," *Journal of Abnormal and Social Psychology,* vol. 65 (1962), pp. 246–53.

[14] P. F. Secord and C. W. Backman, "Interpersonal Congruency, Perceived Similarity, and Friendship," *Sociometry,* vol. 27 (1964), pp. 115–27.

Wizard of Westwood (Coach John Wooden of the perennial national champion, UCLA) would pick up the phone, casually indicate his interest, and the prospect would be gone in a flash.

Experimental and field research confirms these observations. Successful groups attract new members and hold current members better than unsuccessful groups do. In addition, people like and tend to interact with successful individuals more than with unsuccessful individuals.

Most of the bases for interpersonal attraction can probably be explained by either a simple reinforcement or an expectancy approach. Status and success are attractive because high-status, successful people are usually rewarded, both financially and socially. Similarity in backgrounds and attitudes is a basis for attraction because people expect others like themselves to reinforce attitudes and values they already hold. But none of these factors can operate unless people have the opportunity to interact. Parents and governments alike have recognized this basic fact, and restrictions on the movements of people have long been used to prevent undesirable associations.

A Model of Interpersonal Attraction

In Chapter 11 we briefly discussed a model of interpersonal attraction and explained some determinants of employee turnover. This model describes an individual's attraction for a relationship—with another individual, a group, or an organization—as a function of the rewards and costs the individual associates with the relationship.[15]

In this model, *rewards* include all satisfactions and pleasures which the individual derives from a relationship. *Costs* are any factors that operate to inhibit or deter the individual from interacting in the relationship. Costs could include physical effort or mental effort, embarrassment, anxiety, or conflict, as well as financial costs. Distance between the individual and the other party to a relationship is an example of a cost involving physical and mental effort, as well as money. Being required to commute 50 miles a day to work is a cost of many individuals' job relationships.

Three variables are said to determine the individual's attraction

[15] J. W. Thibaut and H. H. Kelley, *The Social Psychology of Groups* (New York: John Wiley & Sons, 1959), pp. 9–30.

to a relationship: outcomes (O), comparison level (CL), and alternatives (A).[16] *Outcomes* are all the rewards and costs associated with the relationship. *Comparison level* is the standard against which the individual evaluates his satisfaction with the relationship; it is the minimum reward-cost position he feels he deserves from the relationship. Outcomes and comparison level are depicted graphically in Figure 12–5. In example (A), the outcomes the indi-

FIGURE 12–5
Outcomes and Comparison Level as Variables Determining Satisfaction

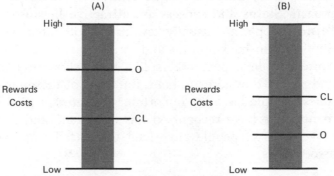

The relative positions of outcomes (O) and comparison level (CL) determine an individual's satisfaction with a relationship. Satisfaction is high if outcomes exceed expectations (A) and low if the reverse is true (B).

vidual receives from the relationship are above his comparison level. According to the model, the individual is satisfied. In example (B), outcomes are below his comparison level; in such a case, he is dissatisfied with the relationship.

Alternatives can be defined as the lowest level of outcomes a member will accept in the light of available alternative models. That is, alternatives are the outcomes the individual would expect to get from his best alternative relationship. A simple example might be an engineer making $15,000 per year who lives in San Diego. Outcomes to his job relationship would be his $15,000 salary, plus whatever other rewards and costs are associated with his present job. Suppose he knew of three other jobs he could get, the best of which paid $16,000 but was in Pocatello, Idaho. In this case

---

[16] Thibaut and Kelley use the term *comparison level of alternatives. Alternatives* is used here as a shorter and less confusing term.

the *alternatives* would be the $16,000 he could get from the Poca-
tello job, plus whatever other rewards and costs he would expect
from that job, including the psychological and financial costs of
moving from San Diego to Pocatello.

The model uses an individual's outcomes, comparison level, and
alternatives to predict his attraction to and dependence on a relationship. Outcomes and comparison level indicate his satisfaction
with the relationship: If outcomes exceed his comparison level, he
is satisfied. If outcomes are below his comparison level, he is dissatisfied. Outcomes and alternatives determine his dependence
on the relationship: If outcomes greatly exceed alternatives, he is
highly dependent on the relationship. If alternatives exceed outcomes, he is not dependent on the relationship for favorable
outcomes.

According to this model, then, dependency is not necessarily correlated with attraction. Under certain circumstances, a person may
be dependent upon a relationship which is not satisfying to him—
he has no better alternatives.

The model can be used to generate the six different outcome–
comparison level–alternative situations depicted in Figure 12–6. In
situation 1, the individual is satisfied with his present relationship
(O > CL), and he is not greatly dependent on it (although O > A,
A would still be a satisfactory alternative, since A > CL). An ex-

FIGURE 12–6
Six Outcome–Comparison Level–Alternative Situations

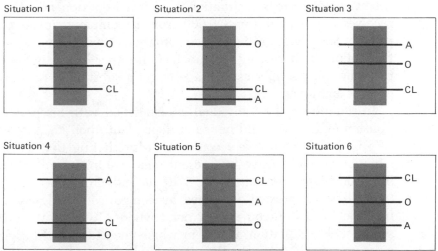

Satisfaction is a function of outcomes and comparison level; dependence is a
function of outcomes and alternatives.

ample of situation 1 might be a new graduate who has several good job offers, at least two of which exceed his minimum criteria. He accepts the best offer but retains an acceptable alternative should this job go sour for some reason (rewards decrease and/or costs increase).

In situation 2, the individual is again satisfied ($O > CL$) with his present relationship, but he is greatly dependent on it, because his best alternative is far below the outcomes of his present relationship ($O > A$). In fact, his best alternative would not be satisfactory ($CL > A$). In such a situation, the individual's dependency on the relationship is said to exceed his attraction for it $(O - A) > (O - CL)$. An example of situation 2 might be the engineer making $15,000 in San Diego. Suppose he loved San Diego so much that he would be dissatisfied with a job in any other location, regardless of salary. If the only engineering job in San Diego which met his salary requirement was the one he already had, then he would be satisfied with it but very dependent upon it.

In situation 3, the individual is satisfied with his present relationship ($O > CL$), but this time he is not dependent on it. His best alternative would not only be very satisfactory ($A > CL$), but he expects it to be even better than his present relationship ($A > O$). It is possible that the individual might leave the present relationship for the greener pastures offered by the alternatives, or he might use his independence as a lever to increase his outcomes from his present position. For example, suppose the San Diego engineer in the example above is in situation 2 (satisfied but dependent), and he receives a job offer for $20,000 from a company opening a new plant in San Diego. Moving from situation 2 to situation 3 gives him the option of increasing his satisfaction either by changing jobs or by using the job offer as leverage to get a substantial raise from his present employer.

In situation 4 the individual is dissatisfied with his present relationship ($CL > O$), and he is not dependent upon it ($A >> O$ and $A > CL$). We would feel confident in predicting that a person in situation 4 would leave his present relationship. In fact, situation 4 often develops from situation 3. If an individual has alternatives better than his present outcomes, his comparison level may increase from below his outcomes to a point where $CL > O$. We often describe such a situation as one in which the individual's aspirations have increased. A World War I song which asked "How ya gonna keep 'em down on the farm after they've seen Paree?" predicted dissatisfaction with the old life for U.S. soldiers who had experienced Paris and other exotic places during the war.

In situations 5 and 6, the individual is dissatisfied ($CL > O$). He is probably also frustrated, since in neither situation is his best alternative satisfactory ($CL > A$ in both situations). The model describes both of these situations as being nonvoluntary relationships: The individual is trapped in a dissatisfying relationship for lack of satisfactory alternatives.

Situation 5 could be an unhappy marriage in which the wife is very dissatisfied but views divorce or separation as dissatisfactory alternatives. She is miserable living with her husband, but she expects that even though she would be better off without him, she would still be miserable. Many a country and western song has lamented such situations.

Situation 6 is probably the worst of all. Present outcomes are not satisfactory, but the only alternatives are worse. A person in prison or a concentration camp might find himself in such a situation: Death may be the only alternative he perceives to prison life.

Predicting what someone in situation 5 or 6 will do is difficult. If possible, he may search for alternatives until a satisfactory ($A > CL$) one is found. If the search is impossible or fruitless, his comparison level may drift downward to a point where it matches either O or A. Such a situation is usually described as one in which the individual has "adjusted to the situation" or has "become resigned to his fate." Once in a while, a person in situation 6 will find the prospect of continued outcomes so bleak that he chooses the alternative; suicide among prisoners is not rare.

SUMMARY

Groups are a pervasive, universal feature of human activity, both within and outside of organizational life. People are attracted to formal and informal groups because they serve a wide variety of functions for individuals. In organizations, groups are particularly attractive sources of identity, security, power, esteem, and accomplishment for individuals.

Individuals are attracted to forming relationships with groups and other individuals by several characteristics. In organizations, the primary bases for interpersonal attraction are frequent opportunities to interact, status, success, and similarities in attitudes.

An individual's attraction to a specific interpersonal or group relationship can be thought of as consisting of two relatively separate components: his satisfaction with the relationship and his comparison level for evaluating his outcomes. Dependence is a function of present outcomes and perceived alternative opportunities.

Because group membership is such a highly reinforcing aspect of organizational life, groups have considerable influence on individual behavior and organizational activity. Managers need to learn to deal with and work with groups as well as individuals. The next chapter describes some important characteristics of groups and their implications for management.

QUESTIONS FOR REVIEW AND DISCUSSION

1. What is the difference between a group and an organization?

2. What functions do reference groups perform for individuals?

3. Would you expect most reference groups in organizations to be formal or informal? Why? Give an example of a formal and an informal reference group for an industrial worker.

4. What would you expect to be the bases for formation of informal groups among (a) medical doctors, (b) managers in a large business organization, (c) police officers, (d) civil service employees in a government agency?

5. List two formal or informal groups to which you belong. What first attracted you to those groups? What factors are primarily responsible for your continuing to belong to those groups?

6. Are attraction to and dependence upon a relationship necessarily related? Explain.

7. Turnover in industry tends to be higher in times of industrial expansion than during recessions. Use the model of interpersonal attraction to explain this tendency.

KEY WORDS

Group	Social validation function
Informal group	Psychological distance
Formal group	Outcomes
Open group	Comparison level
Closed group	Alternatives
Reference group	Dependence
Social comparison function	

Objectives

1. To present a model of group development.
2. To discuss the concept of group maturity.
3. To describe three characteristics of group structure—roles, status, and cohesiveness—and to discuss some of their implications for management.

OUTLINE OF CHAPTER

Group Development
  Developing Power and Authority
   Structures
    Orientation
    Conflict
    Cohesion
  Developing Interpersonal Relationships
   Delusion
   Disillusion
   Acceptance
  Group Maturity
Roles
  Role Set
  Role Conflict
   Types of Role Conflict
   Implications of Role Conflict
Status
  Sources of Status
   Reward Power
   Receiving Rewards
   Personal Investment
  Equity in Status

Cohesiveness
  Sources of Cohesiveness
   Interpersonal Attraction
   Threat
   Severity of Initiation
   Cooperation
   Group Size
  Effects of Cohesiveness
   Communication
   Evaluation
   Hostility and Expressions of
    Aggression
   Conformity and Influence
   Task Performance
Summary
Questions for Review and Discussion

chapter thirteen

Group Development and Structure

DOONESBURY

Copyright, 1973, G. B. Trudeau. Distributed by Universal Press Syndicate.

THE NATURE OF GROUPS commonly found in organizations, the reasons for group formation, and factors which enhance the development of interpersonal relationships and the attractiveness of groups were discussed in the preceding chapter. This chapter will describe the process by which strong groups develop from the first tentative interpersonal relationships. Then three characteristics of group structure which aid the understanding of group behavior in organizations—roles, status, and cohesiveness—will be examined.

GROUP DEVELOPMENT

Groups, like individuals, go through various stages of development once they have been formed. The group development process has been studied intensively in an attempt to discover regular patterns of development. Such knowledge would be useful to both group members and leaders who are interested in increasing the effectiveness and efficiency of groups.

Observations of group processes (and our own experiences) indicate that some groups can behave both effectively and efficiently, while many others are neither effective nor efficient. In fact, though they are formed with strong purposes and nobel intentions, some groups never accomplish anything. This failure could be due to impossible goals, or to lack of ability, or to factors beyond the group's control. But it could also be due to the fact that the group failed to develop to a stage where it could cope with itself and its environment.

Students of the group development process describe it as a struggle to progress from immaturity to maturity, just as developmental psychologists might describe the development of a child. That is, a group must learn a lot about itself and its functioning, sometimes through a painful process before it can cope realistically and effectively with its environment. The development process to be described here is an amalgamation of the processes observed and described by several different psychologists and psychotherapists.[1] In particular, it is based on the process described by participant observations during a five-year study of group development processes.

Developing Power and Authority Structures

There is general agreement that the first major activity of a newly formed group is to get itself oriented and organized. Observers suggest that there are two major obstacles group members must deal with and resolve before the group can reach maturity. The first is members' uncertainties about authority and how power will be distributed among them. Resolving these uncertainties is the major theme of the first phase, which can be broken down into three subphases: orientation, conflict, and cohesion.

Orientation   The orientation subphase of initial group activity is characterized by a good deal of uncertainty. Members are anxious to clarify the group's purpose, their own roles as members, how much they want to commit themselves to the group, and how the group will be structured. Much time is spent trying to define the group's goal, and in relating personal experiences and anecdotes both relevant and irrelevant to the task. The group is usually very dependent upon the formal leader, or someone who assumes leadership in an

---

[1] W. G. Bennis and H. S. Shepard, "A Theory of Group Development," *Human Relations,* vol. 9 (1965), pp. 415–57; B. W. Tuckman, "Developmental Sequence in Small Groups," *Psychological Bulletin,* vol. 63 (1965), pp. 384–99; I. D. Yalom, *The Theory and Practice of Group Psychotherapy* (New York: Basic Books, 1970), chaps. 10 and 11.

informal group. The members seek guidance, direction, and structure from the leader.

Conflict   The conflict subphase usually involves rebellion in one form or another against the direction and guidance of the leader. Some members simply test the leader's authority, power, and decisiveness; others may actually challenge his or her leadership. This is often done subtly by continued questioning of the leader's directions, delays or failures to execute them, or engaging in behavior irrelevant to the group's task. The group may divide into two camps—one subgroup supporting the leader and another not doing so, or one group supporting the status quo and another seeking to restructure the power relationships within the group.

Cohesion   Many groups never develop past the second subphase. Their activities are continually characterized by infighting, rebellion, and foot-dragging. Others move into the third subphase—cohesion—in which the members have worked through their differences and uncertainties regarding power and authority and have developed a structure upon which they agree. The transition to cohesion is often accomplished through the effort of a member who is relatively independent with regard to authority and power—he or she neither fears nor seeks it, and develops the trust of others who are trying to resolve their own problems regarding dependence. The cohesion phase is often marked by feelings and expressions of relief and commitment and comments such as "Now we really are a group."

Developing Interpersonal Relationships

Having resolved their uncertainties regarding authority and power, the group must next overcome a second obstacle on the road to maturity—uncertainty about their relations with each other. In this phase, the members must work through their problems about how close or intimate they will become and how willing they are to reveal and accept each other's differences. Many groups who successfully develop through the first phase make little progress in phase 2, often because of the unwillingness of some members to deal with the emotional aspects of interpersonal relations and individual differences. Resolving these issues is the theme underlying phase 2, in which three subphases can often be observed: delusion, disillusion, and acceptance.

Delusion   The delusion subphase often follows once the group has overcome its difficulties with power and authority. Cohesiveness and harmony are a relief, and the group deludes itself into believing no further problems need be resolved. Any evidence of interpersonal conflict or differences among members is ignored or glossed over, since members are unwilling to recognize that problems still exist. They try to cover up differences and often sacrifice their individual identity or repress personal idiosyncracies for fear of creating problems.

Disillusion   Eventually the group realizes that problems do exist. Some members want to be very open and close to the group; others resist attempts at intimacy and identification. Subgroups form, and feelings that "we're not working together like we should" become evident. One subgroup may consist of members who wish to express their individuality and deal with interpersonal differences. Another subgroup may develop around those who wish "to stick to business" and who refuse to increase their commitment to other members. There may be a tendency to become highly dependent on the leader again as a means of avoiding these interpersonal problems.

Acceptance   Many groups fail to develop beyond the disillusion phase. They settle into a loose federation of subgroups or cliques whose common bond is reduced to working on the group's task. But some manage to deal with and work through interpersonal differences, usually through the informal leadership of one or more members who are not threatened either by intimacy or by the lack of it. In this phase, members discuss differences and reach accommodations on how to deal with them. Subgroups dissolve, and relationships develop around the needs of the group's task and the unique qualifications of each individual. Communications among members are frequent and realistic. The group has reached maturity.

Group Maturity

A group which has developed to maturity essentially is characterized by openness and realism. Some of the characteristics of mature groups are described as follows:

1. Individual differences are accepted, without being labeled either good or bad.
2. Conflict is over real, substantive issues relevant to the group task, rather than over emotional issues regarding group structure or processes.
3. Decisions are made through rational discussion, including and

encouraging dissent. No attempts are made to force decisions or to present a false unanimity.

4. The members are aware of the group's processes and the extent of their own involvement in it.[2]

Group maturity is thought to promote group effectiveness because it allows the group to make full use of its resources. Individual talent and abilities are not withheld from the group's task out of fear, spite, or neglect. Individual effort is directed toward the group effort rather than toward internal power struggles, cliques, or scapegoats.

Most people have probably had little experience with mature groups. In many cases groups do not work out their own power and authority structure but have this structure imposed on them by outside forces. Some members of such a group accept this structure, some are indifferent or apathetic to it, and others reject it by ignoring it, actively trying to overthrow it, or subverting decisions made by those in authority. Look back over your own experiences with student groups or as a member of a group assigned to some class project. Was the power structure accepted by all the members? Were individual differences accepted? How much of the group's time and effort was wasted on activities unrelated to the group task?

It would seem that the characteristics of openness, encouraging dissent, realistic communications, and avoiding false unanimity are particularly important for effective group decision making, which will be the topic of Chapter 15. In that chapter we will see how, lacking such characteristics, groups composed of the best and the brightest individuals can make incredibly disastrous decisions.

ROLES

One characteristic of group structure that is often used in analyzing behavior in and of a group is the set of roles defined for group members. A *role* is a set of expectations about the behavior of someone occupying a given position in a social unit. When we describe someone as "playing the role of the model employee," for instance, we mean that that individual's behavior is consistent with our expectations about the way an ideal employee should behave. Most groups have roles labeled *leader* and *followers,* and the group has expectations about how the leader and the followers will behave. Other typical group roles might be labeled *expert, enforcer, troublemaker,* and *scapegoat.*

---

[2] Bennis and Shepard, "Theory of Group Development."

Role Set

Most individuals occupy several roles. An executive may occupy the roles of president of his company, father of his children, husband of his wife, elder in his church, chairman of a fund-raising drive, director of the hospital board, and lover to his mistress. Certain expectations regarding his behavior develop about each of these roles.

For each role the individual has a role *set*, comprised of those who interact with him in his role and who thus have expectations about his behavior in the role. In his role as president, his role set would encompass employees and stockholders, and customers, officials, and community leaders with whom he interacts. In his role as father, his role set would probably be limited to his children, wife, parents, and his children's teachers. In his role as lover, the role set might consist only of his mistress and perhaps the doorman at her apartment. An individual's role set is important because of the pressures its members often place on the individual in trying to induce him to conform to their expectations.

Role Conflict

The demands of organizational life often create role conflict for the individuals filling the roles. This conflict results from varying expectations as to how the individual is expected to behave in a given role.

Types of Role Conflict   Role conflict can occur in three different forms: intraperson, intrarole, and interrole.

Intraperson Conflict.   A clash between an individual's feelings, values, and attitudes and his or her role can result in intraperson conflict. This type of conflict occurs when something one is expected to do in one's role is incompatible with what one feels one can or should do as an individual.

Intraperson conflict is a quite common source of hesitation, indecision, and misgivings in organizational behavior. A teacher's role may call for him to assign individual grades, and this may conflict with his personal philosophy that grades hinder learning. A politician's role may demand that she associate with, and even be friendly to, people she despises. A supervisor's role may call for dismissing an inept employee, conflicting with her personal feelings about putting someone out of a job. A physician's role may demand that he appear decisive and confident in his diagnoses at times when he is neither. Several examples of intraperson conflict were publicized during the latter stages of U.S. military involvement in Vietnam, when the role expectations for the behavior of pilots conflicted with the personal values of some officers occupying those roles.

Intrarole Conflict. A lack of consensus among members of an individual's role set on how he is to perform that role can produce intrarole conflict. When two or more members of a person's role set express different expectations for his behavior, the occupant of that role finds it impossible to satisfy everyone's expectations.

Intrarole conflict is a common source of strain for occupants of certain positions in organizations. In particular, individuals who occupy either middleman or boundary-role positions are likely to suffer intrarole conflict.

A familiar example of the *middleman* is the first-line supervisor or foreman. The most influential members of his role set are the employees he supervises and his own immediate supervisors. Typically, his employees expect him to act in their best interests, to represent their interests to management, and to protect them from arbitrary management policy and decisions. His immediate supervisors expect him to represent management, to act in the best interests of the organization, and to see to it that management policy is enforced and management decisions are carried out. Other middleman roles subject to intrarole conflict of this type include quality control inspectors, who are often caught between the demands for quality and quantity, and agents, brokers, congressmen, judges, policemen, referees, and umpires.

A *boundary role* is a position which requires the occupant to interact with people outside the organization. A boundary role occupant often spends more time outside the organization than in it, and his success often depends upon the extent to which he can satisfy outside people. Such a person must appear to the outsiders to be acting in their best interests at the same time he appears to the organization to be acting in its best interests.

A good example of a boundary role is the outside salesperson, who may spend 90 percent of his time with his customers. His success may depend on the extent to which his customers will see him as being "on their side" because he makes real or apparent concessions on the organization's behalf, such as price discounts, early delivery, special terms, product changes to customer specifications, or kickbacks. Such a salesperson often finds himself fighting with the home organization on behalf of a customer.[3]

Other examples of boundary roles which generate intrarole conflict for their occupants include union and management labor negotiators, news correspondents, public relations specialists, and foreign diplomats. Certainly during Henry Kissinger's tenure as Secretary of State that position developed into a boundary role in which he often spent more time outside the country than in it, and expectations for his behavior by countries among whom he was negotiating conflicted with expectations for his behavior by many members of Congress and members of his own State Department.

Interrole Conflict. Conflicting expectations for an individual's behavior can arise from the fact that he or she occupies multiple roles. To those who occupy several roles, interrole conflict is familiar. An executive who simultaneously occupies the roles of president, father, husband, church elder, drive chairman, director, and lover could easily find himself in situations in which two or more of his roles demand behavior which conflicts. The demands on his time as president may conflict with his wife's expectations for entertaining guests, his children's expectations for a family vacation, and his church's expectations for attendance.

Examples of multiple roles in which a single occupant would probably be subject to interrole conflict include a mother with a full-time job, a priest involved in politics, a teacher who does research, a college administrator who teaches, and a student-athlete.

Implications of Role Conflict The effects of role conflict can be as mild as slight tension or occasional hesitation, or as severe as complete indecision, acute anxiety and stress, frustration, dissatisfaction, or leaving the position. It is not possible to eliminate role conflict completely as long as the role occupant retains a sense of personal values, has more than one person in his or her role set, or occupies more than one role.

However, some positions provide more opportunities for role conflict than others, as we have pointed out with examples. Both organizations and the present or aspiring occupants of such positions should be aware of the possibilities of role conflict and its consequences. Sometimes the anticipation of role conflict can lead to measures

---

[3] For a brief review of research on boundary roles, see J. A. Wall, Jr., "Some Variables Affecting a Constituent's Evaluation of and Behavior toward a Boundary Role Occupant," *Organizational Behavior and Human Performance*, vol. 11 (1974), pp. 390–408.

which can alleviate it, such as establishing priorities or rules of thumb to reduce the chances of indecision or anxiety. Organizations may seek individuals with demonstrated capacities for coping with psychological stress to fill positions where role conflict is high. Sometimes expectations or duties can be temporarily changed to avoid the pressures of role conflict. For example, "conflict-of-interest" situations which occasionally make local or national news are often simply examples of interrole conflict, such as that experienced by a judge whose court must rule on a case involving an organization he owns or is affiliated with. In such cases conflict is avoided by temporarily removing the individual from one of his roles: The judge removes himself from the case, or the tycoon places his financial holdings in a blind trust before assuming a high public office.

STATUS

Status is a measure of worth conferred on an individual or on a position by some social group. It is the relative standing of that individual or position in the estimation of other people. A person who is granted high status is ranked as more worthy in certain respects than most of the other people with whom he is compared. A job that is described as low status is considered of low value, compared to other jobs in the organization or the profession or trade.

An individual's status may be granted by people in general, or it may be ranked by a single group or organization. A high-status person or position in one culture may have no status to those outside that culture. The world champion bull rider may be the highest status person on the rodeo circuit but just another cowboy to the international jet set. The skills, characteristics, and achievements which give him great esteem among rodeo aficionados are of no value to those in high society.

A few individuals or positions have almost universal high status. Heads of state of powerful countries are generally granted high status outside their own country. Medical doctors are generally accorded high status everywhere; physicians are usually found at the top of the status hierarchy in national polls ranking the esteem of various occupations.

Table 13–1 gives the relative prestige of selected occupations as rated by a large sample of Americans in 1947 and in 1963. It is interesting that the correlations between the two sets of rankings were extremely high, almost 0.99.

TABLE 13-1
**Prestige Rankings of Selected Occupations in the United States,
1947 and 1963**

	Rank	
Occupation	1947	1963
Supreme Court Justice	1	1
Physician.	2.5	2
Scientist	8	3.5
College professor	8	8
U.S. congressman or senator.	8	8
Lawyer	18	11
Architect.	18	14
Psychologist	22	17.5
Member of board of corporation	18	17.5
Civil engineer	23	21.5
Airline pilot	24.5	21.5
Banker	10.5	24.5
Accountant	29	29.5
Factory owner.	26.5	31.5
Economist	34	34.5
Insurance agent	51.5	51.5
Traveling salesman	51.5	51
Bartender	85.5	83

Source: Adapted from R. W. Hodge, P. M. Siegel, and P. H. Rossi, "Occupational Prestige in the United States," *American Journal of Sociology,* vol. 70 (1964), pp. 290–92, by permission of the University of Chicago Press, © 1964 by the University of Chicago. All rights reserved.

Sources of Status

Sociologists and psychologists have studied individuals of various status ranks to determine the general characteristics that seem to confer high status. They have found the following sources of status:

Reward Power People who have the ability to confer upon others rewards which they value are given high status by those others. The value of the rewards and the status of the person conferring them seem to depend upon the scarcity of the rewards. For example, promotions are generally valued by most members of organizations, so superiors who have the power to promote usually are accorded high status. However, if everyone in the organization is regularly and routinely promoted, then power to promote does not in itself confer high status.

Being the sole source of a certain reward usually confers high status. The personnel director of a firm which is hiring new employees during a recession may have high status in the eyes of job applicants. In times of high employment when every company is competing for workers, the personnel director's status may diminish.

Receiving Rewards   Persons who receive rewards valued by a group, class, society, or culture are accorded high status by those who value the rewards. One who is knighted by the queen will be held in high esteem by her subjects, but among those who ridicule or despise monarchy knighthood will be seen as conferring little or no status. Being named "employee of the month" may confer little status on a worker, while getting a $2,000 raise or winning the Irish sweepstakes may raise his esteem considerably in the eyes of his co-workers.

Here too, scarce rewards seem to confer more status than abundant ones. The student who gets the only A in a large class will have more status than if half the class received As. A scientist whose work is published in a journal which rejects 80 percent of the articles submitted will receive higher status for his effort than one whose work is published in a journal which accepts everything submitted to it.

Personal Investment   Incurring high costs can be a source of high status in some circles. People who exert great effort or take great risks to achieve a goal are often accorded high status. An unknown boxer who fights the heavyweight champion gets high status, however fleeting, for the risks he takes. Evel Knievel is a prime example of a person who achieved great status (and, not accidentally, modest wealth) by taking risks few others would dare. Young people the world over have faced the temptations of high status through great risk, from the drag racer of the fifties to the drug experimenter of the seventies, from the young Masai collecting a lion's mane with spear and knife to the young Hungarian attacking a Russian tank with homemade fire bombs.

Sacrifice and seniority are other means of acquiring status through costs. At certain times in various cultures, those who burned the most grain, slaughtered the fattest calf, sacrificed the most beautiful daughter, lost the most sons in battle, or made the largest cash contribution were given highest status. In most organizations, seniority confers status and certain privileges and rewards as well. Seniority may allow one to avoid hard physical work, have first chance at new openings, be the last laid off, call the boss by his first name, or refuse to be traded.

Equity in Status

People in organizations are not as uncomfortable with status differences as one might think. In fact, they seem to be more comfortable interacting in a group when status differences are clear and recognizable. However, status differences can cause problems if they are perceived as in some way inequitable.

We have said that status is a relative thing: One has high or low status in comparison to someone else. In making such comparisons, people tend to look for justification of status differences. Two principles which they are said to apply in such comparisons are called distributive justice and status congruence.

Distributive justice is a principle which suggests that we expect the rewards of each individual to be proportional to his costs or investments.[4] If a person perceives that his rewards and costs relative to his investment in the organization are roughly proportional to those of other members, he feels justified. If, however, he perceives that his rewards are disproportionately small, given his costs and investment, he will feel angry and dissatisfied. As a result of perceived injustice, people may lower their investments, strive to increase their own rewards or to lower those of others, or leave the organization.

Status congruence exists when all the characteristics of an individual in a higher status position are greater than the characteristics of those in lower status positions. Characteristics covered by status congruence include achievements, ability, costs, and rewards. An example of status congruence would be a hospital administrator who has more experience, receives better evaluations, works longer hours, receives a larger salary, has a bigger office, and drives a more expensive car which he parks in a better place than any staff member at the hospital who is not a doctor. Incongruence would exist if a subordinate made more money or had a larger, plusher office.

Status congruence, like distributive justice, seems to make interpersonal interaction easier by reducing uncertainties about how an individual should be addressed. The eccentric millionaire who drives an old clunker and wears cutoffs and sandals to the office often has a good laugh on a new employee who mistakes him for a vagabond. However, the uncertainties introduced by one's status incongruence make it difficult for others to anticipate how he will respond, and this can lead to interpersonal conflict.

Status incongruence can lead to feelings of frustration and dissatisfaction. Individuals low in congruence, especially those who perceive status conferred on them by others to be lower than the

---

[4] George C. Homans, *Social Behavior: Its Elementary Forms* (New York: Harcourt, Brace, 1961), p. 75.

status of their achievements, may react in many ways.[5] Some may advocate or be receptive to changes in the organization which will increase their status congruence. Others may withdraw, fail to participate, or behave in other ways characteristic of dissatisfied individuals, as discussed in Chapter 11. Still others may try to increase those factors that they perceive as too low in status. For example, a highly productive researcher may strive for an office, salary, or influence equal to that of a highly competent administrator.

COHESIVENESS

A characteristic of groups which is especially important for the behavior of their members is *cohesiveness,* or the extent to which the members are attracted to each other and to the group. Obviously, members must be at least minimally attracted, or the group would cease to exist.

Cohesiveness has been described as the sum of the forces acting on the members to remain in the group and as the number and strength of positive attitudes shared by the members. Cohesiveness grows out of the attraction of the members for one another and for the group as a whole.[6]

Sources of Cohesiveness

Cohesiveness in groups can be affected by such factors as interpersonal attraction, threat, severity of initiation, cooperation, and group size.

Interpersonal Attraction   If cohesiveness grows out of the attraction of members for each other, then all the bases of interpersonal attraction we discussed in Chapter 12 ought to influence group cohesiveness. And they do. Groups whose members have lots of opportunity to interact, groups with high status, groups whose members have similar backgrounds and similar attitudes, successful groups, and groups with successful members—all tend to have greater cohesiveness than groups without these characteristics.

---

[5] J. G. Hunt, "Status Congruence: An Important Organization Function," *Personnel Administration,* vol. 32 (1969), pp. 19–27.

[6] This section draws heavily on research reviewed in A. V. Lott and B. E. Lott, "Group Cohesiveness as Interpersonal Attraction: A Review of Relationships with Antecedent and Consequent Variables," *Psychological Bulletin,* vol. 64 (1965), pp. 259–302.

Threat   The effects of threat upon cohesiveness comprise a well-worn story plot: A group of strangers is thrown together in a lifeboat from a sinking ship. Their common fate and mutual dependence swiftly transform these strangers into a strong group united in their desire to survive. Such a plot has a solid foundation in research evidence. Threat is an effective means for producing cohesiveness when the following conditions exist:

1.   The threat comes from outside the group.
2.   Cooperation can help resist or overcome the threat.
3.   There is little or no chance for escape.

There is a good deal of history in the use of threat to increase cohesiveness, even among large numbers of people. Military commanders taking over loose, sloppy, demoralized outfits have successfully pulled the men together by harsh discipline which unites them in their need to cooperate in order to survive the threat posed by the commanders. Such commanders were portrayed in two eminently successful movies of men in combat: Gregory Peck in *Twelve O'Clock High* and George C. Scott in *Patton*. Even national leaders attempt to increase national solidarity through propaganda, and they often succeed. Playing up the threat to national survival presented by some external force can be effective, particularly when that external force is a tangible threat. For example, the Arabs and the Israelis, the Russians and the Chinese certainly have unifying effects on one another.

Severity of Initiation   The story of fraternity hazing which introduced Chapter 12 illustrates a somewhat remarkable human tendency: The more difficult it is to gain admission to a group, the more cohesive the group becomes. This effect can be accomplished in different ways.

One is to set high standards for membership. Schools that require very high grade point averages and test scores for admission, and companies that require excellent grades, superior recommendations, and prior success for hiring, both enjoy a certain status and prestige which rubs off on the members. One effect is to tend to increase their attraction for the group. This same effect can be achieved by making the group members believe they are uniquely qualified or part of an elite.

A somewhat different approach is to require prospective members to sacrifice in order to gain admission. Severe initiation procedures often unite members in the knowledge that each of them has endured the unendurable. The seemingly meaningless initiation rites and pledge hazing practices of fraternities and other secret societies are open to question, particularly where there is danger of physical or psychological harm, but such experiences tend to unite the often disparate group of strangers which endures them together.

Elite military organizations achieve the same results through boot camp and other training experiences. Marines, Green Berets, Rangers, and UDT personnel (frogmen) reflect an esprit de corps which is enhanced by the severity and rigor of the physical and emotional stresses they must overcome in seeking membership.

Cooperation Sometimes the general atmosphere of a group enhances cohesiveness. As we will discuss further in Chapters 16 and 20, reward systems and leadership style are two factors which have been found to affect cooperation.

Tasks or reward systems which promote cooperation between members can lead to increased cohesiveness. Working together for a common goal has a unifying effect on members. In fact, there is evidence that clear, well-defined, and feasible goals can increase group cohesiveness. In one experimental study, subjects were members of groups whose task was to produce and assemble toy houses.[7] Some subjects were clearly informed as to the goal (assembly of houses) and the means to that goal. Other subjects were given only vague references to a goal and how it would be accomplished. Subjects who were given clear goals liked the task more, felt closer to the group, and showed greater concern for their own and the group's performance.

In Chapter 20 we will discuss how democratic leadership styles, when appropriate, can enhance the cohesiveness of groups better than autocratic or other leadership styles can. By "when appropriate" we mean when the situation and the expectations of the group members indicate that democratic leadership behavior is feasible. For example, in discussion groups with plenty of time, democracy might be appropriate and democratic leaders can produce more cohesive groups, as was found in an investigation of 72 governmental and industrial conference groups.[8] On the other hand, democratic or permissive leadership on the part of a military commander under attack would be inappropriate and could lead to group disintegration.

---

[7] B. H. Raven and Jan Rietsema, "The Effects of Varied Clarity of Group Goal and Group Path upon the Individual and His Relationship to His Group," *Human Relations,* vol. 10 (1957), pp. 29–45.

[8] Leonard Berkowitz, "Sharing Leadership in Small, Decision-Making Groups," *Journal of Abnormal and Social Psychology,* vol. 48 (1953), pp. 231–38.

Group Size   The effects of group size on cohesiveness are fairly predictable. As group size increases, cohesiveness tends to decrease. This effect comes about in several ways.[9] As the group gets larger, it is more difficult for a given member to interact with (or possibly even know) all the members. The more members, the more likely that there will be differences in backgrounds and attitudes among the members.

As group size increases, it is also more difficult to get the group to agree on common goals and activities, and expressions of disagreement and dissatisfaction increase. People appear to be somewhat inhibited from such expression in small groups, perhaps out of dislike for hurting others' feelings or fear of lack of support.

Finally, as group size increases, the need for organization and division of labor also increases, and this places certain restrictions on intergroup communication and leads to a decrease in common activities. Perhaps the most telling effect of size on cohesiveness is that, as group size increases, the group tends to break up into smaller groups and cliques.

Effects of Cohesiveness

The sources and determinants of group cohesiveness must be understood because cohesiveness is itself a determinant of group and member behavior. The most important effects are on members' communication activities and task performance.

Communication   Members of cohesive groups communicate with each other more than members of noncohesive groups do. Sharing common ideologies, goals, backgrounds, or attitudes gives cohesive groups a lot to talk about, and such discussion is usually reinforcing.

Communication and social interaction have been found to be both causes and effects of cohesiveness. Interaction increases interpersonal attraction and cohesiveness, and increased cohesiveness in turn leads to greater communication. The increased communication characteristic of cohesive groups is a key to understanding other effects of cohesiveness.

Evaluation   Members of cohesive groups tend to evaluate themselves, the group, and the group's task more favorably than do members of less cohesive groups. A person's acceptance by a strong group

---

[9] E. J. Thomas and C. F. Fink, "Effects of Group Size," *Psychological Bulletin*, vol. 60 (1963), pp. 371–84.

is highly reinforcing; many psychoanalysts maintain that social acceptance is essential to the development of the individual. Because so much information about one's self is communicated by others, the increased communication characteristic of cohesive groups can be an important factor in the development of self-concept and self-esteem. In fact, psychoanalysts who advocate group methods of psychotherapy argue that group cohesiveness, although it is not itself a cure, is "a necessary precondition for effective therapy."[10] Members who are strongly attracted to the group increase their self-esteem, give and receive more communications, and have better outcomes from the therapy.

Members of cohesive groups tend to perceive each other and the group favorably. These tendencies are natural results of similarity and the reinforcement one gets from membership. Unfortunately, these tendencies can lead to perceptual distortion in the form of overevaluation, as discussed in Chapter 6. Overevaluation of one's group can, in turn, create problems for relationships between groups, as we will discuss in Chapter 17.

Hostility and Expressions of Aggression   Members of cohesive groups tend to express more hostility than members of less cohesive groups. This hostility is usually directed toward nonmembers, since cohesiveness increases a member's identification with his group and tends to produce discrimination toward nonmembers as "outsiders." For example, in an experimental study, highly cohesive groups were more cooperative with fellow members than with nonmembers and evaluated fellow members more highly.[11] Such discrimination can lead to overt expressions of hostility. In another study, subjects who had been frustrated and insulted were given the opportunity to administer shocks to friends and outsiders. They shocked outsiders significantly more often.[12]

Conformity and Influence   Cohesive groups are by definition highly attractive to their members. Members tend to like each other and perceive themselves as similar. These characteristics lead members to be relatively dependent on the group for satisfaction, and thus they are susceptible to being influenced.

A good deal of the communication which is characteristic of co-

---

[10] Yalom, *Theory and Practice of Group Psychotherapy*, p. 38.

[11] K. L. Dion, "Cohesiveness as a Determinant of Ingroup-Outgroup Bias," *Journal of Personality and Social Psychology*, vol. 28 (1973), pp. 163–71.

[12] Leonard Berkowitz and James A. Green, "The Stimulus Qualities of the Scapegoat," *Journal of Abnormal and Social Psychology*, vol. 64 (1962), pp. 293–301.

hesive groups concerns things common to the group: goals, attitudes, ideology, values. Such communication increases each member's awareness of group norms and sanctions and reinforces conformity.

One of the interesting ways cohesive group pressures enforce conformity is through communications. Several studies have shown that cohesive groups increase their communication toward a member who is deviating from commonly held attitudes, values, or norms in an attempt to bring him back into line. In one classic study, a confederate was used to express attitudes strongly divergent from the rest of the group's opinions.[13] Communications from the rest of the group quickly were centered on this individual, to the extent that he received five times as much communication as any other group member. This group tendency is so common that you can demonstrate it for yourself. The next time your friends express a common attitude about some subject important to them, argue a different position and see if you don't become the center of their attention quite quickly.

This tendency appears to be specifically directed toward the goal of increasing group solidarity. If the deviant persists in his deviance, there comes a time when the group considers him a lost cause and ceases communication with him altogether. Sometimes this tactic is more effective in reducing deviance than increasing communication is. The deviant may in fact be reinforced by the attention others give him but may find rejection highly punitive.

Figure 13–1 presents a model which suggests how cohesiveness, communication, and conformity are related. Cohesiveness increases the importance and attraction of the group for its members. This increases the dependence of the members on the group and group communication about norms and ideology. The group's attraction gives it power over members; the members' dependence makes them more susceptible to group influence. Power, dependence, and communication increase the influence that the group exerts over its members. This successful influence reinforces the members, increasing their attempts to influence each other. Successful influence reduces deviance, thus increasing similarity. As similarity and communication increase, cohesiveness increases. Small wonder, then, that cohesive groups have been found to have less tolerance for deviance, to attempt to exert more influence on members, and to

---

[13] Stanley Schacter, "Communication, Deviation, and Rejection," *Journal of Abnormal and Social Psychology*, vol. 46 (1951), pp. 190–207.

FIGURE 13–1
Relationships among Cohesiveness, Communication, and Conformity in a Group

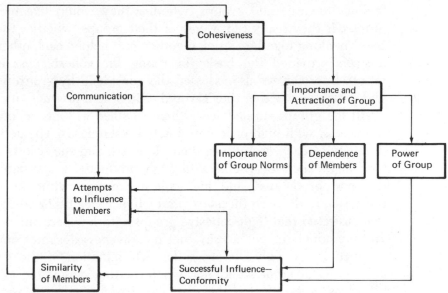

promote greater conformity and uniformity among members' behavior and attitudes.

Task Performance It was once assumed that cohesiveness enhances productivity. In fact, many managers who take over poorly performing groups first attempt to increase group cohesiveness and morale.

Research, however, has shown that the relationship between cohesiveness and productivity is neither simple nor direct. Rather, the effects of cohesiveness on productivity are moderated by group goals.

The goals of cohesive groups are important to them. They are the subject of much of the group's communication and become part of the group's ideology, to which members are expected to conform. Pressures are exerted on deviants, while conformers are reinforced. As a result, cohesive groups are likely to accomplish their goals. *If those goals are consistent with task performance or productivity, cohesive groups will be productive. If those goals are counterproductive* (to sabotage the organization, to avoid work, to get the supervisor fired), then cohesive groups will be nonproductive.

Perhaps the best demonstration of the relationships among cohesiveness, group goals, and productivity was a study of over 200 individual work groups.[14] Members were asked to indicate their feelings toward their groups, whether they would like to change groups, if they really felt a part of their groups, whether the members got along together, stuck together, and helped each other. Their answers provided the basis for rating the cohesiveness of each group. Interviewers also assessed the goals held by group members and evaluated whether they favored or inhibited productivity.

All the groups studied were then classified as high or low in cohesiveness, with high or low productivity standards. The actual productivity of each group was then observed, and the results showed that high-cohesive groups with high productivity standards were the most productive, and high-cohesive groups with low productivity standards were the *least* productive. Since other studies have demonstrated that high-cohesive groups with low performance goals are unproductive, we can say that cohesiveness does not determine productivity; it only increases the determination of the group to achieve its goals or standards, whatever they might be. What cohesiveness does affect is the variance of performance. Norms, communications, and pressures to conform result in less variance in the behavior and performance of members of a cohesive group than of members of a noncohesive group.

SUMMARY

Groups can be observed to progress through several stages of development, from formation to maturity. The two major obstacles they must work through are developing an acceptable power and authority structure and developing an acceptable level of interpersonal relationships. Not all groups develop to maturity; some function with conflicts over power, authority, or interpersonal relations unresolved. Immature groups are less likely than mature groups to make full use of their resources and time.

As groups develop, several structural characteristics take shape. Among the most important are roles, a status hierarchy, and cohesiveness.

Roles are expectations about the behavior of someone who occupies a position. These expectations can come from the individual and from any and all members of his role set. Conflicts often arise

[14] Stanley Seashore, *Group Cohesiveness in the Industrial Work Group* (Ann Arbor, Mich.: Institute for Social Research, 1954).

between the expectations of an individual and those of his role set or among the expectations of different members of his role set. The implications of such conflict in organizations range from hesitation and indecision to stress, anxiety, frustration, erratic behavior, and withdrawal.

Individuals are accorded status for having reward power, receiving rewards, or personally investing in the group or organization. If the different status factors for an individual are perceived to be incongruent or inequitable, problems can arise. Others may find it difficult to deal with him, and he may become dissatisfied, frustrated, or apathetic.

Cohesiveness is the extent to which members of a group become attracted to each other and to the group. It is enhanced by similarity among members and by external threats, initiation rites, and cooperative reward systems. Cohesiveness tends to enhance communications, to elicit hostility toward outsiders, and to induce conformity within the group.

Roles, status, and group cohesiveness are concepts that will show up repeatedly in our discussions of group and social behavior in Part Five. They are particularly relevant to an understanding of communications, group decision making, influence, and leadership.

QUESTIONS FOR REVIEW AND DISCUSSION

1. What are the characteristics of a mature group? How might uncertainties regarding power and authority relationships prevent a group from developing these characteristics?

2. What is the difference between interrole and intrarole conflict? Give an example of some well-known organizational figure who experiences the pressures of both interrole and intrarole conflict.

3. List the members of your role set as a student. Are there conflicts among their expectations for your behavior? If so, how do you tend to resolve these conflicts?

4. What are the implications of status inequities and incongruence for organizations? Give an example of status incongruence that might occur in a classroom situation.

5. Do unions tend to increase or decrease status congruence for their members? Explain.

6. What steps might a manager take to increase the cohesiveness of his department? (Use an example: A product-line supervisor, a political

campaign manager, an athletic coach, a research director, or a military commander.)

7. Why do very cohesive groups tend to exhibit less variation in members' performance than less cohesive groups do?

KEY WORDS

Group maturity

Role

Role set

Intrarole conflict

Interrole conflict

Intraperson conflict

Boundary role

Distributive justice

Status congruence

Cohesiveness

part five

Groups and Social
Behavior in
Organizations

PART FIVE describes several interpersonal and group processes which are important to organizations and explores their implications for management.

Chapter 14 examines the communications process and the factors that influence the direction, frequency, and accuracy of communication in organizations. It describes several characteristics of communication networks, including their structure and functions. An extensive study of research and development organizations is given as an example of how research on communications has been applied.

Chapter 15 compares group decision-making processes to individual decision making. It looks at characteristics of group decision making which result from discussion among members and decision making as a group task. The use of groups as decision makers in organizations is evaluated by examining the effects of group processes on the decisions and on group members.

Chapter 16 deals with three modes of interpersonal behavior: helping, cooperating, and competing. It describes individual and organizational factors which lead to each of these types of behavior and the effects of cooperation and competition on group behavior and productivity.

Chapter 17 discusses organizational factors which can lead to disruptive intergroup conflict. It describes the effects of conflict on groups and organizational reactions to intergroup conflict. It concludes by evaluating methods for reducing and avoiding conflict between groups in organizations.

Chapters 18 and 19 cover organizational influence. Chapter 18 describes resources which enable individuals to exert influence and characteristics which make others susceptible to influence. Chapter 19 describes several influence processes used in organizations and gives an example of the extent to which individuals can be influenced in social situations.

Objectives

1. To examine the communication process and factors which affect its frequency, direction, and accuracy.
2. To discuss the functions, directions, and structures of communications in organizations.
3. To describe the nature of horizontal communications in technical organizations.

chapter fourteen

Communications

"Cathy! Come in, sit down! Have some coffee? Alice, bring Cathy and me some coffee. Let's see, you take it black, right? Sit down, girl, what can I do for you?"

"Well, Mr. Allen—" Cathy Cummings began, determined not to let the size and plush decor of the president's office overwhelm her.

"Jerry, dear! Let's keep it on a first-name basis in this office. Say, how's that little boy of yours? Joshua isn't it? Yessir, Joshua. I make it a point to remember these little details about my best employees. A good trick for you to remember, too."

"Yes, sir. Well, it's about the Hillman project. We've run into a real problem. The—"

"Wait!" said Mr. Allen, rising from his chair and moving around to the side where Cathy was standing. "I don't want to hear it. Now look, Cathy, I promised old man Hillman myself he'd have that new information system operational by August 1st. I'm a man of my word, and that counts for a lot in this business. Allen and Company always meets its deadlines."

"But the—" began Cathy.

"Let me make it perfectly clear. I don't care what you do or how you do it—that's your business. I want that system operational next week on time, regardless of what it takes. We'll make up the extra cost in the service guarantee, anyway," Mr. Allen said with a wink.

"Look, Mr. Allen," Cathy tried, determined to make her point.

"Jerry, dear," corrected Mr. Allen, putting his hand on her shoulder as he walked her to the door. "I don't want to seem harsh. After all, I like you. I took a chance putting you in charge of this group, and I don't think you want to let me down. Not that I'm displeased with your work—I'm not, or you wouldn't be here, women's lib or no. But you've got to be tougher and show more initiative and aggressiveness if you want to survive in this man's world. You don't see any of the other supervisors running to me with little problems.

"Of course," he said, softening his tone as they neared the door of his office, "if you run into anything that you think I can help you with, let me know. You know my door is always open to you, just like it is to all my best people. I enjoy these one-to-one talks. Keeps me from being isolated. I don't ever want to get in a fix by being out of touch with what my people are doing, like Nixon did. My door is always open, OK? Now, any other problems?"

Cathy shook her head. "No, sir, everything's going just fine."

"Great! That's what I like to hear. See you at the staff meeting tomorrow."

Cathy nodded and headed back to the elevator.

IN EVALUATING the exchange of communications between Cathy and Jerry Allen it is apparent this is an excellent example of *one-way communication*. In this type of communication, the receiver of the message has no opportunity to express a reaction to or seek clarification of the message. Every time Cathy tried to communicate, Mr. Allen interrupted. Because she was given no chance to respond to Mr. Allen, he gave himself no opportunity to assess the impact of the understanding of his message. Lack of feedback to the sender is characteristic of one-way communication.

Mr. Allen's comments also are examples of *downward communication*—messages flowing from someone higher in the organization's structure to someone lower in the hierarchy. There is little if any upward communication in the example above; the only time Mr. Allen listened to Cathy was when she told him everything was going fine—just what he wanted to hear.

This incident also points up a problem with upward communications. Most managers, like Jerry Allen, claim to have an "open-door" policy—Subordinates can just walk right in and say what's on their minds. All too frequently, however, these "one-to-one" talks, as Jerry Allen labels them, turn out to be speeches from the boss in which the real message is that he does not want to hear about any problems. Small wonder, then, that Jerry claimed no other supervisors bothered him with little problems. They had probably learned, as Cathy was learning, that his door was open only for pep talks and assurances that everything was going fine.

Problems with one-way, upward, and downward communication are some of the topics that will be developed in this chapter. We will describe the communication process and organization factors which influence it, illustrate several kinds of communication networks and discuss the functions of organizational communications. Finally, several aspects of communications in a particular kind of organization in which both internal and external communications are vital to success will be examined.

THE COMMUNICATION PROCESS

In the example above, Cathy and Mr. Allen talked for several minutes in his office. Many words were exchanged between the two. But how much communication was there?

Consider two definitions of communication. The first is from a cognitive perspective: Communication is the use of words, letters, symbols, or similar means to achieve common or shared information about an object or occurrence.[1] This definition implies that information is something (facts, opinions, ideas, attitudes, values) possessed by one individual, then passed on to another by words or other symbols. If transmitted and received accurately, the receiver then "possesses" the same information as the sender, and communication is said to have occurred.

An operant definition of communication might be: verbal or symbolic behavior by which the sender achieves an intended effect on the receiver.[2] The operant definition avoids the implications of shared information and meanings, concentrating instead on a stimulus-response relationship.

According to the cognitive definition, we cannot say whether Mr. Allen "communicated" with Cathy. Messages were exchanged, but we do not know whether information was shared. It is likely that, while the information that he did not want to hear her problems was shared, information about the reasons for his reluctance was not shared. Certainly, information about the problems which prompted her to visit his office was not shared with Mr. Allen.

According to the operant definition, Cathy definitely failed to communicate with Mr. Allen. The response she intended to evoke can only be speculated upon, but it is certain that she did not intend to evoke hostility, defensiveness, a quick lecture, and the brush-off he gave her.

From a managerial perspective, the operant definition seems to be the more useful one. Communications in organizations are intended to have an effect upon the receivers. When they do not have the intended effect, it does not matter whether "information was shared" or not.

A very simple diagram of the communication process is presented

---

[1] Colin Cherry, *On Human Communication* (New York: John Wiley & Sons, Science Editions, 1961), pp. 2–16 and 217–55.

[2] For a discussion of this approach, see B. F. Skinner, *About Behaviorism* (New York: Alfred A. Knopf, 1974), chap. 6.

in Figure 14–1. The process described includes several elements, terms for which are common to the field of communications.

The process starts with a *source* or sender, the individual who is attempting to communicate with some other person. The first step for the source is to *encode* information. That is, the source translates

FIGURE 14–1
A Model of the Communication Process

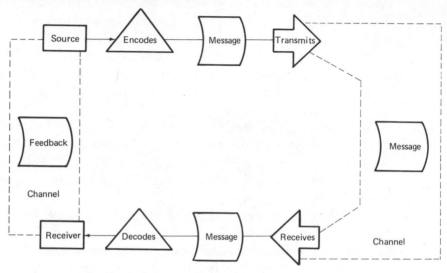

the information into words, signs, or symbols which are intended to have a certain effect (to convey information) to the other person.

The *message* is the physical, observable means by which the source expresses the information. It may be spoken words; written words or symbols; nonverbal behavior such as sign language, gestures, winks, and other "body language"; electronic impulses; Morse code; or other forms of communication, limited only by the imagination and capabilities of the source.

The *channel* is the means through which the message is transmitted. Channels for the spoken word include face-to-face communication, radio, telephone, audiotapes, phonograph records, television, and movie sound tracks. Channels for the written word include any material which can be written on (typically, of course, paper, but virtually every substance has been used to convey written messages, including stone, snow, and slate), or any medium which can visually reproduce the written word, such as television or film projectors.

The *receiver* is the person with whom the source is trying to communicate. He receives the message and *decodes* it. Decoding is the process by which the symbols of the message are interpreted by the receiver. In some cases, such as the use of actual codes, the receiver must go through some physical process of translating the message into some form he can understand. In most cases, decoding simply means interpretation of the message by the receiver.

There may or may not be a *feedback* channel—a means for the source to find out whether the message has been received and whether the receiver has responded to the message as the source intended.

Throughout the communication process, any factor which disrupts, distorts, or in any way interferes with the source's achievement of the desired response in the receiver is called *noise*. Noise can include everything from ambiguous wording of a message to a poor telephone connection or an incompetent receiver.

In the incident described above, Mr. Allen, the source, attempted to change the behavior of Cathy, the receiver. To do this, he encoded his intentions into messages utilizing written words and nonverbal behavior—showing her the door. We do not know how those messages were decoded or even whether they all were received since Mr. Allen made it virtually impossible to receive any accurate feedback. For all he knows, Cathy may have heard almost nothing he said, or she may have kept right on going out the front door, never to return.

FACTORS INFLUENCING COMMUNICATIONS

Empirical studies of communications have usually focused on the direction, frequency, or accuracy of communications as dependent variables.[3]

Factors Affecting Direction and Frequency

Managers and administrators have an interest in the patterns of communication that develop in the organizations to which they belong. Who communicates with whom and how often can be a legitimate concern in many organizational activities. A manager of research and development might want to encourage frequent communications among scientists and engineers; a library director

---

[3] M. E. Shaw, *Group Dynamics: The Psychology of Small Group Behavior* (New York: McGraw-Hill Book Co., 1971), chap. 5.

might want to discourage talking among patrons. Several variables have been found to affect direction and frequency of communication: opportunity to interact, cohesiveness, status, and the two-step flow of communication.

Opportunity to Interact   Obviously, people who find it easy to interact and communicate will do so more often than those who find such activity difficult. Organizations can actively encourage or discourage communications between individuals or groups by manipulating the physical and psychological distance between them. Arranging for people to share common facilities (copying machines, elevators, eating areas, desks) is a common method of encouraging communication. Separate facilities, physical distance, closed doors, walls, indirect lines of communication, and different working hours are devices which will usually discourage communication. Many of these factors are controllable by managers and administrators, and they are more effective than telling people that they should or should not communicate.

Cohesiveness   One of the most consistent effects of increased cohesiveness is an increase in communications. As the group, its goals, and its members become more important to an individual, he will find it increasingly rewarding to communicate with the group. As we have noted, cohesiveness and communication appear to affect each other positively. Communications can lead to an increase in cohesiveness, and cohesiveness increases communications.

Status   People tend to direct their communications to others who are either of similar or higher status. A person communicates with others of similar status because they have common interests, and sharing experiences and attitudes provides reinforcement.

People like to communicate with high-status individuals for at least two reasons. First, they beleive they can increase their own standing in the eyes of others; acquiring the autograph of a famous person may be enough to warrant admiration. To have an audience with the President or the Pope, to meet Raquel Welch or Burt Reynolds, or to have a discussion with the chairman of the board are activities which can confer considerable credit, even in the retelling. Second, they may believe that high-status people are capable of conferring rewards in one way or another. Communicating with people who have reward power is perceived to be a way of increasing one's chances of being rewarded.

The Two-Step Flow of Communication   The rapid diffusion of information among large numbers of people is a phenomenon which used to arouse curiosity but was not well understood. It could be observed that a rumor, idea, or bit of information could be shared by a majority of the members of a community or organization within a relatively short period of time after being introduced, but just how this information was spread was unclear. In the 1930s, the increased use of mass communications media (particularly radio) for business and political advertising gave rise to speculation that the media had a direct influence on the purchasing and voting behavior of the American public. Opportunities were provided for behavioral scientists to study the way such information actually reached and influenced the masses.

Such research on the impact of the mass media during the 1940 Presidential election provided the first clear description of how information is actually disseminated. Most people who changed their voting preferences reported they did so because they were directly influenced not by the media but by personal contacts with others they regarded as reliable sources of information. These personal contacts came to be known as *opinion leaders* because they wield considerable influence among their associates.[4]

Studies of the behavior of these opinion leaders revealed that they are the ones who are influenced by the media.[5] A much greater percentage of opinion leaders obtain their information from the media, and the opinion leaders in turn pass their opinions on to their associates and friends. Thus, information is communicated to large numbers of people, as depicted in Figure 14–2.

Factors Affecting Accuracy

Some of the potential sources of inaccuracy in the communication process are indicated in Figure 14–1 above. Problems in transmitting information or in understanding what is transmitted can cause communication to fail to have the desired impact or to fail to share information accurately.

Problems in Transmission   Certain conditions must be satisfied for transmission to be successful: The complete message must be sent to the intended receiver, and this complete message must be received, undistorted, by the intended receiver in time for it to have

---

[4] Paul F. Lazarsfeld, Bernard Berelson, and Hazel Gaudet, *The People's Choice: How the Voter Makes Up His Mind in a Presidential Campaign* 3d ed. (New York: Columbia University Press, 1968).

[5] V. O. Key, Jr., *Public Opinion and American Democracy* (New York: Alfred A. Knopf, 1961).

FIGURE 14–2
The Two-Step Flow of Communication

Mass Media

Opinion Leaders

General Public

Information flows from the mass media to opinion leaders, and
from the opinion leaders to the general public.

its intended effect. These conditions present numerous opportunities
for error.

1. *The complete message is either not sent or not received.*
Omitting the word *not* from the message "Do not sell these investments before I return" can have disastrous consequences, whether
it is omitted in transmission or overlooked by the receiver.

2. *The message is distorted in transmission.* This is a particular
problem in messages sent via channels that are subject to noise and
interference, such as radio or word of mouth. The tendency for
information passed by word of mouth to lose information at every
point of exchange is called *filtering.* Research has shown that up
to 80 percent of information can be lost in only five exchanges.

3. *The message is not sent to or received by the intended receiver.*
This result can be caused by several factors; channels of communi-

cation may not be open or may be unattended by the receiver. For example, letters sent to people who are out of town or who do not read their mail will be ineffective. Radio calls to police officers who are not monitoring their radio or are out of hearing will likewise fail.

4. *The message fails to arrive on time.* No matter how accurate information is when it is sent, delays in receipt can render it inaccurate or ineffective. An investor trying to buy into an active market using price information from the news media may discover that by the time he receives the information the prices have changed by 20 percent, or a reported advance has turned into a decline.

Certain methods can be used to counteract inaccuracies or failures in transmission. The same message may be repeated or transmitted through several channels or media. Substituting direct, face-to-face communications for indirect methods or providing and using feedback channels can also reduce or correct such errors.

Problems in Understanding   Communications also can be rendered inaccurate because of problems at either the source or the receiver end of the communication process.

Problems at the Source   In preparing a message, the source may omit some information, may fail to say what he means, or may encode a message which can be misinterpreted by the receiver.

Perhaps the most disastrous example of such an error occurred in World War II.[6] Having successfully concluded the war in Europe, the Allies were trying to induce the Japanese to surrender. Japan was divided between those who wished to negotiate a surrender and those who wished to continue fighting until no one was left to fight. The Allies dreaded the prospect of invading Japan itself, estimating that Allied casualties might exceed one million men.

The United States by this time had successfully tested the atomic bomb. The Allies felt that the threat of this weapon might induce the recalcitrant Japanese to accept the terms of surrender, and thus the inevitable tragedy for both sides involved in an invasion could be avoided. On July 21, 1945, the Allies issued the Potsdam Declaration, which called on the Japanese to surrender unconditionally or face the prospect of "prompt and utter destruction." However, no reference was made to the new ultimate weapon which could achieve that destruction. Error No. 1: some vital information was omitted from the message. Consequently the Japanese could only assume

---

[6] Len Giovannitti and Fred Freed, *The Decision to Drop the Bomb* (New York: Coward-McCann, 1965).

this threatened destruction would result from a conventional invasion.

The Japanese government decided to delay its answer and to provide its people with a neutral reaction, in order to give it more time to select the most appropriate response. Premier Suzuki suggested, therefore, that the government "ignore" the Potsdam Declaration for a few days. He meant that they would withhold comment, but the word he used was *mokusatsu,* which unfortunately can be given several shades of meaning—Error No. 2.

The Japanese Cabinet agreed that the official position, for the time being, would be to withhold comment. The next day Japanese newspapers were allowed to carry a government-censored version of the Potsdam Declaration and to report the government's response to be *mokusatsu.* Unfortunately, the Japanese people interpreted *mokusatsu* by its most severe meaning—"to treat with contempt." Other Far East papers and radio broadcasts quickly relayed the news that the Japanese had rejected the Allied ultimatum out of hand. On July 29, Radio Tokyo broadcast Premier Suzuki's official response as *mokusatsu.* To the Allies, this meant that the ultimatum had been rejected as contemptible by the Japanese. The decision was made to demonstrate their ability to enforce the ultimatum's threat to destroy the Japanese homeland. A few days later, the first bomb fell on Hiroshima.

Problems in the Receiver. As we noted in Chapter 6, perceptions can be strongly influenced by the psychological or emotional state of the perceiver. In addition to being unable to comprehend a message, the receiver may misinterpret a communication because he is anxious, agitated, or otherwise predisposed to overlook or read into messages information which is not there. In the case which introduced this chapter, the firm's owner, ensconced in his own office, is trying to communicate with a young, harassed executive involved in the frantic activities of a supervisory job and under the pressures of an important deadline which she obviously had no part in setting. No matter how clear his message, the psychological climate of the receiver makes it highly susceptible to misinterpretation (or even *mokusatsu*).

In attempting to reduce inaccuracies resulting from misunderstandings in a message, the first rule is usually to keep the message simple. Abstract concepts and complex words or codes can be easily misunderstood—and if they can be, they will. A second rule is to reinforce messages with action. Jerry Allen did this—in reverse.

While assuring Cathy that his door was always open, he ushered her out through it. In the World War II example, the Allies clarified their threat to destroy Japan by dropping the atomic bomb. Finally, feedback or two-way communication channels are essential for detecting and correcting misunderstandings. If the source can learn the receiver's interpretation of the message, the source can assess its impact and understanding. Without actively seeking such feedback, a communication source is only guessing if it assumes the message has been received and accurately interpreted.

THE STRUCTURE OF COMMUNICATION NETWORKS

Organizations often affect the channels of communication through which messages flow. They may establish formal communication networks by directing that certain positions must communicate only with certain other positions; communications are often directed to conform to the authority structure of the organization. For example, an employee who wishes to communicate with the general manager may be required to do so through his immediate supervisor. Such "bureaucratic" communication procedures evolve for a variety of reasons: They protect higher level administrators from being swamped with unwanted information, they enhance coordination, and they reinforce the authority structure. Communications may also be restricted by physical barriers, by distance, or by access to transmission and receiving devices such as telephones, computers, and radios.

The pattern of communication channels among positions in an organization is referred to as a *communication network*. Networks may be created by the organization or may evolve in the course of interpersonal interaction. Whatever their basis, communication networks are a fact of organizational life. Different types of networks have been studied for their effects on communications and on the members of the networks.

Effects of Structure on Network Performance

Beginning in the early 1950s, a series of experiments was conducted which used a simple procedure to test the effects of various networks.[7] Five subjects were seated at a table, separated from each

---

[7] H. J. Leavitt, "Some Effects of Certain Communication Patterns on Group Performance," *Journal of Abnormal and Social Psychology*, vol. 46 (1951), pp. 38–50.

other by partitions. Slots in the partitions could be opened or closed by the experimenter to create the communication network desired. Information was transmitted among the members via written messages passed through the open slots.

The group's task was to solve a problem, and each member was given some of the necessary information. No individual alone had sufficient information. The group was required to see that each member was informed of the correct solution when it had been found. In a typical problem each member was given a list of five symbols out of a set of six. The group's task was to discover which symbol appeared on every member's list.

The independent variables studied were several different communication networks, some of which are shown in Figure 14–3.

FIGURE 14–3
Communication Networks Used in Experiments

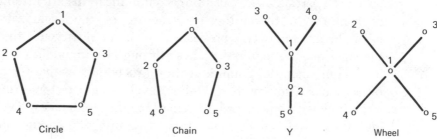

The major differences among the networks is the degree to which they are centralized. The circle network is the least centralized of the four: each position can communicate directly with two other positions on the network. The chain is slightly more centralized: only three positions (1, 2, and 3) can communicate directly with two other positions. The Y network is still more centralized, with only positions 1 and 2 being able to communicate with more than one other position. The wheel is the most centralized. All communications must pass through position 1, which is the only position with direct access to other positions.

The dependent variables studied included the speed and accuracy with which the groups solved problems and frequency of communication, as measured by the number of messages sent. The results revealed a clear superiority for the centralized networks; groups using the wheel network solved problems more accurately than groups using the other networks. Centralization also promoted

efficiency. Groups using the wheel network were quickest to organize; the person occupying position 1 became the leader, assembling
all the information from the rest of the group, solving the problem,
and passing the solution on to the rest of the group. Decentralization
seemed to promote inefficiency. Groups using the circle network
were slowest to organize, sent the most messages, made the most
errors, and tended to be slower to solve problems than groups using
any of the other networks. However, the circle groups tended to
be the most satisfied.

In addition to group performance, the effects of different networks on individual satisfaction and leadership were also studied.
These variables were found to be strongly influenced by the *centrality* of an individual position in the network.

Centrality is measured by the number of communication links
required to reach all other positions in a network. The most central
position in a network is the one that requires the fewest links to
reach the rest of the positions. For example, in the wheel network
the centrality of position 1 is four, while the centrality of each of
the other positions is seven (one link to get to 1, plus two links to
get to each of the remaining three positions). If you calculate the
centrality of each of the positions in the other networks, you can
see that the position labeled 1 is the most central position in the
wheel, Y, and chain networks. In the circle, all positions are equally
central.

Individual satisfaction and activity were positively related to
centrality. Further, the probability of becoming leader of the group
was also a positive function of centrality. Individuals occupying
central positions in the network were more active, satisfied, and
more likely to be named leader of the group than those occuyping
peripheral positions.

Effects of Task Complexity

These initial studies of communication networks produced a flurry
of experimental studies using an ever-expanding variety of networks
and modifying the nature of the group's tasks. The consistency of
these research results with the earlier studies was somewhat mixed.
The relative performance of different networks seemed to vary from
study to study, while satisfaction tended to be consistent.

In a 1964 review of all the experiments that had followed the
initial studies, it was found that those in which centralized networks

produced superior performance had something else in common: The problems confronting the groups were relatively simple, as in the initial studies.[8] However, in studies using more complex tasks, such as sentence construction, discussion, and mathematics, it was found that decentralized networks produced superior performance.

The summary of the results of these experiments presented in Table 14–1 indicates that the complexity of the problem makes a

TABLE 14–1
Comparisons between Centralized and Decentralized Networks Indicating Superiority of Performance on Simple and Complex Problems

Comparison	Simple Problems	Complex Problems
Accuracy		
Centralized made more errors	0	6
Decentralized made more errors	9	1
Time		
Centralized faster	14	0
Decentralized faster	4	18
Messages		
Centralized sent more	0	1
Decentralized sent more	18	17
Satisfaction		
Centralized more satisfied	1	1
Decentralized more satisfied	7	10

Source: M. E. Shaw, "Communication Networks," in *Advances in Experimental Social Psychology*, vol. 1, ed. Leonard Berkowitz (New York: Academic Press, 1964).

difference in the relative superiority of centralized and decentralized networks. Centralized networks tend to be faster and more accurate for simple problems. The most central person assumes leadership, collects all the information, and solves the problem.

However, the organization and centralization which facilitate the accomplishment of simple tasks create problems when the tasks are complex. Complex tasks require considerably more information and communication. If all messages must pass through one central position, that individual may become overloaded—he can't do everything himself. Though the task is more than one person can handle, the structure of the network makes it difficult to distribute the work. In complex problems, the efficiency of centralized networks breaks down. Groups using centralized networks tend to make more

[8] M. E. Shaw, "Communication Networks," in *Advances in Experimental Social Psychology*, vol. 1, ed. Leonard Berkowitz (New York: Academic Press, 1964), pp. 111–47.

errors on complex problems and to reach solutions more slowly than groups using decentralized networks.

Two effects of communication networks remain consistent, regardless of the complexity of the problem. Groups using decentralized networks send more messages and are more satisfied than groups using centralized networks, on both simple and complex problems.

The findings of this research on networks have had several implications for organizations. First, they suggest that the most effective structure for communications depends on the nature of the organization's task. Departments faced with routine, simple tasks, such as clerical departments, might find centralized networks most efficient. Departments faced with complex nonroutine tasks, such as research departments, might find decentralized networks more efficient.

Second, the research suggests that an individual's position in a communication network can directly affect his ability to exert influence. An authority figure who must rely on others for crucial information is dependent upon them. Conversely, a person with no formal power (such as a secretary) who has access to information may become highly influential. The Nixon White House organization during its last years resembled an inverted Y network. Nixon occupied position 5. His lieutenants occupied positions 1 and 2—directly controlling the flow of information to and from the President. As a result, he became isolated, and they were able to wield far more power than their formal positions warranted.

ORGANIZATIONAL COMMUNICATIONS

The importance of frequent, reliable, and timely communications cannot be underestimated. In fact, most managers and students of management recognize how essential communications are and make efforts to improve their understanding of communications systems. There is general agreements that, in order to survive, every organization needs these three things; a goal, the ability to attract resources, and good communications.

Functions of Communications

The importance of good communications is reflected in the functions they serve.[9] One function is simply to provide *information*,

_____

[9] Lee Thayer, *Communication and Communication Systems* (Homewood, Ill.: Richard D. Irwin, 1968), pp. 187–301.

which can help the organization adapt to internal and external changes. For example, information of a local disaster can prepare a community's hospitals for an influx of injured victims, anxious relatives, and aggressive reporters.

A second function is to *command and instruct*. Such informative communications indicate who will do what, where, and how often. For example, a disaster alert will trigger a series of commands and instructions throughout the hospital which will increase the emergency room space and staff, call in additional help, prepare supplies, reallocate other patients, and so on.

A third function is to *influence and persuade*. Such communications are usually directed toward those not directly under the authority of the sender, in an attempt to elicit specific behavior. For example, in responding to a disaster the director of the hospital may communicate with the local police to persuade them of the need for officers to control traffic at the hospital as well as at the disaster sight.

The fourth function of organizational communications is to *integrate. Integrative communications*, which may be directed toward any position within the organization, serve to confirm the states of the various positions and units within the organization and the relationships among them. They may also serve to integrate the organization with its environment.

Integrative communications help to keep the organization running smoothly, regulate the internal communication process, and provide a context for understanding relationships in the organization. Such information is often communicated simply by the way other information is communicated. For example, the authoritative, sharp commands with which a surgeon directs the operating room staff confirm for them that the surgeon is in charge and that their relationship to him is to provide technical assistance and information. Their communications to the surgeon will be informative (e.g., readings on a patient's vital signs, time elapsed) or integrative—confirming the various authority and status relationships within the staff.

Obviously, any message can carry out more than one function. It is not difficult to think of a message accomplishing several functions. For example, the cry "Help!" informs one who hears it that the sender is in trouble, attempts to persuade the listener to provide assitance, and establishes a relationship of victim-helper between sender and receiver.

Directions of Communication

Certain characteristics of organizational communications, including content and function, are associated with the direction in which the message is sent. In the context of the hierarchy of authority in the organization, communications may be vertical (downward or upward) or horizontal.

For the examples in this section we will use the patrol and detective divisions of a small city police force. The patrol division, under Lt. Bunten, consists of 30 officers who patrol the streets in police cruisers, two to a car, and three field supervisors. The detective division, under Lt. Bauman, has 15 investigators, including undercover agents. Lts. Bunten and Bauman both report directly to Chief Nosnar.

Downward Communications[10] Primarily designed to command and instruct, downward communications most frequently contain specific task directives, such as *who* will do *what* and *when*. For example, the chief orders Lieutenant Bunten to beef up patrols in the residential area on weekends, and Lieutenant Bauman to get to the bottom of the rash of streaking incidents around one of the sororities at the local college.

Downward communications also stress procedures and practices—*how* orders should be carried out. Lieutenant Bauman instructs the detective team he assigns to the streaking case to work undercover, posing as streaking enthusiasts.

Somewhat less frequently stressed in downward communications are reasons for instructions and procedures—*why* they have been given. Lt. Bunten may or may not inform his men that the reason for a change in radio procedure is that many citizens are monitoring police broadcasts with special receivers now on sale at the local department store.

Performance feedback is perhaps too infrequently a part of downward communications. We have stressed the importance of feedback in motivation and skill maintenance. Overall crime rate statistics, convictions, and comparisons with other police forces may filter down to the beat patrolmen, or they may not.

Finally, downward communications are sometimes used to confirm relationships or to strengthen commitment. Occasional letters from the chief may underline the authority of the division heads,

---

[10] See Daniel Katz and Robert L. Kahn, *The Social Psychology of Organizations* (New York: John Wiley & Sons, 1966), chap. 9, pp. 239–43.

such as stating that Lieutenants Bunten and Bauman have complete responsibility for maintaining morale and discipline in their divisions. The chief may use occasional visits to briefing sessions as a means of personally communicating to officers the importance of their work and that of the entire force.

How good are downward communications? The question cannot be answered in the abstract, but one of the major problems with downward (or any vertical) communications is filtering—the tendency for only a fraction of a message's contents to be passed on to the next level. One classic study of downward communications in 100 organizations estimated the content of messages sent from the top of organizations through five levels, down to the workers.[11] At each level, significant information contained in the original message was lost. General supervisors received little more than half of the information sent from the top, and foremen less than a third. About 80 percent of the information had been filtered out by the time communications reached the individual workers.

Upward Communications Primarily used to inform, upward communications provide feedback on how downward communications are being carried out. Without this feedback, an organization's effectiveness or even survival is a matter of chance. When one of Lt. Bunten's patrols informs him of suspicious activity, he can assign additional units to the area in time to apprehend three suspects fleeing a house with a carload of stolen property.

Upward communications may also seek to influence and persuade. The detectives assigned to the streaking case daily assail Lt. Bauman with pleas to be reassigned to another case. A patrolman may argue with Lt. Bunten for a chance to set a speed trap for a notorious local dragster.

Upward communications often integrate in that they confirm established relationships. Communications seeking permission to do something are inherently integrative. A patrolman who asks Lieutenant Bunten for permission to find a new partner confirms his subordinate role and the authority of Lieutenant Bunten to assign partners. A detective requesting permission to follow a suspect outside the city limits gives Lieutenant Bauman the opportunity to coordinate the activities of his unit by assigning another unit to maintain surveillance over the house from which the suspect emerged.

Upward communications are obviously vital yet often inefficient,

---

[11] R. G. Nichols, "Listening is Good Business," *Management of Personnel Quarterly*, Winter 1962, p. 4.

for a variety of reasons. One major source of error is filtering; by the time a message is relayed from a patrol unit through the dispatcher to a supervisor, and finally to Lieutenant Bunten, a "minor disturbance" may have become a "riot."

Less immediate communications about the nature of things at the worker level may encounter several other problems in their route to the top. For example, suppose, a certain field supervisor has been seen drinking heavily on the job by one of his men, Officer Dolson, enough so that the patrolman is concerned about the supervisor's ability to function in an emergency. This information may not reach Lieutenant Bunten, who is the only person who can act on it, for several reasons.

First, there may be no precedent for communicating this information. With no established, regularly used channels of information from patrolman to lieutenant, Dolson does not know where to begin. Second, the status differential between the lieutenant and the patrolmen (reinforced by his bars, his larger office, and his private driver) deters Dolson from communicating with Lieutenant Bunten. Third, the officer may fear reprisal for "going outside channels" or from the supervisor himself if he learns that Dolson has reported him. Fourth, Dolson may be uncertain whether his information is really so important, perhaps rationalizing that Lieutenant Bunten must know about the supervisor's drinking problem. Alternatively, Dolson may fear that Lieutenant Bunten will not believe him, particularly if Dolson is known to dislike the supervisor or to exaggerate once in a while.

One of the major problems with upward communications is that organizations typically rely on lower level members to initiate them. Instead of actively soliciting, providing channels for, and rewarding communications, higher level managers usually fall back on devices like suggestion boxes or empty phrases like "My door is always open." The unfortunate result of such devices or policies, when they are not reinforced with action and rewards, is that the suggestion box becomes a receptable for gum wrappers and the boss, like Jerry Allen, hears only what his employees are sure he wants to hear.

To counteract the potential inertia in upward communications, many organizations actively solicit such information. Attitude questionnaires are used to elicit feedback about possible problems and to indicate to employees areas of managerial concern. One benefit of questionnaires is that the reliability of information can be checked. The observations of 50 employees are more likely to be accurate than the observation of a single employee. Interviews with employees who are leaving the organization may provide information which current members are unwilling to relate for fear of reprisal. Contests in which equitable bonuses are awarded for suggestions which lead to significant organizational improvement have appeared to be effective in a variety of forms, although they usually do not attract suggestions like "fire my supervisor," which may be the most significant improvement the organization can make.

Horizontal Communications   Usually intended to persuade or inform, horizontal communications occasionally are designed to integrate. They may occur through formal channels, such as committees or reports circulated throughout the organization. For example, a meeting of all downtown area patrolmen may be called to exchange ideas on reducing the frequency of nighttime burglaries. Occasionally, the report of a patrolman who has identified a burglary suspect may be passed among members of the patrol division for information on the suspect's modus operandi and description.

Most horizontal communication probably occurs informally, as members exchange information while engaging in daily activities or by actively seeking each other out. Word of the supervisor's drinking problem may spread rapidly at a local establishment where off-duty police congregate. Information that the occupant of a certain house has firearms may be radioed from a patrolman who has monitored a colleagues's report of a disturbance at that address.

Horizontal communications are looked on by many management observers as more crucial to success than vertical communications. Certainly they are too crucial for management not to study and influence them. In the following section we will describe one of the most thorough and extensive studies of horizontal communications in ongoing organizations, in order to get an idea of their importance and how they can be influenced. This section deals with communications in research and development organizations.

COMMUNICATIONS IN RESEARCH AND
DEVELOPMENT ORGANIZATIONS[12]

Over the past several years a series of field studies of communications has been carried out by researchers at M.I.T. These studies

---

[12] This section is based on research reported in T. J. Allen, "The Differential Performance of Information Channels in the Transfer of Technology," M.I.T. Sloan School Working Paper #196–66, Cambridge, Mass., June 1966, and T. J. Allen, "Communications in the Research and Development Laboratory," *Technology Review*, vol. 70 (1967), pp. 2–8.

were begun as part of a larger program in the management of research and development activities funded by the National Aeronautics and Space Administration (NASA). Tom Allen, the principal researcher in the communication studies, focused on communications because his prior experience as an electrical engineer had impressed him with the importance of communications to the success of highly technical organizations.

Channels of Communication

The first research question Allen asked in this series of studies was: What channels of communication are most frequently used by scientists and engineers in obtaining technical information for their projects? The subjects were scientists and engineers working in industrial laboratories on government-supported projects dealing with the space program. Communication channels associated with 19 different projects were studied; designs under development included a vehicle to roam the lunar surface, a low-thrust rocket engine for maneuvering manned spacecraft, and a deep-space probe. Every project was being worked on by at least two laboratories independently. Upon completion of a project, the laboratories submitted their designs or solutions to NASA, which evaluated them and selected the best solution for incorporation into the space program.

The method used to study communication channels consisted of weekly interviews with those working on projects. The topic of the interviews was the information that had been used that week in the development of the project, particularly information which could affect the likelihood that one or more alternatives being considered in the project would be used. The object of the interviews was to discover where the scientist or engineer had obtained the information used.

The results showed that eight different information channels were used by laboratory personnel. Four channels had sources outside the company: literature (scientific and technical books and journals), suppliers (sales and technical representatives of suppliers and their publications), customers (representatives of NASA and its publications), and other external sources (consultants and other government agencies). The other four channels were internal to the company: technical staff (laboratory personnel not directly assigned to the project), company research (other projects in the company), analysis and experimentation (information generated solely by engi-

neering analysis, test, or experiment), and personal experience
(ideas recalled directly from memory from use on a similar problem by a project member).

Comparison of the frequency with which each of these channels
was used provided some surprising results. Considering the six
channels of information outside the individual (excluding experimentation and personal experience), it was found that engineers received messages from external channels much more frequently than
from internal channels. The most frequently used information channel for engineers was customers, followed by suppliers, consultants,
literature, technical staff, and company research, in that order. The
finding that literature was relatively infrequently used was a disappointment to many of the companies, which prided themselves on
the size and value of the technical libraries that brought this outside source to their personnel.

However, when only the information that was actually used in
the laboratories' final project designs or solutions was considered,
quite a different pattern of information channel usage emerged.
The ratio of messages used in the final solution to messages received was lower for external channels than for internal channels

TABLE 14–2

**Performance of Information Channels Used by Engineers on Nineteen
Research and Development Projects**

Channel	Use: Number of Messages Received	Efficiency: Ratio of Messages Used in Final Solution to Messages Received
External Sources		
Customers	132	31%
Suppliers	101	33%
Other external sources		
(consultants)	67	48%
Literature	53	40%
Internal Sources		
Technical staff	44	55%
Company research	37	54%

Source: Adapted from T. J. Allen, "Performance of Information Channels
in the Transfer of Technology," *Industrial Management Review*, vol. 8 (1966),
p. 91.

(see Table 14–2). Over half the information received through technical staff and company research was used in the final solution, but
only approximately one third the information received from all external sources was used in the final solution. The most frequently

used channels were the least efficient, and the researchers were curious to know why.

Factors Affecting the Use of Channels

In order to determine why external channels supplied more information, while internal channels were more efficient in providing usable information, a short questionnaire was developed. This questionnaire asked the laboratory personnel to rate each communication channel for its accessibility, ease of use, and technical quality.

The responses to the questionnaire were revealing. External channels were rated as more accessible and easy to use than internal channels. In fact, there was a very strong correlation between rankings on accessibility and ease of use and between the amount of information received from each channel. Clearly, external channels were used more often because they were easier to use.

However, internal channels were rated as providing higher quality technical information than external channels. There was a strong correlation between rankings on quality and the ratio of information used in final solutions to information received for each channel. Thus it became evident that information received from internal channels was used more often because those channels were perceived to provide superior information.

This study uncovered a very inefficient "two-filter" communication process. The first "filter," or criterion for receiving information, was the accessibility and ease of use of the channel through which it flowed, and the second was the technical quality of information. This indicated that the laboratories spent considerable time processing information from low-quality channels. The situation is analogous to a lazy miner who spends most of his time panning the stream next to his camp, even though it yields less than two grams of gold a week. The obvious implication for management from this research was the desirability of making higher quality channels easier to use and more accessible to those who need them.

Communication Networks

The next research question which was examined was: What factors influence communications within a research and development laboratory? A questionnaire was developed which was administered to scientists and engineers working in a small laboratory on direct energy conversion and solid-state electronics, and in a department of a large aerospace firm. The questionnaire asked each member of the laboratory to name those individuals who helped solve technical problems, who belonged to their work group, and with whom they socialized and discussed technical matters.

The information generated by these questionnaires led to a description of the various communication networks in each laboratory. One of the first findings was that high-status members (Ph.D.s) communicated quite frequently among themselves but seldom socialized or discussed technical problems with non-Ph.D. colleagues. Thus in R&D organizations as well as elsewhere, status is an important factor in communications.

A second finding was that there was a strong relationship between social and technical discussion. That is, the social network heavily influenced the network of technical communications. Engineers discussed their work more with friends than with others who were not friends.

A third finding was that the formal organization also influenced the technical communications network. Engineers were more likely to communicate with others in their assigned work group and those who were physically located close to them. Even within the laboratory, accessibility and ease of use were important characteristics of frequently used channels of information: It proved easier for engineers to talk to friends (fewer psychological barriers) and those close at hand (fewer physical barriers).

The Role of Technological Gatekeeper

One unexpected result of the analysis of communication networks within the laboratory was the discovery of a few individuals who were repeatedly named as sources of critical information and were chosen for technical discussion. These few individuals were apparently very important sources of information within the lab, people to whom everybody turned when confronted with a special technical problem or when they came up with a new idea.

The question asked was: What are the differences between these information sources and their colleagues? To answer this question, the individual characteristics and behavior of the information sources were compared to those of their colleagues. The data revealed very little difference in individual characteristics. The sources were neither more intelligent, nor older, nor better educated than their colleagues. Each source, however, had been a member of his laboratory for several years.

The major differences between the two groups were in their behaviors. The sources used many more external information channels than their colleagues did. They used more personal friends outside the laboratory for information, read more technical periodicals and scientific and professional journals, attended more meetings, and published more papers.

This discovery revealed the means by which information outside the laboratory was brought in—via a few people who had extensive outside contacts. These sources, called "technological gatekeepers," act as communication links between the laboratory and the outside world. The process is analogous to the two-step flow of information described earlier in this chapter. The technological gatekeepers are the "opinion leaders" for the laboratory who absorb information from the outside and disseminate it to their colleagues. In organizations such as R&D laboratories, horizontal communications are vital. Physical and psychological variables and individual personnel who facilitate horizontal communications are valuable resources for organizational effectiveness.

SUMMARY

Communication in organizations utilizes verbal and symbolic behavior to achieve some intended effect on others. Good communications is one of the three characteristics essential for any organization.

Studies of organizations reveal that the direction and frequency of communications are affected by the opportunities members have to interact, by cohesiveness, and by status. The accuracy of communications can be affected by transmission problems and by problems in receiving and understanding the message. Many problems can be reduced through repetition of messages, multiple channels, direct face-to-face methods, and provisions for abundant feedback.

The structure of communications networks can affect behavior and performance. Simple, routine information is handled more efficiently through centralized networks. Complex, nonroutine messages are often handled more effectively via decentralized networks, whereby feedback and clarification can be exploited. Individuals who are centrally located in communication networks tend to be more satisfied and more influential than those who are not centrally located.

Downward communications in organizations primarily command and instruct. They are also used to provide information and to confirm relationships or strengthen commitment. Upward communications are primarily used to inform, but they may also attempt to influence and persuade. Most organizations do not have particularly good upward communications, which typically must be actively solicited and reinforced.

Horizontal communications often provide the majority of information used at operational levels. They most frequently occur through informal channels, and therefore they are heavily influenced by physical and psychological distance and interpersonal relationships. In technical organizations, the flow of information horizontally can be influenced by certain individuals who act as technological gatekeepers, serving as links among individuals in the organization and between the organization and the outside world.

QUESTIONS FOR REVIEW AND DISCUSSION

1. Assume you are the manager of a department whose internal communications are too infrequent. What factors would you examine in trying to decide how to increase internal communications?

2. What could be the possible causes of inaccurate communications between (a) a police dispatcher and officers on patrol, (b) between a home office manager and sales personnel in the field?

3. What is the two-step flow of information? How does this phenomenon often show up in technical organizations?

4. Why is status a factor in communications in organizations?

5. How might the complexity of a group's task affect its communications network?

6. Consider the problem of upward communications between students and an instructor. What are these communications primarily used for by (a) the student, (b) the instructor? What factors have inhibited you from making use of an instructor's "open door" policy? What might an instructor do to improve upward communications?

7. Who are the people with whom you most frequently communicate about course work? What characteristics or factors lead you to communicate with them rather than with others?

8. What is the primary function of horizontal communications? What organizational factors might inhibit the flow of horizontal communications?

9. Outline the communication process between the author of this text-
    book and you. What specific elements of that process might result in
    poor communications—error and misunderstanding? Is this process
    one-way or two-way? What could be done to allow for two-way
    communications in writing a textbook?

KEY WORDS

One-way communications   Centralized network
Feedback   Decentralized network
Message   Centrality
Channel   Integrative communications
Noise   Upward communications
Two-step flow   Horizontal communications
Filtering   Technological gatekeeper

Objectives

1. To discuss the important characteristics of the elements of group decision making and the processes that affect them.
2. To evaluate the outcomes of group decision processes as compared to individual decision processes.
3. To describe two alternatives to traditional group techniques.

chapter fifteen

Group Decision Making

THE BAY OF PIGS DECISION

Two days after the inauguration in January 1961, President John F. Kennedy and several leading members of his new administration were given a detailed briefing about the proposed invasion [of Cuba] by Allen Dulles, head of the CIA, and General Lyman Lemnitzer, chairman of the Joint Chiefs of Staff. During the next eighty days, a core group of presidential advisers repeatedly discussed this inherited plan informally and in the meetings of an advisory committee that included the three Joint Chiefs of Staff. In early April 1961, at one of the meetings with the President, all the key advisers gave their approval to the CIA's invasion plan. Their deliberations led to a few modifications of details, such as the choice of the invasion site.

On April 17, 1961, the brigade of about fourteen hundred Cuban exiles, aided by the United States Navy, Air Force, and the CIA, invaded the swampy coast of Cuba at the Bay of Pigs. Nothing went as planned. On the first day, not one of the four ships containing reserve ammunition and supplies arrived; the first two were sunk by a few planes in Castro's air force, and the other two promptly fled. By the second day, the brigade was completely surrounded by twenty thousand troops of Castro's well-equipped army. By the third day, about twelve hundred members of the brigade, comprising almost all who had not been killed, were captured and ignominiously led off to prison camps.

In giving their full approval, President Kennedy, Dean Rusk, Robert McNamara, and other high-level policy-makers in the United States government had assumed that "use of the exile brigade would make possible the toppling of Castro without actual aggression by the United States." The President's main advisers certainly did not expect such an overwhelming military disaster. Nor did they anticipate that the United States government's attempts to disclaim responsibility for the initial air assault would be thoroughly discredited, that friendly Latin American countries would be outraged, that protest meetings would be held in the United States and throughout the world to denounce the United States for its illegal acts of aggression against a tiny neighbor, that intellectuals who had regarded the new administration with bright hopes would express disaffection in sarcastic telegrams ("Nixon or Kennedy: Does it make any difference?"), or that European allies and United Nations statesmen would join in condemnation. None of them guessed that the abortive invasion would encourage a military rapprochement between Castro and the Soviet leaders, culminating in a deal to set up installations only ninety miles from United States shores equipped with nuclear bombs and missiles and manned by more than five thousand Soviet troops, transforming Cuba within eighteen months into a powerful military base as a satellite of the Soviet Union. Had the President and his policy advisers imagined that this nightmarsh scenario would materialize (or had they even considered such an outcome to be a calculated risk), they undoubtedly would have rejected the CIA's invasion plan.

We are given a vivid picture of the President's reactions in Sorensen's *Kennedy,* described by a New York Times reviewer as "the nearest thing we will ever have to the memoirs Kennedy intended to write." When the first news reports revealed how wrong his expectations had been, President Kennedy was stunned. As the news grew worse during the next three days, he became angry and sick at heart. He realized that the plan he thought he had approved had little in common with the one he had in fact approved. "How could I have been so stupid to let them go ahead?" he asked. Sorensen wrote, "His anguish was doubly deepened by the knowledge that the rest of the world was asking the same question."

Arthur Schlesinger, Jr., in his authoritative history of the Kennedy administration, recalled that "Kennedy would sometimes refer incredulously to the Bay of Pigs, wondering how a rational and responsible government could ever have become involved in so ill-starred an adventure." The policy advisers who participated in the deliberations felt much the same way, if not worse. Allen Dulles, for example, was "still troubled and haggard" several days later and offered to resign as chief of the CIA. Secretary of Defense McNamara, when he left the government seven years later, publicly stated that he still felt personally responsible for having misadvised President Kennedy on the Bay of Pigs. All who participated in the Bay of Pigs decision were perturbed about the dangerous gap between their expectations and the realities they should have anticipated, which resulted, as Sorensen put it, in "a shocking number of errors in the whole decision-making process."

. . . The group that deliberated on the Bay of Pigs decision included men of considerable intellectual talent. [Besides the President, there were 15 others, including Dean Rusk, Robert McNamara, Douglas Dillon, Robert Kennedy, McGeorge Bundy, Arthur Schlesinger, Jr., Allen Dulles, the Joint Chiefs of Staff.] Like the President, all the main advisers were shrewd thinkers, capable of objective, rational analysis, and accustomed to speaking their minds. But collectively they failed to detect the serious flaws in the invasion plan.[1]

Scarcely 18 months later, this same group was faced with an even more crucial and threatening series of decisions.

THE CUBAN MISSILE CRISIS

Within a year or so following the Bay of Pigs invasion attempt, the Soviet Union worked out an arrangement with the Castro regime to set up missile installations in Cuba, presumably to be armed with nuclear warheads. More than twenty thousand Russian troops, equipped with atomic tactical weapons, were sent to Cuba to protect the installations. Shortly after detecting missile sites scattered throughout Cuba, United States military intelligence experts estimated that the installations represented about one third of the Soviet Union's entire atomic warhead potential. If fired at American cities, the missiles could kill about 80 million Americans.
 . . . For five days, starting on October 16, 1962, the Executive Committee met continually, often holding formal sessions several times a day, in order to arrive at a strategic plan. At first the best choice seemed to be to threaten a surgical or massive air strike, in the hope that the verbal threat would induce the Soviet Union to withdraw the missiles. But the group recognized from the start that the Soviet leaders might refuse to acquiesce to this threat, and their refusal might lead to a rapid, uncontrolled escalation that would bring on a nuclear war. After debating the alternatives day after day, a majority of the group finally decided on October 20 that the best choice was to institute a naval blockade. This choice, they felt, had the advantage of being a low-level action that would serve as a nonhumiliating warning and would still "maintain the options," as McNamara put it, permitting a gradual, controlled escalation later on, if necessary.
 The crisis continued for another eight days, and the same group continued to meet daily until the crisis was finally resolved by Khrushchev's offer to withdraw the missiles. On October 22, President Kennedy gave his dramatic speech revealing to the world the hitherto secret evidence of the offensive missile sites in Cuba and announcing the United States government's decision to quarantine Cuba. Khrushchev promptly denounced the blockade as "piracy." Eighteen Soviet ships— some of them almost certainly carrying nuclear armaments—continued relentlessly on their course toward the quarantine zone. During the next few suspenseful days the United States repeated its threat to board Soviet ships,

---

[1] Exerpted from Irving L. Janis, *Victims of Groupthink* (Boston: Houghton Mifflin Co., 1972), pp. 15–19. Reproduced by permission © 1972 Houghton Mifflin Company. All rights reserved.

forced several Soviet submarines to surface near the quarantine zone, and actually did board a Lebanese vessel chartered by the Soviet Union. These actions were calculated to postpone a direct military confrontation while demonstrating the firm resolve of the United States government to counteract the missile build-up in Cuba. Then, on October 24 and 25, shortly before reaching the quarantine zone, most of the Soviet cargo ships (including all those with large hatches, presumed to be carrying nuclear missiles) turned around and headed back toward Russian ports.

Despite the success of the blockade, the situation was still considered dangerous because work was continuing on the Soviet missile sites in Cuba, and they were rapidly becoming operational. The Executive Committee began to consider a response that would make its contingency plans operational. These plans involved taking further graduated steps toward more direct forms of military action, possibly resorting to air strikes against the missile sites or even invasion of Cuba. Before taking further action, however, the committee decided that additional warning messages —but not a formal ultimatum—should be sent to the Soviet leaders, urging them to remove the missiles immediately in order to avoid the outbreak of war. As this new crisis was reaching a climax, Khrushchev made it known that the Soviet Union would respond favorably if the United States were willing to make some concessions in turn. The crisis was finally resolved on October 28, when the Soviet leaders agreed to remove the missiles in exchange for assurances that the United States would not invade Cuba.[2]

THE BAY OF PIGS and the Cuban Missile Crisis were incidents in which group decision making was a crucial factor. Indeed, in the past 25 years group decision making has been a crucial factor in the activities of almost every organization. Managers, leaders, and administrators all report increasing amounts of time devoted to various kinds of group decision-making activity. Many are not pleased with the results of such activities; most gripe about the time and effort expended. Yet as the technical and political complexity of organizations grows, decision makers have concluded that group processes are the only way to handle complex problems.

Simply getting a group of several bright individuals together to attack a problem does not mean that the problem will be solved. Group decisions have no guarantee of success or even wisdom. The decisons made by President John Kennedy and his advisors to carry out the invasion of Cuba had catastrophic results for both the invasion force and the United States. Nevertheless, this same group

---

[2] Ibid., pp. 138–45.

some months later handled an even more dangerous problem—The Cuban Missile Crisis—with considerable foresight and skill. As in groups in general, their decisions were neither consistently bad nor consistently good.

REASONS FOR THE TREND TO GROUP DECISIONS

How can the trend toward the increased use of groups to make decisions be accounted for? Individuals have been making decisions throughout history, and many of the decisions that have been recorded were bold, difficult, good, or creative. What can organizations possibly hope to gain by group decision making?

First, most organizations expect groups to make better decisions than individuals; that is, they expect groups to be more accurate or to use better judgment. Particularly as organizations become more complex, as their decisions become more involved and the uncertainties about the problems increase, there is a feeling that a decision can be "too big for one individual." It is believed that somehow the shared knowledge, expertise, and experience of several people will bring about a better decision than if it were left up to one person.

Second, there is a belief that groups are more creative than individuals. Faced with complex decisions requiring innovative solutions, some organizations feel that creativity is enhanced through a group of people of varied backgrounds and experiences working on problems. Some organizations even feel that the group process itself fosters creativity and imagination.

Third, organizations believe that greater commitment from group members to carry out decisions affecting them can be obtained if the members have participated in making the decisions. Allowing members or their representatives to be a part of the decision-making process is seen as an effective way of promoting participation and enthusiasm and commitment for the decisions.

The pressures toward the increased use of group decision making have not all come from the organizational hierarchy; group members have also either suggested or demanded increased decision making by groups. One reason is that they believe better decisions will be made this way. As the education and training of the work force has increased, and as organizations have become more complex, those at lower levels of the organization have developed comparatively greater expertise in specific operations. Such members believe the complexities of many decisions require their expertise, and they see group processes as a means of incorporating it in decision making.

Other pressures result from group members' growing conviction that they have the right to participate in decisions affecting them. The past several years have seen the increasing use of groups that include lower level members to make decisions in all kinds of organizations. In many universities, students participate in decisions involving curricula, faculty selection and evaluation, on-campus housing, and fee increases. Poor people are involved in decisions about the nature and distribution of resources to the needy. Businesses use employee groups to determine decisions ranging from fringe benefits to layoffs. Even some prisons employ representative prisoner groups to make decisions about prisoner recreation and work.

Finally, there is the notion that group decisions are less likely than individual decisions to be biased or to show undue favoritism. This is one of the reasons why the jury system, despite its shortcomings and costs, remains a characteristic of our legal process. Defendants and plaintiffs alike are more willing to accept such decisions as fair and equitable to all parties.

Are these reasons for using groups valid? Do groups in fact make more accurate decisions and better judgments than individuals? Is the group process inherently creative? Do people accept and carry out decisions more readily if they have participated in making them? Are group decisions less biased than individual decisions?

The rest of this chapter attempts to answer these and other questions by evaluating group decision making. First, we will examine the elements of group decision making and the various decision-making processes which can affect them. Next we will analyze whether these elements and processes can reasonably be expected to make group decisions more accurate, more creative, more acceptable, and less biased than individual decisions. We will also examine the evidence of research to consider the likely outcomes of group decision making, its effects on the decision itself and on group members.

ELEMENTS OF GROUP DECISION MAKING

The three basic elements of group decision making are the group, the individuals comprising the group, and the decision. In Chapter 12 a group was defined as two or more individuals who are psychologically aware of each other, who meet from time to time in face-to-face interaction, who share some common ideology, and who come to perceive themselves as a group. It is important to note the characteristics of both the group as a group and the group members as individuals.

As individuals, each member of the group will bring to the decision-making process his or her own knowledge, experience, values, goals, perceptions, attitudes, and motives. This heterogeneity is held to be the source of most of the advantages of group decision making. That is, those who believe groups are more accurate or creative than individuals attribute these characteristics to the diversity of individual members.

As a group, the group will develop certain characteristics, such as group norms, values, and goals, a status hierarchy, size (number of members), communication patterns, leadership, power relationships, possibly even factions and coalitions. At any time these characteristics may be in different stages of development, of course. The medical board of a hospital may have well-established goals and values (maximum patient care regardless of cost), a clear status hierarchy (based on tenure, medical specialty, and professional reputation), and obvious factions (surgeons v. specialists v. general practitioners), but little leadership. A group of friends ordering dinner at a restaurant may have developed norms and values (wine with every meal, exotic rather than everyday foods) and leadership (based on culinary expertise), but no established patterns of communication, factions, or status differentials.

The *decision itself* cannot be ignored in analyzing group decision processes. The decision may be routine (making up a budget) or novel (dealing with a wildcat strike). It may be of vital concern to all members (responding to a threat to the group's survival) or of only passing interest (selecting an agenda for the next meeting). It may vary as to the degree of risk involved, or the uncertainty over possible effects of the decision, or the time available for making the decision.

All of the above factors—the nature of the group, the characteristics of the individual, and the type of decision—will affect the processes of group decision making. These effects take place through the group processes described below.

GROUP DECISION-MAKING PROCESSES

Several different processes relevant to group decision making can take place, as part of two conceptually different behaviors of the decision-making group: discussion among the members and behavior as a group. To facilitate our discussion of these processes, we will use the example of a group of six people who have crash-landed in the desert and are faced with decisions about survival and rescue.

Discussion among Members

Group discussion can be thought of as putting the unique resources of the group (comprised of the characteristics of the individual members) to work. Discussion can lead to such results as sharing information and experience, generating ideas, critical evaluation, bringing in relevant values, developing feelings of participation, and diffusing responsibilities.

Sharing Information   Different group members may have different facts relevant to the decision. The pilot knew the plane was many miles off course. A survivor noted a small mining camp perhaps a hundred miles away. Another noted the exact time of the crash and knew how many hours of daylight remained.

Sharing Experiences   Experiences of members in similar situations may also be relevant to the decision process. One member's experiences with the desert may indicate that searching for water is futile, while another's experience in the army may suggest that water can be obtained from cacti or from condensation. Others' experiences with groups in crisis situations may indicate that it is essential for the group to agree on a leader or that before any decisions can be made, everyone must calm down. The pilot's experience is that air search will not begin for several hours.

Generating Ideas   The varied experiences and information of the members can lead to the presentation of ideas. These ideas can, in turn, stimulate new ideas in the group. One suggests the need for shade to reduce dehydration, and this generates the idea to salvage cargo for constructing a shelter, which in turn stimulates the suggestion to drape parachutes over the airframe. Someone else picks up the idea of using the parachutes both as shelter and to indicate their presence to search parties.

Critical Evaluation   The generation of ideas and suggestions by some of the group may be critically evaluated by others. It is often difficult for an individual to evaluate and question his own ideas, because of pride of authorship. In a group, each member has the others as potential critics, which can be crucial in questioning the assumptions underlying suggestions for action. The pilot may suggest that the group concentrate on survival and leave the rescue to others. The group may then question assumptions underlying his suggestion: that a search will in fact be initiated, that they are not too far off course to be found, that they are more easily spotted at the crash site than wandering around, that a rescue plane can land in the crash terrain.

Bringing in Relevant Values   Individual values will be brought to bear on the decision and discussed in terms of relevance to the situation and congruence with group and societal values. If one member is badly injured, individual values (for one, his life above all others; for another, giving aid to a comrade in need) may be discussed in the context of group values (all for one and one for all) or societal values (the importance of a single human life). These values may bear importantly on decisions to share resources like water or whether to try to walk out to civilization.

Developing Feelings of Participation   Members whose information, experiences, ideas, and values are shared with the group may experience feelings of having participated in the group decision, even if it is not consistent with their own ideas. In a situation like the one described, where one's very survival depends on the decisions made, such feelings of participation may be important to one's psychological state and willingness to carry out the decision.

Diffusing Responsibility   Discussion of alternatives and relevant values can lead each member to feel somewhat less responsible for a decision than if he were required to make the decision alone and without inputs from others. Suppose the group decided to walk out, leaving a mortally injured passenger behind. It might be easier for each member to rationalize that decision, having received support from the group for the position that they would all die if they stayed with the injured passenger, who would die in any event. A single individual who was forced to make the decision on his own would feel the full weight of responsibility and accountability for his judgment. The group realizes it is more difficult to hold each member of a group wholly accountable for its decisions.

Decision Making as a Group Task

Group decision making is not only a discussion among individual members but a task of the group behaving as a group. There are certain group processes and characteristics which can affect decision making as a group task, including individual leadership, group pressures, status differentials, intragroup competition, and group size.

Individual Leadership   The group may have a recognized leader, or some individual may emerge as a leader in the course of the group's deliberations. This individual can exert a great deal of influence over the group's decision processes, or even dominate them. The leader's influence can be particularly critical if his power is based primarily on some source other than expertise in areas relevant to the decision. For example, the decisions and outcomes for the crash survivors would vary greatly depending upon whether a veteran of the desert (expert power) or a novice who happened to have the only gun (coercive power) emerged as the leader.

Group Pressures   Decision-making groups, like any group, will either have norms for the behavior of their members or will quickly establish them. The members will develop certain common ideas as to what behavior is appropriate and what is inappropriate for the group. Depending on the cohesiveness of the group, some members will exert pressure on the others to behave appropriately and not to behave inappropriately, according to these norms. For instance, the survivors may consider it inappropriate for anyone other than the pilot to influence the group. Individual members will feel group pressures, which may be real or imagined, which can influence their behavior in the group decision process. For example, some may feel reluctant to question the assumptions or suggestions proposed by others, for fear of hurting their feelings or of being perceived as hostile or untrusting.

Status Differentials   In any group or social situation, certain individuals are likely to have more status than others. In the course of the decision-making group's activities there may be expressions of status differences ("I've got seniority," "She's only a girl," "He's the strongest and most resourceful"), and feelings of status differences may develop on the part of both high- and low-status persons. These status differences can affect both the content and the evaluation of the group's deliberations. For example, the group may be more receptive to comments and suggestions from high-status than from low-status members.[3]

Intragroup Competition   Rivalry and competition among group members can arise because these members have a history of competing and thus find it difficult to perceive their roles as anything

---

[3] M. E. Shaw, *Group Dynamics: The Psychology of Small Group Behavior* (New York: McGraw-Hill Book Co., 1971), p. 242.

but competitors. Competition can also carry over into the group's deliberations when the members are in fact competitors outside the group's activities; realtors or lawyers who vie with each other in the daily routine of their professions may find themselves thrown together on zoning boards, civic commissions, legislative committees. The nature and distribution of outcomes among group members can also produce competition. For example, if the group members share equally in any rewards (profit, recognition, praise), competition is less likely than if rewards are distributed according to each member's evaluated contribution to the group's decision making.

Group Size   The size of the group can have a number of important implications for decision making. Common sense and research indicate that communications become more complex and difficult as the size of a group increases. If the group consists of three members, there are nine possible communication links (each member can address the other two individually or together). If the group expands to five members, the number of possible communication links jumps to 70 (each member can address four individuals, six pairs, three sets of three, or the rest of the group as a whole).

As the size of a group increases, not only do communications become more complex, but (as noted in Chapter 13) opportunities for a given individual to participate, satisfaction, and cohesiveness all tend to decrease. Another important consequence of larger groups is that the chances increase that cliques or factions will form (the group breaks down into two or more subgroups). Research has demonstrated that, in small groups, groups with even numbers of members (four or six) are more likely to develop factions than those with odd numbers of members (three, five, or seven).[4]

OUTCOMES OF GROUP DECISION MAKING

We have outlined the basic elements of group decision making: the group, individuals who make up the group, and the type of decision to be made. We have briefly described two sets of variables which are likely to moderate the effects of these elements on the primary outcome of the group's deliberations—its decisions. They also can have lasting effects on the members of the group. These

[4] R. F. Bales and E. F. Borgatta, "Size of Group as a Factor in the Interaction Profile," in *The Small Group*, ed. A. D. Hare, E. F. Borgatta, and R. F. Bales, (New York: Alfred A. Knopf, 1955), pp. 396–413.

variables include the presence of and sharing of individual information, experience, ideas, criticism, and values, as well as feelings
of participation and diffusion of responsibility. In addition, they include group characteristics such as leadership, group pressures and
norms, status, competition, and size.

The ways in which these elements and moderating factors can
combine to affect the decisions made by groups, as well as the
members of the groups, will be the topics of the following sections.
Characteristics of the decision which are attributable to group processes and elements are discussed first, with emphasis on how these
characteristics affect the relative merit of individual and group
decision making.

EFFECTS OF GROUP PROCESSES ON THE DECISION

The effectiveness of group decision making can be compared to
individual decision making on several dimensions: accuracy, judgment and problem solving, creativity, risk taking, and the effects
of cultural values.

Accuracy

Because groups have more information and experience available
to them than any individual member does, and because groups have
a built-in critical evaluation potential, we would expect groups to
make fewer obvious errors in decision making than individuals do.
In fact, most comparisons of groups and individuals support that
contention. Some of the earliest comparisons found that groups
were five to six times as likely to correctly solve problems of logic
and judgment.[5] The researcher attributed much of the group success
to critical evaluation of suggestions and noted that most corrections
of errors were made not by the member who erred but by someone
else in the group.

Note, however, that research has shown that experience with a
problem is no guarantee of success. In fact, the wrong kind of experience can hinder rather than help decision making and problem
solving. In one study, engineers with varied experience with design

---

[5] M. E. Shaw, "A Comparison of Individuals and Small Groups in the Rational
Solutions of Complex Problems," *American Journal of Psychology*, vol. 44 (1932),
pp. 491–504.

problems worked on contracts involving similar problems.[6] Some of the engineers had experienced previous success with similar problems, and others had worked on the problems without success. Other engineers had experienced some successes and some failures with similar problems, or had no previous experience with these problems. The researchers found that prior experience was indeed a factor in problem solving, but in a curious way. Engineers with previous successful experience correctly solved 80 percent of the problems, and those with both successful and unsuccessful experience correctly solved 50 percent. However, engineers with only unsuccessful experience solved only 25 percent of the problems, while those with no prior relevant experience were able to solve 43 percent. Clearly, experience can facilitate the group's decision making—if it is the right kind of experience.

Judgment and Problem Solving

We would also expect groups to make better judgments than individuals because of the additional information, experience, ideas, and critical evaluation available to a group. While there is some validity to this hypothesis, the evidence of research is that the relative superiority of groups to individuals is neither clear-cut nor simple. A major review of such research concluded that characteristics of the decision or problem being solved, as well as variables in the group's processes, affect the relative superiority or inferiority of group judgments.[7]

When Groups Are Superior   For certain kinds of problems groups tend to consistently outperform even the best individual members of the group. Such group superiority is found when the problems have multiple parts and the individual members have *complementary* skills and information which they pool.

For instance, solving a complex organizational problem may require unrelated skills and information. The selection of a site for relocating a plant may require information about markets, transportation, suppliers, labor, real estate, energy, taxes, building codes, long-term credit, ecology, and employee morale. It may require

---

[6] T. J. Allen and D. G. Marquis, "Positive and Negative Biasing Sets: The Effects of Prior Experience on Research Performance," *IEEE Transactions on Engineering Management*, vol. EM–11, (1964), pp. 158–61.

[7] H. H. Kelley and J. W. Thibaut, "Group Problem Solving," in *The Handbook of Social Psychology*, 2d ed., ed. Gardner Lindsey and Eliot Aronson (Reading, Mass.: Addison-Wesley Publishing Co. 1969), ch. 29.

psychological, mathematical, and economic skills, memory, attention to detail, and intuition. No single individual will have all that information or all those skills. To the extent that one individual's deficiencies are covered by the skills or knowledge of someone else in the group, the group is likely to make a better decision than even the best individual member.

It is important to note here, however, that group superiority depends on the sharing of information, experiences, and skills. The mere presence of sufficient complementary information and skills is no guarantee that they will be used in making the decision. Certain group processes or characteristics can interfere with the efficient use of group resources.

For instance, if the group is too large, individuals with vital information may never have the opportunity to use it. Even if the group is not large, inefficient communications may prevent the sharing of information, or even the recognition that certain skills or information are available or needed. Individuals low in status congruence (see Chapter 13) may be unwilling to participate or share, and competition or lack of trust among members can also hinder the sharing of information. A veteran salesman may be unwilling to share his experiences for fear of losing a competitive advantage over newer, more energetic salespeople whom he perceives as a threat to his security and prestige. A politician may be reluctant to share information with a committee if he feels some of the members might later use this information against him or his party.

Status differences among members can affect information sharing, processing, and evaluation. Low-status persons may be unwilling to criticize the suggestions of high-status members. The evaluation of the worth of information can be strongly affected by the status of its source. Studies have demonstrated that the participation and influence of members of decision-making groups are directly related to the relative status of members. These effects are primarily due to the human tendency to inflate expectations of performance by high-status individuals[8] and to overevaluate the performance of high-status individuals.

A classic study of status, performance on a game, and evaluation of performance by twelve-year-old boys found that while status and actual performance were not significantly correlated, status and evaluation of performance by the boys were highly correlated

[8] O. J. Harvey, "An Experimental Approach to the Study of Status Relations in Informal Groups," *American Sociological Review*, vol. 18 (1953), pp. 357–67.

($r = .74$ in one group and .68 in the other).[9] That is, the boys over-estimated the performance of high-status members and underestimated the performance of low-status members. In one group of ten, the performance of the boy with the highest status was actually next to last but was ranked as third best by his peers. In the same group, the performance of one of the lowest status boys was actually best but was ranked next to the bottom.

This tendency for status to bias performance expectations and evaluation persists when the status distinctions are irrelevant to the decisions being made. One series of experiments found that status differences affected participation, influence, and prestige in all cases except when the group agreed that a particular status characteristic was culturally known to be irrelevant.[10]

When Groups Are Above Average On certain kinds of problems, groups tend to be better than the average individual, but usually not as good as the best individual group member. This tendency is particularly true in situations requiring judgment or estimation rather than problem solving. Studies of groups acting as juries, estimating numbers of objects, taking true-false tests, and evaluating poems generally have found groups as good as, or better than, the average individual. A review of the nature of the judgments in which groups were better than average leads to the conclusion that such problems have two common characteristics: they require few steps, and the judgments or solutions can be verified—either proved logically or mathematically, or attested to by the fact that a majority of the members agree on the answer.[11]

Although groups tend to be better than the average individual in such situations, there is general agreement that they are hard pressed to outperform the best individual. A review of the evidence concludes:

> The answer to the first question, "Does the quality of group judgment exceed that of the average individual performance of group members?" is therefore a qualified "Yes." The second question, "Does the quality of group performance exceed that of the most proficient member of the group?" must be answered negatively.[12]

[9] Muzafer Sherif, B. J. White, and O. J. Harvey, "Status in Experimentally Produced Groups," *American Journal of Sociology,* vol. 60 (1955), pp. 370–79.

[10] Joseph Berger, Bernard Cohen, and Morris Zelditch, "Status Characteristics and Social Interaction," *American Sociological Review, vol.* 37 (1972), pp. 241–55.

[11] Kelley and Thibaut, "Group Problem Solving," p. 65.

[12] Shaw, *Group Dynamics,* p. 63.

When Groups Are Inferior   Group processes have been found to interfere with decision making and problem solving when the situation requires a sequence of multiple stages, when the problem is not easily divisible into separate parts, and when the correctness of the solution is not easily demonstrated.[13] First, if the problem is not easily broken down, the group's normal advantage of division of labor is lost. Second, if the correctness of the decision is not verifiable, consensus is difficult and the confidence resulting from consensus fails to materialize. Finally, group discussion tends to interfere with the concentration necessary to sequence the stages of the problem correctly.

In summary, the type of problem or decision can moderate the relative effectiveness of groups in judgment and problem solving. Further, the relative success of groups depends on whether the group uses its advantages—information, skills, ideas, and critical evaluation. We have shown how certain group processes, such as status, competition, and pressures, can nullify these advantages. In fact, it has been found that an individual member with complete information can result in *impaired* group performance when the other group members are unwilling to rely on or accept his comments.[14]

A dramatic example of the failure of a group was the inability of the German High Command to make good decisions in the last three years of World War II. Even though German military intelligence, skills, and experience were sufficient to make decisions such as to withdraw from Stalingrad before the entire German Sixth Army was annihilated, fear, jealousy, competition, poor communications, and the individual domination of Hitler prevented such information and experiences from being used advantageously, at a cost of literally hundreds of thousands of casualties.

Creativity

Several individuals together have more ideas and imagination collectively than any one of their number. It seems reasonable, then, to expect this aggregation of ideas, together with a group's advantages in information and experience, to yield a greater quantity and quality of ideas. That is, groups should be more creative than individuals.

---

[13] Ibid., p. 165.

[14] M. E. Shaw and W. T. Penrod, Jr., "Does More Information Available to a Group Always Improve Group Performance?" *Sociometry*, vol. 25 (1962), pp. 377–90.

In 1956 William H. Whyte, Jr. wrote *The Organization Man,* in which, among other things, he spoke of "the current attempt to see the group as a creative vehicle." He pointed out that "fast becoming a fixture of organization life is the meeting self-consciously dedicated to creating ideas."[15]

A good deal of this collective creative effort used one form or another of the *brainstorming* technique developed in 1939 by Alex Osborn of the Madison Avenue advertising agency Batten, Barton, Durstine, and Osborn.[16] The purpose of the technique was to enhance creativity through group discussion. Certain procedural rules were enforced to enhance "free thinking" and to offset group processes that could possibly inhibit creativity, such as critical evaluation. The most important of these rules were:

1. Free-wheeling was encouraged. No idea was to be considered too far-out.
2. Using or building upon others' ideas was supported. No idea was any one member's property. All ideas belonged to the group.
3. There was to be no criticism. Ideas were to be generated and used, but not evaluated.

Osborn's enthusiasm for brainstorming and his agency's success in a creative field enabled him to argue persuasively for the creative potential of such group creativity. Indeed, brainstorming or derivatives of it are in widespread use today in organizations of all sort.

However, the publicity the technique received eventually led to systematic investigation of claims for its effects on creativity. The evidence was not encouraging. In the late 1950s, a research team at Yale pitted four-man brainstorming groups against sets of four individuals working alone.[17] Both groups and individuals were familiarized with the rules of brainstorming and then were given 12 minutes to generate as many ideas as possible about a specific problem. Three problems were used, one seeking ways to increase European tourism, one assessing the assets and liabilities of being born with an extra thumb, and one dealing with problems of increasing school enrollments in subsequent decades.

---

[15] W. H. Whyte, Jr., *The Organization Man* (New York: Simon & Schuster, 1956), pp. 57–58.

[16] A. F. Osborn, *Applied Imagination* (New York: Scribner's 1957).

[17] D. W. Taylor, P. C. Berry, and C. H. Block, "Does Group Participation When Using Brainstorming Facilitate or Inhibit Creative Thinking?" *Administrative Science Quarterly,* vol. 3 (1958), pp. 23–47.

Some have found it surprising that four men working as individuals consistently generated a greater number of nonredundant ideas than did four-man brainstorming groups. As Table 15–1 shows, four individuals produced, on the average, nearly twice as many ideas as a four-man group, on each of the three problems. Judges also evaluated the ideas generated; using their ratings, the researchers found that four individuals produced more "original and qualitatively superior ideas" than did four-man groups.

TABLE 15–1
Average Numbers of Ideas Generated by Four-Man Brainstorming Groups and Four Individuals

	Tourist Problem	Thumb Problem	School Problem
Four individuals	68.3	72.6	63.5
Four-man groups	38.4	41.3	32.6

Source: D. W. Taylor, P. C. Berry, and C. H. Block, "Does Group Participation When Using Brainstorming Facilitate or Inhibit Creative Thinking?" *Administrative Science Quarterly,* vol. 3 (1958), pp. 23–47.

Subsequent research substantiated these findings. Apparently the group process inhibited creativity. Despite rules against criticism, some individuals nevertheless felt inhibited from making far-out comments in the presence of others: One need not be called a fool to feel a fool. Additionally, the researchers noted a tendency for groups to become engrossed in a single area or train of thought, and there was always the problem of individual domination in the group.

Nevertheless, brainstorming and its derivatives have not been abondoned, and some improvements have been made in the technique. While granting that groups may inhibit creativity, it has been pointed out that some group creative activity may be necessary when no one individual has the resources or information needed to solve the problem. One technique designed to alleviate the dangers of individual domination and to overcome the temerity of some members requires each member to speak in sequence or to "pass" if he has no ideas to contribute. The originator of this technique reports a great improvement (more than an 80 percent increase in the number of ideas generated) over other group methods.[18]

[18] T. J. Bouchard, "Whatever Happened to Brainstorming?" *Journal of Creative Behavior,* vol. 5, no. 3 (1971), pp. 182–89.

Risk Taking

Conventional wisdom and folklore saw caution as one definite characteristic of group decisions. One of the traditional axioms of military thought was that individuals, not groups, should make decisions because groups are not capable of the boldness and willingness to take calculated risks that are necessary in a winning military strategy. Another flaw in group decision making which is often cited by military writers is the diffusion of responsibility among the members. Group decision making is proscribed because of the difficulty of holding individual members accountable for group decisions, a flaw which goes against the tradition of individual commanders being accountable for decisions which may affect the lives of their people.

It is interesting that these two weaknesses of group decision making are contradictory. If, indeed, group members feel less accountable for their decisions than do individual decision makers, we would expect groups to be willing to take greater, not lesser, risks than individuals.

This contradiction in theory remained unnoticed until the early 1960s, when J. A. F. Stoner, a student doing research for his master's thesis at M.I.T., systematically tested the hypothesis that group decisions are more cautious than individual decisions.[19] Using a series of cases developed to measure individual propensity to take risk, he administered these cases to individuals, then to groups composed of the same individuals. Each case described an individual faced with a lifelike dilemma, forced to choose between a relatively safe alternative with a moderate payoff and a riskier alternative with a higher potential payoff. Situations ranged from a football team playing for a tie or gambling for a win in a big game to an engineer choosing between a secure job with a big corporation or an uncertain job with a new but potentially more rewarding and exciting company.

Contrary to the hypothesis (and to most people's surprise), the group decisions were consistently more risky than those of individuals. At first, this riskiness was attributed to the nature of the subject population studied: male graduate students in management, who identified with risk taking as a managerial characteristic.

---

[19] J. A. F. Stoner, "A Comparison of Individual and Group Decisions Involving Risk," master's thesis, M.I.T., Sloan School of Industrial Management, 1961.

However, in subsequent research with male undergraduate liberal arts students, female students, and housewives, identical results were reported: Groups took greater risk in their decisions than individuals did.

Spurred on by the consistency of these surprising results, researchers carried out a barrage of studies to understand the so-called risky-shift phenomenon—that individual decisions shift to greater risk following group discussion. In addition to the diffusion of responsibility, other possible causes of the risky shift included notions that leaders of group decisions are inherently greater risk takers than other members, that group decisions tend to shift toward the most extreme decisions of individual members, and that forcing individuals to take as much time in decision making as groups did would result in risky shifts.

Unfortunately, none of these additional explanations received consistent support. In 1967, Stoner carried out a study for his doctoral dissertation which cast serious doubt on the conclusion that groups consistently take greater risk than individuals, as we will note in the following section.[20]

The Cultural Value Effect

Observations of groups engaged in decision making and the observations and reflections of others led Stoner to believe that group decisions are more strongly affected by cultural values than individual decisions are. An individual making a decision can simply apply his own value system or his interpretation of society's value system to a decision and be done with it. However, group decisions call for individuals to propose alternatives to defend their positions. If the defense includes certain values, they are likely to be questioned or evaluated against the group's interpretation of the society's values. Once brought into the discussion, the group's values play an important part in its ultimate decision, as group pressures are directed toward those whose alternatives are not perceived to be in line with theirs.

For example, suppose a jury is deciding the guilt or innocence of a criminal defendant. If the evidence is not overwhelming, a discussion will certainly arise over the values of finding the defen-

[20] J. A. Stoner, "Risky and Cautious Shifts in Group Decisions: The Influence of Widely Held Values," *Journal of Experimental Social Psychology*, vol. 4 (1968), pp. 442–59.

dant guilty and thus removing a dangerous felon from the streets at the risk of convicting an innocent person and violating values of individual freedom. The values of this society, as embedded in our Constitution and still widely held, are that it is better to release a guilty man than to jail an innocent one. If the propositions about cultural values were correct, we would expect juries to evidence some bias in favor of defendants in criminal cases.

In fact, we have evidence to support this hypothesis. In 1966 the University of Chicago Law School published a study of actual criminal cases which compared the jury's decision to the decision that the judge in each case said he or she would have rendered.[21] The results for nearly 3,600 cases involving 600 judges and 42 categories of crime revealed a pattern of jury decisions favoring the defendant. In 14 percent of the cases, both judge and jury agreed to acquit the defendant, and in 58 percent of the cases both judge and jury agreed to convict. But in 19 percent of the cases, the jury acquitted a defendant that the judge would have convicted, and in only about 3 percent of the cases did the jury convict a defendant that the judge would have acquitted.

Research has experimentally confirmed the tendency for groups to make decisions more closely aligned with cultural values, using a set of life-situation dilemmas similar to those described above. However, in the set Stoner used each alternative was associated with a particular value of society.[22] For instance, one situation involved a couple forced to decide whether to abort a problem pregnancy, where further complications in the pregnancy could threaten the mother's life. Associated with the alternative "allow the pregnancy to continue" is the value "the life of a child." Associated with the alternative "abort" is the value "the life of one's spouse." Sociologists maintain that this society values the life of one's spouse over the life of a child. Thus it was predicted that, in this decision involving risk and uncertainty, group discussion and decision processes would result in a decision more consistent with the alternative that had the greater societal value (the life of one's spouse). That is, groups would be more *cautious* than individuals in deciding to allow the pregnancy to continue.

This hypothesis was tested on 32 small groups of housewives and students from M.I.T. and Harvard. The results generally sup-

[21] Harry Kalven and Hans Zeisel, *The American Jury* (Boston: Little, Brown & Co., 1966).

[22] Stoner, "Risky and Cautious Shifts in Group Decisions."

ported the effect of societal values on group decisions. On decisions in which society placed a greater value on the more cautious alternative, groups were more cautious than individuals. For example, on the decision to abort or continue a problem pregnancy, the average individual decided to allow the pregnancy to continue if the doctors rated the chances of successful birth at 80 percent. But the average group decided to allow the pregnancy to continue only if the chances of success were at least 90 percent.

Subsequent research has substantiated the concept that societal values can overcome the tendency for groups to take greater risk than individuals. A study of gambling decisions by individuals and groups revealed that the expected value of a bet affected the relative riskiness of groups over individuals.[23] If the expected value (odds of winning $\times$ payoff $-$ stake) was positive, groups took more risk than individuals. If the expected value of the bet was negative, groups took less risk than individuals.

As a consequence of more than ten years' research, we can conclude that there are at least two forces at work in group decision making under uncertainty.[24] First, a force generated by group discussion of alternatives results in group decisions that are more consistent with widely held values than individual decisions are. Second, a force arising from the diffusion of responsibility and the confidence of certain members results in groups tending to take greater risk than individuals. While the traditional belief that groups are always *more* cautious than individuals has been dispelled, we cannot say that groups are always *less* cautious than individuals—it depends upon the values associated with the alternatives. However, the evidence shows that it is easier to find decisions in which groups take more risk than decisions in which groups take less risk than individuals.

EFFECTS OF GROUP PROCESSES ON GROUP MEMBERS

A number of possible outcomes of group decision elements and processes for members of the groups have been pointed out. We will examine some of these outcomes here, including better understand-

---

[23] D. G. Marquis and H. J. Reitz, "Effects of Uncertainty on Risk Taking in Individual and Group Decisions," *Behavioral Science*, vol. 4 (1969), pp. 181–88.

[24] For a thorough summary of research on group risk taking and several representative studies, see the *Journal of Personality and Social Psychology*, vol. 20 (December 1971).

ing, commitment to carry out the decision, changes in goals, and alienation.[25]

Better Understanding

General Robert E. Lee's success in the Civil War was partly due to the fact that his decisions and orders were seldom misinterpreted by his battlefield commanders. In the confusion of war, Lee was forced to rely on hand-carried, written messages, and he did not have the advantage of feedback provided by modern communication. Therefore he strove to eliminate any possible ambiguity or misunderstanding of his orders. His practice was to draft an order, then call the lowest ranking sentry into his tent to read the order. If, upon being questioned, the sentry clearly understood the order, Lee dispatched it via courier to the intended commander. If, however, the sentry misinterpreted the order, Lee returned to his desk and revised it. The general reasoned that if a sentry could misinterpret an order, so could a company commander, but if the sentry could understand the order, the commander ought to be able to.

Lee realized that a decision, no matter how good, was useless unless executed, and an order could not be executed properly if misunderstood. The principles hold for any organizational decision. In the chapter on communication we stressed the importance of two-way communication for clarity and understanding. If those who are to execute a decision participate in making it, the opportunities for two-way communication are increased, and the chances that it will be misunderstood are diminished.

Commitment

We would expect the feelings of participation that arise from being in on a group decision to strengthen the commitment of group members to executing the decision. If one is allowed to contribute information, experience, and ideas, voice criticisms, and discuss relevant values, one's resistance to carrying out the decision should diminish.

A series of studies with housewives in World War II yielded the first substantial evidence that group decision processes increase

---

[25] Much of this section is based on N. R. F. Maier, "Assets and Liabilities in Group Problem-Solving: The Need for an Integrative Function," *Psychological Review,* vol. 74 (1967), pp. 239–49.

commitment.[26] Government food experts had become concerned about the food buying and using habits of American housewives. Because of a commitment to provide one pound of meat a day for every American in uniform, there was a shortage of most cuts of meat for civilians. However, there was a surplus of offal items—brains, kidneys, and tripe. Although these offal items were nutritious and were readily consumed by Europeans, Americans generally neglected this source of protein. Government research had also documented the nutritional benefits of milk and milk products, orange juice, and cod liver oil.

The problem was to induce housewives to make use of products that they generally ignored. Psychologist Kurt Lewin, often regarded as the father of group dynamics, was retained to oversee the attempts to change the food-buying habits of housewives. He used a number of traditional methods to persuade housewives in face-to-face sessions; most of them involved housewives attending lectures, viewing charts, and listening to panels of experts describe the virtues of the products and exhort them to support the government's efforts. An additional method devised by Lewin involved a group of housewives in discussing the pros and cons of the changes among themselves, with experts available to answer questions.

To test the effectiveness of the various methods, panels of researchers were employed to follow up on the actual food-buying and consuming behavior of the participants at two- and four-week intervals after the sessions. The results, summarized in Figure 15–1, clearly indicate the superiority of the group method. Housewives who participated in group discussion sessions used significantly more offal items, fresh milk, powdered milk, orange juice, and cod liver oil than those who did not participate in such discussions.

Subsequent research has indicated that two important factors contributing to increases in commitment are the group decision itself and perception of a group consensus to carry out the decision.[27] Apparently, agreeing with the rest of the group to carry out the group's decision creates felt pressures to conform, thus increasing the likelihood it will be carried out.

Participation in Decisions   It should be noted that there are several degrees of individual participation in various types of group

[26] Kurt Lewin, "Group Decision and Social Change," in *Readings in Social Psychology*, ed. T. M. Newcomb and E. L. Hartley (New York: Holt, Rinehart & Winston, 1947).

[27] E. B. Bennett, "Discussion, Decision, Commitment and Consensus in Group Decision," *Human Relations*, vol. 8 (1955), pp. 251–74.

FIGURE 15–1

Percentage Increases in the Use of Various Food Products Four Weeks after Lecture or Individual Instruction versus Four Weeks after Group Decision

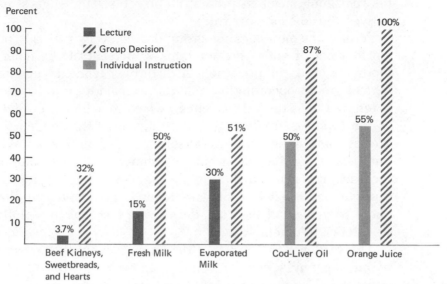

Source: Adapted from Kurt Lewin, "Group Decision and Social Change," in *Readngs in Social Psychology*, ed. T. M. Newcomb and E. C. Hartley (New York: Holt, Rinehart & Winston, 1947).

decisions. In one type of decision the group serves an *advisory* function; the group presents information and debates the alternatives, but the final decision is left up to a single individual. The highest decisions of the Executive branch of the government are usually made this way, with the Cabinet or Security Council providing inputs, discussion, and debate but the President making the ultimate decision.[28] Harry Truman said of such decisions, "The buck stops here."

Even if such a decision process is not specified, it often happens that an apparent group decision is really a rubber stamp. A liability of group decision making is the danger that some individual will dominate the decision because of his status, charm, or power. Unfortunately, there is no evidence that the ability to dominate a group is related to the ability to solve problems or make good decisions.

Decision making by the *minority* is a second type. This often happens in large groups, on issues of interest to only a few members who manage to railroad their program through to the rest of the

[28] A lucid description and analysis of Presidential decision making and the advisory capacity of other members of government is given in Theodore C. Sorensen, *Decision-Making in the White House* (New York: Columbia University Press, 1963).

disinterested members. In such cases, several people (but less than a majority of the group) are strongly in favor of an alternative, and the remaining members present no objections and suggest no alternatives; thus the minority rules.

Perhaps the most common group decision is by *majority*, in which any number of voters greater than 50 percent of the membership binds the group to a decision. A disturbing tendency among members of groups operating on minority or majority rule bases is what is referred to as the valence effect, which may be better understood as the *bandwagon effect*. Research has noted this tendency among groups confronting a variety of solutions to a problem.[29] When the numbers of positive and negative comments for each solution were recorded, it was found that the first solution which elicited 15 more positive than negative comments tends to be adopted by the group about 85 percent of the time, despite the fact that the solution may be inferior to others.

This tendency for the rest of the group to jump on the bandwagon of an apparently popular solution is probably due to pluralistic ignorance. The number of positive comments convinces an uncommitted member that "everybody else" is in favor of the solution, and so if everybody else is for it, he decides to go along with the rest. However, it has been pointed out that a sufficient number of positive comments can be generated by a minority as well as by a true majority.

A fourth type of group decision is *unanimity*, which requires the affirmation of all members. This is the most difficult type of decision to achieve, and it is usually reserved for decisions of great importance to the groups because of the time and energy it requires.

However, many groups and organizations achieve what might be called forced unanimity in their decisions. The appearance of unanimity may be useful as propaganda in presenting a united front to an enemy or a competitor. Leaders often believe unanimity is important to increase group cohesiveness and commitment to the decision. Even after a close and possibly divisive debate, these leaders will push for an unanimous acclamation of the majority decision, using parliamentary tactics and group pressure to coerce dissidents into voting with the majority.

The classic example of forced unanimity occurs every four years in this country at the major political parties' Presidential nominating conventions. After several months of often vicious primary cam-

---

[29] Maier, "Assets and Liabilities in Group Problem Solving."

paigning, the party's nominee is elected by a majority vote of the convention delegates. Usually the vote is close enough that the winner does not achieve a majority until late in the voting session, but then the chairman invariably accepts a motion from the winner's supporters that the convention unanimously accept the nominee by acclamation. The chairman calls for a voice vote, asks for the ayes, and declares the candidate unanimously elected—without even calling for the nays.

The Democratic Convention of 1972 was the epitome of forced unanimity, won in a close election that concluded a particularly bitter campaign with several rivals. The convention's chairperson succeeded in getting the traditional acclamation of the nominee, Sen. George McGovern. The party even managed to persuade the defeated candidates to appear on stage with the nominee, holding hands as a gesture of party unity. These tactics, however, only served to point out the futility of forced unanimity. The show of unity was obviously contrived and probably galling to some of the candidates and their supporters. Soon after the convention, Democrats deserted their party's candidate in droves, refusing to campaign for him and forming "Democrats for Nixon" organizations. Despite his party's significant majority in voter registration, Senator Mc-Govern was defeated by the greatest margin in history, winning the electoral votes of only 1 of the 50 states.

A fifth type of group decision is by *consensus.* As in unanimity, the entire group must favor the same alternative, but a consensus can never be forced. The group must not accept a majority decision unless all objections and alternatives have been explored and all members genuinely feel that the alternative is best.

The advantage of consensus is that, of all types of decisions, it is likely to achieve clear understanding and commitment to the decision. The disadvantage is that it requires even more time and energy than unanimity. Even the strongest advocates of consensus agree that it is a difficult state to achieve. The chapter on group development and structure (Chapter 13) presented a model of group development whose authors describe consensus as possible only in a "mature group, which had evolved through several phases of development, in which members had accepted one another's differences and could deal with conflict at a rational, rather than emotional, level.[30]

---

[30] W. G. Bennis and H. S. Shepard, "A Theory of Group Development," *Human Relations,* vol. 9 (1965), pp. 415–57.

Changes in Goals

A distinct liability of group decision processes is the danger that the goal of the decision-making unit will be changed from making the best possible solution to something less, resulting in one of two conditions. Both are due to intergroup conflict, usually between factions or coalitions representing different viewpoints.

If the factions or coalitions are relatively equal, they may bring about a stalemate in the decision process. Neither side is strong enough to push its alternative through to the entire group, yet neither is willing to permit the adoption of its rival's alternative. Eventually, time creates pressures to arrive at some solution. The goal then changes from making the best decision to making a decision palatable to both factions—a compromise. The problem with compromise is that it is often worse than either of the extremes from which it emerged.

Take for example a finance committee deciding whether to invest in the development of a new product. One faction believes in the product and pushes for a million-dollar budget, and the other is so skeptical of the product that it does not want to give it any funds. Eventually it becomes clear that neither side will win, and the committee has to get on with other decisions. So someone suggests a compromise—say, a $250,000 budget—to which both sides agree. Unfortunately, $250,000 is not enough to develop the product adequately, and the project is started but fails for lack of proper funding. It would have been better either to provide complete funding to guarantee success or to abandon the project entirely. As it was, the compromise resulted in a waste of talent, energy and $250,000.

In the second condition that can be brought about by factions and coalitions in decision-making groups, rivalry becomes so intense that cooperation is virtually impossible. In such cases the goal of the factions which make up the group often changes from making the best possible decision to winning. In some situations it is not rare to find each faction adopting the attitude "I don't care whether our alternative is best for the group or not; we're out to win at all costs."

Effects on Losers

When rivalry between factions becomes as intense as that described above, the factions began to label themselves as "winners" and "losers." One outcome of continuing these processes is the negative effect on the losers. If one faction has suffered a series of setbacks, its members may turn on each other, their leader, or the rest of the group. They may begin to feel alienated from the rest of the group. Alienation may develop into a reluctance to support any of the group's decisions, or even into apathy or withdrawal from other group activities.

TIME AND COST CONSIDERATIONS

An almost certain outcome of group processes is that the decision will be delayed beyond the time required for an individual to make the same decision. First, setup time is required—the group must be assembled, a suitable meeting place located, and an agenda established. Second, startup time is longer—exchanging pleasantries and amenities, dealing with status and power differences, establishing a format for discussion and decision. Finally, group discussion will take longer than the private discussions an individual has with himself.

One of the few instances in which a group decision may require less time is when the individual who would normally make the decision is likely to procrastinate or put off the decision. Sometimes a decision can be speeded up by giving it to a group. Scheduling a meeting and assembling the members can put an end to procrastination.

Group decisions usually cost more than individual decisions. Time is money, particularly when the cost of man-hours invested is included. Except in unusual cases, the number of man-hours required to get a group decision can far exceed that required for an individual decision. If costs of acquiring the meeting place and transportation to the site are included, costs often become prohibitive. For these reasons, the decision-making boards of many professional organizations, composed of people from all over the country, delegate a good deal of their decision-making authority to an executive secretary; the time and cost of assembling the board prevents it from meeting more than once or twice a year.

ALTERNATIVES TO FACE-TO-FACE GROUP TECHNIQUES

Students of decision making have wrestled with the problem of how to obtain the advantages of group processes while avoiding the liabilities. One particular technique which shows promise is the Delphi technique developed by researchers at the Rand Corporation.

The Delphi technique attempts to exploit the additional information, experience, and critical evaluation available to a group, while minimizing potential adverse effects of face-to-face interaction. The Delphi technique can be outlined as follows:

1. A number of experts on the problem to be solved are identified, and their cooperation is enlisted.
2. The basic problem is presented to each expert.
3. Each expert anonymously and independently records his or her comments, suggestions, and solutions to the problem.
4. The experts' comments are compiled at a central location, transcribed, and reproduced.
5. Each expert receives a copy of all the other experts' comments and solutions.
6. Each expert comments on the others' proposals, suggests new ideas triggered by their remarks, and returns these to the central location.
7. Steps 5 and 6 are repeated as often as necessary until consensus is reached.[31]

The advantages of the Delphi technique are fairly obvious. The expertise, experience, and criticism of several individuals can be brought to bear on a problem, and by recycling each member's comments, relevant values can be incorporated and new ideas stimulated. The costs of selecting a common place and time for meeting and for transporting members can be eliminated. Rand has been able to secure the participation of renowned scientists from around the world in work on some of its problems, although the costs of transportation and the problems of scheduling a meeting of these extraordinarily busy people would be prohibitive.

The Delphi technique is not without disadvantages. First, going through several iterations of steps 6 and 7 takes a great deal of time, especially if this must be accomplished by transatlantic mail. Second, considerable effort must be expended in transcribing, reproducing, and transmitting the comments to each member. Third, some control over the decision making effort is lost. Without the pressures of face-to-face interaction, some members are likely to procrastinate in providing their comments and solutions.

---

[31] N. C. Dalkey and Olaf Helmer, "An Experimental Application of the Delphi Method to the Use of Experts," *Management Science*, vol. 9 (1963), pp. 458–67.

A second technique, the Nominal group technique, incorporates some features of brainstorming and Delphi.[32] As in brainstorming, individuals are brought together to work on a problem. The following sequence is followed:

1. Before discussion, each member independently writes down his or her ideas on the problem.
2. Each in turn presents one idea to the group without discussion. Members continue taking turns until all ideas have been presented and written on a blackboard.
3. The group discusses the ideas for clarity and evaluates them.
4. Finally, each member silently and independently ranks the ideas.
5. The idea with the highest aggregate ranking is the group decision.

An experimental study of the Nominal and Delphi techniques examined both the quantity of unique ideas generated and the perceived satisfaction of group members. Students, faculty, and administrators were randomly assigned to seven-person groups which followed Nominal, Delphi, or traditional interaction lines and asked to define the job of student resident counselors in university dorms. Evaluation of the ideas by a panel of judges revealed that both Nominal and Delphi groups generated significantly more unique ideas than traditional groups. The members themselves reported significantly greater satisfaction with the Nominal group technique than with either of the other two.

SUMMARY

The use of groups to make decisions deserves more thought than has typically been given it. Group decisions have potential advantages over individual decisions. There are opportunities for sharing information and experience, for stimulating ideas, for critical evaluation, for applying relevant values, and for generating feelings of participation that are not available in individual decision making. These advantages can result in less error, better judgment, greater understanding and commitment, and decisions that are more consistent with widely held values.

---

[32] A. H. Van de Ven and André Delbecq, "The Effectiveness of Nominal, Delphi, and Interacting Group Decision Making Processes," *Academy of Management Journal*, vol. 17 (1974), pp. 605–21. For a practical explanation of the techniques and their use in organizations, see A. L. Delbecq, A. H. Van de Ven and D. H. Gustafson, *Group Techniques for Program Planning: A Guide to Nominal and Delphi Processes* (Glenview, Ill.: Scott, Foresmen & Co., 1975).

However, certain group processes can limit the achievement of this potential and generate their own disadvantages. Group activity can often lead to individual domination, feelings of status differences, competition, factions, group pressures, and diffusion of responsibility. These tendencies can detract from the quality and creativity of group decisions and the understanding and commitment of its members. They can lead to excessive risk taking, lack of accountability, changes in goals, alienation, delays, and expense. The notion that any group decision is inherently superior to the decision of any individual in the group is simply untrue.

Research in ways to improve group decision processes is continuing. One implication of the research on group decision making is clear. The tendency for organizations to give all important decisions automatically to groups is costly. Before an organization decides to use the group as a tool, as in employing any tool it should have some confidence that the group can utilize its advantages and that these advantages are worth the cost of the group decision-making process.

QUESTIONS FOR REVIEW AND DISCUSSION

1. One of the key elements of most group decision-making processes is discussion among members. What results of discussion might benefit good decision making? What results of discussion might inhibit good decision making?

2. What is meant by "diffusion of responsibility"? What are the implications of diffusion of responsibility for group decisions?

3. Suppose you had to put together a decision-making committee to deal with undergraduate curriculum changes in your college. What factors would you consider in putting together this committee, and why?

4. Given your knowledge of group v. individual decision making, how would you react to a proposal to abolish the present jury system in criminal cases and leave the decision up to a single individual—the judge? Explain.

5. "Groups are more accurate problem solvers than individuals." React to this statement.

6. In selecting members of a decision-making group, a prudent executive would want to consider not only what a potential member might contribute to the group but what the decision-making process might do to the potential member. Explain.

7. What two factors should any manager consider before turning a deci-
    sion over to a group?

8. The Nominal and Delphi group techniques show promise as improve-
    ments over traditional techniques. Under what conditions might an
    organization prefer the Nominal over the Delphi method? Under
    what conditions might an organization prefer the Delphi over the
    Nominal method?

KEY WORDS

Diffusion of responsibility   Consensus
Brainstorming   Delphi technique
Risky shift   Nominal group technique
Cultural value effect

chapter sixteen

Helping, Cooperating, and Competing

Hal Edwards grabbed for the ringing phone, cradled the receiver against his shoulder, and reached for the cigarettes in his shirt pocket. "Miami Farm Implements, Edwards here," he barked, propping his feet on his desk as he lit his first cigarette of the morning.

"Hal, this is Frank Buchman. I'm in a bind and wonder if you could help me out."

Hal chuckled. Frank managed the implement dealership in the next county. Both Hal's and Frank's dealerships were franchises of the same international farm implement manufacturer. While Hal had operated his dealership for 18 years, Frank was new to the business, having bought out the old dealership in Douglas County only 18 months earlier. Frank often called Hal for advice, which the older man was only too flattered to give.

"Sure, Frank, what's on your mind?" Hal replied, dragging on his cigarette and leaning back in his chair.

"Well, Hal, old Bill Crank came by yesterday evening and told me he wanted a new 1700 combine—the whole works. Seems his old one finally gave out on him right in the middle of his bean field. I told Bill that the only one I had in stock was sold, and it'd be about three weeks before I expect the new model on order to get in.

"You know Bill. He wants it right now, and flat told me if I can't get him one by the end of the week he'll go over to Louisburg and pick up that new Harvester outfit they have over there. He's just ornery enough to do it, too."

Hal dropped his feet off the desk and sat up. Uh oh, he thought, I know what's coming next.

"Hal, what I need to know is, will you transfer me that 1700 you showed at the county fair last week? Then I'll send that new model I've got on order to your place when she comes in."

Hal's mind labored as he crushed out his cigarette. I need time, he thought. "Frank, I'd like to help you out, but I've got somebody pretty interested in that combine myself right now. Let me check with him first. If he's just shopping around or in no great rush, we might work something out. What say I get back to you before supper?"

"Great, Hal, I appreciate it. Hope you can help me out. It'd be a big boost to me to sell two of these babies in one season. Besides, I'd sure hate to see old Bill driving a Harvester. He's not exactly uninfluential in these parts. I'll wait for your call."

Hal dropped the receiver back in place and reached for a pencil. What a deal! Here he'd just about sewed up the company's contest for spring sales. He and Edna were already planning their trip to the Azores, which the company provided, all expenses paid, for the district winners.

And now this kid Buchman comes up with two combine sales in one week! Let's see now . . . a 1700 series, with auxiliary equipment, might go as high as $65,000! Two of these would surely top $115,000, and that would put Frank's franchise dangerously close, if not past, Hal's own figures, with less than two weeks left in the contest.

The trouble was, Hal liked Frank. Frank was no smart-aleck youngster—he worked long and hard to build up his business. And he trusted Hal and gave Hal the kind of respect his expertise deserved.

But Frank's sales wouldn't be near Hal's without Hal's help. And now Frank was asking him, in effect, to cut his own throat! Of course, Frank probably had no idea how close their sales totals actually were, but still. . . .

It's a strange fact, Hal thought. Here I'm being asked to cooperate with somebody who turns out to be my closest competitor. On the one hand, I'd like to help the boy out. On the other hand, I deserve that Azores trip! Wonder what I ought to do?

HAL EDWARDS faces a problem not uncommon in many organizations. He sees himself in a system in which he is expected to cooperate with another member of the organization, but that other member is also a competitor.

Both Hal and Frank are vying for the same prize—a trip to the Azores. Such situations produce competition. But the company wants Hal and Frank to cooperate. Transferring inventory to help other dealers short on stock is highly encouraged by the company, as it allows increased sales without excess inventory.

The company wants both competition, to provide individual incentive for high sales, and cooperation, to avoid lost sales opportunities and to reduce costs. From Frank's point of view, cooperation is rewarding. If Hal transfers the combine, Frank gets a big sale and Hal gets a newer model to replace the transfer. From Hal's point of view, cooperation is self-defeating; Frank's sale decreases Hal's chances of getting the Azores trip. Hal feels he's being asked not just to cooperate but to slit his own throat—to help another at considerable cost to himself.

This chapter covers several types of social behavior which are common among people working in organizations—helping behavior, cooperation, and competition. These modes of behavior will be defined, and differences among them will be illustrated by several examples. We will describe factors which tend to elicit these behaviors, compare the relative effectiveness of cooperation and competition, and discuss one particular response to a competitive situation: the formation of coalitions.

HELPING BEHAVIOR: ALTRUISM

The social-psychological term for helping behavior is *altruism*— behavior which helps another without external rewards for the helper. In Hal Edward's view, he was being asked to be altruistic, to help Frank Buchman at no gain to himself. In fact, he would be helping Frank at the risk of personal loss. If Frank sells the combine, Hal may lose the contest and the free trip to the Azores.

Altruism usually involves at least some cost to the helper, such as the physical, mental, or emotional effort involved in helping someone else. Hal's previous attempts to respond to Frank's requests for advice were also altruistic; they helped Frank, and they cost Hal at least some time and effort in replying.

Helping behavior can mean a great deal to an organization. Informal assistance to other members, groups, departments, or plants, even at some cost to the helping unit, can provide a smoother and more immediate response to organizational problems than waiting for the organization's bureaucracy to respond to the situation.

In many organizations, altruism plays a bigger role than might be suspected. Employees are expected to be helpful to clients or customers even though a sale is neither imminent nor likely. Departments are expected to help another department out of a bad situation, cover up for another's failure, take over another's "problem" employees, pass on vital information, and lend out equipment, even though this behavior is not explicitly rewarded either by the organization or by the recipient of the help.

Helping behavior is often mislabeled cooperation. Cooperation means working together for some joint goal or mutual benefit, as we will note in the section on cooperation and competition. What the organization or the department in trouble may call cooperation is really altruism—they expect help, though there are no obvious benefits to the helper.

Helping behavior went largely unresearched until a notorious incident in March 1964. A young girl named Kitty Genovese, returning to her home in Queens, New York, at 3:00 A.M., was attacked by a man with a knife. Her screams of terror attracted the attention of no fewer than 38 respectable, law-abiding citizens, her neighbors in the Kew Gardens apartment complex. These 38 people watched in horror as her assailant stalked and assaulted her in three separate attacks lasting over half an hour. Yet not one of the neighbors came to her aid; none even called the police. Only after the assailant had left and Miss Genovese was dead did a single individual go to the telephone.

The story received nationwide attention and provoked a new interest in helping behavior. Most of the research has focused on the conditions under which one individual might reasonably expect to receive help from another.

Determinants of Altruistic Behavior

Most of the research on altruism has been experimental attempts to isolate factors which increase or decrease the likelihood of a helping response. These include social norms, models, the presence of others, and the dependency of the person needing help.

Social Norms One plausible reason why individuals provide help to others is that society expects such behavior. "Social responsibility" implies the obligation to assist others in need of help. Certainly the notion of helping others is an important tenet of most major religions. It is also a basis for the collective actions of nations and governments, ranging in this country from the Marshall Plan through Medicare to the acceptance and care of Vietnamese refugees.

Nevertheless, attempts to demonstrate that social responsibility norms elicit altruistic behavior have largely failed.[1] Many studies of altruism have found that most helpers are not thinking about social norms or what they ought to do when responding to a request for help. Studies in which certain potential helpers were preached to or reminded of their social responsibilities found these subjects gave no more help than potential helpers who were not reminded of them.

---

[1] J. R. Macaulay and Leonard Berkowitz, eds., *Altruism and Helping Behavior* (New York: Academic Press, 1970), pp. 4–6.

Models Helping behavior seems to be particularly responsive to models. Studies of both children and adults have found that charitable contributions and assistance to victims increase when potential helpers observe another person contributing, sharing, or helping. Individuals, uncertain as to what they should do in a novel situation, are particularly susceptible to the influence of others. Imitation is one way out of such a dilemma—do what others do.

The influence of models has been found in a variety of situations. Volunteers for an experiment increased when potential volunteers observed someone else volunteer.[2] Donations to a Salvation Army bell ringer increased when a confederate dropped some coins in the pot in the view of potential donors. Offers to help a woman change a flat tire increased when passing motorists had just witnessed another motorist being helped.[3]

The effects of a model can be subtler than simply eliciting perfect imitation. One set of studies was designed to test the effects of a model who explicitly refused to donate to a "worthwhile" appeal.[4] Contributions were solicited on a public thoroughfare, in one case by a Santa Claus figure seeking money for Volunteer for America and in another by students soliciting funds for the relief of starving Biafrans. In one condition, a woman model walked up to the solicitor, commented about its being a good cause, and made a donation. In the refusal condition, the woman studied the request, remarked that she did not want to give, and walked off without making a donation. A third condition used no model at all.

In one study, 15 percent of those who witnessed the model donating made a contribution, 20 percent of those who witnessed the model refusing made a contribution, and only 5 percent of those who witnessed no model made a contribution. In another study, 40 percent of those who witnessed a model donating and 36 percent of those who witnessed a model refusing to donate made a contribution, compared to only 2 percent of those who witnessed no model.

We can understand the effects of the model who donated as imitation. But why did donations increase when the model refused to donate? The experimenter suggests that the model lowers restraints against public action—that people somehow feel inhibited from any

---

[2] Milton Rosenbaum and R. R. Blake, "Volunteering as a Function of Field Structure," *Journal of Abnormal and Social Psychology*, vol. 50 (1955), pp. 193–96.

[3] J. H. Bryan and M. A. Test, "Models and Helping: Naturalistic Studies in Aiding Behavior," *Journal of Personality and Social Psychology*, vol. 6 (1967), pp. 400–407.

[4] J. R. Macaulay, "A Shill for Charity," in Macaulay and Berkowitz, *Altruism and Helping Behavior*, pp. 43–59.

public reaction to another's plight. Seeing someone else respond, either positively or negatively, somehow breaks the ice and makes it easier for the observer to respond.

Presence of Others   The suggestion that people generally feel inhibited from public reaction to another's request for help seems to be borne out in studies of the effects of the presence of others in helping behavior. One of the startling facts of the Kitty Genovese murder was that each of the 38 witnesses was aware of at least some of the other witnesses. Subsequent accounts of attacks and accidents have revealed that the adage "There's safety in numbers" is not necessarily true: Victims often go unaided despite the presence of large numbers of bystanders.

In order to study systematically the effects of the presence of others on helping behavior, several realistic experiments were designed.[5] In one experiment, an "accident" occurred in the presence of subjects who were either alone or with another subject. The subjects, who had responded to a company's offer to participate in a survey for pay, filled out some forms at the request of a female company representative, who then went into an adjacent office. Suddenly the subjects heard a loud crash, like a chair collapsing, and a scream as the representative seemed to fall to the floor, moaning that her ankle hurt and "I can't get this thing off me." In response to her plight, 70 percent of those who were alone in the testing room responded positively, most by directly going to help her, a few by calling out to see if she needed help. However, only 8 of the 40 subjects who were with somebody else in the testing room responded!

What accounts for the fact that the victim was more likely to receive help when only one, rather than two, potential helpers were present? Interviews with the subjects after the accident indicated that those who did not help felt the accident was not serious, or that someone else would come to her rescue, or that she would be embarrassed. Whether these were rationalizations or not is hard to determine. However, the results have been replicated in other studies.

For example, college students waited for an interview in a small room, either alone or with two others.[6] After a few minutes, smoke began to seep into the room through a vent, enough to cloud the

[5] Bibb Latané and J. M. Darley, "Bystander Intervention in Emergencies." In Macaulay and Berkowitz, *Altruism and Helping Behavior,* pp. 13–27.
[6] Ibid.

room and obscure vision. While 18 of the 24 subjects who waited alone left the room to report the smoke, only 3 of the 24 people waiting in groups reported it. Clearly, social inhibition prevented their response. The presence of others makes action less, rather than more, likely.

In most situations, bystanders or witnesses untrained to respond to such emergencies will hesitate, in a state of indecision. If by themselves, they tend to interpret the situation as serious, realize they alone can respond, and usually do so. In the presence of others, each witness interprets the others' indecision as a sign that the situation is not serious. Not wishing to appear a fool by overreaction, or figuring that someone better trained than he should respond, his own hesitation eventually becomes inaction, and the victim's plight goes unheeded.

Dependence of Victim   If one's interpretation of the seriousness of a situation affects one's response to a request for help, we would expect more help to be given to people whose situations make them highly dependent on assistance from others. Research tends to support this expectation. The more serious a victim's plight, the more likely he is to receive help. Interestingly enough, females seem to be more sensitive than males to differences in another's plight; they are much more likely to give help when the victim is highly dependent. Differences in the frequency of help given by males in varying conditions are not so great.

In one experiment a male telephone caller sought the assistance of strangers whose number he had reached accidentally.[7] He indicated that he had just used his last dime and asked the recipient of the call to relay a telephone message to a third party. In the low-dependency condition, the message was about a meeting to be held in 30 minutes. In the high-dependency condition, the message was that the caller was stranded at the airport and needed a ride.

Overall, 62 percent of the females called responded to the caller's plight by calling the third party. However, the high-dependent caller received help significantly more frequently from females than did the low-dependent caller. Nearly three quarters of all females helped the high-dependent caller, but only one half helped the low-dependent caller. Males, on the other hand, did not differ significantly in the percentages who helped the high-dependent and the low-dependent caller.

[7] L. D. Baker and H. J. Reitz, "Blindness, Situational Dependency, and Helping Behavior," *Proceedings of the American Psychological Association,* 1973, pp. 803–4.

In summary, an individual is more likely to help another when he alone is available to help, when the other is highly dependent on assistance, or when he has recently observed a model actively responding to a request for assistance. Social responsibility norms appear to have little effect on helping behavior, and the presence of others definitely reduces the chances that help will be given. In fact, prior experience does not appear to enhance greatly the prospect that a witness will come to another's aid. Eleven years after the Kitty Genovese incident another murder was committed in the Kew Gardens complex. On Christmas morning a 25-year-old model, Sandra Zahler, was beaten to death in her apartment.[8] A neighbor in the next-door apartment admitted that she had heard the sounds of a fierce struggle and the girl's screams of pain and terror, but she did nothing because she believed that the building superintendent had heard the fight and would investigate or call police. The neighbor revealed that she had lived in Kew Gardens for many years and even recalled having heard the scream of Kitty Genovese.

Implications for Organizations

What are the implications of helping behavior for organizations? First, it seems that people often fail to help others because they do not know others' needs, are unaware of how much others depend on them, or do not know how to help. This suggests that managers interested in increasing altruistic behavior ought to make it clear to their employees what the relevant needs of others are, why they are dependent upon these employees for help, and how help can best be given.

Second, managers interested in altruism ought to practice what they preach. We have noted the positive effects of models on helping behavior, and a manager is usually an effective, high-status model for workers. A manager who visibly goes out of his way to assist a worker, another manager, or a customer provides important cues that helping others is an appropriate and desirable response.

Of course, organizations concerned with helping behavior ought to see to it that such behavior is occasionally reinforced, or at least not punished. In Chapter 14 we described technological gatekeepers as individuals whose assistance is extremely helpful, throughout a laboratory. In some organizations, however, the control system discourages gatekeepers from assisting those outside the project to

---

[8] *New York Times,* December 27, 1974, p. 1.

which they are assigned. If reward or control systems in effect make helping behavior difficult or unrewarding, employees will find alternatives which are less difficult or more rewarding. These alternatives may range from competition to apathy.

COOPERATING AND COMPETING

In the case which introduced this chapter, Hal Edwards had to decide whether he would cooperate with or compete against his young friend Frank Buchman. Cooperation and competition are two forms of social interaction that have received considerable attention over the past few years. The notion that competition is the best (healthiest, most productive) mode of activity, particularly in the world of business, has been questioned and debated with increasing intensity, if not intelligence. Certainly America's experiences with societies whose successes are based on systems that are much less competitive internally than ours is have given us cause for concern. In any event, the size and power of our federal government, national unions, and big business make our own system something less than a purely competitive free-market form.

At the interpersonal or intragroup level, cooperation and competition are two of the modes of behavior available to workers and managers; they are not the only ones, however. Altruism, which we have already discussed, is a third mode, and individual noncompetition is a fourth.[9]

Differences between Cooperation and Competition

The differences among cooperation, competition, and individual noncompetition are apparent in their generally accepted definitions. *Cooperation* can be defined as two or more people working together for a common goal or mutual benefit. *Competition* is two or more people vying with one another for some relative individual gain. *Individual noncompetition* is two or more people working independently against some external standard.

The major differences among these three modes of behavior lie in their goals or objectives. In cooperation the notion of mutual, compatible goals is dominant. A cooperative situation is one in which

---

[9] L. K. Hammond and Morton Goldman, "Competition and Non-Competition and Its Relationship to Individual and Group Productivity," *Sociometry*, vol. 24 (1961), pp. 46–60.

one person's achievement of his goal facilitates the others' achievement of their goals.[10] One member of the group can become successful only if the other members become successful. For example, consider a group whose goal is to solve a complex problem. Each member of the group has some unique expertise or experience which lends itself to the solution, so the problem is broken down into subproblems assigned to various members. As any one member successfully accomplishes his or her part, the whole group moves closer to its goal. Further, anything one member does to facilitate the solution of another member's subproblem also makes it more likely that the former will achieve his own goal.

The major difference between cooperation and altruism is in the outcomes to the helper. One who helps another and, in so doing, helps himself is being cooperative. One who helps another without benefit to himself, or at some personal cost or sacrifice, is being altruistic.

A manager who takes time away from his own work to help another manager who has an unrelated problem is being altruistic. He gives such help at a cost—the time he spends helping the other manager will have to be made up. A worker on an individual piece-rate system who leaves his machine to show a new employee how to position some material is being altruistic—downtime on his machine costs the experienced employee money.

On the other hand, a manager who sends some of his people to help another department out on a joint project involving both departments is cooperating. By assisting the other manager, he comes closer to his own goal of completing the project. A basketball player who passes off to another teammate is cooperating—his teammate's basket brings closer the team objective of winning the game. A suspected criminal who testifies in court for the police against his accomplices in crime is cooperating with the police—as he helps them convict criminals, he helps himself escape from a prison sentence.

In competition the notion of individual, interdependent goals is dominant. For instance, there may be a fixed amount of rewards available, so that the more one individual gets, the less others get. Companies vying for a share of a consumer market are competing. If Ford increases its share of the new-car market, the share available for the other automobile manufacturers goes down. If the National Science Foundation budgets $100 million for research projects, researchers around the country are competing for those funds. When

---

[10] Morton Deutsch, "An Experimental Study of the Effects of Cooperation and Competition upon Group Processes," *Human Relations,* vol. 2 (1949), pp. 199–232.

one researcher gets his or her project funded, the chances for others to be funded decrease.

Competition may also result from unique goals. There is only one Academy Award for each category of movie; if one director gets the prize, all the other directors nominated cannot get it. Thus they compete. If only one of the five corporate vice presidents will eventually be named president, the vice presidents are in competition for that office. Whenever individuals are evaluated by comparison against each other, competition ensues.

Individual noncompetition occurs when individuals are evaluated against some external standard and have individual, independent goals. A professor who grades his students against certain academic standards and awards grades on a certain basis (say 90% = A, 80% = B, and so forth) is establishing a noncompetitive situation. A professor who grades on a curve, on the other hand, encourages competition. Management by objectives, whereby a manager establishes with each of his employees a specific goal for that employee, can be set up as a noncompetitive system. The employee is evaluated by his individual goal accomplishment rather than his performance relative to other employees.

In summary, cooperation and competition are only two of the modes of social behavior available to people working in organizations. Cooperation and competition are often discussed as if employees either cooperated or competed with each other and had no further alternatives. Under certain conditions, however, they may behave altruistically or remain independent but noncompetitive. This is an important point to remember in considering the effects of cooperation and competition on individual and group behavior.

Some Effects of Cooperation and Competition

We have noted that cooperation requires working together for mutual benefit, while competition involves striving against another for individual reward. We would therefore expect individuals to behave and feel differently while cooperating than they do while competing. A number of studies, mostly experimental, have uncovered several differences between cooperating and competing groups.

The initial study, which has had a major impact on theory and research in this area, involved ten groups of five students.[11] The groups met once a week for three hours to solve puzzles and discuss human relations problems.

---

[11] Deutsch, "Effects of Cooperation and Competition."

The independent variable was group internal orientation—cooperation v. competition. Competition was induced in five groups by ranking each member on the basis of his contribution to the group effort. The highest ranked member of each group was rewarded by being excused from preparing a term paper and receiving an A for the assignment. In the other five groups cooperation was induced by ranking each *group effort* against the other four. All members of the highest ranked group were excused from the term paper and awarded an A. These five groups, then, had internal cooperation, while competing externally against other groups.

Four observers recorded and evaluated several dependent variables, including task functions (seeking information, coordinating), group functions (behavior intended to strengthen the group), and individual functions (behavior benefitting only the individual—aggression, domination, seeking recognition, and so forth). In addition, observers gave each group an overall rating on communications, involvement, productivity, and other relevant behavior. The results of the experiment revealed significant differences between the cooperative and competitive groups in several different categories of behavior.

In individual behavior, members of cooperative groups helped each other more and obstructed each other less than members of competitive groups. Members of cooperative groups also were more agreeable to each other's ideas, rated each other's contributions higher, and were more friendly to each other than members of competitive groups. However, there were no differences between the two types of groups in interest and involvement in the task.

In group behavior, cooperative groups worked together more and had more coordination of their efforts than competitive groups. In addition, there was more specialization of activities within cooperative groups—less duplication of effort by members. Cooperative groups expressed significantly less trouble in communicating within the group, both in getting ideas across and in being understood.

In terms of productivity the results were mixed. Cooperative groups took less time to solve puzzles and wrote more lengthy solutions to the human relations problems. In addition, the product of cooperative groups was evaluated by judges as qualitatively better. On the other hand, no differences were found between the two types of groups in ratings of individual productivity or in learning. Despite other consistent differences in individual and group behavior, the superiority of cooperative groups in productivity was not as clear as expected. We will return to a more thorough discussion of the effects of cooperation on group productivity at the end of this section.

Since this original study, scores of experiments have tested the effects of cooperation v. competition on individual and group behavior. Some areas in which significant differences have been found include attitudes within the group, risk taking, and attribution.

Attitudes within the Group   Members of cooperative groups are more friendly toward one another, evaluate one another's efforts and contributions more highly, and tend to be more antagonistic toward outsiders. In other words, they display more of the characteristics we usually associate with cohesiveness (see Chapter 13) than do individuals competing against one another.

Risk Taking   There is some evidence that cooperating individuals will take greater risks in decision making than competing individuals.[12] This may be due to greater feelings of solidarity and confidence among members of cooperative groups.

Attribution   The reactions of group members to group success or failure can vary according to the cooperative or competitive orientation of the group. In one study, pairs of subjects cooperated or competed in a task, and their performance was evaluated against a prior established goal.[13] When they exceeded the goal, both cooperating and competing individuals attributed their success to themselves. Failure produced differences in attributions: Cooperative subjects who failed to meet their goals attributed failure to their partners, whereas competing subjects who failed to meet their goals attributed the failure to the situation. The same phenomenon is often observed in sports, where members of a team (requires cooperation) often turn on each other or their manager when they have a disappointing season. In individual competition, such as track and field, one can only blame one's self or the situation (a wet track, a poor start, the muggy weather).

Factors Affecting Cooperation and Competition

It is common, even chic, for editorial writers today to attack what they perceive to be a deficiency in cooperation in American culture.

[12] Michael Lupfer, Mark Jones, Lionel Spaulding, and Richard Dreher, "Risk-Taking in Cooperative and Competitive Dyads," *Journal of Conflict Resolution*, vol. 15 (1971), pp. 385–92.

[13] R. J. Wolosin, S. J. Sherman, and Amnon Till, "Effects of Cooperation and Competition on Responsibility by Attribution after Success and Failure," *Journal of Experimental Social Psychology*, vol. 9 (1973), pp. 220–35.

To this "deficiency" they attribute rising crime, falling productivity, and their own conclusion that "something is terribly wrong in America."

Whether there is indeed such a deficiency or whether competition can be causally related to crime rates or feelings of malcontent can be left to editorial speculation. There are observed effects of cooperation and competition on productivity, and these will be discussed later in this chapter. But perceptions of a decline in cooperative behavior do raise an interesting question: What factors make cooperation a more likely response than competition; that is, why do people cooperate rather than compete, and vice versa? These factors can be classified as individual characteristics, characteristics of others, or organizational characteristics.

Individual Characteristics   One reason for cooperative rather than competitive behavior might be the individual. Three personal characteristics have received the most research attention—age, sex, and culture.

Age.   Studies of cooperative and competitive behavior among different age groups in several different countries indicate that both responses are learned at an early age. Children are likely to compete at an earlier age than they will cooperate; they begin to compete around the age of four and to cooperate around the age of six.[14] Both types of behavior tend to increase with age. The important conclusion is that cooperative and competitive responses develop at an early age, across cultures, and that both are learned.

Sex.   Sexual stereotypes suggest that males are more competitive than females. There is some evidence to support this stereotype. For instance, a study of sex and age differences (from seven years through college) indicated that females tend to avoid being directly competitive, and competitive behavior increases with age among males.[15] Studies of young children, however, have not found differences between the sexes in cooperation and competition.

Given the evidence that cooperation and competition are learned, we can attribute differences between older males and females to the tendencies for children to be reinforced for behavior consistent with sexual stereotypes. That is, girls are likely to be rewarded for coop-

---

[14] Harold Cook and Sandra Stingle, "Cooperative Behavior in Children," *Psychological Bulletin*, vol. 81 (1974), pp. 918–33.

[15] W. E. Vinacke and G. R. Gullickson, "Age and Sex Differences in the Formation of Coalitions," *Child Development*, vol. 35 (1964), pp. 1217–231.

erating and discouraged from competing, whereas boys are encouraged or rewarded for competition and aggression.[16]

Culture. Obviously, if cooperation and competition are learned, we would expect differences in cultural background to influence individual tendencies to cooperate and compete. Nationality is one such variable. People from different countries often exhibit differences in cooperation and competition under similar conditions.[17] For example, Anglo-American children were found more competitive than Mexican children, children of an Israeli kibbutz, and Belgian children. Blackfoot Indian children displayed more cooperation than Canadian and Israeli children. American adults were found to be more competitive than Belgian adults.[18] While insufficient research has been carried out to permit ranking various cultures as more cooperative or competitive than others, it is clear that different nationalities place different values on the two modes of behavior, and these cultural emphases are reflected in behavioral differences between people from different cultures.

Urban-rural differences within a country also affect cooperative and competitive tendencies. Rural environments tend to stress helping one's family and one's neighbor, while urban environments are more likely to emphasize individual achievement and independence. These emphases are borne out by studies comparing urban with rural American children, urban Afro-, Anglo-, and Mexican Americans with Mexican villagers, and urban with kibbutz Israelis. In all these studies, rural children were found to be more cooperative than their urban counterparts.[19]

Comparisons of cooperative and competitive responses of black and white Americans have yielded mixed results. Some studies found blacks more cooperative, some found whites more cooperative. The findings have been too contradictory to allow any conclusion to be drawn about differences between the two races in cooperative and competitive tendencies.

Characteristics of Others   In addition to an individual's own tendencies to cooperate or compete, other persons in a given situation

---

[16] Herbert Barry, Margaret Baron, and Irwin Child, "A Cross Cultural Study of Some Sex Differences in Socialization," *Journal of Abnormal and Social Psychology,* vol. 55 (1957), pp. 326–32.

[17] Cook and Stingle, "Cooperative Behavior in Children."

[18] C. G. McClintock and S. P. McNeel, "Cross-Cultural Comparisons of Interpersonal Motives," *Sociometry,* vol. 29 (1966), pp. 406–27.

[19] Cook and Stingle, "Cooperative Behavior in Children."

will influence his ultimate response. Whether he cooperates or competes with another person depends in part on characteristics of the other person. If he finds the other person to be *similar* to himself or to be otherwise *attractive,* he is more likely to cooperate with him than if he finds the other different or unattractive. All those variables we have discussed as affecting interpersonal attraction (Chapter 12) can influence tendencies to cooperate.

Others besides the potential partner or rival can influence cooperative or competitive responses. There is good evidence that models can play a big part in determining the extent of cooperation. In Chapter 19 we will discuss how people often learn new responses, or learn how to respond in novel situations, by observing how another (the model) responds and the consequences that follow this response. Cooperative behavior is often learned in this way. For example, a new employee who sees his boss go out of his way to cooperate with another manager is more likely to cooperate himself than if his boss had avoided or openly been hostile to his colleague's request for cooperation. There is abundant evidence that people tend to imitate high-status, successful, and rewarded models. Thus it is difficult to overestimate the impact of superiors' cooperative or competitive responses on employees' tendencies, just as parents' cooperative or competitive tendencies are likely to rub off on their children.

Organizational Factors   Certain factors in the organizational environment can affect tendencies toward cooperation or competition. These include task characteristics, communication, time pressures, and reward systems.

Task Characteristics.   The characteristics of the task or situation can enhance the likelihood of either a cooperative or a competitive response. Some tasks are so *interdependent* they almost preclude competition. Two climbers ascending the face of a mountain have to cooperate: The situation requires that while one climbs, the other controls the safety rope and can catch the climber should he fall. There is no way they can race to the top. Held together by 100 feet of rope, their joint survival depends upon their cooperation. There are scores of tasks in which competition is irrational, dangerous, or impossible, such as flying an airplane, performing surgery, building a bridge, handling a steer, or making a double play. We do not say that perfect cooperation is ensured in such instances; it must be remembered that cooperation and competition are only two possible modes of social behavior. Just because the second baseman is not competing with the shortstop on a double play does not mean he is cooperating. He may fail to cover the base or to make a good throw, and thus do neither.

Other tasks are so arranged as to make cooperation unlikely, if not impossible. In order to cooperate, one needs to know what one's potential contributions are, what assistance one's partner requires, and the overall task requirements. Two policemen unaware of each other's presence at the scene of a crime will be unable to cooperate in apprehending the criminal. One plant with an oversupply of labor cannot cooperate with another plant experiencing a labor shortage without information that the second plant needs people.

On the other hand, some tasks are too *independent* to allow for cooperation. It is difficult for the sales office in Beirut to cooperate with the sales office in Moose Jaw, Saskatchewan. It is difficult for an engineer in one project to cooperate with an engineer totally involved in a different project, even if they are in the same plant. Their skills and knowledge requirements may be so specialized they preclude a transfer from one project to the other.

Communication. Because cooperation requires the exchange of information between partners, we would expect communication to affect cooperative responses. Tasks which make communications difficult are likely to result in less cooperation, and increasing communication should enhance cooperation. These expectations are supported by research. In one study, women played a two-person game under various conditions of communication.[20] Members of some of the pairs were allowed to communicate, some only to see each other, some only to speak to each other, and some to see and speak to each other. Cooperation increased as the ability to communicate increased.

Time Pressures. Under severe time pressures, requirements for good communication can make cooperation a frustrating mode of behavior. One feels a tendency to try to do everything one's self, rather than to cooperate with others. In extreme conditions, panic can blind individuals to the needs and potential contributions of others. At the closing of a crowded nightclub, the 500 patrons can easily file out three entrances in a few minutes by allowing each other room to maneuver, assisting each other through crowded doors, and so forth. However, should a fire break out, panic can result from individual perceptions that the longer they remain inside the more likely they are to perish. Lack of cooperation and the ensuing competition to get out first have resulted in tragedies like the Cocoanut

<hr>

[20] H. Wichman, "Effects of Isolation and Communication on Cooperation in a Two Person Game," cited in Cook and Stingle, "Cooperative Behavior in Children."

Grove night club fire in Boston in 1942, in which 474 persons died. The chief loss of life resulted from screaming, clawing crowds wedged so tightly in the exits that no one could escape, and so they died of smoke inhalation.

In an experiment designed to replicate the effect of time pressures, each subject in a group of 15 was required to remove an aluminum cone from a bottle by a string attached to the cone.[21] Only one cone at a time could be pulled through the narrow bottleneck. If subjects cooperated with each other and took turns withdrawing their cones, all could be withdrawn in a very short time. However, if subjects competed and everyone tried to get his cone out as fast as possible, the bottleneck became jammed, and no one got out.

The experiment was run under two conditions. In the high-incentive condition, water seeped into the bottle through an opening in the base. Subjects were instructed to get their cones out before they got wet. A subject who withdrew his cone before it got wet was awarded 25 cents, while a subject whose cone got wet was fined 10 cents. In the nonincentive condition, no water was admitted to the bottle, and no rewards or fines were administered.

In the 20 groups assigned to the nonincentive condition, where subjects were encouraged to cooperate, no serious jams developed. All the cones were successfully withdrawn in times ranging from 10 seconds for the fastest to 59 seconds for the slowest group. In the 16 groups assigned to the high-incentive condition, with the water slowly rising in the bottom of the bottle, serious jams occurred in almost every case, and most subjects were unable to withdraw their cones at all.

Reward Systems. Experiments such as the one described above suggest that reward systems have a powerful influence on cooperation and competition, as they do on other kinds of behavior. Examples of incentive systems which seem to reinforce one mode of behavior over the other are abundant.

Any system in which group members share more or less equally in rewards given for group accomplishment would seem to reinforce cooperation. Researchers may receive equal credit for the success of a joint project, such as Drs. John Bardeen, Leon Cooper, and John Schrieffer of the University of Illinois, who shared the 1972 Nobel Prize in physics for their work on superconductors. Reporters may

---

[21] Alexander Mintz, "Non Adaptive Group Behavior," *Journal of Abnormal and Social Psychology*, vol. 46 (1951), pp. 150–59.

receive equal credit for a joint investigation, such as Donald L. Bartlett and James B. Steele of the *Philadelphia Enquirer,* who shared the 1975 Pulitzer Prize for national reporting for their investigations of the Internal Revenue Service.

Cooperation is reinforced in such cases because individual rewards are dependent upon group or team success, and cooperation is essential to group success. There is little or no incentive to compete when group members share more or less equally in the group rewards, and differences in their individual performances are neither rewarded nor recorded.

A system in which group members are differentially rewarded based on their relative performance seems to reinforce competition. A department head who annually gives the biggest salary increase to his best rated performer incites competition. Organizational systems in which only the best individual member of a group of managers is promoted to the next level foster competition.

Increasing the differences in rewards tends to increase competition. Suppose two groups of nine management trainees each were told that their relative performance in the company training program would affect certain of their outcomes. For group 1, the incentive system is as follows: the highest performer will get a $300 bonus, the next four will get $200 each, the next two $100 each, and the last two $50 each if they successfully complete the program. This system provides for moderately different rewards, which should produce a fairly spirited brand of competition among the trainees.

For group 2, the reward differentials are increased. The highest performer will get an $800 bonus, the second best will receive $400, third will get $200, and the lowest will be terminated from the company's employ. In this system we would expect fierce, serious, even bitter competition.

Competition is reinforced under systems of differential rewards because individual performance is rewarded. Any individual moves closer to his goal as his own performance improves or as others' performances decline. There is no incentive to cooperate—to work together—because cooperating means helping another achieve his goals, and if the other moves closer to his goal, the helper's chances of achieving his own goal are reduced. An example is two players trying out for the same position on a team. If one player helps the other learn the position, the first player does it at his own expense. The more the second player learns, the lower are the first player's chances of getting the position.

Coalition Formation

In competitive situations involving more than two persons (or units), conditions sometimes make it advantageous for some of the individuals to cooperate with one another. In politics, for example, two minority parties may agree to support each other's candidates and programs. This agreement often enables them to elect officials and pass legislation over the opposition of a third party that is more powerful than either of them.

Such an agreement forms a *coalition:* two or more persons who cooperate or combine their resources in order to increase their outcomes relative to another person or persons. For a coalition to occur, there must be at least three parties involved in some competitive situation in which cooperation or coordination between some of the parties is possible.

In many competitive situations involving three or more parties, cooperation among any of them is infeasible or unlikely. Where the task is independent, that is, where the behavior of one party has little or no effect on the behavior of the rest, coalitions are infeasible. For example, it is difficult to conceive of two runners forming a coalition to defeat a superior runner in the 100-yard dash, except by tactics (bumping, tripping) that would lead to their disqualification. Salesmen on a bonus plan or production workers on individual piece-rate incentives would find it very difficult, and probably unrewarding, to form a coalition against some of their colleagues.

An additional condition is necessary before coalition formation can be a real behavior option: the possibility that cooperation will result in outcomes superior to any outcomes possible by individual action.[22]

Political life provides abundant examples of coalitions, particularly in democracies where so many parties have evolved that no single party can ever command the support of a majority of the people or a majority of the elected representatives. Italy and Germany are good examples of countries run by coalition governments.

The same principle holds in democratic processes below the national level. In any decision-making system in which the majority rules, the possibility for coalitions exists. Coalitions frequently determine who are elected to honorary organizations, or the slate of officers for clubs and professional organizations, or which programs will be funded or policies adopted by the board of directors.

---

[22] M. E. Shaw, *Group Dynamics—The Psychology of Small Group Behavior* (New York: McGraw-Hill Book Co., 1971), p. 106.

Coalitions may even form on occasion to restrict competition. For example, cartels may be formed to fix prices, combine resources, support legislation, or withhold resources in order to drive out or keep out competitors. Allegations that the major oil companies recently conspired to "create" an oil shortage were based on the recognition that such cooperation among competitors would enable them to drive the independent oil companies out of business. (Whether those allegations are true or not remains to be proved.) The incentive for coalitions exists in many industries in which no single company dominates the industry but several companies enjoy a sizable minority share of the market.

Coalitions, then, are temporary alliances between individuals, groups, organizations, or nations whose long-run goals may be very different, but who see short-run benefits in joining resources against other parties. It is not unusual for one party to seek coalitions with others whose value systems are diametrically opposed, temporarily ignoring those differences for the duration of the coalition. The classic example was Russia in World War II, which first formed an alliance with Germany against Poland, and later entered into an alliance with the United States and Britain against Germany.

Most of the research on coalitions has attempted to predict the formations of coalitions. In particular, researchers have tried to develop a model to predict which of the possible coalitions in a situation is most likely to form. Interestingly enough, this research has ignored most individual characteristics and values of coalition members, under the assumption that the major determinant of coalition formation is the division of resources among the parties. Two theories of coalition formation have evolved from this research: the minimum-resource and anticompetitive theories.

Minimum-Resource Theory   Envision a number of rivals, none of whom has a majority of resources which would enable him to dominate the outcomes of a situation. According to minimum-resource theory, the coalition most likely to form is the one that can dominate the situation with the smallest total amount of resources.[23]

For example, suppose a corporate board of directors consists of five members. Each member owns or controls several hundred of the corporation's 2,800 outstanding shares of stock. Member A controls 700 shares; B, 600 shares; and C, D, and E each control 500 shares. With 2,800 shares being voted, it would take over 1,400 votes to control a decision. No single member controls over 700

---

[23] W. A. Gamson, "A Theory of Coalition Formation," *American Sociological Review*, vol. 26 (1961), pp. 373–82.

shares, so coalitions are attractive alternatives to simply fighting it out.

There are several possible majority coalitions. All four-party coalitions control a majority of the votes, as well as three-party coalitions among ABC, ABD, ABE, ACD, ACE, ADE, BCD, BCE, BDE, and CDE. Of all those possible coalitions, the one that requires the minimum total resources is CDE, which would control 1,500 votes, the smallest majority possible in this situation.

Experimental studies of coalition formation tend to support the predictions of minimum-resource theory. In one series of studies, three persons were involved in competitive games in which collaboration was possible.[24] In one condition, A had three units of power, B and C each had two units. Although all two-party coalitions are possible, BC requires the fewest resources (four). In another condition, A had four units of power, B had three, and C had two. Again all coalitions are possible, but BC (five units) requires the minimum resources. As Table 16–1 shows, the coalition BC was formed far

TABLE 16–1
Number of Coalitions Formed in Three-Person Situations

Resource Distribution Situation	Coalitions Formed			No Coalition
	AB	AC	BC	
A = 3, B = 2, C = 2	13	12	64	1
A = 4, B = 3, C = 2	9	20	59	2

Source: Adapted from W. A. Gamson, "A Theory of Coalition Formation," *American Sociological Review*, vol. 26 (1961), pp. 373–82.

more often than either of the other two possible coalitions in both situations.

The reasoning behind the predictions of minimum-resource theory is that members prefer the majority coalition in which they will be relatively strongest. The assumption is that the profits of the coalition will be divided among the members in proportion to their relative strengths, an assumption further supported by evidence. Thus, in the situation where A's resources equal 4, B's equal 3, and C's equal 2, BC is the coalition most preferred by both B and C. B prefers C to A as a partner, because B is stronger than C but weaker than A, and thus stands to reap a greater share of the payoffs from

---

[24] W. E. Vinacke and A. Arkoff, "Experimental Study of Coalitions in the Triad," *American Sociological Review*, vol. 22 (1957), pp. 406–15.

the coalition with C than with A. C prefers B as a partner, because his resources are 40 percent of a BC coalition but only 33 percent of an AC coalition. C would thus expect to profit more from the BC coalition.

Anticompetitive Theory   A second theory, based on the relative strengths of members of the winning coalition, has been called anticompetitive theory.[25] This theory recognizes that sometimes members are concerned with maintaining good interpersonal relations among coalition members. They therefore prefer coalitions where competition or rivalry is minimized, specifically those in which resources are equally divided. This avoids hard feelings on the part of the weaker members who receive smaller shares than the stronger partners.

In a three-person situation with resources distributed so that A = 4, B = 4, and C = 2, anticompetitive theory would predict an AB coalition, whereas minimum-resource theory would predict an AC or a BC coalition. The predictions of anticompetitive theory have been supported by research using female subjects.[26]

As was pointed out earlier, males tend to be more competitive than females, at least partially because of their socialization experiences. In situations where it is possible, anticompetitive theory might predict coalition formation among females more accurately than minimum-resource theory.

Productivity under Cooperation and Competition

A major question arising from the differences between cooperation and competition is which mode of behavior is more productive. Early studies comparing cooperation with competition found cooperation to be more productive. These were popular findings, because the social scientists felt that cooperation produced several positive side effects—friendlier relations among group members, less duplication of effort, more communications, and so on.

Subsequent research, however, produced evidence of cases in which competitive groups outproduced cooperative groups. Out of a total of 24 studies investigating the relative effectiveness of cooperation and competition, 14 found that competition resulted in greater group productivity, while 10 found cooperation more pro-

---

[25] Shaw, *Group Dynamics*, pp. 108–9.

[26] T. T. Uesugi and W. E. Vinacke, "Strategy in a Feminine Game," *Sociometry*, vol. 26 (1963), pp. 75–88.

ductive.[27] These conflicting results at first appeared irreconcilable, but a careful review of the research revealed a major difference in the tasks of the groups studied.

Some of the tasks involved discussing and solving complex problems (one was the experiment requiring subjects to withdraw cones from a bottle). These tasks could be classified as highly interdependent. That is, the behavior of each group member affects the others, and any individual success depended on what others did. In discussing problems, for example, if one member was talking, the others had to remain silent. In complex problems, information had to be shared for a successful solution. In the cone-and-bottle experiment, members had to take turns in order to complete the task.

In each of the six studies classified as highly interdependent, differential rewards had a negative effect on group productivity. That is, competition was dysfunctional, and cooperation more productive, on highly interdependent tasks.

The other tasks, however, involved no such interdependence. These tasks required members to do such things as add numbers, cancel letters, carry and sort objects, read, print, and unscramble words. In all of these tasks, each member's behavior was relatively independent of the rest of the group. That is, each member could add, cancel, carry, sort, read, print, and unscramble without any assistance or interference from anyone else. In 14 of the 18 studies classified as independent, differential rewards had a positive effect on group productivity. That is, competition enhanced productivity.

The conclusion is that the relative effectiveness of cooperation and competition depends on the nature of the group's task. Reward systems should be compatible with task requirements. Because an interdependent task requires cooperation, a system of shared rewards, which tends to induce cooperative behavior, should produce the highest productivity on these tasks. A system of differential rewards, which tends to induce competition, is not compatible with interdependent tasks because it can produce behavior which interferes with the nature of the task. In competition, each individual strives to outperform others, and relative performance is important. One can improve one's position either by improving his own performance or by hindering the performance of others. For example, I can improve my chances for promotion either by working harder or by sabotaging the work of my rivals.

---

[27] L. K. Miller and R. L. Hamblin, "Interdependence, Differential Rewarding, and Productivity," *American Sociological Review*, vol. 28 (1963), pp. 768–77.

In interdependent tasks, it may be that one's individual contributions, while advancing the group effort, will detract from others' opportunities to contribute. In basketball, everyone likes to score. But when any one player is handling the ball or shooting, the rest of his teammates cannot do so. It may be best for the team's success if one player does most of the shooting, but as his scoring average goes up, the others' decline. In a discussion group, one member may make a particularly good point. While he is talking, the rest of the group must listen. If there is competition among the members of such groups, individuals may be induced to prevent each other from performing at their best. One way to improve a player's scoring average relative to a teammate's is to keep the ball away from him. One way to make more contributions to group discussion than the others is to talk so much that no one else has a chance.

In this way, competition can elicit behavior which is contrary to a group's successful accomplishment of an interdependent task. If basketball players refuse to pass the ball to one another, if discussion group members refuse to yield the floor to their colleagues, then the group's performance suffers.

An independent task, however, does not require cooperation. Competition is not incompatible, because the nature of the task is such that each individual can produce independently of the others. A group of salespeople, each with his or her own territory, provides a good example of independent tasks. The behavior of each salesperson is independent of the others; one person's sales do not detract from the sales of the rest of the force. In such cases, differential rewards can increase group productivity.

SUMMARY

Interpersonal behavior in organizations can take a number of different forms. Individuals or groups may help each other, cooperate, or compete, as well as behave independently of each other. These modes of behavior differ from each other in the situations which produce them and in their effects on individual and group behavior.

Helping behavior, or altruism, means providing assistance without external reward, and usually at some cost to the helper. Helping behavior is important to consumer-oriented departments and to service organizations in general. Within an organization, helping behavior among departments or units often makes it possible for the organization to respond more smoothly, efficiently, or quickly to opportunities and problems than usual bureaucratic procedures would allow. Altruism is enhanced when potential helpers understand the needs of others, the extent of their dependence, and the means by which they can be helped. Helping behavior is made more likely when potential helpers have seen others providing assistance in similar situations.

Cooperation and competition are both learned at early ages, and the frequency of both forms of behavior increases with age. Cultural background affects individual tendencies to cooperate or compete, as reflected in the evidence that males tend to compete more than females and that people from rural areas are more likely to cooperate than urban dwellers.

Organizations can encourage either cooperation or competition in several ways. Interdependent tasks and shared reward systems increase the likelihood of cooperative responses. As with helping behavior, cooperation is also enhanced by imitation: Managers who visibly cooperate with others encourage their subordinates to do the same. Competition is more likely to develop among individuals who are dissimilar and who are under time pressures. Organizational reward systems in which rewards are not shared but are proportional to relative individual performance or performance evaluations encourage competition.

Managers should be aware of the implications of task design, reward systems, and their own example for cooperation and competition within their organizations. Cooperative groups tend to be more friendly and cohesive and to communicate better than competitive groups. When tasks are interdependent and rewards are shared, cooperation enhances productivity. When tasks are independent, differential rewards encouraging competition can enhance productivity.

QUESTIONS FOR REVIEW AND DISCUSSION

1. What is the difference between helping behavior and cooperation? Give an example of an organization that might particularly depend on both forms of behavior for success.

2. Explain the effects of the presence of others on helping behavior.

3. From your knowledge of interpersonal attraction and group formation, predict the conditions under which an individual would be more attracted to a competitive than to a cooperative group.

4. Is scapegoating (placing the blame for failure on someone else) more likely to occur within cooperative or competitive groups?

5. Describe three tasks in an industrial setting that could be classified as interdependent and three that could be described as independent.

6. Classify each of the following organizational rewards as *differential, shared,* or *neither*. Explain.
   a. Group bonus
   b. Individual bonus
   c. Across-the-board merit wage increase
   d. Pension system
   e. Paid vacations based on seniority
   f. Promotions based on seniority
   g. Promotions based on comparative performance evaluations
   h. Executive privileges (private secretary, car, etc.)

7. Identify the nature of the tasks and reward systems experienced by (*a*) a member of a world champion professional baseball or football team, (*b*) a member of a unionized college faculty, (*c*) a sales representative on commission who has an exclusive sales territory.

8. Predict the coalition most likely to form if resources were divided so that A had five units of power, B, C, and D each had four units, and E had three units.
   a. A minimum-resource coalition
   b. An anticompetitive coalition

KEY WORDS

Altruism
Cooperation
Competition
Individual noncompetition
Coalition

Interdependent tasks
Independent tasks
Shared rewards
Differential rewards

Objectives

1. To evaluate conflict in organizations and to discuss organizational factors which lead to intergroup conflict.
2. To describe the effects of conflict on groups and organizational reactions to intergroup conflict.
3. To evaluate methods for reducing the negative consequences of conflict and to suggest ways of avoiding them.

chapter seventeen

Conflict

"I'm sorry, Dr. Baker. As much as I'd like the job, I just don't think I want to be the supervisor in hematology as long as this battle is going on." With that, June Travis, composed but visibly upset, turned and walked away.

She's right, thought Dr. Susan Baker, sitting on the edge of the desk. She'd be caught right in the middle of a fight that's been going on for too long now. It's up to me to do something about it, but what?

Dr. Baker was the director of the pathology laboratory in a large city hospital. The laboratory was organized along functional lines into sections, staffed by trained medical technologists and technicians, all women. Two of the most important sections, hematology and chemistry, shared the same room. In fact, when the lab had expanded and remodeled its facilities ten months ago, it had been designed to facilitate cooperation and sharing of personnel between hematology and chemistry as work loads varied.

Unfortunately, that cooperation had never come about. Instead, the sections avoided helping each other; members of both groups seemed to go out of their way to be hostile. At breaks or at lunch the women tended to stay with their own section members. There was occasional interaction between members of either section and technicians from other sections, but even this was infrequent.

As far as Dr. Baker could determine, it all started out as a personality conflict between Betty Campbell, a medical technician, and Frances Jones, the chemistry supervisor. Betty had worked for the laboratory for five years. In the first three years of her employment she rotated from section to section on a scheduled basis typical for new technicians. In all her assignments her work was extremely good. She worked hard and willingly assumed responsibility.

Two years ago Betty rotated into the chemistry department, where she encountered a definite conflict between her lifestyle and that of her supervisor. Briefly, Betty was young, attractive, single. Dr. Baker guessed that Betty would be described as a "swinger" in terms of her outlooks on sex and social behavior. Her vivaciousness and quality of work made her a strong informal leader, particularly among the younger technicians. Frances, on the other hand, had been with the laboratory for 12 years and chemistry supervisor for 6. She was middle-aged, and although not prudish, definitely disapproved of Betty's lifestyle and had occasionally complained to Dr. Baker about Betty's "bad influence" on the lab's younger employees.

During her assignment in chemistry, Betty had expressed the opinion that Frances was not well qualified to be a supervisor. Further, she claimed that Frances was deliberately showing bias against her in various ways. Betty's work deteriorated, and her attitude became negative and cynical. As a result, her performance evaluation for that period, made by Frances and approved by Dr. Baker, was quite low.

After the evaluation, there was considerable discussion among Betty's fellow workers, generally very critical of Frances and the administration for submitting such a "biased" evaluation when Betty had clearly been an excellent employee. Betty asked to be transferred to the hematology section and has remained there since. She meanwhile has retained much of her cynical attitude toward the chemistry department; she is highly critical of the chemistry supervisor and chemistry technologists in general. At the same time she emphasizes her own abilities and high degree of competence in hematology.

Regarding her technical ability, the laboratory administration agrees with her. Betty's work in hematology has been back to her usual high level. She continues to be well respected and has many friends in the laboratory. On the matter of Frances and the chemistry section, however, she remains unchanged.

Frances continues to run a good chemistry section. However, her opinion of Betty as a bad influence and undesirable member of the lab also remains unchanged. This personal conflict has spread throughout the two sections, creating larger problems.

For one thing, it has prevented any real sharing of personnel between hematology and chemistry, since there remains a very strong wall between the two departments which is based on ill feelings between Betty and Frances and their various supporters in the two sections.

This had a detrimental effect on recruiting a supervisor in hematology. The long-time supervisor had resigned approximately two years previously and had been replaced by Mary Higgins, a highly trained hematologist from a prominent hospital in the East. Mary, however, met with great antagonism and criticism from the five technicians and technologists in hematology. Although Mary displayed a lack of tact in handling this situation, the eventual outcome was that she felt she no longer could cope with the situation, and after one year she resigned. Since that time, for eight months, the department has been without a formal supervisor. June, a young medical technologist who the administration feels has great potential as a supervisor, has been an unofficial leader in the department, but she has made it clear that she does not feel she can be the official supervisor in the face of the problems she could expect if she were given real authority.

A third effect of the conflict between the departments is that new personnel being rotated through hematology or chemistry become polarized and are forced to take sides. On several occasions the laboratory administration has noted that well-recommended people produce poorly in chemistry and show bad attitudes which they trace to their exposure to Betty's philosophy.

Dr. Baker ruefully admits that she has deliberately avoided stepping into the situation, because she had assumed that Betty's transfer to hematology would significantly ease the conflict. Obviously something more drastic has to be done. She couldn't afford to lose June, or any other bright and qualified people. Either Betty or Frances would have to go.

CONFLICT IN ORGANIZATIONS often follows the pattern experienced in Dr. Baker's lab. It starts off as a personality conflict between two competent people. As a result of circumstances, one of them takes some action which hurts the other, and the conflict escalates. Both parties seek and get sympathy from their friends and close associates at work, and before long, two departments, project teams, or sections are at war. Meanwhile, administrators have glossed over or ignored the spreading conflict in hopes that it would go away, until one day it becomes apparent that the work of the organization has been disrupted.

THE NATURE OF CONFLICT IN ORGANIZATIONS

In an organization, conflict can be described as a breakdown or disruption in normal activities in such a way that the individuals or groups concerned experience difficulty in working together. In the case of the pathology laboratory, the hematology and chemistry departments were not only failing to work together but were openly feuding. The work of the laboratory was severely disrupted.

Not all conflict in organizations is so disruptive. Some interpersonal conflict is inevitable in any organization where people have a diversity of backgrounds, interests, and talents. In fact, the absence of any conflict would suggest an organization that is too tightly run or whose members are too homogeneous for its own good. Individual differences will inevitably produce some conflict—but they will also produce the flexibility, creativity, and specialization necessary for modern organizations to survive.

There is evidence which supports the assertion that not all conflict is bad. In one study, 64 research and development project groups were observed through questionnaires and interviews.[1] Some groups worked in a government laboratory doing basic and applied research in aerodynamics, and the rest did development work in an industrial laboratory. The performance of each group was measured by ratings of productivity and creativity by scientists, engineers, and supervisors and by the number of patents and papers produced by each group. Two types of conflict were measured by questionnaire: *interpersonal* (dislikes, distrust, prejudice), and *technical* (disagreement on objectives and methods).

The results revealed that only among the government project groups was conflict a significantly negative factor in group performance, and this was true only for interpersonal, not technical conflict. In fact, positive correlations between technical conflict and performance were found in the government labs, although the correlations were not statistically significant. In the industrial groups, there were no correlations between performance and either interpersonal or technical conflict.

This chapter focuses on disruptive conflict—conflict that significantly impairs the work of the organization. We will focus in particular on intergroup conflict, the most common form of disruptive conflict in organizations. Conflict between individuals usually can be resolved or at least avoided through transfer, scheduling, or termination of personnel. Conflict that is not resolved or avoided typically escalates to intergroup conflict, as the protagonists elicit sympathetic followings. Conflict between an individual and a group usually lasts only a short while; most frequently the group either wins over the individual or the individual abandons the fight psychologically (becomes apathetic) or physically (quits). Occasionally the individual will form a group of his own, and the conflict will escalate to the intergroup level.

In this chapter we start with a model describing the most frequent causes of intergroup conflict and then consider the effects of conflict within and between groups. We discuss the possible and likely reactions of individual managers and organizations to conflict among subordinate groups and analyze tactics for resolving intergroup conflict. Suggestions for preventing disruptive conflict in organizations conclude the chapter.

---

[1] W. M. Evan, "Conflict and Performance in R&D Organizations." *Industrial Management Review*, vol. 7 (1965), pp. 37–45.

WHY DO ORGANIZATIONS EXPERIENCE CONFLICT?

The cause of conflict has been a subject for speculation throughout the history of organizations. There are those who claim that conflict results from poor communications; if everyone simply understood everyone else, conflict would cease to exist. There is no doubt that communications problems lead to conflict, but all conflict is not the result of poor communications. Figure 17–1 presents a model of the numerous factors that can lead to intergroup conflict within an organization.[2]

Interdependence

To the extent that two groups, sections, or departments are interdependent within an organization, opportunities for conflict between them are present. Such interdependence can arise in several different forms, such as the *dependence of one group or the other*, situations requiring considerable *association between the parties*, and the *need for consensus*.[3]

An example of dependence would be an accounting department's reliance on the data processing department for fast and accurate processing of accounting data to be used in reports and decision making. Increased association is often required among groups or departments in a time of crisis or organizational stress; for example, the Watergate crisis precipitated a good deal of association among members of the Committee to Reelect the President and the White House staff. The need for consensus is required in several decision-making procedures involving participation by more than one group, section, or department. Passage of a bill through Congress requires the consensus of both the House of Representatives and the Senate, groups whose views on legislation often differ considerably. These differences are worked out, not through direct confrontation between the two groups but through a joint committee composed of members of both houses.

Interdependence in organizations stems from two characteristics of all organizations: limited resources and the pressures of time.

---

[2] This model is based heavily (with a few modifications) on the model described in J. G. March and H. A. Simon, *Organizations* (New York: John Wiley & Sons, 1958), pp. 121–29.

[3] These three factors are listed among the antecedent conditions of conflict by Alan C. Filley, *Interpersonal Conflict Resolution* (Glenview, Ill.: Scott, Foresman & Co., 1975), pp. 9–12.

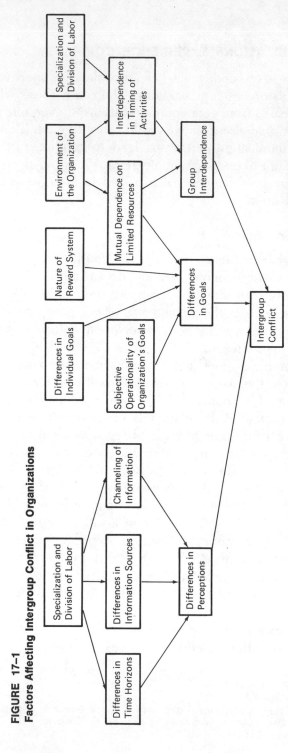

FIGURE 17–1
Factors Affecting Intergroup Conflict in Organizations

Source: Adapted with modifications from J. G. March and H. A. Simon, *Organizations* (New York: John Wiley & Sons, 1958).

Mutual Dependence on Limited Resources Every organization operates with a finite amount of resources: money, personnel, and equipment. This fact of organizational life means that subunits in the organization will be interdependent. What one subunit gets in terms of budgets, personnel allocations, or equipment use, the other subunits cannot get. If a university is given the authority to add 50 new faculty members, then the various colleges and departments in the university will all be dependent on those 50 positions to fill all their needs. The more positions given to the school of engineering, the fewer are left for arts and sciences, education, or business.

As dependence on the same resources increases, so does the likelihood for conflict. In response to that tendency, organizations often attempt to decrease mutual dependence through allocation procedures. If a company were run strictly on a cash basis, departments would be in a constant state of conflict as they maneuvered to get access to the day's or week's cash receipts in order to pay their employees, buy equipment, or settle expenses. *Budgeting* has the effect of encapsulating conflict over money. Budgets do not eliminate conflict, but they reduce conflict over funds to a more orderly process with specific procedures and rules, limited to a few months of each fiscal year. Once each department has been allocated its share of the budget, its attention and energy can be shifted from fighting for its share to other activities.

Decentralization of resources is another means of reducing mutual dependence on limited resources. If subunits and departments are forced to share the same computer, typing pool, maintenance crew, or transportation pool, the chances of intergroup conflict are increased. One way to minimize such conflict is to give each department its own secretaries, maintenance personnel, transportation, and computer consoles.

Of course decentralization of resources increases duplication and the possibility of excess idle resources. A pool of ten secretaries may be kept reasonably busy by five departments, but it may take three or four secretaries to handle the peak work load produced by any one department. Therefore, 15 departmental secretaries may be required to handle the work of 10 pool secretaries. Decentralization, then, may be relatively more expensive; reducing the opportunities for intergroup conflict has its price.

This is how the organization's environment influences conflict. If the environment in which the organization operates is wealthy and easily exploited, then the organization will have sufficient resources to decentralize and to otherwise reduce mutual dependence by providing abundant resources to satisfy the needs of all departments. For example, an army of a country with many healthy young citizens who are sympathetic to the military, backed by a legal system of enforced military service, should experience few internal conflicts over personnel. There is a wealth of human resources available to fill every unit's quota of personnel needs. A company with a monopoly on a product in great demand by an affluent, growing population is in a similar situation. Expansion and growing profits lessen internal conflicts over limited resources.

As the environment changes due to a decrease in affluence, drying up of resources, or competition, then the organization is forced to reduce resources allocated to each subunit, increasing mutual dependence and chances for conflict. Observe the effects of the recession of the midseventies on school districts, for example. During the prosperous sixties teaching and administrative staffs mushroomed, and new programs were funded without question. When the recession began eating into state and local tax revenues, budgets had to be cut back, programs terminated, and faculty laid off, and there ensued fights among the various interest groups over whose budgets would be cut the most and whose programs would suffer least.

Interdependence in Timing of Activities   The second major characteristic of organizational interdependence has to do with timing and scheduling. The closer two groups or departments are in terms of timing or scheduling, the greater the likelihood of conflict between them. In a hospital, surgery cannot begin until certain tests have been performed on the patient and analyzed and reported by the pathology department. Pathology depends on the attending physician to initiate requests for tests; surgery depends on pathology to perform and report. Thus the pathology department often finds itself in the center of conflict as it tries to cope with the demands of surgery for the service which it needs in order to function.

Charting the flow of work through the organization can reveal several areas where conflict is likely. Any two units adjacent to one another in the flow of work are likely to be interdependent in timing and scheduling. As an example, consider the chart in Figure 17–2, which depicts the flow of work through a portion of a meat-processing plant.

In the operation depicted in Figure 17–2 cattle carcasses are purchased by the processor, and work begins at the receiving dock, where the carcasses are weighed and accepted by the receiving de-

FIGURE 17-2
Steps in Processing Beef into Sausage: A Typical Operation

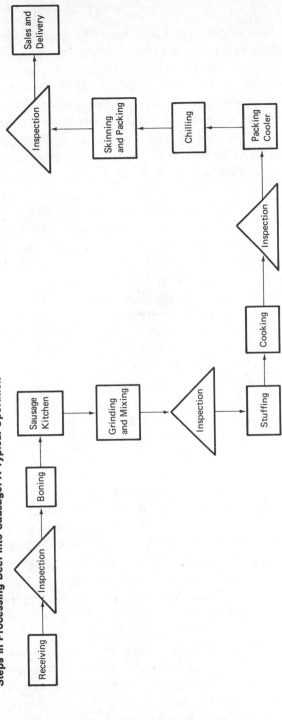

partment and inspected by federal meat inspectors. If passed by the inspectors and if the weights conform to the shipper's bill of lading, the carcasses are then sent to a large cooler for boning, where skilled workers remove the bone, gristle, and excess fat. The boned meat is sent to the sausage kitchen, where an expert sausage maker weighs and grinds the meat and mixes in the correct amount of spices, preservatives, and water. This mixture is again subjected to inspection for standards in meat, fat, and water content and then sent through large machines which stuff the material into paper-thin casings, in which they are cooked. After cooking, the product is placed in a cooler to be chilled and then sent to the skinning room, where machines remove the casing. The product is packaged and weighed, again with federal inspection for weight and labels, and the inspected packages are put into large cases for delivery to groceries.

At several steps along this line, various subunits are highly dependent on the work of other units in order to do their own. Inspectors cannot inspect carcasses which receiving has not unloaded, and receiving cannot accept carcasses which inspection has not examined. Opportunities for conflict are high. The sausage kitchen crew cannot prepare meat for stuffing unless it has been boned, and the workers who operate the smokehouses have nothing to cook if the sausage kitchen falls behind. The skinning and packing department cannot process bad products, and sales cannot deliver unpacked meat. Thus the greatest opportunities for conflict exist between sales and packing, between the sausage kitchen and boning, and between receiving and inspection.

A number of factors affect the degree to which two departments are interdependent in timing and scheduling. *Specialization* of functions in organizations is characteristic in industry, medicine, government, and education. While it facilitates skill and efficiency, it also produces greater interdependence. Sausage production is a highly interdependent activity because people and machines specialize in each of the steps which turn beef carcasses into hot dogs. The greater the specialization, the greater the interdependence, and the greater the opportunities for internal conflict.

Conflict arising from specialization becomes particularly acute if the organization's external *environment* becomes unpredictable. If the meat processing plant cannot reasonably predict the demand for hot dogs or the supply of beef carcasses, scheduling gets more confused and interdependence increases. If only half the expected tonnage of carcasses is delivered, everyone soon runs out of work and the organization ceases to operate. If no sales are made, the meat storage coolers become filled with product and no one has room to operate. Organizations try to increase the predictability of their environments, both indirectly through the use of sales and supply forecasting and more directly through sales goals and campaigns and long-term purchase agreements. Where possible, some organizations increase predictability through vertical integration, buying up and controlling both their sources of supply and their major customers.

Another device for reducing interdependence in the timing of activities is the use of inventories. If there is a cooler full of inspected carcasses waiting when the boning department starts to work, that department's dependence on receiving and inspection is diminished considerably—at least for that day. If there is a large finished-goods inventory waiting to be sold, sales personnel will not be in the packing room yelling for something to sell. Most organizations, whether they produce products or services, find ways to create inventories to reduce timing problems. Hallways full of patients waiting to be X-rayed and lines of students waiting to register for classes are examples of work-in-process inventories of service operations.

Differences in Goals

Organizational subunits with differences in goals are more likely to experience conflict than those with similar goals, other things being equal. Differences in subunit goals arise out of four characteristics of organizations: mutual dependence on limited resources, competitive reward systems, differences in individual goals, and organizational goals which are only subjectively operational.

Dependence on Limited Resources   Differences in goals are not so apparent or important when resources are abundant and subunits are independent. Each unit can go its own way, pursuing, at least to a relative degree, its own goals. But when resources dry up and mutual dependence increases, differences in goals become more apparent and more crucial. When universities were affluent, students supported increases in faculty salaries and faculties supported decreases in student tuition. When university budgets dried up, students demanded that available funds be channeled to scholarships and maintaining tuition levels, while faculty supported tuition hikes to fund faculty salary increases.

Competitive Reward Systems   It has been pointed out that organizational reward systems are seldom designed to be internally consistent. Rather, they develop by bargaining and independent activities which make it likely that competition will be directly reinforced or that conflict will be inadvertently rewarded.[4]

In some instances, of course, competition is deliberately encouraged for purposes of increasing levels of effort. However, as Chapter 16 points out, competitive reward systems not only elicit a motivation to produce but a motivation to block or inhibit others' productivity, if the task and circumstances permit.

Beyond deliberate competition, the organization may reward one department or unit for behavior which inherently conflicts with the goals of another. For example, production departments are typically encouraged to produce large quantities at minimum cost. Quality control, however, is encouraged to minimize the shipment of defective parts. Production's goals are achieved by a high-speed, uninterrupted flow of goods through manufacturing processes. Quality control goals are achieved by slower, more expensive production procedures with frequent interruptions for inspection. The two departments are rewarded for conflicting behaviors.

Differences in Individual Goals   Group and departmental goals, of course, are the products of individuals. An organization staffed with people who bring similar individual goals to it will have less intergroup conflict than one whose members bring a variety of goals. Therefore, factors such as the organization's recruitment and selection procedures can influence the diversity of individual goals and, ultimately, the likelihood of internal conflict.

For example, an engineering organization which recruits only engineering graduates of the local state university is bringing into the organization individuals who, because of their common educational experiences, are similar in many ways. Conversely, a professional baseball team composed of high school dropouts and college graduates, of rural whites, urban blacks, exiled Cubans, and Latin Americans, is likely to find itself with several cliques with very different lifestyles and goals. To be sure, the demands for talent may require recruiting among diverse groups. Diversity of membership has both its advantages and its costs, an organizational fact of life to which the Democratic National Party can testify.

Subjective Operationality of Organizational Goals   Organizations with clear, well-defined, objectively operational goals can reduce

---

[4] March and Simon, *Organizations*, p. 126.

intergroup conflict by appealing to the organization's overall mission. A quarrel between ambulance drivers and emergency room staff can be settled by subordinating the activities of each to the overall goal—save the patient's life.

Not all organizations have developed clear, objective goals. In some cases, the organization's mission has never been easy to define. In other cases, clear goals become fuzzy as the organization grows in size, power, and scope. Not so many decades ago, an elementary school could define its goal as simply to teach students between the ages of 6 and 16 the basic elements of reading, writing and arithmetic. Today's elementary school systems publicize such overall missions as nurturing and developing each individual student's skills and abilities to the maximum potential, thereby creating well-educated, well-informed, and well-rounded future citizens prepared to cope with the demands of a complex and ever-changing society. Lofty goals, to be sure, but neither clear, operational, nor well defined. They are open to the subjective interpretation of whichever groups happen to be assessing the goals. The lofty goal expressed above can be viewed as a mandate for such divergent and often conflicting activities as sensitivity training, varsity athletics, sex education, physical education, local control, central administration, federal control, forced busing, school lunch programs, the new math, and if time and space permit, reading and writing.

To further confound the issue, subjectively operational goals create ambiguous jurisdictions in which two or more groups have related responsibilities.[5] The boundaries over these related responsibilities are often unclear, and this provides opportunities for conflict. The conflicts over boundaries between the parents' and the schools' responsibilities in the education of children, and between local and federal responsibilities for the integration of schoolchildren, are vivid examples of this effect.

Differences in Perceptions

The third major source of intergroup conflict in organizations is differences between groups in their perceptions of reality. Differences in perceptions precipitate disagreement and make joint decision making and cooperation difficult. These differences are primarily, but not completely, attributable to communication problems.

---

[5] Filley, *Interpersonal Conflict Resolution,* p. 9.

Channeling of Information   Division of labor and specialization of functions are characteristics of modern organizations which enable the efficient production of goods and services. Because each unit, section, or department has its own special function, only some of the information available to the organization is directly relevant to its activities. For efficiency's sake, organizations develop communications systems which channel relevant information to the department that needs it—often to the exclusion of the rest of the organization. To return to the example of the meat processing plant, information that a trainload of beef carcasses had been derailed en route to the plant would be directed only to the purchasing and receiving departments.

Unfortunately, this channeling of information for efficiency's sake leads to differences in perceptions among departments. Knowing that an expected shipment of meat has been delayed, the receiving department adjusts its work pace and slows down, much to the consternation of the boning department. The boning department is under pressure from the sausage kitchen to step up production because of an increase in demand which has not been communicated to purchasing and receiving.

Independent Sources of Information   As departmental specialization and sophistication increase, organizational subunits develop their own independent sources of information, both formal and informal sources. The marketing department employs market researchers and consumer behavior analysts to provide information about trends and developments in markets; the finance department uses economists, financial analysts, and tax specialists to provide information about the company's financial environment; manufacturing employs research and development scientists and engineers and (occasionally) industrial spies to keep abreast or ahead of competition in manufacturing techniques.

Each of these major departments is tuned into a specialized, highly trained information network that is very different from the others. Because perceptions are based on information received, each department is likely to develop very different perspectives about what is going on. It is possible, for instance, that marketing's sources indicate the time is right for a major effort to increase the market share of color television sets, while finance's sources indicate that funding any large program would be prohibitively expensive, and manufacturing believes that a major breakthrough in production is imminent which would allow substantial savings in the production of sets. Each piece of information indicates to the department that has it a move entirely different from those suggested by the others' information.

Differences in Time Horizons   Perceptions of the world and the priorities assigned to alternative activities can be highly colored by the time perspective taken. A person who has only a few months to live is likely to assign priorities to work and pleasure that are quite different from someone planning for a long future.

The nature of the tasks performed by people in different units, sections, and departments and the nature of different positions in organizations contribute to differences in the time horizons of the individuals who occupy them. In a manufacturing organization, the time perspectives of top management may be five years, of research and development ten years, of marketing one to two years, of manufacturing six to nine months, of foremen one to a few weeks, and of workers a few hours or days. With such widely different time horizons, it is not surprising that problems important to workers are dismissed as trivial by executives, and those crucial to top management are dismissed by workers. Differences in time horizons are certainly not limited to industry. In colleges and universities, the administration might focus on time horizons of three to five years, tenured faculty would have considerably longer perspectives (number of years to retirement), nontenured faculty would not look beyond the year when they will be granted or denied tenure, and students would not project much beyond their expected graduation date.

Differences in Goals   Of course, the fact that each department has different goals can contribute to differences in perceptions, and vice versa. A flaw in the production system may be viewed quite differently by manufacturing personnel, whose goal is to maximize output, and quality control, whose goal is zero defects. Similarly, the goals of tenured faculty have longer time horizons and are likely to differ from those of nontenured faculty.

To summarize, intergroup conflict in organizations stem from three major characteristics of modern organizations: interdependence, differences in goals, and differences in perceptions among the groups which make up the organization. Each of these characteristics, in turn, is affected by policies and practices of the organization and by the environment in which they operate. To a certain extent, then, internal conflict is affected by factors which the organization can influence. In many cases it comes down to a tradeoff between specialization and division of labor on the one hand and intergroup conflict on the other.

EFFECTS OF INTERGROUP CONFLICT

In an effort to understand more about disruptive intergroup conflict and how to resolve it, behavioral scientists have analyzed how intergroup conflict affects groups experiencing it. In what is generally regarded as the pioneer study of the effects of conflict on groups, 12-year-old upper middle-class boys were selected for a summer camp.[6] After two days together, the boys were divided into two separate groups, the Bull Dogs and the Red Devils. The groups were housed in different areas of the camp and engaged in all subsequent activities separately.

Once the two groups had developed, hostility and conflict between them was engendered by manipulation and competitive situations. As the competition and conflict persisted and increased, observers noticed changes in the behavior of the boys toward their fellow group members and toward members of the other group. These changes, categorized into changes within and between groups, have subsequently been noted in other studies of intergroup conflict. In fact, these effects are so reliable that they could be produced easily in classroom demonstrations.[7]

Changes within Each Group

The changes that may take place within groups as a result of intergroup conflict include the following:

1. *Cohesiveness increases.* We have noted that group cohesiveness increases in the face of an external threat. Competition and conflict produce the same effect; the rival group is seen to be a common threat to the status of the group and the members' prestige. As cohesiveness increases, individual differences are forgotten. The group becomes more attractive and important to the members, and their loyalty to the group is increased.

2. *The group becomes more task oriented.* "Playing around" decreases as concern for defeating or meeting the challenge of the

[6] Muzafer Sherif and Carolyn W. Sherif, *Groups in Harmony and Tension* (New York: Harper & Bros., Publishers, 1953).

[7] E. H. Schein, *Organizational Psychology*, 2d ed. (Englewood Cliffs, N.J.: Prentice-Hall, 1970), p. 97.

other group increases. There is less concern for individual satisfaction and more for accomplishing the group's task.

3. *Leadership becomes more autocratic.* Crisis situations often produce in groups not only a tolerance for less democratic methods but a demand for strong, active, controlling leadership. Responding to these feelings and the group's concern for task accomplishment, leaders of groups in conflict tend to behave more autocratically toward their members, issuing orders and making individual rather than group decisions.

4. *Organization and structure become more rigid.* In conjunction with increasing autocracy and concern for task accomplishment, everything "tightens up." Rules are made and enforced, decision making becomes structural and centralized, responsibilities are assigned and carried out. Individual efforts are monitored and coordinated.

5. *Unity is stressed.* As a result of the threat and increased cohesion brought on by conflict, members are expected to demonstrate their loyalty and conformity to their own group. Deviant behavior is tolerated less, and friendliness with members of the opposing group is viewed with suspicion, if not hostility. Personal sacrifice for the group is highly rewarded.

Examples of these effects of conflict on group behavior are readily found in the world of international politics. Observe what happens to a country when it begins to perceive an increasing possibility of war with another country. Citizens living in other countries return home. Interest and support for government human resource programs decline as military programs are pushed. Individual liberties such as freedom of movement and occupation become less important as military conscription begins and workers are pushed into (or volunteer for) defense work. Economic controls are tightened or imposed, and bureaucracies are established to administer them. Fraternization with the enemy is grounds for official as well as unofficial sanctions; loyalty oaths are demanded; spies are shot. Rallies, parades, and "spontaneous demonstrations" are staged. Personal sacrifices are demanded and rewarded. Dictatorships or near dictatorships are likely to arise, as the country closes ranks around a strong leader.

Changes between Groups

Conflict also causes certain changes in the relationships between the separate groups:

1. *Perceptions of the other group become negative.* The rival group is seen as hostile or evil, rather than a neutral force or object of indifference, and derogatory labels and names are assigned to its members. In the boys' camp experiments, rival groups called each other "pigs" and "bums." Negative stereotypes of the rival group develop; its strengths are minimized, its weaknesses overestimated. As World War II approached, Americans confidently predicted a quick victory over Japan because, they said, "The Japanese all have weak eyes" and thus could neither shoot nor fly effectively.

2. *Selective perceptions increase.* Not only does stereotyping of the rival group occur, but distortions in the form of positive and negative halo effects (see Chapter 6) develop. One's own group is seen as doing no wrong; the rival group is seen as doing no right. Negative information about one's own group is discounted; positive information about the rival group is ignored. In debates or confrontations between representatives of the conflicting groups, members of each group are likely to hear only what they want to hear. They listen closely to their own representative and ignore or scoff at the rival group's representative.

3. *Hostility and aggression increase; communications decrease.* As conflict grows, members avoid interaction and communication with members of the rival group. There are some exceptions: Occasionally individuals will seek out members of a rival group either to confirm their stereotypes of that group or to display loyalty to their own group by hostility and aggressive acts toward the rival group.

The development of conflict in the late 1960s between groups of citizens divided along antiwar and military victory in Vietnam philosophies provided countless examples of these changes in intergroup behavior. One group was called "peaceniks," "traitors," "cowards," and "commies"; the other, "pigs," "facists," and "murderers." Stereotypes emphasizing the most bizarre characteristics of each group were supported by the rival faction, and reinforced with cartoons, slogans, and other gimmicks. Those who opposed the war, were stereotyped as dirty, drug-crazed, immoral cowards. Those who supported it were stereotyped as ignorant, materialistic, prejudiced warmongers. The groups even mocked each other's symbols: The flag was burned or worn as patches, or changed by replacing the field of stars with other symbols. The peace symbol was portrayed on bumper stickers as "the footprint of the American chicken." Communications between rival group members decreased; even within families, parents and children took up opposite sides. Hostility and aggression between groups escalated, as members of both groups sometimes openly sought confrontation and egged each other on to acts of violence.

In most organizations, of course, intergroup conflict seldom develops to the stage of physical aggression, although union-management conflicts are not without a history of occasional violence and bloodshed. But labeling, stereotyping, decreasing communications, and subtler forms of aggression and hostility, such as name calling and interference with work, are typical reactions to intergroup conflict in all organizations. Such effects make conflict resolution extremely difficult.

HOW DO ORGANIZATIONS REACT TO INTERGROUP CONFLICT?

Organizational reaction to internal conflict can take several forms, and there is little evidence to suggest that one form is more likely than another. It has been argued, however, that nonintervention tactics are likely to be tried before the organization attempts to intervene directly.[8]

Nonintervention Approaches

Managers and administrators are likely to avoid direct intervention in intergroup conflict, at least initially, for two reasons. First, they may be highly uncertain about the possible consequences of any direct intervention. Second, they do not want to admit that conflict exists and is so serious that it exceeds the capacity of the conflicting parties to resolve it themselves.

Perhaps the most used tactic is simply to *ignore* the conflict and hope that it will not prove seriously disruptive or that it will eventually resolve itself. This is the tactic initially used by Dr. Baker in the case discussed at the beginning of this chapter. Unfortunately, as happened in that laboratory, the conflict often does not fade away but grows and envelops more and more people.

A second nonintervention approach is to encourage the involved parties to confront their differences and work them out among themselves. This approach assumes that the conflict is based not on major personality differences but on substantive issues which the parties are capable of recognizing and which they have sufficient incentive to resolve.

---

[8] March and Simon, *Organizations*, p. 131.

The processes used by conflicting groups to resolve their own differences fall into one of four major categories: problem solving, persuasion, bargaining, and politics.[9]

Problem Solving   We have described a problem as an obstacle to a goal. In order for two conflicting parties to resolve their conflicts through problem-solving methods, they must agree on the goal. If there is agreement on some specific goal, then information can be gathered, alternative solutions proposed, and alternatives evaluated until one that solves the problem to the satisfaction of both parties is found.

A fairly common example of conflict amenable to problem solving is in the area of hiring. One faction within a department insists on hiring a female or a minority group member to fill a new position; another faction insists on hiring someone with high qualifications, regardless of sex or ethnicity. If both parties agree that a common goal is to hire someone with high qualifications, then extra resources can be used in the search process until a candidate who is highly qualified and who happens to be female or a minority group member is found.

Persuasion   Sometimes agreement is not so easily reached. No immediate common goals can be found. The parties are forced to search for some higher level objective which they both agree on and then attempt to persuade each other that their approach makes a greater contribution to that goal. Persuasion assumes that group subgoals, although different, are flexible enough to be changed to meet some larger objective.

For example, one division of a large recording company deals in classical music, another in country and western. There is conflict between the two over budget allocations and use of recording studios and equipment. Their immediate goals are not easily reconciled. The classical division is to record and sell the highest quality classical music at minimum losses. The country and western division is to maximize income by recording and distributing large-volume country and western records. In searching for higher level goals, they find agreement on a goal of survival for the corporation. Because of inflation and recession, the classical division may be persuaded that diverting additional resources to the country and western division may be the best way of maximizing income and guaranteeing that the organization will survive the financial situation, making it possible to produce and sell classical music in the future.

---

[9] Ibid., pp. 129–31.

Bargaining When disagreement over goals is fixed and common higher level goals cannot be found, conflict resolution moves into nonanalytic modes of bargaining and politics. Persuasion and appeals to reason are abandoned in favor of compromise, threats, bluffs, gamesmanship, and side payments.

Bargaining is defined as the process by which two or more conflicting parties agree as to what each will get and each will give in some transaction. Side payments are rewards given by one side for a significant concession by the other. For example, a group of congressmen may agree not to actively oppose a bill they disfavor if the bill's proponents will support the appointment of the congressmen's candidate for a high-level appointment.

For bargaining to be a feasible solution, there must exist the possibility of agreements in which each party would be better off (or at least no worse off) than if no agreement were made. In addition, more than one such agreement or position must be possible, to allow for bargaining and compromise to take place.[10]

The classic examples of bargaining are derived from negotiations between management and employees over labor contracts. The goals of the two parties are different and fixed: management's is to maximize net income (minimize costs), and labor's is to maximize employee benefits and income. The conditions of bargaining are met in that both parties are usually better off by having a contract than by having no contract. Without a contract, employees cannot work and earn income, and the organization is seriously hindered or prevented from operating. Both parties usually have a wide number of possible agreements in mind which will be generally acceptable to each other, although obviously some agreements are more favorable to one party than to another. Side payments often take the form of management making some major concession in return for labor's dropping some other point of contention. For example, management offers to make the union representatives look good if the representatives agree not to press for a reduction in the work week that year.

Threats have been historical weapons in bargaining attempts to induce major concessions from rival groups, from student threats to boycott classes to Hitler's threat to invade Czechoslovakia and Poland. One problem with the use of threat is that it must be credible to work; and to be credible, threats sometimes need to be carried out, as Hitler found to his eventual dismay.

---

[10] Morton Deutsch and R. M. Krauss, "Studies of Interpersonal Bargaining," *Journal of Conflict Resolution,* vol. 6 (1962), pp. 52–76.

The use of threat sometimes provokes a reaction not of concession but of counterthreat, as is often manifested in international "saber rattling." One experimental study of the effects of threats on bargaining actually found threat to be counterproductive.[11] Games were developed with monetary payoffs to opponents, who could bargain with each other to increase their payoffs. In some cases neither party was given the means to threaten the other. In another condition, one party was given the means to threaten the other (unilateral threat). In a third condition both parties had the means to threaten each other (bilateral threat). The results revealed that the highest joint payoffs occurred when neither party could threaten. The lowest payoffs occurred in the bilateral threat condition, which often resulted in a deadlock which cost both parties dearly. A common finding was that the use of threat provoked hostility, aversion to cooperation, and counterthreat rather than concession.

Politics   Occasionally parties become so inflexible that neither side is willing to concede. In such cases bargaining, which requires flexibility in the form of two or more possible agreements, is impossible. There are no illusions about common goals or compromise. Both parties are determined that one will win and one will lose.

Resolution then shifts to a power struggle. The field of conflict usually grows, as both sides seek outside support. Powerful third parties may be called in to take one side or the other. For example, disputes between various stockholder factions (e.g., the board of directors and stockholders angered over company policies or losses) may reach the point where the only resolution is at the annual meeting. Both sides solicit the votes and proxies of as many stockholders as they can reach, and the issue is decided in favor of whichever side has the most support.

Organizations prefer for conflict to be resolved by analytic rather than nonanalytic modes. For one thing, the use of bargaining and politics is an admission of fixed differences in goals, which is seen as detracting from the preferred rationality of organizational design and management. For another thing, bargaining and politics often result in win-lose situations in which the balance of organizational power shifts, creating a period of uncertainty. Of course, bargaining and politics can also result in situations where all parties lose, as when management and labor fail to agree on a contract and the result is both lost profits and lost wages.

---

[11] Ibid.

Intervention Approaches

There are several ways in which management can directly intervene in conflict. Some methods deal with the symptoms of conflict, some attempt to settle the conflict, and some seek to eliminate the sources.

Dealing with Symptoms   Smoothing over or repressing conflict are two methods which deal with the symptoms or effects of conflict. *Smoothing over* involves the use of reward power: conflicting parties are given some incentive to control conflict and to avoid open clashes. *Repressing conflict,* a more familiar reaction, involves the use of coercive power. Conflicting parties are threatened with punishment for allowing conflict to disrupt the organization's work.

For example, Dr. Baker could have offered the hematology and chemistry departments incentives in the form of bonuses, days off, or fringe benefits for working together. Alternatively, she could have threatened to "fire the lot of them" if they continued to annoy each other and to refuse to cooperate.

Deterring or detracting the parties' attention from conflict is another method of dealing with symptoms while ignoring the causes. Expansion and growth provide opportunities to detract conflict by giving the parties so much work to do that they have no time for conflict.[12]

In Dr. Baker's case this approach would be questionable because it is the departments' refusal to cooperate that is interfering with work, as it is. If the departments recognized that the only way they could handle the increasing work volume was through cooperation, this method might work, providing they were more interested in task accomplishment than in fighting.

Attempts to Settle the Conflict   Establishing rules which limit the conflict to an acceptable level or field is called *encapsulating* conflict.[13] Nations have encapsulated conflict by formal agreements banning the use of gas and germ warfare, establishing rules for the treatment of civilians and prisoners of war, and tacit prohibitions against the use of nuclear weapons. Managers sometimes encapsulate conflict by establishing sales or production contests with specific rules, in the hope that competition will provide an outlet for the conflict in a way that will facilitate, rather than obstruct, work.

---

[12] K. E. Boulding, "Organization and Conflict," *Journal of Conflict Resolution,* vol. 1 (1957), pp. 122–34.

[13] Amitai Etzioni, "On Self-Encapsulating Conflicts," *Journal of Conflict Resolution,* vol. 4 (1964), pp. 242–49.

Democratic means are occasionally employed. The manager or leader allows the larger group or organization to settle an issue of conflict by a vote. This approach is sometimes used in less formal organizations or in those in which the leader or manager has little position power, and membership is voluntary. For example, conflicts over which of competing delegations to the 1972 Democratic National Convention were to be seated were settled by votes of the convention delegates.

A problem with encapsulating or voting on conflict issues is that they typically intensify win-lose situations. The loser often becomes dissatisfied with its role in the organization and lowers its commitment. In 1972, Mayor Richard J. Daley's Illinois delegation was unseated by a delegation challenging it under the rules of the McGovern Commission. As a result, Daley's powerful political machine ignored George McGovern in the 1972 Presidential race, and McGovern was soundly beaten in traditionally Democratic Illinois.

Eliminating the Sources   A drastic but sometimes effective means of dealing with intergroup conflict is the *removal of key figures* in the conflict. This method, which centers around the personal animosities of two or more strong individuals, is a viable alternative in Dr. Baker's case. There are at least two problems with this approach. First, the key people often are very valuable or productive employees, and the manager must balance their loss against the effects of conflict. Second, there is a danger that removal will leave a smouldering resentment or create "martyrs" around which the conflicting parties will continue to rally even after the martyrs have been removed. Senator Thomas Eagleton, whose failure to reveal treatment for mental illness prior to accepting the Vice Presidential nomination caused great conflict in the Democratic Party, was eventually removed from the ticket by McGovern. However, the methods of his removal (he was forced to resign despite McGovern's public assurances that he backed Eagleton 1,000 percent) caused widespread disaffection with McGovern's candidacy.

Restructuring the organization is effective when the source of conflict is structural, as it often is. Conflicting groups can be relocated, task responsibilities redefined, hierarchies decentralized. Occasionally the conflicting groups are merged into one group. This usually resolves the conflict, but in most mergers one group feels that it has actually been subordinated to the other. The merger of the American and National football leagues several years ago is an example of a successful restructuring which reduced the negative consequences of conflict, such as overlapping markets and self-defeating bidding wars for players.

REDUCING THE NEGATIVE CONSEQUENCES OF CONFLICT

A number of tactics aimed at reducing the disruptive effects of conflict have been developed and tested in research. All of these tactics are intuitively appealing; on the surface, they should work. Unfortunately, most of them are relatively ineffective.

Relatively Ineffective Tactics

Tactics designed to reduce conflict which have not proved effective include increasing intergroup contacts, promoting contacts between leaders, propaganda, and distraction.

Increasing Intergroup Contacts   One way of overcoming tendencies for interaction to decrease and stereotyping to increase would seem to be by increasing contacts between conflicting groups. Unfortunately, when such groups are brought together members are more likely to use the occasion to demonstrate loyalty to their own group and aggression toward the rival group, and to reinforce their stereotypes of the other. Some evidence of this has appeared in the results of forced busing to achieve integration, particularly among high school youths. Proponents of busing can argue that over the long run, forced integration will work, and the eventual long-term benefits will overcome intermediate-term hostilities. Most organizations, however, cannot afford intermediate-term hostilities.

Promoting Contacts and Negotiations between Leaders   A device which is often attempted by nations who wish to reconcile, or at least mask, differences is providing for contacts between leaders which can open the way for negotiations. There are two major problems with this tactic. First, successful negotiations require concentration on the issues and flexibility to maneuver. Individual leaders who negotiate are typically so much in the public view that they can only partially concentrate on negotiating and must direct considerable attention to projecting the "correct" image (e.g., a tough, shrewd bargainer) to the group they lead.

In one study, 62 groups who were paired off against one another in competition became deadlocked over some issue. The groups were given full access to information about one another's positions and then elected representatives to negotiate a settlement. In only 2 of the 62 groups did representatives compromise sufficiently to reach an agreement. The other 60 representatives remained steadfastly loyal to their group's position, despite the fact that impartial judges had no trouble deciding which group's position was logically superior.[14]

The second problem with this tactic is that in such negotiations each rival group focuses its attention on its own leader and ignores the rival group's leader (or pays attention only in order to find fault). In another experimental study, conflicting groups were brought together to hear elected representatives of both groups state their own group's position.[15] Subsequent questions revealed that the groups felt they had equivalent knowledge of both positions. But tests showed that 161 subjects knew significantly more about their own group's position, while only 9 knew equivalent amounts about both and only 1 knew more about the rival group than his own.

Propaganda   Allowing groups to exchange positive information about one another would seem to be a way of breaking down negative stereotypes. However, perceptual distortion usually overcomes the effects of positive information or propaganda. Loyalty hinders the acceptance of positive information about the rival group or its cause.

Distraction   Distracting the groups from conflict by improving their overall environment has limited, short-term effects. For example, Dr Baker might have temporarily diminished the intensity of departmental conflict by remodeling the laboratory. However, such distractions usually prove to be at best very short-term deterrents to conflict.[16]

Relatively Effective Tactics

Three different approaches have been found to provide more than temporary relief from the negative consequences of intergroup conflict: locating a common enemy, negotiations between powerful subgroups, and determining a superordinate goal. None of these is simple or easily carried out.[17]

---

[14] Robert R. Blake and Jane S. Mouton, "Loyalty of Representatives to Ingroup Positions during Intergroup Competition," *Sociometry*, vol. 24 (1961), pp. 177–83.

[15] Robert R. Blake and Jane S. Mouton, "Comprehension of Own and of Outgroup Positions under Intergroup Competition," *Journal of Conflict Resolution*, vol. 5 (1961), pp. 304–10.

[16] Sherif and Sherif, *Groups in Harmony and Tension*.

[17] Schein, *Organizational Psychology*, pp. 99–100.

Locating a Common Enemy   In the same way that external threats can increase cohesiveness within a group, an external threat or enemy confronting two groups can induce them to forget their differences in order to deal more effectively with a common opponent. Success of this tactic requires that the groups perceive the threat as difficult to avoid or escape and that they perceive joint efforts as superior to individual efforts.

In the boys' camp experiments described earlier, conflict between the two rival groups was alleviated by a challenge to an all-star baseball game by another camp.[18] The best players from both groups were selected to meet the challenge, and the attention of the members of the group shifted from their own conflict to defeating the rival camp.

Some types of enemies or threats seem to be more effective than others. Immediate tangible threats from a clearly recognizable enemy, such as a military invasion, a union strike, an employee lockout, a government investigation, or an attempted takeover, can successfully induce the threatened parties to cooperate. Less immediate, less tangible threats, and those where the cause is difficult to pin down, are less successful. For example, world hunger and environmental pollution may ultimately kill more people than all wars and diseases, yet they have failed to elicit international cooperation on the scale of NATO or the Warsaw Pact.

Negotiations between Powerful Subgroups   We have pointed out that individual leaders have difficulty in negotiations because of their well-founded concern for maintaining a proper image with the groups they represent. But groups of representatives who have been empowered to negotiate can overcome such anxieties.

It may be true that negotiators feel more secure in groups and are thus willing to take the risks necessary to work through differences. Negotiating through teams also makes it possible for some, if not most, negotiating to be done away from the careful scrutiny of the public eye. Thus concessions can be made and then dressed up to look like gains in order to save face for the negotiators and the groups they represent.

According to experienced labor negotiators, the real negotiations are carried out in small groups behind closed doors, and what appears to go on between the leaders in public is merely propaganda, or attempts to elicit public sympathy. Certainly the Nixon administration employed the strategy of public negotiations and summit

---

[18] Sherif and Sherif, *Groups in Harmony and Tension,* chap. 10.

conferences to attract public attention, while the real negotiations and concessions were carried out privately by small groups. This strategy resulted in the end of direct American–North Vietnamese conflict and in a lessening of conflict between the United States and both the Soviet Union and Communist China.

Determining a Superordinate Goal   The most successful tactic used to resolve conflict between groups in the boys' camp experiments was devising a set of superordinate goals.[19] Having successfully produced two cohesive, rival groups which displayed all the within-group and between-group characteristics described above, the experimenters attempted several methods to reduce the negative consequences of conflict: hostility, aggression, name-calling, stereotypes, refusal to cooperate. Contacts between groups and between leaders, distractions, jointly attended movies and programs had little effect in altering hostility. Finally a series of superordinate goals was devised—goals which were thought to be important to both groups and which required their cooperation. These included finding and fixing a break in the camp water supply, choosing and renting a movie, pushing a stalled truck supplying camp food, and preparing a joint meal. Successful cooperation between the two groups had the effects of lowering tension and hostility, blurring lines between the groups, lessening the tendency to compete, increasing friendships across group lines, and reducing stereotypes.

All of the superordinate goals used to reduce conflict had the following characteristics:

1. They were very attractive to both groups.
2. They required cooperation; no group could possibly have achieved them by itself.
3. They were successfully accomplished.

We can conclude that the use of superordinate goals to reduce conflict is successful but difficult. It requires considerable imagination and some control over resources to devise a superordinate goal which meets these three criteria—strongly attractive, requires cooperation, and attainable.

PREVENTING INTERGROUP CONFLICT

Intergroup conflict within an organization can escalate to a point where effectiveness is severely impaired. Because conflict, once it

---

[19] Sherif and Sherif, *Groups in Harmony and Tension,* pp. 159–96.

flourishes, is so difficult to resolve, the thoughtful manager will consider ways to prevent conflict from getting out of hand in the first place.

Certain characteristics of modern organizations create conditions which can lead to disruptive conflict. Specialization, division of labor, interdependence, tight schedules, and communication channeling are here to stay. To a certain extent, an imaginative manager can modify some of these characteristics if conflict is a problem, but they cannot be eliminated. There are certain precautions, however, which may serve to defuse the intergroup conflict which these characteristics promote.[20]

Establishing *clear, operational, feasible goals* for the organization can channel energy away from conflict. Emphasizing total effectiveness rather than individual group effectiveness can promote cooperation rather than rivalry. The contribution of groups, sections, and departments to overall effectiveness and to the effectiveness of other groups should be measured so it can be *recognized and rewarded.* This will encourage cooperation and altruistic behavior across group lines.

Communications and interaction between groups should not only be facilitated but encouraged and rewarded. Projects or programs requiring the joint efforts of members from several groups can reduce stereotypes and labeling. The rotation of members among groups reduces group identification and provides individuals with insight into the problems and processes of other departments which should facilitate cooperation.

Competition need not be abandoned, but it should be evaluated carefully to see whether the benefits of increased effort and productivity would not outweigh the costs of conflict and diminished cooperation. Where competition is not clearly called for, win-lose situations should be avoided. At the least, managers should be very skeptical of extremes in differentially rewarding groups (such as winner take all).

SUMMARY

Not all conflict in organizations is harmful. Disagreements over goals and methods are healthy indications that people are alert and

---

[20] This section is based (with modifications) on Schein, *Organizational Psychology,* chap. 5.

interested in their work and can provide a spark for innovative and creative behavior. However, organizational conflict between groups can become disruptive to the point of severely limiting organizational effectiveness.

Intergroup conflict in an organization is increased by interdependence, differences in goals, and differences in perceptions. These characteristics are in turn influenced by specialization and division of labor, recruiting and communication practices, and the nature of the organization's environment.

Intergroup conflict produces changes within a group. These include increased cohesiveness, greater concern with the task, more structure and centralization of authority, and emphasis on group unity and member loyalty. Relations between groups also change as conflict increases. The rival group is seen as an "enemy," and negative stereotypes about its members develop—name-calling, hostility, and aggression increase. Perceptions of both the rival group and one's own group are distorted. Communication and interaction between groups decrease.

Organizations react to conflict in a variety of ways. By not intervening, a manager depends on the groups involved to resolve conflict through problem solving, persuasion, bargaining, or politics. The mode they use will depend in part upon whether group goals are shared or flexible. Managers may directly intervene by attempting to smooth over or repress conflict, deter or encapsulate it, transfer personnel, or otherwise restructure the organization. Only the latter two methods deal directly with the conflict; others attempt to treat or alleviate symptoms of conflict.

Of the several tactics developed to reduce the negative effects of intergroup conflict, only three have been found to be really effective. These include locating a common enemy (which has the effect of moving conflict to a higher level), negotiations between powerful subgroups, and establishing a superordinate goal.

Disruptive conflict can be prevented to a certain extent by promoting overall goals, cooperation, and interaction and by avoiding win-lose situations.

Managers can exploit the productive advantages of division of labor, specialization, and competition while still avoiding or at least minimizing disruptive intergroup conflict. However, to do both a manager is going to earn his salary in terms of both effort and ingenuity. He has a good idea of what needs to be done; the problem is in finding feasible ways of doing it.

QUESTIONS FOR REVIEW AND DISCUSSION

1. What are the three major characteristics of intergroup relations which lead to conflict in organizations?

2. In what ways do specialization and division of labor affect the likelihood of conflict in an organization? Give an example to support your statement.

3. Why is conflict more likely when resources are scarce than when they are abundant?

4. Explain the effects public negotiations between leaders can have on reducing the negative consequences of intergroup conflict.

5. Locating a common enemy tends to be a relatively effective short-term tactic for reducing the negative consequences of conflict between groups. Speculate upon some likely long-term effects of this tactic.

6. What is the major difference between persuasion and bargaining as devices for groups trying to work out their differences? Which tactic is likely to be tried first? Why?

7. An organization can experience both too little internal conflict and too much internal conflict. Explain.

8. What are the characteristics of a superordinate goal? Try to construct a superordinate goal meeting these characteristics which might be effective in reducing the negative consequences of conflict between groups in some organization with which you are familiar.

9. Throughout this chapter goals have been mentioned as important factors leading to, reducing, and preventing conflict. What are some reasons why it might be difficult for a manager to come up with a set of clear, operational goals for his or her department?

KEY WORDS

Interpersonal conflict   Problem solving
Technical conflict   Persuasion
Subjective operationality of goals   Bargaining
Encapsulating conflict   Politics
Superordinate goal

Objectives

1. To describe the concept of influence as arising from a relationship between two parties.
2. To discuss the resources of agents of influence which increase their power.
3. To discuss the characteristics of targets of influence which increase their susceptibility.

chapter eighteen

Influence and Power

At last it was time to sing the battle song:

The Airman's color is the color of the cherry blossom.
Look, the cherry blossoms fall on the hills of Yoshino.
If we are born proud sons of the Yamoto race,
Let us die fighting in the skies.

Then the final toast. The *sake* glasses were raised and the cry surged: *Tennoheika Banzai!* (Long live the Emperor). The *Kamikaze* were saying *sayonara* now, laughing and joking as they climbed into their obsolete planes—antiquated fighters, even trainers. The old planes didn't matter, though. It was a one-way trip. The smiles? They might remain on some of these faces to the very last. For others, those smiles began to fade as they settled into their cockpits. Maybe for a few the fear cloud would not settle until the enemy convoy loomed. And what was courage? I never knew. Who was the most courageous—the man who felt the least fear or the man who felt the most? But just then I could think of only one man.

. . . The lead slab in my chest was heavy now, weighing me down, crushing my words. "Tatsuno . . . I . . . " Our hands met in an icy clasp. Nakamura stood by, looking down. Nakamura, a better friend than I, was giving me this final moment.

"Remember . . . " the words came, "how we always wanted to fly together?" I looked into his eyes and bowed my head.

"I will follow you soon," I whispered. . . .

Tatsuno was leading the last V in an all-but defunct navy plane—a Mitsubishi, Type 96.

Already the twelve had opened their cockpits, and fluttered their silk scarves in the wind. Always the wind—the divine wind. Ahead and beneath them the first flak was beginning to burst in soft, black puffs, and the tracers were red lines reaching for the heavens.

Now . . . we seem to be almost on top of them! I am sweating, watching. The lead *Kamikaze* dives, dropping vertically into a barbed-wire entanglement of flak. He'll never make the carriers; that seems obvious. Instead, he's heading for a cruiser near the fringe. For a moment it looks as if he'll make it. But no—he's hit, and it's all over. His plane is a red flare fading, dropping from sight.

Everything is a blur now—a mixture of sound and color. Two more of them go the same way, exploding in mid-air. A fourth is luckier. He screams unscathed through the barrage, leveling inside the flak umbrella near the water. A hit! He's struck a destroyer right at the water line. A bellowing explosion, then another and another. It's good! It's good! The ship is in its death throes. It can't stay afloat—water plunging over the bow, stifling it. It up-ends and is gone.

Now I'm losing track of the flights. They've been scattered. The two trailing formations are forging in through the lethal blossoms. Everywhere, incredible sound and confusion. One of our planes is skimming low across the water, gunfire kicking up a thousand spouts around him. He's closing the gap, aiming straight for a carrier. Straight in—he'll score a direct hit. No, no, they got him. He's bashing into the stern, inflicting little damage.

The defense is almost impregnable. Only a gnat could penetrate that fire screen now. Two more suicides stab at the same carrier and disintegrate, splattering the water. Others have dropped like firebrands into the sea. Impossible to keep track at all now. So far I can be certain that we have sunk only one ship.

Already, only a few planes left. It's hard to discern some of them against the murky horizon. Two planes, an advanced trainer and a Mitsubishi fighter, have swerved back toward us. We circle above them, watch them complete their arcs and head back in. That Mitsubishi! It's Tatsuno! Yes, I'm positive. He was in the last V—the only navy plane!

The two of them are diving, knifing for the convoy's core. Suddenly the trainer plane next to him is hit, virtually clubbed from the sky. His wing and tail rip off, and he corkscrews insanely away, out of my line of vision.

Tatsuno is alone now, still unhit, making a perfect run, better than they ever taught us in school. Tatsuno! Tatsuno! Fire spouts from his tail section, but he keeps going. The orange fingers reach out. His plane is a moving sheet of flame, but they can't stop him. Tatsuno! A tanker looms, ploughing the leaden liquid. They're closing! A hit! An enormous explosion rocks the atmosphere. For a curious instant embers seem to roll and dance. Now a staccato series of smaller bursts and one mighty blast, shaking the sea like a blanket. The tanker is going down. Gone. No trace but the widening shroud of oil.

That was my friend.[1]

IN THIS MANNER Yasuo Kuwahara describes the day he escorted his lifelong friend Tatsuno to a fiery death as a Japanese suicide pilot in World War II. Both Kuwahara and Tatsuno had experienced pain

---

[1] From *Kamikaze* by Yasuo Kuwahara and Gordon T. Allred. Copyright © 1957 by Gordon T. Allred. Reprinted by permission of Ballantine Books, a Division of Random House, Inc.

and seen death as combat veterans of the Japanese Air Force. On that fateful day in 1945 these two kamikazes were only 17 years old.

It is probably difficult for you to imagine yourself in Kuwahara's place—obeying, without complaint, an order to fly with your closest friend on a last mission in which he will destroy himself by deliberately crashing into an enemy ship. Further, Kuwahara knew with certainty that his own time to die for the Emperor would come within weeks.

While we may find his story incredible, it was not unique. In the last ten months of the war, over 5,000 young Japanese pilots obeyed the final order to die the death of a kamikaze. How could so many individuals be influenced to make the ultimate sacrifice in an obviously losing cause?

To a large degree, much of the influence can be attributed to various socialization processes these pilots underwent—from childhood through combat training—that resulted in their internalizing values which made the act of self-destruction honorable, glorious, and inevitable. We will consider this example of extreme influence in some detail in Chapter 19, which discusses socialization and internalization as processes of influence.

Influence and such related concepts as power, authority, and conformity are the subjects of this chapter and the next. This chapter describes influence as a relationship between two parties, the *agent* and the *target* of influence. Characteristics of agents and targets are discussed in some detail. The next chapter will examine and provide examples of several types of influence processes. It concludes by discussing the implications of human influenceability for organizations.

WHAT IS INFLUENCE?

It is useful to make distinctions among some concepts which are commonly used in discussing influence. *Influence* is a process—the process of affecting the behavior of others. In any influence process, there are two parties. For the sake of consistency and clarity, we will refer to the one exercising influence as the *agent* of influence and the one whom the agent is trying to influence as the *target* of influence. Obviously, the agent can be an individual (a teen-ager trying to influence a parent to let her use the family car), a group (several workers trying to influence a new worker to have a beer with them), or an organization (a welfare organization trying to influence its caseworkers to evaluate cases more objectively). The target can be any number of people; an individual, many individuals, a group, an organization, a crowd, a nation, a mob. The earth's entire population can be conceived of as the target of influence of certain agents, such as churches, prophets, and leaders of movements concerned with such ideas as ecology and population control.

Other terms that are often used in conjunction with influence are power, authority, control, and conformity. *Power,* the capacity to influence others or to affect others' behavior, accrues to an agent because of his resources, like strength, wealth, or knowledge. *Authority* is legitimate power, one of the several different kinds of power available to an agent. Authority is conferred upon an agent by an organization˙ (such as a government) or by the people (as in an election, or by custom and tradition).

Control is an extreme form of influence in which the agent not only influences the target to behave in a certain way but enforces limits to that behavior. For instance, traffic experts seek to do more than just influence drivers to slow down. In order to achieve their objectives of safety and movement, they enforce both maximum and minimum speeds on interstate highways. Government economists (with less success than traffic experts) also seek to control behavior. For instance, they establish acceptable limits on the twin economic evils unemployment and inflation, but those limits are seldom achieved simultaneously.

Conformity is the objective of influence—the yielding of the target to the agent's wishes. The word is usually used to indicate that the target has succumbed to the influence of a group or organization. Conformity implies a notion that the target changes his behavior to go along with the group or organization—or behaves differently from the way he would have in the absence of influence. Thus conformity is distinguished from *uniformity,* which indicates several people behaving similarly for reasons other than group or organizational pressure. For example, like everyone else you may be wearing shoes today to protect your feet and keep them warm. This is uniform behavior. If, however, you are wearing shoes today not because of health reasons but for fear of being ridiculed if you go barefoot, you are conforming to group standards for dress. Sometimes there is a fine line between uniformity and conformity. The point is, however, that not all uniformity is evidence of conformity. That is, just because several people are behaving similarly does not indicate that they are targets of some agent of influence.

CHARACTERISTICS OF AGENTS AND TARGETS OF INFLUENCE

We have said that influence is a process involving an agent and a target in some sort of social relationship. The word *relationship* is important here, for the amount of influence an agent can exert on a target is contingent upon the *agent's resources relative* to the target's and upon the *target's dependency relative* to the agent. The greater the agent's relative resources, the more he is able to influence the target. The greater the target's relative dependency, the more he is influenceable.

The Agent's Resources

The resources which give an agent the ability to influence the target—the target's bases of power—can be classified according to the type of power they bestow upon the agent. Social scientists have enumerated five types of power: reward power, coercive power, legitimate power, referent power, and expert power.[2]

Reward Power   An agent has reward power over a target when the agent controls resources which are valued by the target. The agent can induce the target to conform by offering to share a valued resource with the target if the target complies (a company induces its customers to pay their bills early by offering them a 5 percent discount off bills paid within ten days). Or the agent can skip the offer and simply reinforce the target when the target happens to perform as the agent desires (a nurse gives extra attention and care to a patient who follows her instructions, takes medicine promptly, and causes her no trouble).

One of the important things to understand about reward power is that the agent's resources must be of value *to the target.* Many agents who believe they have great reward power are in fact able to exercise little influence because their targets do not place much value on the agent's resources. For example, if a patient values privacy over a nurse's attentiveness, she may have to search for a new source of influence.

Conversely, it is possible for an agent to have reward power of which he is unaware. That is, the agent may have resources which

---

[2] This classification was developed by R. P. French and B. H. Raven, "The Bases of Social Power," in *Studies in Social Power,* ed. Darwin Cartwright (Ann Arbor: University of Michigan Press, 1959), pp. 150–67.

he considers worthless but which others find very reinforcing. This situation often results in the agent's inadvertently reinforcing undesired behavior. For example, a policeman picks up a drunk some night and takes him in to the station to sleep it off. To the policeman, riding in a police car and sleeping in the drunk tank are not highly valued, but the drunk may find the attention and shelter very reinforcing. If so, the policeman may eventually find the drunk waiting for him on his beat on a regular basis.

It is also possible for an agent to have reward power—temporarily—by claiming to have control over resources which he really does not have. As our discussion of expectancy theory in Chapter 4 indicated, if the target expects to be rewarded for complying with the agent, the target may be influenced—for a while. Many con games operate on this principle. A con artist convinces his target (referred to as a "mark" in the language of such operators) that he will share a large sum of ill-gotten money with the mark if only the mark puts up his life savings as evidence of good faith. The mark goes to the bank, withdraws his savings, gives them to a third party for safekeeping, and then waits for his reward. Unfortunately, he eventually discovers that the third party was an accomplice of the con artist, that the con artist, the accomplice, and the mark's life savings have vanished, and that his only reward is a painful, costly lesson on the consequences of greed. In such a case, we could consider the con artist's resources to be his abilities to judge people, appear credible, talk fast, and ignore conscience.

Coercive Power An agent has coercive power over a target when the agent has resources which enable him to cause the target to have unpleasant or aversive experiences. These experiences could include both inflicting pain (as a physical beating or a verbal tongue-lashing) and removing reinforcers (as in removing freedom by incarceration or removing job security by firing).

An agent can induce conformity by directly punishing nonconformity. A soldier is put in the brig for going AWOL, a hoodlum is beaten for informing on an accomplice, a doctor is shunned by colleagues for unethical behavior. An agent can also induce conformity by an "offer" to punish nonconformity, that is, by threat. As with reward power, an agent without resources can temporarily induce behavior by claiming to have those resources, that is, by bluff.

A supervisor may threaten to fire a worker who continues to

ignore his orders; the worker may comply if he values his job and if he thinks the supervisor may actually be able to fire him. A valuable scientist may threaten to leave a job for a better offer unless given a big raise; the company may comply if it considers that the scientist is valuable, has an offer, and is willing to leave.

The problem with offers, threats, and bluffs is that they only work for a while—eventually a target will call the agent's bluff. If the supervisor cannot fire the worker, or if the scientist has no other job offer, these agents may lose much or all of their power over the target and have to suffer the consequences.

Hitler's initial threat in the late 1930s successfully induced other nations to succumb to his will—for a while. The drawback to the use of threat is that its success may seduce the agent into using it once too often. A threat will eventually be answered. Hitler was apparently shocked when England and France responded to his last threat, the invasion of Poland, by declaring war on Germany. Eventually, he paid the highest price for his miscalculation.

Legitimate Power   An agent has legitimate power over a target when the agent possesses attributes or resources which cause the target to perceive that the agent has the right to influence him, and the target has the obligation to obey. These attributes or resources are of a wide variety and may come from a number of sources.

First, a group or culture may bestow legitimate power upon those who possess certain physical attributes or skills. In some societies, elders have legitimate power over younger members. In many cultures males have legitimate power over females, but in others females have legitimate power over males. In most organizations seniority gives a measure of legitimate power over those who have been around only a short time. In all these cases, legitimate power reflects the values of the group, culture, or organization.

Second, an agent's position in a social structure may give him legitimate power over other members who accept the structure. Upon joining an organization one makes a sort of psychological contract with the organization which implies acceptance, at least tentatively, of its hierarchical structure. Therefore, a foreman has legitimate power over subordinates, a judge has legitimate power over those in court, a coach has legitimate power over players, a surgeon has legitimate power over members of the operating team.

Finally, one can acquire legitimate power by being designated as the agent of a person or persons in power. In a democracy, the citizens may bestow a great deal of legitimate power on one of their number by electing that person to fulfill the duties of sheriff, councilman, mayor, tax collector, constable, school board member, senator, member of parliament, or president. Alternatively, one may acquire legitimate power by being designated as a trustee, executor of another's estate, deputy, acting chairman, secretary of defense, or simply as "the guy in charge 'til I get back."

One of the problems with legitimate power is that there is often confusion or disagreement about the range or scope of that power. That is, the two parties may generally agree that one has legitimate power over the other but they will disagree as to the specific behaviors the agent can rightfully order the target to perform. An executive can rightfully expect a supervisor to work hard and diligently; may he also influence the supervisor to spy on rivals, spend weekends away from home, join an encounter group? A coach can rightfully expect his players to execute specific plays; may he also direct their life styles outside the sport? A combat officer can rightfully expect his men to attack on order; may he also direct them to execute civilians whom he claims are spies? A doctor can rightfully order a nurse to attend a patient or observe an autopsy; may he order her to assist in an abortion against her will?

Much of what is written today about the erosion of authority really concerns its range or limits. Not too many decades ago, managerial authority was virtually unbounded. It was accepted as legitimate for plant owners to dictate the social relationships, political behavior, and religious activities of their workers. Today management's range of legitimate power is significantly more restricted to organizationally relevant activities. Most employees feel obligated to obey only those directives that relate to the efficiency or effectiveness of their job performance.

Referent Power   An agent has referent power when he possesses attributes which cause the target to be strongly attracted to or identify with the agent. Such attributes include personal attractiveness, fame, and charisma.

Much has been written about referent power and those who possess it, with the usual conclusion that while "some people have it and some don't," it is difficult to explain *why* some have it and some do not. Comparisons are made between famous persons which suggest that it is easier to agree on who has referent power than to explain why they have it. For instance, Arnold Palmer and Jack Nicklaus are both millionaires because of their golfing skills. Even though Nicklaus is generally acknowledged as the greatest golfer of all time, Palmer is the one with whom the public identifies. John Kennedy and Lyndon Johnson were both Democratic Presidents during the sixties. Although Johnson had years of experience wielding power as Senate majority leader, he was never able to generate the referent power that Kennedy enjoyed. Muhammad Ali and Joe Frazier have both been heavyweight boxing champions of the world. Ali is a Black Muslim, refused to be inducted into the armed forces, and publicly berates his opponents while praising himself—characteristics which the American public generally does not condone. And yet Ali's referent power completely overshadows that of Frazier, whose background is much "straighter."

The kind of behavior referent power often elicits is imitative behavior. The target identifies with or is attracted to the agent so strongly that the target wants to be like the agent and so imitates his behavior. The next chapter will show that the personal characteristics most likely to encourage imitation are status, experience, and success. In organizations with clearly defined status hierarchies, therefore, junior members who desire success are likely to imitate successful senior members. This kind of imitation is functional for the organization as long as the conditions that made senior members successful have not changed. Unfortunately, it is often true that the behavior of high-status, successful members may be dysfunctional for junior members and for the organization. This is particularly true when the rewards for success are perceived by junior members as successful behavior itself.

For example, a senior executive of a corporation may spend a good deal of time heading civic campaigns, making speeches, and entertaining at his club. He does these things because he enjoys them, because his success and status have put him in demand for such activities, and because his high salary enables him to carry them out with style. A young manager who tried to emulate this executive's highly visible behavior, however, would eventually discover that his attempts were neither functional for nor rewarded by the organization. A senior faculty member may spend a lot of time consulting with outside organizations and serving on university committees, but a nontenured faculty member who imitated such behavior could find himself denied tenure because committees and consulting left him no time to carry out research.

Referent power can influence a wide range of behaviors. A target may consider anything an attractive or charismatic agent does as worthy of imitating. Such an agent may influence targets and behavior unintentionally and unknowingly. Joe Namath was probably not aware of the thousands of high school and college players who began sporting white football shoes after he introduced them to professional football.

The fact that referent power can influence behaviors and targets that are unintended as well as intended induces most societies and organizations to exert pressures on the high-status member to adhere strictly to "appropriate" behavior. Such pressures are a cost of high status.

Expert Power   An agent is said to have expert power when he possesses attributes which lead a target to perceive that he has valid knowledge which can be useful. There are several criteria for expert power.

First, the target must perceive the agent as credible; that is, he must believe the agent really knows. An agent must have some history of demonstrated knowledge or skills or possess attributes which the target associates with the possession of knowledge or skills. One who has a doctor of medicine degree may be given expert power in medical matters by a sick person. One who is wearing greasy overalls, carrying a tool kit, and driving a tow truck may be given expert power in automobile repairs by a stranded motorist. One who is the boss's private secretary may be given expert power in organizational secrets by a curious subordinate.

The target must also perceive the agent as trustworthy—believe that the agent is not trying to deceive him. Trust may result from a history of or reputation for honesty or from lack of evidence of any reason to be dishonest, or it may simply require "an honest face." Television advertisers continually search for personalities who are highly trusted to give credibility to advertising claims by endorsing the products. Long-time performers like Henry Fonda and Arthur Godfrey are rated as highly trustworthy by television viewers, perhaps because viewers believe men with so much money could not be induced to publicly endorse an inferior product.

Finally, the target must perceive the agent's knowledge or skills as useful. One who knows more than anyone else in the world about the sexual behavior of the duckbilled platypus would not have expert power over the whole world, but only over certain zoologists (or, occasionally, the owner of a wayward platypus). Obviously, changing conditions can cause an agent's expert power to wax and wane. The coming of electricity via rural electric cooperatives to midwestern farms reduced the expert power of experts in the design and repair of windmills, which were for years a major source of energy in rural areas of the Great Plains. Now, however, the energy and pollution crises have returned to these windmill experts a measure of their former power; governments and private concerns are funding research into the potential of using clusters of windmills to supply low-cost pollution-free energy.

A necessary caution about expert power is that an agent can lose it by abusing it. One who claims expertise in an area outside his real area abuses his expert power and can lose credibility. Dr. Spock lost a good deal of credibility as a pediatrician by claiming to be an expert in foreign affairs. Jane Fonda lost credibility as an actress by claiming to know more about North Vietnamese treatment of American POWs than the POWs themselves.

One can also lose expert power by using it. If I teach you everything I know about trout fishing, I will have expert power in that area over you no longer, for you'll know everything I do about trout fishing. If a secretary knows more about the boss's files and schedule than the boss does, the secretary has some expert power. If the secretary organizes and arranges that information to make it instantly and easily available to the boss, the secretary may gain gratitude but lose expert power. One of the most common complaints of low-ranking employees is that "the boss never tells me anything." One obvious reason why bosses are reluctant to share all their knowledge is the fact that knowledge is power—until it is shared.

Expert power, especially in contrast to referent power, is quite limited in its range and, more than any other form of power, highly dependent upon the target's perceptions. Even if one in fact communicates valid knowledge useful to a target, the agent may fail to influence the target because he does not accept his expertise, or does not believe him, or is not convinced the knowledge is useful. When middle-class welfare administrators are perceived as lacking knowledge and experience of ghetto living, when federal governments are perceived by citizens as knowing the truth but not sharing it, when teachers are perceived by students as dispensers of valid but irrelevant knowledge, their expert power is considerably diminished.

Interaction among Sources of Power   The five sources of power are not completely independent of one another. The way the agent uses certain powers can affect the extent of his other powers.

The use of reward power, for example, can increase referent power, in that people are attracted to and like those who reward them. The appropriate use of reward power—specifying desired behavior and rewarding it when it occurs—may also increase expert power by heightening the agent's perceived credibility and knowledge. That is, he is perceived as doing what he says he will do and as capable of distinguishing desired behavior from undesired behavior.

The use of coercive power tends to decrease referent power, in that people tend to avoid those who administer punishment or withhold rewards. The judicious use of coercive power—specifying undesired behavior and punishing it when it occurs—can increase expert power. Such use heightens the perceived credibility and expertise of the agent. As with the appropriate use of reward power, the agent is seen as one who does what he says and who is capable of distinguishing undesired from desired behavior. A colleague who once flunked a graduate student for plagiarizing was subsequently praised by his other students for being sharp enough to detect the cheating and "having the guts to do something about it." These students implied that the plagiarizer did the same in other classes and that they disapproved, but they felt that detection and action were up to the faculty. It is not uncommon for subordinates to be disappointed in and resent a manager who lets others "get away with murder" in the performance of their jobs.

The possession of legitimate power can increase referent power. Legitimate power is often a mark of high status and honor, and people are attracted to high-status individuals. Possessing legitimate power can also increase expert power, in that targets often associate positions of authority with expertise in the field. Applicants assume that the director of the license bureau is familiar with all the laws regarding licensing in that state; customers assume the head mechanic knows a lot about automobile engines; students assume the instructor knows the subject being taught. Of course, these assumptions may be inaccurate. The director of the license bureau may be a political appointee, selected for the size of a campaign contribution; the head mechanic may be the garage owner's brother-in-law; and the teacher may be substituting for the regular instructor.

Referent power can probably increase most of the other powers. People place more value on rewards given by attractive than unattractive individuals. Attractive people are attributed more legitimacy and more expertise than they perhaps deserve because of a halo effect.

Expert power most directly affects legitimate power, at least in this society. We more rapidly accept the authority of those who have expertise and are more willing to accept a system in which knowledgeable individuals wield the authority. Expert power also affects referent power. One who uses expertise judiciously and who accepts the limits of his expertise can increase his attractiveness. One who refuses to share expertise, who claims more than he has, or who flaunts it can lose attractiveness.

A good way to review this section is analyze your own bases of power in some position. If you are working or hold an office in some organization, what bases of power do you have over your subordinates, your peers, your supervisor? How could you go about increasing these powers? If you are currently not in any such position, think of yourself in the job or role you would like to have immediately after graduation, and ask yourself the same questions.

Characteristics of the Target

Characteristics which are associated with a target's influenceability include the target's dependency on the relationship, uncertainty, and individual traits related to personality characteristics, intelligence, age, and culture.

Dependency   Other things being equal, the greater a target's dependency on his relationship to the agent, the greater the target's susceptibility to influence by the agent. First, the target may perceive the rewards he can obtain from the agent as being uniquely valuable. This type of dependency has been immortalized in songs ("No love like your love"), in advertising ("Where else can you get style, comfort, power, and fuel economy for only $2,195?") and in recruiting ("If you want to swim on a national championship team, there's no place but Indiana"). Dependency may also increase when the target cannot escape the relationship ("You and me are gonna be sharin' the same cell for a long time, buddy") or if the target has no alternative relationships ("Who else would hire a broken-down old bum like you?"). Thus, when a target cannot escape a relationship, perceives no alternatives, or values the agent's rewards as unique, the target is highly dependent and very influenceable.

Uncertainty   The greater a target's uncertainty as to the appropriateness or correctness of a behavior, the greater his susceptibility to being influenced to change that behavior. A series of experiments including more than 600 subjects confirmed this relationship.[3] A typical subject was asked to make judgments, some concerning facts and logic, others concerning opinions and attitudes, and then to indicate how certain he felt about those judgments. Later, the subject was led to believe that four other persons like himself agreed on a judgment different from his. He was then given an opportunity to change his judgment to conform to the group's judgment. The results clearly indicated how conformity increases with uncertainty (see Table 18–1).

TABLE 18–1
Uncertainty and Conformity on Judgments

Certainty of Subject about Initial Judgment	Percent of Subjects Who Changed Judgment to Conform to Group
High	15
Medium	24
Low	36

Source: Adapted from David Krech, R. S. Crutchfield, and E. L. Ballachey, *Individual in Society* (New York: McGraw-Hill Book Co., 1962), p. 510.

Personality Characteristics   A number of personality characteristics have been hypothesized as related to influenceability. Research has found that individuals who cannot tolerate ambiguity or who tend to be highly anxious are more susceptible to influence than others. People with very strong needs for affiliation are particularly susceptible to group influence. The personality characteristic most heavily researched in studies of influence is self-esteem. Although we would expect individuals low in self-esteem to be more easily influenced than those high in self-esteem, research does not bear this out.[4] Studies have found both positive and negative relationships between self-esteem and influenceability. If the two variables are consistently related, the relationship is more complex than originally suspected.

Intelligence   Evidence about the relationship between intelligence and influenceability is mixed.[5] On the one hand, more intelli-

---

[3] David Krech, R. S. Crutchfield, and E. L. Ballachey, *Individual in Society* (New York: McGraw-Hill Book Co., 1962), p. 510.

[4] W. J. McGuire, "The Nature of Attitudes and Attitude Change," in Gardner Lindzey and Elliot Aronson, *The Handbook of Social Psychology*, 2d ed. (Reading, Mass.: Addison-Wesley Publishing Co., 1969), vol. 3, pp. 250–51.

[5] Ibid., p. 249.

gent persons appear to be more receptive to communications than others. That is, they are willing to listen. On the other hand, high intelligence is often associated with high self-esteem and may result in a resistance to influence. Most studies of conformity find the relationship between intelligence and conformity to be negative. That is, the greater one's intelligence, the less one tends to conform.

Of course, if the full range of human intelligence is taken into account, we would find a change in the relationship. Those with very low levels of intelligence would be unable to understand the influence attempts, and thus they could not conform.

Age   Studies of influence and persuasibility have been the focus of a research group at Yale University for some time. Reviewing the evidence of their own and others' studies, this group concludes that susceptibility to influence increases in young children up to about the age of eight or nine. From that age suggestibility decreases with age until adolescence, when it levels off.[6]

Culture   Culture can affect persuasibility in two different ways. First, certain cultures may emphasize individuality, dissent, and diversity (e.g., the French), while others may emphasize cohesiveness, agreement, and uniformity (e.g., the Japanese). Thus we would expect individuals raised in different cultures to vary in their influence-ability according to the emphasis of their society. In support of this hypothesis, a series of experimental studies found French students to be less likely to yield to group pressures than Norwegian students.[7]

Second, cultures can establish different norms for conformity to different roles. This is especially true in sex roles. In this country (until recently, at least), the male role has been viewed as more aggressive and independent, while the female role has been viewed as more submissive and dependent. Such norms have become deeply imbedded in the culture; aberrant behavior on the part of boys is tolerated much more than that of girls. A case in point: A major U.S. brokerage firm recently came under fire because of a question on a test it administered to job applicants. The question asked which qualities are most important in a woman. An answer of "dependency" was worth two points, while an answer of "independence" or "intelligence" received a zero.[8] Such cultural pressures are one reason most

---

[6] C. I. Hovland and I. L. Janis, eds., *Personality and Persuasibility*. New Haven, Conn.: Yale University Press, 1959.

[7] Stanley Milgram, "Nationality and Conformity," *Scientific American*, vol. 205 (1961), pp. 45–51.

[8] *Wall Street Journal*, February 26, 1974, p. 1. The company promised to drop the question in the next revision.

studies find that females conform more often than males in group-
pressure situations.

SUMMARY

Influence is the process of affecting the behavior of other people.
An agent's success in influencing a target is directly related to the
agent's resources relative to the target's resources and to certain
characteristics of the target.

An agent's resources can be classified as reward, coercive, legitimate, referent, or expert power. Each of these types of power arises
from a somewhat different type of dependency relationship between
the agent and the target. However, these bases of power are interdependent in that the way a target uses one type of power can affect
other types. For instance, the use of reward power can increase referent power.

Experiments in influence have found that certain characteristics of
targets increase their susceptibility to influence. A target who is
highly dependent upon an agent is more susceptible to influence than
one who is not highly dependent. A target highly uncertain about a
decision or act is more susceptible to influence than one who is certain. Intelligence, age, culture, and a few personality characteristics
have also been found to be related to one's susceptibility to influence.

Perhaps the most important implication for management to be
drawn from this chapter is that the ability to influence (power) is
not absolute but depends on the relationship between agent and
target. Rewards are effective instruments only if they are rewarding
to the target. Punishments are effective only if they are truly aversive
to the target. Legitimate power requires that the target perceive an
obligation to obey. Expertise is effective only if the target perceives
it to be credible and useful. A manager who fails to assess his employees' traits and resources carefully is likely to overestimate his
ability to influence them.

In the next chapter we will examine several processes by which
agents influence targets and give some examples of the extent to
which individuals can be influenced.

QUESTIONS FOR REVIEW AND DISCUSSION

1. Power is not absolute, only relative. Comment on this statement.
2. Can one have influence without power? Can one have power without
    influence? Explain.

3. What are likely to be the primary bases of power of the following agents: (*a*) a foreman in a union shop over his employees, (*b*) a medical doctor in private practice over her medical staff, (*c*) a field sales representative over the vice president of sales, (*d*) a graduate student over a faculty member.

4. In what ways can the use of coercive power affect other bases of power?

5. Investigations occasionally reveal widespread corruption in an organization in which perhaps an entire department is "on the take" or stealing from the company or public. Use the concepts of dependency and uncertainty to explain how an entire department can become involved in such activity.

6. Research has found rather consistent differences between male and female subjects in their susceptibility to influence. Would you expect these differences to persist over the next 20 or 30 years? Explain your answer.

KEY WORDS

Influence

Authority

Control

Agent

Target

Conformity

Uniformity

Reward power

Coercive power

Legitimate power

Referent power

Expert power

Objectives

1. To describe several processes by which agents influence targets and the processes which induce targets to conform.
2. To illustrate the extent to which individuals can be influenced by others.

chapter nineteen

Influence Processes
and Conformity

"*This one's for keeping a neat and tidy cubicle at all times and this one's for not tying up lines with personal calls and this one's for not horsing around at the water cooler.*"

Drawing by H. Martin; © 1975 The New Yorker Magazine, Inc.

THE CONCEPT OF INFLUENCE as a relationship between agents and
targets of influence, which was established in Chapter 18, is expanded in this chapter, which describes the processes through which
agents influence targets. Examples of the extent to which influence
processes can be successful are also provided.

PROCESSES OF INFLUENCE

Influence processes can be classified as either institutionalized or
uninstitutionalized.[1] The process of socialization, whereby the individual acquires the attitudes, values, and norms he or she must have
to function as a member of a social unit, can also be either institutionalized or uninstitutionalized. From the perspective of the target,
there are three influence processes which induce the target to yield
to the influence of an agent: compliance, identification, and
internalization.

Institutionalized Influence

Institutionalized processes are carried out by agents occupying
positions which have been designated by society to exert influence.
The targets of institutionalized influence have likewise been designated by society to be influenced. Thus, parents are designated to
imbue children with the values of their society; educators are designated to prepare students for particular roles in life. Wardens are
designated to rehabilitate criminals, and therapists are designated to
rehabilitate patients. Personnel managers are designated to orient
new employees to "the company's way of doing things." Coaches are
designated to improve the performance of athletes.

Because the agents and targets of institutionalized influence processes are designated by society, the agents of such influence have
legitimate power as a common basis. Society expects the agents of
institutionalized process to exert influence and their targets to obey.
Of course these agents may exert other types of power and may be
expected to do so. Parents are expected to use reward power, educators to provide expertise, coaches to exert referent power, and wardens to coerce.

Institutionalized influence processes may take a number of forms,

---

[1] This classification scheme was conceived and is described in detail in Warren G.
Bennis, Edgar H. Schein, Fred I. Steele, and David E. Berlew, *Interpersonal Dynamics*
(revised ed., Homewood, Ill.: Dorsey Press, 1968), pp. 333–48.

including education, role training, therapy, and rehabilitation. Such influence is usually expected to be one way, from agent to target. Institutionalized influence has as its goal fundamental, lasting change in the target's behavior.

However, because these processes depend heavily on legitimate power, the range of behaviors which an agent may seek to influence is limited by the norms of the society which designates his role. Teachers are expected to educate children in the three R's but may encounter resistance from parents if the curriculum is broadened to include sex, drug, and moral education. Ministers, priests, and rabbis are expected to influence the moral development of people but not their voting behavior. Management development trainers are expected to influence the way trainees deal with employees and customers but not the way they deal with their children. Doctors are expected to influence patient behavior in recovering from and avoiding illness and injury but not in making investments or paying taxes.

Uninstitutionalized Influence

Not all influence processes are formally designated and sanctioned by society or have as their goal lasting, basic changes in the target's behavior. Uninstitutionalized influence processes occur when both agent and target accept their roles voluntarily.

We can classify these types of processes according to the target's inclination to be influenced. When the target is presumed to have at least some resistance to the agent's planned change, the agent employs some form of *persuasion, selling,* or *seduction.* Thus a customer persuades (changes behavior by reasoning or argument) a supplier to give him an extra month to pay his bills. A real estate agent sells (induces someone to pay money in exchange for goods or services) a couple a home more expensive than they originally intended to buy. A con man seduces (entices by means of a lure) a retired couple into giving him their life savings.

When the target is willing or eager to be influenced, the agent then employs tactics such as *informal role training, coaching,* or *consultation.* A machine operator may coach (train by demonstrating a method or series of steps) a new worker in a time-and-energy-saving way of handling the machine. An aspiring writer may consult (seek professional advice) with a famous author for help on a manuscript.

A good deal of informal role training takes the form of *imitative behavior,* whereby a person aspiring to successful or improved per-

formance of a role adapts his behavior to conform with that of someone already in that role. Circumstances under which an individual
imitates a model, and characteristics of models who are imitated,
have been the subject of much research.[2] This research is of particular interest to organizations in that models are powerful sources of
influence in role training, and also because organizations may have
little control over the models which members choose to imitate.

Imitation tends to occur when an individual encounters a novel
situation in which he is very uncertain about what behavior on his
part would be appropriate. The first time a person is invited to dine
at the home of persons from another culture, it is likely he will carefully observe his hosts' eating and table manners for clues as to how
he should behave. If the hosts remove their shoes, eat from a common dish, or refrain from conversation, he will probably find himself
doing the same.

Imitation also tends to occur when one discovers that behavior
which was once appropriate is no longer appropriate (instead of
being rewarded, one is now punished). The office clown whose jokes
about the boss are always good for a laugh may slink silently back
to his desk when his latest joke is met with an anxious silence. The
rest of the office's behavior cues him that, for some reason, joking
about the boss is inappropriate at that time. The situation has
changed—perhaps the boss just died or just walked into the office,
or the grapevine reports the clown is to be fired that day.

In either event, individuals are inclined to imitate in the face of
uncertainty. Imitation can take three forms. First, one can learn new
ways of behaving; a novice learns how to operate a computer console
by observing an expert. Second, one can learn a new application for
previously learned behavior; a manager discovers that employees respond positively to a pat on the back by observing the results when
other managers do so. Third, one can learn to avoid or suppress behavior. A salesman who observes a customer resisting another's hard
sell approach may adopt a soft-sell line with that customer.

Why do people imitate? There are explanations to fit all the basic
approaches to understanding behavior: cognitive, psychoanalytic,
and reinforcement.[3] A cognitive explanation is that people imitate
because they associate a model's behavior with the outcomes of the

---

[2] J. P. Flanders, "A Review of Research on Imitative Behavior," *Psychological Bulletin*, vol. 69 (1968), pp. 316–37.

[3] M. E. Shaw and P. R. Costanzo, *Theories of Social Psychology* (New York: McGraw-Hill Book Co., 1970), chap. 3.

model's behavior (reward or punishment), mentally encode that behavior, then reproduce it when conditions are appropriate. A psychoanalytic approach proposes that man has an inherited instinct to imitate. A reinforcement explanation proposes that humans are reinforced from birth for imitating (e.g., babies learning how to smile and talk) and thus develop a generalized tendency to imitate.

Regardless of the explanation, the inclination to imitate is pervasive and powerful. The characteristics of individuals whom others choose as models are somewhat diverse. However, one thing most models seem to have in common is that their imitators perceive them to be more competent than themselves, at least in the situation about which the imitator is uncertain. This competence is often inferred from other characteristics of the model which people tend to associate with competence. For instance, prior success, socioeconomic status, and seniority have all been found to increase the likelihood that models who possess those traits will be imitated.[4]

The most important and obvious, yet sometimes overlooked, characteristic of a model is his or her availability. Organizations need to be aware of the persons who are available as models for upward-aspiring members to emulate. If the only visibly successful senior people appear to spend more time on lunches, drinking with the president, or entertaining at the club, there is a very real possibility that such behavior will become imitated, insofar as possible, by junior members. This problem of availability of models has received a good deal of attention from urban sociologists, who attribute much juvenile criminal behavior in ghetto areas to the relative unavailability of successful "straight" male models and the relative availability of successful, high-status models who are pimps, pushers, or rip-off artists.[5]

Socialization

Socialization refers to all those processes by which an individual acquires the attitudes, values, and norms necessary to function as a member of a social unit. It includes both "learning the ropes" and acquiring a commitment to the group or organization. The individual is socialized by both institutionalized and uninstitutionalized processes.

[4] Flanders, "Research on Imitative Behavior."

[5] Charles Keil, *Urban Blues* (Chicago: University of Chicago Press, 1966), pp. 198–202.

A child's primary socialization into society comes through his or her family; the child may learn to value love and sharing at home. From an institutionalized source of influence, school, the child acquires values and attitudes toward learning, authority, and competition. The child is also subject to uninstitutionalized sources of influence such as peers, acquaintances of his parents, and the mass media. Peers may provide attitudes and norms regarding sex and honesty; parents' friends, attitudes toward drinking and smoking; television, attitudes toward wealth, violence, and pollution. Given the variety and availability of these sources of socialization and the susceptibility to influence of preadolescent children, it is likely that a child will have formed a strong set of values, norms, and attitudes with which to confront the world by the time he or she is nine or ten years old. If these sources happen to be consistent in the values and attitudes they offer and reinforce, his socialization may be quite resistant to change.

Organizations attempt to control the socialization processes to which their members are exposed. They are concerned not only that new members "learn the ropes" but that they learn the proper (from the organization's perspective) ropes and acquire a commitment to the organization. There is good reason for organizations to be concerned about these processes. Evidence abounds that ill-planned or inconsistent socialization of members can be related to high turnover. There is less evidence that socialization directly affects member efficiency.

However, organizations control only a portion of the socialization of their members, just as parents control only a portion of the socialization of their children. Orientation programs, management training, employee handbooks, and apprenticeships are some of the means which organizations use to socialize members. The influence of coworkers and clients of the organization may be beyond the organization's awareness and control, however. A nurse may be formally trained to be warm and sympathetic to patients but may learn from other nurses and the patients themselves that the only way to cope with the duties and emotions of nursing is to maintain a detached, businesslike demeanor.

Rites and rituals are often important to socialization.[6] Many socialization processes involve the transition of the target through various stages, steps, or phases. A college football player goes from

---

[6] Erving Goffman, *Relations in Public* (New York: Basic Books, 1971), chap. 3.

high school recruit to freshman to junior varsity to varsity status. A manager goes from prospect to management trainee to staff assistant to department manager. A college professor goes from graduate student to nontenured faculty to tenured status. A physician progresses from medical school student to intern to resident to private practice. These stages of socialization into a profession, organization, or culture are often marked by rites and rituals which symbolize the passage from one phase to the next. Such rites serve not only to facilitate the individual's abandonment of his old status or identity and assumption of his new role, but also to reconfirm the norms and values of the society and to give those who have not reached a certain stage something to aspire to.

All societies have developed rituals to mark the important events of life, such as birth, puberty, marriage, and death.[7] Some of these rituals are complex and ornate. The student's passage through the educational system is marked by graduation exercises, the conferring of degrees, and the wearing of caps and gowns. Acquiring the key to the executive washroom and admittance to the executive dining room are indications that a manager has made it to the top. Scouts acquire badges, wear different uniforms, and learn new signs and salutes as they progress through the various phases of scouting. Military promotions are awarded with insignias and exercises including bands and parades and the entire battalion as an audience; dishonorable discharges are marked by the removel of insignia and uniforms, and the battalion turns its back to the separated individual. The importance of these rites and rituals is evidenced by the amount of information about norms and values which cultural anthropologists can discern from their study.

Processes Inducing Targets to Conform

If influence processes are examined from the target's perspective, it is possible to distinguish three basic reasons why a target of influence yields to an agent of influence. A different influence process has been associated with each of those reasons: compliance, identification, and internalization.[8]

---

[7] See Philip E. Slater, "On Social Regression," *American Sociological Review*, vol. 28 (June 1963), pp. 339–64.

[8] Herbert C. Kelman, "Compliance, Identification, and Internalization: Three Processes of Attitude Change," *Journal of Conflict Resolution*, vol. 2 (1958), pp. 51–60.

Compliance   The process whereby the target yields to the agent because he expects either to be rewarded or to avoid being punished by the agent is called compliance. The target is induced to conform not because he expects the behavior itself to be appropriate, correct, or satisfying, but because he expects some extrinsic reward from the agent for so behaving. For example, a baseball player may bunt when his manager orders it even though he would rather swing away, and even though he expects the play to fail. He obeys because he fears he will be fined or benched if he does not comply with the manager's orders. A politician says what his audience wants to hear, not because he believes what he is saying but because he expects his statements to bring him cheers and votes.

From the influence agent's perspective, obtaining compliance from a target requires two conditions. First, the agent must control the outcomes for the target; that is, he must have either reward or coercive power, or both, over the target. Second, the agent must have opportunities for surveillance over the target's behavior; that is, he must be able to determine whether or not the target complies, so as to appropriately reward or punish him. The target also must believe that the agent exercises surveillance over him.

These conditions can make compliance a rather expensive proposition from the agent's point of view. He must have sufficient resources relative to the target to be able to reward or punish, but perhaps the most expensive requirement is for surveillance. One of the reasons why police states are not greatly successful, although they hold overwhelming reward and coercive powers, is the impracticality of complete surveillance over every citizen's activities. George Orwell's *1984* presents a plausible methodology for such surveillance (two-way televisions in all homes and buildings, plus an extensive citizen-spy system), but few countries could afford such a system—unfortunately, the United States is one of them.

Identification   The process whereby the target is influenced by the agent because the target expects the induced behavior to help him establish or maintain a satisfying relationship to the agent is called identification. The target is so strongly attracted to the agent that he is willing to be influenced by the agent just because he likes or identifies with him. The target does not necessarily believe the behavior is correct, appropriate, or satisfying, but he believes that the act of conforming itself will be. It is not the content of the behavior but being influenced by the agent that is satisfying.

Identification can occur in the form of imitative behavior. The target identifies with and wants to be like the agent, so he imitates the agent's behavior as a means of expressing this identification. Young children may imitate the behavior of their parents to an amazing, and sometimes dangerous, extent, even when the outcomes of the behavior are unpleasant. They will drink beer or coffee, grimacing all the while at the bitter taste, just to be like Mommy or Daddy. Adults will pick up the mannerisms, speech habits, and dress styles of those they consider particularly attractive. For example, a huge demand for rocking chairs resulted from news of President John F. Kennedy's fondness for his.

Identification can also take the form of reciprocal role behavior, in which the target sees his role as accepting the agent's influence, likes that role, and therefore conforms because to do so is part of a satisfying role. Many lasting relationships are formed in which one party plays the dominant role and the other plays the subservient role. Both parties find the roles satisfying, and so their dominant and compliant behaviors persist, not because the subservient party believes in the behavior (he may hardly consider the nature of the behavior at all) but because he wants to obey the dominant party. Many marriages and boss-subordinate relationships may reach this state.[9]

The two requirements for identification are attraction and salience. The relationship with the agent must be attractive to the target; obviously, identification is facilitated when the agent has referent power over the target. Further, the induced behavior will be performed when conditions make the behavior salient or relevant to the relationship. For example, a young lawyer may adopt positive attitudes toward capital punishment which are expressed by a judge whom she greatly admires. When the lawyer is with the judge, or shortly thereafter, she is likely to express those attitudes. At a cocktail party, when her relationship with the judge is farthest from her mind, she may express indifference or even a negative attitude toward capital punishment. However, suppose the relationship should be made salient, as when someone says, "Say, Joan, you're a good friend of Judge Bernem, and he's a strong advocate of restoring the death penalty. How do you feel about it?" We would then expect the lawyer to argue in favor of capital punishment.

Internalization In the process of internalization, the target is influenced by an agent because the target perceives the induced behavior to be congruent with his own value system. He conforms

---

[9] See Eric Berne, *Games People Play* (New York: Random House, 1964).

because the behavior itself is intrinsically rewarding, not because the agent will reward him for conforming. The target is interested in the *content* of the behavior. He perceives it as directly satisfying a need, or solving a problem, or morally correct, or otherwise appropriate. For example, if your boss tells you to take the day off and go fishing because you've been working too hard, you may do so even though you neither like nor respect him, and even though he'll neither reward you for going fishing nor punish you for going back to work. You obey simply because you like to fish and you believe he knows when you've been working too hard. You anticipate satisfaction from the content of the behavior—relaxing and fishing are rewarding in themselves.

The two requirements for internalization are that the agent must be credible and the behavior must be relevant. The target must first perceive that the agent indeed "knows what's good for him." This implies that the agent has expert and/or legitimate power over the target. If you believe your boss doesn't know when you're overworked and is merely trying to get rid of you for the day, you may refuse to take the day off to go fishing. Second, the behavior must be perceived as relevant to the issue. In the example, the issue is your physical and mental state, and you easily perceive overwork, relaxing, and fishing as relevant to the issue. Suppose, however, the boss had said, "You've been working too hard. I want you to drink this six-pack of beer today while you're working." Even though you might like beer and believe that you had been working too hard, you would be hard pressed to see what beer drinking had to do with it, and thus you might take the beer home instead.

Figure 19–1 summarizes the distinctive features of each of the three processes of influence discussed above. The power used by the

FIGURE 19–1
Characteristics of Three Influence Processes Inducing Targets to Conform

Process	Agent's Power	Target's Reason for Conforming	Source of Target's Satisfaction	Necessary Conditions
Compliance	Reward Coercive	To gain reward or avoid punishment	Outcomes administered by agent	Surveillance by agent
Identification	Referent	To establish or maintain a relationship	Conforming or being influenced	Salience to relationships
Internalization	Expert Legitimate	Behavior is seen as consistent with values	Content of induced behavior	Relevance to issue

This figure is based on the models described in Herbert C. Kelman, "Compliance, Identification, and Internalization: Three Processes of Attitude Change," *Journal of Conflict Resolution,* vol. 2 (1958), pp. 51–60.

agent will determine which process occurs and, ultimately, the conditions under which the target will perform the induced behavior. If the agent uses reward or coercive power, the target will comply only when he perceives his behavior as under the agent's scrutiny. If the agent uses the attractiveness of the relationship to the target, the target will tend to perform as desired whenever the relationship is made salient to him. If the agent is able to get the target to internalize the behavior, it should occur whenever it is appropriate or relevant.

Internalization is thought to be the most powerful process. It is the state toward which most agents aspire, primarily because of the cost of surveillance. A parent wants children to play safely, not merely in the parent's presence but wherever the children may be. A teacher wants students to study, not just in the classroom but at home. A supervisor wants workers to work diligently and correctly, not only when he's out on the shop floor but when he's in the office or out of the plant.

How do agents and targets get to a state of internalization? One way is for an agent to select targets whose value systems are already congruent with what he wants them to do. Organizations can do this by carefully explaining to prospective members what the member will be expected to do, in the hopes that those who do not want to do these things will choose not to join. There are some problems with this strategy, in that the prestige or monetary rewards associated with membership in the organization may cause recruits to exaggerate their professed agreement with the organization's values or plans for them. Thus some organizations attempt to uncover prospective members' "real" values and attitudes through other screening devices, such as interviewing, psychological testing, and letters of recommendation.

Another alternative is to employ a well-designed socialization process in which compliance and identification processes are consistently used to reinforce desired behavior, to the extent that the target eventually internalizes behavior which he has often been rewarded for performing, for which he has often been punished for not performing, and which he has often seen others he admires performing. Most people internalize such behaviors as brushing teeth after meals, washing before and after eating, and using proper table manners as the result of intensive processes of compliance and identification exercised by parents, older brothers and sisters, and teachers.

RESPONSES TO INFLUENCE

To what extent can people be influenced by others? How well do compliance, identification, and internalization work? This section will give you some idea of how susceptible most people are to influence by others by describing some famous studies of conformity.

Studies of Perception

A set of experiments was designed by S. E. Asch to test the effects of group pressure on individual judgment.[10] Subjects were given the task of judging which of three lines on a card was the same length as a fourth line on another card, as indicated in Figure 19–2. Sub-

FIGURE 19–2
Typical Set of Lines Used in Experiments on Group Pressure and Conformity

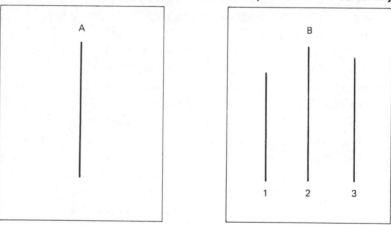

Subjects in Asch's experiments were asked to indicate which of the three lines on card B was the same size as the line on card A.

jects were given several such sets of lines to judge. This was a very simple objective evaluation task, as evidenced by the fact that subjects who performed this task *by themselves* made virtually no errors.

To test the effects of group pressure, groups of seven to nine subjects judged the sets of lines, each subject giving his decision in the presence of others, one at a time. In fact, however, all but one of the group were the experimenter's paid confederates, who had all been instructed earlier to give incorrect responses on certain sets.

[10] S. E. Asch, "Effects of Group Pressure upon the Modification and Distortion of Judgments," in *Groups, Leadership, and Men,* ed. Harold Guetzkow (Pittsburgh: Carnegie Press, 1951), pp. 177–90.

Thus, only one of the group was a true subject, and it was arranged that he give his response after the rest of the group had responded. For this subject, then, there were two sources of information as to the correct answer: what he saw, and the unanimous opinion of the rest of the group. Each subject evaluated 30 sets of lines in the group situation. On 18 sets, the confederates had been instructed to give the correct answer. They did, and so did the subject. On 12 sets, however, the confederates gave the wrong answer. The subject's response on these 12 sets was the dependent variable of interest.

In 37 percent of the judgments made on the 12 crucial sets, the subjects conformed to the unanimous opinion of the rest of the group instead of giving the obvious correct answer! Not every subject conformed, however. About one quarter successfully resisted group pressures and gave the correct answer in every case. Another third of the subjects conformed at least half of the time, and some subjects said whatever the rest of the group said every time.

While the extent of conforming behavior in these experiments was fairly great, we might say that 37 percent conformity is not unreasonable, given the fact that the naive subject was confronting the unanimous opinion of seven or eight others. When researchers varied the size of the group in later experiments, however, they found that the frequency of conformity was just as great when the group was as small as four members—one subject and a unanimous majority of three. Size of the group was not so important a variable as unanimity was. In further studies, with eight-person groups, one of the confederates was instructed to always give the correct answer. Given this additional support, subjects were able to resist the pressures of the rest of the group nearly 95 percent of the time.

These experiments demonstrated rather dramatically that face-to-face peer group influence can in fact significantly affect individual behavior, even to the extent of causing individuals to deny the relatively objective evidence of their own eyes. If objective behavior is so influenceable, to what extent is more subjective behavior influenceable?

Studies of Conformity

The findings on perception touched off a series of investigations of conformity, including a large-scale study using five-person groups.[11] In this study, subjects responded to a series of questions

[11] R. S. Crutchfield, "Conformity and Character," *American Psychologist*, vol. 10 (1955), pp. 191–98.

after first being given the "responses" of another four. In fact, the responses of the other four had been manipulated by the experimenter so that on certain questions a subject was confronted with a unanimous opinion which was clearly ridiculous or incorrect. Despite the fact that the subjects were not subjected to face-to-face group pressures, they exhibited a high percentage of conforming behavior. Some examples of the extent of conformity are given in Figure 19–3. The first column gives the percentage of individuals

FIGURE 19–3
Examples of Conforming Behavior in Non-Face-to-Face Groups

	Percent Who Agreed	
Item	*Privately*	*When All Four Others Agreed*
I doubt whether I would make a good leader.	0% (military officers)	37% (military officers)
Free speech being a privilege rather than a right, it is proper for a society to suspend free speech whenever it feels itself threatened.	19% (college students)	58% (college students)
Subversive activity is the most important problem facing our country today.	12% (females)	48% (females)

Source: R. S. Crutchfield, "Conformity and Character," *American Psychologist,* vol. 10 (1955), pp. 191–98.

who *privately* agreed with the statement. The second column gives the percentage of subjects who agreed when confronted with the unanimous opinion of four others that the statement was true.

It was concluded that the unanimous opinion of small groups can induce substantial conformity from a variety of individuals over a variety of subjects, even when the individual opinions are not given in a face-to-face group situation.

A Study of Obedience

Perhaps the most controversial and certainly the most dramatic study of conformity was by Stanley Milgram in the early 1960s.[12] Forty males between the ages of 20 and 50 were hired to partici-

---

[12] Stanley Milgram, "A Behavioral Study of Obedience," *Journal of Abnormal and Social Psychology,* vol. 67 (1963), pp. 371–78.

pate in an experiment for which they would be paid $4.50. Among the subjects were workers, sales and businessmen, and professional people.

Each subject was told he was participating in an experiment on the effects of punishment on learning. His task was to teach a 47-year-old man a series of word pairs by reading a list of these words to him and then quizzing him. Whenever the learner (actually a paid confederate of the experimenter) failed to give the correct answer, the teacher (the naive subject) was to punish him by administering an electric shock.

The subject was introduced to the learner and taken to a separate room where he watched the learner strapped into an electric-chair apparatus, complete with electrodes. The subject was then taken to an adjacent room consisting of a shock generator and an intercom for communicating with the subject. The shock generator consisted of a series of 30 lever switches in a line, each labeled from 15 to 450 volts, in 15-volt increments from left to right. Each group of four switches was also labeled, from left to right, as follows: Slight Shock, Moderate Shock, Strong Shock, Very Strong Shock, Intense Shock, Extreme Intensity Shock, Danger: Severe Shock. The last two switches, labeled 435 and 450 volts, were simply marked XXX.

Before beginning, the subject was given a sample 45-volt shock from the generator, to give him an idea of what the learner might experience. The subject was then told to begin reading the words and quizzing the learner, and to punish the learner for failure to respond correctly. Importantly, the subject was told to move one level higher on the shock generator each time the learner failed to answer correctly, and to announce the voltage level before administering the shock.

The subject then undertook the task in the presence of a white-coated experimenter. At any time the subject hesitated to administer the shock, the experimenter used a sequence of mild inducements to encourage him to continue:

1. Please go on.
2. The experiment requires that you continue.
3. It is absolutely essential that you continue.
4. You have no other choice, you must go on.

If the subject still refused to continue after inducement 4, the experiment was terminated. Of primary interest was the maximum level of shock a subject would administer before he refused to go any further. In fact, of course, the learner was a confederate of the experimenter and actually received no shocks but followed a script prepared for him to convince the subject of the authenticity of the shocks. The script included failing to respond at all to the subject's quizzing after the 300-volt shock level, and pounding on the wall after the 300-volt and 315-volt shocks. After the 315-volt shock, nothing more was heard from the learner.

It was hypothesized that very few if any subjects would administer any shock beyond the level of Very Strong, and that virtually no one would administer shocks through all the levels. In the course of the experiment it was indicated that the subjects were convinced of the reality of the situation and the shocks they administered. As Milgram noted,

> Many subjects showed signs of nervousness . . . especially upon administering the more powerful shocks. . . . Subjects were observed to sweat, tremble, stutter, bite their lips, groan, and dig their fingernails into their flesh. . . . Fourteen of the 40 subjects showed definite signs of nervous laughter. . . . Full-blown, uncontrollable seizures were observed for 3 subjects.[13]

Despite the subjects' acceptance of the authenticity of the experiment, the learner's failure to respond after 300 volts, and the mildness of the experimenter's exhortations to continue, the researchers were stunned at the results of the experiment, indicated in Table 19–1. Not a single subject refused to administer shocks of less than 300 volts. The great majority of the subjects continued to administer shocks to the end (450 volts) of the series, although they expressed great reluctance to do so and fears for the safety of the learner, and they exhibited numerous signs of severe psychological stress.

Although we may take issue with the ethics of this experiment, it demonstrated just how influenceable people can be. Even though the experimenter's powers were limited to legitimate and expert (he neither had nor pretended to have any means of rewarding or punishing subjects), he was able to induce each subject to behave in a bizarre and harmful way. His power was perhaps augmented by the fact that the subject had no other source of information. Like the subjects in the perception and conformity experiments discussed above, the subject here was faced with a unanimous majority against

---

[13] Ibid., p. 375.

TABLE 19–1
Distribution of Breakoff Points Where Subjects Refused to Administer Shocks

Verbal Designation and Voltage Indication	*Number of Subjects for Whom This Was Maximum Shock*
Slight shock	
15	0
30	0
45	0
60	0
Moderate shock	
75	0
90	0
105	0
120	0
Strong shock	
135	0
150	0
165	0
180	0
Very strong shock	
195	0
210	0
225	0
240	0
Intense shock	
255	0
270	0
285	0
300	5
Extreme intensity shock	
315	4
330	2
345	1
360	1
Danger: Severe shock	
375	1
390	0
405	0
420	0
XXX	
435	0
450	26

Source: Stanley Milgram, "A Behavioral Study of Obedience," *Journal of Abnormal and Social Psychology,* vol. 67 (1963), pp. 371–78. Copyright 1963 by the American Psychological Association. Reproduced by permission.

him, although in this case it was not a unanimous majority of seven or four, but one (the experimenter).

As you can see, people forced to behave in very subjective or uncertain situations are highly susceptible to influence. One may suspect that what one is about to do in such a situation is inappropriate, immoral, unethical, disloyal, or dangerous, but if everyone else involved is doing it or encourages it, one may very well succumb to their influence. Recognizing this tendency should help you understand certain kinds of collective behavior:

- Drug use among high school children (Mom and Dad and all my friends do it in one form or another.)
- Expense account padding among business and professional people (My boss and colleagues all do it.)
- Driving ten miles over the speed limit (I'm just keeping up with the traffic.)
- The taking of kickbacks from contractors and builders by state officials (It's the history of the job—everyone has always done it.)
- Accepting huge campaign donations from corporations, unions, and special interest groups by candidates (It's the only way anyone ever gets elected.)
- The My Lai massacre (Everyone says they're the enemy; everyone else is shooting.)
- Mass political murder in Hitler's Germany, Stalin's Russia, Mao's China, and more recently, Nigeria and Uganda (My leader says they're enemies of the state, my friends say they're less than human, the state has made it official policy, everyone else is shooting.).

AN EXAMPLE OF A SOCIALIZATION PROCESS: WHAT MAKES A KAMIKAZE PILOT?

Now that we have described and analyzed human influence processes and what makes them work, we can go back to the story that introduced the preceding chapter[14] and try to understand the forces that brought two 17-year-olds to obey willingly a squadron commander's order to take their own lives.

First we must consider the culture in which they were born and raised. According to the national religion of Shintoism, all authority, whether it be military or parental, comes from the Emperor, who is not a mere man, but divine. There was also the revered national tradition of the samurai—the seven warriors who fought against overwhelming odds and whose code was never to surrender—to accept death before dishonor.

Yasuo Kuwahara was raised in a family which believed in and practiced the national religion and honored the samurai tradition. Yasuo first brought honor to his family by winning the national

---

[14] Yasuo Kuwahara and Gordon T. Allred, *Kamikaze* (New York: Ballantine Books, 1957).

glider championships when he was 15 years old. Shortly thereafter, he was drafted by the Imperial Air Force, much to his father's delight. His father felt that a fighter pilot was the modern samurai, with a unique opportunity to gain great honor in battle. He stressed to Yasuo the courage and nobility of the family ancestors and of the Japanese fighting man in general, pointing with pride to the few Japanese who had been taken prisoner by the Americans and with disdain to the thousands of Americans who had surrendered to the Japanese at that stage of the war.

By the time Yasuo reported for basic training he had internalized the values of respect for authority, devotion to the Emperor, courage, and honor. The institutionalized processes that had influenced him came from his family, religion, and education, and the uninstitutionalized processes were those of his peer group, including Tatsuno, his friend since preschool days.

Basic training for Imperial Air Force recruits was designed to intensify the values of authority, devotion, courage, and honor. In recruit training, the slightest real or imagined infraction of rules or hesitation to obey was punished with a variety of physical abuses which included being beaten with a baseball bat, fists, and bamboo rods, kicked in the face with hobnail boots, and other tortures and humiliations. To "instill the fighting spirit" and to teach the recruits to endure pain without whimpering, regular sessions involving being beaten unconscious with clubs or boots, being forced to smash each other's face with fists, and having noses and teeth broken were endured. The *hanchos* explained such punishment as essential in turning raw recruits into samurai and making them unafraid c. pain, difficulty, and death.

Not everyone survived. During Yasuo's training, nine recruits committed suicide, but the suicides served to strengthen the others' resolve to survive and avoid dishonor. Upon graduation, the recruits saw their experiences as making them a special elite, aware that the weak are expendable. Their strong affection for the Imperial Air Force is another example of a phenomenon we discussed in Chapter 13: The more severe the initiation, the greater the liking for the group.

Throughout the six grueling months, the recruits were constantly reminded that their only purpose in life was to serve their Emperor and their country, and that to die in battle for the Emperor is one's greatest opportunity for honor. On leave after graduation, these ideas were reinforced for Yasuo by his father and when he was honored by a special convocation at the high school from which he had graduated only months before. When he left home again to report to flight school, 250 students and a brass band gave him a send-off. His father's parting words were "Remember now that your life is no longer your own. If you should ever fall into dishonor . . . do not return to bring unhappiness and shame upon us. Live proudly, fight gloriously for the Emperor. Should you die . . . I will have a grave prepared."[15]

Flight school was more of the same. Punishment continued, including beatings with a whip, and for Yasuo a four-day solitary confinement in which he was repeatedly beaten unconscious for "dishonoring" his *hancho*. Upon graduation, Yasuo was elated to learn he had been picked for fighter school—something every trainee desired but only one of three achieved. The commanding officer's graduation speech exhorted the new pilots to dedicate their lives to dying valiantly for the cause, which at that time (October 1944) was becoming quite serious for the Empire.

Although the kamikaze concept had still not emerged, Yasuo's fighter training included regular suicide practice. It was understood by all that the pilot of a disabled plane would crash into an enemy vessel rather than abandon his aircraft. Thus, the pilots routinely practiced diving at the airfield's control tower from various heights and angles. Eventually they were able to dive at painted outlines of ships, pulling out only 60 feet above the ground. Finally, they learned to dive with their eyes closed.

On October 25, 1944, a young newly married lieutenant accepted the honor of becoming Japan's first kamikaze and plunged with a 550-pound bomb into an American ship in Leyte Bay. The initial successes of the kamikaze, the training and socialization of men like Yasuo, and the Shintoist philosophy that "honor is heavier than mountains and death is lighter than a feather" resulted in the suicide deaths of over 5,000 such pilots over the next ten months, in a futile attempt to change the course of the war.

So we can come to understand kamikazes like Tatsumo and Yasuo, not as the "fanatic, mad Japs" they were made out to be in wartime propaganda but as the targets of a lifelong socialization process in which both institutionalized and uninstitutionalized influence processes gradually shaped their behavior toward an almost inevitable tragic conclusion. From one point of view, we might evaluate this socialization as being incredibly successful. From another, we might

---

[15] Ibid., p. 71.

say that these processes and others that brought the Japanese to a militant expansionist posture which demanded unquestioning devotion to authority did not achieve the goals of the society. Instead, they resulted in the destruction of the Empire, incredible suffering and loss of life, and unconditional surrender.

Therein lies the problem for organizational influence and socialization. Such processes must be effective if the organization is to function efficiently. Yet if they are too effective, if all questioning and dissent are stifled, then not only will creativity diminish, but the organization may find itself embarked on a path from which it cannot veer because everyone unconditionally subscribes to the organization's goals. An organization with a completely effective socialization process cannot afford to have goals that are not completely right.

SUMMARY

Influence processes can be institutionalized, such as education, rehabilitation, and socialization, or they can be uninstitutionalized, like persuasion, selling, and seduction. Depending upon the powers used by the agent, influence can take different forms. Compliance requires surveillance of target behavior. Identification works when the target sees the induced behavior as relevant to his relationship with the agent. Internalization is the most difficult to achieve but has the widest scope of influence.

People are demonstrably susceptible to the influence exerted by others, especially when the appropriateness of their behavior is subjective, they are uncertain, and they face a unanimous majority. But even when behavior is not so subjective and the unanimous majority is only a single other person, people can be strongly influenced by authority and expertise. An intense, prolonged socialization process can even influence large numbers of people to the ultimate conformity: self-destruction.

The first implication for management is the need to be aware that influence processes, both institutionalized and uninstitutionalized, are continually going on in any organization. Because of this, only in a closed institution (one from which there is little or no escape, in which members' interaction with the outside world is limited, and which has a great deal of power relative to the members) is it likely that a completely successful socialization of members will be achieved. Often uninstitutionalized processes such as those exerted by peer groups will counteract the institutionalized processes of the organization.

Managers can be of better service to their organizations if they do not demand complete allegiance to all organizational norms and values but try instead to achieve a sense of "creative individualism." This has been advocated not only for subordinates but for managers as well.[16] Rather than conforming to all values and norms (or rebelling against them), the individual adopts only those norms absolutely essential to his functioning in the organization. At the same time he maintains a sense of identity which enables him to both question the organization's goals and work creatively for them.

QUESTIONS FOR REVIEW AND DISCUSSION

1. What type of power do agents of institutionalized influence processes have in common? Why?

2. Why do people imitate others? What factors increase an individual's inclination to imitate a model?

3. What functions do rites and rituals play in a socialization process?

4. In what ways were you socialized into the college or university you are now attending? How might the socialization process have been improved?

5. Compare the relative costs of compliance and internalization as influence processes for an organization.

6. What would you expect to be the primary organizational influence process in (a) a prison, (b) a medical surgery team, (c) a missionary group, (d) a research team, (e) a military unit in combat, (f) a military unit in peacetime, (g) a labor union, (h) a commercial cargo ship?

7. Why do organizations try to socialize their members? What factors make socialization particularly difficult for industrial organizations?

KEY WORDS

Institutionalized influence
Uninstitutionalized influence
Imitation
Socialization

Compliance
Identification
Internalization

---

[16] E. H. Schein, *Organizational Psychology*, 2d ed. (Englewood Cliffs, N.J.: Prentice-Hall, 1970), pp. 78–79.

part six

Leadership and
Changing Behavior
in Organizations

20
Leadership Behavior and Effectiveness

21
Changing Behavior in Organizations

THE PRECEDING parts of this book have been based on the premise that behavior in organizations can be observed, measured, evaluated, diagnosed, and influenced. Part Six concludes by viewing how the manager seeks to influence behavior as a leader and as an agent of change.

Chapter 20 deals with leadership behavior and effectiveness. It describes what we know about leaders and patterns of leader behavior, after decades of research. Factors which influence leadership, and some common effects of different patterns of leadership behavior, are discussed. The chapter concludes by presenting two models which describe leadership effectiveness as dependent upon certain characteristics of the leader, the subordinates, and the situation.

Chapter 21 discusses the problem of how behavior in organizations can be changed. It describes the sources of pressure on managers to change behavior and presents a model for overcoming resistance to change. The argument that behavior change results from changing people, changing their environments, or both is presented. The chapter concludes by presenting and evaluating several methods currently being used to change behavior in organizations.

Objectives

1. To discuss conclusions drawn from research on traits and behavior of leaders.
2. To describe those factors in an organizational setting that can influence a leader's behavior.
3. To examine the effects of certain leadership behaviors on subordinate satisfaction and performance.
4. To present two models of leadership effectiveness.

chapter twenty

Leadership Behavior and Effectiveness

In the summer of 1955, I was working for the North Harbridge Railway to earn money with which to pay for my next year of college. Quite a few college students in the area worked for the company every summer, doing cleanup work and laying track; but the majority of the men doing this work were permanent employees between the ages of 20 and 25. There were three other college men in the gang I was assigned to, and the four of us became quite close friends. The rest of the gang consisted of eleven fellows about 20 years old, from poor families, most of them without a high school diploma, and all of them tough and hard as nails. Our foreman was a fellow of about 35, who was known around the plant as a taskmaster of the first order. We knew him only by the name Chick. With the exception of our foreman, all of us had been hired at the beginning of the summer and were on the same basis, except that the four of us who were college students did not intend to continue our employment after the end of the summer as did the others.

I always worked with the three other college students, Mac, Jack, and Doc, because we could carry on interesting conversations and swap stories, which helped pass the time and make the job more enjoyable. In addition, the rest of the gang seemed fairly tight-lipped, in their own close group, and little, if at all, interested in talking with us. I made an effort to work harder than some of the other fellows, because I had gotten my job through a friend of one of the bosses and felt I had an obligation to him. The summer progressed this way into early August. I frequently talked with the foreman, and we often joked or hurled friendly insults at one another, The rest of the crew did not very often engage Chick in this sort of banter, but they all seemed to get along with him well enough. Occasionally when he had messages to deliver to various parts of the plant, or other crews needed an extra man for an emergency job, Chick would send me; but ordinarily I worked with my regular crew and did the same work as they did. On one occasion, Chick sent Mac, Jack, Doc, and me on an emergency job to clean up some track where a "spill" (coal had spilled from a car and blocked the track) had occurred, and placed me in charge of the group.

Then, in the second week in August, Mac, Jack, and Doc quit working so as to remain deductions on their father's income taxes as dependents. Thereafter, I spent more time talking to Chick, asking him questions about the plant and "shooting the breeze." I was able to do this and still hold up my end of the work, but I noticed some of the others on the crew seemed to resent it and become cooler than usual toward me. I didn't worry about this, as they had never been very friendly, and I was satisfied that I was doing a satisfactory job. Chick sent me on an increasing number of errands and jobs in various parts of the plant, I think, because he knew that I was interested in learning more about the plant. Some of these jobs involved nothing more difficult than walking around oiling switches, which meant I was my own boss for the day. On other occasions the jobs Chick sent me on were emergencies, in which case the work was considerably more difficult than my regular job.

The rest of the crew grew steadily cooler to me and frequently made snide remarks about "getting a soft touch from the boss," even when I was sent out on some of the tougher jobs. Adding to this atmosphere was the fact that when I went on these special jobs, I always had time to wash up before reporting back to the time clock, which the rest of the crew generally did not have the opportunity to do. Seeing me cleaned up when they came in at the end of the day did little to change their opinion of how hard I was working. I continued to ignore their attitude, for I knew I would only be working for another month and then would probably never see any of them again.

One very hot morning, Chick asked me if I would like to go outside the plant during lunch for a couple of beers. This was something he had always forbidden the crew to do; and as it was very hot, I readily accepted. Thereafter, we used to follow this practice about three or four times a week. This only served to make matters worse, and some of the crew became quite hostile toward me in their statements and actions. This bothered me quite a bit, as most of them were bigger than I was and considerably tougher due to the "struggle for existence" type of environment in which they had been brought up. One of them even went so far as to warn me that it might not be wise for me ever to let him catch me alone, or at least "when there weren't any bosses around."

One morning in early September, Chick told me to take four of the crew and the truck to another section of the plant to clean up a load of coke dust that had been spilled on the tracks. I wanted to think of some excuse for not going, because I was afraid of what might happen or that the men might just refuse to work for me. However, I felt I owed it to Chick to accept the responsibility he had delegated to me. I could think of no logical excuse except the truth, and I refused to lose face in this way. Chick told four of the fellows to get into the truck and go with me, and informed them that I was to be their boss for the remainder of the day. They climbed into the back of the truck, and we set off for our new job. On the way to the other side of the plant, I tried to think of some way to gain their co-operation, but could not. I realized that if I did the wrong thing, we would get little, if any work done and that I might collect a few bruises for my troubles as well.

When we arrived at the coke spill, I explained to them what we had to do, and we started working. It was a blistering hot day, and coke dust is the dirtiest stuff imaginable to work with. The crew didn't like it at all, and it wasn't long before they were spending more time leaning on their shovels than using them. I also heard several remarks relating to what they thought of me and had several sneers passed in my direction. I realized that something had to be done or we wouldn't begin to finish the job, and we might all get in a good deal of trouble. I had continued to work while the others leaned on their shovels. At that moment, one of them made a very nasty remark about me and my relationship with the boss. With this, I completely lost my temper.

"Why, you dirty s.o.b.'s" I yelled. "I don't give a damm what you think of me; but as long as you're working for me, you're going to work your tails off, and anyone who doesn't like it can take his timecard and get the hell out! Now get to work, or get out!" I shouted this at the top of my lungs, and they all stood staring at me. I turned around and began to shovel as hard as I could, half expecting to get a shovel over my head.[1]

WHAT HAPPENED NEXT? Did the men respond as the young foreman half expected, with a shovel on his head? Did they walk off the job? Did they ignore him? Or did they just laugh at him? Before you read on, write down how you think the work crew responded to the young foreman's outburst.

If we define leadership as *the process of influencing a group to-ward the achievement of a goal,* then we would describe the young foreman's behavior at the coke spill site as a *leadership attempt.* The goal for the work crew set by Chick was to get the coke dust spill off the tracks. The young foreman's first leadership attempt was simply explaining to the crew what had to be done. Its effectiveness was minimal—a little work and a lot of hostility, not much progress toward the goal.

His second attempt included an assertion of authority ("you're working for me"), a statement of his expectations ("you're going to work your tails off"), a threat ("get to work, or get out"), and an example (he began to shovel as hard as he could). What was the result? The young foreman's story concludes as follows: "A few min-

---

[1] *The Young Foreman,* copyright © 1961 by the President and Fellows of Harvard College.

utes later, the five of us were working like demons, and we accomplished more that day than our whole crew of eight ever had done before." The young foreman's second attempt was effective. He successfully exerted leadership—he influenced the group to achieve the goal of cleaning up the tracks.

Why was his leadership effective? Was he simply a "natural-born leader?" Was it because "people like that" (the work crew) only understand fear? Was it because the situation called for aggressive, autocratic leadership? By the end of this chapter you should be able to give a plausible explanation for the young foreman's success.

In this chapter we are going to examine leadership in much the same order that it has been studied over the past 75 years or so. First we will look at the *leader as a person* and summarize the evidence provided by the trait theory of leadership as to what kind of person makes a leader. Then we will look at the *behavior of leaders*. Next we will take a somewhat broader view of leadership by examining the *factors* that can affect the way leadership is exercised, such as the leader's superiors, the nature of the groups, characteristics of the leader himself, and the situation in which the group is operating. Finally, we will consider two models or theories of leadership effectiveness which propose that the most effective leadership behavior depends upon certain elements of the situation.

THE CHARACTERISTICS OF LEADERS

Think of ten individuals who, in your opinion, are examples of an outstanding leader. They may be current or historical, but only real, not fictional, people should be included. Write down the names and go over your list to look for personal traits and characteristics which these leaders all have or had in common. Look for physical characteristics (height, fitness, sex, race) and personality characteristics (dominance, extroversion, empathy). What about intelligence—were they all extremely intelligent or all of average intelligence?

If your list of outstanding leaders is similar to most students', it contains some of the following names:

Jesus Christ	Martin Luther King
Adolf Hitler	Napoleon Bonaparte
Mahatma Gandhi	Dwight D. Eisenhower
Mao Tse-tung	Moses
Franklin D. Roosevelt	Joan of Arc

Winston Churchill   Vince Lombardi
Golda Meir   Abraham Lincoln
Ralph Nader

You will probably find it is much easier to generate a list of outstanding leaders than it is to discover personal traits or characteristics they have in common. Look at the above list. What kinds of physical traits could these leaders be said to share? Some, like Napoleon, were short; others, like Lincoln, were tall. Some, like King, had a pleasing personal appearance; others, like Lombardi, were not so attractive. Some were female, some male. Some were Oriental, some Western. Some were physically fit. Others, like Roosevelt and Eisenhower, were crippled or often ill.

As to intelligence and personality traits, Roosevelt and Lombardi were dominant, but Eisenhower and Gandhi were not. Some, like Churchill and Joan of Arc, were outgoing. Others, like Lincoln, were quiet, almost shy. Most were psychologically healthy, but some, like Hitler, were not. Some were noted for their intelligence; many were not.

What, then, can we conclude about the nature of a leader? From this exercise, not much. The purpose of the exercise was to demonstrate what more than 50 years of research into the nature of the leader have concluded: It is probably fruitless to search for a single trait or set of traits which distinguishes leaders or potential leaders from the rest of the population.

The so-called *trait theory* of leadership basically assumed that leadership, like intelligence, is a personal trait which some individuals have and others do not have. For many years, research was directed toward trying to identify traits or characteristics which actual leaders have in common. Had this research been successful, organizations seeking leadership could use a simple strategy: Look for individuals with traits that are characteristic of outstanding leaders, and hire them.

The trait theory persisted for some 50 years; researchers first investigated one trait, then another, then patterns of traits, searching for the key characteristics which would identify leaders. However, beginning around 1950 several reviews of the research suggested that trait theory is, at best, of marginal use in understanding leadership. The research had failed to demonstrate a consistent, definite relationship between leadership ability and either physical traits, personality characteristics, or combinations of the two.

An excellent summary of these reviews can be found in the *Hand-*

book of Social Psychology.[2] Some studies have found leaders to be
taller, but others have found them shorter. Some have found leaders
to be heavier, others lighter. Some have found leaders to be in better
health, but others not. Some have found personal appearance to be
important, but the nature of the appearance (e.g., clean-cut or slov-
enly) and its importance for leadership depend on the situation and
the group to be led.

Personality characteristics have been equally inconsistent as predictors of leadership. While well-adjusted personalities are highly
valued by most groups, personality adjustment is not an efficient
predictor of leadership. There is some evidence that dominant individuals are likely to become leaders, but the likelihoood seems to
depend on the particular situation. Even the evidence on extroversion is equivocal. Apparently, extroverts are more likely to *be elected*
as leaders. The effects of authoritarianism seem to depend on the
nature of the group to be led—some followers seek authoritarian
leaders, while others avoid them.

Not all the investigations have been completely fruitless. The evidence seems to suggest that empathy or interpersonal sensitivity is
a desirable leadership trait. Leaders somewhat consistently rate
higher than followers in self-confidence, although certainly the
accomplishment of achieving and maintaining a leadership position
can increase one's self-confidence, and thus the causality of the relationship can be confounded. It is difficult to determine whether self-
confidence makes leaders or whether leadership increases self-confidence. Finally, the relationship between intelligence and leadership
appears to be consistent enough to warrant some generalization.[3] On
the average, leaders appear to be more intelligent than their followers. However, the difference in intelligence is apparently not too
great. That is, one who is far superior intellectually to a group may
be so far removed from the group in interests that he is unacceptable
as a leader and may be unable to communicate well with the rest of
the group.

In summary, looking at leadership as a trait of the leader has not
been a particularly efficient or effective means of understanding leadership. The ability to lead is apparently *not* an individual trait which
some have and others lack. Intelligence, self-confidence, and sensitivity may be useful traits for leaders to have, but they are likely to

---

[2] C. A. Gibb, "Leadership," in *The Handbook of Social Psychology*, 2d ed., ed.
Gardner Lindzey and Eliot Aronson (Reading, Mass.: Addison-Wesley Publishing Co.,
1969), vol. 4, pp. 216–28.

[3] Ibid., pp. 217–18.

play a small role in leadership effectiveness when all other factors, such as the group and its task, are considered. Therefore we must turn from analyzing the traits of leaders to analyzing leadership behavior.

THE BEHAVIOR OF LEADERS

If leaders are not much alike in appearance and personality, are they at least alike in their behavior? What things do leaders do that set them apart from their followers? Are certain ways of behaving as a leader more effective than others? These are the kinds of questions that have led to the study and classification of leadership behavior. In this section we will examine the behaviors and functions of leaders which have been identified and the styles of leadership that seem to be most prevalent.

The obvious, most frequently used method of learning about leadership behavior is simply to observe and record the behavior of individuals functioning as leaders in both natural and laboratory settings. By observing and recording leadership behavior in a variety of settings, social scientists gradually came to perceive certain patterns of behavior, based on the relative frequency or intensity of different behaviors carried out by leaders. For instance, some leaders frequently consulted their groups when making decisions; others never did. Some leaders spent much time organizing the work, others spent much time dealing with workers' personal problems. Some were intensely involved in evaluating and criticizing work; others behaved no differently from their workers. As recognition of patterns of leader behavior grew, these patterns or *styles* of leadership became objects of study themselves. Some of the most prevalent patterns or styles are discussed below.

Authoritarian, Democratic, and Laissez-Faire Leadership Styles

One of the dimensions upon which leadership behavior has been classified is the locus of decision making in the group. Some leaders make all or almost all the decisions regarding the group's activities; this leadership behavior is typically classified as *authoritarian*. Other leaders delegate a great deal of decision-making responsibility to the group itself; this type of leadership behavior is classified as *democratic*. In other groups, neither the leader nor the group makes many decisions. Individual behavior is left up to the individual; the leader in essence abdicates his leadership role. This kind of leadership behavior is called *laissez-faire.*

One of the early, classic studies of leadership behavior investigated the effects of authoritarian, democratic, and laissez-faire leadership behavior on group performance and satisfaction.[4] Groups of boys were assigned to recreation leaders who had been trained to behave in an authoritarian, democratic, or laissez-faire style. Primary differences in the behavior of the leaders were as shown in Figure 20–1.

FIGURE 20–1
Differences in Behavior of Various Styles of Leaders

Behavior	Authoritarian	Democratic	Laissez-Faire
Policy determination	Solely by leader	By group's decision	No policy—complete freedom for group or individual decision
Establishment of job techniques and activities	Solely by leader	Leader suggests—group chooses	Up to individual
Planning	Solely by leader	Group receives sufficient information to obtain perspective needed to plan	No systematic planning
Establishment of division of labor and job assignments	Dictated by leader	Left to group decision	Leader uninvolved
Evaluation	Leader personal in praise and criticism	Evaluation against objective standards	No appraisal—spontaneous evaluation by other group members

Source: Based on K. Lewin, R. Lippitt, and R. K. White, "Patterns of Aggressive Behavior in Experimentally Created Social Climates," *Journal of Social Psychology,* vol. 10 (1939), pp. 271–99.

In this study, ten-year-old boys met in groups of five regularly after school to engage in hobby activities under the direction of one of the three types of leaders. The leaders were rotated among the groups every six weeks, so that each group experienced each type of leadership. All groups met in the same place and had the same materials and same activities.

---

[4] Kurt Lewin, Ronald Lippitt, and R. K. White, "Patterns of Aggressive Behavior in Experimentally Created 'Social Climates'" *Journal of Social Psychology,* vol. 10 (1939), pp. 271–99.

In observing the behavior and production of the boys over 18 weeks, the researchers found certain behaviors were characteristically associated with each of the three leadership styles, as shown in Figure 20–2.

FIGURE 20–2
Characteristic Behaviors of Groups with Different Styles of Leaders

Behavior	Authoritarian	Democratic	Laissez-Faire
Dependent, submissive demanding attention	Most	Little	Least
Aggression to leader	Most	Little	Little
Friendly, confiding	Least	Most	Moderate
Group-oriented suggestions	Least	Most	Moderate
Playing around	Least	Moderate	Most
Reaction in absence of leader	Stopped working	Continued to work	Horseplay
Number who quit	4	0	0
Preferred leadership style	Democratic	Democratic	Democratic
Quantity of output	Most	Somewhat less than autocratic	Least

Source: Based on K. Lewin, R. Lippitt, and R. K. White, "Patterns of Aggressive Behavior in Experimentally Created Social Climates," *Journal of Social Psychology*, vol. 10 (1939), pp. 271–99.

Although the behavior of the boys was close to the expectations of the researchers, they were somewhat surprised at the relatively high productivity of the authoritarian-led groups. They expected the democratic-led groups to be both more satisfied and more productive, perhaps because this is the kind of leader for whom the researchers themselves would have preferred to work.

Other studies also have shown that democratic styles of leadership are not always the most effective, as we will discuss in more detail later. In fact, democratic leadership behavior is not always the most satisfying for the group members, although we might like to think so. There are many individuals who prefer to leave the decision making to the leader, either because such leadership behavior complements their own personalities (e.g., low need for independence, high on authoritarianism) or because of the situation (e.g., a crisis calling for fast action).

In one study of 488 managers of consumer loan offices, the highest job satisfaction was found among subordinates high on authoritarianism who worked for bosses who had little tolerance for freedom.[5] In another study of over 1,000 workers, worker satisfaction with leadership style depended upon the situation.[6] Workers whose jobs required a great deal of interaction with their superiors and whose work was highly independent were most satisfied with authoritarian leaders. An example of such a job might be a policeman on patrol.

Showing Consideration and Initiating Structure

Two other dimensions of leadership behavior that have been studied extensively are the extent to which the leader's behavior is directed toward either getting the job done or caring for his or her subordinates. If we think of a group as working at some task to achieve its goal, it can be expected that success will depend on the group's making progress toward the goal and on its staying together. For instance, an advertising group planning a sales campaign needs both to work on the campaign and to obtain satisfactions for the group which will keep it working on the campaign. Since employee turnover, absenteeism, and tardiness are strongly affected by worker satisfaction, it is not surprising that much leadership behavior can be classified as exhibiting concern for subordinate satisfaction, as well as for task performance. There are also other reasons for being concerned with subordinate satisfaction, including a general concern for the welfare of others, satisfaction from making people happy, and fear of rejection.

Studies and classifications of leadership behavior along these two dimensions originated with a list of some 1,800 leadership behaviors generated by the Personal Research Board at Ohio State in the late 1940s.[7] These behaviors were eventually sorted by statistical analyses into two categories which accounted for most of the leadership behavior described by the subordinates:

1. *Showing consideration* for workers: This dimension included behavior indicating mutual trust, respect, and rapport with subordinates. A leader who showed much consideration was described as one who frequently:

[5] Henry Tosi, "Effect of the Interaction of Leader Behavior and Subordinate Authoritarianism," *Proceedings of the Annual Convention of the American Psychological Association*, vol. 6, part 1 (1971), pp. 473–74.

[6] V. H. Vroom and F. C. Mann, "Leader Authoritarianism and Employee Attitudes," *Personnel Psychology*, vol. 13 (1960), pp. 125–40.

[7] J. K. Hemphill, *Leader Behavior Description* (Columbus, Ohio: Ohio State University, 1950).

- Helped his subordinates with personal problems
- Put subordinates' suggestions into operation
- Treated subordinates as his equal
- Stood up for his subordinates

and as one who seldom

- Refused to compromise
- Asked for more work than could be done
- Refused to explain his actions
- Insisted that everything be done his way

2. *Initiating structure* for the subordinates: This dimension included behavior organizing and defining the work, work relationships, and goals. A leader who initiated a great deal of structure for his subordinates was described as one who frequently:

- Assigned people to particular tasks
- Emphasized meeting deadlines
- Expected workers to follow standard routines to the letter
- Stressed being ahead of competition

and who seldom

- Waited for new ideas to come from the group
- Let subordinates do their work the way they thought best

Employee-Oriented and Production-Oriented Behavior

At about the same time the Ohio State researchers were studying the leadership behavior dimensions of showing consideration and initiating structure, a similar research program at the University of Michigan's Survey Research Center also came up with two dimensions of leadership behavior which they labeled *employee oriented* and *production oriented.*[8]

Employee-oriented behavior includes taking an interest in individual employees and their personal needs, encouraging two-way communications, developing supportive personal relationships with subordinates, and avoiding punitive behavior. Production-oriented behavior concerns planning, establishing goals, giving instructions, checking on performance, stressing production, and similar acts.

It is apparent that there is a great deal of similarity between showing consideration and employee-oriented behavior. There is also

---

[8] Daniel Katz, N. Maccoby, and N. C. Morse, *Productivity, Supervision and Morale in an Office Situation* (Ann Arbor, Mich.: University of Michigan, Survey Research Center, 1950).

a great deal of similarity between initiating structure and production-oriented behavior, although the latter includes a somewhat broader range of behaviors. For our purposes, two factors of the research are important. First, two different categories of leadership behavior were uncovered, one dealing with concern for the task and the other dealing with concern for the subordinates. Second, these two categories do not appear to be diametrically opposed. This fact is important because it was originally believed that concern for the task and concern for subordinates were opposite ends of the same continuum. That is, leaders were thought to behave either in ways that are directly related to the task or in ways related to the welfare of subordinates, as shown in Figure 20–3.

FIGURE 20–3
Original Concept of Leadership Behavior: One Dimensional

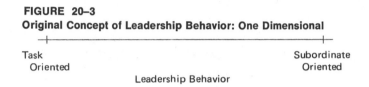

If leadership behavior were unidimensional, as depicted in this figure, then leadership styles would be either task oriented or subordinate oriented: A leader could not be both task and subordinate oriented. If this were true, it would have important implications for organizations with respect to such practices as leadership development and training. For example, if an organization felt that some of its managers needed to behave in a more task-oriented fashion and trained them to do so, they would risk making these managers less subordinate-oriented.

To appreciate the problems organizations would face if task- and subordinate-oriented leadership behavior were opposite ends of the same continuum, consider a parallel problem in another field. Suppose it were discovered that verbal skills and quantitative skills are opposite ends of the same continuum (they are not). Schools and parents would then be faced with a dilemma: If the curriculum emphasized verbal skills, students would develop these skills, but their quantitative skills would deteriorate correspondingly. Or if quantitative skills were emphasized, verbal skills would suffer.

Fortunately, neither quantitative and verbal skills nor task- and subordinate-oriented behavior are diametrically opposed. In fact, one review suggests that the two behavior dimensions are either independent or *positively* related.[9] Out of 24 studies in which subordinates were asked to describe their supervisor's behavior, 13 found a significant positive relationship between showing consideration and initiating structure for subordinates, 9 studies found no relationship, and only 2 studies found the two dimensions to be opposed (negatively related). Further, in the nine military organizations studied, showing consideration and initiating structure were significantly positively related in eight organizations, and unrelated in the ninth.

The important conclusion is that it is possible for leaders to exhibit concern *both* for the task and for the subordinates, and they can increase (or decrease) their behavior along both dimensions at the same time. Therefore, it is more appropriate to depict these leadership behavior dimensions as in Figure 20–4 (rather than as in Figure 20–3).

FIGURE 20–4
Leadership Behavior Dimensions: Revised Concept

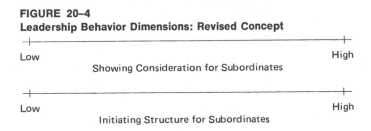

Thus it is possible for an individual leader to show little consideration for subordinates and at the same time initiate little structure for them—that is, he does not exert much leadership at all, as a laissez-faire leader might behave. It is also possible for an individual leader to initiate considerable structure for his subordinates and at the same time show them a great deal of consideration; such a leader would appear to be quite active relative to his laissez-faire counterpart. Or a leader could be high on one dimension and low on the other, or in the middle on both.

A more graphic portrayal of the possibilities is provided by the Managerial Grid® that has been developed out of certain research on leadership styles.[10] This research indicates that managers can be found for any area of the Grid (see Figure 20–5), ranging from those

---

[9] Peter Weissenberg and M. H. Kavanagh, "The Independence of Initiating Structure and Consideration: A Review of the Evidence," *Personnel Psychology*, vol. 25 (Spring 1972), pp. 119–30.

[10] Robert R. Blake and Jane S. Mouton, *The Managerial Grid* (Houston: Gulf Publishing Co., 1961).

FIGURE 20–5
The Managerial Grid

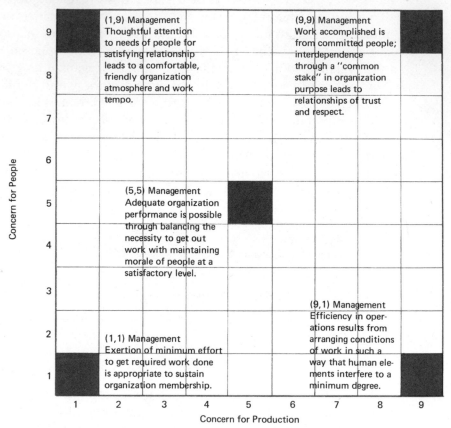

Source: Robert R. Blake and Jane S. Mouton, *The Managerial Grid* (Houston: Gulf Publishing Co., © 1964), p. 10. Reproduced by permission.

who exhibit a great deal of concern for both aspects of leadership, referred to as 9,9 leaders on the Grid, to those exhibiting almost no concern at all, or 1,1 leaders.

DETERMINANTS OF LEADERSHIP BEHAVIOR

One of the problems with concentrating on the leader rather than on leadership behavior is that one's perceptions of leadership can become distorted. Early research on leadership, which focused on the leader, suffered from a sort of myopia in that it left the impression that leadership is a one-way street—the leader influences the group. It was assumed (or at least never questioned) that the leader autonomously determines his own style of leading and imposes it on the group, which is then influenced to behave in a certain way.

What this one-way concept failed to account for was why the leader behaves as he does. Only as researchers of leadership behavior began to ask that question did they acknowledge that leadership behavior, like other behavior, is not determined by the leader autonomously but is the product of many forces acting on the leader and influencing him to behave in different ways. Looking at leadership as determined by forces outside the leader is sometimes referred to as the *situational* approach to leadership: The leader's behavior is seen as a function of the situation in which he finds himself.

The situational approach can be illustrated by an analogy from the sports world. In major league baseball, sportscasters indulging in hyperbole can lead us to believe that a good pitcher dominates the game. The impression is given that the pitcher, cool and aloof on the mound, is the sole agent of influence. This impression might be reinforced by a closeup shot of Tom Seaver shaking off his catcher's sign or Nolan Ryan challenging a batter to hit his fast ball. Their behavior is portrayed as being almost independent of external sources of influence, just as leadership behavior was formerly believed to be independent of the situation.

But when great pitchers explain their behavior, it becomes apparent that a number of factors influence what they do on the mound. The first source of influence is the batter's characteristics—his size and where he stands in relation to the plate, his tendencies, strengths, and weaknesses. Other sources of influence are the situation—base runners and number of outs—and the dimensions of the ball park and the weather. Then there are superiors (the manager's instructions) and peers (the catcher's sign, fielders' strengths and weaknesses). Another factor is the pitcher himself—his confidence, feelings, and repertoire of effective pitches. Finally, the pitcher is influenced by the batters' responses to his pitching—whether they are hitting his curve ball or not, for instance.

Examined in this light, the pitcher, who may appear to dominate the game, is nevertheless heavily influenced by a number of other factors, some of which he can affect, but others which are beyond his control. In the same way a leader who appears to be in control of the situation may in fact find that his behavioral options are strongly affected or constrained by a number of factors.

Seven potential sources of influence on leadership behavior which parallel the sources of influence in the baseball analogy can be distinguished. These are the subordinates, the task, policy and climate, superiors, peers, the leader, and subordinates' responses.

Characteristics of Subordinates

As characteristics of the batter influence the pitcher, so do characteristics of subordinates influence the leader. A leader may be inclined to supervise closely workers who are ill trained or lack experience, or to delegate responsibility to those who understand and accept his objectives and are willing to undertake such responsibility. He may be inclined not to trust, or to remain aloof from, subordinates who are different from him in terms of background, age, sex, or other personal characteristics. He may tend to be patronizing to those whom he perceives as inferior or dependent.

The Task

The number of outs and the presence of base runners can limit a pitcher's options. Similarly, the group's task can place certain constraints on leadership behavior. The task may be quite structured, such as an assembly-line job. Since the goal is clear (assemble 1,000 wheelbarrows per day) and the paths to the goal have been determined (attach two handles and three wheels to the frame with these nuts, bolts, and washers according to this diagram), the leader may be inclined to be very directive. That is, he tends to tell each person exactly what to do and then see that he does so. If the task is unstructured, his tendencies may be different. If the goal is to come up with a new concept in television news reporting, for instance, then neither the goal nor the steps to it are easily defined. The leader may be inclined to facilitate the group's work by providing them with resources, freedom, guidelines, incentive, and encouragement, rather than being directive.

Organizational Policy and Climate

As the dimensions of the ball park and the weather can influence a pitcher, factors like organizational policy and climate can be sources of influence on the leader's behavior. Organizational policy might be strict about fraternizing with employees, including students on curriculum committees, or using physical punishment. An organizational climate which produces a general feeling of well-being and success may influence leaders to be less autocratic and more benevolent, whereas a climate of crisis might encourage tendencies toward more directive, centralized, and autocratic leadership behavior, as in the energy crisis of the 70s. Research has shown that in times of crisis, subordinates expect and even demand directive and autocratic leadership. If the leader's behavior does not meet these expectations, he is in danger of losing his position.[11]

Superiors

The manager's orders can influence a pitcher's approach to the game; similarly, a leader's superiors can influence his or her approach to leadership. The superiors may have a personal preference for a particular leadership style. Among industrial firms TRW, for instance, stresses a very democratic, team-oriented, empathetic approach. A study of leadership training demonstrates the extent of the influence of superiors.[12] A group of foremen from the International Harvester Company were sent to a leadership training program which had the objective of increasing the extent to which they showed consideration for their workers. The training program was a success; shortly afterward, the foremen were found to be significantly more considerate toward their workers. However, the long-term effects of the training program were to a large extent determined by the foremen's supervisors. Foremen who returned to work for supervisors who were themselves considerate continued to rate highly on showing consideration. Those who returned from the training program to work for supervisors who were low on showing consideration for subordinates, however, eventually became even less considerate than they had been before the program.

The influence of superiors on leadership behavior can be explained in several ways. First, one usually perceives one's superior as having a great deal of power over what happens to one and thus is susceptible to the superior's expectations and direct attempts to influence behavior. Second, one may, consciously or unconsciously, imitate the leadership style of one's superiors. As we noted in earlier chapters, one way to learn "proper" behavior, including leadership behavior, is by imitating those who are successful and influential.

---

[11] R. L. Hamblin, "Leadership and Crises," *Sociometry,* vol. 21 (March 1958), pp. 322–35.

[12] E. A. Fleishman, "Leadership Climate, Human Relations Training, and Supervisory Behavior," *Personnel Psychology,* vol. 6 (1953), pp. 205–22.

These are characteristics likely to be attributed to one's immediate superiors.

Peers

As a pitcher's teammates can influence his delivery, a leader's peers can influence the way he handles his job. A leader's contemporaries are a source of a great number of potential reinforcers (friendship, recognition, support, esteem), and as such they can exert a great deal of influence regarding the extent to which the leader conforms to behavioral norms which they consider important. Faculty members are often subjected to peer norms regarding grading curves ("You're not giving enough C's and D's"), classroom procedures ("Case courses are anti-intellectual"), and student relationships ("You're not spending enough time in office hours"; "You're spoonfeeding your students"; "You ought to get to know your students' names"). In industry, attempts to increase consideration or reduce structure may be met with resistance from one's peers ("If you let your people come in at all hours, we'll all have to do it"; "You can't give a second coffee break because pretty soon my workers will be asking why they can't have one, too").

The Leader's Own Characteristics

A pitcher's own skills and feelings may influence his choice of pitches, and a leader's characteristics obviously influence his leadership approach. One such source of influence may be his assumptions about the nature of people at work. Three common sets of assumptions about the nature of man have been identified by Edgar Schein.[13]

The *rational–economic man* model assumes that people at work are basically passive, find work distasteful, are primarily motivated by economic gains, have goals contrary to those of the organization, and are untrustworthy. A manager who subscribes to this model tends to structure work greatly, design out employee feelings as irrational, establish tight control systems, and use economic incentives.

The *social-man* model assumes that work has lost its meaning to people through industrialization and the division of labor, and people at work are basically motivated by social needs and are

---

[13] Edgar H. Schein, *Organizational Psychology*, 2d ed. (Englewood Cliffs, N.J.: Prentice-Hall, 1970), pp. 55–76.

greatly influenced by peer groups. A manager who subscribes to this model will tend to be greatly concerned with employee feelings and with attending to their needs. He is likely to show consideration and sympathy and to use group incentives.

The *self-actualizing-man* model assumes that people enjoy work, can be creative and self-controlled, can integrate their goals with those of the organization, and have needs for autonomy and independence. A manager with such a view of subordinates is likely to try to discover how to make work more meaningful and fulfilling to his workers. He may use job enrichment and job enlargement strategies, while delegating increasing responsibility to workers.

A second set of personal characteristics has to do with the leader's skills and self-image regarding different leadership styles. Some people may find a directive, autocratic mode of leadership to be totally incompatible with their self-image; they feel very uncomfortable in such roles and cannot play them convincingly. Others may not be anxious to delegate authority or may feel uncomfortable in dealing personally with subordinates. There are other people who apparently can move in and out of different leadership styles freely, comfortably, and convincingly (like the pitcher with a wide variety of pitches), and have confidence in each of them. Such leaders can more easily fit their approach to the situation.

Subordinates' Responses

The final source of influence on leader behavior to be discussed lies in the response of subordinates to the leader. The influence a subordinate exerts on the way a leader tries to influence him is known as *reciprocal causation.* The process of reciprocal causation is at work in leadership situations in the same way a pitcher's decision to throw an inside fast ball can be influenced by the fact that the batter missed that same pitch badly during his previous turn at bat.

There is evidence that certain personality characteristics of followers are compatible with, and evoke, certain leadership behaviors. For instance, authoritarians and egalitarians seek different kinds of leadership. Whereas authoritarians seek direction and authority and like high-status leaders, egalitarians do not generally indicate such preferences.[14] Subordinates in compatible groups (e.g., authoritarian

[14] F. H. Sanford, *Authoritarianism and Leadership* (Philadelphia: Institute for Research in Human Relations, 1950).

followers and leader) are more secure than those in incompatible groups.[15] Leaders who behave autocratically are more likely to emerge from authoritarian than nonauthoritarian groups, and leaders who behave less autocratically are more likely to emerge from nonauthoritarian groups.[16] In one study, authoritarian and nonauthoritarian groups of subordinates were assigned to leaders who had either a high or a low tolerance for freedom.[17] Satisfaction and participation were highest for authoritarians working for supervisors with a low tolerance for freedom. However, the nonauthoritarians working for supervisors with a high tolerance for freedom were the least satisfied and participative. This indicates that some degree of direction and structure is expected of every leader.

Besides being influenced by the expectations of subordinates, leadership behavior can also be affected by subordinate task performance. In the early decades of research, the role and power and mystique of the leader were so greatly emphasized that writers assumed that the direction of causality was from leader to subordinate. However, in 1966 a longitudinal study of the performance of research scientists and engineers suggested that the relationship is not so clearly a one-way street.[18] As Chapter 2 noted, a longitudinal study facilitates inference of the direction of causality between variables. In this study of research scientists, the evidence indicated that the performance of the scientists exerted greater influence on the leadership style of their superiors than the superiors exerted on the scientists. To use the baseball analogy, the batters were overpowering the pitchers.

Encouraged by the study of research scientists, an experimental study of office supervisors tested the proposition that subordinate performance influences leadership behavior.[19] Individuals were hired to supervise Job Corpsmen working as secretaries. These corpsmen were really confederates of the experimenter who had been programmed to perform either very competently or very incompetently.

[15] W. Haythorn, A. Couch, D. Haefner, P. Langham, and L. Carter, "The Behavior of Authoritarian and Equalitarian Personalities in Small Groups," *Human Relations*, vol. 9 (1956), pp. 57–74.

[16] Sanford, *Authoritarianism and Leadership*.

[17] Tosi, "Leader Behavior and Subordinate Authoritarianism."

[18] G. F. Farris, "Organizational Factors and Individual Performance: A Longitudinal Study," *Journal of Applied Psychology*, vol. 53 (April 1969), pp. 87–92.

[19] Aaron Lowin and J. R. Craig, "The Influence of Level of Performance on Managerial Style: An Experimental Object-Lesson in the Ambiguity of Correlational Data," *Organizational Behavior and Human Performance*, vol. 3 (November 1968), pp. 440–58.

The competent "secretary" typed 17 two-page letters and envelopes, containing a half-dozen minor errors, in one hour. The incompetent "secretary" typed only 11 one-page letters and averaged six major errors per letter.

Half the supervisors were given the competent secretary to work with, and the other half were given the incompetent secretary. The researchers then systematically observed the behavior of the supervisor once the competence of the secretary had been established. Observations were made of supervisory behavior showing consideration (allowing the secretary to make a personal long-distance phone call), initiating structure (giving specific directions as to how the letters should be typed), and supervising closely (time allowed for coffee break).

The results clearly demonstrated how subordinate performance can affect supervisory behavior. First, supervisors prescribed much closer supervision for incompetent than for competent secretaries and behaved accordingly. Compared to supervisors of competent secretaries, supervisors of incompetent secretaries were less likely to authorize coffee breaks or to allow breaks to exceed ten minutes, and they were more likely to remind the secretary of his mistakes, to criticize him for taking unauthorized breaks, to threaten or command him to end unauthorized breaks, to enter the secretary's office to check on him, and to spend more time there.

Second, supervisors prescribed and initiated more structure for incompetent than for competent secretaries. Compared to supervisors of competent secretaries, supervisors of incompetent secretaries were more likely to insist that the secretary type letters, envelopes, and addresses in a prescribed way rather than the way the secretary desired. They also were more likely to refuse to accede to the secretary's request to change tasks.

Finally, supervisors showed less consideration for incompetent than for competent secretaries. Compared to supervisors of competent secretaries, supervisors of incompetent secretaries were less likely to allow personal long-distance phone calls, to enter the secretary's office just to visit, to accept the secretary's offers of friendship, and to assist the secretary in getting a date and finding local night spots.

To summarize this section, Figure 20–6 depicts the seven sources of influence on leadership behavior. It is important to realize that these sources can exert conflicting pressures on a supervisor. Just

FIGURE 20–6
Sources of Influence on Leadership Behavior

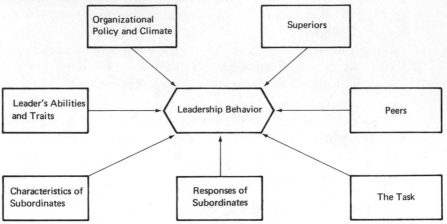

as a baseball pitcher may find himself in a position in which the situation calls for a fast ball, but he feels his curve ball is working better, while the catcher signals for a slider, so a leader may find himself facing a set of conflicting pressures. Poor subordinate performance and an impatient superior can create pressures for close supervision and increased structure, contrary to the expectations of subordinates and the self-image of the leader. This is a situation in which a leader earns his pay.

Nevertheless, it must be remembered that leadership is an interactive process. Although a leader may face conflicting pressures from a variety of sources, he still retains the ability to influence many of those sources. Ultimately, he can choose some leadership strategy within the constraints of the situation. The awareness of potential sources of pressure should help the leader to select an effective strategy to meet the constraints.

LEADERSHIP EFFECTIVENESS

The effectiveness of individuals occupying leadership positions in organizations is of concern to the organization, to subordinates, and to the leader. Is the leadership helping or hindering the group, department, or organization in achieving its goals? Is it leading to subordinate satisfaction or to dissatisfaction, to group cohesiveness or to disintegration, to greater creativity or to conformity?

Effects of Democratic and Authoritarian Styles

Because our culture has traditionally placed higher values on democratic than on authoritarian leadership, certain biases can be detected in the research on the effects of these leadership styles. Much of the research appears to be designed to *prove* that democracy is superior to autocracy, rather than *to test* that proposition. Many equivocal research results have been described as unequivocally demonstrating that democratic methods are more effective in every respect. As Mammy Yokum says in the comic strip "Li'l Abner," "Good is better'n evil, becuz it's nicer." In leadership, the assumption is "Democracy is better'n autocracy, becuz it's nicer."

There is a good deal of evidence to support the contention that, to most people in our culture, democracy is nicer. Investigations, both in the laboratory and in ongoing organizations, usually find that subordinates have higher morale, stronger commitment, greater initiative, and more group cohesiveness under democratic leadership than under autocratic leadership. These positive effects of democracy are particularly evident in certain kinds of tasks, such as problem solving and decision making, and among subordinates who expect and desire democratic leadership.

Note that we said these positive effects *usually* result from democratic leadership. In times demanding speed and efficiency, and especially crisis situations, authoritarian leadership can result in greater subordinate morale and more positive attitudes than democratic leadership. As one reviewer of leadership research puts it, "Authoritarian leadership is practically demanded under such circumstances."[20]

As to the effects of authoritarian and democratic leadership styles on performance and productivity, democracy seems to lead to greater productivity in some situations. One study followed the behavior of employees in nine state agencies in Ohio over a twelve-month period.[21] The supervisors in these agencies were rated on such leadership behavior dimensions as representation, interacting, setting standards, emphasizing goals, allowing participation, giving direction, and enforcing rules. The results indicated that leaders who supervised in the most democratic fashion enjoyed the greatest commitment and initiative from both individual subordinates and groups

[20] Gibb, "Leadership," p. 263.

[21] S. C. Latona, "Leadership Styles and Productivity," *Training and Development Journal*, vol. 26 (August 1972), pp. 2–10.

of subordinates, and they also had the highest producing sections.

An experimental study of group problem solving had similar results.[22] In this study, over 100 teams of students were formed to solve personnel problems, with one student acting as the foreman and three students acting as workers in each team. The researchers observed the way the leader of each team presented the problem and the extent to which the leader shared his information with the rest of the team. The tendency was for the most acceptable, innovative, and highest quality solutions to come from groups in which leadership behavior promoted democracy, information sharing, and interaction.

Authoritarian leadership has likewise been found productive in a number of situations. In an experimental study of leadership and stress, male undergraduates were given either structured or unstructured tasks to perform in four-man groups.[23] Some groups were forced to work under stress, while others worked under nonstressful conditions. The group leaders had been trained to behave in either a democratic or an authoritarian manner. Regardless of the task, groups not under stress performed better under democratic than under authoritarian leaders. However, groups who were under stressful conditions performed better under authoritarian leaders.

We must conclude, then, that democratic leadership behavior is "nicer" than authoritarian behavior, but it is not necessarily more productive. However, the effects of leadership style on both satisfaction and productivity appear to be dependent on such factors as the nature of the subordinates, the type of task, and the control of the leader over his or her subordinates.

Effects of Initiating Structure and Showing Consideration[24]

As you might expect from the classification of leadership behavior as initiating structure or showing consideration, the former affects productivity and the latter affects satisfaction. However, these effects

---

[22] N. R. F. Maier and M. Sashkin, "Specific Leadership Behavior That Promotes Problem Solving," *Personnel Psychology*, vol. 24 (Spring 1971), pp. 35–44.

[23] L. L. Rosenbaum and W. B. Rosenbaum, "Morale and Productivity Consequences of Group Leadership Style, Stress, and Type of Task," *Journal of Applied Psychology*, vol. 55 (August 1971), pp. 343–48.

[24] This section is based on research reviewed in E. A. Fleishman, "Twenty Years of Consideration and Structure," in E. A. Fleishman and J. G. Hunt, *Current Developments in the Study of Leadership* (Carbondale: Southern Illinois University Press, 1973), pp. 1–40.

are not exclusive and are not simple. They can interact with one another, and they can vary with the situation.

In general, most studies have found that showing consideration increases morale and favorable attitudes on the part of subordinates. Where turnover and grievances are concerned, the relationship is not quite so simple. Very low frequencies of considerate behavior are associated with high turnover and many grievances. As the frequency of consideration increases, turnovers and grievances decrease—up to a point. As consideration increases from moderate to high levels, there is little or no additional effect on turnover and grievances.

The effects of initiating structure appear to be less consistent. In part, this may be due to the moderating effects of other variables, including showing consideration. Supervisors who are well above average in initiating structure generally have high productivity but also have a high number of grievances. In times of great pressure for productivity, such as trying to reduce backlogs of orders or meet seasonal production requirements, such supervisors are highly valued and rated by their supervisors. However, the effects on turnover and grievances are not linear. The frequency of initiating structure can increase from low to moderate levels with little or no change in turnover and grievance rates. But as the frequency continues to increase to the intense ranges, turnover and grievances increase markedly.

If we put these data together, we might infer that, if the interest is in keeping turnover and grievances low, there are upper limits to the degree one should show consideration. However, closer studies of the interactive effects of these two dimensions of leadership behavior are somewhat more illuminating.

In studies of foremen in International Harvester plants it was found that the effects of initiating structure as reflected in subordinate grievance rates were moderated if consideration was shown.[25] Foremen who seldom showed consideration had high grievance rates, regardless of the extent to which they initiated structure. Those who showed a great deal of consideration tended to have low grievance rates, regardless of how much they initiated structure. For foremen who were about average in showing consideration, it was found that grievances increased if they increased their emphasis on initiating structure. The relationships are roughly as depicted in Figure 20–7.

---

[25] Ibid., pp. 22–23.

FIGURE 20–7
Relationships between Employee Grievance Rates and Initiating Structure
by Supervisors

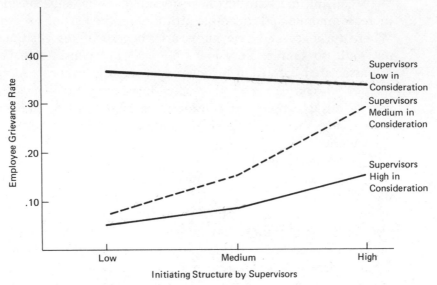

Source: E. A. Fleishman and E. F. Harris, "Patterns of Leadership Behavior Related
to Employee Grievances and Turnover," *Personnel Psychology*, vol. 15 (1962), pp. 43–56.
Reproduced by permission.

Similar relationships were found among these foremen when turnover was the criterion. Apparently, a supervisor who is high in initiating structure can reduce the negative effects on turnover and
grievances by increasing consideration for subordinates. However, a
supervisor who is low in consideration cannot reduce grievances and
turnover by reducing emphasis on initiating structure.

These findings lead us to expect that leaders who are either high
in both dimensions or low in both dimensions would experience
significantly different results. A frequent hypothesis has been that
leadership behavior high on both dimensions will yield greater subordinate satisfaction and productivity than any other leadership
style. Recent evidence, however, fails to support this hypothesis.[26]
A major study measured leader behavior, subordinate satisfaction,
and job performance criteria for 2,474 members of seven different
organizations, including industrial, health, public, and service orga-

[26] L. L. Larson, J. G. Hunt, and R. N. Osborn, "The Great Hi-Hi Leader Behavior
Myth: A Lesson from Occam's Razor," *Proceedings of the Academy of Management,*
1975, pp. 170–72.

nizations. In some of the 14 samples studied, subordinate satisfaction was highest for leaders high in both showing consideration and initiating structure. However, there was no support at all for the hypothesis that such leadership yielded the greatest productivity.

So you can see that, while showing consideration tends to affect satisfaction and initiating structure tends to affect productivity, the overall effects are more complex and interactive. Leadership behavior which exhibits little of both dimensions is likely to be ineffective in achieving productivity, morale, or good ratings for the supervisor. That is, "impoverished" or laissez-faire leadership will do little except conserve the leader's energy. A leader who is high in showing consideration, however, can vary his emphasis on initiating structure to fit the situation, as in responding to changes in pressure for productivity. Although more research is needed to clarify the effects of these leadership dimensions, it appears that showing consideration is a good strategy, if the climate, time pressures, and expectations of subordinates permit.

A CONTINGENCY MODEL OF LEADERSHIP EFFECTIVENESS

A contingency model of leadership effectiveness attempts to combine elements of both trait and situational theories.[27] According to this model, developed by Fred Fiedler, certain elements of a leadership situation moderate the effectiveness of certain leadership traits. To put it another way, the relative effectiveness of leadership traits is determined by how favorable the situation is for the leader.

Elements of the Situation

The contingency model states that three elements of any leadership situation determine the favorableness of the situation for the leader: leader-member relations, task structure, and position power of the leader.

Leader-Member Relations   Whether the leader's relations with the rest of the group are good or bad is considered the key element in determining how favorable a situation is for the leader. If he gets along well with the group, if they hold him in high regard, if he is accepted as the leader, then this element of the situation is quite favorable for the leader. If he does not get along with the

[27] For a more complete discussion of the model and research testing it, see F. E. Fiedler and M. M. Chemers, *Leadership and Effective Management* (Glenview, Ill.: Scott, Foresman & Co., 1974).

group, is not held in high regard, or is not accepted, then this element of the situation is unfavorable. It is argued that a well-liked and respected leader can exert influence over the group far beyond the extent of his legitimate, reward, and coercive power.

Task Structure   The more a task is structured, the more favorable is the situation for the leader; it becomes relatively easy for the leader to determine what should be done, by whom, and for what purpose. There are four characteristics of structured tasks:

1. Decisions about the tasks can be evaluated objectively.
2. The goal is clearly understood by the group.
3. There are few, rather than many, ways to accomplish the task.
4. There are few, rather than many, correct solutions to the problems.

Position Power of the Leader   The leader's position power is comprised of four of the five basic types of power discussed in Chapter 18—legitimate, expert, reward, and coercive (the exception is referent power). A position such as that of an infantry battalion commander in combat carries a great deal of authority, reward, and coercive power. Such a position, which would be labeled *strong* in terms of the model, is considered very favorable for the leader. A position such as the chairman of a fund-raising drive would be labeled *weak* in terms of the model: It has little authority and less reward and coercive power over the volunteers on whom the leader must rely. This kind of position would be relatively unfavorable for the leader.

Overall Favorableness of the Situation   The combination of these three elements determines the favorableness of the situation for the leader. The model describes eight different situations which range from very favorable to very unfavorable for the leader. A very favorable situation would be one in which the relationships between the leader and the rest of the group are good, the task is structured, and the leader's position power is strong. An example of such a situation would be a well-respected director of a hospital laboratory; the tasks (running tests on tissues and specimens) are structured, and the director's authority, reward, and coercive power are all strong. A very unfavorable situation would be one in which the relationship between the leader and the rest of the group is poor, the task is unstructured, and the leader's position power is weak. An example of such an unfavorable situation would be an unpopular chairman of a temporary fact-finding committee composed of his peers; the task is unstructured and the leader's position is weak.

The Leader's Traits

The key aspect in this contingency model, traits of the leader himself, is measured by a questionnaire which asks the leader to describe his least preferred co-workers (LPC). The description includes such dimensions as cooperative v. uncooperative, friendly v. unfriendly, self-assured v. hesitant, and interested v. bored. Some leaders describe their least preferred co-workers in very negative terms (low LPC); others describe them in both good and bad terms (high LPC). Research suggests that high–LPC leaders are concerned with maintaining good relationships in the work situation and seek status and esteem. High–LPC leaders are described as more cognitively complex than low–LPC leaders, whose basic goal is to accomplish the task. High–LPC leaders show great variability in their behavior as the situation changes.[28]

Group Effectiveness

The final component of the contingency model is the relative effectiveness of the group. The effectiveness criterion per se depends on the group's task. Some that have been used are the bombing range score of B–29 crews, the won-lost records of basketball teams, the tonnage produced by open-hearth steel shops, sales and inventory control of service stations, net income of small cooperative corporations, accuracy of land-surveying teams, and ratings on a variety of decision-making and problem-solving group tasks.

Validity of the Model

The contingency model predicts that leaders with certain traits will be relatively more effective than other leaders in certain situations. The evidence summarized in Figure 20–8 suggests this might be true. In some kinds of situations (very favorable or very unfavorable for the leader), groups with low–LPC leaders are more effective than groups with high–LPC leaders. In other situations

[28] R. W. Rice and M. M. Chemers, "Personality and Situational Determinants of Leader Behavior," *Journal of Applied Psychology*, vol. 60 (1975), pp. 20–27.

FIGURE 20–8. Correlations between Leaders' LPC Scores and Group Effectiveness Plotted for Each Situation

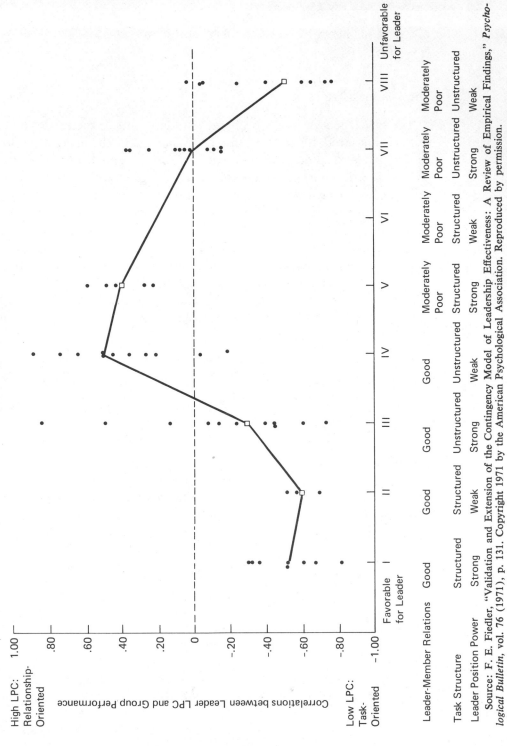

Source: F. E. Fiedler, "Validation and Extension of the Contingency Model of Leadership Effectiveness: A Review of Empirical Findings," *Psychological Bulletin*, vol. 76 (1971), p. 131. Copyright 1971 by the American Psychological Association. Reproduced by permission.

(moderately favorable for the leader) the reverse is true: groups with high–LPC leaders appear to be more effective.

Other research has less consistently supported the model. While the observed relationhips are often as predicted, they are seldom significant. One massive study tested the model in two large organizations—an electronics manufacturer with over 5,000 employees and a teaching hospital with a staff of 1,000.[29] The relationships between LPC and group effectiveness were almost all as the model predicted (except for situation VI, in which low–LPC leaders were more effective). However, only the relationship in situation III was statistically significant.

Field studies of the model generally support the proposition that the relationship between leadership style and group effectiveness is moderated by the favorableness of the situation for the leader.[30] However, data from laboratory studies have been less supportive of the model.[31] Therefore, although the model is an extremely promising vehicle for resolving much of the confusion over leadership effectiveness, the need for further research to clarify these inconsistencies is clear.

A PATH-GOAL THEORY OF LEADERSHIP EFFECTIVENESS

A very different theory of leader effectiveness, developed by Robert J. House, is based on the expectancy theory of motivation described in Chapter 4. It views the leader as potentially a key variable in affecting subordinate perceptions of the instrumentalities and valences of work behavior.[32] The leader affects these "paths" between work behavior and worker goals by:

1. Determining what kinds and what amounts of extrinsic rewards are available.
2. Recognizing and rewarding achievement.
3. Supporting subordinates' efforts to achieve work goals.
4. Assigning and delegating tasks.

[29] Walter Hill, "The Validation and Extension of Fiedler's Theory of Leadership Effectiveness," *Academy of Management Journal*, vol. 12 (March 1969), pp. 33–47.

[30] F. E. Fiedler, "Validation and Extension of the Contingency Model of Leadership Effectiveness: A Review of Empirical Findings," *Psychological Bulletin*, vol. 76 (August 1971), pp. 128–48.

[31] Ibid., p. 141.

[32] R. J. House, "A Path Goal Theory of Leader Effectiveness," in Fleishman and Hunt (eds.), *Study of Leadership*, pp. 141–78.

5.   Enhancing subordinate satisfaction, reducing stress, and re-
     moving barriers which frustrate goals.

Some Propositions of Path-Goal Theory

The path-goal theory has been used to derive a number of hypotheses about the effects of certain kinds of leader behavior on
subordinate performance and satisfaction. Among the more important are the following.

First, the effects of a leader's showing consideration and initiating
structure on subordinate satisfaction and performance depend on
whether or not the task itself is satisfying and whether the task
demands are clear or ambiguous. For tasks that are satisfying,
showing consideration will have little effect. In unsatisfying tasks,
consideration will offset dissatisfaction. Regarding ambiguity, the
more ambiguous the task, the more will initiating structure enhance
subordinate satisfaction and performance. For unambiguous tasks,
initiating structure may prove to be dissatisfying.

Second, where factors in the environment produce stress, showing
consideration will reduce dissatisfaction. If stress comes from external forces and tasks are ambiguous, initiating structure will increase subordinate security and satisfaction.

Third, where leadership is authoritarian or punitive, initiating
structure will decrease subordinate satisfaction.

The basic proposition of path-goal theory is that certain leader
behaviors will be effective in situations where those behaviors
facilitate the subordinates' paths to work-related goals.

Validity of Path-Goal Theory

Results of studies testing the propositions of path-goal theory
have been mixed. One study considered relationships between
leader behavior and subordinate satisfaction and performance at a
university medical center.[33] In unambiguous tasks (food service,
janitor, and building services), initiating structure by the leader was
dissatisfying. As the theory predicted, structure in such jobs is re-
dundant. In ambiguous tasks (administration), initiating structure
was satisfying, since structure removes ambiguity and provides a
clearer path to subordinates' goals. However, the predicted effects

[33] A. D. Szilagyi and H. P. Sims, Jr., "An Exploration of the Path-Goal Theory of
Leadership in a Health Care Environment," *Academy of Management Journal,* vol. 17
(1974), pp. 622–34.

of initiating structure on job performance did not appear. The theory suggests that initiating structure should facilitate subordinate performance both when tasks are clear and when they are unclear. This study found that initiating structure and subordinate performance were negatively related for all occupational skill levels studied.

A study of civil servants, project engineers, and military officers likewise yielded mixed results.[34] As predicted by the theory, relationships between leader consideration and subordinate satisfaction depended on task structure. Consideration was more satisfying when tasks were structured than when they were not. However, the effects of initiating structure were opposite those predicted by the theory: Initiating structure was more satisfying when tasks were structured than when they were unstructured.

Like contingency theory, path-goal theory is a promising approach to understanding the complexities of leadership effectiveness, but much more research is needed to refine and further validate the theory.

SUMMARY

The study of leadership is interesting and yet confusing. We seem to have been more proficient at discovering the misconceptions of leadership than the principles of leadership.

First, we know that leaders cannot confidently be selected on personal or personality traits independent of the situations. The concept that leaders are born and not made is unsupportable.

Second, we know that it is misleading to conceive of the leader apart from the group. The principle of reciprocal causation indicates that leaders can be influenced by groups just as the leaders themselves influence their groups.

Third, we know that the leader is not autonomous from the situation. Leadership behavior is susceptible to a number of sources of influence, including superiors, peers, subordinates, climate, the task, and characteristics of the leader himself.

Fourth, we know that there is apparently no one best way to lead. Some leadership behavior is better than none, but we cannot say that democratic or relationship-oriented leadership is always more productive or more satisfying than authoritarian or task-

---

[34] J. E. Stinson and T. W. Johnson, "The Path-Goal Theory of Leadership: A Partial Test and Suggested Refinement," *Academy of Management Journal*, vol. 18 (1975), pp. 242–52.

oriented leadership, even if we limit our discussion to American culture. The most effective leadership behavior appears to depend on characteristics of the leader and the situation, including the nature of the task and characteristics of the subordinates.

This implies that until we know a great deal more about leadership, the best leadership strategy may be founded on this advice:

> Perhaps the most important implication is that *the successful manager must be a good diagnostician and must value a spirit of inquiry.* If the abilities and motives of the people under him are so variable, he must have the sensitivity and diagnostic ability to be able to sense and appreciate the differences. Second, rather than regard the existence of differences as a painful truth to be wished away, he must also learn to value difference and to value the diagnostic process which reveals differences. Finally, he must have the personal flexibility and the range of skills necessary to vary his own behavior.[35]

QUESTIONS FOR REVIEW AND DISCUSSION

1. Select some leadership position in an organization with which you are familiar. What would you look for in selecting an individual to fill that position? Defend each selection criterion you mention.

2. What is the difference between an authoritarian leadership style and initiating structure?

3. What is the difference between a democratic leadership style and showing consideration?

4. Which determinants of leadership behavior would you expect to be most powerful in (*a*) a military organization, (*b*) a research organization, (*c*) a professional sports organization?

5. "The most effective leaders show great concern both for the task and for people." Comment on the validity of this statement.

6. Describe the characteristics of a situation which would be considered very favorable for a leader. Give an example of such a situation.

7. Describe the characteristics of a situation which would be considered very unfavorable for a leader. Given an example of such a situation.

8. If the contingency model described in this chapter were valid, what would be its implications for organizations?

[35] Schein, *Organizational Psychology*, pp. 70–71.

9. If the path-goal theory proved to be valid, what are some implications which could be drawn for organizations?

10. Why did the young foreman's second leadership attempt work?

KEY WORDS

Trait theory	Rational-economic man
Authoritarian style	Social man
Democratic style	Self-actualizing man
Consideration	Reciprocal causation
Initiating structure	Contingency model
Situational approach	Path-goal model

538

chapter twenty-one

Changing Behavior in Organizations

DEALING WITH CHANGE is the essence of a modern manager's job. Much of the utility of the material in this book for managers and potential managers lies in its application to changing behavior. Managers who seek to *improve* some major dependent variable, such as performance, efficiency, effectiveness, creativity, accuracy, turnover, satisfaction, or communications, are looking to change one or more independent variables in order to bring about the desired improvement. Managers who seek to *maintain* current levels of one or more of these dependent variables must also deal with independent variables which are subject to change beyond their control. These managers must exert counterforces to maintain the independent variables or change other variables to offset the impact of changes in those they cannot control.

For example, a highly successful business organization like the National Football League must react to changes in public taste, general economic conditions, and the strength of competition such as rival football leagues and major league baseball and hockey. The effectiveness with which the NFL reacts to these changes with changes of its own determines whether or not the league will successfully maintain its current and potential profitability.

In this chapter we will look at factors which lead to the need for changing behavior in organizations. We will then outline a simple model for overcoming resistance to change which identifies the elements a manager might manipulate to produce change, and discuss some of the techniques appropriate for each element. Some of the more popular methods of change will be introduced, and examples of their success will be given.

PRESSURES FOR CHANGE IN ORGANIZATIONS

Managers are faced with an abundance of factors which can dictate the necessity for changes in behavior. From the manager's viewpoint, an important aspect of any of these factors is the degree to which he can influence it. For example, in certain circumstances competition can produce a need for organizational change. The editor of a weekly magazine may find pressures from competition so strong that major changes in content or reporting must be made. The editor of a city newspaper, however, may have no competition or have sufficient power over potential competitors or advertisers that competitors' behavior can be virtually ignored.

Sources of pressure to change can be classified as either external or internal to the organization.

External Sources of Pressure

Like any organism, an organization needs to acquire and process external resources in order to survive. This means it must be able to attract resources such as capital, labor, equipment, and knowledge, and it must be able to market what it produces, either goods or services. External sources for change are thus any factors outside the organization which modify the organization's ability to attract resources and to produce or market its goods or services. These factors include competition and changes in the economic environment, the labor force, the consuming public, the physical environment, and the legal environment.

Changes in the economic environment of the early 1970s dictated a myriad of changes in organizational behavior. Many organizations were forced to find ways to induce their employees to step up productivity, without the prospect of large economic rewards to which they had become accustomed. Some were successful; in 1975, Eastern Air Lines pilots agreed to fly an extra five hours per month without additional pay to help the company cope with financial difficulties. Others were unsuccessful; the World Football League folded, although it tied players' and coaches' salaries to box office receipts.

Changes in the labor force were particularly evident during the Vietnam buildup of the mid 1960s. When defense firms with lucrative government contracts drained the supply of skilled labor from nondefense work, other firms found it necessary to increase emphasis on recruitment and training just to maintain current levels of performance.

Changes in the tastes and abilities to pay of the consuming public have been reflected in the American automobile industry's change to smaller, more economical cars. This change, while grudingly made, was spurred on by the pressures of competition, as foreign manufacturers proved successful in their efforts to produce and market small, economical cars to the American public. It was also abetted by changes in the legal environment, as both federal and state governments began to legislate changes in automobile pollution and fuel economy requirements. Change in the physical environment, such as the depletion of oil reserves and damage to the ozone layer, continue to bring pressures on organizations to change such behaviors as hours worked, manufacturing methods, and accounting procedures. Technological change is usually reflected in competition.

Internal Sources of Pressure

Sources of pressure to change which arise within an organization include administrative changes, technological changes, and changes in people. Administrative pressures include factors such as goals, deadlines, and reward or policy changes. For example, a university administration's decision to abandon the honor system requires many changes in student and faculty behavior. Breakdowns in technology and the introduction of new technology frequently require short-term changes in behavior. If a computer system malfunction terminates the management information system, behavior must change or stop. A major disaster such as a fire or explosion requires long-term changes in production behavior, until facilities are repaired or rebuilt.

We have emphasized throughout this book the concept of individual differences and variability. People in organizations change in abilities, interest, and motivation. Workers who become surfeited with fringe benefits require changes in reward systems to maintain low turnover rates. Aspiration levels increase as workers compare their outcomes to those of peers outside the organization. Such changes may require new projects, decentralization, or expansion to maintain people's levels of effort and loyalty. Pressures for change also can come from the managers themselves, as they seek to readjust behavior in their organizations to reflect changes in their own aspirations, values, interests, or abilities.

Organizational Requirements for Change

In order to cope with these various sources of pressure for change successfully, organizations must have clearly defined goals, adequate communications, and adaptability.[1]

Goals Goals are essential because changes in the organization's effectiveness or efficiency in meeting its goals are often the first clues that changes must be made. If a company with a $100 million profit objective makes only $20 million, a hospital with an expansion plan of 100 beds can afford only 50, a college's enrollment figures are 750 below its target, or a football team with designs on the Super Bowl fails to make the playoffs, it is an indication that all is not well. The failure of each of these organizations to meet its goal suggests the need for change.

Communications Communications serve two functions for organizations facing pressures for change. First, communication of organizational goals throughout the organization, so that all members share and understand them, improves the organization's ability to sense changes which might affect those goals. Second, communications permit feedback from different parts of the organization about internal or external changes which may have to be initiated at high levels of the organization. If a municipal health department's goal of avoiding epidemics is clearly understood by its field staff, evidence of a possible outbreak of influenza can be communicated to the department head quickly enough to permit the department to mobilize its resources (change) in order to control the epidemic.

Adaptability Organizations which can sense and communicate the need for change must be able to diagnose the appropriate reaction and carry it out. Adaptability requires a capable decision-making process and a reasonable degree of flexibility. The process of adaptation has been broken down into six stages:

---

[1] These characteristics closely parallel those proposed by Warren G. Bennis: a sense of identity, capacity to test reality, and adaptability. See W. G. Bennis, "Toward a 'Truly' Scientific Management: The Concept of Organizational Health," *General Systems Yearbook* 7 (Ann Arbor, Mich.: Society for General Systems Research, 1962), pp. 269–82.

1. Sensing a change in the internal or external environment.
2. Communicating information about that change to those parts of the organization that must deal with it.
3. Changing the organization (if necessary).
4. Stabilizing the change while controlling its undesired by-products (e.g., costs, turnover, delays, dissatisfaction).
5. Marketing new goods or services to those affected by the changes.
6. Evaluating internal and external feedback regarding the success of the change.[2]

For example, in 1974 major American automobile dealers sensed a change in the consuming public's willingness to buy big, expensive new cars. This information (sales figures) was communicated to corporate headquarters, which changed standard production procedures in 1975 by building their own compacts, rather than selling imports. Undesired by-products (leftover 1975 inventory) were dealt with through a program of cash rebates on 1975 models, with higher rebates for more expensive models. In the fall of 1975 the new 1976 compacts were marketed, and sales profits figures were compared with projections to evaluate the success of the change.

PROBLEMS IN CHANGING BEHAVIOR IN ORGANIZATIONS

Change the Person or Change the Environment?

Part Two of this book introduced the basic concept that behavior is a function of the individual interacting with the environment. In equation form this relationship is stated as

$$B = f(P, E).$$

The fact that human behavior is a result of both personal and environmental characteristics means that changes in behavior in an organization can result from changes in either the personnel or the environment in which they operate. Further, a manager seeking to produce change must consider that, because there is an interaction between the person and the environment, changing the environment is likely to produce changes in the individuals who work in it. For example, changing to a technically more efficient production

---

[2] E. H. Schein, *Organizational Psychology*, 2d ed. (Englewood Cliffs, N.J.: Prentice-Hall, 1970), pp. 119–24.

system may arouse such resentment and fear that workers will sabotage it, as they did at the Lordstown Vega plant (see Chapter 11).

Change Abilities or Change Motivation?

Part Two also introduced the concept of human performance as a
function of ability and motivation. This suggests that managers
seeking to change levels of performance must diagnose whether
the desired change is best achieved by changing the ability of the
individuals involved, changing their motivation, or both. Changes
in both ability and motivational levels can be accomplished either
by changing the persons involved or the environment in which they
work, as we will note later in this chapter.

Change Individuals or Change Groups?

Parts Four and Five described the importance of groups for
people who work in organizations and considered the amount of
influence which groups, particularly informal groups, exert over behavior in organizations. Evidence suggests that managers concerned
with changing behavior should consider not only the physical environment of those whom they wish to change but the social
environment as well. The management literature is replete with
cases of change programs which failed, not because they were ineffective at the individual level but because the changes that were
produced could not withstand the peer group and other social pressures to which changed individuals were subjected.

Resistance to Change

Do individuals and groups "naturally" resist change? The difficulties many organizations have encountered in establishing successful long-term changes in behavior have been attributed by
some writers to something they call "resistance to change." Resistance to change is described as if it were an enduring personality
characteristic common to most members of organizations.

However, labeling behavior does not explain it, and attributing
behavioral tendencies to personality characteristics does nothing for
managers who must deal with it. As we pointed out in Chapter 6,
outside observers give more credit (or blame) than is warranted
to individuals in explaining their behavior. It might be more fruit-

ful to look to the environment in attempts to explain resistance to change.

Sources of Resistance Rather than being attributable to personality characteristics, the causes of resistance may be rooted in the experiences or past reinforcement history of those facing change. It is not unreasonable to assume that a good deal of change in organizations is planned for the organization's benefit at the individual's expense, or at least with individual interest secondary. Lower level members of organizations may have had direct experiences which have led them to associate change with negative consequences, such as working harder for the same or even fewer rewards.

Further, most members of organizations have vested interests in the status quo. They adapt to the organization's environment and learn how to cope with it, developing behavioral patterns which enable them to obtain satisfactory levels of outcomes and whatever reinforcers are available, while avoiding as many unpleasant outcomes as possible. In terms of the model developed in Chapter 12, those who have remained in the organization have managed to cope so that their outcomes exceed their comparison level. Change means uncertainty—abandoning the certainty of whatever satisfactions they now obtain for the uncertainty associated with the new way of doing things. Uncertainty that one will be as satisfied after the change as before, plus the effort perceived as necessary to learn how to cope with the new system, add up to resistance to change. In this light, resistance is not a flaw in worker personality but a psychologically sound behavioral tendency which is based on past experiences.

This proposition is supported by a list of those areas in which resistance to change is most likely to occur:[3]

- Changes that are perceived to lower status
- Changes that cause fear
- Changes that affect job content
- Changes that reduce authority or freedom of acting
- Changes that disrupt established work routines
- Changes that rearrange group relationships
- Changes that are forced without explanation or employee participation
- Changes that are resisted because of mental and/or physical lethargy

---

[3] B. J. Hodge and H. J. Johnson, *Management and Organizational Behavior: A Multidimensional Approach* (New York: John Wiley & Sons, 1970), pp. 432–33.

Of all these areas, only the last suggests that resistance is due to some employee shortcoming. The other areas imply changes which either decrease employee outcomes (lowered status, reduced freedom, disrupted routines and relationships) or increase the probability of decreased outcomes. Under such circumstances, resistance to change in the form of absenteeism, turnover, apathy, stubbornness, decreased productivity, or even sabotage should not be surprising.

A Model for Overcoming Resistance to Change

Many changes in organizational behavior are either resisted or short-lived because the methods used to bring about the change failed to deal with its complexity. A model of the change process which attempted to deal with this complexity was developed by Kurt Lewin, some of whose research was discussed in Chapter 15.

Lewin described behavior patterns, habit, or work routines as persisting because of a set of forces acting on the individual or group. Some of these forces reinforce the routine, some oppose it, and eventually a behavior pattern develops in which the sum of the forces acting on it offset one another. For example, a worker develops a routine production standard averaging 200 units per day because at that level the forces to increase the level (incentive pay, pressure from the supervisor, feelings of accomplishment) offset forces to decrease the level (fatigue, peer group pressure, feelings of autonomy). Effective change therefore requires a program which deals with these forces throughout the change process. Lewin proposed a change process consisting of three phases, which he labeled unfreezing, moving, and freezing.[4]

Unfreezing   According to Lewin, behavioral patterns or routines, including those developed at work, do not persist independently of an individual's self-concept or lifestyle; rather, they become integrated with other aspects of his or her emotional, cognitive, and behavioral characteristics. Attempting to change behavior without dealing with the aspects of an individual's environment which support that behavior invites resistance or backsliding.

The first step in a change program is to induce the target to want to change by "unfreezing" or rearranging the environmental context which supports the target's current level of behavior. Some of

[4] Kurt Lewin, "Group Decision and Social Change," in *Readings in Social Psychology* (3d ed.), ed. E. E. Maccoby, T. M. Newcomb, and E. C. Hartley (New York: Holt, Rinehart & Winston, 1958), pp. 197–212.

the mechanisms which might be used include removing reinforcement for the current behavior, inducing guilt or anxiety about the current behavior, making the individual feel more secure about change by reducing threat or barriers to change, removing the individual from the environment which supports current behavior, or physically changing the environment in which he is behaving.

For example, a program designed to change a manager's leadership style could provide him with feedback that his current style is ineffective or inappropriate. It could involve changing his office location to make him more or less accessible to his employees. It could remove him from the situation and provide a "safe" climate in which he can experiment with alternative behaviors by sending him to a training program conducted away from the premises.

Moving or Changing   Once a target's current behavior pattern has been unfrozen, the new behavior must be learned; the target moves from the old to the new behavior. The target develops new responses through coaching, modeling, demonstration, or any of the several influence processes discussed in Chapter 19. The new behavior is practiced and corrected until a desired level of performance is reached. For example, changes in production techniques designed to increase levels of productivity typically are followed by initial decreases in productivity as workers adapt to and modify the changes and engineers work out "bugs" in the technology. Eventually, productivity returns to and surpasses previous levels to some target level, as depicted in Figure 21–1.

Refreezing   Refreezing means to stabilize and integrate the changed behavior. Refreezing is most effectively accomplished by providing the individual with a social and physical environment which will support the changed behavior. This includes providing the individual with feedback about his or her performance and reinforcing that performance when it is satisfactory.[5]

Analysis of change programs which failed to take hold frequently point to failure to provide an environment which reinforces the change. Examples include failures of supervisory training in industry[6] and of the Chinese brainwashing of American POWs in Korea.[7]

---

[5] For a detailed discussion of the three-stage model of the change process, see W. G. Bennis, E. H. Schein, F. I. Steele, and D. E. Berlew, *Interpersonal Dynamics* (2d ed.) (Homewood, Ill.: Dorsey Press, 1968), pp. 338–66.

[6] E. S. Fleishman, "Leadership Climate, Human Relations Training, and Supervisory Behavior," *Personnel Psychology,* vol. 6 (1953), pp. 205–22.

[7] E. H. Schein, Inge Schneider, and C. H. Barker, *Coercive Persuasion* (New York: W. W. Norton, 1961).

FIGURE 21–1
Typical Productivity Curve before and after a Change in Production Techniques

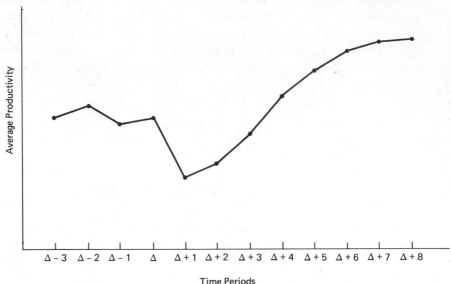

Time Periods

The change in production technique is depicted as occurring in time period Δ.

CHANGING PEOPLE

We have said that behavior change can be accomplished by changing people, by changing their environment, or both. Organizations can change the ability levels of their personnel either through recruitment and selection of new members or through training current members.

Recruitment and Selection

One way for an organization to change its mix or level of abilities and motivation is in its recruitment and selection of new members as discussed in Chapter 5. Before these can be effective methods of change, however, the organization must decide whether its goals are to bring in new or higher levels of ability, interest, or motivation, and what costs it is willing to pay for these changes.

Once the organization has selected the objectives of its recruitment and selection program, several steps are necessary to implement it successfully:

1. Determine how to measure or predict the ability, interest, or motivation of job candidates.

2. Identify the population from which members will be recruited and selected.
3. Select candidates on these bases.
4. Validate the selection criteria by evaluating performance and correlating performance data with selection criteria.[8]

The two basic measurement techniques used by most organizations are testing and interviewing.

Testing   As a selection device, testing in this country got a big boost from the military in both World Wars. Over the course of its long history, psychologists, industrial psychologists, and personnel departments have developed tests for selecting personnel on a wide variety of bases.[9]

General-ability tests typically measure quantitative and language skills. A major user is the military, which uses the General Classification Test to set minimum cutoff scores for enlistment.

Intelligence tests such as the Wechsler Adult Intelligence Scale are often used by business and industry for managerial selection.

Aptitude tests attempt to measure an individual's ability to learn. Some, such as clerical tests, focus on specific jobs or skills. Others measure a more general aptitude for learning. These range from the Law School Admissions Test and the Graduate Management Admissions Test to the more general Scholastic Aptitude Test, widely used by colleges and universities to select students for admission.

Skill tests measure an individual's ability to perform a job. The assumption is that the applicant has already learned the skill. Typing tests, aircraft simulators, and professional football training camps are all examples of skill tests.

Interest tests attempt to match an applicant's interests with characteristics of the jobs that the organization is seeking to fill. The Strong Vocational Interest Blank is the dominant test in this area.

Personality tests attempt to measure certain individual predispositions such as dominance—submissiveness, stability—instability. Some tests are designed to measure the strength of individual needs. The Thematic Apperception Test attempts to measure an individual's need for achievement, affiliation, and power. Of all the types of tests, personality tests are perhaps most controversial because of the high variance in their ability to predict success. One survey of research

---

[8] E. B. Flippo, *Principles of Personnel Management,* 3d ed. (New York: McGraw-Hill Book Co., 1971), chap. 8.

[9] For a thorough discussion of testing, examples of tests, and problems, see J. D. Dunn and E. C. Stephens, *Management of Personnel* (New York: McGraw-Hill Book Co., 1972), chap. 8.

relating personality characteristics to job success found that correlations between predicted success and actual success ranged from
+.50 to —.40.[10] The negative correlations indicate that some of these
personality tests were not only poor predictors or success but actually
discriminated against applicants who were successful and in favor of
applicants who were less than successful.

Problems in Testing. Among the problems with testing, the most
crucial are validity and discrimination. *Validity* is the extent to which
the test accurately predicts job success. Hundreds of tests which
logically would seem to predict specific job success are in fact unable
to demonstrate their usefulness. Nevertheless, many organizations
persist in their use.

Organizations which fail to validate their tests run the risk of
spending a good deal of money for a program which keeps out good
employees and lets in poor ones. To increase confidence in a test's
validity, organizations often perform *cross-validation* tests. This technique consists of randomly assigning a majority of applicants to a
validation group and a smaller number to a cross-validation group.
Correlations between test scores and job success for both groups are
computed and compared, to hedge against the possibility that one
group was not really representative of the population of interest.
For example, aptitude tests were developed for a computer technology training organization to predict students' success in learning
programming and computer maintenance.[11] Applicants were tested
and assigned to validation samples of 209 programmers and 75 maintenance personnel, with cross-validation samples of 106 programmers
and 24 maintenance personnel. Correlations between aptitude tests
and grades in the program were positive and statistically significant
for all four groups, ranging from +.40 to +.67. Such results support
the usefulness of these tests for selecting students for computer technology training.

Discrimination is the problem that certain tests may have different
validities for different groups of people. For example, a general-
ability test may be a valid predictor of job success for white workers
but not for black workers. In such a case, an organization which uses
the test for job selection may unfairly discriminate against capable
black workers.

---

[10] E. E. Ghiselli and R. P. Barthol, "The Validity of Personality Inventories in the
Selection of Employees," *Journal of Applied Psychology*, vol. 37 (1953), pp. 18–20.
  [11] J. A. Fossum, "An Application of Techniques to Shorten Tests and Increase
Validity," *Journal of Applied Psychology*, vol. 57 (1973), pp. 90–92.

The Civil Rights Act of 1964 and the Equal Employment Opportunity Act of 1969 specifically forbid the use of tests which discriminate against minority groups. Further, they require organizations doing business with the federal government to demonstrate that their selection tests are valid and do not discriminate. The results of this program have been mixed, with some organizations being forced to drop or revise selection procedures. A review of 13 studies of black-white differences in validity of selection procedures, covering occupations ranging from dental workers and general maintenance to welders and psychiatric aides, found little evidence of differential validity between ethnic groups.[12] In only 7 of 60 instances were significantly different validities found between black and white workers. However, 100 of the 160 validity coefficients computed in these 13 studies were not significant, either for blacks or whites. This suggests that the organizations using these tests were wasting time, money, and talent on their efforts to select successful employees.

Interviewing Practically all organizations require personal interviews for prospective employees. Unfortunately, the popularity of interviewing as a selection device is not paralleled by evidence of its validity. One problem is that the interviewing process provides a stressful environment, which may distort the communication process between the interviewer and the interviewee. Second, the subjective nature of interviewing heightens the probability of perceptual distortion and bias. Third, the frailty of most people's ability to recall makes the reliability of interviewing highly tenuous. Fourth, because perceptions are influenced by the context or frame of reference in which they occur, the sequencing of interviewees may play an important part in how a job applicant is appraised. An average applicant may look especially good if he is interviewed immediately after a particularly poor group of applicants, but the same applicant may look relatively bad if he is sandwiched between a set of particularly qualified applicants.

To demonstrate some of these problems with interviewing, 80 subjects watched videotaped interviews of job applicants and rated them in terms of their qualifications for the job of office systems salesman.[13] Each student watched three videotapes and evaluated

---

[12] V. R. Boehm, "Negro-White Differences in Validity of Employment and Training Selection Procedures," *Journal of Applied Psychology*, vol. 56 (1972), pp. 33–39.

[13] K. N. Wexley, G. A. Yukl, S. Z. Kovacs, and R. E. Sanders, "Importance of Contrast Effects in Employment Interviews," *Journal of Applied Psychology*, vol. 56 (1972), pp. 45–58.

the three applicants interviewed in the tapes. Of particular interest were ratings of the third applicant, performed after the subjects had evaluated two others.

Some of the applicants were highly suitable, some unsuitable, and some of average suitability. The results clearly showed that the interviewers' frame of reference rather than the applicants' suitability played the major role in evaluation. The mean rating of an average applicant whose interview followed two highly suitable applicants was 2.5 on a 9-point scale; the mean rating of the same applicant when his interview followed two unsuitable applicants was 8.1 on the same 9-point scale! Such contrast effects could explain 80 percent of the variance in ratings of an average applicant.

Almost every personnel textbook sets forth a number of principles for interviewers to follow to increase the reliability and validity of the process. One of the most common suggestions is the use of more than one interviewer as a check on perceptual distortion or bias of any single individual. Despite such precautions, interviewing does not appear to merit the widespread popularity it enjoys.

Training

In addition to replacing personnel as a means of changing behavior, organizations also can change current personnel through a variety of training techniques. As with recruitment and selection, the first step in a training program must be to identify which aspects of behavior are to be changed: skills, abilities, routines, motivation, or interest. The techniques used include socialization, formal and informal training, management development, and sensitivity training.

Socialization   Virtually every organization uses some formal socialization techniques. Socialization processes (see Chapter 19) are used by the organization to develop the attitudes, values, and behavior necessary for its members to function effectively. In practice, formal socialization processes can include a wide variety of activities. Rigorous entry requirements may instill feelings of camaraderie and pride among those who pass them. Personnel manuals and brochures provide general guidelines for behavior and propaganda designed to increase the employees' attraction to the organization. Rites, rituals, and reward systems may be effectively used to shape employee behavior.

Formal and Informal Training   Besides general socialization processes, specific techniques are also used to change the skills and techniques of performing jobs. *On-the-job training* typically relies on a coaching relationship in which an experienced employee runs through the rudiments of a task, both verbally and physically, for a new worker and then observes and corrects the new employee as he or she learns the task. For many routine or machine-assisted jobs, this informal method seems to be adequate. A punching machine operator describes his introduction to the task as an "all-time minimum of job training." He was assigned a machine, at which the superintendent and an older operator gave a few demonstrations, and was warned to keep his hands clear of the descending hammer. "After a short practice period," he said, "I was left to develop my learning curve with no other supervision than afforded by members of the work group."[14]

Formal training programs are typically used to develop more complex skills, when large numbers of people are to be trained, and when attitudes and motivation are important targets of the change process. These programs may run from a single exercise designed to familiarize personnel with new products and processes to a year-long program in science or technology conducted by an outside contractor.

Management Development   In the post–World War II era there has been a trend toward the use of formal training programs to developing managerial skills. A number of major companies conduct such programs with their own personnel; others use outside consultants or draw on the facilities of colleges and universities. Management development programs may vary from regular one- or two-hour sessions per week to a full year's master's degree program in business, such as that offered by M.I.T. for promising executives from large organizations.

One example of a short-term management development program was conducted for two groups of managers from nine departments of a large urban medical center.[15] The program consisted of two phases. In Phase I each manager actively participated in several role-playing exercises during 4½-hour workshop sessions held on two consecutive days. The managers played the role of supervisor, and especially trained graduate students played various subordinate roles. Each manager was given a list of effective and ineffective supervisory

[14] D. F. Roy, "Banana Time," *Human Organization*, vol. 18 (Winter 1959–60), pp. 158–68.

[15] K. N. Wexley and W. F. Nemeroff, "Effectiveness of Positive Reinforcement and Goal Setting as Methods of Management Development," *Journal of Applied Psychology*, vol. 60 (1975), pp. 446–50.

behaviors relevant to each exercise. During the course of the role playing, each manager was given specific feedback and verbal reinforcement for his or her performance. At the end of each exercise, managers were assigned specific goals for their next exercise, such as showing no favoritism, delegating responsibility, and discussing significant details for a job assignment with a subordinate.

In Phase II each manager filled out a daily behavioral checklist to record his or her own managerial behavior on the job. Some of the 30 checklist items included praising a subordinate for good work, giving a subordinate an immediate answer to a question, and avoiding the temptation to interfere with the way a subordinate handled an assigned task.

Measures of managerial behavior and subordinate satisfaction were collected 60 days after the completion of training. Results revealed that the consideration and integrating behavior of the trained managers and the absenteeism rate of their subordinates were both significantly improved over a control group of managers who went through a different program.

Sensitivity Training One of the most widely used personal-change techniques in organizations today is sensitivity training, which has taken on many forms in practice. The essence of its design is to bring individuals into an unstructured small-group situation for sessions ranging from a few hours to days. Under the guidance of a professional trainer, the members explore their own behavior and feelings via verbal and nonverbal behavior, relying heavily on group dynamics techniques and feedback from one another. The objectives are to increase members' awareness of:

1. Their own feelings and the feelings of others.
2. The complexity of the communications process.
3. Genuine differences among people in their needs, goals, and ways of approaching others.
4. Their own impact on others.
5. How groups function and the consequences of certain kinds of group action.[16]

At least in part, these objectives have helped make sensitivity training a popular management development technique. Many organizations experiencing problems in communications, cooperation, coordination, or other types of interpersonal behavior have turned

---

[16] E. H. Schein and W. G. Bennis, "What Is Laboratory Training: Description of a Typical Residential Laboratory," in Schein and Bennis, *Personal and Organizational Change through Group Methods: The Laboratory Approach* (New York: John Wiley & Sons, 1965).

to sensitivity training as a means of improving personal and organizational effectiveness.

However, a recent review of 100 studies found much more evidence of the effectiveness of sensitivity training at the personal level than at the organizational level.[17] The studies reviewed all compared the effect of 20 or more hours' training on the attitudes or behavior of a training group and some control group. The review concluded that sensitivity training:

1. Frequently leads to changes in self-evaluation, typically (but not always) toward a trainee's ideal self-concept.
2. Temporarily induces trainees to perceive their behavior as less controlled by others and more controlled by themselves.
3. Had no consistent, predictable effects on openness or prejudice toward others; in some cases trainees showed more openness, in some more prejudice, and in others no change in either variable.
4. Was likely to increase participative leadership behavior by trainees temporarily.
5. Tends to produce at least short-term improvement in some communication skill.
6. Changes others' perceptions of trainees, usually in positive directions.

Studies of the effects of sensitivity training on the ways in which an organization operates rather than on individuals typically have found some effects. Targets of change in these studies included openness, trust, candor, communications, and leadership behavior. The majority of the programs were in industry, a minority in school and hospital settings. In 12 of the 13 studies, significant effects on organizational behavior were attributed to the training. However, in two of the studies the effects were the reverse of those intended (less confidence, acceptance, trust, help seeking and giving), and in several others the effects fell short of the program's goals.

The relative lack of success of sensitivity training in improving organizational effectiveness contrasts with its effectiveness in changing individual behavior. This paradox is reflected in the popularity of the method despite disappointment about its results. A national survey of 225 large firms (over 1,000 employees) supports this contrast.[18] Over half the firms surveyed used sensitivity training as part

---

[17] P. B. Smith, "Controlled Studies of the Outcome of Sensitivity Training," *Psychological Bulletin,* vol. 82 (1975), pp. 597–622.

[18] W. J. Kearney and D. D. Martin, "Sensitivity Training: An Established Management Development Goal?" *Academy of Management Journal,* vol. 17 (1974), pp. 755–60.

of their management development programs, but they ranked sensitivity training lowest in effectiveness among eight development techniques. The rank order of effectiveness is shown in Table 21–1.

TABLE 21-1
Rankings of Effectiveness of Management Development Tools among 225 Firms

Technique	Frequency with Which Technique Was Ranked:		Mean Rank
	First	Second	
On-the-job experiences and job transfers	158	17	1.4
Seminars	39	62	2.4
Conferences	23	52	2.8
Other	10	10	2.8
In-basket technique	10	6	4.3
Role playing	11	4	4.4
Quantitative techniques	6	12	4.5
Sensitivity training	4	5	5.3

Source: Adapted from W. J. Kearney and D. D. Martin, "Sensitivity Training: An Established Management Development Tool?" *Academy of Management Journal*, vol. 17 (1974), p. 757.

Transferability of Training to the Job A major problem with training as a means of changing behavior is whether what is learned is transferred effectively to the job. This is a particularly acute problem for off-the-job training in which trainees are removed from the job site, given specialized instruction, and then returned to the job site. The newly learned behavior is often not "frozen," in Lewin's terms. When subjected to the forces at work back on the job, the trainee's behavior changes away from what he or she has learned. This may explain why on-the-job experiences and job transfers were rated as most effective in the survey described above.

Transferability has been a special problem in sensitivity training. New methods and skills are learned in the relative safety of the group experience. Back on the job, these new skills are frequently not reinforced, and old behavior patterns reemerge.

CHANGING ENVIRONMENTS

The second major category of methods for changing behavior in organizations is changing the physical or social environments of those whose behavior is to be altered.

Behavior Modification

Behavior modification is a change technique based on the principles of the operant model described in Chapter 4. In the equation $B = f(P, E)$, behavior modification emphasizes changing E (the environment) to change behavior. The principles of reinforcement theory are followed in that correctly learned new behavior is reinforced, while undesirable behavior is not.[19]

An important feature of behavior modification as applied to organizations is the analytic model used to determine an appropriate change strategy. This model is presented in Figure 21–2. In step 1 the behavior to be changed is identified, and its frequency is recorded in step 2. Step 3 applies reinforcement principles by examining behavior processes to find discriminating and reinforcing stimuli which act on the target behavior. In Lewin's terms, step 3 identifies the forces which maintain the target behavior and which must be "unfrozen."

Step 4a develops a strategy which considers all organizational environment variables: structure, processes, technology, groups, and the task itself. This step recognizes that several environmental variables may have to be changed in order to unfreeze the target behavior and allow the new behavior to be learned and refrozen. For example, improving assembly-line productivity may require not only new machinery but a new supervisory structure (e.g., more decentralization), a new communications process (e.g., to offset noise) and a reshuffling of groups (to maintain social reinforcement on the job).

Step 4b applies the appropriate reinforcement procedures to help shape and bring the new behavior to the desired level. Step 4c provides feedback on the success of the program, and step 4d applies the schedule of reinforcement appropriate for maintaining the new behavior once it reaches the desired level (freezing the new behavior).

Thus the behavior modification model closely follows the principles of the operant approach and of Lewin's unfreeze-move-refreeze model for changing behavior.

In one industrial application of behavior modification, groups of nine first-line production supervisors in a medium-sized manufactur-

---

[19] Fred Luthans, *Organizational Behavior* (New York: McGraw-Hill Book Co., 1973), pp. 521–23.

FIGURE 21–2
A Model of Organizational Behavior Modification

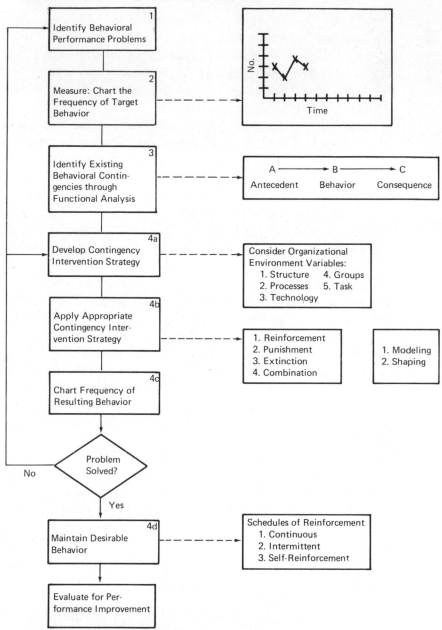

Source: Fred Luthans and R. Kreitner, "The Management of Behavioral Contingencies,"
Personnel July–August 1974, pp. 7–16. © 1974 by AMACOM, a division of American
Management Association.

ing firm were put through a series of ten 90-minute training sessions in behavior modification principles.[20] During these sessions they applied the model to behavior problems in their own departments and carried out the resultant change programs on their own work groups. By the end of the training program the direct labor effectiveness of their departments had improved by nearly 11 percent, compared to a 0 percent increase in the departments of nine supervisors who served as a control group. These differences persisted throughout a three-month posttraining observation period.

Goal Setting

One aspect of the organizational environment which has received considerable attention in behavior-change programs is the setting of goals toward which individuals and groups can strive. Much of this interest developed from empirical studies which showed that individuals tend to perform at higher or more effective levels when they are working toward specific goals than when they are not. In this area, a goal is defined as "a level of performance whose attainment is associated with 'success' and nonattainment with 'failure.'"[21]

A review of the research on the effectiveness of goal setting provides consistent evidence that setting specific, clear goals generally improves both individual and group performance more than merely defining responsibilities or encouraging people to improve.[22] Six aspects of goal setting have been identified:

1. Setting specific goals.
2. Allowing subordinates to participate in setting their own goals.
3. Providing employees with feedback on progress toward performance goals.
4. Providing peer competition for goal attainment.
5. The relative difficulty of goals.
6. Acceptance of goals by subordinates.

---

[20] Robert Ottemann and Fred Luthans, "An Experimental Analysis of the Effectiveness of an Organizational Behavior Modification Program in Industry," *Proceedings of the Academy of Management, 1975,* pp. 140–42. For a review of foundations and applications of behavior modification in organizations, see C. E. Schneir, "Behavior Modification in Management: A Review and Critique," *Academy of Management Journal,* vol. 17 (1974), pp. 528–48.

[21] A. C. Stedry and Emanuel Kay, "The Effects of Goal Difficulty on Performance: A Field Experiment," *Behavioral Science,* vol. 11 (1966), pp. 459–70.

[22] R. M. Steers and L. W. Porter, "The Role of Task-Goal Attributes in Employee Performance," *Psychological Bulletin,* vol. 81 (1974), pp. 434–52.

Of these six attributes, the first and the last are more consistently related to performance improvement.[23] Setting specific goals that are accepted by subordinates has been demonstrated in both laboratory and field studies to be an effective method of behavior change. The effects of participation and feedback appear to be complexly related to individual differences. The effects of competition (see Chapter 16) depend on the nature of the task and the reward systems involved: it is effective when quantity rather than quality of performance is most important, when tasks are independent, and when differential rewards are used. Research on goal difficulty tends to show that moderately difficult goals are more effective than easy or impossible goals, but so many exceptions have been reported that no safe conclusion can be drawn.

The effectiveness of goal setting as a behavioral change program has been demonstrated in the lumber industry.[24] Questionnaires administered to 292 pulpwood producers indicated that goal setting, when accompanied by supervision, is strongly correlated with high productivity and a low number of injuries. A subsequent analysis of 892 pulpwood producers found that producers who set production goals and actively supervised their employees had the highest production in terms of cords of wood produced per man-day of production (3.14), compared to 2.96 cords for those who set goals without active supervision and 2.56 cords for those who supervised without setting goals.

A subsequent field experiment in a related industry (logging) provided further support for goal setting.[25] Six company logging operations were studied, the target being to increase the net weight of 36 trucks transporting logs from woods to the mill. Because each tree differs in size, the number of trees which constituted a full load was a matter of judgment.

Analysis revealed that trucks had been averaging only 60 percent of their legal net weight, an expensive waste of space and time for the company. Researchers, management, and the union decided that 94 percent was a difficult but attainable goal. This goal was assigned to the drivers, whose responsibilities included loading the truck to the maximum legal weight.

---

[23] Ibid.

[24] W. W. Ronan, G. P. Latham, and S. B. Kinne III, "Effects of Goal Setting and Supervision on Worker Behavior in an Industrial Situation," *Journal of Applied Psychology*, vol. 58 (1973), pp. 302–7.

[25] G. P. Latham and J. J. Baldes, "The 'Practical Significance' of Locke's Theory of Goal Setting," *Journal of Applied Psychology*, vol. 60 (1975), pp. 122–24.

Within four weeks performance had improved to 80 percent capacity. It dropped to 70 percent after another four weeks, but within six weeks it had climbed to 90 percent, where it remained over the next six months. Company accountants concluded that the additional performance gained would have required a quarter million dollars worth of new trucks alone, had it not been for the goal-setting program. This study demonstrated the effectiveness of goals with the two important characteristics of specificity and acceptance. The goal was specific at 94 percent and was agreed upon by both union and management.

Management by Objectives

A variation of goal setting which has increased in popularity is management by objectives (MBO). This technique incorporates the attributes of specific goal setting, participation, and feedback into a system of performance appraisal in what often turns out to be a company wide behavior-change program. The essential features of MBO are:

1. Effective goal setting and planning by top levels of the managerial hierarchy.
2. Commitment of the organization to this approach.
3. Participation of subordinates in setting goals.
4. Frequent performance review (feedback).
5. Some freedom in developing means for achieving objectives.[26]

Under companywide MBO programs, objectives at all levels of management and employees are set with reference to the overall organizational goal. Goal setting starts at the top and works down, with each level setting goals consistent with those of the next highest level.

MBO, while difficult and time-consuming to implement, has demonstrated success in changing behavior. In one production firm productivity had been declining at an average rate of 0.4 percent per month. After MBO was instituted, productivity increased at an average rate of 0.3 percent per month. Managers involved in the program attributed the improved productivity to performance appraisal, better planning, and better communications resulting from MBO.

---

[26] S. J. Carroll, Jr., and H. L. Tosi, Jr., *Management by Objectives: Applications and Research* (New York: Macmillan Co., 1973), p. 3. This book provides an excellent review of MBO applications and a detailed study of the authors' own research on MBO.

However, they expressed negative feelings about the amount of subordinate participation in goal setting and about the amount of paperwork involved.[27]

MBO has been applied with varying success outside industrial settings, as in hospitals and educational institutions. In one study, MBO was instituted in a university which had 9,000 students and 600 faculty members.[28] One year after it was incorporated the MBO program was evaluated by questionnaires to the faculty, who perceived the greatest improvements to be in understanding department goals and priorities and in developing professional objectives. Only about one third of the respondents believed university productivity had improved because of MBO.

Despite evidence of its effectiveness in industrial settings, there is resistance to MBO, partly because, to be fully implemented, it involves a major time-consuming effort throughout the organization. The most frequent criticisms from managers who have been involved in MBO are:

1. It takes too much time.
2. Subordinates are incapable of participating in goal setting.
3. It erodes managerial authority.
4. There is an unwillingness to plan ahead.
5. MBO is a weapon for forcing behavior change on unwilling managers.
6. There is a dislike for providing regular feedback and performance review to subordinates.
7. Too much paperwork is involved.[29]

For these reasons, MBO is still undergoing revisions and evaluation as a major change program.

Organization Development

The increasing pressures for change outlined at the beginning of this chapter have led some organizations to seek to do more than simply react. Their needs have led organizational change to be institutionalized into an activity which has been labeled organization development (OD). OD is a continuing effort by organizations, typi-

[27] A. P. Raia, "Goal Setting and Self-Control," *Journal of Management Studies,* vol. 2 (1965), pp. 34–53.

[28] Y. K. Shetty and H. M. Carlisle, "Organizational Correlates of a Management by Objectives Program," *Academy of Management Journal,* vol. 17 (1974), pp. 155–60.

[29] Carroll and Tosi, *Management by Objectives,* pp. 49–52.

cally with the help of outside consultants, "to uncover and remove attitudinal, behavioral, procedural, policy, and structural barriers to effective performance across the entire sociotechnical system, gaining in the process increased awareness of the system's internal and external dynamics so that future adaptations are enhanced".[30]

The objectives of OD are not only to react effectively to pressures for change but to actively seek avenues for changing the organization. The goals are to secure greater employee effectiveness and satisfaction and to increase the organization's abilities to change. Some of the concepts on which OD is based include:

1. The unfreeze-move-refreeze model described earlier in this chapter is an effective means of overcoming resistance to change.
2. Learning is most effective when it occurs within the natural work group.
3. Behavioral systems are interrelated; change must consider the interdependencies of the environment.
4. OD consultants should help the rest of the organization to learn and to adapt.
5. OD is not merely a program but a continuous monitoring of the organization's systems and processes.[31]

In practice, OD may use any of the methods described in this chapter to change behavior through changing people and their environment.

SUMMARY

Managers in contemporary organizations are constantly confronted with perceived or actual pressures to change behavior. These pressures may arise from within the organization as people, technology, and administration change, or they may come from outside it in the form of competition or changes in the labor force, or the economic, legal, or physical environments.

Managers facing the need to change behavior must choose among the alternatives of changing people or their environments, of changing abilities or motivation, and of changing individuals or groups. Resistance to change often occurs because members see the change as

---

[30] R. E. Miles, *Theories of Management: Implications for Organizational Behavior and Development* (New York: McGraw-Hill Book Co., 1975), p. 191.

[31] Ibid., pp. 192–93.

likely to lower rather than improve their outcomes, or as entailing more trouble than it is worth. In designing a change program, managers should therefore consider the forces acting to maintain current behavior as well as those likely to act on the changed behavior.

One approach to changing behavior is to change people. Recruitment and selection can be used to bring new skills, abilities, and interests into the organization. Training can increase the skills, abilities, and interests of those already in the organization. Among the most frequently used techniques are socialization, on-the-job training, management development, and sensitivity training. Each method has its own advantages and disadvantages.

The second major approach to changing behavior is to change the environment: the technology, structure, systems, tasks, and social environments in organizations. Major methods include behavior modification, goal setting, and management by objectives. The field of organization development has emerged as an activity in some organizations that see the value of preparing for and facilitating organizational change.

QUESTIONS FOR REVIEW AND DISCUSSION

1. Identify some internal and external sources of pressure for change within the college or university you are attending.

2. Why are goals and communications important requirements for organizations faced with pressures to change?

3. Identify some conditions under which it might be easier to change people rather than their environment.

4. Suppose a sales manager were concerned over the poor sales performance of sales personnel. How might the manager decide whether to try to change the ability or the motivation of the sales department?

5. How does Lewin's model of change deal with resistance to change?

6. What are the major limitations of testing and interviewing?

7. Describe an informal training program you have been through. Was it effective? Have you retained the skills you acquired? If so, how; if not, why not?

8. Discuss the problem of transferability in training. What training method discussed in this chapter is likely to have (*a*) the greatest problem and (*b*) the least problem with transferability?

9. What are the similarities between (*a*) behavior modification and

management by objectives, (*b*) goal setting and management by objectives?

10. What major elements of the environment are explicitly examined in a behavior modification approach to change?

KEY WORDS

Adaptability	Test discrimination
Resistance to change	Management development
Unfreezing	Sensitivity training
Refreezing	Behavior modification
Tranferability	Management by objectives
Test validity	Organization development

Index

Index

A

Ability and
   individual differences, 111–14
   performance, 74
Absenteeism and
   job satisfaction, 276–77
   operant model of motivation, 98
Actuarial approach, 220–21
Adaptability, 542–43
Administrative man, 168–69
Affiliation, and joining groups, 297
Affective component of attitudes, 257
Age differences and
   cooperation, competition, 414
   creativity, 222–25
   individual decision making, 171–72
   target of influence, 475
Aggression and
   conflict, 446–47
   group cohesiveness, 329
Ahistoric, 69, 87–88
Alcohol and individual decision making,
   174–75
Allocation, 161
Alternatives
   and interpersonal attraction, 306–9
   types of, 190–91
Altruism
   and cooperation, 403, 410
   defined, 403
   determinants, 404–8
   implications, 408–9
Appraisal; see Evaluation and Program
   appraisal
Aptitudes and performance, 112
Asch, S. E., 490
Association and attitude formation, 259
Attitude model of behavioral intentions,
   76–79
Attitudes
   and cognitive approach, 53
   components, 256–61
   consistency, 258–59
   functions, 260–61
   similarity, 303–4

Attitudes—*Cont.*
   sources, 77–78, 259–60
Attribution and
   cooperation, competition, 413
   perception, 137–40
   performance evaluation, 147
Authority, 464
   and group development, 314–15
Autonomy and creativity, 247
Avoidance behavior, 58

B

Bandwagon effect, 392
Bargaining, 449–50
Bechterev, V. M., 88
Behavior modification, 557–59
Behaviorally anchored rating scales, 149–
   51
Behavioral component of attitudes, 258
Behaviorism, defined, 88–89
Belief, 77, 258˙
Between-subjects design, 32
Bisociative act, 208
Blauner, Robert, 271
Boundary role, 319–20
Bounded discretion, 182–83
Bounded rationality, 168
Brainstorming, 383

C

Case study method
   defined, 24
   example of, 24–26
Causes of behavior, 93–95
Change
   environment, 556–62
   individual, 548–56
   organizational, 539–64
Classical conditioning, 55
Coalitions
   anticompetitive, 423
   defined, 420
   formation, 420–23
   minimum resource, 421–23

569

This book has been set in 11 and 10 point Caledonia, leaded 2 points. Part numbers are 24 point (large) Helvetica Medium and part titles are 24 point (small) Helvetica. Chapter titles are 18 point Helvetica Medium and chapter numbers are 24 point (small) Helvetica Medium. The size of the maximum type page is 30 by 46 picas.